AF544978

ELECTRONIC COLOR SEPARATION

Dr. R. K. Molla
Professor, Printing Technology
West Virginia Institute of Technology

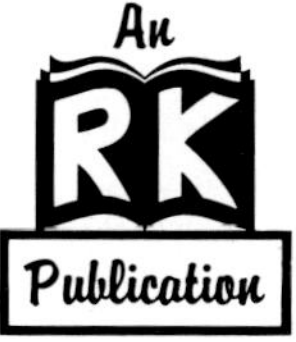

R. K. Printing & Publishing Company
120 Fifth Avenue
Montgomery, West Virginia 25136

PRINTED IN THE UNITED STATES OF AMERICA

International Standard
Book Number: 0-9620453-0-6

Library of Congress
Catalog Card Number: 88-90902

Printing: Chapman Printing Company, Parkersburg, West Virginia
Typesetting: S. Rosenthal & Co., Cincinnati, Ohio
Binding: Arcata Graphics, Kingsport, Tennessee

To my wife Faizun
Her patience and encouragement have
made this project a reality

Foreword

The years since the end of World War II have been the Golden Age of Printing. In 1950, when the word **printing** was spoken, it meant **letterpress.** In fact, if Johann Gutenberg, who invented letterpress printing in 1440, returned to the average print shop in 1950, he could have stood at a type case, set type and proofed it in much the same way he printed his famous Bible 500 years earlier. Letterpress had not advanced much.

Things began to change in 1950. The Fotosetter, introduced by Harris Intertype at the U.S. Government Printing Office in 1948, was setting type photographically and the first commercial electronic scanner for making color corrected separations was introduced in 1950 by PDI, a subsidiary of Time-Life. Web offset printing was attracting attention, and both Harris and Miehle were distributing advertisements of the same subject printed on one side by letterpress and the other side by offset lithography with crossovers by both processes. Soon the term printing was used to describe all three major printing processes — letterpress, offset lithography and gravure — because often you couldn't tell the difference between them without a magnifying glass.

It took over 20 years, into the 1970's, however, before phototypesetting and electronic scanners gained acceptance in the printing industry. In 1970, 75% of the type set in the U.S. was still cast metal. The video display terminal, introduced in 1970, simplified corrections so that phototypesetting and electronic typesetting have finally almost completely replaced cast metal type. Digital electronic enlargement by Crosfield and electronic dot generation by PDI and Hell increased the use of electronic scanners so they have become the preferred means for producing corrected color separations. In 1977, 320 scanners in the U.S. were used to make about 20% of the color separations made. In 1987 the 3,000 scanners in North America made almost 90% of the color separations produced! This is close to the saturation point for scanner use, as about 10% of the subjects for color reproduction cannot be handled on scanners.

The explosive increase in the use of scanners has created a tremendous demand for scanner operators. Training, especially of scanner operators, has suddenly become the most critical requirement in the printing industry. This book by Dr. R. K. Molla is an important contribution to the training world and will help alleviate this crisis. It will not only simplify training but will develop scanner operators with improved skills and basic knowledge of the principles of color imaging and reproduction.

The role of educational institutions in training the future generation of the work force for the printing industry is expanding. Since the use of color in printing is growing at an unprecedented rate, it is important that the latest techniques and equipment developed for color reproduction advances made in this area are integrated in the curricula of graphic arts educational programs. Electronic Color Separation by Professor Molla is an ideal textbook for teaching the latest techniques of color separation and correction. Its numerous illustrations, a simplified content and reproductions of actual scanner control panels make it possible to teach the principles of color scanner separation, even for schools without scanners.

Dr. Rafiqul K. Molla, Professor of Printing Technology at West Virginia Institute of Technology, has been teaching printing in the U.S. and Bangladesh, his native country, since 1963. He has personally operated the four scanners that are featured in his book — Crosfield Magnascan 645, Dainippon Screen SG 608, Hell Chromagraph 399ER, and Royal Zenith 200-S. These are four basic popular designs of scanners in current use.

The next generation of color scanners and their new peripherals will be sure to include presetters, previewers, cameras for scaling and rotating images, layout programmers, and tint inserting devices. Newer scanners use digital image processing and some use colorimetric image recording in place of conventional R,G,B. The scanners Dr. Molla describes in this book are basic designs that will remain in current use for some time before they are replaced by the next generation. The foundation of basic knowledge of scanners in this book will make it easier for operators to learn the principles and operation of the future scanners.

Electronic Color Separation by Professor Molla contains 17 chapters, 288 pages and is printed on 100 lb. coated stock to enhance the 320 illustrations, a third of which are in 4-color. The 17 chapters cover the basic scanner mechanics and functions, set up, halftones, copy evaluation, calibration, adjustments, correction for color cast, tone reproduction, color correction, gray balance, unsharp masking, under color removal, under color addition, gray component replacement, color communication and a discussion of the basics of digital image processing. This book is recommended reading for scanner operators, pre-press managers and anyone involved or interested in color image processing.

Michael H. Bruno
Graphic Arts Consultant
Nashua, New Hampshire

Preface

The volume of color printing has increased rapidly during the last decade and is continuing to expand. The color scanners have significantly contributed in this growth by providing quality separations to the industry at an acceptable cost. The inventions and innovations in this area have also provided the impetus to the color electronic prepress systems (CEPS) which appear to be the trend of the future. This book is written to provide a basic understanding of the concepts, principles and skills necessary for the operation of a color scanner.

The thought of writing this book first occurred in the early '80s when the author was pursuing his doctoral study at the West Virginia University. While conducting research for the dissertation, he found that there was a lack of simplified training material available for a student or for a prospective scanner operator who wanted to get into the exciting and challenging field of scanner operation.

This book is intended for the scanner operators, prepress technicians, high school and post high school students, sales personnel and anyone with an average graphic communications background who wants to learn the principles of color scanner operation. The content is simplified with appropriate examples and illustrations wherever possible. In addition, some of the concepts and principles of scanner operation which apply to conventional separation as well, are also discussed so that persons with background in conventional separation can relate their knowledge to the specific functions in the scanner.

The selection and organization of proper content for such a publication was a real challenge. In making these crucial decisions, the author drew upon his experience in teaching color for the last 15 years; upon the input of more than 300 scanner operators, experts and trainers who participated in his doctoral dissertation; and upon the suggestions of his colleagues and students at California Polytechnic State University and West Virginia Tech. Whenever time permitted, he consulted personally with technical experts of the major scanner vendors and graphic arts suppliers while the manuscript was being prepared.

The content is organized into seventeen chapters. Chapter 1 deals with some of the basic concepts and principles of color separation, evolution of color scanners, advantages of electronic scanning over conventional separation and the current advances made in the technology. In Chapter 2, the reader becomes familiar with the basic construction and functions of several types of drum scanners. Chapter 3 deals with the important mechanical aspects of the scanner set up and operation. Chapter 4 is exclusively dedicated to the principles of halftone — both conventional halftone and electronic dot generation. The basic principles of tone reproduction are covered in this chapter. The discussion in Chapter 5 concentrates on problems with originals, copy evaluation, photographic emulsion characteristics, the scanner's response to color and various scanning aids available to the scanner operator for the optimum set up. A discussion on both input and output calibrations for a scanner is presented in Chapter 6.

Chapters 7 through 15 deal with a detailed presentation of eight specific adjustments available in most scanners. These adjustments are needed to correct for the deficiencies in the originals, printing conditions and to adjust for the special requirements of the customer. Chapter 16 deals with communication in color reproduction which includes the various production steps, processes and materials where communication is essential for optimum efficiency. The techniques and methods available for effective communication including prepress proofs as the visual communication tool are also presented in this chapter. Chapter 17 is dedicated to the concepts and fundamental techniques of digital image processing; several color retouching and pagination systems are briefly described in this chapter.

The discussion in the chapters is supplemented by the reproduction of control facilities available in four different scanners: Crosfield Magnascan 645, Dainippon Screen SG-608, Hell 399ER and RZ 200-S. During the presentation of various functions, the control panels of the DS SG-608 and Hell 399ER are reproduced part by part during each related discussion. However, for the Crosfield Magnascan 645 and RZ 200-S, the entire panel is reproduced each time and the buttons in the panel relating to the specific functions are highlighted with tints, enlarged and reproduced separately for clarity. Other such illustrations are also reproduced similarly when specific controls are shown along with the entire panel or group of controls.

The author chose the four scanners because they represented a cross section of the different types of drum scanners available in the industry. Once the readers become familiar with the adjustment capabilities available in these scanners, they should have no problem in relating their knowledge to other types of scanners.

All possible precautions were taken to insure the accuracy of the content. The discussion relating to each of the four brands of scanners was checked for accuracy with an experienced operator or expert familiar with the particular equipment in question. The author welcomes comments from the readers which may help to improve the next edition of this book.

R. K. Molla
West Virginia Tech
Montgomery, West Virginia

Acknowledgement

During the months of researching and writing this book, the author was fortunate to get a large number of friends, scholars, experts, well wishers and industry representatives involved in this publication. He owes sincere appreciation to the following companies for their generous support in the specific areas of production as indicated below:

Arcata Graphics: Bindery
Chapman Printing Company: Printing
DuPont De Nemours Co.: Proofing materials
Eastman Kodak Company: Jacket cover
Hoechst Celanese Corp.: Proofing materials
S. Rosenthal & Company: Typesetting
Westvaco Paper Co.: Paper

Many thanks are offered to those friends and well wishers who provided encouragement and active support for this project:

Bill Campbell, Chapman Printing Company
Cam Hitchcock, DuPont De Nemours Company
Charles Rinehart, Eastman Kodak Company
Harold Sterne, Rosenthal & Company
Fran Welch, Westvaco Paper Company
Bob Wilcox, Arcata Graphics

The author is greatly indebted to those who reviewed the manuscript during its preparation; without their thoughtful input, this book would have been less complete and less accurate:

Joyce Anderson, Eikonix Corporation
Mike Blum, California Polytechnic State University
Dudley Boden, Crosfield Electronics
Paul Borth, International Prepress Association
Marta and Stahly Brown, Stamar Studios
Richard Condon, Eastman Kodak Company
Scott Cornish, USA Today
Mike Ditchen, West Virginia Tech
Gary Field, California Polytechnic State University
Don Hutcheson, Royal Zenith Corporation
Werner Knepper, Hell Graphic Systems
John McReynolds, X-Rite Company
Steve Mott, California Polytechnic State University
Art Procter, Hoechst Celanese Corporation
Charles Rinehart, Eastman Kodak Company
Brad Ross, Crosfield Electronics
Mark Tonkovich, Hell Graphic Systems
Steve Walker, DuPont De Nemours Company
Gary Worthington, PROSE Writing and Editing
Janet Worthington, West Virginia Tech
M. Yamada, Dainippon Screen Mfg. Company

His gratitude is offered to the following persons for granting permission to reproduce illustrations, photographs and other related copyright materials:

Dudley Boden, Crosfield Electronics
Deborah Bongiorno, Rochester Inst. of Technology
Ed Boudreau, Scitex
Timothy W. Combs, Fuji Photo Film
Ed Friedlander, Royal Zenith Corporation
Sylvia Ingwersen, Dr. -Ing. Rudolf Hell GmbH
Faith A. Kluntz, BYTE
Dennis E. Mason, DS America
Charles E. Sack, Hell Graphic Systems
Enrica Santelli, Royal Zenith Corporation
Richard Warner, Graphic Arts Technical Foundation

Special thanks goes to Mark Eaton and Karl Mayer of Chapman Printing Company, Bill Lovisek, John Reh and James Walsh of Hell Graphic Systems for the color separations; Kay Cook, Cris Buckley and Libby Oliver of West Virginia Tech for corrective typesetting; Wendy Preston, Tom Vincze, Patty Garrison and Cris Lantz, his students at CalPoly for some of the drawings and photographs; other students, Rich Berry of CalPoly, Tamara Tatu and Paul Mornault of West Virginia Tech for the helpful suggestions during the writing of the manuscript; Joann Toney, also from West Virginia Tech for the help in various areas of production; and Jerry Walker of Jarret Printing Company for printing the last 16 pages.

The author would like to recognize an outstanding educator, teacher, friend and author, Dr. Edward C. Pytlik, Professor, Department of Technology Education, West Virginia University. Authorship of a book had never been an ambition even in his wildest dreams. If this publication meets the slightest criteria in this respect, then the credits must go to Dr. Pytlik. The author still remembers Ed Pytlik's endless patience in trying to teach him how to write while advising the dissertation.

Last, but not the least, his deep appreciation to Bob Gillespie, President; Tom Jones, Vice President; Martha Shouldis, Dean; and Jack Nuckols, Chairman, West Virginia Institute of Technology for their encouragement during the preparation of the manuscript.

Special Notice

To Whom It May Concern

In this publication, control facilities available in four different scanners are discussed and the panel pictures are reproduced to illustrate the concepts and principles of electronic color separation. These scanners are Crosfield Magnascan 645, Dainippon Screen SG-608, Hell 399ER and Royal Zenith 200-S. The illustrations have definitely helped to raise the quality of this publication and have made electronic color separation easier to understand. The author expresses his sincere gratitude to the four scanner vendors for providing generous help, support and granting permission to reproduce the various illustrations and control panels. It must be indicated here that during the preparation of this manuscript, there was no intention whatsoever on the part of the author, implied, expressed or otherwise, to present one of the scanners as better than any other. It is possible that some positive qualities of one or more of each of the scanners may have been unintentionally left out. However, it is re-emphasized that the purpose of this publication is not to compare the quality of the scanners, but to explain the various concepts of electronic separation and their relationship to different types of scanners. A section consisting of the names and addresses of various equipment manufacturers and vendors follows the bibliography at the end. If the reader is interested in learning more about particular equipment, then he/she should contact the appropriate company to get the information.

The four scanners used in the publication are superior in quality and they were state of the art equipment at the time of the writing. However, the scanner technology is constantly changing; new models are being introduced every year incorporating the latest innovations for consistency and predictability in the separations and convenience in the operation of the equipment. In the next edition, the author plans to update the content through consultation with the scanner vendors and experts in the industry. Consequently, information on the latest equipment and techniques will be incorporated in the content.

Sincerely,

R. K. Molla

Contents

Chapter 4 HALFTONE 79

Chapter 5 COPY EVALUATION AND SCANNING AIDS 97

Chapter 6 BASIC CALIBRATION 113

Chapter 7 SPECIFIC ADJUSTMENTS 127

Chapter 8 CORRECTION FOR COLOR CAST 129

Chapter 9 TONE REPRODUCTION 137

Chapter 10 COLOR CORRECTION 167

Chapter 11 GRAY BALANCE 191

Chapter 12 UNDER COLOR REMOVAL (UCR) 203

Chapter 13 UNDER COLOR ADDITION (UCA) 211

Chapter 14 GRAY COMPONENT REPLACEMENT (GCR) 215

Chapter 15 UNSHARP MASKING (USM) 225

Chapter 16 COLOR COMMUNICATION 241

Chapter 17 INTRODUCTION TO DIGITAL IMAGE PROCESSING 253

Chapter 1
Introduction: An Overview

Human eyes behave as if they contain three color receptors. Each receptor is sensitive to one of the three colors of the visible light: red, green, and blue. The color the eyes see in an object depends on how much red, green, and blue lights are reflected to the eye. Black results when no light is reflected. All the reflected red, green, and blue lights produce white. Equal amounts of reflected red, green, and blue lights in different proportions will produce white or various shades of gray with no dominant color.

Color pictures frequently contain hundreds of small areas of distinctly different colors. To print such pictures using each color ink would be impractical. Fortunately, most colors of the original can be reproduced by printing a mixture of only four colors: cyan, also known as process blue; magenta, also known as process red; yellow; and black. Cyan absorbs red, magenta absorbs green, and yellow absorbs blue; these three inks are printed in various proportions on white paper to reflect the same proportion of red, green and blue as the original. Black is printed to increase contrast and make up for the deficiency of the inks.

During printing, each printing color is transferred to the paper by a separate printing plate. To make these printing plates, four negatives or positives are required, each recording densities for the varying amounts of cyan, magenta, yellow, and black it will carry. Making these negatives or positives is called *"color separation."*

The use of only four colors to reproduce thousands of colors is possible because the eyes are basically responsive to three broad sections of the spectrum (visible white light): red, green, and blue. The many distinctly different colors that are seen in a picture are simply mental interpretations of varying proportions of red, green, and blue signals transmitted to the brain through the optic nerves.

To understand color separation, it is essential to have a basic knowledge of the color itself. To know color, some of the natural and fundamental behavior of light must be understood, because without light there is no color.

LIGHT AND COLOR

Definition of Color

Color can be defined as a sensation or as an object that absorbs different wavelengths of light to different degrees. As a sensation, the first definition is psychological and as an object, the second definition is physical. The color is seen as a result of the physical modification of light by colorants, observed by the human eyes, and interpreted in the brain. As such, the production of colors requires three things: (1) a source of light, (2) an object which it illuminates, and (3) the eye and the brain to perceive the color.

THE SOURCE — THE LIGHT

Light is a form of electromagnetic radiation which travels in a wave form similar to the ripples caused by tossing a stone into a pond. Light waves are the same as radio waves, but they are much smaller. Only a very narrow band of the light rays is visible; on one side of the band are the infrared rays, and on the other side are the X-rays and Gamma rays. Each of these types of energy has a unique frequency. The wavelength of visible light lies between 380 to 770 nanometers (nm). (A nanometer is about one billionth of a meter.) These rays, also called the visible spectrum, show a gradual color change as seen in a rainbow or through a prism. The spectrum can be divided into six groups of colors: violet, blue, green, yellow, orange, and red. Each of these colors has different wavelength, violet has the shortest, and red the longest (see Figure 1.1).

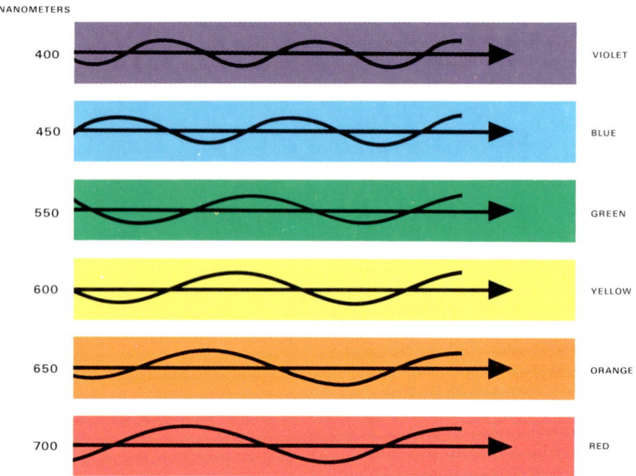

Figure 1.1. Wavelengths of different components of the white light

Color Temperature of a Light Source

Color temperature is assigned to any light source by matching it visually against a light radiating from a heated black body. The best radiator is an absolute black body which absorbs all the radiation that falls on it. As shown in Figure 1.2, a small cavity in a graphite block serves as a practical black body. Any light that enters the hole is reflected many times from the walls and is partly absorbed at each reflection until no light remains. The radiation that escapes from the hole is called the black body radiation.

When the black body is heated, the spectral distribution emitted by the body depends on the Kelvin temperature of the black body and not on the material of which it is made. Kelvin temperature is the temperature of the black body plus 273 degrees Celsius. The system is named in honor of its developer Lord Kelvin.

Color temperature may be assigned to any light source by matching it visually against the light radiating from the heated black body. For example, when the color of the light radiating from the black body at a certain temperature matches

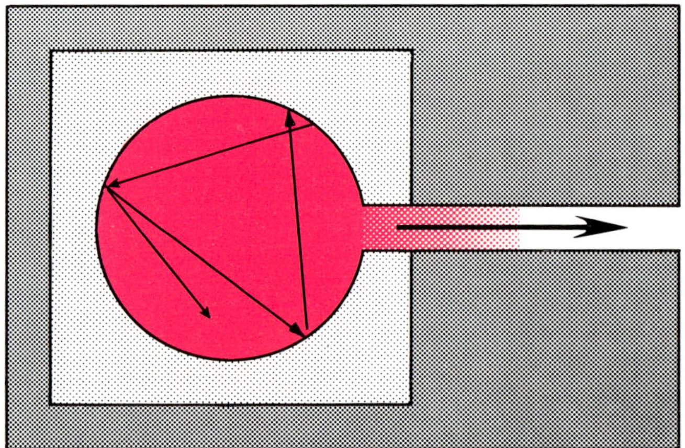

Figure 1.2. A black body radiation

the color of any other light source, then the source is said to have the same color temperature as the black body radiation. At a low temperature (below 800°K) only infrared radiation results. Table 1 represents the approximate color temperature of different sources of light.

TABLE 1

Light Source	**Color Temperature** (Degrees Kelvin)
Clear blue sky	12,000 to 27,000
Overcast sky	7,000
Daylight fluorescent lamp	6,500
Blue flash lamp	6,000
Sunlight	4,300 to 6,500
White flame carbon arc	5,000
Clear flash lamp	3,600
Photoflood	3,480
Gas filled tungsten filament lamp	3,200 to 2,865
House lamp	2,400 to 2,700
Candle flame	1,500 to 1,900

The higher the temperature, the bluer the light; the lower the temperature, the redder the light. In color work, a balanced or neutral output of the light is required. When the light source contains equal amounts of red, green, and blue lights, it is neutral. A neutral output is obtained with a color temperature of approximately 5,000°K.

Light Behavior

The second requirement for the production of color is the colored object. When a light strikes an object, it will reflect, transmit, or be absorbed by the object (see Figure 1.3). Absorption depends in part on the chemical components of pigments and dyes which will absorb certain frequencies of

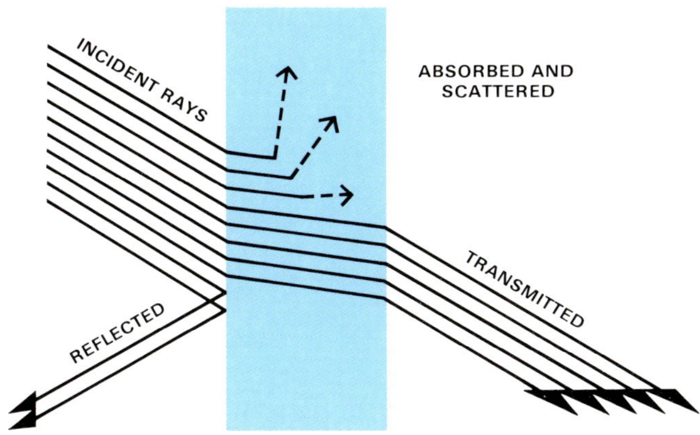

Figure 1.3. Light behavior when a beam of light strikes a thick sheet of glass

light. Objects which reflect or transmit light do so in one of three ways: diffusely, specularly, or by scattering. A reflective or translucent object with low gloss will diffusely reflect or transmit light. This occurs when the reflected or transmitted light travels in all directions. However, when a surface increases in smoothness, becomes glossy, the light will be specularly reflected, that is, reflected in only one direction (see Figure 1.4). Similarly, a clear transparent object will

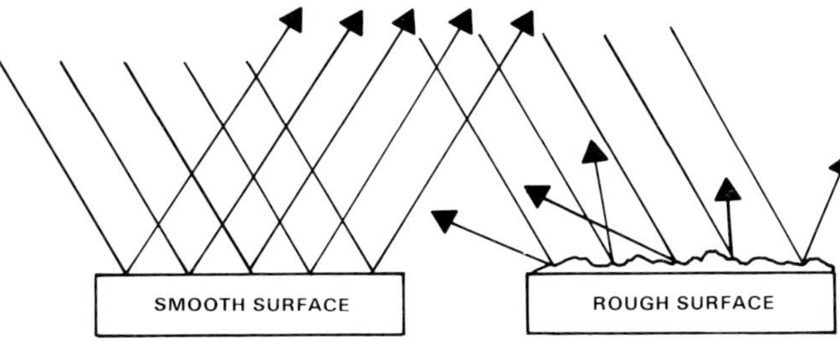

Figure 1.4. Reflection of light from smooth and rough surfaces

transmit light specularly. Examples of the scattering of light are the blue appearance of the sky and the red appearance of the same sky during sunrise and sunset. These colors are caused by the effects of the atmospheric particles on sunlight. Still there are other ways that objects may affect light: they are by refraction, diffraction, interference and polarization.

As shown in Figure 1.5, refraction is the bending of a light ray when it crosses the boundary between two different materials, as from air into water. This change in direction is due to a change in speed, light travels faster in empty space and slows down upon entering matter. An example is the dispersion of sunlight into the rainbow or spectrum colors by a prism.

Diffraction is the bending of light waves around the edge of an obstacle. However, the amount of bending is very small, about one fifty-thousandth of an inch.

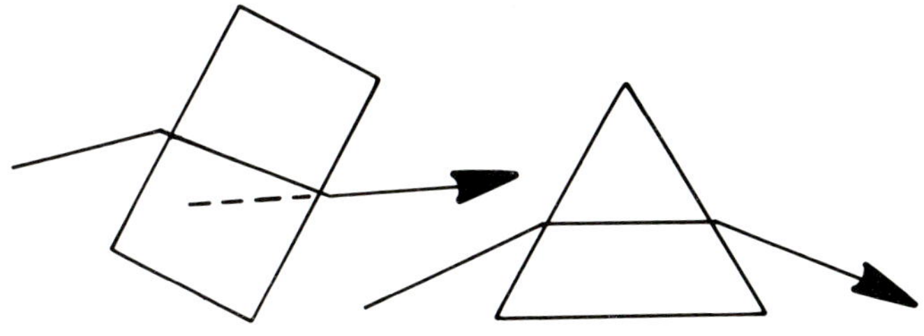

Figure 1.5. Refraction of light when it passes through two different materials

Interference is an effect that occurs when two light waves of equal frequency are superimposed. This often happens when light rays from a single source travel by different paths to the same point. If the two waves meet out of phase, the result is a wave whose amplitude (peak value) is the difference of the original amplitudes. This is called destructive interference. If the two waves are in phase, they may combine to form a new wave of the same frequency. The process of forming this new wave is called constructive interference (see Figure 1.6).

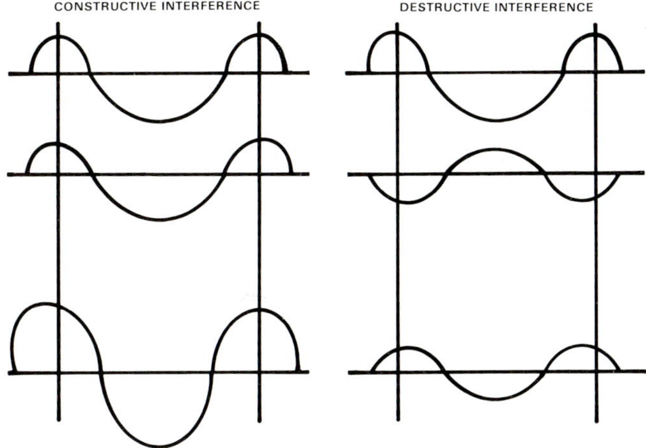

Figure 1.6. Effect of light interference

Polarized light waves are restricted in their direction of vibration. Normal light waves vibrate in an infinite number of directions perpendicular to their direction of travel. When the components of vibration are present in only one direction, the light is plane polarized. This is explained with Figure 1.7. Some sunglasses utilize this principle.

All colors are produced by selective absorption, and reflection or transmission. Substances do not reflect, transmit or absorb the same proportions of all light waves. For example, as shown in Figure 1.8, a red apple reflects only the red rays of the visible spectrum, so when white light strikes it, the apple only reflects the red and absorbs the other visible

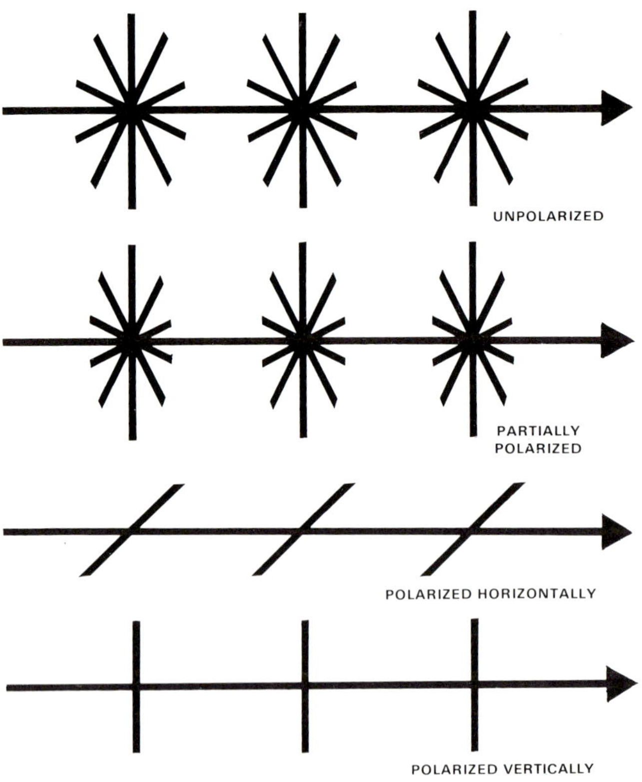

Figure 1.7. Lights with different degrees of polarization

rays. The same principle is applied to the production of color by selective transmission as shown with the example of a glass of wine in Figure 1.8.

If a white light is directed towards a white sheet of paper, the reflected light appears to be white if the sheet reflects all colors uniformly. When transparent colored inks are printed on a white sheet of paper, part of the white light is absorbed by the ink. The remaining light that is reflected by the paper through the ink is the only color seen. When all the light is blocked or absorbed, nothing is seen. This absence of color is defined as black.

COLOR PERCEPTION

The final requirement for the production of color is the human perceptor. Not only do humans respond physically to radiant energy, but their response is also dependent on other conscious responses and behaviors such as attention, memory, motivation, and emotion. Considering all the variables in light sources and objects which alter the appearance and quality of color, adding the human perceptor makes it difficult to define color accurately.

There is no single or universal system for the classification and specification of color that takes into account all the factors that affect perception. However, from time to time, attempts were made to classify and specify colors. A brief description of only the important ones will be presented here.

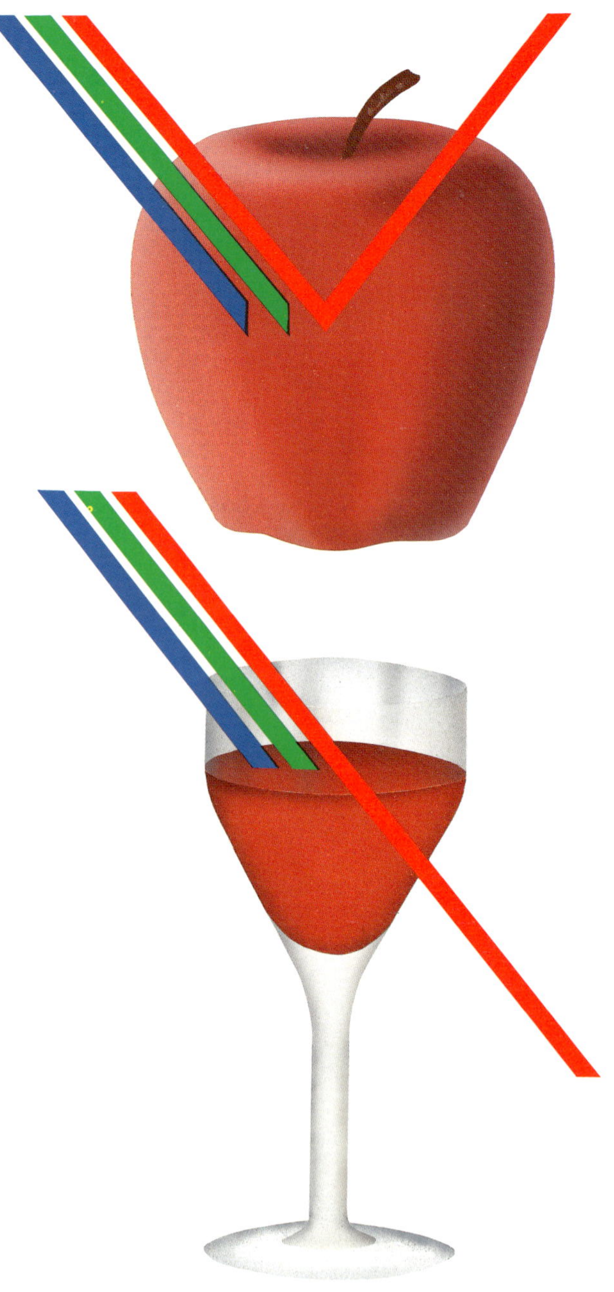

Figure 1.8. The red apple and the red wine absorb the green and blue portions of the white light; the apple reflects the red and the wine transmits it.

ISCC — NBS

One way to classify color is to use a descriptive adjective for each color such as strong, vivid, dark, pale, etc. For example, the relationship between dark and vivid green are the same as between dark and vivid red. This is the basis of the ISCC — NBS (Inter-Society Color Council — National Bureau of Standards) system of color names.

Munsell Color System

This system arranges all colors on the basis of their appearance and classifies colors according to hue, chroma, and value. These are often termed as the three dimensions of color. Often defined by a scientist, light has three attributes: dominant wavelength, luminance, and purity. These definitions are directly related to the three dimensions — dominant wavelength corresponds to the hue of a color, luminance to the brightness, and purity to the saturation (see Figure 1.9).

Hue is the name of the color which places the color in its correct position in the spectrum. For example, if a color is described as blue, it is distinguished from yellow, red, green, or other colors.

Saturation refers to the degree of hue in a color — it is that quality of color which enables an observer to state how strongly colored it is. A neutral white, gray, or black is considered to have zero saturation. As such, saturation may also be referred to as how much it differs from a neutral gray. Closer to neutral it has less saturation; away from neutral, it has more saturation. Saturation is a color sensation by which one can distinguish a hue as being pale or rich, weak or strong. For example, a jacket may be dull green, bright green, or brilliant green depending on the differences in saturation.

Brightness is the term used to describe differences in the intensity of light reflected from or transmitted by the colored image. It is the primary visual sensation by which one can detect the presence of light. For example, a shirt may be described as dark blue or light blue. The hue of the shirt is blue, but the terms dark or light distinguishes the brightness of one shirt from the other.

Colorant Mixture

This system of classifying colors is a colorant-mixture plan and is used effectively in specifying ink colors. It depends on the systematic mixture of pigments or dyes. The method utilizes a limited number of dyes or pigments to develop a full range of colors by systematically varying the proportions of the basic pigment or dye. A PMS® color swatch book used by the printers to specify printing inks is an example of this type.

CIE

In all the above systems, colors are subjectively compared to color standards available for each particular system. However, in 1931, an objective approach of color specification was first adopted as an international standard by the Commission Internationale d'Eclairage (CIE) as the stimulus-response system for colorimetric specification. To reduce the variability, the CIE adopted certain specified conditions for color specification. These include standard light sources, standard viewing conditions, and standard observer. According to the CIE system, a color description requires a set of three numbers, designated as tristimulus values denoted as x, y and z. These numbers correspond roughly to the relative amounts of red, green, and blue lights reflected by a colored object.

COLOR MEASUREMENT

There are three basic methods of measuring and specifying color:

1. By visual comparison — The visual comparison can be done with a standard set of color material such as in a Munsell System under standardized viewing conditions.

2. By measurement through three filters — A densitometer normally contains the filters to measure color. The method is simple and satisfactory if the sensitivity of the instrument for the various colors of the spectrum is properly related to the eye. However, in color reproduction, it is preferable to use an instrument whose spectral sensitivity corresponds to that of the photographic material used in the color separation process.

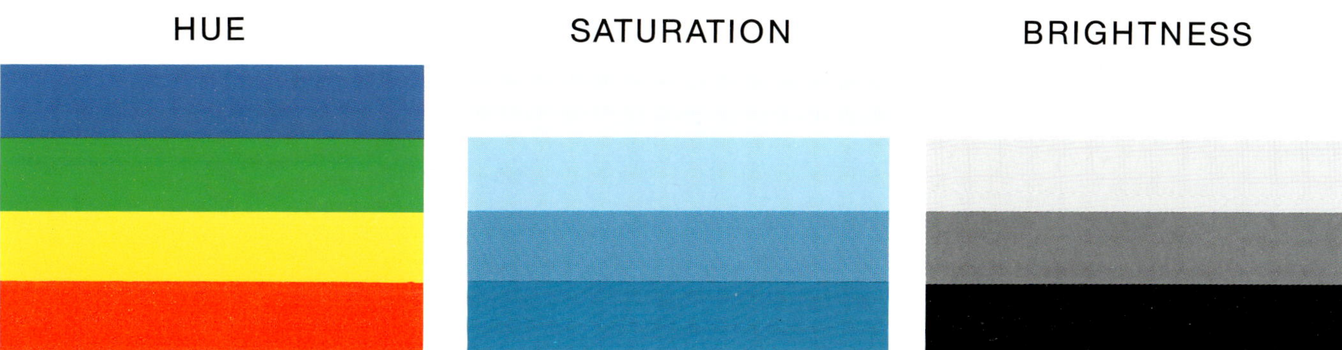

Figure 1.9. Three dimensions of color

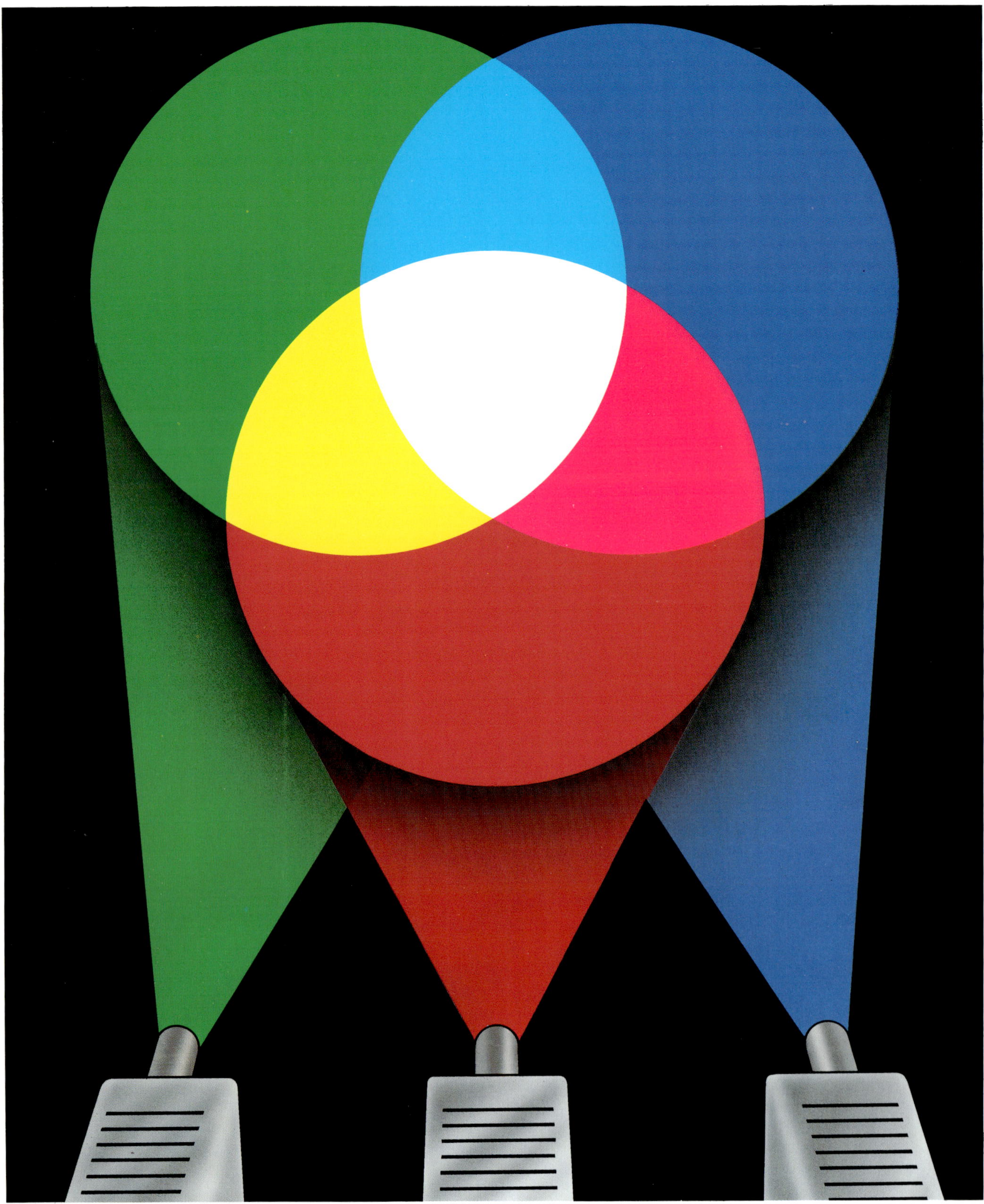

Figure 1.10. The additive color mixing — red, green, and blue lights are combined to produce other colored lights

3. By spectrophotometry — Spectrophotometry is the measurement of each wave length of light reflected or transmitted by an object. This measurement gives a more detailed description of the light absorption properties of the object. The amount of light reflected at each wave length of the visible spectrum can be plotted to give a spectrophotometric curve. The curve is an accurate representative of the colored object and a set of numbers can be calculated from the curve to represent the color of the object.

COLOR MATCHING

The most common method of identifying color within a "color space" is a three-dimensional geometry. The three color attributes — hue, saturation, and brightness — are measured, assigned numeric values, and plotted within the color space. The latest color matching system based on human perception is known as the CIE-UCS (Commission Internationale d'Eclairage- Uniform Chromaticity Scale). In color reproduction it is known as uvL space. The uvL space is concerned with predicting color changes as the human eye perceives these changes. In practice, the uvL space is not perfectly uniform, but it does represent an improvement on the CIE chromaticity diagram.

Metameric Color Matching Problems

Metameric color matching is a problem faced by personnel in the production steps of process color reproduction. Under one lighting condition, two colors make a perfect match, but look quite different under another. Many printers have had the experience of carefully matching colors in the pressroom, and after comparing the finished job in sunlight, finding that it did not look like the color sample at all.

PROCESS COLOR REPRODUCTION

So far the description involves the perception, description, and measurement of color. But how do they relate to the reproduction of color? A brief discussion on the various concepts and principles of light and color relating to process color reproduction follows.

Color Mixing

Two natural phenomena of light, additive and subtractive color mixing principles, are at the core of four color process reproduction. The additive principle is based on the properties and characteristics of colored light. When white light is projected on a screen from a projector fitted with colored filters, various colored lights produced by different filters can be combined to make other colored lights (see Figure 1.10). The components of the visible light (spectrum) are red, green, and blue, and these three colors can also be combined in pairs to make other colors. The combination of blue and green lights will make cyan (blue-green), red and blue will make magenta (blue-red), and red and green will make yellow. Color television works on this principle; the variety of colors seen on a television screen are actually a combination of three projected lights — red, green, and blue.

In the subtractive principle, one or more colors from the white light can be subtracted or removed by absorption as shown in Figure 1.11. A color filter or a layer of colorant, like a printing ink, absorbs some light, and the remaining colors are reflected to the eyes. For process color reproduction, colorants are selected in such a way that each absorbs approximately one of the three components of the white light. The process inks used are cyan, magenta, and yellow; cyan absorbs red, magenta absorbs green, and the yellow absorbs blue. The inks are transparent and they can be combined in any proportion. When they are printed on white paper, they can be made to reflect various amounts of red, green, and blue.

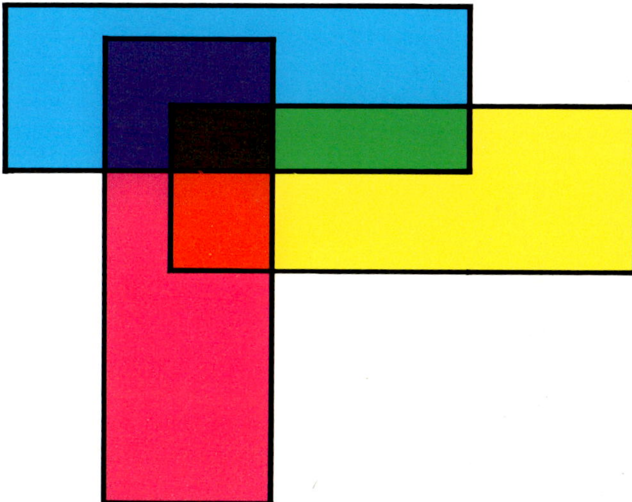

Figure 1.11. The subtractive color mixing — cyan, magenta, and yellow inks are printed on white paper to selectively absorb and reflect components of the white light

In the additive principle, the primary colors for the visible spectrum are red, green, and blue lights; whereas, in the subtractive principle, the primaries are cyan, magenta, and yellow colorants or pigments (see Figure 1.11). They are called primary colors because they cannot be produced by combining two colors of the same group..Other characteristics of these primary additive and subtractive colors are when any of the two primaries are combined from one group, they make a primary color for the other group. For example, when red and green lights are combined, they make yellow light; similarly, when the cyan and yellow inks are printed together on white paper, they reflect green. When all three primary additive lights are combined, they produce white. On the other hand, when the cyan, magenta, and yellow inks are combined, they subtract all the colors of the visible light and produce black.

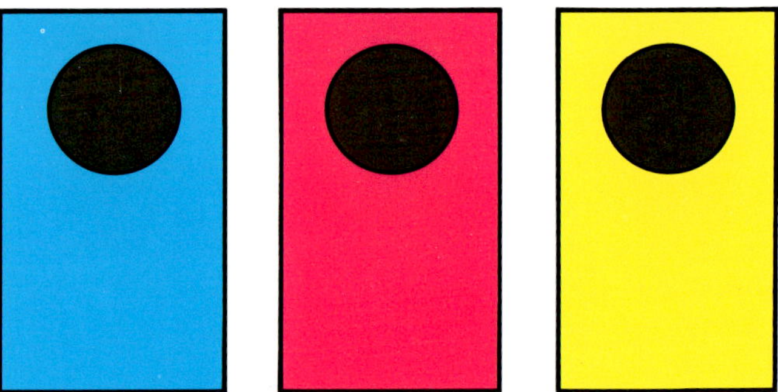

Figure 1.12. The effects of placing red, green, and blue filters over cyan, magenta, and yellow pigments

Complementary Colors and Separation Filters

Since an object reflects or transmits various proportions of red, green, and blue, it is assumed that to reproduce the same object, various combinations of cyan, magenta, and yellow pigments can be printed on a white substrate to simulate the object by reflecting the same amount of red, green, and blue. These colorants will selectively absorb and reflect the various combination of the three colors of the white light. When two of these colorants are combined, they become complementary to the third colorant. For example, when magenta and yellow are combined, they become complementary to cyan, because magenta and yellow (red) when combined with cyan will absorb all the light and consequently produce black.

A transparent color filter transmits its own color and absorbs the other colors. The color which is absorbed by the filter will be sensed as black by the eye or photographic emulsion and will be a clear image on a negative. The panchromatic emulsion will be sensitive to the light transmitted through the filter. It will be the black metallic silver and nonimage areas in the negative. Consequently, when red is used as a filter and placed in the light path of cyan (blue and green light) through this filter, the photographic film emulsion will see the cyan as black. This will become an image on the film. Similarly, the green is complementary to magenta and blue is complementary to yellow, and when the green and blue filters are used, the film will record the magenta and yellow clear images on the film respectively (Figure 1.12).

These natural phenomena of color make possible a combination of one or more of the three colorants in various proportions. They absorb and reflect various proportions of red, green, and blue light to match the colors reflected or transmitted from the copy. For example, a reproduction of red is made possible by printing magenta over yellow — the magenta ink absorbs the green, the yellow ink absorbs the blue, and the remaining color is red.

In reproduction using only three printing inks, the additive and subtractive principles are responsible for many color sensations. To match the reproduction with the original, it is assumed that the ink mixture reflection from the reproduction matches the red, green, and blue balance of the original colors. All the colors are already reflecting from the white paper in equal balance. To print any particular color does not require that an ink matches this color. What is required is that some proportions of the three transparent inks are printed. The inks act like partial filters during reflections of the red, green, and blue lights from the white paper to the eyes. Therefore, process color reproduction can be justifiably termed as taking color away, rather than putting color on paper.

The major objective at the color separation stage in process color printing is to produce three separate images on film which contain information for each of the major printing colors: cyan, magenta, and yellow. The initial procedure for doing this is similar in both conventional and scanning processes. The process consists of illuminating the original copy with a balanced white light and then separating three images by placing red, green and blue filters in between the copy and the film. Figure 1.13 is a simplified diagram of the various steps in four color process reproduction.

Halftones

Except gravure, no printing process can print varying thicknesses of ink to match the various shades of the original. Instead, when photographs or color pictures are reproduced, they are broken into tiny dots of different sizes by means of a halftone screen. Each area in the picture is converted into proportional dot sizes to give the same visual appearance as the original (Figure 1.14). The dots are so small that the human eye cannot distinguish each dot separately. In a color picture, a shade of red can be achieved by printing different proportions of both magenta and yellow dots. Depending on the areas of the paper covered by these dots, they will absorb different proportions of green and blue lights respectively, leaving only a shade of red light reflected from the paper. Similarly, green is created by overprinting yellow and cyan;

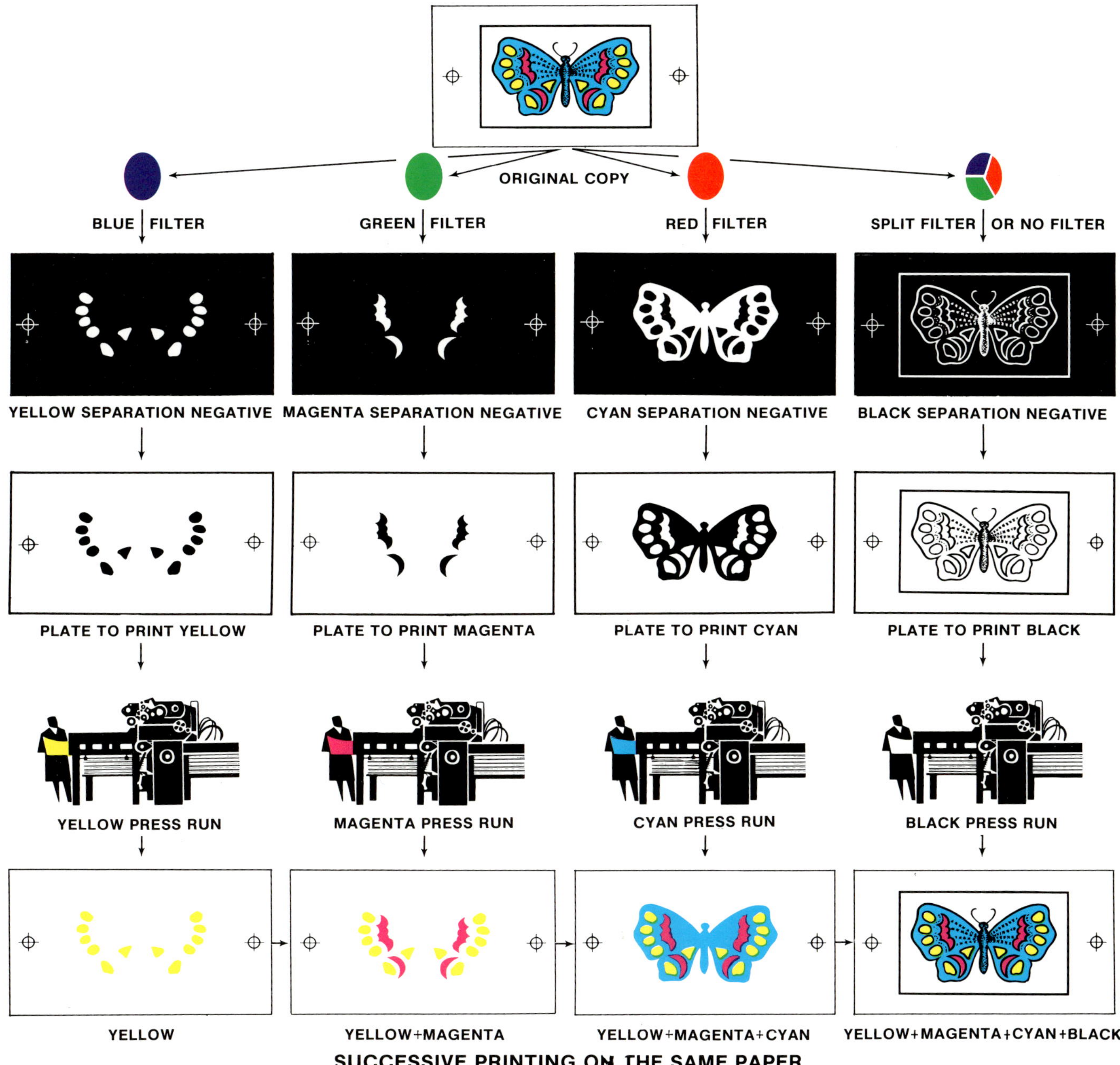

Figure 1.13. Production flow of a simplified process color reproduction

blue is formed with magenta and cyan. Varying the sizes of these dots alters both the hue and the lightness or darkness of the colors desired (see Figure 1.15).

Black Separation

In theory, black is produced on the press sheet when layers of cyan, magenta and yellow inks are overprinted, thus absorbing all the visible lights reflected from the paper. However, in practice, the printing inks do not absorb all of the available lights. A reddish-brown color rather than black is produced when the three colors overprint. This is because of the impurities in the process inks — more red, rather than a balanced overprint of the three colors is reflected to the eyes. Therefore, a black record of the original copy is needed for reproduction. The black printer, when added to the cyan,

Courtesy E. I. Du Pont De Nemours Co.

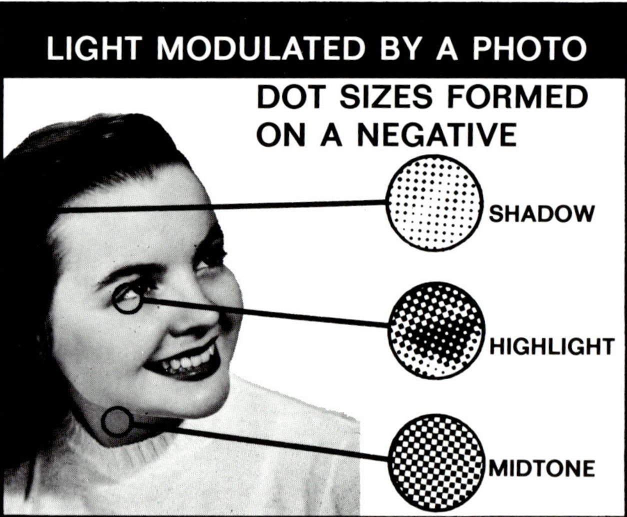

Figure 1.14. Enlarged portion of a halftone reproduction showing the dots produced in the highlight, middle-tone, and shadow areas in a negative

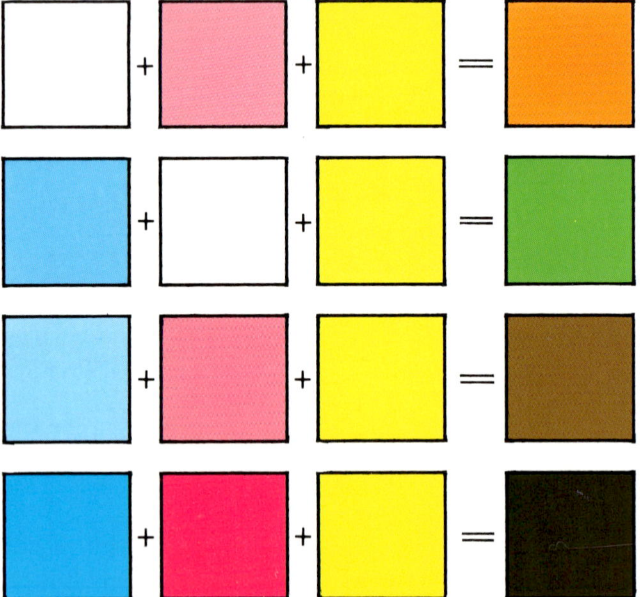

Figure 1.15. Production of various shades of colors by combining different proportions of cyan, magenta, and yellow

magenta, and yellow, will enhance the contrast of the final reproduction by making the dark shadow areas darker. Printing black over the three color reproduction will make the white areas appear whiter and will add detail and improve contrast in the shadow areas.

History of Color Separation

The printing of colored illustrations from wooden relief blocks using colored inks can be traced back to the fifteenth century. These early printings consisted of numerous blocks, virtually one for every color contained in the original picture.

Color as a sensation was not recognized until physicist Thomas Young read a paper to the Royal Society of London in 1802, explaining that a human retina possessed three different kinds of nerves which when stimulated caused a reflex of the respective nerve elements sensitive to violet, green, and red. At a later date, after Niepce had taken the first photograph and the other pioneers had established the early photographic processes, the famous Scottish physicist James Clerk Maxwell (1831-1879) wrote:

> It is almost a truism to say that color is a sensation, and yet by recognizing this simple fact Thomas Young clearly realized, nearly forty years ago, that the science of color must therefore be regarded as essentially a mental science. (Burden, p. 345)

Maxwell was the first person to employ the newly developed process of photography as a means for determining the relative amounts of red, green, and blue lights present in any color. He demonstrated the photographic procedure before the Royal Institution in London on May 17, 1861.

The idea of photographic color reproduction also appealed to two Frenchmen, Du Hauron and Cros. Working independently and unaware of Maxwell's experiment, their work and ideas during the year 1868 were very similar.

Du Hauron culminated his early experiments with the idea of a screen consisting of primary colored dots or lines coated with panchromatic emulsion — a photographic emulsion which is sensitive to all colored lights. In one of his many disclosures, Du Hauron suggested a triple sandwich, three suitably sensitized photographic emulsions assembled in layers. This arrangement was the forerunner of the integral tripack films. Du Hauron also invented a three-color camera in which three color-separated negatives were made simultaneously. Du Hauron wrote the following in an application for a French patent:

> We obtain by the aid of the photographic camera three negatives of the same object, the first negative through a green colored glass, the second negative through a violet colored glass, and the third negative through a orange-red glass. Then transparent positives are made by the pigment or a similar process by the aid of chromolithography, woodburytype or a toning process. From the first negative a red print is made, from the second a yellow print, and from the third a blue print. When the three prints are superimposed and thus combined we obtain a finished print which is a polychrome reproduction of nature. (Burden, p. 347)

The present state of the color separation technology has been the result of a two phase evolution during the last fifty years. The first phase consists of an improvement in the conventional method of color separation — separations done in a camera, in an enlarger, and with the contact method. These improvements have been attributed to the development of fast photographic emulsion, improved masking materials for color correction and tone reproduction, improved light sources for copy illumination like carbon arcs and pulsed xenon, and finally, the improvements in the quality of the contact screens. Parallel to these developments is the rapid conversion from letterpress to the offset printing process. The improvement in the design and speed of the offset press has further helped to attain excellence in the conventional method of color separation and reproduction.

The other phase resulted from the incorporation of sophisticated electronics and computers in the techniques and processes. During the last decade, with the introduction of color television and improved imaging on the screen, there has been a greater demand for realistic color in consumer packaging, magazines, newspaper, and virtually in all other facets of the printing industry. At this time, it seemed that the conventional method of color separation had reached a point where it fell short of meeting the demand for more, better, and cheaper color required by the industry. During the last decade, with the advent of microprocessor chips and memory devices, the scanner technology has emerged as a viable alternative to the conventional separation. The scanners gained immediate acceptance for the efficiency and accuracy in the production of color separations. Although scanners are expensive at the present time, the trend shows that the price of this equipment will be substantially lowered in the foreseeable future and may be affordable to a medium or even a small size printing plant within the next few years. Improvements and new innovations in the technology are continuing. Electronic dot generation devices, floppy disk drive units with expanded computer memory and functions, a usable storage of fixed gradations of different curve characteristics on floppy disks, and the use of gray component replacement (GCR) are but a few of the latest advances made in this direction.

THE LIMITED ACCURACY OF PROCESS COLOR REPRODUCTION

Color reproduction in the graphic communications industry is a complex process of division and reassembly. It starts with a continuous-tone original. Four sets of screened separations are made, plated, and printed on white paper with cyan, magenta, yellow, and black inks in registration. Then the reproduction is compared with the original for accuracy in color and for other details.

The following problems demonstrate that it is almost a miracle that the goal of matching the reproduction with the original is ever achieved:

1. The density range between the whitest paper and the darkest ink printed on that paper will rarely be over 1.50 when measured with a reflection densitometer. However, the difference in density of an original between the brightest highlight and the darkest shadow will frequently exceed that range. Consequently, no matter how expensive the press, paper, or inks are, often it is not possible to reproduce the range of density or shades from the copy to the press sheet.

2. Four-color reproduction starts with a continuous-tone original, but the separations are screened. The conversion to halftone from continuous-tone copy is necessary because the press can print only one density of ink; i.e., either it will print solid ink or leave the white of the paper. For halftones, the shades of the copy are broken down into various size dots proportional to the original tones. However, it is difficult to match the converted halftone print with a continuous-tone original. The dots are made tiny, with hopes that when the reproduction is seen, the entire area is seen as an integrated continuous-tone image rather than the individual dots.

3. The third major problem comes from the deficiency or contamination of the process inks. It is not that the ink or the dye manufacturer was not concerned about the dust, dirt, or other contaminants during the manufacturing of the ink, but simply that he could not make a pure ink which will be cost effective, will run smoothly in the press, and will do exactly what it is supposed to do. The cyan falls short of its expected theoretical performance: it absorbs less red, but it also absorbs some of the other two colors which it is not supposed to do; it acts as if it is contaminated with the other inks. The same is true for the magenta and yellow. It is as if the process ink cans were left open and someone got into the press room, put a dab of one ink into the other cans, mixed them up and left!

Other problems in process color reproduction include: an increase in dot size during printing compared to the original dot size on the plate (also called dot gain), ink trapping (when a coat of ink is printed on the top of another coat, the first coat does not accept all of the second coat), an imperfection in the color separation filters, and the paper quality (coated, uncoated, or newsprint).

In reality, four-color process reproduction is a compromise, because thousands of colors seen in the original are reproduced with only three or four inks. These few inks have to be combined and printed on the white paper in such a way that every spot of the reproduction reflects the same amount of red, green, and blue lights as the original. This is a difficult task, and a compromise is needed between perfect and practical aspects of the reproduction. Breaking up the continuous-tone original into dots for halftones, using a set of deficient process inks, gaining dots on the press, and other similar problems add to the impossibility of obtaining the desired reproduction.

Manual Color Correction

Much of the color correction in lithography and other graphic arts processes for the aforementioned deficiencies had traditionally been done manually. In the 1920's and 1930's, color separation of fine art calendar pictures sometimes took as much as a week's time to retouch for color correction.

Manual color correction in lithography is done by local dot etching (reducing the size of the dots by chemicals) on halftone separation negatives or positives; in photoengraving, by local work on plates; and in photogravure, by hand retouching of continuous-tone negatives or positives.

Color Correcting by Masking

Most of the problems in color reproduction discussed earlier can be successfully corrected by a technique called photographic masking. Masking involves the making of a weak image of the original on photographic film, and then placing this film in the optical system in registration with the original when making the separation negatives or positives. A detailed explanation of the photographic masking is presented in the chapter "Color Correction."

Masking methods are designed to carry out three functions: (l) to color correct for the ink deficiencies; (2) to control the density range (contrast) of the original and thus bring the range within the limits of the reproduction process (also called tone compression); and (3) to enhance the detail of the printed reproduction.

While manual color correction had been a dominant force in the past, photographic masking has gradually become increasingly popular because it takes less time than manual correction. With masking, normal color reproductions can now be accomplished without any hand correction.

COLOR SEPARATION SYSTEMS

Depending on how they are accomplished, color separation methods are classified into three main categories: direct screen color separation, indirect color separation, and electronic scanning.

Direct-Screen Color Separation

Direct-screen separations are made by exposing the copy directly to a panchromatic film emulsion through a gray halftone screen. The most popular equipment for making direct-screen separations are enlargers, cameras, and contact frames. Figure 1.16 is a flow diagram of a direct-screen separation.

The modern technique for the direct-screening of color transparencies dates from 1963 and is based upon the work initiated by F. R. Clapper of Eastman Kodak Company. The introduction of gray contact screens, improved masking materials, light sources, and various innovations in the equipment made direct screening attractive and economically feasible.

Condenser-type enlargers fitted with a high intensity pulsed xenon light source are available from several manufacturers. Optional equipment includes a push-button exposure console and electroluminescent panels for flash exposure. Process cameras with good construction, built-in pin register, vacuum back, balanced light, and high quality color corrected process lens are also used in the industry for direct-screen separation.

In direct-screen separations, exposures are made on fast panchromatic litho film. Masks with dye coupled materials or silver emulsions are used for color correction.

When the direct-screen separation is made in an enlarger, the mask is made in contact with the original using a pin register system to minimize problems associated with registration. After the mask is processed and dried, it is left in contact with the original transparency in the enlarger head throughout the separation procedure. In a camera, the mask is made by projecting the image onto the masking film using the pin register system. The separation films are then exposed through the masks, both positioned on the camera back. Since the same pin register is used for positioning and exposing the developed mask, there is no registration problem. The efficiency and acceptance of the system is such that little or no further correction is necessary after processing, and the color-corrected separations become ready for platemaking.

Indirect Color Separation

With indirect color separation, the halftone negatives or positives are not made directly from the original copy, but from intermediate continuous-tone separations. The use of continuous-tone negatives makes possible the broader use of masking procedures for tone control and color correction. Figure 1.17 is a flow diagram of an indirect separation.

Indirect color separation negatives are made in a camera, in an enlarger, or in a contact frame under a point light source. Masking principles for indirect separation are usually the same as the direct-screen separation — to reduce the tonal range, to enhance the detail, and to color correct for the ink deficiencies of the original.

Electronic Scanning

With all the problems of process color reproduction, matching the reproduction with the original is often consid-

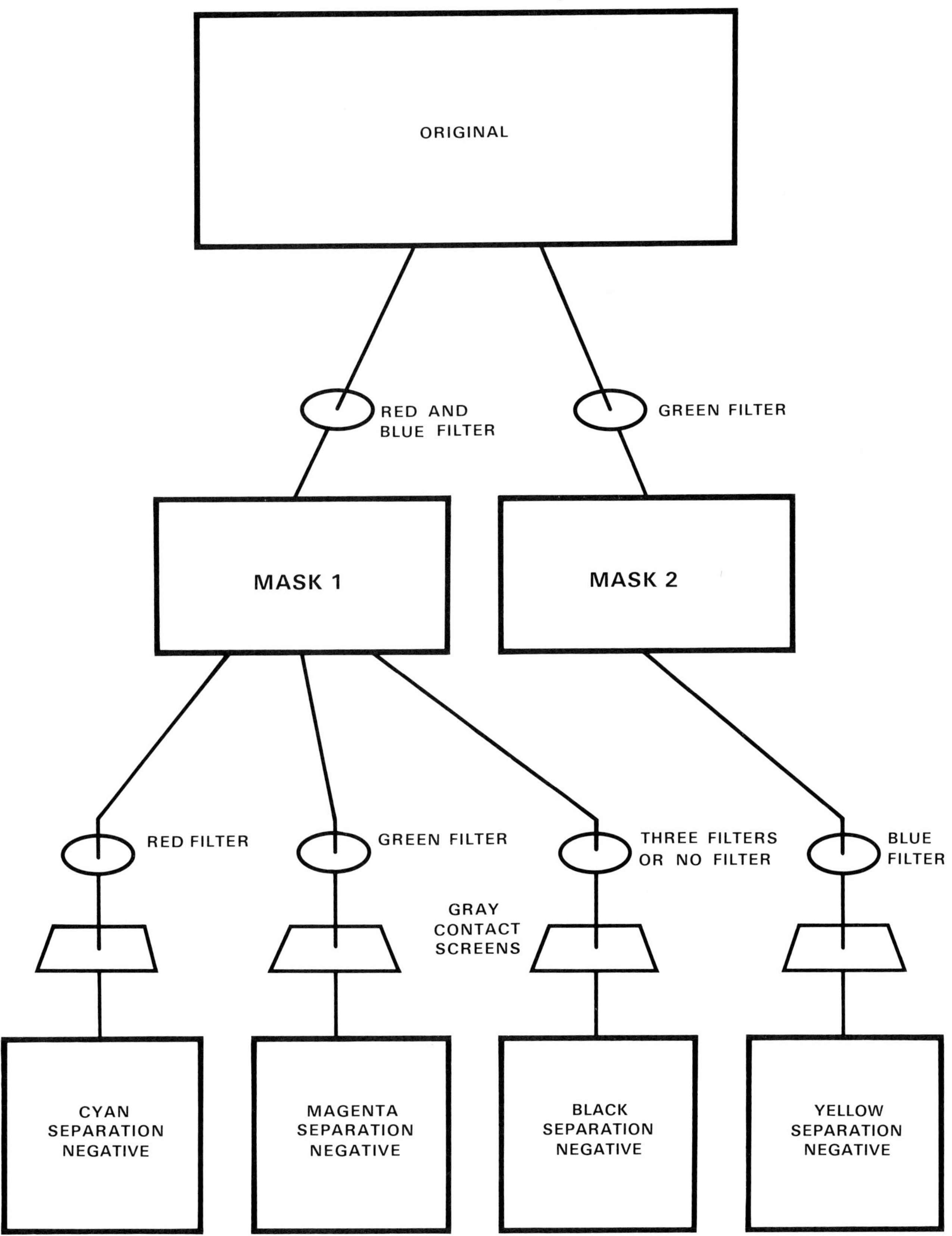

Figure 1.16. Flow diagram of a direct-screen separation

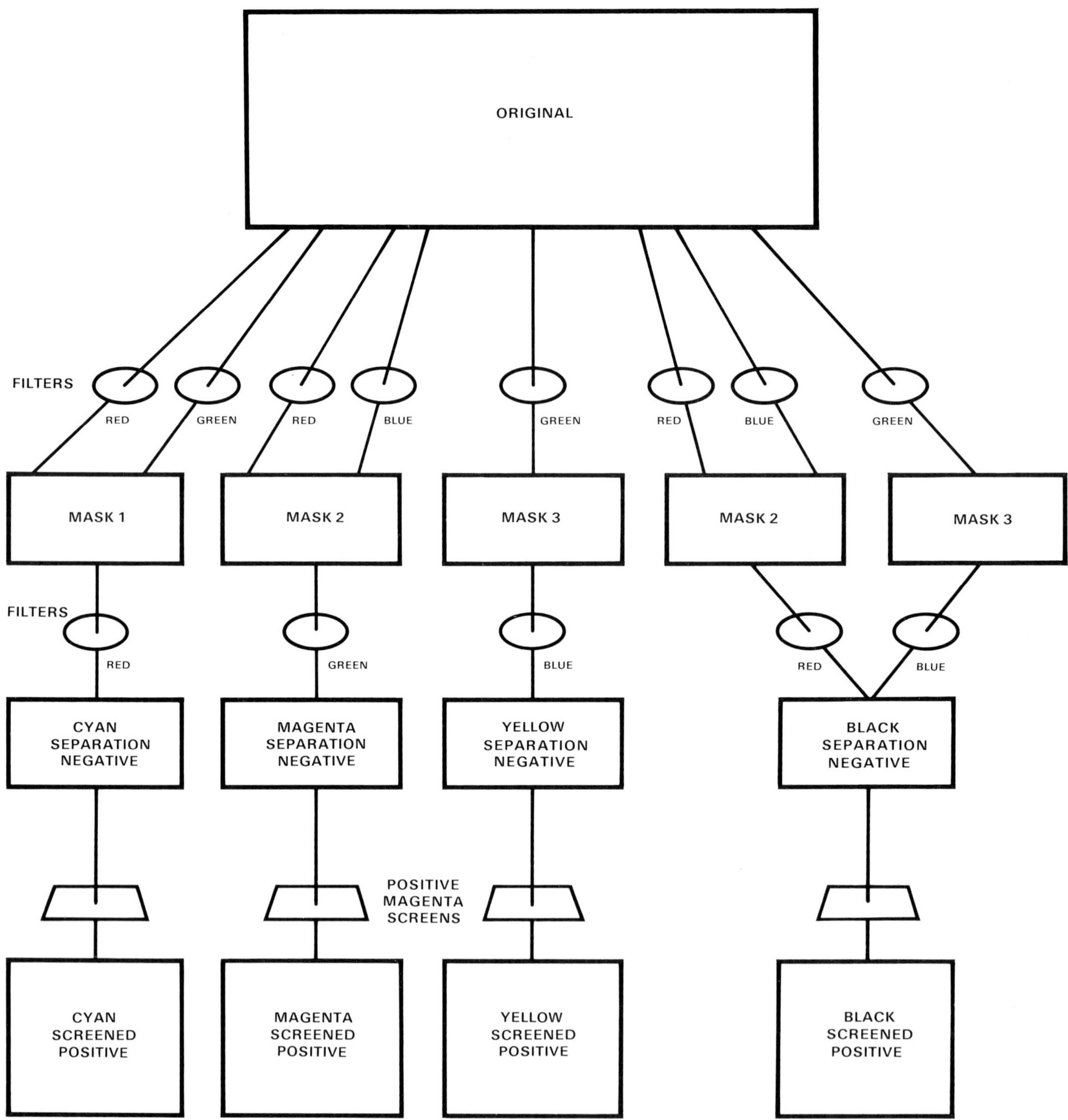

Figure 1.17. Flow diagram of an indirect separation

ered a miracle. However, during the last two decades, the development of computers and their involvement with the scanner technology in color reproduction has helped this miracle to happen.

The scanner radically differs in the technique for the separation of colors from the conventional equipment. Instead of exposing the entire copy at a time, the scanner analyzes, scans, and exposes a fine line of the original at a time. As shown in Figure 1.18, after the original and the film are mounted on the scanning and the exposing drums, a minute

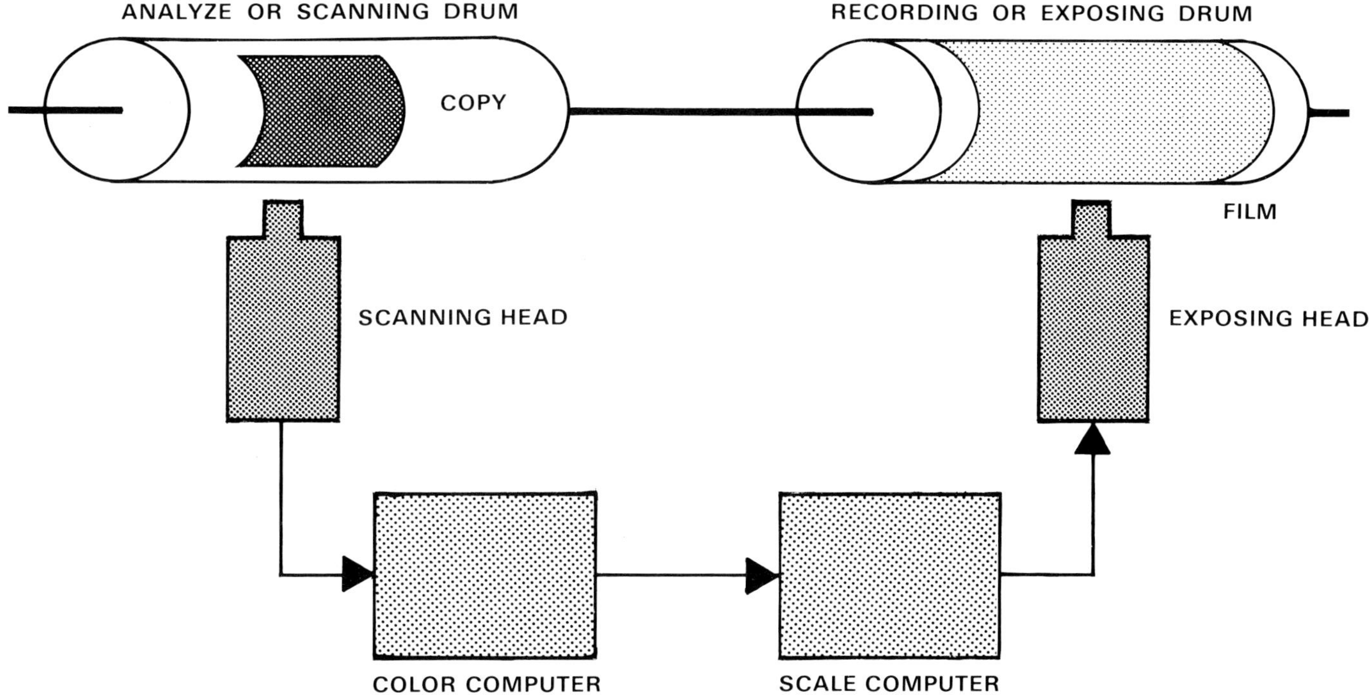

Figure 1.18. Principles of operation of a typical drum scanner

spot of copy is illuminated by the scanning light, which is split up and transmitted through the red, green, and blue filters containing information relating to cyan, magenta, and yellow ink values. As the drum rotates, the copy is scanned in a helical pattern, the information from each line of the copy passes through the computer, which in turn controls the exposure on the film. Each scanned line is modified by the computer to correct for different copy and printing variables according to the settings used in the operator's control panel.

An earlier survey by the Graphic Arts Technical Foundation indicates that the percentage of separations done on scanners in this country has grown from 35% in 1979 to 80% in 1983, a 230% increase in a span of only 4 years. And it is forecasted by many industry experts that color scanners will account for over 99% of all color separations by the year 2000. Another recent survey by the Graphic Arts Technical Foundation also indicates that process color printing has nearly doubled during the last 12 years. Curiously enough, in the mid '70s, the United States ranked well behind Europe and Japan in the overall acceptance of the latest technology; in 1976, 65% of all color separations in Europe were done on scanners, 95% in Japan, and this country accounted for only 35%. But the U.S. is catching up because of the necessity for faster, cheaper, and more accurate separations.

LIMITATIONS OF THE CONVENTIONAL METHOD

What is it in the new technology that the previous one did not provide? Before this question can be answered, a discussion on the limitations of the conventional color separation is in order. The following are some of the major problems with the conventional separation:

1. Conventional separation is an inefficient process compared to the other areas of process color reproduction. The indirect process is more flexible in terms of quality, however, it is a slow and expensive process.

2. Color correction by photographic masking is often a compromise. Some colors cannot be adequately corrected without affecting the other colors.

3. Because of the inadequate color correction by masking, hand correction is often needed for critical colors. This procedure is time consuming and the quality of the separations may be affected by human factors.

4. Attaining flexibility for tonal adjustments for different types of originals is difficult to achieve in conventional separation.

5. Conventional direct-screen separation normally uses high contrast panchromatic emulsion which is extremely sensitive to changes in room temperature, humidity, and process conditions. It is difficult to obtain consistent results using this type of emulsion with normal exposure and development. Handling the film in total darkness poses additional

problems.

MAJOR ADVANTAGES IN ELECTRONIC SEPARATION

In view of the above difficulties in the conventional separation, the following can be listed as the major advantages of electronic scanning:

1. Both conventional separation and electronic scanners use films and optical devices to produce images. However, in the conventional method, the entire picture is recorded at one time; whereas in the scanner, one small fraction of the picture is scanned and exposed at a time, thus providing better control and flexibility.

2. Tone control and correction possibilities are more versatile in scanners than in the conventional system. This is extremely useful, particularly with difficult originals which may require a lot of highlight or shadow contrast.

3. Color correction is more versatile in scanners than in the conventional equipment. In many cases the scanner can be programmed to correct certain difficult colors; e.g. flesh tones, wood tones, etc. without affecting any of the other colors in the original.

4. The factors which effect gray balance also effect tone reproduction and color correction. In a scanner, these effects may be quantified and compensated for at the separation stage quickly and inexpensively.

5. Under color removal (UCR) is much easier to achieve in a scanner, because there is no need to use any special masking steps as there is with conventional equipment.

6. Generation of the black printer in a scanner is far cleaner than in the photographic process. The scanner can be programmed to generate black only in the neutral areas of the original where all three colors are equally present; consequently it may be printed right through the entire tone scale without making the colors dirty. With the advent of better computers, generation of a full range black is possible in the scanner which can replace the gray components of the process colors. This concept is called gray component replacement (GCR). When separations are made with appropriate GCR adjustment, only a bare minimum of the process colors are required to be printed with a full range black for optimum results. GCR shows numerous advantages in the controlling of costs and production efficiency in the process color reproduction.

7. Any required degree of unsharp masking is possible in a scanner to preserve fine details in the separations.

8. Emphasis for highlight or shadow details is possible independently in the scanner.

9. The advent of the electronic dot generation scanners has significantly simplified and speeded up the steps. Without a contact screen, scanning is much faster, and because of direct laser exposure, cheaper films and less critical rapid access processing can be used for economy.

10. There is a wider enlargement and reduction capability in a scanner since the introduction of the digital computers. In some of the latest scanners, it is now possible to scan together a group of transparencies which has different color and tone characteristics.

11. With the introduction of several recent innovations, the scanner became more versatile, flexible, predictable, consistent, and easier to operate than ever before. Some of these latest innovations include: unlimited expansion of the scanner's capability with the use of an independent programmable computer and floppy disk drive; the incorporation of on-line and off-line monitors to check and adjust for the accuracy in the separations before exposing; the use of a totally digital set up for pinpoint consistency and predictability; the use of programmable halftone dot shapes and sizes stored on a floppy disk; and, the programming of simple stripping functions on a floppy disk.

Complete automation in the controlled production of color separation, color correction, and tone reproduction is the ultimate goal in full-color reproduction. The limiting factors in the desirable reproduction of a full-color subject are the need to the use of a halftone screen, the inability of a press to print exactly as desired, and the deficiency of the printing ink. However, the techniques for measuring these limiting factors are available, and make automatic color separation and correction possible. The single most important advance in scanning is the replacement of photographic masking by electronic masking. A scanner reduces the time required for the production of a set of separations from several hours to a few minutes. In addition, scanning provides the advantages of consistency and flexibility.

BASIC PRINCIPLES OF A SCANNER

The basic principles of a color scanner are similar to that of a photographic facsimile transmission system. However, in a facsimile system the receiver might be a great distance from the transmitter, but the scanner combines the transmitter and receiver in one piece of equipment. The transmitter in this case is the scanning unit and the receiver is the exposing unit. The computer connects the two units which in turn processes the input signals from the scanning unit to produce the output signals for the recording or exposing unit.

Figure 1.19 is a flow diagram of a drum scanner. The original copy to be scanned is a transparency or a reflection copy. For the transparency, a lamp within the scanning drum focuses a minute spot of white light onto the original; the transmitted light outside the drum passes through three color separation filters — red, green, and blue via the scanning lens. Each filter is attached to a photomultiplier which trans-

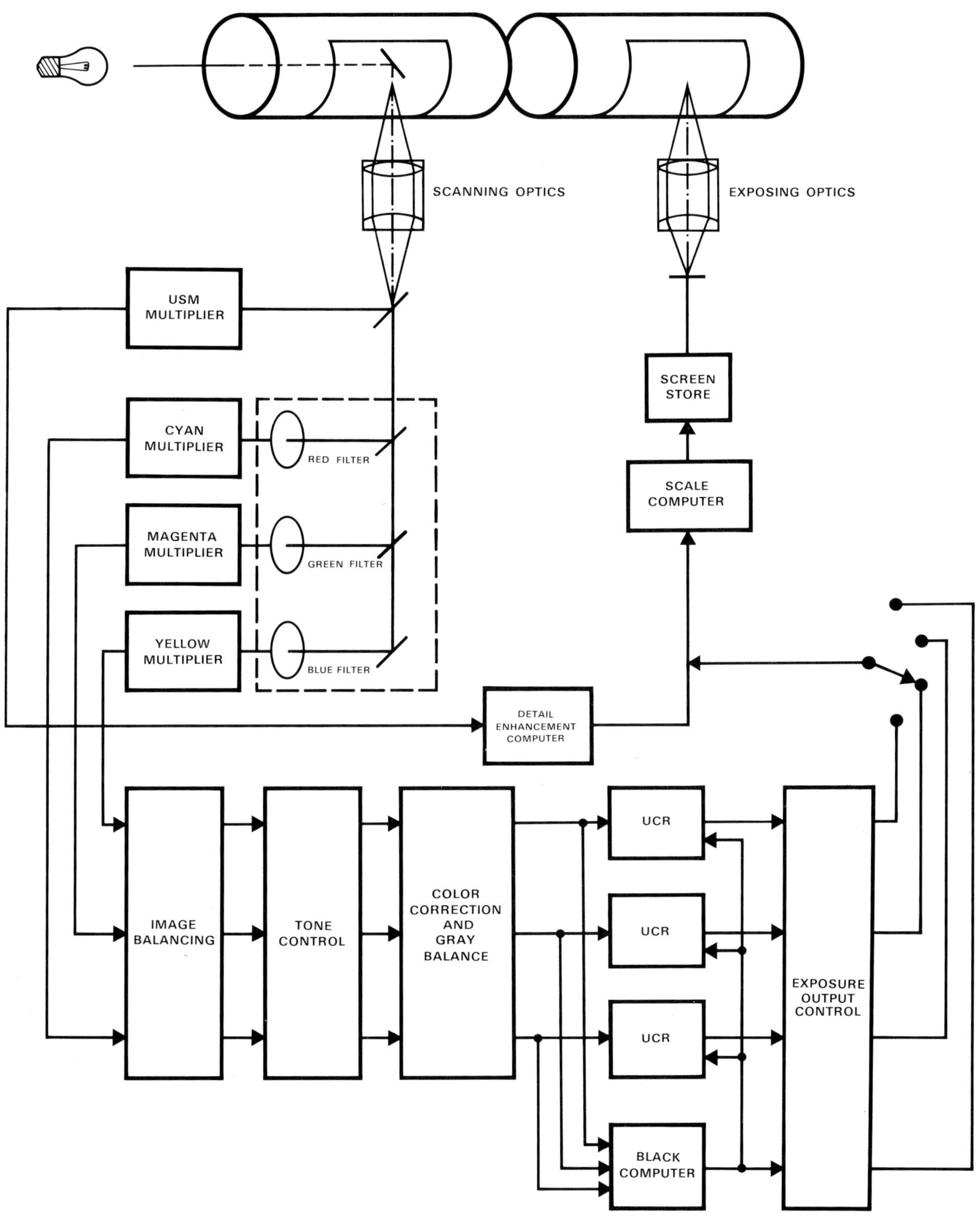

Figure 1.19. Flow diagram of a typical drum scanner

forms light intensity into electrical voltage and creates the input to the computer. The computer calculates the amount of ink required for each color separation — the signal through the red filter representing the cyan separation, the signal through the green filter representing the magenta separation, and the signal through the blue filter representing the yellow separation. The ink requirement is interpreted by the computer in terms of dot values or densities, and each signal is modified according to the predetermined requirements of color correction. The above principle is applied to a reflective copy as well, except that the copy is illuminated by a reflective light source.

With a four-channel computer, the requirements of the black printer are calculated at the same time with corresponding undercolor removal. This calculation includes the reducing of the three colors in the neutral areas of the original and replacing them with black ink. The computer controls the intensity of the exposing lamp on the exposing side of the equipment so that the scanned spot of copy is exposed on the film with greater or lesser density (or dot area) on each separation.

Some of the latest scanners can produce all four color separations simultaneously during a single operation, but most of the earlier scanners produced only one separation at a time. The scanners which produced only color-corrected continuous-tone negatives or positives without screening or enlargement are commonly known as second generation scanners. Those of the first generation are equipped only for color correction of separations. The latest generation of scanners are additionally equipped for enlargement, electronic dot generation, improved signal processing by the color computer, and other expanded capabilities.

HISTORY OF A COLOR SEPARATION SCANNER

With its reliance on high level electronics technology, the scanner seems very much a creation of the 1970's, yet in fact, the technology is almost 100 years old. The inventions and innovations which resulted in the creation of a scanner started with the development of photo-transmission system patented by Alexander Bain of England in 1843. The first practical transmission of pictures based on the selenium photoelectric cells was developed in 1902 by a German physicist, Arthur Korn. American Telephone and Telegraph Company invented and introduced the first wire photo service in the United States in 1925.

The first patent for a color-separation scanning device was obtained by Alexander Murray and Richard Morse. Murray, a native of Scotland, came to the United States as a boy and studied art and chemistry. Murray was hired by Eastman Kodak Company to do research in their engraving department where he developed "Chemical Retouching," which later became known as dot etching. After being transferred to the Kodak Research Laboratories, he improved the photographic masking methods. The first drum scanner was constructed by Murray and Morse from an ordinary engineering lathe in 1937. About the same time, Arthur Hardy of the Interchemical Corporation and F. L. Wurzburg, a professor of M.I.T., independently developed a device for photomechanical scanning. Later the scanner section of the company was taken over by RCA. Although the machine was abandoned, but for some time the computer section was used for analyzing color separation errors. In 1946, Time Inc. picked up the prototype from Kodak and continued its development. In 1949, the first workable scanner was built for Time by the Austin Co.; this scanner subsequently became known as the Austin Scanner.

Also during the 1940's, Printing Developments Incorporated (PDI) was formed and began to produce a steady stream of new developments related to plates, blankets, chemicals, and other graphic arts materials. Still very much a research tool, the scanner was nevertheless operational, and the second machine Model H-R (named after its PDI creators Hall and Ross) came out in 1950. These early machines were huge; they worked with vacuum tubes, took several hours to warm up, and took more than two hours to make a set of continuous-tone color separations which could not be enlarged or reduced.

Despite all the drawbacks, there was sufficient interest to encourage Time to install six H-R machines by August, 1950. The Penrose Annual carried a feature on the scanner in Time Springdale in its 1951 issue complete with some of the earliest printed samples of *"unretouched"* scanned color. At that time the item caused a sensation and encouraged other manufacturers to look at the possibilities.

However, the heat produced by a roomful of hot vacuum tubes was not an ideal situation for a color separation system — even if the demand was there. Letterpress was the dominant process at the time, and several companies were developing machines for electronically engraved metal blocks for letterpress. There was particularly a great need for faster black and white newspaper engravings. The wirephoto, or Hell-Schreiber, as it appeared on the patent literature of 1929, was an established piece of equipment, so why could not a similar principle be used for engraving blocks for letterpress?

First on the scene in 1949 was the Fairchild Camera and Instrument Corporation with its Photoelectric Engraver built on the basis of experimentation by Walter Howey, editor of Randolph Hearst's American Weekly. Like the PDI machine, it was based on a lathe arrangement with an input cylinder and an output cylinder. The image dots, however, were burned into a plastic material by a red-hot stylus. A few years later Fairchild produced an enlarging and reducing machine, the Scan-A-Sizer that had flat copy input and a cylindrical plate holder capable of a high quality 120 line-screen, black-and-white output.

Newspapers also provided the impetus for Dr. Ing Rudolf Hell's Klischograph which used a hardened steel stylus to engrave letterpress plates in metal or plastic. This employed a totally flat operation having both the original and plate material mounted on a common slide to produce same size output. The first machines, introduced in 1953, were single color, but color sets became available shortly afterwards. The "Vario" version of the Klischograph was introduced at a later date. The vario had enlargement and reduction capabilities.

The importance of these machines for the development of more sophisticated scanners can hardly be overemphasized. They brought electronics into the craft of printing. Vario Klischograph installations, including the new "Vario" model, went well over the 10,000 mark, and many of these survive to this day, some are more than 20 years old. The original principle of an electronically controlled stylus, now made of diamond, is the basis of current Helioklischograph direct engraving systems for gravure. Klischographs even made the transition into litho by the replacement of printing surfaces with an orange coated thin plastic sheet, "Nolar," to produce a shallow engraved separation.

An interesting diversion from the original scanning concept of reducing picture information to an electronic signal and then modifying it to compensate for ink deficiencies (masking) came at IPEX in Europe in 1955. There, Hunter-Penrose introduced its HPK Autoscan which attempted to modulate a light spot traversing the original. Each color separation was produced in a normal camera lens/filter set up except that the illuminating light spot made color corrections by increasing its intensity to give a corresponding increase in density on the film in the areas of colors. The Autoscan also incorporated the enlarging and contact screening of the separations on the scanner.

A BACKGROUND OF MAJOR SCANNER COMPANIES

Since the introduction of the first color separation scanner, the equipment has undergone some major changes. The main focus of these changes is in the areas of flexibility in the equipment to adapt to a wide variety of originals, consistency and predictability in the separations, and ease of operation of the equipment. A handful of companies are responsible for bringing those changes with new inventions and innovations. Because of the dedicated research and aggressive development efforts by these companies, the scanner has grown from a wishful alternative of the conventional separation to a massive technology within a span of only 20 years. Never in the history of printing has a single technology been expanded and accepted so rapidly. A background of each major company which has contributed to the development of the modern scanner will be discussed here.

Crosfield

Crosfield Electronics, firmly on the forefront in the manufacture of modern scanners, enjoyed rapid expansion during the last decade. The present growth and success of the company are due to an aggressive group of researchers. Founded in 1947 by John F. Crosfield in England, in 1974 the company became part of the De La Rue Group of the United Kingdom. De La Rue is a famous name in the manufacture of postage stamps, bank notes and similar security government documents.

In the United States, Crosfield Electronics, Inc., was first established in 1976 in Chicago with a small office and four people. Activities then were limited to the sales and service of press control equipment in North America. By 1980, however, the rapid expansion in the color scanning side of the business prompted Crosfield to take over from a previous distributor, the Ruthographics Division of Sun Chemical, the direct sales and service of those products in the USA and Canada. The company's investment in the region was further increased by the acquisition of LogEscan Systems, Inc., in the same year. Today Crosfield Electronics, Inc., employs more than 180 people in the head office in Glen Rock, NJ, and various other offices in North America and Canada.

Right after the establishment of Crosfield Electronics in the mid-forties, the company introduced the Autotron, an automatic register control for the press. The first color scanner, Scanatron MK1, was developed by Dr. Crosfield in 1955 using a cathode ray tube and a flying spot scan similar to that used in a television. The first machine was installed by Sun Printers in England in 1959. In this model, color separation negatives still had to be made conventionally on a glass coated with light sensitive panchromatic emulsion; however, from the negatives the Scanatron produced corrected screen positives. In the following years, about 80 Scanatrons were installed; the last one was in production in Austria until well into the '70s.

The true separating scanner was developed by Crosfield in 1964. The Diascan 101, which in its 1967 updated version was named Diascan 2000, gave a limited number of fixed enlargements. But the real breakthrough came in 1969 with the introduction of the Magnascan 450, the first enlarging/reducing drum scanner capable of producing fully corrected screened or continuous-tone separations to the required size in a single step. The machine became an instant success, and over 100 Magnascans were installed during the following two years. A faster version, the 460, was introduced in 1971 and continued with modifications until the model 510 replaced it.

The first commercially successful scanner, the Magnascan 550 launched in 1975, was of an entirely new design, exposing four color separations simultaneously. For the first time a built-in digital computer controlled tone and color calculations and automated the setup procedure for the 550.

In the spring of 1981, Crosfield launched a new generation of color scanners, modular in design, the Magnascan 530 and 540, with separate input and output units under sophisticated microprocessor control. These were followed a year later by the Magnascan 640 series, offering a choice of output options including electronic screening and floppy disk storage for all setup information. Crosfield claims that this modular system could grow from a low cost machine to a sophisticated full page composition system for both pictures and text.

In addition to the Magnascan 570 Electronic Page Composition System in 1977, Crosfield later developed the Studio 800 series and the Lasergravure 700. The later uses a laser beam to engrave gravure cylinders. The company also acquired LogEscan, now Crosfield's Data Systems Inc., and its laser platemaking products for offset printers combined with remote transmission facilities.

Courtesy Crosfield Electronics

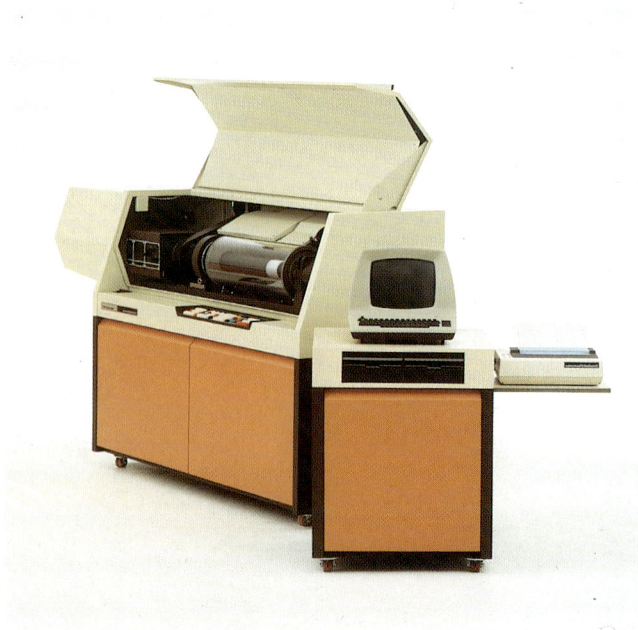

Figure 1.20. Crosfield Magnascan 645 scanning unit with Scanner Data Terminal

The current line of Crosfield scanners include the Magnascan 645 (the top of the line), 635, 625, and 610 series. All models are offered in "S," "E," and "M" versions. "S" is conventional contact screening; "E" stands for electronic dot generation; and "M," for larger format with electronic dot generation. All these models are modular in design and can be expanded and upgraded to any level with the addition of appropriate hardware and software. The Magnascan 645 series uses an independent Scanner Data Terminal for multiple original setup, simple page make-up, and floppy disk data storage. The current models are totally digital with separate input and output units. Other options include the Magnaplan page composition system, which is available on the 645IE/M. It is equipped with electronic dot generation that allows a number of pictures, tint blocks, and borders to be positioned within a defined background area. The Scanview previewing terminal provides for the viewing and correcting of scanned images on a high resolution color monitor. The Scanset workstation sets up job data totally off-line from the scanner. The Scanscale contains a microprocessor controlled projector for image scaling, rotation, and cropping.

Another innovation, claimed by Crosfield, is the soft edge around their laser generated electronic dots for conventional dot etching. The dots are dense enough to be produced solid if no etching is required; however, a maximum of 15% of the dots can be reduced by dot etching without affecting quality. This is made possible by an exclusive electronic masking method during the generation of laser dots.

Crosfield Electronics Limited has won three Queen of England's Awards for Technological Achievement for the application of electronics to the printing industry and for the Magnascan 450 and 550. Three more Queen's Awards were received for export achievements.

Dainippon Screen (DS)

With the solid reputation as one of the topmost manufacturer of graphic arts products, Dainippon Screen (DS) was the latest company to enter the scanning scene during the 1960's. Started in 1934 and incorporated in 1943 in Japan, DS is the world's leading integrated manufacturer of image reproduction equipment and systems for the graphic arts industry. The company's products for the graphic arts industry include electronic page make-up systems, electronic color scanners, industrial process cameras, automatic film processors, step and repeat machines, proof presses, densitometers, and other related equipment.

Through the application of its basic technologies, DS is also a major supplier of shadow masks and ultrafine metal meshes for use in color television picture tubes and other electronic applications. In addition, DS offers a range of products for other industries including textile and office equipment.

Dainippon had its scanning origins firmly in letterpress engraving, dating back to 1959 with the Autograver. The Scanagraph followed in 1966, one of the earliest scanners made by the company. The first scanner introduced in the US by Dainippon Screen in 1977 was a fixed size table-top continuous-tone model SG-1000. This was followed by a series of conventional-screen machines — SG-601, SG-603, SG-606, SG-606II, and SG-701. Model SG-701 was modular in design. All these machines had halogen lamp input and helium neon red laser output. It is interesting to note that Dainippon Screen is the only scanner manufacturer which has used red lasers in most of their scanners rather than the traditional argon blue lasers. The company claims that the red laser is cheaper to produce, lower in price, almost maintenance free, and lasts longer. However, faced with the problem of traditional red-safelight working habit of the operator with blue laser, the company, at a later date, introduced several models with blue laser output in some of their electronic dot generation machines.

The first electronic dot generation scanner introduced by Dainippon Screen was the SG-708, which is actually a modified SG-701 with the addition of a laser unit. The first blue laser scanner was the model SG-808, introduced in Drupa 82 followed by a larger version of the same model SG-888 (26" x 40"). The company claims that this model was unique in that two selective unsharp masking photomultipliers were incorporated to avoid undesirable lines for different subjects with different colors. In 1984, Dainippon Screen first introduced the lowest cost electronic dot generation scanner, model SG-608, with a red laser output. A larger output version of the same model, SG-688 was introduced in 1986.

Courtesy D.S. America, Inc.

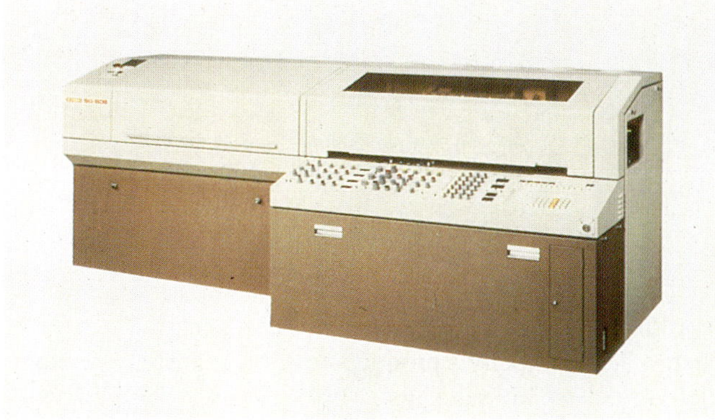

Figure 1.21. Dainippon Screen SG-608 scanner

The latest scanners introduced by Dainippon Screen are models SG-757 and SG-777. Both are blue laser electronic dot generation scanners with composing and automatic film loading facilities. SG-777 is available with an optional exposing head so that two portions of the same film can be exposed at once. This scanner is one of the world's largest output scanners with a film size of 65.8" x 47.2". The model SG-757, smaller in format than the model SG-777 (32" x 44") is the first scanner introduced by DS with full digital controls for all functions. An off-line computer is used to enter the picture information digitally. This feature allows the operator to set up all functions ahead of time and store the data on a floppy disk. As soon as one job is completed, the operator simply changes the drum and immediately starts the new scanning. Other features of these two models include the presetting and storing of up to 64 sets of data on a single floppy disk. Additional notable features of the SG-777 include the composing and/or simple stripping functions for generating outputs in rectangular form from several copies scanned successively as well as those for flat tints, keylines, border tint generation, and overlapping.

A significant innovative feature in the DS scanners is a 10-beam direct drive laser for all their electronic dot generation scanners instead of the conventional 6-beam fiber-optic laser found in other scanners. DS claims that each dot is produced by two and one-third rotation of the drum and consists of 529 pixels or elements. In other conventional scanners, each dot is produced by two rotations of the drum and has 144 pixels or elements. DS further claims that because of this factor, dots produced by their scanners are smoother, have better shapes, and allows the use of conventional screen angles and rulings. There are 28 different dot shapes available on floppy disks for several models of Dainippon Screen scanners.

Hell

One of the very few companies which are credited with the development of modern scanners is the Hell Company of Kiel, Germany. The history of the Hell Company was shaped over a period of many years by the personality of one man: the founder of the company and the man who gave its name, Dr. Ing Rudolf Hell. In 1927 he received a doctorate for his work on a "radio-direction-finder-indicator" for air navigation, and during this period, he also invented the image dissector for television. Dr. Hell founded the firm Berlin-Babelsberg to produce his latest telecommunication invention, the "Hell-writer." By the end of the war, Hell was employing a workforce of more than 1000. However, after the destruction of his factory during the war, the company moved to its new premises in Kiel. Hell next worked on Morse-code machines and the legendary Hell Writers. From 1951-53, Hell entered the field of reproduction technology with the development of new machines, the Klischographs. At this time, Dr. Hell concentrated on two main areas, electronics for image telegraphy and reproduction technology. Through further application of the principle of electronics for the scanning and recording of reproducing the originals, he invented digital typesetting from an electronic memory. In 1971, Dr. Hell withdrew from active management of the company and sold the interest to Siemens.

The evolution of Hell scanners is a fascinating story. During the '50s, the company introduced the Colorgraph, the first experimental flat-bed scanner ever built by Hell. In the early '60s, the company introduced three models — Chromagraph C 285, Chromagraph C 286, and Chromagraph C 287, all of which were continuous-tone and same size drum scanners, differing only in input and output sizes. The scanners became immediately popular for their design and engineering excellence. The machines were compact for the output size, the controls were logically laid out, and were easier to operate than the other scanners available at that time. Even today, 20 years after their introduction, the same design principle is used in most Hell scanners with only minor modification. In 1967 the Combi-Chromagraph was introduced which allowed a limited picture make-up through the addition of a second input drum.

In the same year, the first Hell direct-screen scanner with enlarging capability was introduced with the Vario Chromagraph C296. The success of this machine had proved the engineering and creative capability of Dr. Hell in the design of scanners. Vario Chromagraph C296 was actually a modified version of the earlier model C286. Even the basic set up and steps for same size continuous-tone separation for both models remained the same. However, the novel feature of the 296 is a special scanning attachment for enlarging purposes. The transparency holder moved up and down instead of rotating during scanning, and a mechanical enlarging mechanism with adjustable arms for guide bevels were added. A rotary tube-drive with different cams for different enlargement ratios were attached, and the operator could view and adjust the enlargement ratios with two microscopes fitted at the top of the scanner. The enlargement ratios in the 296 could be varied from 170% to 2000%. The machine became an instant success as an enlarging direct-screen scanner, and because of the low cost and simplicity of operation, hundreds of C296 are still in use all over the world.

But the biggest landmark for color scanners was the launching of the Hell DC 300 digital enlarging and reducing scanner in 1970. The DC 300A was introduced first. It was a single channel machine with a xenon lamp for analyzing and scanning, but it did not have a white alignment control. With the introduction of DC 300B, two images could now be recorded in one pass (duplo), and white alignment control was incorporated with or without color compensation. The DC 300 had little resemblance to earlier models, was faster, and incorporated many more control refinements. With the introduction of laser generated halftone dots on the ER version in 1973, the DC300 remains one of the most popular scanners ever built in the decade.

Chromagraph C299 was introduced later. It is a direct-screen enlarging scanner with a more sophisticated color computer and a special digital scale computer for enlargement, reduction, and other specific functions. An optional argon laser light source was offered later for this unit and was designated Chromagraph 299L. However, 299L still remained a conventional contact-screen scanner. Its advantage is its faster speed because of the laser exposing light source.

Other Hell developments include the models DC 350, C399, CP 341, and CP 340, differed only in input and output sizes and specific functions. The ER versions of the same models designate electronic dot generation.

The introduction of Hell DC 360 and DC 370 with monitor controls offers greater flexibility and system compatibility. The DC 370 offers the color computer in both digital and analog versions. Hell claims that the options provide the operator with different possibilities for optimum performance. Since a wide range of originals has to be optimized on an individual basis, a continuous analog technique could be used wherever they are proved adequate; however, where interchangeability is required for different scanners or when repeat color computer settings are needed, they can be done with digital mode. Most of the Hell scanners provide electronic screening, multicolored separation in a single pass, software controls of screen programs, gradation memory of up to 40 gradations, job storage, CCR (GCR) reproduction, and the compatibility to connect the Layout Programmer LP 307 and Scale Programmer SC 2000. The LP 307 allows entire pages to be structured from rectangular elements completely independent of the scanner. All the data stored on a floppy disk is converted by the Hell scanners into the separations. The SC 2000 is able to determine the reproduction scale, specify the image section and position the transparencies at the desired angle; the scanner then uses the data for the scanning work.

Courtesy Hell Graphic Systems, Inc.

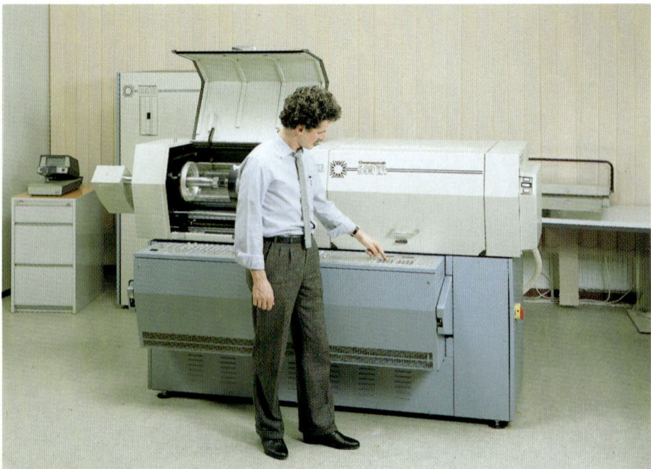

Figure 1.22. Hell 399ER scanner with Electronics Cabinet

The latest scanners in the Hell family are the all digital DC 380 and a larger version CP 345. Important features of the

DC 380 include: a color monitor with menu display for all color computer functions, an operating keyboard for color correction settings, an electronics cabinet with digital color computer, and the floppy disk drive which allows operation with off-line job preparation units.

During the '60s, most of the Hell scanners in the United States were marketed through RCA (Radio Corporation of America). HCM (Hell Color Metal), Inc., was formed in 1959 with the studio and corporate head office in Great Neck, New York, to market Helio-Klischographs and their Color Metal Champion offset presses. The distribution of Hell scanners was taken over from RCA and added to the product line in the late '60s. The name of the company was changed to Hell Graphic Systems, Inc., in 1985, and in 1986 the company moved its corporate headquarters and other facilities to a new building in Port Washington, New York. The success of Hell in the United States has been synonymous with a name, Mr. Charles E. Sack, President of the company in the United States since 1968. Because of his aggressive marketing policy, unreserved support for training and education, and a competent staff of sales and technical personnel, Hell has been a popular name in the field of scanning. His efforts have also contributed in the rapid adaptation of scanner technology in this country during the last two decades. Mr. Sack retired from the company in April, 1987. Hell Graphic Systems, Inc., has other regional offices in Atlanta, Chicago, Dallas, Los Angeles, and Toronto, Canada.

Royal Zenith

The early '60s saw another scanner manufacturer on the scene, K. S. Paul, who had previously been an agent for Fairchild. Printing Development Incorporated (PDI), having made the decision to set up a worldwide network of studios rather than sell equipment outright, took on the agency for the K. S. Paul scanner with considerable success, selling approximately 160 machines throughout the world between 1965 and 1969. The United Kingdom was an important market, taking an additional 60 machines during the same period. In 1969, having joined forces with Linotype, K. S. Paul, renamed as Linotype Paul, launched the model 204 scanner, which, after many modifications, was still in production in 1982. Linotype-Paul's most important development, the Linomask, came out in 1973. This technique allows groups of transparencies to be mounted together on the input drum and individual adjustments of highlights and color balance up to a maximum of 16 subjects are possible.

Linotype-Paul had considerable impact at the Drupa exhibition in 1977 where it introduced the Linoscan 3040, which, besides being the lowest priced reducing and enlarging scanner on the market, was also the most compact. More than any other development, the 3040 demonstrated the effect of the microprocessor in reducing a roomful of electronics to a unit no wider than a doorway.

The last scanner manufactured by Linotype-Paul was the Linoscan 4050-E, a faster version of the 3040. The 4050-E allowed two-color scanning in one pass and claimed to pioneer a unique "5th color" circuit for over-saturated reds. Both the 3040 and 4050-E departed from the conventional scanner theory in their use of a single-channel analysis system. It is claimed that the design overcomes problems due to photomultiplier drift, and eliminates the unnatural "black line" unsharp masking effect by enhancing each color signal independently.

In 1983 Linotype-Paul sold its U.K. scanner interests to Itek Color Graphics, and at the same time Royal Zenith Corporation began marketing Itek scanners in the United States under its own name. The Royal Zenith 4050-E was joined in 1984 by the larger model 200-S, a four-color-at-a-time scanner. Another innovation claimed by Royal Zenith is the first integrated video previewing system. The system contains a color video monitor which receives its signal from the scanner's computer and allows the operator to make a quick prescan of the original and see a simulated press proof on the video screen in less than a minute. Changes made to the scanner's controls can be previewed in seconds, effectively eliminating guesswork from the setting-up task, and permitting the first practical option to scan from color negatives, which appear to be positive on the preview screen. Flexible software allows the screen characteristics to be altered to simulate paper color, ink hue, dot gain and trapping for any three or four-color printing process. The 200-S is also the first Royal Zenith scanner to offer the option of electronic dot generation output as well as conventional separations with

Courtesy Itek Colour Graphics

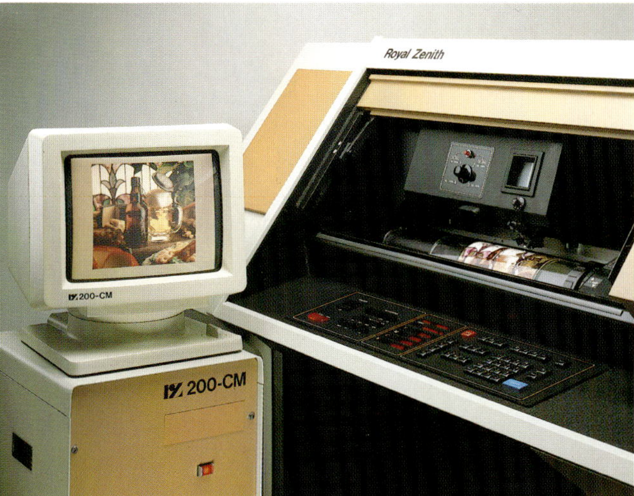

Figure 1.23. Royal Zenith 200-S scanner with 200-CM color monitor

contact screens. At the Drupa 86, Itek Color Graphics unveiled their latest scanner, Model 210-L with color monitor 210-CM. The model is similar to 200-S except that an argon laser electronic dot generation unit is a standard feature with the scanner, and an improved color monitor. The monitor is menu driven and has a wide range of features. These features include split-screen functions to compare changes made to the original, progressive display of colors, and ink and paper mapping where electronically generated calibration wedges are proofed to the customer's standard.

EIKONIX-KODAK and SCITEX

The history of technology is a history of aggressive research and development. Innovative individuals and groups have been relentlessly placing forward new ideas for the betterment of the existing technology. Eikonix-Kodak and Scitex share this ongoing venture and without discussing the contribution of these two companies, the history of the scanner technology will be incomplete.

Eikonix

Founded in 1968, Eikonix Corporation is a leader in the field of digital imaging. Initially, the company specialized in developing custom digital electro-optical systems for the government. Later, these changing technologies were transformed into components and systems for the commercial marketplace.

Eikonix introduced its first commercial digital imaging camera system in 1980. Product development efforts led to a series of camera systems based on a linear 2048-element photodiode array and a 4096-element charge coupled device (CCD) array. In the early '80s, Eikonix identified the prepress segment of the graphic arts industry as an emerging vertical market into which integrated digital imaging systems could be sold. In 1983, the Eikonix DESIGNMASTER 8000 was introduced as the first all-digital color electronic prepress system (CEPS).

The DESIGNMASTER 8000 is a modular and interactive system. It represents a new approach in CEPS technology by using red, green, and blue filters in combination with a photodiode array to simulate the response of the human eye. Featured in the DESIGNMASTER 8000 is a unique color space technology called uvL. This technology is based on the color attributes of hue, saturation, and luminance and allows the system and operator to see color in the same way. The result is an accurate color reproduction from previewing to printing. And uvL provides a cost-effective alternative to traditional YMCK-based systems since it saves time, labor, and materials.

The basic components of the DESIGNMASTER 8000 include: the Model 8701 Input Digitizer; the Model 8101 Color Editing Console; the Model 8601 Laser Beam Recorder; and associated electronics.

The Input Digitizer is a flatbed scanner that captures all the true colors and detail of reflective and transmissive originals. It scans and digitizes an original and stores it on a hard disk. Once scanned, infinite versions of the same picture can be created without rescanning. The original remains on the disk until erasure.

The Color Editing Console is used to make a variety of changes to the image and to view the image as it will appear on the proof or printed piece. A high-quality color monitor provides real-time (simultaneous) response and makes possible the most comprehensive, precise rendering of an image. All calibration, input, and output tasks are controlled with a puck and tablet that interact with simple-to-use menu displays.

Some of these menu options include removing or introducing a cast — in a local area or overall — adding or subtracting unsharp masking, silhouetting, increasing or decreasing contrast, and cloning. The editorial menus are so simple to operate that a person with a basic understanding of color can edit an image with a minimum of training.

The final step in the color separation process is accomplished with the Eikonix PAGE MANAGER page composition software. Page assembly and output specifications, such as screen ruling and positioning, are selected from menus. Pages can be created at a fraction of the time it would take to strip them manually.

Once the image has been edited, it is ready for the Laser

Courtesy Eikonix Corp.

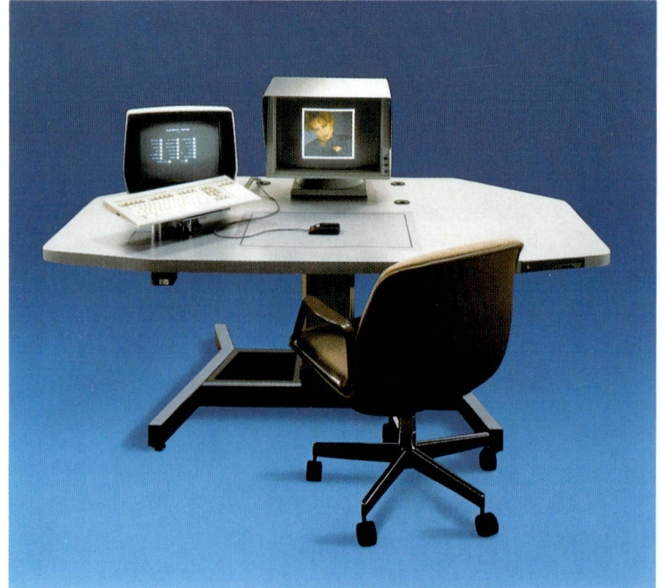

Figure 1.24. Eikonix-Kodak Designmaster 8000

Beam Recorder (LBR). The LBR is a self-contained output writer equipped with a rotating drum. The drum accepts a 20x24 inch sheet of film with the flexibility to expose large separations l-up, or smaller separations 4-up.

In 1986, the Eikonix Digital Graphic Arts Camera and Input/Output Workstation were introduced as optional equipment. The graphic arts camera scans large format images, including reflective artwork, three-dimensional objects, and objects up to three inches high. The Input/Output Workstation is a multitasking and multi-user device that significantly increases productivity.

Eikonix Corporation is headquartered in Bedford, Massachusetts. In 1985, Eikonix became a wholly-owned subsidiary of Eastman Kodak Company.

Courtesy Scitex America Corp.

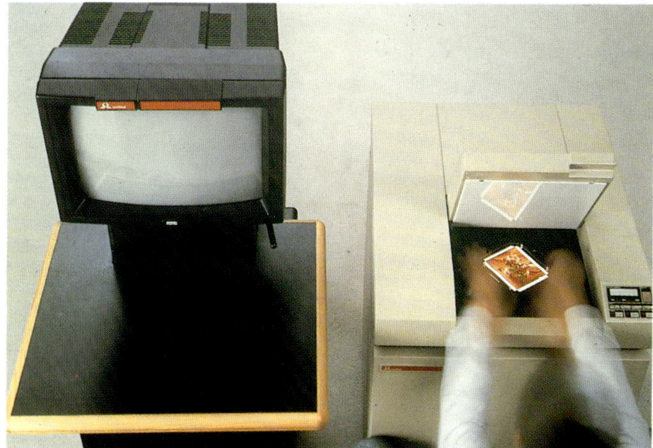

Figure 1.25. Scitex "Smart Scanner"

Scitex

Based in Israel, Scitex has been a world leader in computer imaging technology. With the introduction of its Response-300 System in 1979, Scitex became a prestigious name in the electronic color prepress field. With the Response System, Scitex automated the otherwise a complex time-consuming manual tasks of prepress. After color pictures are recorded electronically on a color separation scanner, the resulting digital data is transferred to the Response, and color correction, retouching, and other complex manipulation of the images are accomplished by viewing the changes on the video screen in real time. Using the system, different photos can be combined and individual details can be changed at will. For example, a model's eye color, make-up or nail polish can be altered on the Response to match her dress.

Scitex has also made a significant contribution in the newspaper and magazine industry to speed production deadlines. Satlight is one of the major innovations in the Scitex line; a transportable color separation scanner, which transmits color photographs over telephone lines from remote locations to a Response System in the home editorial office or production center. The Scitex Raystar, a high speed plotter introduced in 1985, enables publishers to get pages to press faster and to improve overall productivity. The Raystar produces complete color separation films for a full-size newspaper page in minutes. Catalog and magazine publishers use the Scitex Vista to design and layout pages. Vista enables publishers to combine color photos, graphics and text quickly and make changes flexibly without disrupting production deadlines.

The major contribution of Scitex in the scanner technology is its introduction of "Smart Scanner" in Drupa 86. The scanner incorporates the latest advances in digital scanning technology utilizing a flat-bed design. Its high resolution charged coupled device (CCD) optics can detect an enormous amount of picture data, about 7,200 spots per inch. The "Smart Scanner's" all-digital controls, special color computer and automatic calibrating mechanism virtually eliminate set up time. Pre-scan and post-scan color assessments and modifications are carried out on the Softproof Viewer. This high resolution console lets the operator make cropping, rotation, and sizing decisions. Global and local corrections can be carried out interactively with changes appearing on the monitor. With an electronic cursor, it is possible to determine highlight and shadow points and to adjust for color casts, tone, and gray balance curves.

Images scanned on the "Smart Scanner" can be transferred electronically to a Scitex interactive color work station for further digital color enhancement and page assembly. Final output is via Scitex's high-resolution Raystar and Eray Laser Plotter or to a conventional drum scanner, via an interface.

In the USA, Scitex America Corporation is located in 8 Oak Park Drive, Bedford, Mass. Other Scitex affiliates are located in Japan and Europe.

SCANNERS AND DIGITAL COMPUTERS

The most significant single advance in scanner technology after the transistor improvements is the use of digital computers. These computers were originally introduced to overcome one of the serious disadvantages in the earlier scanners: the problem of enlarging and reducing in a scanner. In those scanners, enlargement and reduction worked on the principle of changing the speed and size of the input drum in relation to the output drum. However, this method had very limited success. With digital computers, the analog signal from the color computer output is converted into digital data, and the information for each scanning line across the entire copy is stored temporarily in the computer memory. This data is then played back to the exposing head at a speed in proportion to the scanning cylinder diameter depending on the required enlargement or reduction. The process can effectively stretch or compress the image in the circumferential direction of the exposing cylinder. Then the crossfeed or axial speed of the scanning head is changed in relation to the exposing head to match the enlargement ratio on the other direction.

However, it was not long before some of the other advantages which occurred from capturing information in digital form started to be realized. For example, the facility to assign x-y coordinates to the transparency, or various parts of it, made possible the automatic generation of a color or tint within a position as long as it is of a simple rectangular geometric shape. A digital computer memory also permits scanning several transparencies which are out of balance with each other. This function allows the operator to balance them by individual controls so that they are all scanned together. Other benefits include electronic cropping of the original, automatic exposure of register marks and gray scales.

More important advantages of digital technology are found in some of the latest digital scanners. With the advent of faster and efficient digital computers, the use of these computers for signal processing has grown rapidly during the last decade. With a set or list of preprogrammed values, a digital computer computes the dot sizes required to reproduce an original point by point during scanning and exposing the film. When the copy is positioned for the scanning light and a specific program is called, the values are displayed at the digital panel. Using the keyboard, the operator can enter the required changes in the control unit. The control unit compares and calculates the changes in accordance with a list of preprogrammed values and displays the data or sends it to the next station for further processing.

The other important aspect of the digital technology is the interchangeability of data. This has made it possible to exchange or to transmit data from one location to another for identical output. Satellite transmission of data to different locations for identical output from a central unit is an example. The rapid expansion and utilization of digital image processing such as electronic pagination and retouching systems are also made possible by digital technology. In the electronic page make up and retouching systems, digital computers are exclusively used to record the data on a magnetic media for further manipulation. Normally each original or copy is digitized from the output of a video camera or a scanner and stored on disks. The data is then played back on a color monitor; various copies are assembled and/or required changes or retouching functions are accomplished by using a digitizer and a computer terminal. A full page or section consisting of various originals, type matters or illustrations is then stored on magnetic disks, and a composite film containing the entire page or section is later generated in the scanner. Another important development is the setting up of any original, off-line from the scanner and storing all data on a magnetic disk. For scanning, the copy and the disks are replaced, and the proper data are recalled. The latest development in the charge coupled devices (CCD), which are currently being used in the flat-bed scanners, uses digital technology. It is predicted that digital hard copy color proofing will replace the present hard and soft copy proofing for several reasons — they will be consistent, predictable, and cost effective.

Controversy exists as to the extent of digital technology to be used in scanners. Traditionally, the signals generated from the photomultipliers are processed with an analog color computer for color correction, gradation, under color removal, etc. However, after the signal is processed with the analog device, the data is then stored digitally for further processing. Most of the digital application in these scanners is in the exposing section, like scaling or formatting, output film size, registration marks, etc. However, now there are scanners in which all signals are processed digitally once they are digitized from the analog signals generated by the photomultipliers.

The argument in favor of total digital technology insists that digitization provides unlimited flexibility and simplicity in the setting up of a color computer in addition to making it easy to store and retrieve data. This provides the scanner operator the advantage of standardizing all the functions in the operation of a scanner. It is claimed that digital technology is robust. There is no misunderstanding regarding the data at the scanner end, and as such, set ups are interchangeable between scanners. It is further argued that the trend in the communication technology shows a gradual transition towards using totally digital technique. For example, multiple satellite transmission and retrieval of data in the graphic communication industry can be fully and effectively utilized only with digital technology.

The argument in favor of analog color computer claims that the photomultipliers used in the scanner as signal sensors are analog devices. These sensors are the most sensitive and unstable devices in the scanner. Since the analog computer is more stable than the photomultipliers or the log amplifier, digitization does not provide additional advantage. It is further claimed that the fundamental problem with digitization is that it is not continuous, and so data is being thrown away during the process of numbering the steps. Solid state analog computers are stable, with less than 1% variation in the output, reliable, inexpensive, and they are continuous similar to the original picture to be scanned. Another point often indicated is that the potentiometer type controls in an analog computer provides a clearer picture of an adjustment to the operator than the adjustment with pushbutton controls in a "black box" type digital computer.

ELECTRONIC DOT GENERATION SCANNERS

One of the significant advances in color scanning is the innovation of electronic dot generation devices. In the contact screen scanners, direct screening is done with a contact screen on the output drum. One of the main disadvantages is that the speed of the machine is slowed down quite dramatically because of the reduced light intensity falling on the film. Now this is changed with the introduction of the laser, which produces the halftone dots directly on the film.

The laser, which is a very high-intensity and directional light source, is operated at a constant intensity. Combined with various devices, it modulates the area exposed at each point on the film. The result is a complete set of screened separations ready for platemaking. The main advantage of electronic dot generation scanners lies in the advantage of producing dots directly from the laser beam rather than through the screen. Halftone dots produced through the conventional screens have fringe areas around the dots because of the characteristics of the screen. As such, the processing of the film becomes critical and a slight inconsistency may change the result. However, when a laser light beam is producing a dot, the light does not spill, and it produces a hard dot with almost no fringe. This makes the processing non critical. The cheapest films, in conjunction with rapid access processing can be used for an electronic dot generation scanner without affecting the quality.

CURRENT TRENDS

Scanner technology has changed so rapidly during the last decade that it has become unpredictable in nature. Competition among manufacturers has resulted in new innovations which constantly improved the quality of the scanners. Compared to the scanners of yesteryear, the drum scanners of today are unbelievably faster, more flexible, and predictable. The modern scanner provides programmable electronic dots of any shapes and sizes, a bank of preprogrammed data individually adjusted for a variety of customers, production of multiple separation after the scanner is initially set up,and similar features. At this time, the technological trend seems to be in two broad areas: (1) the expansion of the capability of the scanners by interfacing them with other peripherals, and (2) the addition of features which make the operator's job easier.

In addition to color separation, scanners are currently being used both as an input and as an output device for the electronic image processing system. Several originals required for a page or a section can be scanned line by line in a scanner and digitized for manipulation in the image processing hardware. After the data is manipulated and the images are processed and assembled, the scanner is again used to generate a composite film for the entire page or section which reduces the stripping operation to a minimum.

Another exciting development is the color computer's capability to remove gray component from the three colors and replace it with a full range black (GCR). The concept is old, but has been revitalized with the incorporation of new microprocessors in the color computer. All scanners available at this time are offering this feature, but the industry has yet to extract the full potential of this development.

Further research is needed to explore the full potential of analog and digital technology. Digital technology has been with the scanners for some time, but only at the output end. However, it seems that the technology is slowly moving towards other areas as well. The Hell 370 is an example where both technologies are utilized to their full potential. Possibly in the future, both analog and digital scanners will be available to meet the diversified needs of the market.

Video display terminals for data are the newest addition to some scanners. In the Crosfield Magnascan 645, Dainippon Screen SG 777, Hell DC 370 and DC 360, video terminals are added to simplify job set ups. Most of the computer software in these scanners are menu driven, the operator enters data through the keyboard, and sets up all job parameters while observing the display.

Another new development is the presetting of data input off-line to be used later with the scanner. Dainippon Screen's Data Setter DS-700 allows the operator to use the peripheral which includes a scanning drum adapter, a key board, and a monitor. The Data Setter stores settings for subsequent jobs on a floppy disk. Scanner set up can then be performed by simply placing the disk onto the scanner's disk drive and recalling the proper data. Since this can be done while scanning another job, downtime can be substantially reduced with the use of these peripherals.

Another development often called soft proof is the use of a high resolution color video monitor with which the operator can preview the result of a computer setting on the scanner. Crosfield introduced the Scanview previewing terminal which provides the viewing and the correction of scanned images on the monitor for its 625, 635, and 645 series scanners. The terminal has an editorial control panel which provides the same functions and modes of operation as the scanner with which the operator is familiar. Royal Zenith offers 200-CM for their 200-S and 210-CM in their 210-L scanners. The image is produced on the on-line high grade video monitor after a quick prescan of the copy is done. Then the image is adjusted by the operator to match any desired printing process. The operator gets an accurate picture of how the final printed piece will look, including the effects of press variables like dot gain, ink density, and trapping. The effect of any scanner control instantly appears on the screen. Made by a Japanese company named Toppan, Scan Proof is a previewer made exclusively for Dainippon Screen scanners. The previewer takes the image signal directly from the scanner and shows the operator exactly how the image will look when it is reproduced. The manufacturer claims that the system provides a remarkably accurate simulation of the process colors and allows users to adjust for the specific printing characteristics of their own equipment. At Drupa 86, Gramag Ag, a Swiss company introduced a previewer, the Scanvision, which can be connected to all standard color scanners and shows a soft proof before or after the exposure of the separation films.

One of the significant developments in recent times is the facility available for a limited job assembly off-line from the scanner, stored on a disk, and then generating a composite film from the scanner. Hell LP 307 Layout Programmer and the Scanner Data Terminal of the Magnascan 645 allow the operator to structure limited page assembly functions completely independent of the scanner. The Scanset workstation by Crosfield has also been specifically designed for the speedy set up of a job data totally off-line from the scanner. With this unit, it is possible to position a number of transparencies, tints, and borders without tying up valuable scanning time.

FUTURE OF THE TECHNOLOGY

Scanner technology has become the most rapidly changing field in the entire realm of printing. It not only created a greater demand for more color printing by making it less expensive and technically more perfect, but it also created a market for more and better technology. Many of the forward strides made in the field of color scanner technology are attributable to the utilization of computers, and specialists are predicting larger and faster units in the future. Many of the developments in the scanner technology have speeded up the process of electronic page assembly with fully computerized stripping. These electronic page make up systems have utilized many of the innovations of the scanner technology. It is predicted that in the near future, with advanced digital computers, will come automatic plate exposing directly in the scanner.

There has been and will continue to be a significant growth of color printing in this country. The rapid transition from conventional to electronic color separation has played a major role in this growth. As for economics, the cost of a set of color separation did not increase over a period of time and this phenomenon in a high inflation economy is significant. The scanner became one of the single most profitable pieces of equipment in the entire industrial printing plant.

It appears that the color scanner will dominate in the production of four color separations. Primarily because of the cost savings that will result from the accuracy and the repeatability of the computer as used in the color scanner. As in so many other instances, computers have replaced or supplemented individual skills. Scanner technology radically changed a way in which a heretofore time-consuming and unpredictable step was accomplished.

One of the major developments in color scanner technology in the past few years is the introduction of CCD (charge coupled devices) technology in flat bed scanners and electronic prepress systems. The Eikonix-Kodak Corporation first introduced CCD technology in the Designmaster 8000 to capture and manipulate images in digital form. Scitex in their Satlight portable color scanner and DuPont in their latest monochrome scanner have utilized this technology successfully. The CCD replaces the conventional photomultiplier sensing device. The technology is only about 5 years old, and it is expected that further refinement will make it a common input system for color scanners, cameras, and pagination systems for capturing information in the digital form. In the near future, it may replace the photomultipliers which are claimed to be one of the unstable sensing devices in the image processing systems.

In some scanners, the use of color video monitors has substantially reduced the time and film usage. It has also made the operator's job easier. However, the soft-proof images on the monitors are not ideal for customer approval and this has somewhat limited the potential for their extensive usage in the future scanners. Even when a monitor is used to show the image to the customer for approval, complaints are heard that some customers like to use the monitor as an experimental tool and tie up the valuable scanner time. These monitors will be strictly used as a prescan analysis system and will not be substituted as hard copy proof, digital proof will be a dominant proofing system in the future.

As long as the original can be wrapped around the scanning cylinder, the motion of the rotary drum and electronic dot generation by laser seem to offer the most efficient and convenient methods of exposing the film. However, it seems that more and more digital technology will be used in the future scanners for ease of operation, consistency, and predictability. Scanners are becoming more modular in design, and add-on modules are being offered by several scanner manufacturers to upgrade the equipment. The modular approach adapts easily in the existing scanner to an electronic preparatory system. Another functional approach of the modular concept is to incorporate user serviceable facilities in the scanner. When the equipment fails, with this approach the user will be able to perform a series of simple diagnostic steps to locate the faulty plug-in board or module and replace it. As of this writing, several scanner manufacturers are planning to incorporate such facilities in their future scanners to cut down scanner down time and service cost. More standardization in the steps, techniques, and processes will be the wave of the future to cut down cost in scanner productivity.

Chapter 2
Basic Mechanics of a Scanner

HOW THE SCANNER WORKS

Basically a drum scanner can be divided into three sections: the scanning section, the electronics or computer section, and the exposing section. The concept of operation of a typical drum scanner is explained on page 31 with Figure 1.18. In the scanning section, the original transparency or the reflection copy is mounted on the scanning drum (also called an analyze drum), while the photographic film to be exposed is mounted on the exposing drum (also called recording drum). A small spot of light illuminates the copy and is projected through or reflected from the original. As the scanning drum rotates, a very fine line of copy is scanned by the light spot for every revolution. After a line is scanned, the light spot and the optical system will move exactly the same distance as the width of the scanned line, and the drum will continue to rotate in a helical or spiral pattern until the entire original is scanned.

Light from each spot of the scanned copy is transmitted through an optical system which is enclosed in a unit called the scanning head. Figure 2.1 shows the signal path in a typical scanner. The spot of light is split into four beams by beam-splitters in the scanning head. Three beams are used for the red, green, and blue signals, and the other one is used as an unsharp masking signal. Each of the three beams passes through a color separation filter and is focused onto three photomultipliers (usually referred to as multipliers) which convert them into electrical signals. In the RZ 200-S, only one multiplier is used for all three color signals. The other beam is focussed onto a separate multiplier; this signal is used to manipulate the main color signal to enhance details in the reproduction. However, in the Crosfield Magnascan 645, the unsharp masking signal is simulated from any of the three color signals, and no unsharp masking beam is needed for detail enhancement.

The scanning and the exposing drums rotate, and depending on the color content of each line of the original being scanned, there will be a constant change of electrical signals generated by the multipliers which are fed into a color computer. The computer can be analog or digital depending on the model and brand of scanner used. For example, Hell 399ER and Dainippon Screen SG-608 scanners process the signals with an analog color computer; however, the Crosfield Magnascan 645 and the Royal Zenith 200-S use a digital color computer. The signals at the multiplier output are uncorrected color separation signals and can be compared to a set of uncorrected camera separations. Inside the color computer, adjustments are made for a particular printing condition or for the specific nature of the original. As a result of these adjustments, the output signals generated by the color computer will be corrected, modified, and will be different from the input signals. The signal from the color computer is then fed into a scale computer which controls the reproduction size.

The scale computer controls the signal for exposing the film, the signal has to be stretched or compressed in both circumferential and cross-feed or axial directions of the exposing drum depending on the enlargement or reduction required (see Figure 2.2). In an analog computer, the corrected

Courtesy Hell Graphic Systems, Inc.

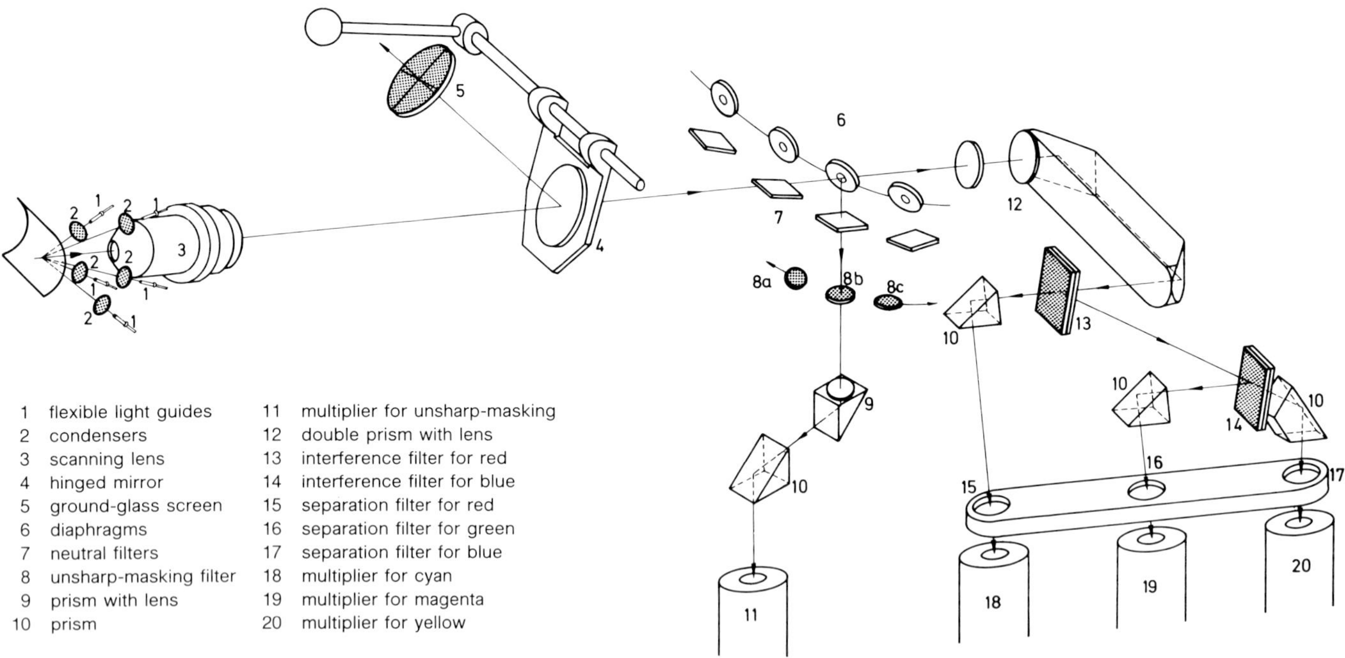

Figure 2.1. Signal path inside the scanning head of a typical drum scanner

signal generated by the color computer is continuous or analog. An analog signal cannot be stretched or compressed electronically; however, limited mechanical enlargement is made possible by changing the ratio of the circumference of the input and output drums. In most scanners, the signal is digitized by an analog to digital converter at this point and then stored temporarily in the memory (often called a store). The picture signal is then retrieved (called back) from the memory with the aid of an exposing pulse. It is then played back on the exposing drum at a slower speed for enlargement and faster speed for reduction during operation. The digitized signal is then reconverted into an analog signal for contact screen or continuous-tone separations. These signals are directly connected to an exposing lamp which will glow at different intensities at different strengths of the signal. For electronic screening, however, the digital signals are used directly to operate the dot generator. The scale change in the crossfeed or axial direction is performed by the different speed ratios of the exposing and scanning heads; the scanning head moves faster or slower compared to the exposing head depending on the enlargement or reduction. For example, during a 200% enlargement, the scanning head will move exactly half the speed of the exposing head, and conversely, for a 50% reduction, the head will move twice as fast as the exposing head.

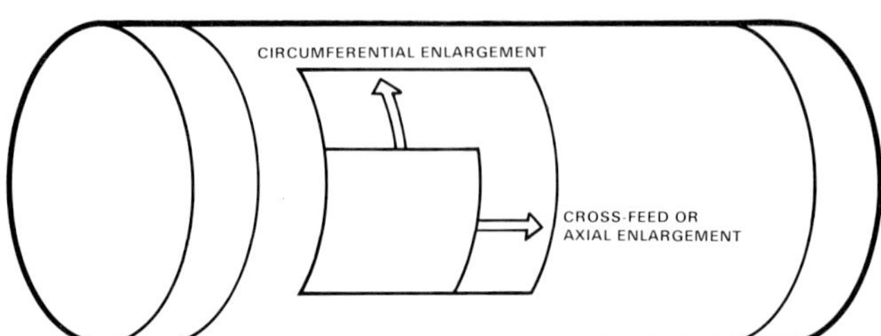

Figure 2.2. Circumferential and axial (also called horizontal or cross-feed) enlargements

Depending on the type of scanner, the method of exposure will vary. Scanners for contact screen and continuous-tone separations use an exposing lamp which will glow at different intensities if it is connected to a variable electrical voltage. Since the electrical output signal from the computer will be proportional to the color content of each line of the copy being scanned, there will be a continuous variation in the signal. This signal, in the form of electrical voltage, will continuously change the intensity of the lamp. The film passes by in front of the exposing lamp and will result in different density or dot sizes.

The electronic dot generation scanners use a laser light source to produce the dots directly on the film. As indicated earlier, the digital signals at the scale computer do not need to be reconverted back into analog signals for electronic screen-

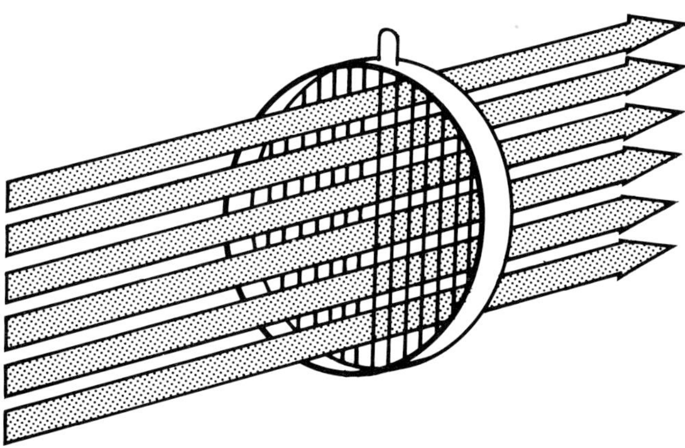

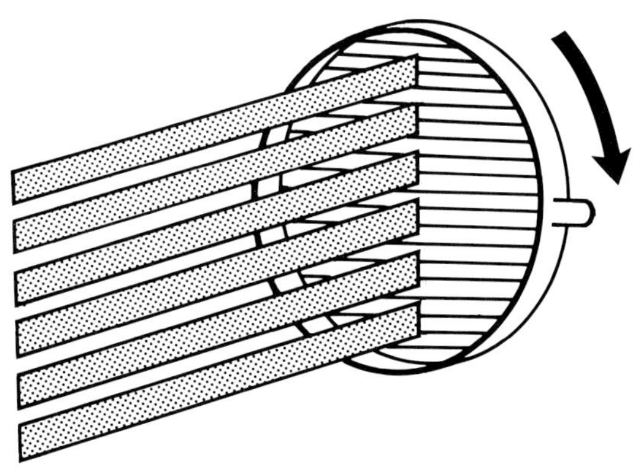

Figure 2.3. A polarization filter is used to allow a directional light similar to a laser to pass through or stop by applying defined electrical or acoustical signals

ing. These signals are used to control an electro-optical crystal modulator. In its simplest form, the modulator is a liquid crystal polarization filter. Since the laser light is directional and polarized, the light through the filter is allowed to transmit or be stopped by changing the polarization level of the filter. When a defined electrical voltage is applied to the filter for a certain polarization level, it will let the laser beam pass through for exposure. Then another defined voltage is applied to change the polarization level of the filter so that it stops the light passing through the filter (see Figure 2.3). However, in the Dainippon Screen scanners, the polarization level of the filter is controlled by an acousto-optical device. In most scanners, the major laser light source is split into several sources, and they are guided through fiber optics into a modulator for each. Several fine butted lines along with more than one revolution are used to make a single dot on the film. This is illustrated with Figure 2.4.

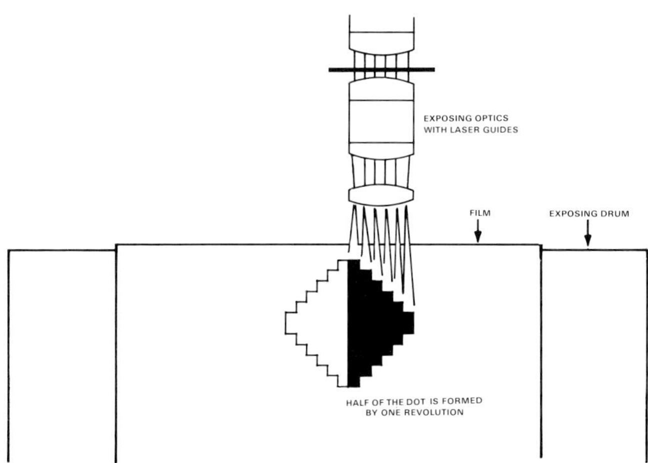

Figure 2.4. Formation of an electronic dot with six laser sources and two revolutions of the exposing drum

MECHANICS AND FUNCTIONS — A DETAILED EXPLANATION

Mechanical, electrical and optical analyses as well as a functional description of each of the three sections of a scanner relating to the flow of a signal are presented in detail in the following paragraphs.

SIGNAL FLOW IN THE SCANNING SECTION

The scanning section, often referred to as analyze section, can be divided into several sub sections on the basis of optical, mechanical, and electrical means of processing a signal.

Scanning Lamp: Depending on the brand of scanner, various types of lamps are used for illuminating a copy. For example, in both the Hell 399ER and DS SG-608, a halogen lamp is used for analyzing and scanning the original; however, in the Crosfield Magnascan 645, a xenon lamp is used for the same purpose. In the RZ 200-S, the same xenon lamp is used for analyzing, scanning, as well as exposing the film.

Different size scanning drums are needed for a variety of originals and for different enlargements and/or reduction. When a scanning drum is changed, it alters the plane of the original. As such, the optics of the light which illuminates the original has to be adapted for different drums to focus a minute spot of copy for the scanning optics. A center optics tube containing the light source provides illumination for the transparency on the scanning drum (see Figure 2.5). Three scanning drums and an optics attachment for each of the drums are provided for the Hell 399ER. The Magnascan 645 uses two drums and two selectable optics for the drums. On the RZ 200-S, the two scanning drums are of the same circumference; they differ only in length. The enlargement and

Courtesy Hell Graphic Systems, Inc.

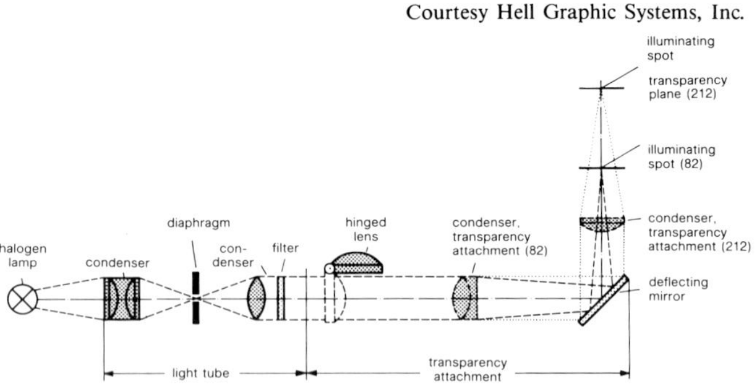

Figure 2.5. Center optics tube for illuminating the transparency during analyzing or scanning

reduction functions of this scanner are affected by the speed ratios of the scanning and exposing drums — the speed of the exposing drum is constant, but the scanning drum speed changes to accommodate the different enlargements and reductions. Three scanning drums are standard for the DS SG-608; however, the same light tube for illuminating the transparency is used for all three drums. The scanning optics assembly is moved at different positions to accommodate for the size and focusing plane for each drum. When properly positioned, a signal lamp lights up indicating that the scanning optics assembly is correctly focused for the particular drum in use.

The lamp for illuminating a reflection copy on the drum uses a separate optics system and is shown in Figure 2.6. The beam is focused directly or through a group of fiber optic cables to the collector lenses forming the illuminating head around the scanning lens. These lenses project the light at an angle on the copy surface which reflect back to the scanning lens.

Scanning or Analyze Head: The illuminated spot of the original passes through a group of scanning optics which is mounted on a scanning head. The scanned light beam is reflected through 90 degrees by a prism onto a dichroic assembly. The assembly consists of interference filters, prisms, and separation filters to separate the signal into red, green, and blue components. These separated light beams are then focussed onto the multipliers (see Figure 2.1).

In the RZ 200-S, no beam splitter or colored filters are

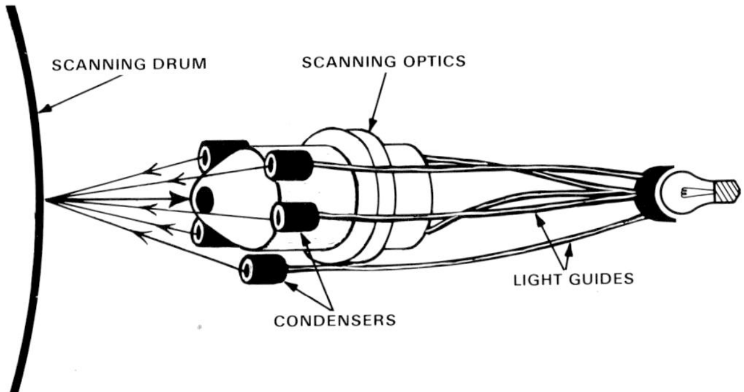

Figure 2.6. Light source and optics for illuminating a reflection copy in a scanner

used for separating the original signal into cyan, magenta, and yellow content for the three multipliers. Instead, the xenon analyzing light beam is passed through a prism to produce a spectrum containing the red, green, and blue lights. The spectrum is then projected on a spinning disk. The disk separates the red, green, and blue lights on the successive revolution of the scanning drum (see Figure 2.7). In other words, for each of the successive scanning drum revolutions, the spinning disk sends the multiplier each of the cyan, magenta, and yellow signal content of the original. The light, after passing through the original, is focused by the analyzing lens through a multiple lens turret onto a small aperture; this is the sharp aperture of the main multiplier. The remaining light is reflected onto a second multiplier and is used for unsharp masking.

In the RZ 200-S, the alternate lines of cyan, magenta, and yellow components of the original are scanned and stored, and are then recalled moments later for processing by the color computer. This sequential method of color analysis allows the 200-S to use just two multipliers instead of the conventional four, one for processing the color channels and the other one for processing the unsharp masking beam.

The final effect of the unsharp masking signal depends on the size ratio of the main aperture and the unsharp masking aperture and the color of the unsharp masking beam. The ratio of the aperture sizes will vary for different degrees of detail enhancement required for various enlargements and reductions. In most analog scanners, several sets of main and unsharp masking apertures are provided to vary the ratio of the two aperture sizes for different enhancement needs. All Hell scanners provide a rotating aperture wheel to select a different combination of main and unsharp masking apertures. In the DS SG-608, the proper combination of the main and unsharp making apertures are selected by placing an appropriate metal insert in the scanning head. In the Hell 399ER and DS SG-608 scanners, selectable color filters are also provided on the scanning head for the unsharp masking

Courtesy Itek Colour Graphics

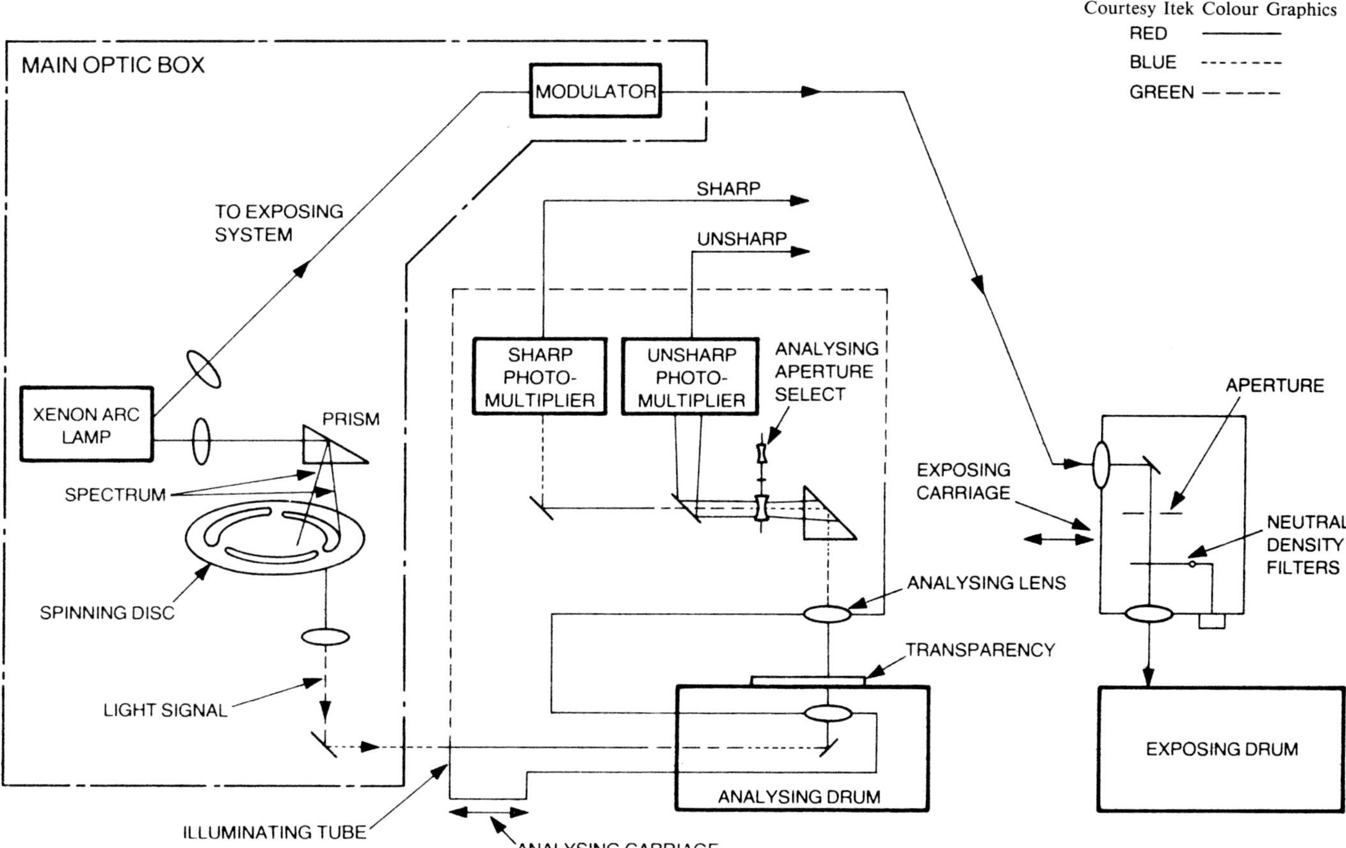

Figure 2.7. Optical system of the Royal Zenith 200-S

beam. This provides the detail enhancement in the borders of selected colors, if needed. However, because of the design principle, no color filter is required for the unsharp masking signal in the RZ 200-S. The same separation color is used for the unsharp masking channel during each separation. Similarly in the Magnascan 645, a special digital circuit converts each color signal into an unsharp masking signal during scanning.

Different scanning optics are normally used for different diameter drums. In the Hell 399ER, three separate scanning optics are provided for the three drums. However, in the DS SG-608, the same scanning optics is used for all three drums. The optics remains fixed; however, the scanning head is moved to different positions to accommodate for the size of the drum and focusing of the original. In the Crosfield 645, the two interchangeable lenses are inserted into the center optics or ray tube which is fixed. A fixed pickup lens is moved in or out to accommodate the large and small scanning drums.

Other controls on the scanning head include a knob for selecting a neutral density filter to control the intensity of the scanning light before it reaches the multipliers, and a lever or knob for precise focusing of the optical system on the transparency or reflection copy planes. In most scanners, a pivoted mirror is also provided in the scanning path for the observation of the enlarged scanning area on a ground glass screen. In most of these scanners, this mechanism is used to cut off scanning light transmitting through the scanning optics so that a total dark shadow can be created for the multipliers to set a zero reference.

Signal Flow in the Scanning Head

When the light from the original reaches the multipliers, each will produce a small electrical current which will be proportional to the amount of the separation signal. In the Hell 399ER, RZ 200-S, and DS SG-608 scanners, these analog signals are directly fed into the input of the color computer for further processing. However, in the Magnascan 645, these analog electrical signals from the multipliers are converted into digital signals and fed into the digital color computer for processing.

SIGNAL PROCESSING IN THE COMPUTER

Analog and Digital Computers

The two types of signal processing — analog and digital, have a large impact on the design and operation of a scanner. In an analog device, à physical means changes the values in the signals in a continuous fashion without breaking or separating the signals. A system that plays records or cassette tapes is an example of an analog system. As shown in Figure 2.8, continuous varying signals of audio tones from the record or tape pass through the pickup or tape playback head into the amplifier and out through the speaker. The electrical signals have provided an "analog" or analogy of the sound signals. Other examples of typical analog quantities are time and temperature. Time changes continuously as indicated by the continuous rotation of the hour, minute, and second hands on a typical clock. Temperature in a thermometer also varies continuously. The liquid level rises and falls smoothly with the heat or cold. In other words, any quantity that varies continuously and represents an infinite number of minute values can be considered to be analog. The analog signals in a computer are in electrical voltage, and a continuous resistor type potentiometer control is used to change the electrical signal to higher or lower values (see Figure 2.9).

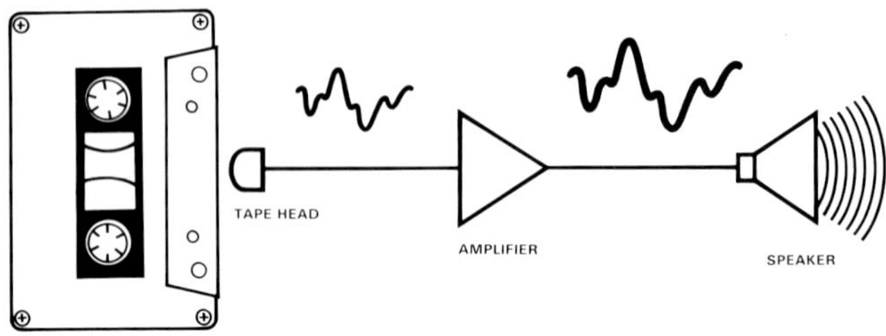

Figure 2.8. Analog sound amplification from a cassette tape

In contrast to an analog device, digital quantities exist or vary in clearly discrete increments or steps. For example, the pulse rate of a person is expressed in digital value. Money, like coins or bills is digital in nature as it can change only in increments of dollars and cents. While many quantities are analog in nature, virtually any analog quantity can also be represented digitally. In the previous examples of clocks and thermometers, the time and the temperature can also be represented digitally. A digital clock or a digital thermometer represents the time and temperature in digital forms.

Numbers are the primary language of all digital equipment. The data processed by digital devices, including computers, are usually numerical in nature. Digital equipment uses a special number system to represent quantities and process them. "Processing" refers to the way the data are handled or manipulated. Examples of processing are storing, retrieving, sorting, transmitting, etc. A digital system that uses only two symbols or digits to represent the quantities, 0 and 1, is called the binary number system. Binary numbers are more easily and quickly processed than other numbers and virtually all digital equipment uses binary numbers.

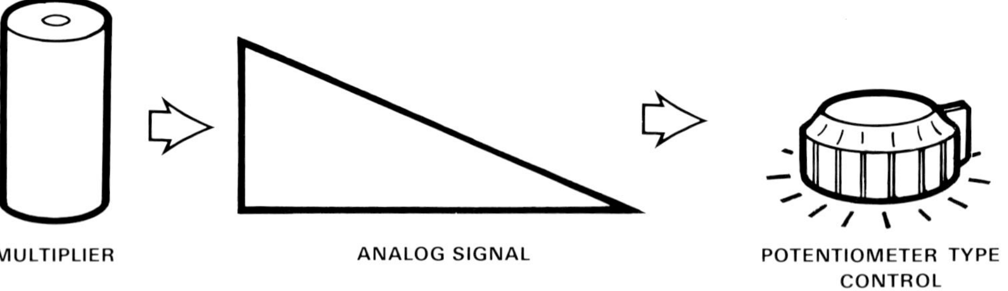

Figure 2.9. Concept of analog signal processing in the color computer of a scanner

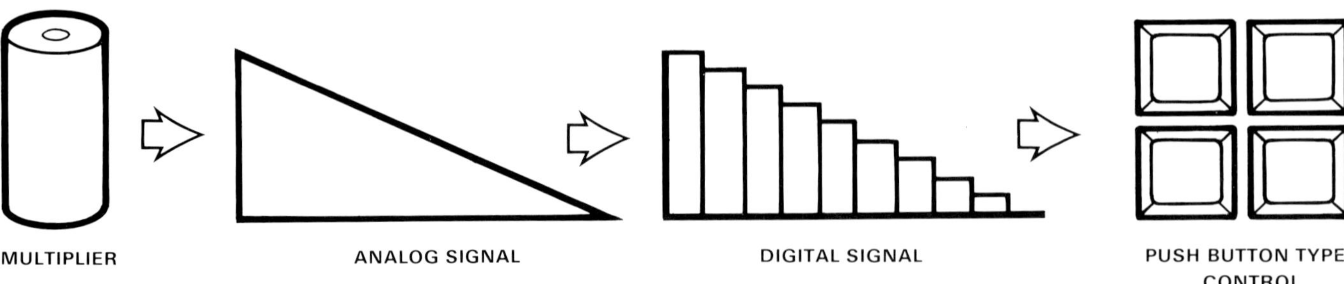

Figure 2.10. Concept of digital signal processing in the color computer of a scanner

Figure 2.10 shows the concept of digital signal processing in the scanner. As presented in the diagram, the signal generated by the multiplier is an analog or continuous signal. This analog signal is converted into a digital signal by breaking the continuous-tone signal into several steps and then numbering those steps. In this example, only 10 steps have been shown, however, in an actual situation there are many more steps.

These step numbers are then coded with only two digits, 0 and 1. Table 2 shows how the numbers 0 through 9 are coded with only two digits. Subsequently, the computer works only with these coded values.

TABLE 2

0	1	2	3	4	5	6	7	8	9
0	1	0	1	0	1	0	1	0	1
0	0	1	1	0	0	1	1	0	0
0	0	0	0	1	1	1	1	0	0
0	0	0	0	0	0	0	0	1	1

Figure 2.11 is a block diagram of an analog computer. All the computer functions in a scanner involve complex mathematical computation. However, in an analog computer, this computation is fairly simple because it is performed by the physical change of the electrical voltage. By the turn of a potentiometer, an increase or decrease of the electrical voltage results. The effect of these changes can be observed or measured in an analog or digital panel. Once the potentiometers are set, the time to process the signal generated by the original during scanning can be very short; in fact, it can be as fast as the travelling speed of an electrical signal (approximately 1,86,000 miles per second). As a result, in an analog scanner, the scanning speed is not dependent on the computational speed of the color computer, but is limited only by the speed of the light sensitive materials (film emulsion) in relation to the exposing lamp.

To perform the same functions, the digital computer has to determine the values of cyan, magenta, yellow, and black for each point of the original during scanning. The speed of the computation required for each point of a fast moving original and concurrently supplying this information to the exposing unit for exposing the film have to be extremely fast. One of the earliest digital computation methods is based on the Neugebauer Equations. During scanning, the look up table, which contains data for red, green and blue filter values, is searched by the computer for the cyan, magenta, yellow, and black values for each point of the original being scanned. The

Courtesy Hell Graphic Systems, Inc.

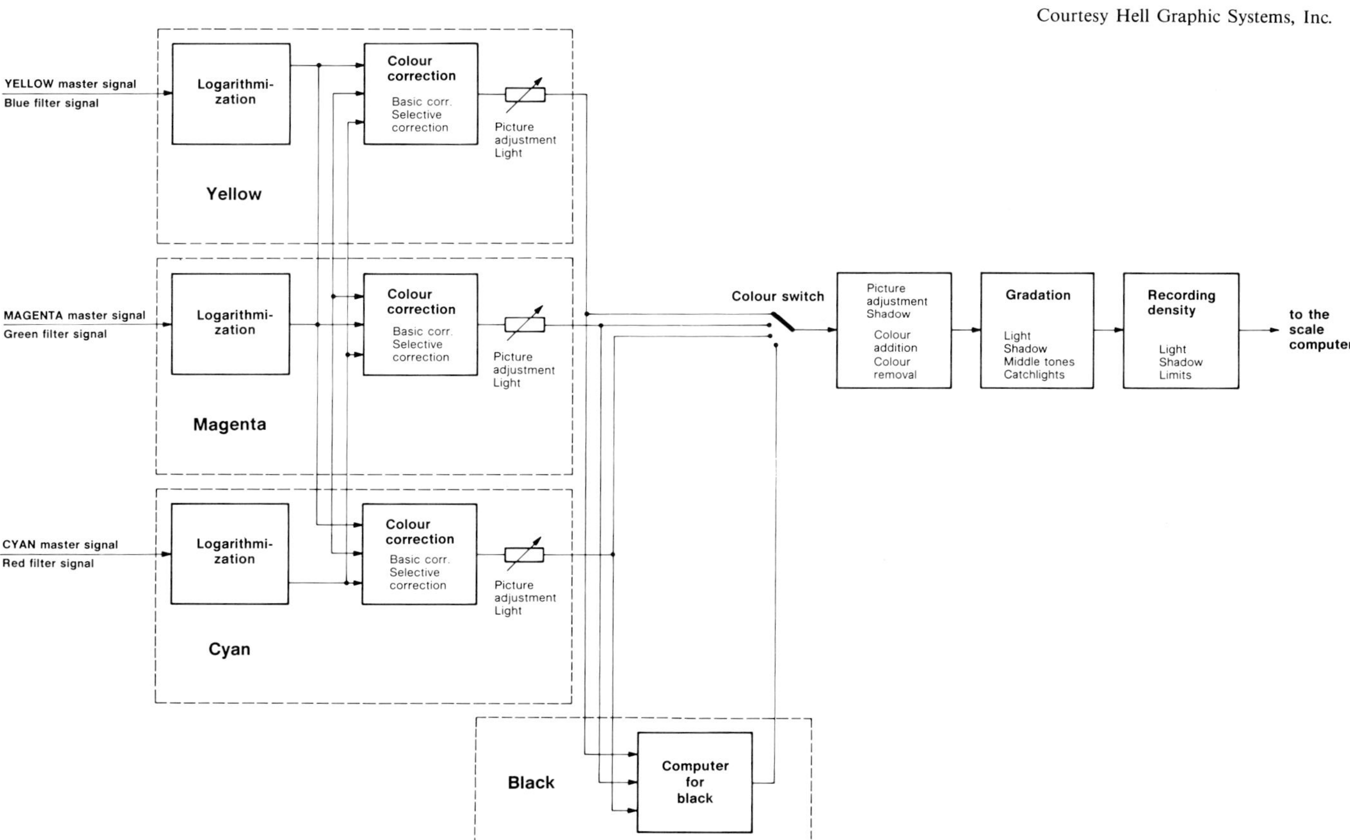

Figure 2.11. Block diagram of a typical analog color computer

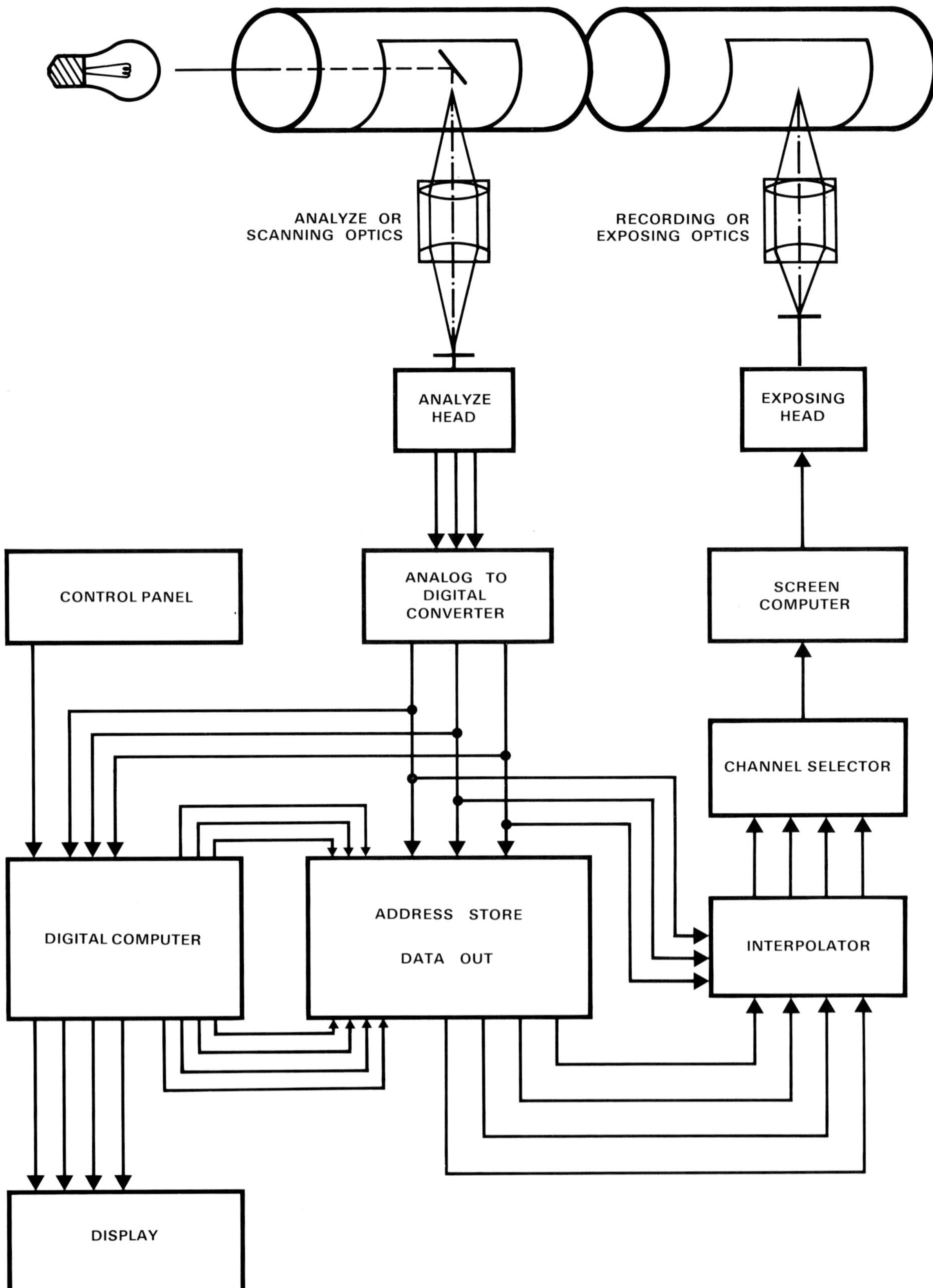

Figure 2.12. Block diagram of a typical digital color computer

digital computer was not fast enough to compute the values of the original while it was rotating, and the scanning speed of the scanner had to be slowed down considerably to adapt the approach.

With the advent of faster, more efficient digital computers, new memory devices with exotic names such as EPROM, DRAM, CMOS, etc., and new innovations in the field, the use of these computers for signal processing has grown rapidly during the last decade. The revised version of Neugebauer Equation and other faster and efficient methods of digital computation are adapted successfully in some of the latest generation of scanners. One of the significant developments is Crosfield's approach to digital computation in its current models of scanners. The analog signals from the multipliers are converted into digital signals, and the computer is first programmed for color and tone values within definite parameters by normal computation with a set of trial colors. These trial digital "coarse" values, also called basic values (BV), are stored in the form of red, green, and blue filter signals, together with their yellow, magenta, cyan, and black printing values as computed by the tone and color correcting programs. A job is set up in the scanner and the necessary tone and color adjustments are made for the reproduction of the original. These adjusted "fine" values, also referred to as customer values (CV), are applied to the basic or coarse values to come up with a new set of values, called "job values." These job values are the final values applied to the job. If the "coarse" values do not contain the exact "fine" values, the "coarse" values are interpolated to achieve the approximate "fine" values. Interpolation is the technique of finding an approximate value from two or more values when the precise value is not available in the table. This interpolation technique is performed by the computer automatically. The advantage of this technique is that there is no searching of a look up table for the vast amount of data. Instead, a small amount of preprogrammed values are searched for each and every point of the copy being scanned, resulting in faster computation.

Digital computers work with a set of preprogrammed values. With a set or list of preset values, the computer is asked to compute the dot sizes required to reproduce a point on the copy being scanned. Software packages on floppy disks are available from the scanner manufacturer with updated programs to perform a specific set of functions. When a point on the copy is positioned in front of the analyze light and the appropriate button for a specific function is pressed, the values are displayed at the digital panel. Using the keyboard, the operator can inform the control unit of the required changes. The control unit compares and calculates the required changes in accordance with a list of preprogrammed values and displays the data or sends it to the next station for further processing.

Figure 2.12 is a simplified block diagram of a digital color scanner adapted from an earlier Crosfield patent. The light rays from the original containing the cyan, magenta, and yellow signals are converted from analog to digital signals. The three signals are connected to the digital computer as well as to the digital storage and an interpolator. If the stored values do not contain the required values for a specific need, automatic interpolation takes place between the stored values and the interpolator to find the exact values. The store and the interpolator provide three output signals for the cyan, magenta, and yellow printer values and also a fourth signal for a black printer. The black printer value, however, is derived from the values of the cyan, magenta, and yellow signals. A channel selector receives the four signals and selects the one which corresponds to the separation to be made on the light sensitive film. This digital signal is then converted into an analog signal for contact screen or continuous-tone application, or in the case of electronic dots, is used directly to control the modulator for exposing the film. For the preliminary loading of the storage with the matrix of output values, a control panel enables parameter values to be set in accordance with the system characteristics and the characteristics of the original to be reproduced. These parameter values are then entered into the digital computer which is programmed to provide the required output-input relationship. A display permits the effect of this relationship and the effect of the parameter settings to be inspected before the matrix of output values is calculated by the computer and entered into the memory store of the computer.

The analog and digital computers can be easily distinguished by the design of the operator control panels (see Figure 2.13). For analog signal processing, a large number of continuously variable potentiometer type controls are available for setting the values. In the digital computers, the operator adjusts various functions of the scanner by pushbutton controls. The pushbutton keyboard is the medium by which the operator communicates with the scanner. Each keystroke or a proper sequence of keystrokes form a part of a command sequence which specifies the control or controls to be adjusted.

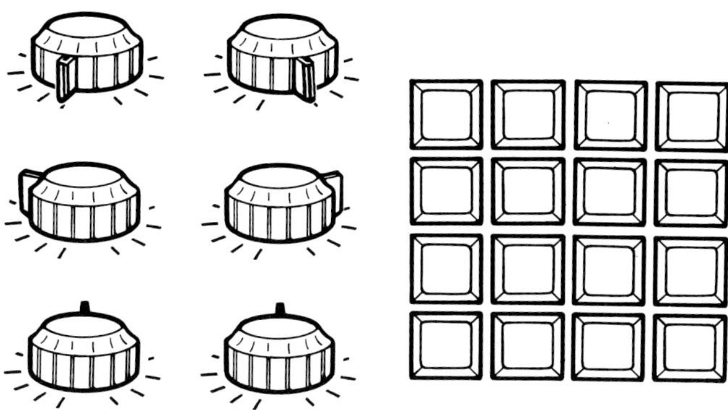

Figure 2.13. Potentiometer and pushbutton controls in the analog and digital color computers

Scanners may require more than one type of computer for signal processing. For example, the Hell 399ER and DS SG-608 use an analog color computer; however, they also use digital signal processing for scaling, for some mechanical functions, and for the control of a supplemental computer such as the electronic screen computer. The RZ 200-S uses digital technology to process the analog signal. The Crosfield Magnascan 645 is an all digital scanner. The analog signal from the multipliers are converted into a digital signal and from this point, all signal processing as well as the form of the signal itself are digital.

SIGNAL PROCESSING IN THE COLOR COMPUTER

White Alignment or Autobalance

The initial step in the processing of signals is to calibrate the computer to balance the multipliers. This calibration of the scanner can be compared to the calibration of a densitometer: it must be zeroed before an accurate reading can be taken. Similarly, the output ranges of the multipliers are adjusted for a minimum density and a maximum density. When the circuits are balanced for these outputs, the scanner acts like a densitometer, reading the continuously variable copy density and generating a balanced output within these density limits. The other objective of the calibration is to have identical output from the multipliers for given minimum and maximum densities. After the calibration, a balancing circuit monitors the input versus output signals of the multipliers and makes adjustments for any discrepancy. For example, if for the same input values, the output of the green filter multiplier is different than the others, the balancing circuit will bring the output of this multiplier to the same level as the others.

Depending on the brand of scanner, the basic input calibration is designated with different names. For example, in the Hell 399ER scanners, they are called WHITE and BLACK ALIGNMENT; in the Magnascan 645, RZ 200-S, and DS SG-608 scanners, they are called AUTOBALANCE. The steps to perform this basic calibration are simple in all scanners. To calibrate for a highlight, the scanning light is positioned for a neutral white area, and the designated button is

Courtesy D.S. America, Inc.

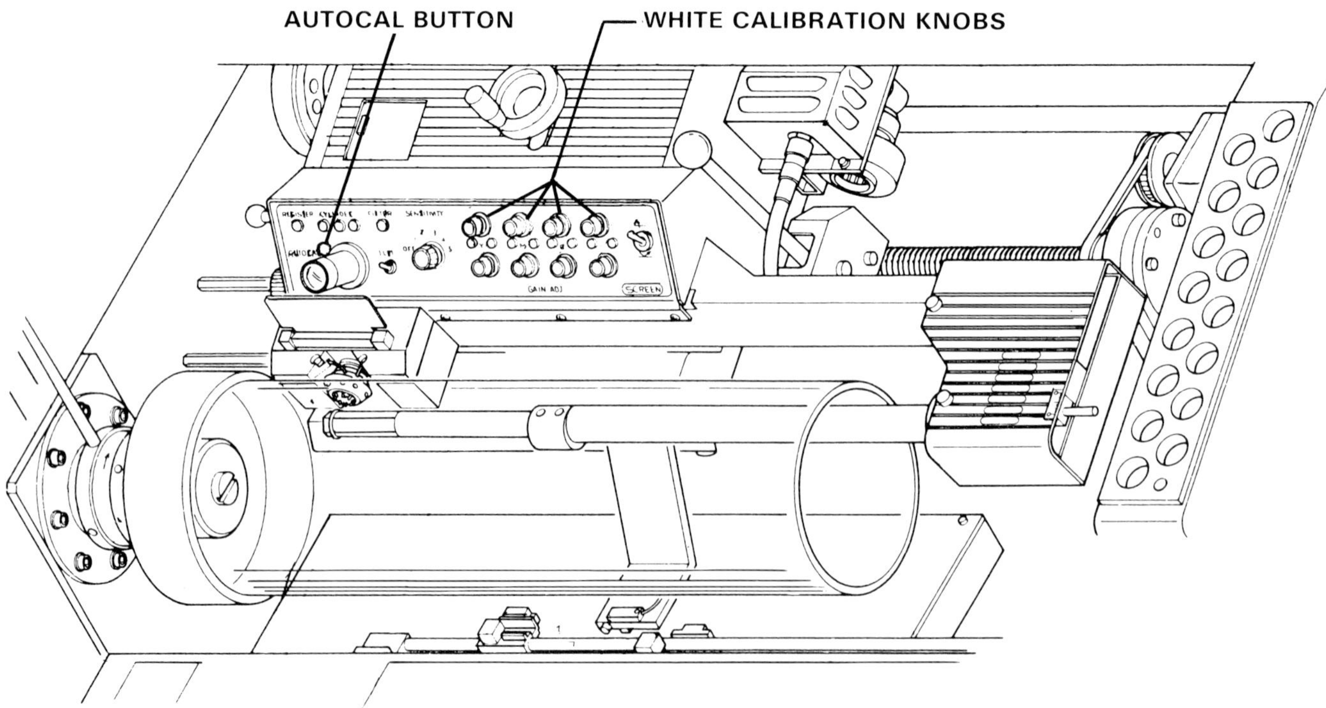

Figure 2.13a. AUTOCAL button at the DS SG-608 scanning head. The button works in conjunction with the Reference WHITE CALIBRATION control knobs. These knobs can be used for adjusting the sensitivity of the photomultipliers. When any highlight (copy highlight, gray scale, or the transparent cylinder) is placed in the scanning light path and the AUTOCAL button is pressed, an automatic calibration of the photomultipliers takes place. The correct calibration is indicated by the lights situated under the WHITE CALIBRATION control knobs going out. A value of 100 is also obtained on the digital meter for correct Autocalibration when the meter switch is at the AUTOCAL position

pressed to balance the circuits. Normally for a transparency, a clean scanning drum, and for a reflection copy, a highlight step of the gray scale are used for this calibration. To calibrate for shadow, the scanning light is cut off before reaching the multipliers and thus adjustments are made for the maximum shadow.

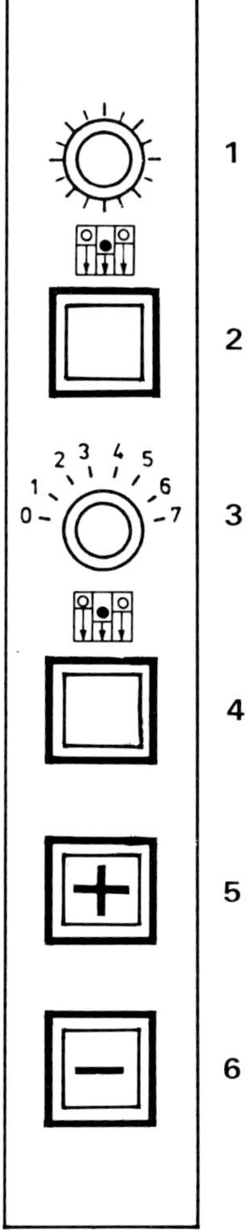

Figure 2.14. WHITE ALIGNMENT panel in the Hell 399ER. Control 1 is used to simulate neutral density ranging from 0.0 to .70 for the WHITE ALIGNMENT. Control 2 is used in conjunction with Control 1 to reduce any color cast in the highlight during White Alignment. Control 3 is a color cast reduction switch, and when used in conjunction with Control 4, it removes various proportions of color cast. Push buttons 5 and 6 are used to increase or decrease density or dot percent values after the White Alignment is performed

In the DS SG-608, the calibration is performed by first placing a neutral point (a clean scanning drum, an internal highlight density, or a highlight step of the copy) in the scanning path and then pressing the designated pushbutton AUTOCAL. The button works in conjunction with WHITE CALIBRATION controls. The correct calibration is indicated by the lights going out which are situated under the WHITE CALIBRATION control knobs. When the METER switch is in the AUTOCAL mode, pressing the AUTOCAL button shows a digital display of 100, indicating that the calibration for the highlight is completed. However, if the multipliers are not balanced properly, one or more lights under the WHITE CALIBRATION knobs will glow. Calibration steps are similar in the Hell 399ER scanner. The accuracy of the calibration is first checked by predesignated numbers (60) which appear on the display panel for each channel indicating that the multipliers are balanced for equal output. In addition, an unsharp masking value of 0 indicates that the difference between the main signal and the unsharp masking signal is zero when the two signals are from a surface with the same density values. After the White Alignment is performed, an electrical range value of 100 is assigned for all the color channels. The shadow calibration for the multipliers is performed by cutting off the scanning light transmitting through the scanning head and assigning a lower electrical range value, 0 in the Hell 399ER and 40 for the DS SG-608. The next and the last step of the basic calibration is to assign appropriate dot values for the highlight and shadow points for the three colors and black. To perform AUTOBALANCE in the Magnascan 645, the clear cylinder is positioned for the scanning light and the AUTOBALANCE button is pressed. The balancing function proceeds and is performed automatically for both highlight and shadow. A correct balance is indicated by a bleep sound, and the Alphanumeric display will revert to the monitor mode indicating that normal operation may continue. In the RZ 200-S, a clear drum is positioned for the scanning light and a RESET button is pressed for automatic calibration of the multipliers. A detailed discussion on the scanner calibration is presented in the chapter "Basic Calibration."

In most scanners, the WHITE ALIGNMENT or AUTOBALANCE functions are conveniently used for eliminating any minor color cast in the highlight area of the copy. When any highlight area is positioned for the scanning light during this calibration, the multipliers are automatically balanced for equal output, as if a neutral area has been used for this calibration. As a result, the colored highlight will appear as neutral in the reproduction. Most scanners use this as a color cast compensation circuit for originals with a neutral highlight having a minor color cast.

It may be emphasized here that before this basic input calibration is performed, all adjustments which affect the scanning light must be set before they reach the multipliers. These adjustments include the selection of the scanning aperture, the color filter for unsharp masking, and the neutral density filter on the scanning head. Any change in the light value falling on the multipliers because of such a change will necessitate a new calibration.

In an analog computer, after the circuits are balanced, the signals from the multipliers are converted into logarithmic density values by a log amplifier. This is a mathematical conversion, but the physiology of the human eye with respect to sensitivity and color perception are also considered during this conversion. The analog signals are transmitted via the low noise amplifiers to the input stages of the color computer. However, for digital signal processing, the analog signal is converted into digital signal by a converter.

Color Correction

Various Concepts of Color Correction

Different principles exist for the correction of color with both analog and digital computers. Popular among those are the electronic masking methods in which the electronic computation is performed by taking into account the unwanted absorption characteristics of the process inks. The other type is the use of Neugebauer Equations in which a look up table is generated containing a vast amount of data for each and every possible point on an original. During the scanning of the original, the table is searched for proper values for each point. The Masking Equation approach is normally used in an analog computer and a Neugebauer look up table approach is used with a digital computer. Recently the Neugebauer approach has been modified to speed up the computation. With this approach, the equations are "presolved" and the solutions are stored as software in the form of a small look up table to be used by the digital computer. This makes it possible to compress and limit the number of data. The job input values are then used to search the look up table to find the appropriate output values. Interpolation techniques are used when a precise value is not found in the tables.

The Masking Equation approach is popular in analog scanners and produces high quality results. In this case, the color value is computed by an overall approach, which means that when a color correction is performed, an automatic correction will take place for the entire separation for that color. The major disadvantage in this approach is that, except for the highly saturated primary and secondary colors, some secondary and tertiary colors do not produce the best results when mixed in different proportions. As a result, supplementary color correction controls are added to the scanner to allow for the independent adjustment of these colors without significantly influencing the other colors.

The basic steps for color correction in both analog and digital computers are identical. Color correction is performed by first placing a saturated patch of color in the scanning light path and then changing the values of the wanted and unwanted colors by the appropriate controls. Two types

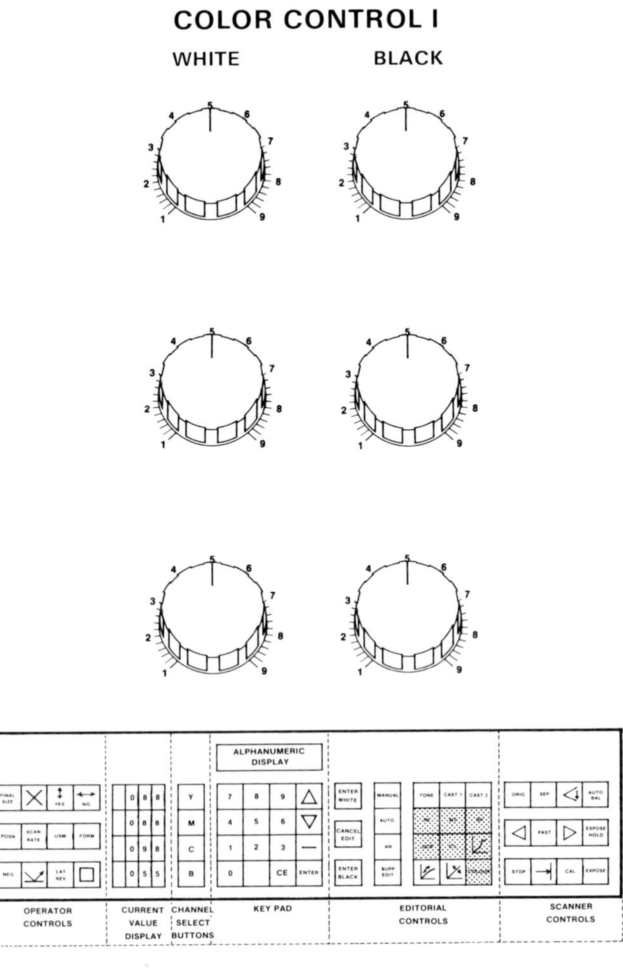

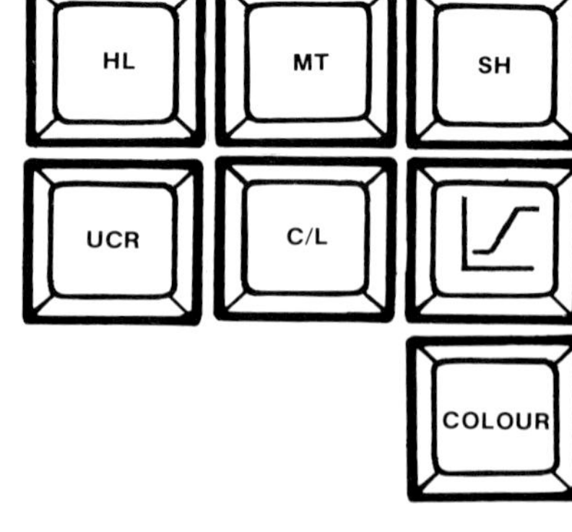

Figure 2.15. Basic color correction panel of the DS SG-608 and color correction push button controls in the Magnascan 645. In the DS SG-608, the required amount of unwanted color is set with the White Color correction knobs and the required amount of wanted color is set with the Black Color correction knobs. In the Magnascan 645, the six color correction buttons have dual functions: HL: Red; MT: Yellow; SH: Green; UCR: Cyan; C/L: Blue; and ∟/: Magenta. The color correction function is activated by pressing the push button designated as COLOUR. Otherwise they operate according to the functions marked on their faces. Each of the six buttons specify which color in the original is to be adjusted, and the position of the channel select buttons Y, M, C, and B specifies the separation which is affected by the adjustment

of corrections can be done for each basic color — black color, also called wanted color, and white color, also called unwanted color. The black and white colors may be compared to the main separation color and the masking unwanted color in a conventional separation. For example, when cyan is the separation color, the yellow and magenta (green and blue filter masking signals) are the mask colors; when magenta is the separation color, cyan and yellow (red and blue filter masking signals) are the mask colors; when yellow is the separation color, cyan and magenta (red and green filter masking signals) are the mask colors. The extent of correction will depend on the intensity or the signal level of the mask, and this level is adjusted with the corresponding correction controls in the scanner for the white (unwanted) and black (wanted) colors.

As indicated earlier, with most color computers, additional color correction controls are available for correcting narrow bands of colors. They are provided to correct the colors selectively, i.e. without appreciably influencing the adjacent colors. This correction affects all colors of limited saturation while leaving the neutrals and highly saturated colors unaffected.

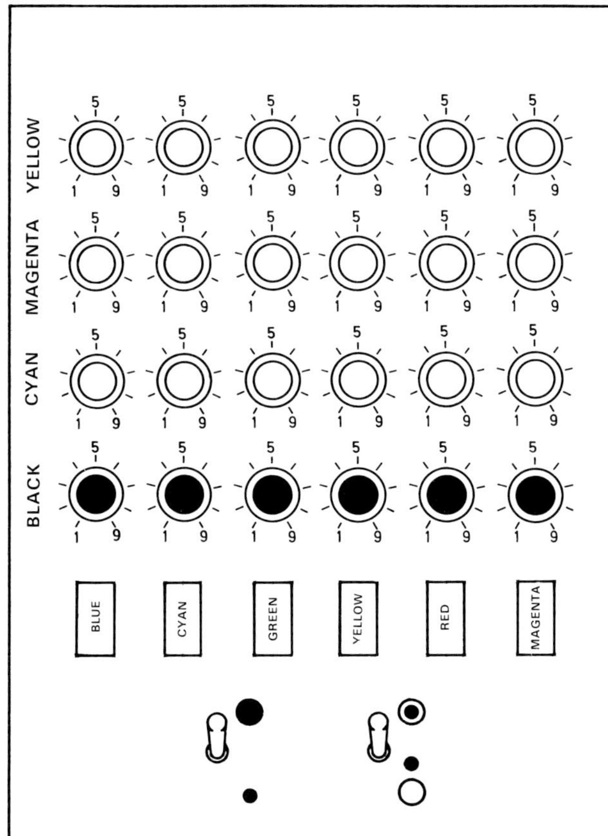

Figure 2.16. SELECTIVE COLOR CORRECTION panel in the Hell 399ER. Each of the four horizontal rows of knobs represent cyan, magenta, yellow, and black channels. The six controls for each channel correct the corresponding colors shown below the controls. The toggle switch at the bottom left activates either the effects of the above color correction controls or a fixed factory calibrated color correction value. The toggle switch at the bottom right either selects a strong or a weak correction

In all analog computers, a change of color value is obtained by turning the potentiometer knob towards increasing or decreasing value. A saturated color from the copy or a standard color patch is positioned for the scanning light, the separation channel which needs to be affected by the change is selected, and the values of any of the primary or secondary colors are monitored and changed as desired. For example, if more yellow is needed in the green area, a green color is positioned for the scanning light, the yellow color channel is selected, and the yellow is added by the black color controls monitoring the values on the panel. However, in a digital computer similar to the Magnascan 645 and RZ 200-S, the color correction is accomplished in a slightly different way. If a change is desired that is different from a normal color correction program already stored in the computer memory, first appropriate calibration number is used to recall the specific color correction program. Then the color correction function is executed by entering predetermined values or by increasing or decreasing the values. Normally there are six keybuttons available for color correction in these two scanners, one each for the cyan, magenta, yellow, red, green, and blue. The six buttons specify the color of the original to be affected and the channel select button specifies the separation being affected by the adjustment. For example, in the Magnascan 645, to reduce magenta in green, first the color correction program is called, a green color of the original is positioned for the scanning light, and the green color correction button is pressed. A display on the panel shows the color correction value, and a specific value can be entered in the magenta channel or the displayed value can be increased or decreased by a pair of designated push buttons until the required number is reached. Similarly in the RZ 200-S, color correction is performed by either subtracting or adding the percentage desired for the yellow, magenta, cyan, blue, green, and red. For example, if more yellow is desired in red, the desired percentage is entered with the yellow key while the scanning light is positioned for a red area of the original.

Image Adjustment

Image Adjustment, also called Highlight and Shadow Density Setting or Enter White and Enter Black, is an electrical adaptation of the computer to the highlight and shadow range of the copy. In other words, each time an original is scanned, the computer must be informed of the density range of that original so that appropriate dot values are produced for the copy. The function of the image adjustment also involves the compression of tones so that proper tonal values can be obtained within the range of the copy. To accomplish image adjustment, the highlight and shadow density values for each copy are entered into the computer. To perform these functions in the Hell 399ER, first the scanning light is positioned for the copy highlight or the equivalent step on a gray scale, and an electrical range value of 100 is assigned for all the color channels. Then the scanning light is positioned on the darkest shadow step of the copy, and a range value of 0 is assigned. In the DS SG-608, the density values for the highlight and shadow are set by two knobs in the predesignated density values, and a range value of 100 is set for the highlight and 40 for the shadow during the AUTOBALANCE function. These two highlight and shadow density set knobs have a highlight range from 0 to 1.0 and a shadow range from 1.3 to 3.3 density values. The copy may also be used for this calibration by placing the scanning light for the highlight and shadow, assigning values of 100 and 40 for these two areas respectively, and then assigning the appropriate dot values. However, when an exact or facsimile reproduction of the copy is desired, the standard values used during the WHITE and BLACK ADJUSTMENT or AUTOBALANCE should be kept the same.

In both the Magnascan 645 and the RZ 200-S, first an appropriate spot of the copy is positioned for the scanning light; a specific program is recalled for this function, and the highlight and shadow density values are assigned. This function is called ENTER WHITE and ENTER BLACK in the Magnascan 645. In both the scanners, any color cast in the highlight and/or shadow can be neutralized during the entering of these values if the original scene contains any neutral highlight.

After the image adjustment, the black portion of the separation is automatically computed by the black computer when the separation of the three corrected colors are in progress. However, at this stage, some of the computer functions, which are involved in the modification or change of the shadow areas of the original are again introduced. Examples of these functions are gradation, under color removal (UCR),

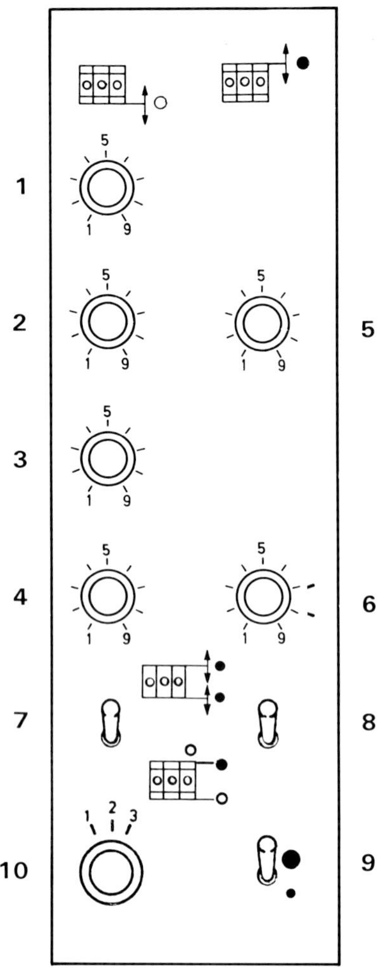

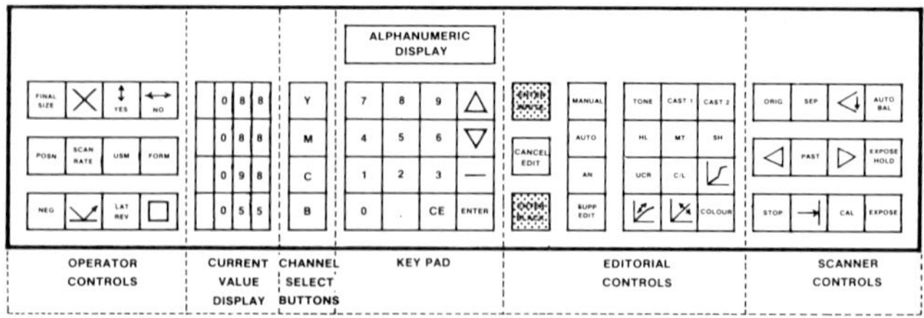

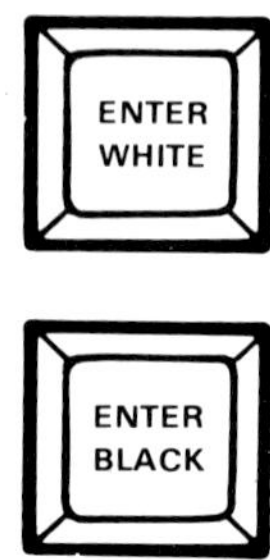

Figure 2.17. IMAGE or PICTURE ADJUSTMENT controls in the Hell 399ER and ENTER WHITE/ENTER BLACK pushbutton controls in the Magnascan 645. In the 339ER, controls 1 through 4 are used for electrical adaptation of the photomultipliers to a selected white level by assigning a value of 100. Controls 5 and 6 are used to assign a minimum value of 0 for the image shadow - Control 5 is for the cyan, magenta, and yellow separations and Control 6 is for the black separation. With toggle switches 7 and 8, the effects of the above image adjustment controls can be deactivated, if necessary. With toggle switch 9, the density range of the original can be adapted for the computer - large dot for a large range and small dot for a small range. Control 10 is a 3-position black separation switch to select any one of the (i) uncorrected, (ii) split-filter, or (iii) corrected black. In the Magnascan 645, ENTER WHITE and ENTER BLACK pushbuttons are used to enter the highlight and shadow density values of the original. These values must be entered before other specific adjustments or editorial retouching controls are used

under color addition (UCA), and gray component replacement (GCR). (A detailed discussion of these functions are presented in the related chapters.) In addition to these shadow functions, a gray balance function is also introduced at this point by assigning different dot values for the three colors along the entire range of the gradation curve.

Gradation

During image adjustment, the computer is adapted for the copy highlight and shadow, and the minimum and maximum dot percentages are assigned for these two points. The purpose of the gradation control is to provide an optimal tone compression resulting in a customized tone curve for each original while the highlight and shadow density points are adapted for each copy. Each gradation adjustment can be done manually for each copy by assigning dot values for the appropriate aim points. In some scanners, the aim points remain fixed, the gradation curve shape is changed by increasing or decreasing the dot values for each fixed aim point density. Several curve parameters can also be stored in the computer memory for different applications. After the highlight and shadow density points are entered for the copy, any of these fixed preprogrammed curves can be called which will produce a customized curve within the highlight and shadow limits. In the DS SG-608, three sets of four controls are provided for each of the cyan, magenta, yellow, and black to control the highlight, middle-tone and shadow contrast. After the highlight and shadow dot values are set, a pair of reference switches are used to assign appropriate dot values for the fixed quarter-tone, middle-tone, and three-quarter-tone aim points. An optional Function Generator is available for the DS SG-608 which can be used for the storage and

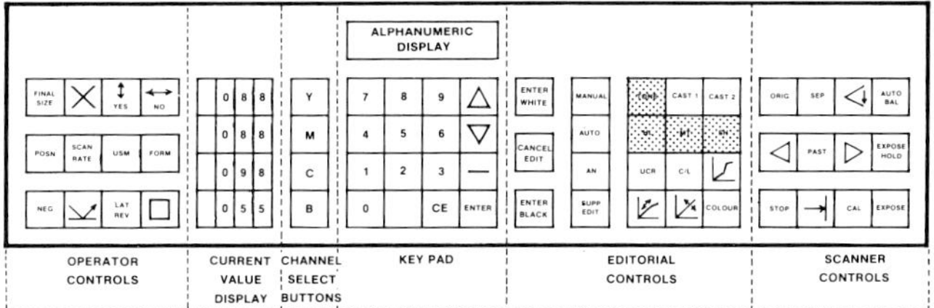

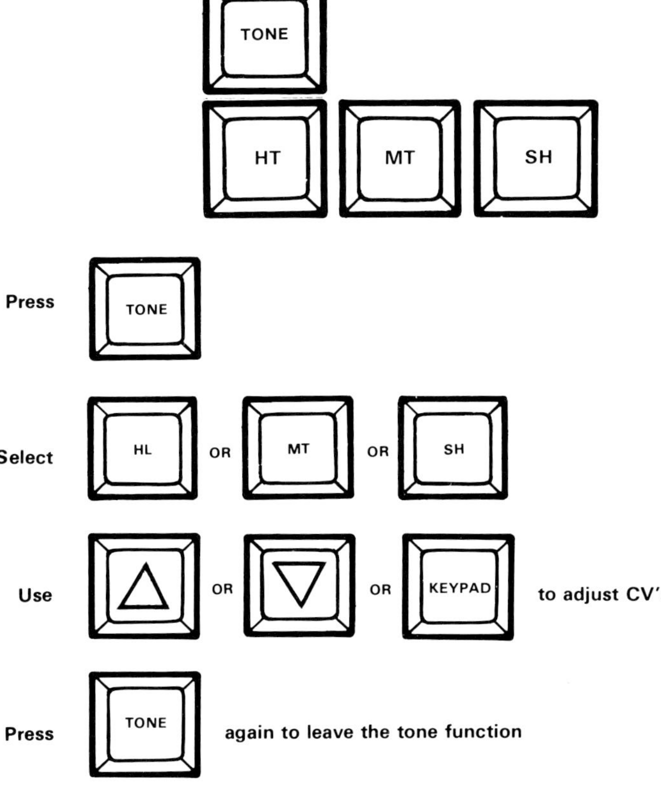

Figure 2.18. Gradation panel in the DS SG-608 (left) and Magnascan 645 (top). Also shown is the operating sequence for adjusting tone in the Magnascan 645. In the SG-608, the quarter-tone, middle-tone and shadow GRADATION knobs are used to adjust the three-color dot percent values for the fixed aim points. These aim points for the quarter-tone, middle-tone, and three-quarter-tone are activated with a pair of Reference switches. When all controls are set at midpoint as shown in the illustration, and when the BLACK GRADATION knob is set at 0 (see Figure 2.21), the tone curve will represent a factory calibrated standard gradation curve. In the Magnascan 645, once the push button TONE is pressed, equal and simultaneous adjustment of the tonal curves in all three color channels can be made while maintaining gray balance. Changes can also be made individually in the highlight by selecting the HL button, in the middle-tone by selecting the MT button, and in the shadow by selecting the SH button

retrieval of up to 4 different preprogrammed gradation data. In the Hell 399ER, 20 preprogrammed fixed gradations with different curve shapes are available on a floppy disk, any one of which can be recalled after the highlight and shadow values are entered for the copy. In addition, a maximum of 18 gradation curves can be customized and stored on a floppy disk for special application. A set of manual controls is also provided to adjust individually any fixed gradation curve, if needed, or for manual gradation adjustment. In the Hell 399ER and DS SG-608, values for gray balance are introduced at this point by maintaining a difference of dot sizes between the three colors along the entire curve. In the 399ER, a set of three controls is provided to affect the relative dot percentage of the three colors for proper gray balance.

In the RZ 200-S, the gradation is adjusted by the highlight and middle-tone controls along with a range setting. The range control is designed to provide the correct change of gradation to accommodate long-range or short-range transparencies without adjusting the middle-tone position. However, a control is also provided to change the contrast of the middle-tone, if necessary. A highlight gradation control is provided to emphasize highlight for a high-key copy. Initially a gray balance program is produced and stored in the memory which can be recalled and changed if desired.

In the Magnascan 645, the tone values for highlight, middle-tone, and shadow can be individually adjusted in relation to a set of preprogrammed values. Once the proper values for highlight and shadow points are entered, an increase or decrease of the displayed values are made until the desired change is achieved. Once the gradation is adjusted for the placement of the middle-tone, it is automatically calculated and placed for the range of any original. A gray balance is achieved by producing a 16-step electronic gray scale using a set of basic values for the three colors. When the proper magenta and yellow tone values for gray are found in the printed scale in relation to cyan, the values are entered into the computer. All curves are then automatically extrapolated from this program for gray balance.

The signal is further processed to change the gradation for catchlight drop out, if necessary. In the Hell 399ER, four controls are provided for this function, three for each of the process colors and a starting point control to adjust the catchlights at a certain point on the gradation curve. Similar controls are also provided in the DS SG-608. A set of controls can be used to boost or limit the highlight in the area brighter than the set highlight. A program named Highlight Flip is used in the RZ 200-S to expand the difference between highlight and catchlight resulting in the dropout of dot values in the catchlight areas. A similar program is provided in the Magnascan 645 to attain five different slopes to dropout catchlight at different highlight density points on the copy. There are two parameters for the catchlight adjustment in this scanner. A breakpoint can be set to designate where the dropout will start, e.g. 5%, 7%, etc., and then the slope is set which affects the degree of dropout.

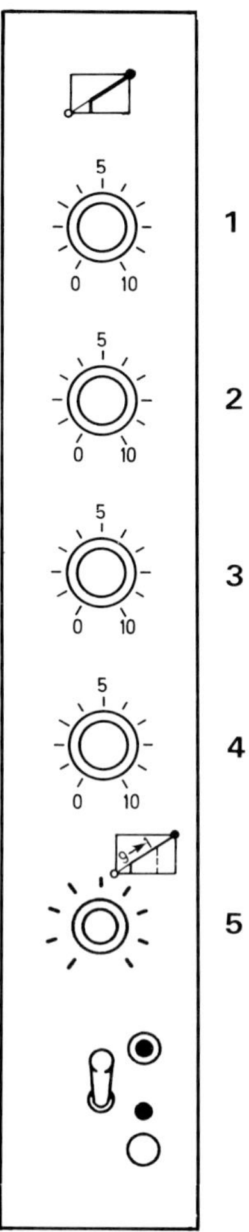

Figure 2.19. Catchlight panel in the Hell 399ER. Controls 1 through 4 are used to adjust the intensity of dropout in each color. Control 5 is the Starting Point Control on the gradation curve from which the dropout will be effective. The toggle switch at the bottom activates (when up) or deactivates (when down) the effects of the above controls.

UCR, UCA, and GCR

After the gradation adjustment, the signal in the shadow regulator stage is adjusted for under color removal (UCR), under color addition (UCA), and gray component replacement (GCR). In both the Hell 399ER and DS SG-608, the extent of removal or addition of colors in the neutral areas is controlled by a set of knobs to adjust the level for each color. In addition, in both the scanners, starting point controls are provided to select a point on the gradation curve from which the UCR/UCA will be effective. In the RZ 200-S, a UCR key is provided to reduce the color in neutral shadow areas. The same control can be used for REVERSE UCR, a function similar to UCA control in the other scanners. The range of black can be changed from a skeleton to a full range by entering the required dot values into the program during the highlight and range adjustment. The UCR and PCR (Polychromatic Color Removal, a GCR version of Crosfield) programs of the Magnascan 645 are integrated into one set of functional controls. PCR is set with a function button on the key panel. "Normal" UCR (without PCR) can be performed as well and is accessed via a "Calibration Number." The two cast controls provided in this scanner can be used to add or subtract any or all of the three colors individually to neutralize any area/areas of the copy.

At this point, the signal is connected to the GCR function of the computer. In the DS SG-608, a black gradation control knob is provided. When the control is set to 0, the black gradation curve becomes linear; however, it can be gradually increased to a full-range black by turning the control clockwise. An ICR switch (Integrated Color Removal — GCR version of Dainippon Screen) affects the achromatic color separation. When this switch is activated along with a higher position of the black gradation knob, the black gradation curve becomes full range and at the same time it causes the three separation colors to decrease in tone values. In the Hell 399ER, with a CCR (Complementary Color Removal, GCR version of Hell) control, the tone values of the complementary colors can be continuously reduced from a full to a 0 value in proportion to black for an achromatic structure. In addition to the built-in CCR function in the 399ER, a different GCR function called PCR (Programmed Color Removal) is available as an optional hardware to customize any GCR function for a specific printing condition.

In the RZ 200-S, PIR (Programmed Ink Reduction, Royal Zenith's version of GCR), a graduated program of reduction of color and correspondingly an increment of the black are introduced by a preprogrammed control. In the Magnascan 645, several operating functions are provided for PCR. Once

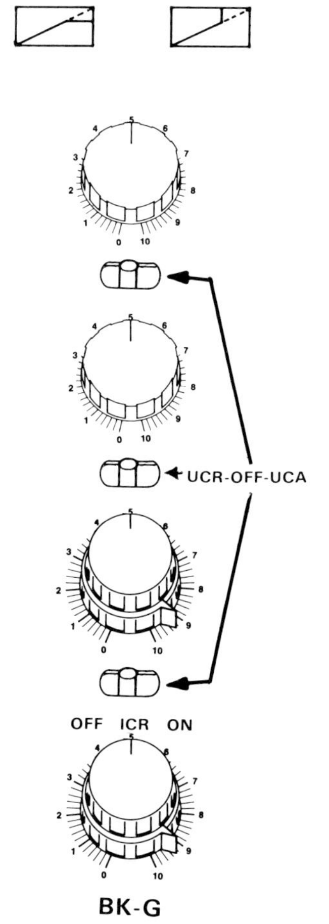

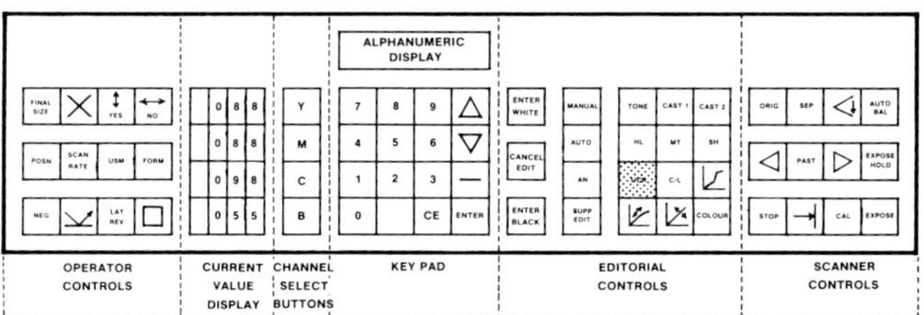

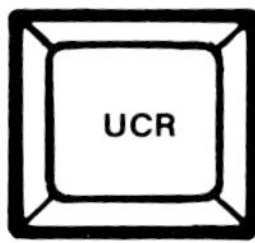

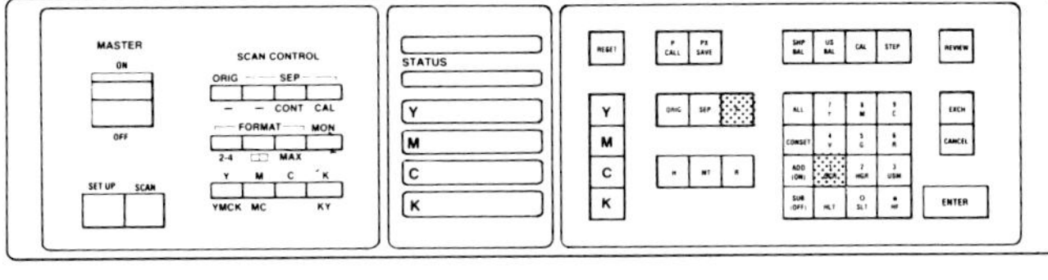

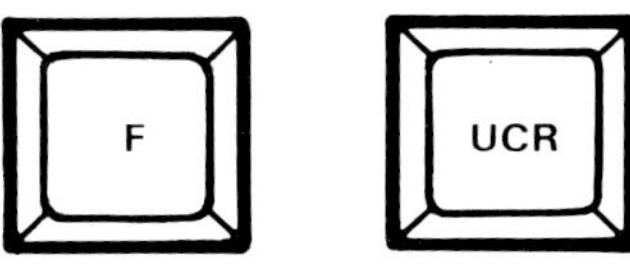

Figure 2.20. UCR and UCA panels in the DS SG-608, Magnascan 645 and Royal Zenith 200-S. In the SG-608, the three UCR/UCA set knobs are used to set the amount of UCR or UCA. The third UCR/UCA set knob is also a dual-function knob; the position of the outer knob determines the point on the gradation curve from which UCR/UCA will be effective. The three UCR-OFF-UCA select switches at the bottom of each knob select either UCR or UCA functions. The dual-function control at the bottom of the panel is the BLACK GRADATION/ICR knob. The outer knob sets the black tone and the inner knob sets the ICR; when the function of ICR is activated, UCR works in conjunction with the black gradation. In the Magnascan 645, after the UCR button is pressed, the function of UCR is accessed via a Calibration number, and then the operator enters a break point and a slope of the black gradation curve. In the 200-S, adjustments for UCR is made with the F and UCR keys. The same keys can be used for UCR or UCA individually for a single or for all colors. Adjustments for the black UCR are made with the K and UCR keys. The black gradation curve can be adjusted for skeleton or full-range black.

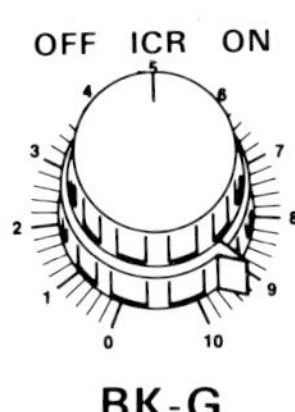

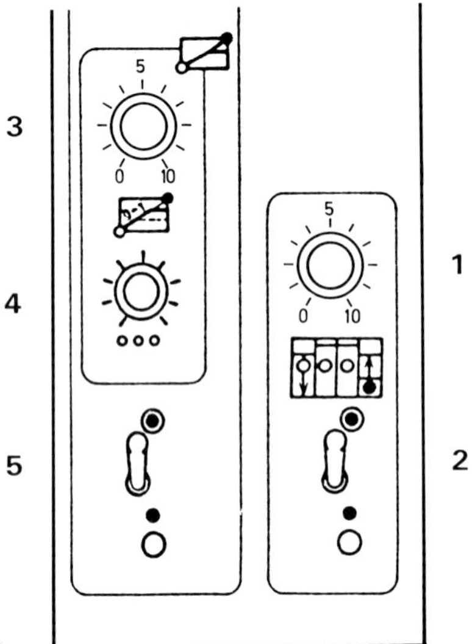

Figure 2.21. Controls for GCR in the DS SG-608 and the Hell 399ER. In the SG-608, when the ICR is activated, turning the BK-G knob causes the black separation curve to change from skeleton or linear to a full range black and the UCR amount of the three colors is reduced from 100% to 0% in step wise fashion. In the 399ER, with Control 1, the complementary color can be infinitely reduced from 100% to 0% for GCR reproduction. The toggle switch 2 is used to activate or deactivate the effects of Control 1. When the CCR is activated, the function of the UCR (Control 3) is simultaneously switched to UCA. Control 4 is used to set the starting point for UCR/UCA. With UCA intensity control (Control 3), cyan, magenta, and yellow can be added to reinforce black. Toggle switch 5 is used to activate or deactivate UCR/UCA

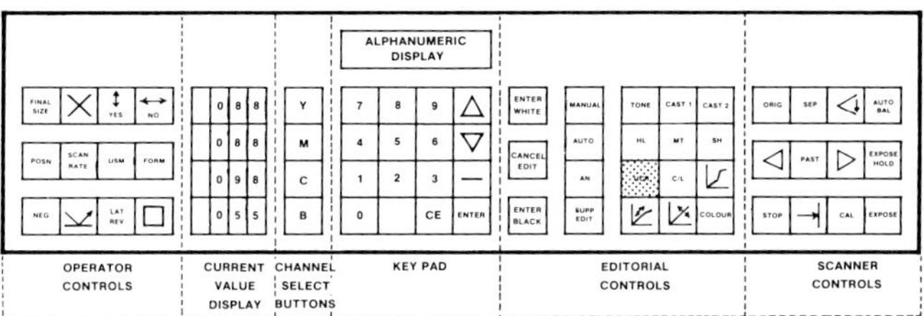

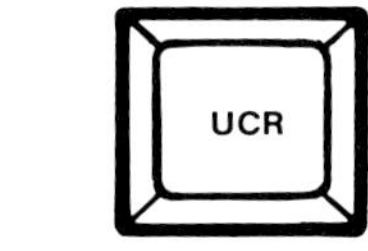

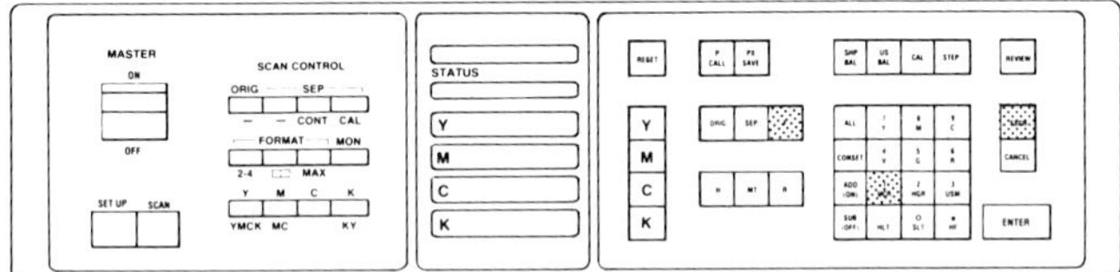

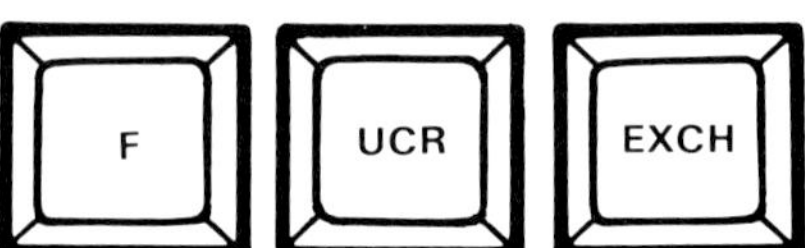

Figure 2.22. Controls for GCR in the Magnascan 645 and the Royal Zenith 200-S. To enter PCR in the Magnascan 645, the UCR button is first pressed, and after the "YES" button is pressed to answer question, the gain value for PCR appears on the Alphanumeric display. With the KEYPAD, a 3-digit decimal value is selected and entered for the proportion of PCR required. In the RZ 200-S, the function of P1R is selected by the F EXCH key sequences. Then the amount of PIR is set by the F UCR controls

the PCR program is entered, the proportion of color can be increased or decreased in relation to a basic value and the black. With another program, the maximum overprinting of dot values can be determined to alter the PCR values. In addition, with an editorial control, the weight of the black can be balanced with the weight of the color under black. Two separate programs are provided for these functions, one for the weight of black and the other one for the weight of color under black.

Unsharp Masking Adjustment

It was indicated earlier that during the initial White or Autobalance adjustment, the output of the three process color multipliers are balanced. During the same calibration in the analog scanners, the multiplier for the unsharp masking signal is also balanced. When the adjustment is performed by positioning the scanning light spot for a uniform flat surface, there should be no difference between the main and the unsharp masking signal values. During this calibration in the Hell 399ER, a value of 0 on the display panel indicates that there will be no detail enhancement for such a flat uniform surface.

In all scanners, elaborate controls are provided to enhance the details in the reproduction using the unsharp masking signal. In most scanners, detail enhancement is performed mechanically by changing the ratio of the unsharp masking aperture and the main scanning aperture. Electronic detail enhancement is accomplished by using controls designated for these purposes. The Hell 399ER provides five intensity controls for the increase or decrease of details in the highlight, quarter-tone, middle-tone, three-quarter-tone, and

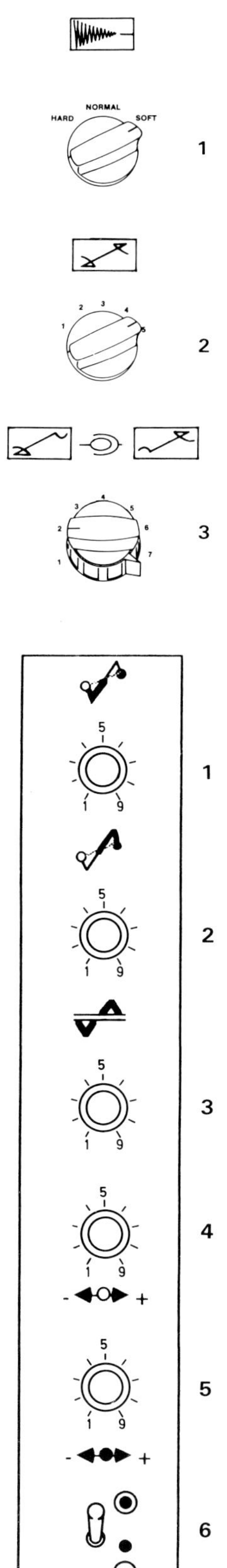

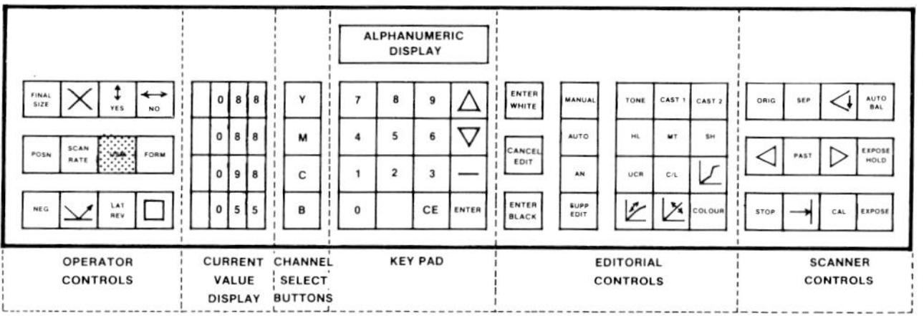

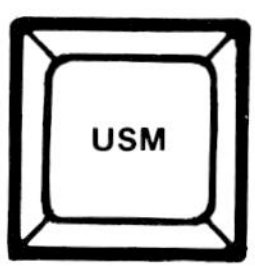

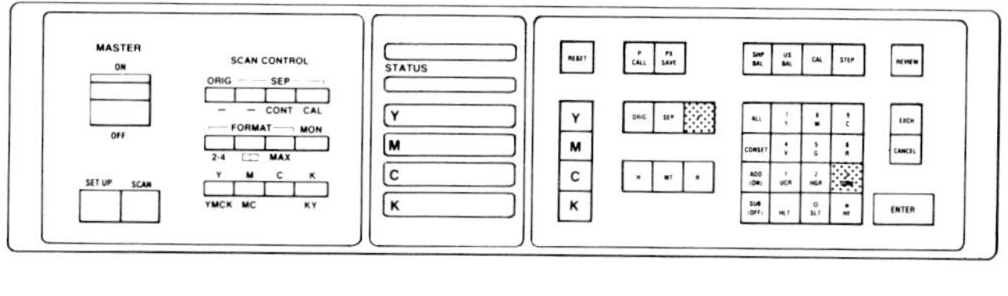

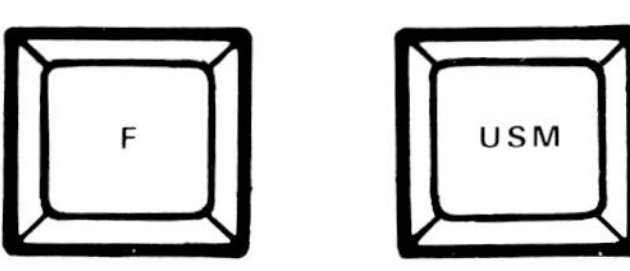

Figure 2.23. Electronic unsharp masking controls in the DS SG-608, Hell 399ER, Magnascan 645, and RZ 200-S. In the SG-608, Control 1 is used for the adjustment of graininess in 3 steps; Control 2 is used for the adjustment of details in both highlight and shadow; Control 3 is a dual-function knob, the inner knob controls the enhancement of details in the highlight and the outer knob controls the enhancement in the shadow. In the 399ER, Controls 1 and 2 are used to adjust detail enhancement in the highlight and shadow respectively. Control 3 is used to set the starting threshold for highlight and shadow detail contrast. Controls 4 and 5 are used to increase or decrease details in the quarter-tone and three-quarter-tone areas. The toggle switch (Control 6) is used to activate or deactivate the effects of the above controls. In the Magnascan 645, The USM pushbutton is used to enter USM SHARP and USM SMOOTH - the SHARP function will enhance and the SMOOTH function will smooth out any unwanted density variations. Other USM functions in this scanner can also be entered using a calibration number. In the RZ 200-S, the USM is selected by two sets of control setting numbers; the first set defines the amount of the sharpness and the second set assists in automatically reducing noise and grain problems while retaining enhancement in the important areas

shadow. Another control is provided to minimize the effect of detail enhancement in certain density ranges or areas of the copy, such as emulsion grains or skin blemishes. Similar controls are also provided in the DS SG-608 to increase or decrease the detail enhancement and to minimize the effect on specific areas of the copy. With the optional Function Generator, several unsharp masking programs can be stored for use with different types of copy. In the RZ 200-S, the electronic unsharp masking control is programmable by key command sequences. In this scanner, the unsharp masking beam is color selective, i.e., it is generated individually for each color. The grain reduction function is programmable and can be selected within the range of 0-9, 0 being the position where there will be no effect on grain, and 9 being the smoothest effect. In the Crosfield Magnascan 645, unsharp masking effect is simulated electronically, and as a result, the use of the unsharp masking signal and the multiplier are completely eliminated. Any of the three color signals can be used for the simulation of unsharp masking, and can be switched from one color to another to reduce unwanted lines or fringes around the density or color change. Programs for several functions to control the effect of unsharp masking are provided in the Magnascan 645 to enhance, smooth, reduce, and unbalance the enhancement in the light and dark edges, if necessary. The unsharp masking is selected by depressing the USM button and then selecting any level from 0 through 9.

SCALE COMPUTER

The corrected and enhanced picture signal from the color computer is fed to the scale computer. Here the signal is digitized for size change and temporarily loaded into a main memory. The rate of the loading/unloading speed of the digitized data will depend on the speed of the scanner as well as the enlargement and reduction scales. These expanded or compressed signals are fetched or retrieved from the computer memory with the aid of an exposing pulse. If the exposure is for contact screen or continuous tone separation, these digitized signals are converted back into continuous analog signals to supply electrical voltage to operate the glow lamp. These continuous signals are then fed to the final exposing stage for enlargement or reduction in the circumferential direction of the exposing drum. For electronic dot generation scanners, however, these digital signals are directly used to drive the screen computer for exposing the film with a laser. However, in the RZ 200-S, the speed of the exposing drum remains fixed, but the speed of the analyze drum changes to accommodate for different enlargement and reduction in the circumferential direction.

A fixed mechanical enlargement is also possible by replacing the normal scanning drum with a smaller drum. This will change the ratio of diameters of the scanning and exposing drums and will result in a mechanical enlargement at the exposing drum for each revolution (see Figure 2.24). In most scanners, a suitable combination of both mechanical and electronic enlargements are used for optimal results. The smallest diameter scanning drum should be used wherever possible; mechanical enlargements will have favorable effect on picture definition.

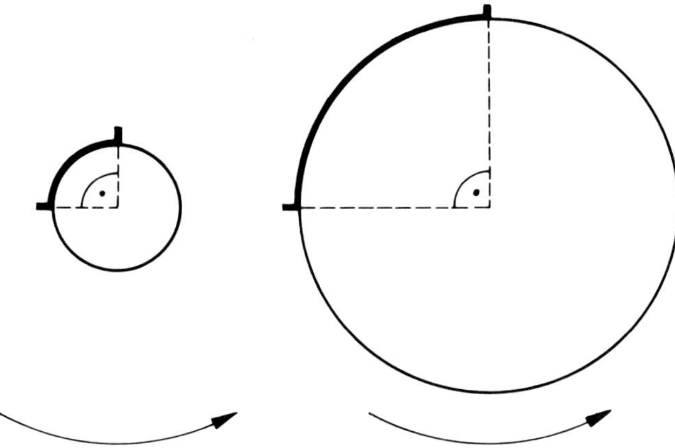

Figure 2.24. Cross sections of small scanning and large exposing drums showing mechanical enlargement in the circumferential direction

Figure 2.25 explains the principle of electronic enlargement and reduction in the circumferential direction. The process of a 200% enlargement and a 50% reduction are shown in the diagram. First, the signal supplied by the color computer is digitized. This is accomplished by dividing the entire density range into a finite number of steps so that a definite density step is assigned to each value of the continuous signal coming from the color computer. The example in the diagram shows only 25 density steps; in an actual situation, however, there will be many more steps. The density steps are then loaded into a main memory. The memory has a fixed quantity of numbered locations and the content of each location can be retrieved by entering the designated number. Thus each location can be compared to an address. The data at that address may be called storage data which are actually the various density steps.

The upper line of the store represented in the figure contains the first 21 addresses, and the stored density step in each address is stored in the lower line. By means of a precisely timed device called the write clock, the corresponding density step is again read out of the main memory and converted back into a filtered signal voltage. This output voltage controls the film density board, which supplies voltage to the exposing section. The concept of electronic digital enlargement is further explained with Figure 2.26. Using the keyboard, the control unit is informed of the required change in scale. The control unit calculates the required scanning and recording pulses and informs the memory unit of the required output. The memory unit reads out the pulses at the required speed.

Courtesy Hell Graphic Systems, Inc.

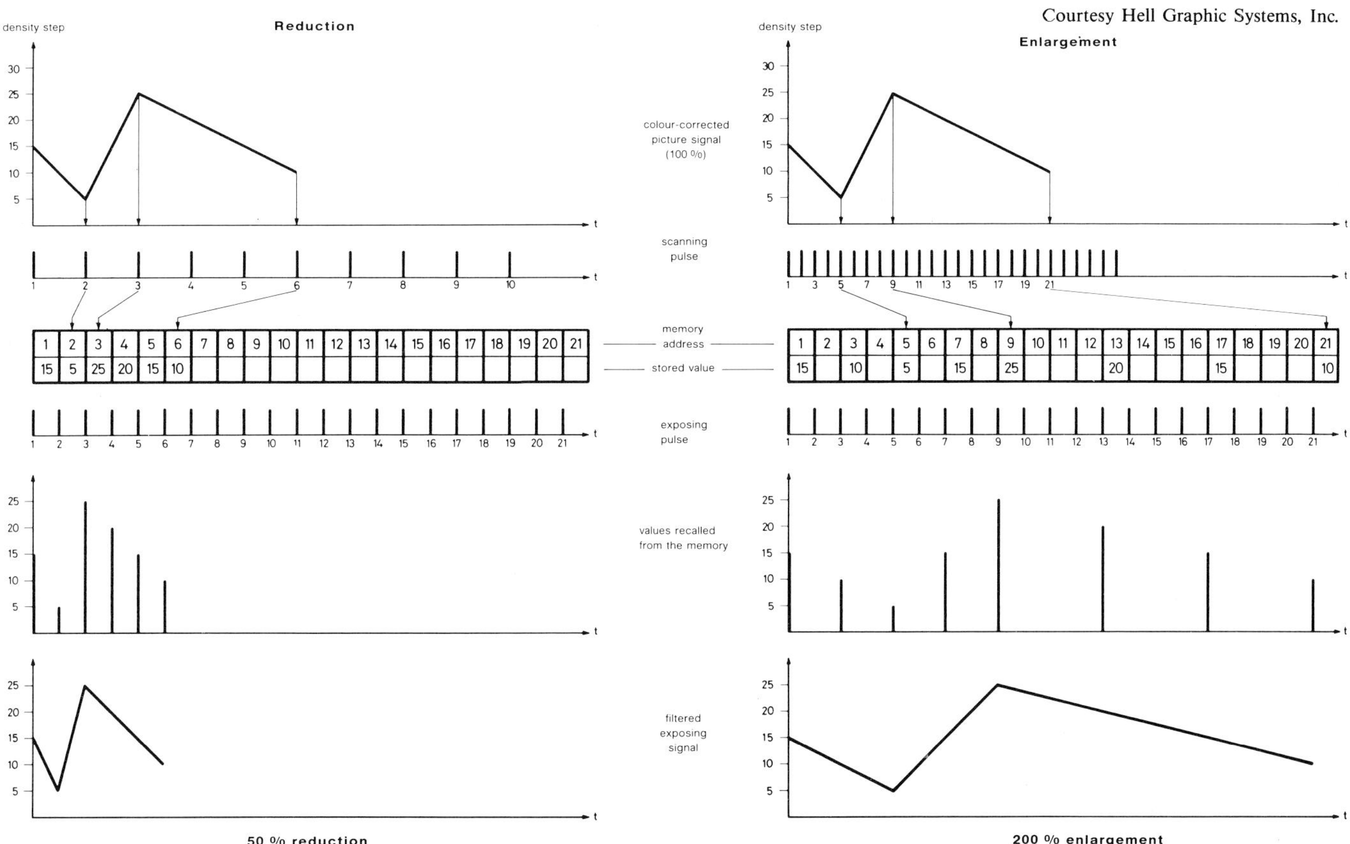

Figure 2.25. Principles of digital enlargement and reduction in the circumferential direction of the exposing drums

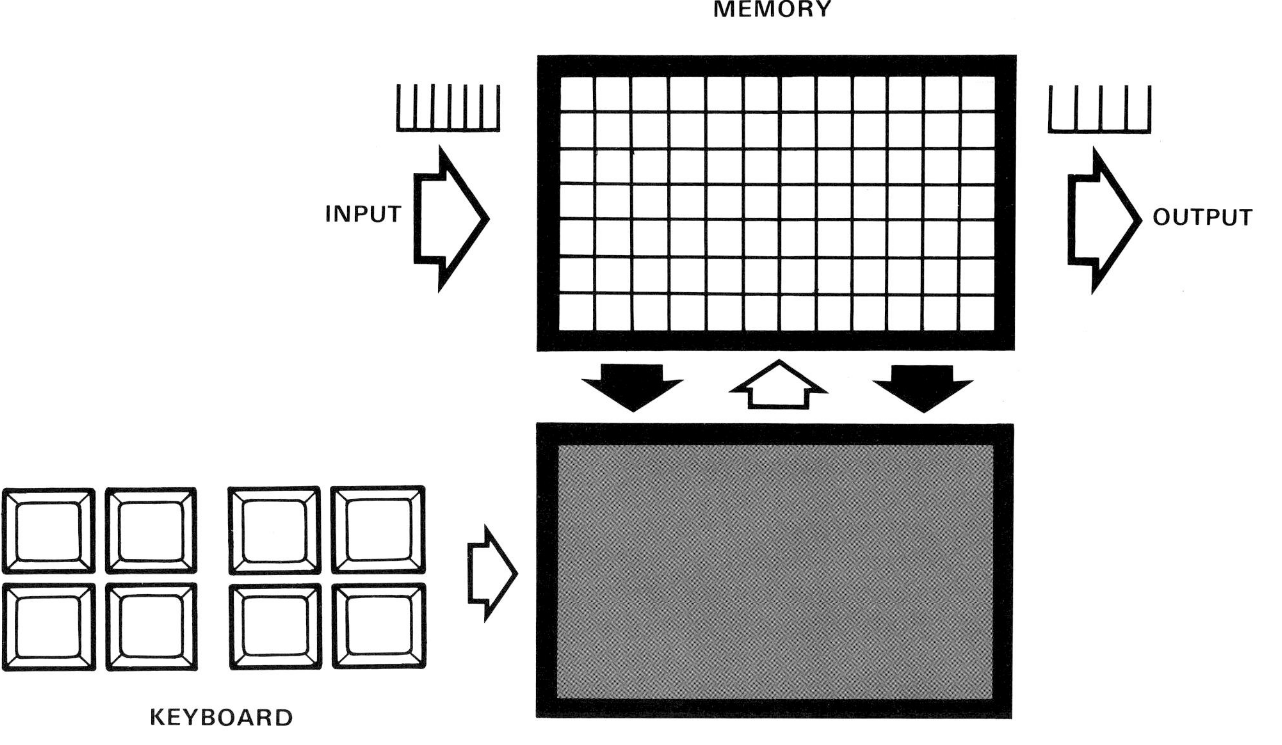

Figure 2.26. Functions of scale computer for digital enlargement and reduction

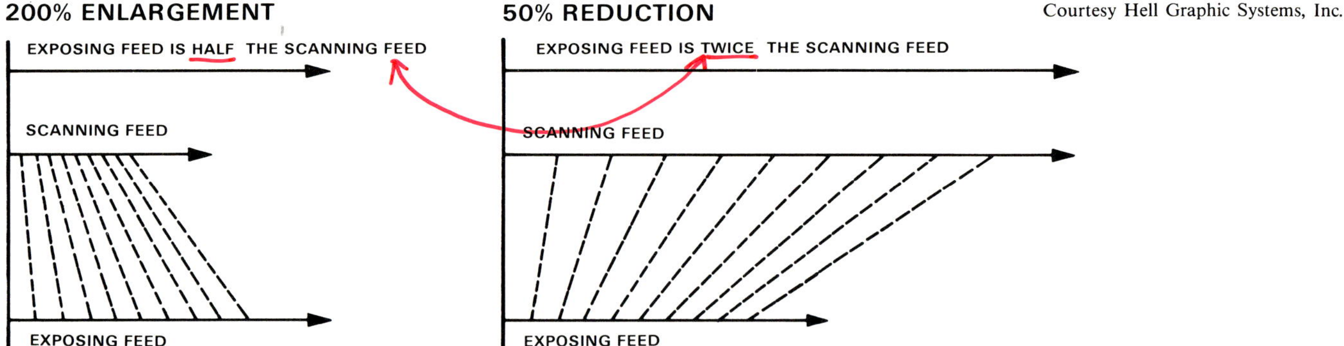

Figure 2.27. Principles of horizontal (also called axial or cross-feed) scale adjustment

The enlargement or reduction in the cross-feed or axial direction is accomplished by purely mechanical means and is explained in Figure 2.27. The cross-feed of the exposing head depends upon the required number of lines per inch or cm. Once the enlargement/reduction percentage and the exposing line width data are entered into the computer, the ratio of horizontal or axial travel rate between the scanning and exposing lamps can be determined. The axial speed of the exposing head remains constant for a certain feed-rate and line ruling; however, the axial speed of the analyze/scanning head becomes slower or faster in relation to the exposing head. For example, for a 200% enlargement, the scanning head will travel half the speed of the exposing head, and as a result, the exposing head will produce twice the exposing lines compared to the scanning lines, and vice versa for reduction. Both heads are driven by stepping motors.

In all scanners, data entry for the scale change is simple and consists of entering the scale percentage values and a measured size of the film to be exposed. In the Hell 399ER, two panels display the input data for both cross feed and circumferential directions. During scanning, these panels also display the length of the film being exposed. The DS SG-608 control panel includes a pair of manual digital counters for setting the magnification, as well as a pair of stretch switches for different horizontal and vertical magnifications. In the Magnascan 645, programs are provided to input the final size, enlargement/reduction and the start and stop position of the picture. In the RZ 200-S, the enlargement is set by means of two thumbwheel counters; their functions are identical for the horizontal and vertical enlargement but are independent. In all these scanners, anamorphic distortion, i.e. a different magnification of the image in each of the two directions is possible.

In both analog and digital types of scanners, the functions of the digital scale computer can be expanded to control other functions as well. Most mechanical and electrical functions which are not related to the functions of the color computer are also controlled by the digital scale computer. These functions include generating register marks, borders around the separation, positioning the separations on the film, etc. The additional signal processing unit normally contains an additional computer with memory and a screen computer. Most of the functions of the additional signal processing unit containing the disk drive unit are controlled from the scale computer panel. The functions of the screen computer, such as screen rulings, screen types, screen systems, etc. and film linearization steps are also controlled from the scale computer panel. However in Magnascan 645, the screen information, such as dot shapes, screen rulings, etc., are an integrated part of the scanner computer. In this scanner, the external computer with floppy disk drive is exclusively used for the storage of Basic Values (BV) and Customer Values (CV) for the digital color computer.

ADDITIONAL COMPUTER WITH DISK DRIVE

Most electronic dot generation scanners provide an additional computer with a disk drive unit for storage, retrieval, and control of certain functions of the scanner. Depending on the design and extent of functions to be processed, one or more disk drive units are incorporated. These units serve three major functions:

1. In most scanners, a basic program disk is used to control the function sequences in the scanner. When the machine is turned on, this program is loaded into the main memory and all the basic functions are automatically initiated in proper sequence. The program allows the required keyboard functions to be activated so that any entry and follow-up functions via these keyboards are processed correctly. This process is called Initial Program Loading or Initialization. With this process, a basic setting for the different color computer functions, such as linearization, gradation, etc., are also loaded into the memory. These programs and functions are usually predetermined and supplied as a package by the scanner manufacturer. Any alterations or amendments can be done by simply replacing the disk.

2. The second purpose for using a floppy disk is to record

any change which is consequently a deviation from the basic values. These changed values can be used immediately or are saved on the disk to be used at a later time. Once the basic setting is loaded into the main memory, new values are entered via the operator panel of the color computer. For example, the gradation settings for each job can be very time consuming. A variety of gradations consisting of different curve shapes can be stored under different job numbers or names and recalled at any time. The loading of jobs into the memory and the recording of a new job on the disk are simple; they are done by pressing a button.

3. In the analog scanners, most of the electronic dot generation functions are processed by the screen computer and controlled by a floppy disk. Once the proper values for the exposing optics, light, and film linearization are achieved, they are recorded on the disk for future use. The screen computer also stores the various screen configurations such as screen angle, dot shape, screen system, etc. on a disk under a variety of job names or numbers.

In the Hell 399ER, the additional computer, the "Electronics Cabinet" contains a single disk drive unit, a digital scale computer with memory, and a screen computer with a second memory for electronic screening. A program on the disk serves for the initial set up, spaces for the storage of different sets of data under different job names or number, and it also contains the functions of the screen computer. The Scanner Data Terminal in the Crosfield 645 contains the systems computer with two disk drive units with an optional video display unit and a printer. The left hand disk stores the system's programs, the system diagnostics, the operator manual extracts, and memory facilities. The other disk contains the records of job parameters (job files) and customer data. However, in this scanner, all the electronic screen information is an integral part of the main scanner computer. As an integrated unit, a screen computer with a single floppy disk drive unit is located under the operator panel of the DS SG-608 scanner. Referred to as Dot Generator, the entire exposure package consists of a recording head, a controller, a floppy disk drive, and a laser adjust switch on the control panel.

THE EXPOSING SECTION

From the scale computer, the picture signal is fed into an electronic circuit where the selection of a negative or positive output is made by pressing a button. This circuit controls the output amplifier which supplies the current for the exposing lamp. At this point the relationship of this current from the computer to the output voltage can be changed so that a linear relationship can be obtained between the film density and the computer voltage. For this purpose, in most scanners an electronic gray scale is generated from this point to test for optimum film linearization.

There are various ways to expose a piece of film. In the contact screen or continuous-tone scanner which uses a glow lamp, light from the exposing lamp reaches the exposing drum via a set of exposing optics. However, the RZ 200-S uses a constant intensity pulsed xenon light source for exposing a set of contact screen separations (see Figure 2.7). Similar to the electronic dot generation scanners, the light source is used in conjunction with an electro-optical modulator for controlling the intensity of light reaching the contact screen and film emulsion.

During the electronic dot generation, the picture signal is fed into a screen storage memory system which contains preprogrammed screen dots for the different density values and for the different screen angles (see Figure 2.28). The loading of this store with the screen information takes place by means of the main computer memory or the floppy disk. The disk reads the screen information and passes it to the screen store. From the position of one or more of the four (C, M, Y, K) color separations in progress, the screen store determines the screen angle to be used. For the final exposure, the main laser beam is divided into several smaller sections by splitting mirrors, usually a row of six to ten beams. Supplied with this information, a digital signal moves from the screen store to the modulation unit where it controls the electro-optical modulator with two specified electrical signals, one for the opening and the other for closing the modulator crystal. In the DS SG-608, however, an acousto-optical signal is used to control the crystal. The laser source next to this unit delivers a light beam of constant intensity. The modulator constantly stops or allows the light beam to pass through it and expose the film at various lengths of time for dots with different sizes and shapes.

A functional diagram of electronic screening in a Hell scanner is presented with Figure 2.29. In all electronic dot generation scanners, more than one revolution of the exposing drum forms a dot. For each revolution of the drum, a group of small lines produced side by side by the beams form one half of the screen dot. The second half of the dot is exposed during the second revolution of the exposing drum. However, in the current models of DS scanners, more than two revolutions are used in conjunction with 10 laser beams for a more defined dot (see Figure 2.30).

In most continuous-tone and contact screen scanners, the scanning line width can be varied from a coarse 250 to a very fine 2000 lines per inch. The greater the number of scanning lines per inch, the more details will be picked up from the copy, and as a result, there will be more resolution on the separations. A higher resolution in the separations can be obtained in an electronic dot generation scanner in several ways. Examples of exposures for fine resolution taken from a Hell screen resolution program are shown in Figure 2.31.

Courtesy Hell Graphic Systems, Inc.

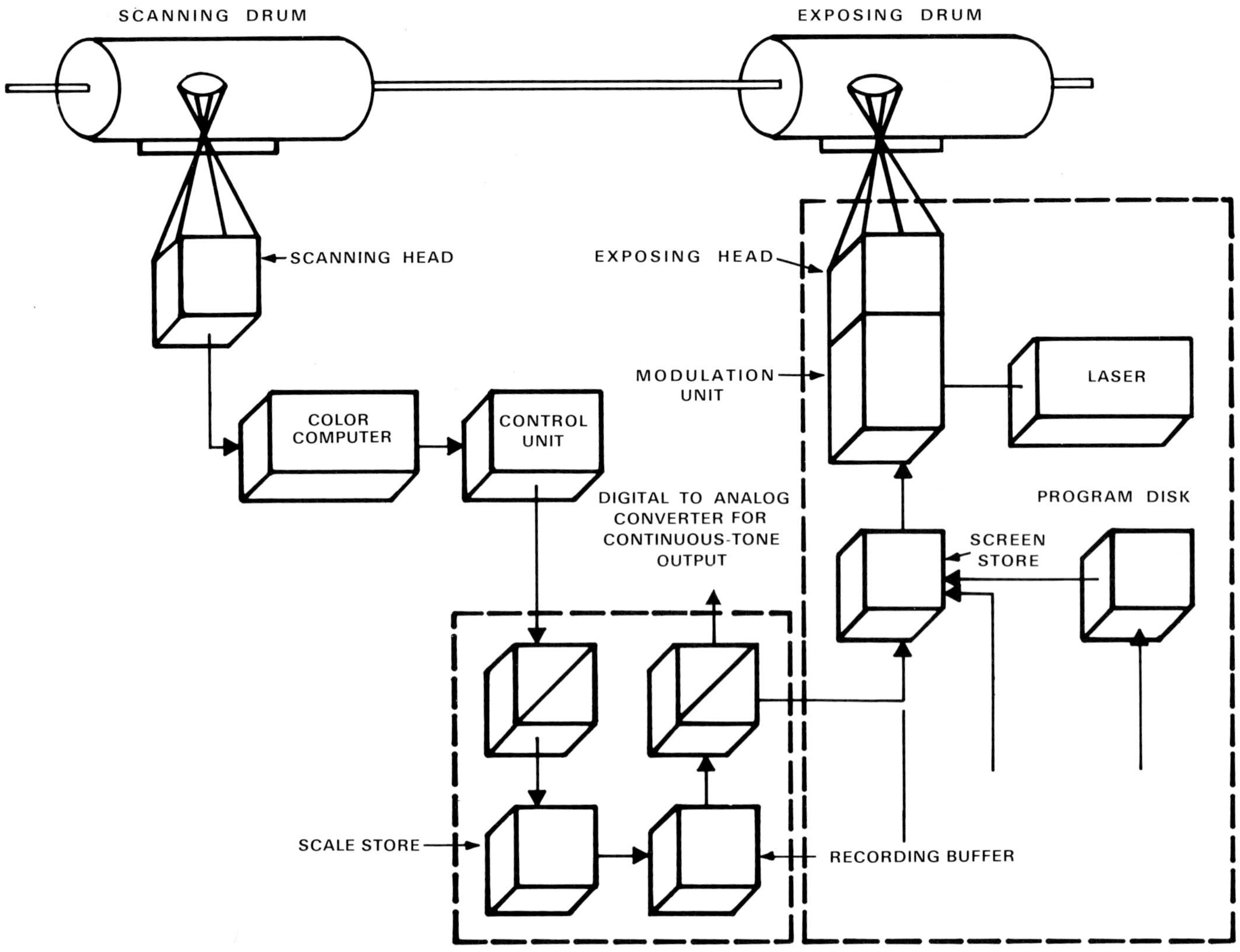

Figure 2.28. Block diagram of electronic screening in a Hell scanner

Diagram A is a normal scan, the dots are formed with six-fiber exposures. In Diagram B, the dots are formed with only three fibers and the width of each set of exposed lines remained the same as the normal six-fiber lines. However, in this mode, four rotations of the scanning drum are employed for a single dot instead of a normal two-revolution that resulted in greater resolution because of finer scanning line widths. In Diagram C, each dot is exposed with four revolutions and six fibers; however, the width of each exposed line is decreased by adjusting the zoom value. This has increased dot resolution considerably. It should be emphasized at this point that resolution on the film will also depend on the selection of screen ruling — the finer the ruling, the better the resolution.

The final exposing unit consists of an exposing drum with a vacuum to hold the loaded film, and the optical systems for exposure. The initial step to set up the exposing optics in relation to the photographic film emulsion are about the same for all scanners. The exposure optics in the Hell 399ER consists of a set of three zoom lenses in order to be able to produce all the screen rulings provided within a single screen system. The focus of the exposing lens depends on the aperture size and the applied zoom value of the intermediate lens system. The finer the screen to be exposed, and the longer the focal distance of the intermediate lens system, the smaller is the area and greater is the need for critical focusing adjustment. The initial set up includes the optics tests for zoom and light values for each screen system and ruling. After the optimal values are found, they are entered into the computer and saved on the floppy disk. The linearization scale is then exposed for all the four screen angles, the individual steps of the scale are analyzed, and the dot values are determined and loaded into the main memory.

The Magnascan 645 consists of an independent exposing unit which is completely separated from the scanning unit.

BASIC PRINCIPLES, TECHNIQUES, AND STEPS TO PRODUCE A CONVENTIONAL HALFTONE

Halftone Screen

Breaking the continuous-tone shades into thousands of tiny dots is made possible by a device called a halftone screen. Screens may be broadly divided into two different types: glass screens and contact screens. Over the years, the glass screens were replaced by contact screens for several reasons — glass screens are heavy, cumbersome, expensive, and breakable. On the other hand, the contact screens are flexible and are easier to handle. They are made by a special dye depositing process. Thousands of tiny beehive like compartments or cells are made on a stable clear plastic base. Each compartment or cell is vignetted: that the center of each cell is almost clear, but gradually the dye gets denser and darker towards the edges. The darkest points are the four corners of each cell (see Figure 4.8).

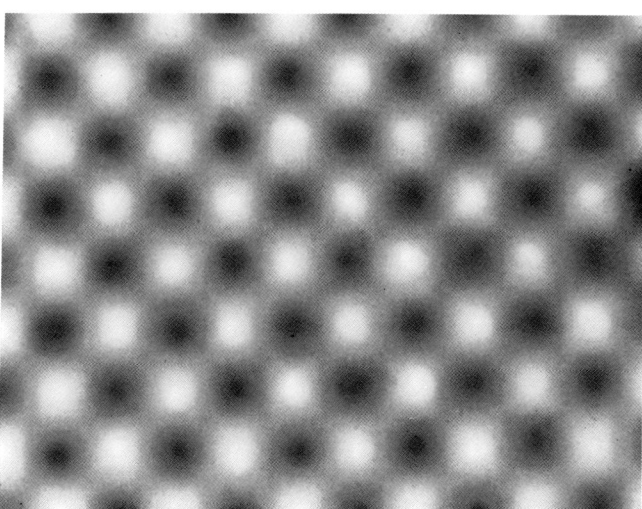

Figure 4.8. Section of an enlarged contact screen

How dots are formed by the screen

Glass screens consist of two pieces of ruled glass cemented together so that the opaque rules or lines on one piece of glass cross the lines of the other piece at a 90 degree angle. The rulings are etched into the glass and filled with pigment. When the crossline screen is placed in front of the sensitive materials at a specified distance, the dots are produced by the lights transmitted through the screen. The size and shape of the dots on the negative vary according to the various amounts of light reflected or transmitted by different sections of the copy.

When a dye emulsion of the contact screen is placed in contact with a film emulsion and is exposed to a source of light through the screen base, it will produce dots on the film. The size of the dots will depend on the intensity of light reaching the film emulsion through the screen. As indicated earlier, each vignetted cell of a contact screen is clear in the center, so a stronger white light will pass through the center of each cell quite easily, and it will possibly transmit through the entire vignetted portion of the screen, except the dark opaque areas. When the light intensity is weak, it may transmit through the center of each cell, but the darker vignetted portion of the cells will block the weak light and prevent its penetration. As a result, the strongest light will expose most of the film, but it will leave tiny areas of the four corners of each cell. On the other hand, the weak light will leave most of the film unexposed except for the tiny areas of the centers of each cell (see Figure 4.9). When the film is processed, the areas of the film which are exposed from the whitest area of the copy (brightest light) will be entirely black except for the tiny clear dots. For the weak light from the darkest area of the copy, most of the areas will remain unexposed and will become clear except for the tiny black dots.

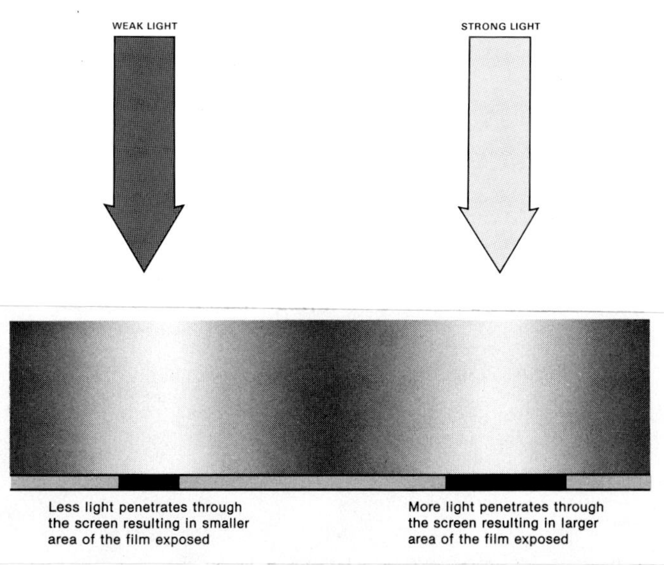

Figure 4.9. Cross section of an enlarged contact screen showing how different size dots are produced from varying intensities of light

A continuous-tone copy such as a photographic print has tones ranging from the whitest highlight to the darkest shadow. When a copy is placed on a copy board and illuminated, the different tones will reflect various intensities of light; the highlight area will reflect the most and the shadow the least. As such, when the film is properly exposed through a screen using a continuous-tone copy and processed, the highlight areas of the negative will be totally dark except the tiny clear dots, and the shadow areas will be clear except for the tiny black dots. However, there are other shades or tones in a copy ranging from the light gray to the dark gray. Depending on the different intensities of light reflecting from these areas, more or less light will be transmitted through each of the vignetted cells to expose the film resulting in different size dots (Figure 4.5 on page 82).

Requirement of Different Exposures for an Optimal Halftone

The technique involving the shooting of a halftone negative for optimal reproduction has some severe limitations. The major one is the limited range of the screen — the smallest printable dots for highlight and shadow that can be produced by a screen with a single exposure. Since a wide range of copy with various density ranges is brought into a shop, a screen with fixed range cannot be used if the smallest highlight and shadow dots are to be produced for all copy. As a result, in addition to the main exposure, two more exposures are used for shooting a halftone. They are flash and bump exposures. The flash exposure compensates for the shadow area limitation of the screen. If the copy shadow is too dark to reflect enough light to penetrate through the screen to create the smallest shadow dots (clear area with tiny black dots in a negative), an exposure from an external light source is used to help produce those tiny dots for the darkest shadow area of the original. Consequently, a flash exposure expands the screen range. On the other hand, when the highlight area of the original is not bright enough to reflect enough light to produce those tiny highlight dots in a negative with the main exposure (solid black area with tiny clear dots), a no-screen exposure from the copy, often called bump exposure is used to reinforce the main exposure to reduce the size of the dots in the highlight areas. However, a combination of different main and bump exposures can also be used for the placement of middle-tone dots at different positions on the tone reproduction curves. Consequently, bump exposure compresses screen range. The effects of flash and bump exposures are shown in Figure 4.10. There will also be a need to adjust the main exposure for different types of copy. The main exposure cannot be a fixed exposure; it has to be adjusted for different highlight density to produce the smallest dots in the highlight. The main exposure has to be increased for copy with higher than ideal highlight density (lesser white in highlight will need more exposure time to produce the smallest highlight dot in the negative) and vice versa for a copy with lower than ideal highlight density.

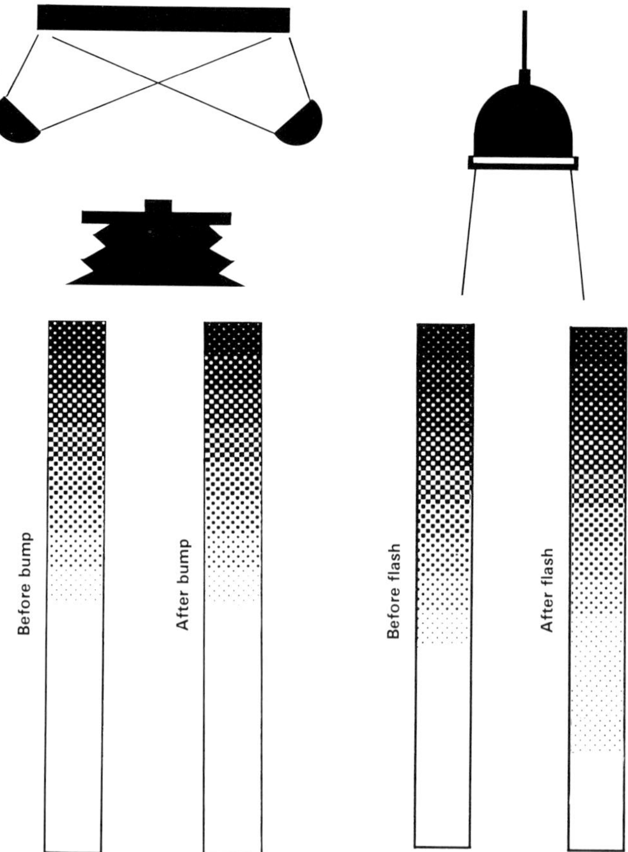

Figure 4.10. Effect of flash and bump exposures on halftone

Calibration of the Darkroom

Every darkroom condition will be different in terms of equipment, lighting, screen, film, and processing conditions. Once ideal exposures and processing conditions are found for shooting a quality halftone using standard copy, accommodations can be made for other types of originals by varying the exposures. Ideal exposures for a specific darkroom condition are determined by first establishing the basic exposure times for each of the main, flash, and bump exposures. These basic exposures are established by first finding the Screen Range or Basic Density Range (BDR) — the density range within which the screen is capable of producing the smallest dots in the highlight and shadow with only one main exposure. A gray scale with known density values for each step is used for this calibration, and by trial, an exposure is found which produces the smallest printable highlight and shadow dots within a certain density range. The basic flash time is calculated in the dark room by finding an exposure time with an external light source which produces the smallest printable shadow dot. A basic main exposure is established by finding the exposure which produces the smallest highlight dot for a standard highlight density, for example, a density of 0.0.

Once the above basic exposure times are established for a certain darkroom, camera, and screen, the exposure for an original is determined by first measuring the copy range (shadow density minus highlight density) and the highlight density to find out how much the original deviates from the standard. Then the new main, flash and/or bump exposures are calculated for the particular original. Several calculator type dials or charts are available to find a new set of exposures for each original. As long as the screen, film, chemistry, lights, and processing conditions are not changed, the same basic calibration values can be used over and over to shoot a quality halftone for each and every original.

When some advanced light integrators are used, the main, flash, and bump exposures need not be calculated by the operator. Once the basic values are obtained for a specific darkroom condition and after the values are stored into these integrators and new copy values are entered, the exposure values are automatically calculated and produced by these integrators. In some of the more advanced computerized light integrators, once the basic and changed values are entered, the computer automatically computes and exposes the copy using one or more of the three exposures. Carlson Sharpshooter is such a device for controlling exposures for a halftone (Figure 4.11).

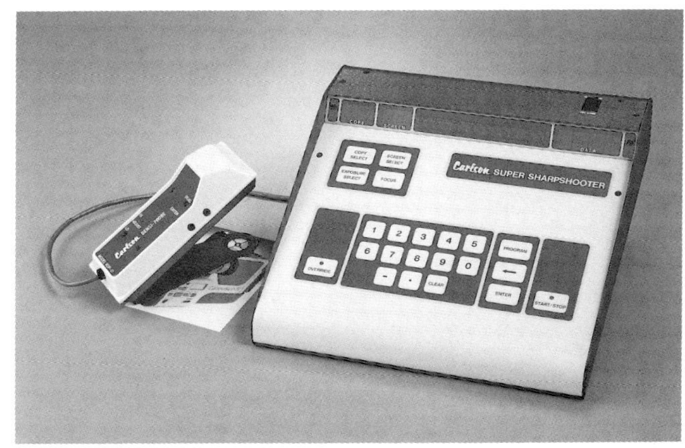

Figure 4.11. A Carlson Sharpshooter with probe for automatic halftone exposure control

Courtesy Eastman Kodak Company

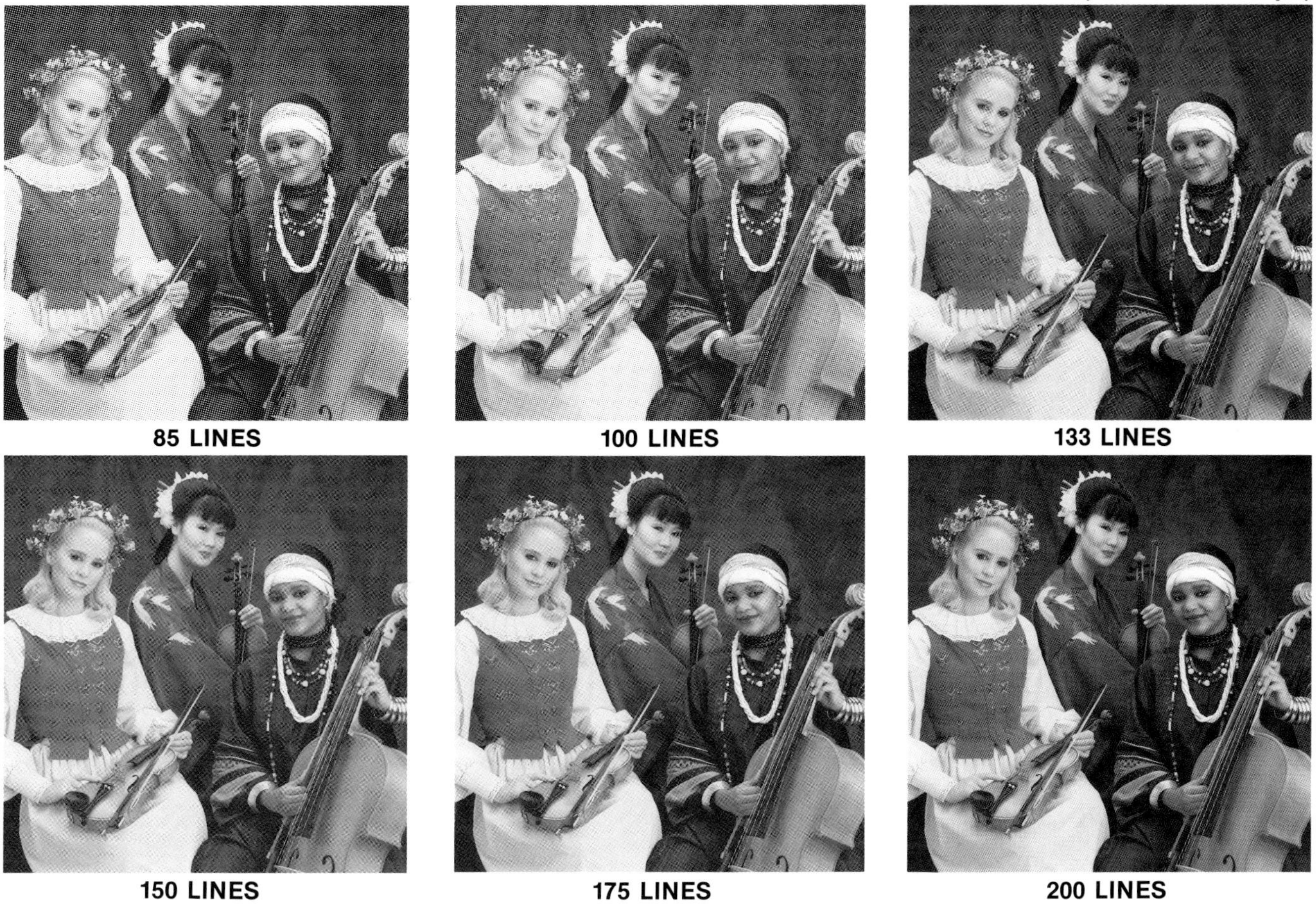

85 LINES

100 LINES

133 LINES

150 LINES

175 LINES

200 LINES

Figure 4.12. Halftones with different screen rulings

Screen Types for Conventional Separation

Based on application, a contact screen may be classified into several different types:

Color: Contact screens are available in two colors: magenta and gray. Magenta contact screens are mostly used for black and white work and to make positives from color separation negatives. Filters can be used to control the magenta screen range. A yellow filter will extend the screen range and a magenta filter will compress it. Gray contact screens are mostly used for direct-screen color separation for its neutral color.

Negative and Positive Screen: Contact screens are used for producing both negatives and positives. However, because of the tone reproduction requirements, negative and positive screens are made differently. Negative halftones are made with a negative contact screen, and a positive screen is used for exposing halftone positives from continuous-tone negatives. Negative screens are mostly used for black and white halftones and direct-screen separations. The positive screens are used for indirect separations.

Screen Ruling: Screen rulings refer to the number of lines of dots per inch. Contact screens are available in a wide range of rulings from a coarse 65 lines per inch to an extremely fine ruling of 300 lines per inch. For example, a 120 line screen will produce 14,400 dots per square inch. The use of the screen ruling will depend on the type of job, printing method, and the quality of the paper stock. For example, coarse rulings are normally used for printing halftones in newspapers. The fine rulings are used for high quality jobs such as catalogs and advertisement brochures. Figure 4.12 contains several halftones produced from the same copy with different screen rulings.

Dot Shape: Dot shape describes the shape of an individual dot or group of dots formed by the contact screen. A dot may be square, round, elliptical, or may have texture effects. Elliptical dots are used for smooth tone rendition in a halftone reproduction. Texture effect screens are used for special effect halftones. Figure 4.13 shows a variety of dot shapes that can be generated in an electronic scanner.

Screen Angle: Screen angle is an angle measured from the base of the screen to a line formed through the diagonally-opposite corners of the dot pattern. Because the screen pattern is least noticeable at a 45 degree angle, this angle is used for single color work. When more than one color is to be printed, the screen angle must be changed for each color, otherwise an undesirable pattern called "moiré" will result from overlapping the dots produced by different angles (Figure 4.14). An accepted set of angles for process color reproduction is 90° for yellow, 75° for magenta, 105° for cyan, and 45° for black (see Figure 4.15).

Screen Range: Screen range refers to a range within which the screen is capable of producing the smallest printable dots in the highlight and shadow with only one main exposure. Screen range will depend on the density of the dye used for a particular screen and will vary from one screen to another. Even screens from the same batch made by the same manufacturer may vary in range.

Courtesy D.S. America, Inc.

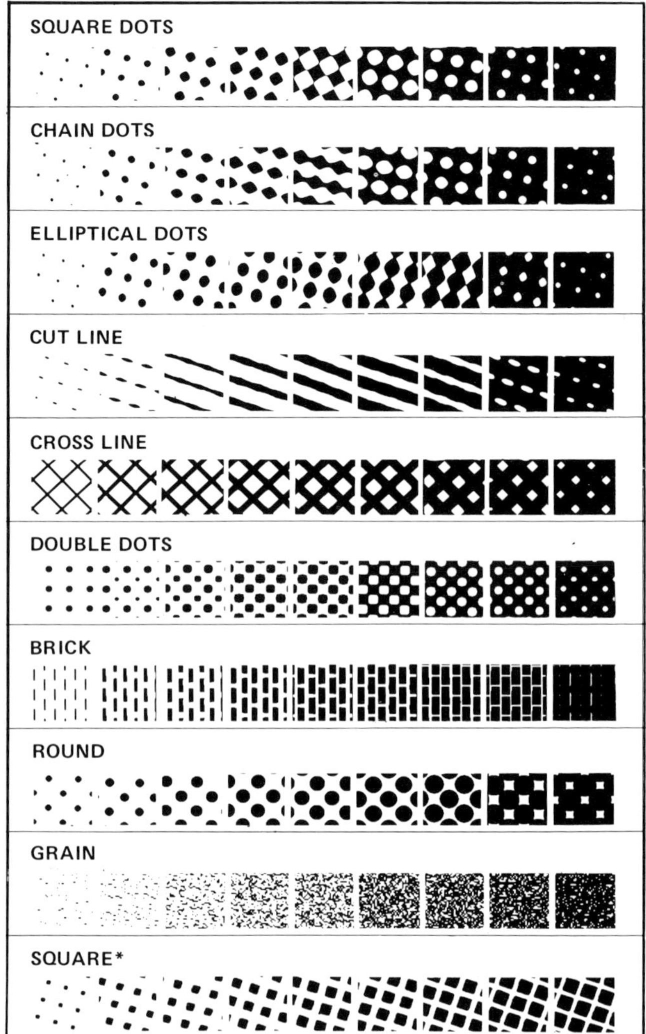

Figure 4.13. Examples of various dot shapes that can be generated in some DS scanners

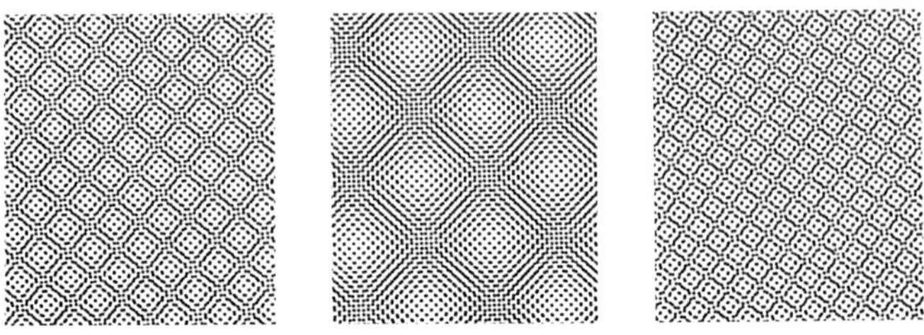

Figure 4.14. Example of "moiré" patterns

Screen Speed: Screen speed is the difference between the exposures necessary to produce halftones of equal value with different screens. The speed of each screen will depend on its transmissive characteristics — its light stopping ability. Gray contact screens of equal characteristics are faster (more light will be transmitted through the screen) than the magenta contact screens. Screens made for scanners are faster than screens used in cameras. Contact screens for scanners have less density with greater light transmitting ability so that a faster drum rotation can be achieved.

CONTACT SCREEN HALFTONE IN A SCANNER

For conventional direct-screen separation in a scanner, a gray halftone contact screen is used. The principle of halftone dot formation in a scanner and that of a camera is same. However, the technique of producing the halftone dots on the film is different in the scanner than in the conventional camera. As illustrated in Figure 4.16, in a camera, the original is exposed through an optical system. The proper exposure will depend on the exposing light intensity and the length of time the film is exposed. On the other hand, in a scanner one line of copy is scanned and exposed for every rotation of the scanning and exposing drums.

The scanning light transmits through the copy while it is rotating, and after each line is scanned, the scanning head moves to each subsequent line to be scanned. After transmitting through each line of copy, the scanning light passes through the scanning head and is received by the photomultipliers which convert the light signal into electrical signal. Depending on the intensity of light received by the photomultipliers for each line of copy, the intensity of the electrical signal will also change for that line. These electrical signals are constantly fed into the color computer, and the output is connected to the exposing lamp. After the adjustments for color correction, tone reproduction, gray balance, and other such changes of the signal at the computer stage, the modified signal at the computer output supplies the current for the exposing lamp. At the final exposing section, the lamp is constantly changing its intensity while the film is passing by and the sizes of dots will be proportional to the light signal being supplied by the copy.

In a camera, different types of exposures such as main, flash and bump can be used to control the dot values in a halftone. In the scanner, however, only one lamp is exposing the film to produce the range of dots. In some scanners, a pre-exposure lamp is used to supplement the main exposing lamp

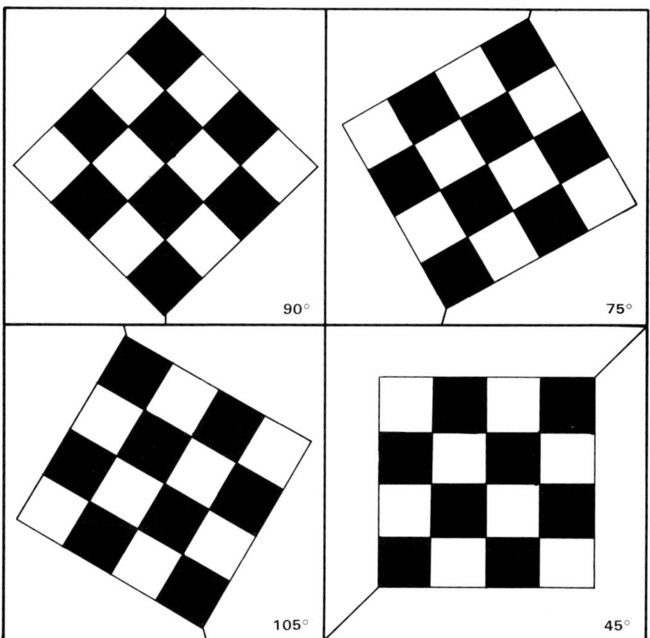

Figure 4.15. Normal screen angles used in four-color process printing

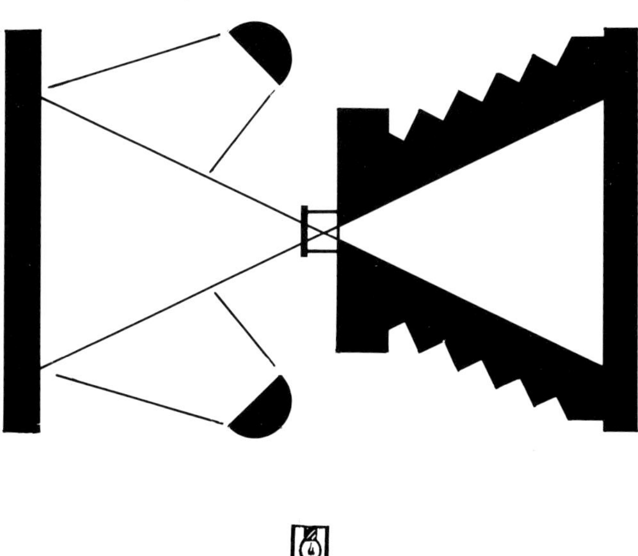

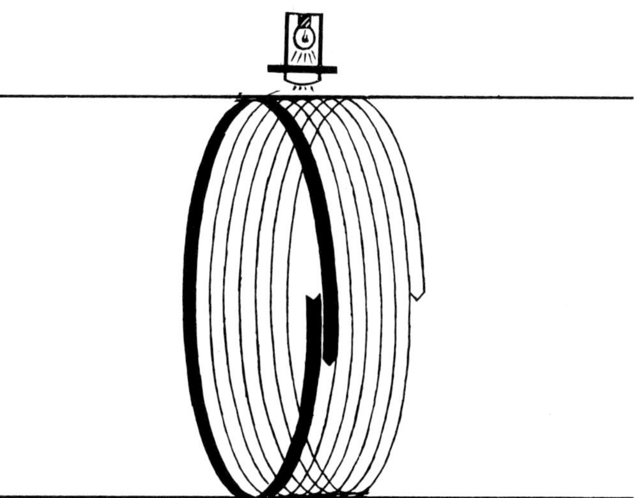

Figure 4.16. Principles of conventional camera and scanner separations

and is useful when a low intensity lamp like a glow lamp is used for exposure. In the scanner, a single lamp is capable of producing a range of dots for both the highlight and shadow because of a constant variation of intensity produced by the lamp during exposure while the film is passing by.

Calibrated gray scales are used for the initial set up in both conventional separation and scanning. During the initial calibration in the scanner, a proper electrical output from the photomultipliers for a given highlight and shadow steps of the gray scale are adjusted to produce the required density or dots for the different density values of the scale. Once the values are found for a certain film emulsion and processing conditions, the results remain consistent and predictable as long as the variables do not change.

Some contact screen scanners similar to the RZ 200-S are equipped to produce more than one separation in a single pass or on a single film. Specially designed contact screens are available with two or four sections, each section containing a different screen angle.

ELECTRONIC SCREENING

Problems of Conventional Screening in a Scanner

For black and white halftone and conventional color separation, the contact screens work well in a camera, enlarger, or in the contacting equipment, but they seem to have limited the capabilities of an electronic scanner. The following are some of the limitations using contact screens in a scanner:

1. It is difficult to manufacture four screens which are matched in density, range, and rulings for scanner use. These variables can be easily compensated for in conventional color separation or halftones, but the frequent calibration of the unmatched screens is needed in a scanner for predictable results, is not practical.

2. The density of the screen cuts down the intensity of the light exposing the film and limits the speed of the scanner. Only the fastest litho films can be used for contact screening in a scanner.

3. Because of the vignetted pattern of the contact screen, dots made with these screens have fringe areas. This non-reproducible fringe consists of a partially exposed latent image towards the periphery of each dot, and the exact size of the final dots will largely depend on the processing conditions. In other words, dots will vary in size if exact processing conditions like developing time, temperature, freshness of developer, etc., are not strictly maintained.

4. The mechanical wear and tear on the contact screens and any dust trapped in between the film and the screen may cause additional problems in the separation.

Background of Electronic Screening

In the '60s, when the color separation scanner began to occupy a good share of the color separation market in Europe and the USA, scanner manufacturers were researching an electronic process for screening color separation. According to RCA publications, American trials involved the use of a cathode ray tube in a scanner. One approach was to form a halftone dot by making a spot on the cathode ray tube screen move outwards in a spiral path from the center. The size of each generated dot is dependent on the point where it stopped during its outward travel. Another way of producing the dots was density modulation as a function of the interval between halftone dots of equal size. Light image areas or the highlight recorded only a few dots. However, in the shadows, a large number of dots of equal size covered nearly the whole area. This process resulted in the local frequency modulation of equal size halftone dots.

In 1969 in the Soviet Union, the Bronch-Breuvich Institute for Electrical Telecommunication Technology in Leningrad demonstrated a cathode ray system capable of recording halftone images on a rotating drum. This method recorded 125 lines per inch; however, it could expose only 1200 halftone dots per second. This exposure speed was considered slow for a rotating drum scanner. At the IPEX in 1971 in London, Printing Developments Incorporated (P.D.I.) of the United States presented the first electronically screened color separation with the halftone dots recorded in a 0 degree orientation.

At the DRUPA 72, Dr. Ing Rudolf Hell GMBH produced and showed the first set of four color prints made from a set of electronically screened color separations. New screen angles were realized by digital electronics on the Hell Chromagraph DC 300 and exposed by laser beams. Originally the DC 300 scanners were not equipped to produce electronic dots; the laser unit was added to the existing scanner at a later date.

Since its introduction in the early 1970s, the electronic dot generation units has almost totally replaced the conventional screen in all popular brands and models of scanner. All the currently manufactured models of Crosfield, Dainippon Screen, and Hell scanners are equipped to produce electronic dots with laser. So far, only Itek Colour Graphics Limited of United Kingdom (Distributed by the Royal Zenith Corporation in USA) was producing scanners for generating dots with conventional screen. However, at the DRUPA 86, the company introduced their latest model Itek 210-L (RZ 210-L in the US) with an electronic dot generation device made by Isomet, the makers of PDI scanners.

Advantages of Electronic Screening

There are many advantages of using laser light and electronics to produce halftone dots on the film. The following are some of the important ones.

1. Screen rulings are simply provided by pushbutton selection. They may vary from 65 lines to 200 lines or higher. Each screen is electronically matched so that no compensation or calibration is necessary for any screen because of a change.

2. Scanning speeds are much faster than the speeds of the contact screen scanners. In contact screen scanners, light has to penetrate the screen to expose the film, so a major portion of the light is lost during this process.

3. The film is exposed by a focused and polarized laser beam with a sharp cutoff point between exposed and unexposed areas. As a result, the dots produced by a laser beam are hard and contain little or no fringe. The developing variables are almost eliminated and the scanner predictability is achieved without concern for processor activity. Even if there are variations in the processor, such as feed speed, temperature, or chemical activity, etc., only the density of the dot will change, but not the size.

4. A cheaper film with noncritical rapid access processing can be used for producing electronic dots.

5. All four separations can be exposed on one piece of film without stopping the scanner if the final size is small enough to fit into the size of the film being used.

However, some disadvantages of electronic screening are as follows:

1. Since the laser dots are mostly produced by 12 or more lines of laser beams for each dot, it is difficult to produce small highlight or shadow dots that are smooth. Dots in these areas often take unusual shapes compared to the smooth dots produced by the contact-screen.

2. Some "moiré" problems were experienced in the earlier electronic dots when the separations were printed.

3. The cost of a laser as well as its maintenance are comparatively higher than in the contact screen system.

4. The laser dots provide very limited dot etchability.

Comparison of Signal Processing in the Two Types of Dot Producing Scanners

When the signal processing is compared in contact screen and electronic screening, there is no difference at the scanning and color computer sections of the scanner. The signals from the multipliers are fed into the color computer, and adjustments for color correction, tone reproduction, etc. are made at this stage. The corrected signal from the color computer is fed into a scale computer where the signal is digitized for size modification at varying rates for the selected enlargement or reduction. From this point onwards, the signal processing is different for these two types of screening.

For contact screens and continuous-tone separations, the digital tone values are reconverted into an analog continuous signal which is connected to the exposing lamp. Depending on the various intensity of the signal, the exposing lamp glows at a different brightness. But for electronic screening, the digital tone values, which are stored at varying rates at the screen store, do not require any conversion from digital to analog. These signals are fed into the screen store which contains all the different percentages of dot sizes required for different tone values along with the screen shapes and angles. In most scanners, the information is stored on a floppy disk and can be recalled at any time.

Techniques of Electronic Screening

Unlike the usual process of generating screen dots by means of contact screens, electronic dots are the result of a combination of optical and electronic processes. The process by which the laser dots and other halftone functions are generated by the optical and electrical methods in the scanner is described below.

Figure 4.17 explains how the laser light path in a typical Hell electronic dot generation scanner forms the screen dot. The light beam (1) emitted by the laser passes to a beam

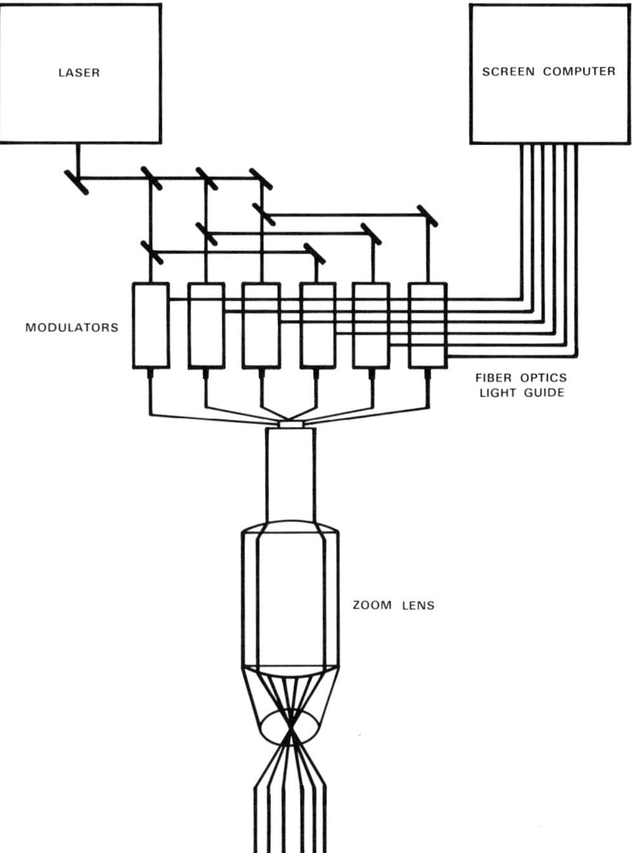

Figure 4.17. Exposure of electronic dots by six laser sources

splitter (2) where it is divided into six individual beams. Each of these light beams is connected to a modulator (3) from which it is passed via fiber optics light guide (4) to the recording or exposing lens (5). From the lens it passes to the separation film where all the single elements of the screen dot are exposed (6).

Laser

A laser beam is the result of amplification of only one frequency of light, hence the acronym LASER: Light Amplification by Stimulated Emission of Radiation. A laser beam is a highly concentrated light source and is directional. It is also coherent. The light emitted has only one wavelength with a single phase, and it is polarized. This decisive property of a laser light source is used electro-optically or electro-acoustically with a modulator to switch the beam on and off during the exposure of the film.

Two types of laser sources are currently available to use in a color scanner: the argon-ion laser and the helium-neon laser. The argon-ion laser produces a blue-green light which matches the spectral sensitivity of the orthochromatic film. The helium-neon laser produces red light and requires a panchromatic film for exposure. However, a special red sensitive emulsion is being used in the red laser scanners. Presently all scanners manufactured by Crosfield, Hell and Royal Zenith employ an argon-ion laser; scanners manufactured by Dainippon Screen are equipped with either an argon-ion or the helium-neon.

Modulator

Fundamentally, a modulator is an electro-optical polarization crystal filter. These filters are constructed using the same principle employed in producing the filters used in applied photography. The main characteristic of these filters is that they let through the light of only a specified oscillation level. When an electro-optical or acousto-optical modulator is used, the level of polarization is controlled by turning the modulator on and off to let the light pass through or stop. Since laser is polarized light, it may be switched on and off during exposure by controlling the polarization level. It is switched off if the polarization filter is placed vertically towards the polarization level of the laser light. During the generation of dots, the modulator crystal is supplied with a defined voltage or sound signal to allow light in a particular plane of vibration to pass through. Since the wave trains of the polarized laser beam have single plane, it will pass through. When another control voltage or sound signal is applied to the modulator, the plane of vibration of the crystal is rotated, thus blocking the laser beam (see Figure 2.3 page 47). This means that the light can be switched on and off optically with the precision required for exposure cycles. Modulators have been effectively employed in contact screen scanners where a pulsed xenon light source is used for exposing. In these exposing devices, the xenon light source remains constant and it is collimated or concentrated to a sharp focal plane to make it directional as the laser light source.

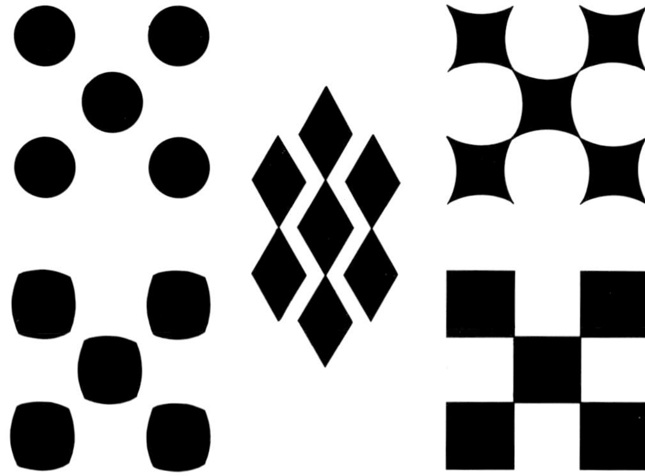

Figure 4.18 A few popular halftone dot shapes

Dot Shape

The selection of dot shape affects the smoothness of the halftone reproduction. In the highlight and shadow areas, the dots will be very close to round no matter what dot shape is selected. However, the shapes of the dots will have a profound effect on the middle-tones. Figure 4.18 shows a few popular basic dot shapes used in the industry.

Test results indicate that there is a sudden jump in density around the 50 percent halftone dot when the square dot screen is used. The uneven density distribution is in the corners, and this is due to uneven ink spreading on the press in these corners. However, with an elliptical dot, the 50 percent dot joins only at the two ends and reduces the jump considerably. The effect of elliptical dots becomes more noticeable in the skin tone where a smoother rendition of tones takes place than when square dots are used. The use of elliptical dots also eliminates small undesirable details such as graininess, facial blemishes, retouching marks, etc.

By switching the laser elements on and off at any point in an electronic dot generation scanner, the shape of a screen dot can be changed. As shown in Figure 4.19, the six spots of lights lie one beside the other and form a line as wide as these six elements. In the screen systems, which use two sets of lines consisting of 12 elements per dot, this line width corresponds to the width of the half of a screen dot. The length of the dots is determined by the length of each laser element exposing the film and is controlled by the electronic switching of the modulator crystal. For example, when the length of the dot equals the width, it becomes a square dot. Examples of producing different types of dots are shown in Figure 4.19. In electronic screening, it is also possible to arrange the halftone dot shape to be different in various tone values, for example, square dots for the highlight, elliptical for a 50% tone, and round dots in the shadows.

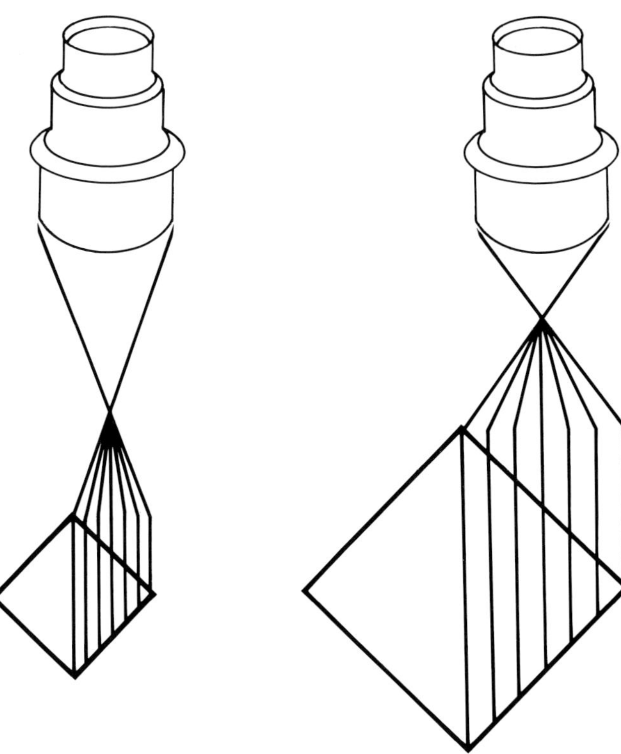

Figure 4.20. Two different screen rulings formed by adjusting the focal planes of the same zoom lens

Screen Rulings

For different rulings, the size of the dots has to be changed. For example, in a 100 line screen, there are 100 lines of dots per inch. To change this to a 150 line screen, the size of the dots has to be reduced so that 150 lines of dots can be accommodated into one inch. For contact screens, separate sets of screens containing different rulings are used to change the size of the dots. For electronic dots, this is done by purely optical and electronic methods. Most electronic dot generation scanners use a zoom lens with a continuous range of focal lengths to change the width of each beam for smaller or larger screen rulings (see Figure 4.20). The length of each dot is then controlled by the screen computer by reducing or increasing the exposure time. The preselected zoom value allows the projected size of light beams to be altered. The exposing line width for each rotation of the drum can be adjusted to correspond with the exposing width of the laser elements. This is called feed-rate, and the rate is inversely proportional to the screen width. The recording time will depend on the screen ruling. For example, it is twice as long for a 200 line screen as it is for a 100 line screen.

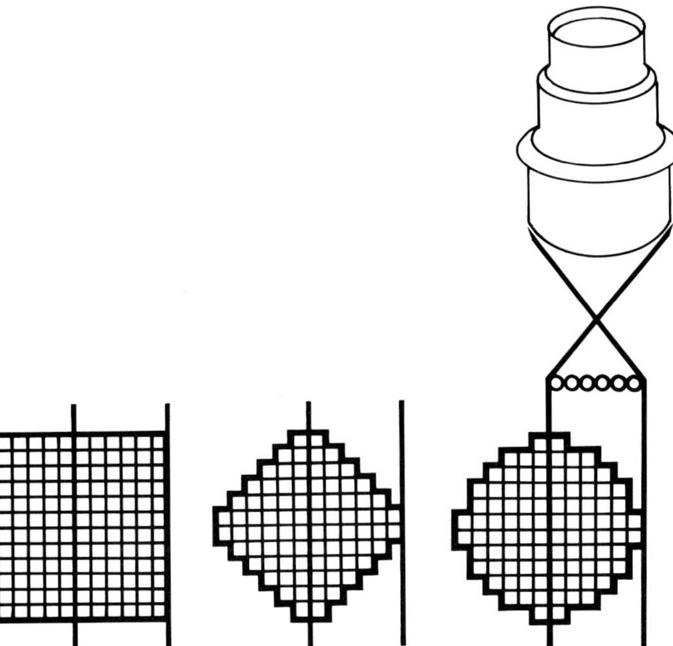

Figure 4.19. Formation of different dot shapes by electronic screening

Range of Dot Percentage

Depending on the density of each line scanned, the dots recorded on the film will vary in size. As indicated earlier, for laser dots, the size variation is affected entirely by computers and electronics. The percentage of dots ranging from 0 to 100 is divided into hundreds of small sections and stored in the computer or on a floppy disk. These sections can be compared to a pyramid shape density mound (see Figure 4.21). The base of the mound corresponds to a 100% screen dot. The peak of the pyramid with an area of 0 corresponds to 0% dot. The entire pyramid is divided. For example, in a Hell laser unit, there are 256 divisions or steps with each plane of the section corresponding to a particular screen percent value. This data is also stored as elliptical, square, round, or any other shape corresponding to the shape of the dots desired. Depending on the modulation of the laser light, a different

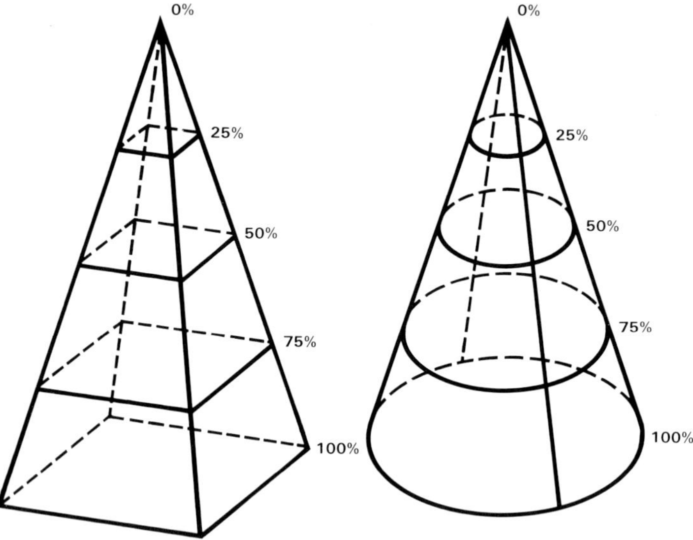

Figure 4.21. Density mounds for square and round dots

percentage of dots along with the corresponding shape will be produced on the film.

Screen Angles

Selection of proper screen angles for each of the separations plays an important role in the smooth rendition of tones in the reproduction. For single color work, a 45 degree angle works best, because the dot formation at this angle is least noticeable to the eyes and provides an illusion of continuous-tone. For process color work in which four sets of dots are superimposed, the screen angle for each color has to be at least 30 degrees apart to avoid the "moiré" pattern. However, for four different screens, this poses a problem. When placed 30 degrees apart, only three screens can be accommodated within the maximum limit. As such, the dominant colors such as cyan, magenta and black are placed 30 degrees apart; however, the yellow is placed within 15 degrees from the two dominant colors. Because yellow is not a dominant color, the "moiré" patterns caused by the superimposition of the yellow is not normally noticeable. The following are the normal screen angles for four colors: black — 45 degrees, magenta — 75 degrees, cyan — 15 or 105 degrees, and yellow — 90 degrees. However, in special situations the screen angles are interchanged. For example, a normal skin tone contains heavy magenta and yellow, and normal screen angles of 75 degrees for the magenta and 90 for the yellow may show a "moiré." However, a 45-degree screen angle for the magenta and 90 for the yellow will make a difference of 45 degrees in the normal angles, eliminating the "moiré." In an original with dominant skin tone, this change of angle will provide smoother tone rendition with least "moiré."

Preangled screens are available for contact screen scanners. In the electronic dot generation scanner, the angle of the screen for each color is changed by a novel computer function designated as the rotation and displacement calculation. The angle of the first screen dot of each line is calculated at the beginning of each line as specified via an electronic pulse. When the dots are superimposed one above the other for each screen angle, the distance between the dots of two screens are always the same, so the other dots are calculated from the displacement along the x and y axis.

Figure 4.22 shows the examples of four screen angle dots that are produced by simply changing the distance of each set of dots in relation to the other. In example A, a screen angle of 0 degree is produced by recording the dots periodically in each exposing line with a vertical/horizontal dot pattern. In example B, the halftone dots are located in the intervals between two neighboring dots of the previous exposing line and a 45 degree screen angle is produced. For two more screen angles which will be compatible with this exposing line system, two mirror images on both sides of the zero degree angle at the vertical scanning direction are obtained by producing dots at the angles of 18.4 degrees. This is shown in examples C and D. Instead of a normal 15 degree angle, the earlier electronic dot generation scanners used about 18 degrees because of the variation in the screen rulings for different colors. However, with the introduction of 10-beam laser dots, precision optics, and computer programming, normal screen angles are now being produced in most of the current scanners.

Courtesy Hell Graphic Systems, Inc.

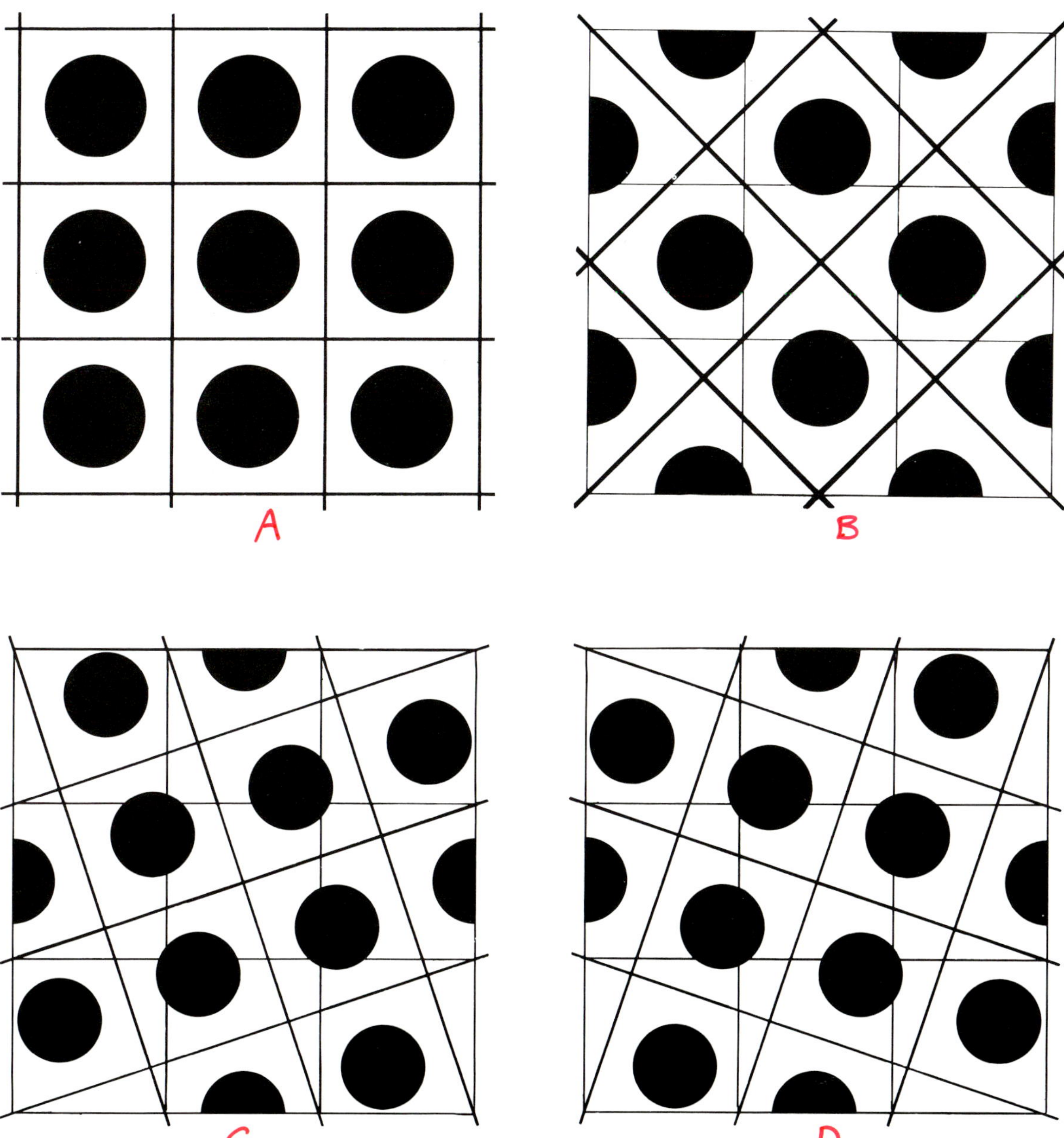

Figure 4.22. Concept of producing electronic dots in four different angles in a Hell scanner

Chapter 5
Copy Evaluation and Scanning Aids

Many people in the industry feel that the scanner operator should have a comprehensive background in photography. Some even go so far as to suggest that a background in photography will be more important than a background in graphic arts for the person who runs the scanner. There are many good reasons for this belief. The printing conditions for a specific shop can be standardized and, in turn, can be translated into specific adjustments in a scanner, but it is difficult to standardize the original for scanning. For example, ten different types of color transparency films may be photographed for a neutral balance, and when viewed with a standard 5000°K transparency viewer, all would appear identical in color quality and neutral balance. However, when all ten originals are color separated in the scanner with identical adjustments, the results obtained in the reproduction probably will not be the same. This results from the characteristics of the different color dyes which constitute the various film emulsions. Although the dyes appear to be visually identical, the scanner optics and electronics see them differently. So, the operator needs to treat each transparency separately if an optimal result is required in the reproduction. It will be important for him to know whether the transparency is Kodak Ektachrome or Fujichrome, even whether it is Kodachrome 25 or 64.

The problem discussed above is often compounded by the fact that there may be hundreds of other variables associated with an original and many of them may be subjective in nature. Important among those are color cast, over or under exposure, short or long tonal range, desaturation, graininess, and unsharpness, to name a few. The objective of the scanner operator is to evaluate each original critically for its unique characteristics and adjust the scanner so that a set of optimal quality separations is obtained for that particular original. However, to be successful in this respect, it is necessary to understand the various problems associated with an original and their relationship to the correction facilities available in a scanner. A scanner is a flexible and a creative tool. With the correction potentials available in a modern scanner, the possibility for generating an acceptable set of separations for most originals is there. However, without an understanding of the variables present in the original, the possibility of making a wrong decision is also there.

COLOR AND TONAL PROBLEMS OF THE TRANSPARENCY

Most originals, especially a transparency, have the tonal range and saturation that exceed the capabilities of the printing process. To adjust the tonal range, the scanner operator will compromise for an optimal "tone compression" in a certain tonal range of the original, which is expected to be visually indistinguishable by the viewer when the reproduction is compared with the original. He will also adjust for an optimal saturation for one or more colors without affecting the gray balance. However, no matter how accurate the adjustments are, the reproduction will never match the original, especially for transparencies which contain an unusual range and saturation.

Problems with Reflective Originals

The density range of a photographic print is similar to the range obtained on a press sheet. As a result, the saturation and tonal range in the reproduction is much easier to obtain from a reflective copy than with a transparency. However, noncompatible dyes used for retouching a photographic print may pose a problem. The manufacturer of photographic materials recommends the type of retouching dyes that should be used with the prints. Additional problems may arise from original art pigments and dyes. Some colors may "fluoresce" and may give pigments a brighter visual appearance. The copy can be checked for fluorescence under a ultra violet light source. When working with original artwork, the scanner operator should test the pigments to see if they are accurately reproducible. This may be done by generating a set of separations in the scanner with normal set up and then making a proof for visual evaluation.

Color Cast

Another common problem associated with the original is a color cast. There are two types of cast normally present in the original, local and overall. Local color distortions, or hue changes are produced when an unsuitable background or a reflecting surface throws a color cast over flesh tones or other colors. On the other hand, an overall color cast results from incorrect processing and/or incorrect lighting condition when the film was exposed. Genuine color shifts may also result from the use of outdated films and improper film storage. Local color casts are difficult to remove without affecting the quality of the separations. Modern scanners provide facilities for the partial or complete removal of overall color casts. However, the decision to remove a color cast will depend on the customer requirements.

Exposure

The quality of the original will depend on the proper exposure received by the photographic emulsion. An overexposed transparency or photograph will have an washed out effect in the entire original and the colors will appear desaturated. A properly exposed transparency will have a highlight density of approximately .25 and will have good shadow details. The scanner operator can lighten up a slightly dark transparency, but cannot add detail that is not in the overexposed copy. In this respect, a slightly underexposed transparency possibly will be better and risk-free. However, when the shadow details are overly important, even a slightly underexposed transparency may be unacceptable.

Contrast

All originals have two types of contrast — the overall picture contrast and the detail contrast. The picture contrast refers to the range of the highlight and shadow density. Higher density range will produce higher contrast and lower density range will produce lower contrast. However, the detail contrast within the image elements refers to the edge definition of small details. The detail contrast is independent of the overall contrast and is not affected by the larger contrast. The detail contrast consists of variation of density within the image areas such as blades of grass, the thread in a ball of knitting materials, leaves of a tree, etc. In a scanner, the overall image contrast is maintained, changed or improved by the tone reproduction controls, whereas, the detail contrast is maintained or enhanced by the unsharp masking controls.

Grain

Graininess is the small variations of local density in the areas where the observer expects to see a uniform density value. These variations are caused by individual particles (usually silver halide crystals) of the developed image on the photographic materials. These measured variations are often expressed as granularity. In photographic materials, the faster emulsion contains larger crystals and a slower emulsion contains smaller crystals. When the emulsion material is processed, larger crystals in the faster films give larger dye deposits that are more visible in the enlargements than the small dye deposits associated with small crystal in slower films. Graininess becomes more apparent with the degree of enlargement.

The finest grain is generally obtained with slow-speed films. For example, Kodachrome ASA 25 emulsions contain one of the finest grain materials. The problem arises when high speed emulsions are used to capture action photographs such as sports pictures. However, these types of originals are normally used by newspaper or other news media, and the main consideration is the news value. While good color reproduction will enhance the editorial pages, the news value of a picture is the overriding factor, an up-to-the-minute news photograph, taken under bad lighting conditions and known to be technically poor, cannot be discarded if it is the only one available. However, the requirements will be different for other purposes. For example, in advertising, the main consideration is correctness of color reproduction and fine grain. The color of a new car or the brand color of a paint needs to be reproduced exactly.

Unsharp Originals

Unsharp originals are caused by either incorrect focusing

of the camera lens, the movement of the subject, or camera movement during the exposure of the film. The use of a faster shutter speed or the use of a tripod when exposing the original photograph will help to improve sharpness related to motion. This defect cannot be corrected in the scanner.

Enlargement and Reduction Factors

Contrary to the principles of conventional camera separation, a reduction will tend to lose detail in the scanned separations than with an enlargement. The reason is that while the exposing width remains the same, the enlargement and reduction are adjusted by setting the axial or horizontal speed of the scanning head. For an enlargement, the slower axial speed covers a narrower width of each scanned line that contains greater definition than if there is a reduction (see Figure 5.1). However, in most scanners, finer resolution in the separations can be maintained by using a "fine" mode. Examples of increased definition in scanner separations are shown in Figure 2.31 on page 70.

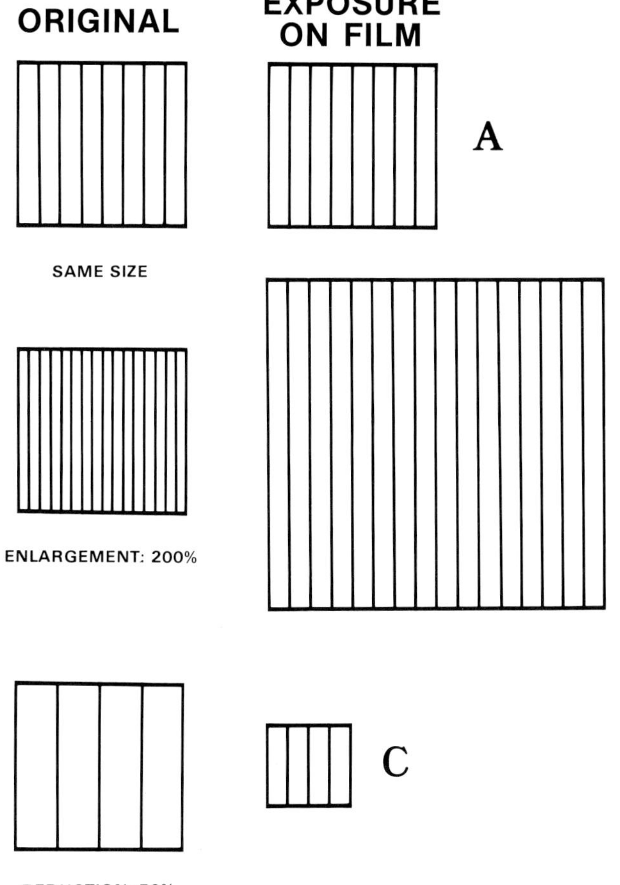

Figure 5.1. Diagram showing the change of scanning line widths in relation to the fixed exposing line widths for axial or cross-feed scale changes

Key Classification

Depending on the main interest area, an original can be classified as high-key, low-key, or normal. In a high-key original, the main interest is in the highlight area, in a low-key it is in the shadow, and in a normal-key, the interest is in the entire original. By manipulating the adjustments in the scanner, the interest areas are normally emphasized in the reproduced tones; however, this occurs at the cost of other tonal areas. In other words, since the reproduction has a limited range, one area can be emphasized only when portions or all of the remaining areas are de-emphasized.

Originals without a Certain Tone

In some cases, an original may not contain a certain tone, for example, a true highlight. This is not necessarily because the original is underexposed, for the photographer may have been trying to achieve a certain effect. With these originals, the highlight is normally set up in the scanner using a gray scale.

Specular Highlights

When lights reflect from a polished or mirror surface, such as metal, glass, or water, specular highlights occur. These highlights should not contain any dots in the reproduction. If these highlights are used as normal highlights in the separation, the reproduction will have dark tonal characteristics.

Second Originals

In some color reproduction departments, it is a popular practice to photograph rigid reflection copy on transparency materials when the original cannot be wrapped around a cylinder. There are several problems associated with this practice. Because of the limited gamut (the entire range of the color) of the dyes, the color of the original may not be accurately registered on the film. Additional problems arise when some of the pigments in the original "fluoresce" and reflect ultraviolet light which will appear brighter and different. The angle of the incident light which is used to photograph the original may also affect the outcome. Specular highlight may result from an area of the original; however, the effect may be minimized by using a polarizing filter during the photographic exposure. If the surface of the original has a texture, it may also register differently on the film because of the angle of lighting. If the reflective surfaces from the surrounding areas of the original are not controlled when it is photographed, flare will also deteriorate the quality.

Duplicate Transparencies

Quite often a duplicate transparency is received for scanning. These duplicates (often referred to as dupes) may lack certain details, density, and saturation of the original transparency. The quality of the duplicate will depend on several factors. Since the reversal duplicate films have a very narrow latitude in exposing and developing, a slight variation in those factors will result in a poor quality. If the duplication is made by enlarging the original, the result will also depend on the quality and focusing of the enlarging optics and color adjustment in the filtration.

Transparency Handling

Transparencies are easily damaged, and therefore, need careful handling and protection. The main enemies are scratches and fingermarks. These are often invisible when viewed, but appear in the color separations, particularly when enlarged. Both of these defects are more serious when they occur on the emulsion side of the transparency. Transparencies should be handled carefully by the edges and protected by cellophane sleeves.

HOW IMAGES ARE FORMED ON FILMS

Reversal Images on Transparencies

The image formation on the film follows two basic principles of color: additive and subtractive color mixing, the same principles which are used in color printing. The reversal film consists of three layers of emulsion, each layer is sensitive to about one third of the visible spectrum — red, blue and green. When the film is exposed, the lights of each color produce an invisible latent image on each of the three layers. During the first development of the film, each latent image is converted into a metallic silver negative image. The density of these negative images will depend on the amount of each primary color received by the emulsion from the original scene or object. Positive color images are created by a reversal process which consists of a second exposure by light or by a chemical agent. During the first development, not all the silver was deposited in the negative. By the second exposure and development, black and white positive images are formed on the emulsion. As in the first development, the developer is oxidized as it converts the exposed silver halide into black metallic silver. The oxidized developer combines with chemical couplers to produce dyes, forming three positive color images in the metallic silver positive images. Each layer of the dye produces a color which is complementary to the color it received — yellow is formed in the blue-sensitive layer, magenta in the green, and cyan in the red.

In the final stage, all the metallic silver is bleached out which leaves only the positive color images in each layer. When a beam of white light is projected through these layers, the color on the screen is produced by the subtraction of colors. For example, to produce blue, only cyan and magenta are formed, and they subtract the red and green lights from the white light. Varying mixtures of dyes in the transparency produce the entire range of colors. Black is produced where all three colors are subtracted, and white is produced where no color is subtracted by the dyes.

Color Negative for Print

The negative that is used to make color prints works in the same manner as the reversal film, but with one important exception: it is processed into a negative of the subject. This means that the light areas of the original scene becomes dark in the negative and vice versa for the dark areas of the original. The colors also appear as their complementary hues.

Similar to reversal films, when a color negative film is exposed, the red, green, and blue sensitive layers of the emulsion record latent images that are developed into black and white negatives. Unlike the reversal films, color negatives are developed only once and a black-and-white negative image is first produced in each emulsion layer. During this development, a color dye is combined with each black-and-white negative image. The dyes are cyan, magenta, and yellow — the complements of red, green, and blue. Once the silver is bleached out, the three layers show the subject in superimposed negative dye images. The color negative has an overall orange color or "mask" to compensate for the distortions that would have occurred during the photographic printing.

When light is transmitted through the color negative, the layers of subtractive primaries absorb all the original colors of the image and transmit their complementaries. For example, where there is a red spot in the original, there will be a cyan dye in the negative and it will allow the blue and green lights to pass through for the red. Similarly, blues and greens in the original appear as yellow and magenta, their complementaries, in the negative image.

A color positive is made by printing the color negative image on a three-layered emulsion which is similar to that of the film except that it has a paper background. The print is developed by a process similar to the negative — each layer of the exposed emulsion develops into a black-and-white silver positive image corresponding to each primary color and the dyes are formed with this positive image. The result is three positive images — each consisting of the dye plus silver. In the last step, the silver is bleached out leaving only the color images.

FILM TYPES AND CHOICES FOR TRANSPARENCIES

The two main groups of transparency films available are Kodachrome, which has color dyes added at the time of processing, and all other films including Ektachrome, contain the color dyes in the film emulsion. The first group of films include Kodachrome 25, 64 and 200; Kodachrome 25, 64 and 200 Professional; and Photoflood-balanced Kodachrome 40 Type A. The second group is commonly referred to as "E-6 Type" emulsions, named after the Kodak color processing system. All E-6 films can be processed with E-6 chemicals in the home darkroom or by most professional or custom labs. However, Kodachrome films require complex, multiple-step processing, and are therefore available only through Kodak or major photofinishing labs.

There are advantages and disadvantages in both film types. Because the silver in Kodachrome film is bleached out during processing and replaced with dyes, images appear almost grainless. By contrast, E-6 films display more grain and slightly less image sharpness when compared with Kodrachrome films. However, the E-6 films can be more conveniently processed by local labs, and have the advantage of "pushability," or raising the effective film speed by extending development.

Compared to the negative films, reversal films have a very narrow exposure latitude and need the correct exposure for a "saturated" slide in which the contrast of the colors is optimal. For a slide film, overexposure will render a washed out and desaturation effect for most of the colors. The end use of the slide will also determine how exposures should be made. In general, slides for reproduction should have open tones, without over bright highlights or deep shadow areas.

The need for the correct exposure for a slide film cannot be overemphasized. The use of a lightmeter with an understanding of how the various types of lighting affect the result will help in determining the optimal exposure. Most professionals use a bracketing technique, in full, half, or even one-third-stop steps in an effort to capture the right color and tone. Bracketing is accomplished by adjusting the camera's exposure compensator dial or by manually moving the camera's aperture-control ring or shutter-speed dial. With tight bracketing, at least one exposure out of several will be good enough to bring out the quality of color and tone which was sought.

Difference in Various Brands

The most significant difference among the various brands of film materials are their color responses. These differences are due to the following two factors:

1. Even though manufacturers design films so they will respond equally well to the three primary colors — red, green, and blue under controlled laboratory conditions, each film may respond somewhat uniquely in practical situations, especially when the light conditions vary considerably from the laboratory standard.

2. The balance between the intensity of color dyes — cyan, magenta, and yellow — that make up the color slide image — varies between brands according to the manufacturers' interpretation of what is most pleasing to customers. Because of cultural differences, this interpretation varies considerably among films made in different countries, even brands made for different parts of the same country. For example, what is considered to be an accurate skin-tone reproduction, varies from the East Coast to the West Coast of the United States. Californians find a browner, more suntanned skin-tone natural, while New Yorkers prefer pinker-appearing complexions.

Guide for the Selection of a Film

The first step in the selection of a film should be based on whether it will be photographed in daylight/electronic flash or tungsten illumination. Films are available for both types of lighting. The next step is to decide on the appropriate film speed. A good general rule is to select the slowest film speed that the subject and light level will allow if the measurable qualities of fineness of grain and sharpness are important. Next comes the brand. Personal taste plays a large role in the choice of a brand. Some photographers, for example, prefer a warm color balance, others a cool balance, while something in between is likely to satisfy the majority. Personal taste is also involved with another dimension of color balance which can result in image characteristics that favor one of the primary or the complementary colors. To some degree, this aspect of choice also varies according to the subject characteristics. For example, a film that has a warm balance and reproduces yellows and reds with exceptional saturation might be favored for photographing people. But a completely different interpretation and a cooler color balance may be more appropriate for a snow scene.

Standardizing Originals

Over the years, the question of standardizing the originals for scanners has been raised. There is a new hope that this hurdle may be overcome in the near future by the fact that a cross between conventional photographic principles and electronics is now possible with the advent of the digital technology. Negatives or slides can be electronically optimized and reproduced on photographic paper or transparency materials. Eastman Kodak and Laser Color have been working on systems that use lasers as the light source for exposing prints.

Three other companies — Agfa, Fuji and Konica — announced different approaches. Their systems are based on the use of newly-developed cathode ray tubes (CRT) as the light source. With the CRT printers, the image is taken off-line for electronic processing to improve prior to the actual exposure of the prints. With a digital image processor, the technician can manipulate the image for any type of correction which includes color, tone, sharpness, and even suppression of grains.

Digital proofs and second originals are already a reality. Hell CPR 403 is such an unit (Figure 5.2) that produces continuous-tone images on print paper or transparency materials after the image is corrected. These images appear better than the original photographic images in terms of color, sharpness, and grain. However, these are large and expensive units and are used mostly for complex image processing in the page make-up and retouching systems. The same type of small systems may be available in the near future to generate standardized originals from a variety of copies for consistency and a greater efficiency in the separations in a scanner.

Courtesy Hell Graphic Systems, Inc.

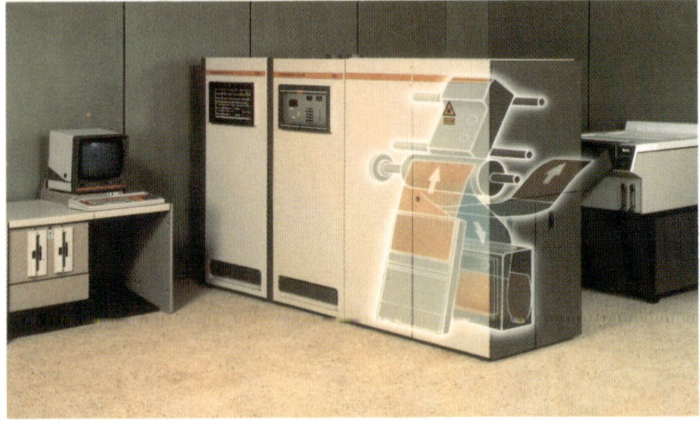

Figure 5.2. Hell CPR 403 Color Proof Recorder

THE SCANNER'S RESPONSE TO COLOR

Eyes and the Photomultipliers

Before an objective approach can be taken for evaluating an original for reproduction, the color response of the scanner in relation to the color response of the human eyes must be understood and considered first. Any light or photoreceptor, such as film, photomultipliers, CCDs, or the eyes, has a spectral response. For a given amount of light energy at a specific wavelength, the photoreceptor has a specific level of response. The eyes, as well as the photomultipliers, produce small amounts of currents when exposed to lights. The current from the eyes goes to the brain, but, in the case of photomultipliers, they are amplified to a more convenient level in the computers. However, the level of current produced by the eyes and the photomultipliers in a scanner are not identical for a given wavelength of light. As a result of this difference, several problems are encountered in both photomechanical and scanner separations. Color patches that look identical to the eyes may not be seen as such by a photographic lens in a camera or the optics/photomultipliers in a scanner because their spectral response is different than that of the eyes.

An eye is assumed to have three types of color receptors. Each receptor is sensitive to a particular range of wavelength of light. However, because of the spectral characteristics of the human eyes, two colors may appear identical under one lighting condition but different under another lighting condition. This problem is called metamerism, and the colors in question are called metameric colors. For this reason, two colors may appear visually identical, but may separate differently in the scanner. The spectral response of the scanner depends on several factors: the absorption characteristics of the scanning optics, prisms, mirrors, filters, and the type of illuminating light source. Because of these factors, the response will differ from one scanner to the other.

Differences in Emulsion Dye

Color photographic materials consist of three layers of light sensitive emulsions and after exposure and processing, form cyan, magenta and yellow dyes. Different color reflective and transparency materials such as Agfachrome, Fujichrome, Ektacolor, Kodachrome, Ektachrome, etc. consist of different dye sets. Although the visual differences of the processed emulsions may not be apparent, however, optics and electronics of a scanner may see these differences significantly.

Dye differences in various emulsions can lead to problems when more than one transparency is ganged for separation on the scanner. Figure 5.3 shows the sensitivity curves of the eye's three light receptors and the spectral dye density curves for the Ektachrome 200 and Kodachrome 64 film emulsions. Although both color patches corresponding to the set of spectral dye density curves shown will be seen as neutral by the eyes, they will be seen differently by the scanner because they differ in spectral composition. As a result, the set of separations corresponding to these original film gray patches will not be the same and consequently will not reproduce neutral.

Effect of UV Light Absorber

Another problem is caused by the presence of different amounts of ultraviolet light absorbers in the transparency films. In the earlier days, professional photographers used ultraviolet light absorbing filters. They did not want their images on film distorted by the ultraviolet radiation visible to the film. An example will be a fabric in the original scene which

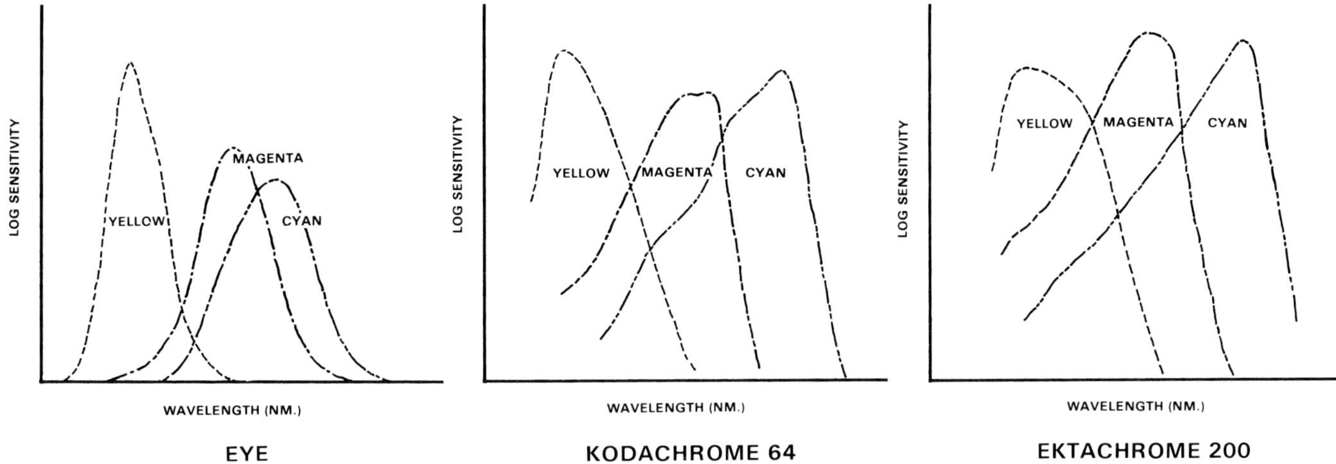

Figure 5.3. Sensitivity curves of the eye's three light receptors and various Kodak film emulsions

reflects ultraviolet light, it will reproduce bluer than it looks. If the fabric is blue, the effect will be minimal. However, if the fabric is of any other color, the additional blueness may cause a neutralizing effect or a color shift in the visual color. Neutral and near-neutral colors are mostly affected by such a shift because their saturation is low. For example, a black tuxedo made of synthetic material may come out blue in a color photograph. These effects may be reduced by using an ultraviolet light absorbing filter, such as Kodak Wratten filter No. 2B over the lens or over the light source, if practical. However, presently, in most cases, the film designers meet the customer's needs by incorporating the filters right into the film. The film absorbs any ultraviolet radiation so that it plays no part in exposing the image. However, the absorbers placed in the film materials during manufacturing are generally not completely removed from the transparencies when the image is processed. In addition, the level of the ultraviolet absorber dye varies in coating from one film to another. The eyes are not sensitive to the ultraviolet light dyes and are not affected by the spectral response. However, in the scanner, the photomultipliers are generally sensitive to ultraviolet light as well as visible light. To solve similar problems in a scanner, Kodak recommends the use of an ultraviolet radiation filter in the scanning light path located on the scanning head to reduce the potential variability in the reproduction of color transparencies. (Kodak Bulletin # Q-500-4, Ultraviolet Absorption in Color Reproduction).

Kodak Color Reproduction Guides

Each and every scanner has a unique set of "eyes" — they are the separation filters, optics, and the photomultipliers. Thus each individual scanner has a unique response to the original it scans. It is impossible to suggest a specific adjustment for each scanner. However, aids are available to study the response of a scanner to help adjust for an optimal response. Such an aid is the Kodak Color Reproduction Guide, Q-60 Kit. The kit consists of test objects on different Kodak Reversal Films and color print materials. Using these guides, scanner operators have a visual aid in their efforts to fine-tune the scanner's adjustments. The test target of the selected Kodak color material is mounted on the color scanner, separated and proofed, using proofing conditions that matches the printing condition. The proof is visually compared with the original target under standard viewing conditions. The objective is a visual match between the target and the proof. If a match does not exist, appropriate adjustments are made to the scanner controls. The target is rescanned and a second proof is made and visually compared to the Q-60 target. Once a visual match is achieved the scanner settings are recorded and used each time that particular Kodak color material is scanned as an original. Test images of other color materials are mounted on the scanning drum and color correction controls are adjusted until the color values for a specific area become the same as those recorded from the original color emulsion(see Figure 10.20, reproduction of Kodak Transparency Guide).

STANDARDIZED VIEWING CONDITIONS

Viewing Problems

Color is a psychophysical sensation, the quality that is perceived by the brain will depend on the interaction of several variables such as the pigment of the object, the light source which illuminates the object, and the mental condition of the observer. However, the physical quality of the color will be mainly dependent on the two aforementioned factors — the pigment of the object and the light which illuminates it. Portions of the light will be absorbed by the pigment or dyes and the remaining part will be reflected or transmitted to the eye. The amount of various wavelengths which will be absorbed or reflected will depend on the composition of the original light source which illuminates the object, and the light reaching the eyes will vary if the composition of the source changes.

The influence of surrounding colors is another problem area. Human perception of brightness, saturation, and even hue can be affected as the human eyes adapt to the presence of another surrounding color. As such, the colors are always seen in relation to one another. This interaction has always been realized by the advertising agencies and printers, and they emphasized the need to control and specify the viewing conditions.

The color of any transparency will look different under a different composition of light with which it is viewed. Direct sunlight is a fairly well-balanced mixture of all the rays in the visible spectrum and never changes; however, the mixture of the rays that finally reach the earth does change. On a clear day, more blue rays will be present than on a dull one. Towards evening, the light becomes more yellow or orange because the blue rays are scattered and lost in the atmosphere. As a result, when viewed in daylight, the colors in a transparency will appear different at different times of the day, times of the year, and even during different weather conditions. When a transparency is viewed with artificial light such as a tungsten filament bulb, it will have more red rays than blue. Similarly, light from a daylight type fluorescent lamp will have more blue and yellow rays than red or violet.

It is evident from the above discussion that the actual physical quality of the original or the reproduction will be mostly dependent on the viewing conditions. The nonstandard light may be the source of disagreement on the quality of the color among the production personnel, the customer, and the salespersons. This problem is solved by the American National Standards Institute (ANSI) which has established a set of conditions for appraising color quality in the graphic arts. The following are some of the viewing standards set forth by the ANSI.

Viewing Transparencies

For a 4 X 5 inch or larger transparency, the American National Standards Institute (ANSI) recommends that the transparency should be illuminated by diffused light and surrounded by an illuminated area of 2 inches wide on at least three sides. The surrounding area must be evenly illuminated and should not exceed four times the transparency area. For viewing a smaller sized transparency, any illuminated area in excess of this ratio should be covered with an opaque gray border of about 60% reflectance. The transparency viewer should be placed within the reflection viewing booth so that the surface of the transparency illuminator is illuminated by the standard light.

Viewing Prints

For viewing prints, the light should be placed in such a way so that it does not make specular reflection from any part of the print to be viewed. The surface areas that the print is placed upon immediately surrounding it should be a matt neutral gray of about 60% reflectance. The level of illumination of the print viewing plane should be about 200 foot candles with even illumination. External light sources should not constitute more than 5% of the total illumination on the viewing area. Surfaces surrounding the viewing area such as walls, ceilings, floors, etc. should be baffled so that there will be no undesirable light falling on the samples while they are being viewed.

The ANSI Standards are now accepted worldwide as the standard viewing conditions. The light source for illumination is recommended to be 5000°K. The required color rendering index (CRI) of the light is 90-100, which means that the light source will contain 90-100 percent of all wave lengths of the visible spectrum from 400-700 nanometers. It has been recommended that a typical small transparency should be viewed on a small format ANSI viewer. It has also been recommended that the light source should have a minimum warm up time of about five minutes and the bulbs should be changed for every 2500 hours of operation. Figure 5.4.shows a color viewing booth with the small transparency viewer.

Until recently the ANSI was still recommending a color temperature of 7500°K for viewing press sheets. The reason was that the light at 7500°K is much bluer than at 5000°K that makes it easier for the pressman to assess visually the yellow ink on white paper. However, with a four or five-color press, all colors are printed in one pass, and the yellow does not need to be evaluated separately. As such, a 5000°K is more appropriate and ideal for the press room, for the press sheet will be viewed under the same conditions that the customer and others in the plant will use. The consistency of the color temperature of the viewing light is important when visually comparing the press sheet and the transparency.

It may be emphasized at this point that some magnification is needed for the critical study of a 35 mm transparency, otherwise some of the faults may not be noticed. On the other hand, if the magnification is too great, the granular structure of the film will become visible and this may be confused with unsharpness. For a critical evaluation of a small transparency, about six times magnification will be suitable. This can be obtained with a linen tester, or a large magnifier with a color corrected lens that can be mounted permanently on

Courtesy GTI Graphic Technology, Inc.

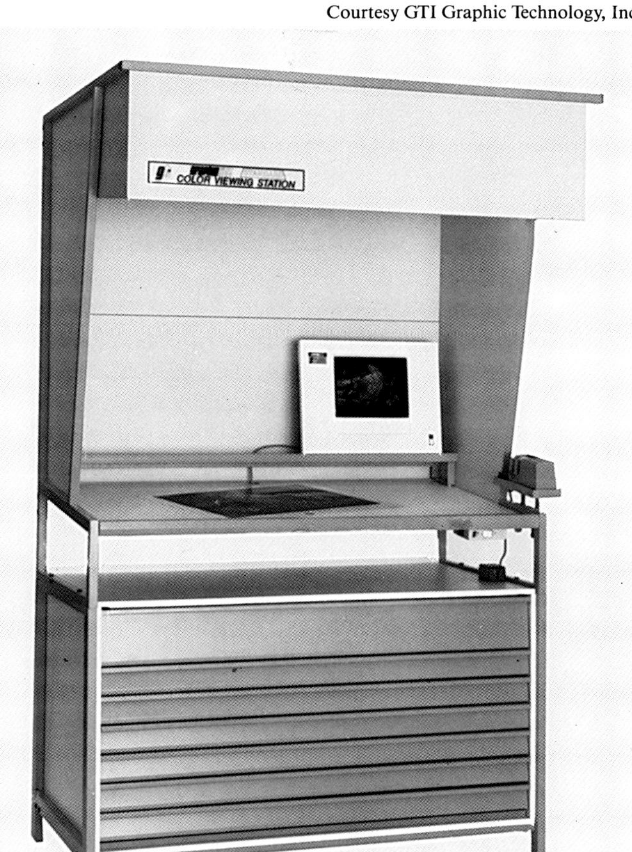

Figure 5.4. A color viewing booth with transparency viewer

the viewer for this purpose.

Size differences between the original and the reproduction may create a major problem. For a given tone reproduction curve, enlargements tend to look lighter in the middle-tones while reductions tend to look darker. This can be solved by moving the larger image away from the eyes in an attempt to equalize the image size. Using a transparency projector to assess the difference in quality because of size changes can be effectively used for visual evaluation. In practice, if the enlargements tend to lighten up the original in the middle or other tonal areas, a tone reproduction curve that results in the closest resemblance of the reproduction with the original can be selected.

As indicated earlier, communicating color still remains subjective in nature, and sometimes it may be difficult to reach a consensus about a color, even when viewed under the same viewing conditions. In this situation, an accurate color measuring device such as a colorimeter or a spectrophotometer should be used as the ideal communicating tool. However, when a visual evaluation is preferred by the customer, a set of Kodak color compensating filters (CC) can play a very important role. These transparent color filters are available in stepped increments of saturation values for both primary and secondary colors, and can be used to assess the quality of a transparency, a reflective original, or the reproduction. The filter is placed over or is viewed through after holding it at a certain distance from the object (see Figure 8.1, page 130). The correct value of the CC filters can be selected that gives the customer what he/she wants, and this information can be communicated to the scanner operator. For example, if the transparency has a greenish cast, the customer may view it through a 20 CC magenta filter which gives him what he expects in the final results. The information is then sent back to the scanner operator who then visually assess the changes by viewing through the filter. It is also possible to correct the color cast in the scanner by placing the CC filters over the original on the scanning drum and adjust the scanner through the CC filters. However, this procedure may need some trial and experimentation. It should be realized that a common reference point reduces the number of variables in any process. Standards are nothing more than agreed upon reference points that are common to all the people involved in the process. With so many variables in the reproduction of color, standardization in any step of the process will assure consistency and efficiency.

COMMUNICATION ABOUT THE ORIGINAL

So far the discussion has focussed on the most important of all production tools, communication. The scanner cannot be successfully operated as an isolated piece of equipment. It must be thought of as a small part of the entire color reproduction system. Any change in any step of the system will necessitate a change in the set up of the scanner. The scanner operator normally receives the original copy with the attached form specifying what the customer wants. The form is the communicating tool and should have all the completed information required for that original. The scanner operator will set up the scanner on the basis of this information. It should be clear, concise, and free from ambiguity. The following information is typical of what should be included with the original:

1. Enlargement / Reduction
2. Negative or positive
3. Line screen: (85/100/120/133/150/175/200)
4. Copy Emulsion (Kodachrome/Ektachrome/Fujichrome, etc.)
5. Emulsion speed (ASA 100/200/400 etc.)
6. Sharpness required (below normal/normal/excess)
7. Color Cast: (local/overall): removed/partially removed/ keep as is
8. Interest area in the copy: High-key/Low-key/Normal/ others (specify)
9. Open-up tones: Quarter-tone/Middle-tone/Three-quarter-

tone/shadow.

10. Copy match?
11. Any specific color match?
12. UCR/GCR Percent

Press Information:

1. Press to be used to print the job .
2. Paper to be printed on: Newsprint/Glossy coated/uncoated/other (specify).
3. Standard dot gain: C: , M: , Y: , K: .
4. Ink quality: Standard / Others . (bluish magenta, etc.)

The above is a typical list of information needed by the scanner operator to help in the correct setting on the scanner. However, this information will vary from shop to shop and can be custom tailored to the shop's own requirement.

PRE-SCAN ANALYZING DEVICES

Possibly the most critical step in the setting up of a scanner is to evaluate the original for optimum results in the separations. Even an experienced operator may make wrong decisions, and the adjustments in a scanner may not always produce the expected results. Consequently there are more remakes, backlogs, and scanner down time. Most pre-scan analysis systems will aid the scanner operators in making objective decisions to set up the scanner for consistent and predictable results with reduced scanner down time, increased productivity, and efficiency.

In a scanner department where a wide variety of originals is received for scanning, and where the time is premium, any of the pre-scanning devices will be cost effective. It will help the scanner operator to set up quickly and accurately. The greatest advantage, however, is that a pre-scanning device will help standardize the scanner set up. Considering all the variables involved in process color reproduction and the cost of scanner down time, a pre-scan device will prove its worth within a short period of time. It must be emphasized at this point that the scanner provides the flexibility and potential to adjust a reasonably degraded original for acceptable results. But this very flexibility provided by a variety of controls in a scanner also makes it more vulnerable to a wrong adjustment.

The pre-scan devices for copy evaluation range from the simple visual assessment of the original to the most sophisticated digital image processing system. Most of the pre-scan off-line devices are used to analyze the original before it goes to the scanning drum. Some are used on the scanner while the copy is being analyzed by the scanning light of the scanner. These devices take advantage of the modern computers with preprogrammed software to compute the characteristics of the separations required for the type of original and the printing conditions. In this type of device, the densitometer is integrated with the system and is used to measure the lightest highlight and the darkest shadow. Information such as low-key, high-key or normal-key are entered into the system. A few manufacturers provide reference original samples to help the operator decide the type of an original. Once the characteristics of the original are entered, the device will select an optimal curve from the memory for that particular original.

Most of the pre-scan and post-scan devices normally generate optimal tone reproduction data after considering several characteristics of the original, the paper to be printed on, and the press variables. After the printing conditions are optimized, these data can be stored as density values. Several sets of such data may be stored for different printing conditions, and the operator may recall data that corresponds to the exact condition. After the characteristics and the aim point values of the original are entered, the computer calculates the optimal curve and generates density or dot percent values for each of the process colors. In some of these devices, optimal color balance may also be preprogrammed. When a copy is analyzed, the computer will generate the values required for optimal color correction. Color cast of the original may also be considered at this point. These are mostly comparison devices. Depending on the preprogrammed values, when a new set of values are entered, the computer compares the new values with the fixed preprogrammed values and comes up with an optimal set up values for the scanner. As such, the accuracy of these devices will depend on the accuracy of the set of preprogrammed values.

A color video monitor, often called soft proof, may be used as a pre-scanning device. Normally a quick scan of the original is performed, and then played back onto the video monitor. With the monitor, it is possible for the operator to assess visually the effect of the scanner adjustment on the original by viewing the changed image on the monitor while changing the scanner control and generating a set of corrected separations. These video monitors may be an integrated part of the scanner as with the Royal Zenith CM-210 monitor, or they may be added to the scanner as a separate unit.

With the advent of more and more digital technology in color scanners, it is now possible to mount the copy on a separate drum and make adjustments with a peripheral unit. The adjustment parameters are then saved on disks, and later the drum containing the original is replaced, and the disk is used to generate the separations. Because of the interchangeability of the digital data, it is now possible to set up a job on one disk while scanning another job. Scanner set up is performed by simply placing the disk into the scanner's disk drive and recalling the data. The Data Setter DS-700, manufactured by Dainippon Screen and used for the DS Scanagraph SG-757 scanners, has this capability.

The others are mostly image capturing digital devices. A video camera or a scanner's output is converted into digital data and the information is stored on a magnetic media. With a keyboard control and a computer with memory and disk drives, the digital information is then converted into an analog signal and played back into the monitor. While the image is viewed on the monitor, all types of manipulations are performed to make the image acceptable. These devices are normally used in the electronic retouching of pagination systems. They are extremely useful to assemble, merge, retouch or convert the images into any geometrical shapes or sizes. These are necessary for the composition of pages or other purposes where several images of different shapes or sizes are required. All the data are recorded on magnetic disks and are transferable from one station to another.

Many pre-scan and post-scan devices are available in the market. Further information on the devices can be obtained directly from the manufacturers. Software for a few devices is available for only a certain brand or brands of scanners. The selection of a system will depend on the requirements and the suitability of the device for a specific need. Any of the systems described will optimize quality and production time and eliminate waste. More importantly, it may be used as a communication and standardization tool for the people involved in the production of color. It is emphasized that the list is not complete, for excellent devices are being offered continually by the manufacturers.

Colortune Viewer

This is a small, portable, computer controlled viewer with which the transparency can be corrected for color balance while it is being viewed. Starting with a standardized white viewing light, the operator can add or subtract one or more of the cyan, magenta, and yellow colors by simply adding or subtracting their values. The changes in color are then translated into corresponding changes in dot sizes in the screened separations. The actual process of correcting the separations are done by using a conversion chart from the display of the viewer or fed into a pocket computer. The computer displays those readings which consist of the dot size changes required to alter the highlight, middle-tone, and shadow areas of the separations.

Courtesy Colortune Corp.

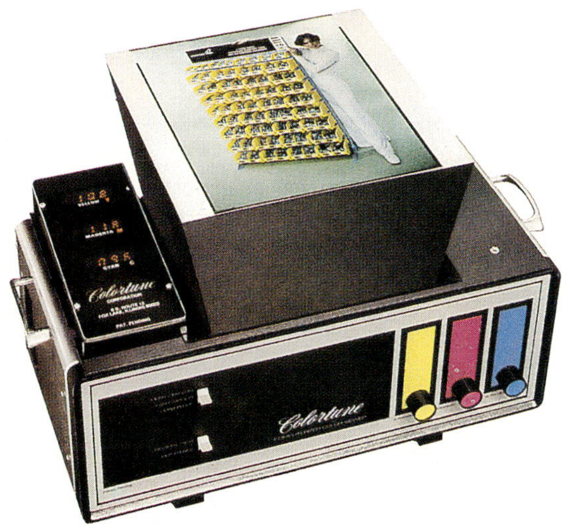

Figure 5.5. Colortune Viewer

Chemco C.A.P.S.

This is an off-line pre-scan evaluation system designed to improve scanner operations. The original copy is classified with the aid of the C.A.P.S. reference transparencies and/or reflection prints into one of three categories: high-key, important middle-tones, and important shadow details. After the subject matter has been referenced to one of these three categories, it is then further broken down to overexposed, underexposed, or normally exposed and high contrast, normal contrast, or low contrast. This information is then keyed into the C.A.P.S. subprogram. After all the data concerning copy, customer, size, and printing processes are entered into the computer, the scanner settings for the original are then determined in dialogue with the program. On the basis of the input data and of the densitometrically established minimum and maximum densities, the computer generates the programming for gradation, color correction, gray balance, and under color removal. The computer output is a printed data sheet which contains all the information as to how this particular job should be set up in the scanner.

X-Rite 410

The problems with most analyzing devices which uses a densitometer is that it measures a larger spot of the copy compared to the scanner which measures and scans point by point, a much smaller area. This problem becomes extreme in shops where the workload is mainly consisted of 35mm transparencies. The newest pre-scan analysis system, the X-Rite 410 Color Transmission Densitometer solves the problem by using a .5mm aperture to measure the copy like the scanner does. The 410 can simultaneously read and display values for all colors (red, green, and blue) for fast pre-scan analysis. The densitometer's viewing optics allows accurate positioning of the copy and the calibrated crosshairs simplify targeting of small highlight and shadow areas. Once the density measurements of highlight and shadow areas are determined, this data can be sent directly to the scanner or set up console, via an interface. The optical and spectral characteristics of the 410 can be custom calibrated to match the input of any Hell, Crosfield, or DS scanners.

Courtesy X-Rite

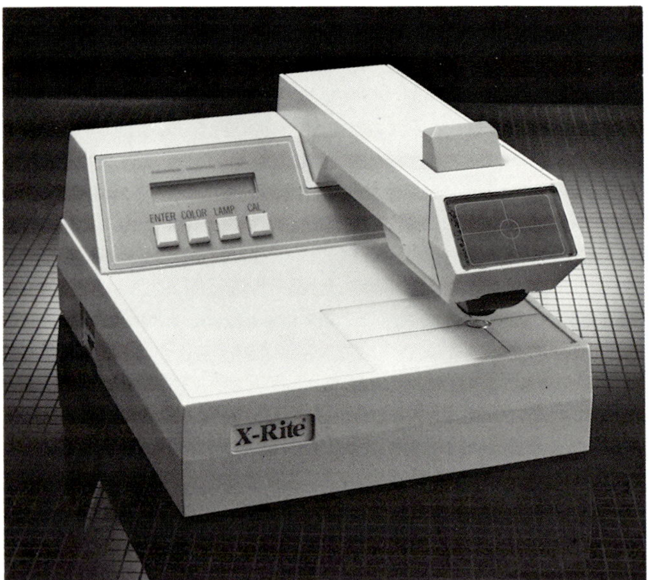

Figure 5.6. X-Rite 410 Transmission Densitometer

DuPont Image Manager

This is a computer based pre-scan analyzing system that analyzes transparencies and produces the optimal scanner aim points for proper gradations and balanced color separations. The Image Manager also keeps track of all pending and completed jobs, thus providing detailed reports on the flow of work. The unit produces a scanner setting report for each transparency and produces special reports that can assist in job management.

The Image Manager analyzes a transparency in the following manner:

1. The Image Manager scans the entire area to be reproduced and breaks it up into thousands of "pixels" or picture elements. It then measures the intensity of each pixel.

Courtesy E. I. Du Pont De Nemours Co.

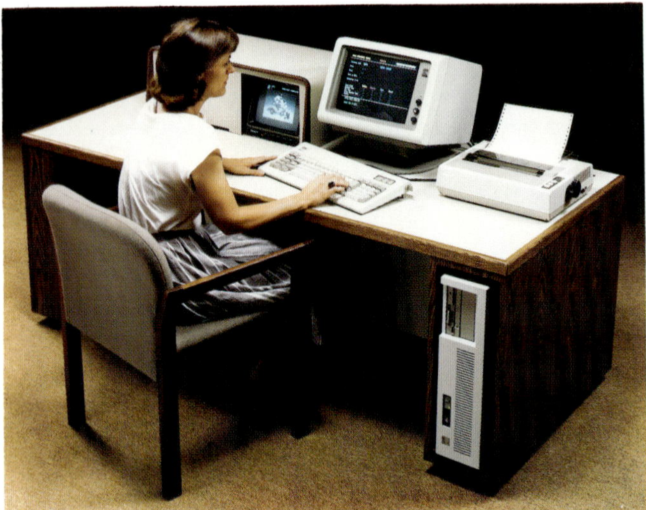

Figure 5.7. DuPont Image Manager

2. The system finds the brightest pixel in the image and asks the operator if that is a minimum density highlight. If not, the operator adjusts the highlight level while viewing the results of the adjustments on the monitor.
3. The system then computes the optimal gradation for this particular image and the customer's preferences such as Clean and Bright, Facsimile, Lighter, or Darker.
4. The reproduction characteristics of the customer's press and stock are used to establish the scanner aim points for optimal reproduction.
5. The resulting scanner aim points are then printed on a form along with all other relevant information for this image, including calculated magnification or reduction percentages.

Scancal

This pre-scan analyzing device employs CCD linear array processing for image analysis. The main feature of the unit includes an infinitely variable amount of RGB or YMC color correction to eliminate or modify color cast in the transparency.

Courtesy Chesley F. Carlson Co.

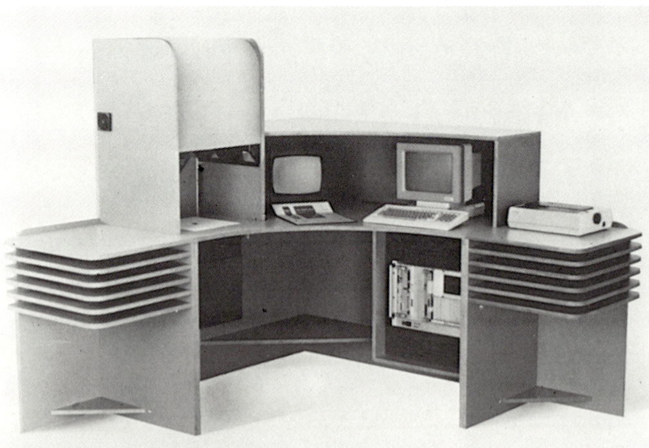

Figure 5.8. Carlson ScanCal

The image analyzing system consists of a Photo Diode Array camera with a zoom lens. During the analysis of the originals, the system digitizes the copy and displays it on a high resolution monochromatic monitor. The highlight is displayed, but it can be changed by the operator. When the desired highlight is defined, an "enter" key is pressed and the system automatically moves to the darkest shadow density. The same procedure is followed in determining the shadow desired. When both the highlight and shadow are defined, the system performs a 50 cell frequency histogram and computes the required tonal distribution curve required to reproduce the modified original. The tonal distribution curve is then matched as closely as possible to the stored gradations in the scanner. An image is displayed on a second monitor that shows a gradation curve using dot values for various aim points. However, at this point the operator has three options — to accept the computer-generated match, to match the tonal distribution curve exactly, or to manipulate all values to change the curve.

Colorcomp

The Colorcomp pre-scan analysis system is used to analyze an original before it goes to the scanner. The measured data is then fed into the computer which automatically generates data for adjustment in the scanner for the optimal quality separations. The major difference, however, is that the Colorcomp utilizes a spectrophotometer for the measurement of color rather than a densitometer. The spectrophotometer renders more accurate information on the characteristics of the original than is possible with a densitometer. The system makes a print from the data which includes the gradation curves for the scanner operator to input into the scanner control panel. The unit can also be used to analyze press sheets and proofs for color matches.

Data Setter DS-700

The Data Setter DS-700 permits data presettings to be entered off-line for use with the DS SG-757 scanner. The unit consists of a scanning drum adapter, CRT display, disk drives, and a keyboard. While scanning one job, the operator can use this peripheral to store settings for subsequent jobs on a floppy disk. Scanner set up can then be performed simply by replacing the drum, placing the disk into the scanner's disk drive, and recalling the proper data. The DS-700 can be used to preset data for gradation, color correction, unsharp masking, UCR/UCA, ICR, and other variables affecting the separations. A CRT display simplifies set up and automatic input error checking helps prevent input mistakes. Scanner settings for up to 64 different set ups can be stored on a single floppy disk for easy processing and storage.

Courtesy D.S. America, Inc.

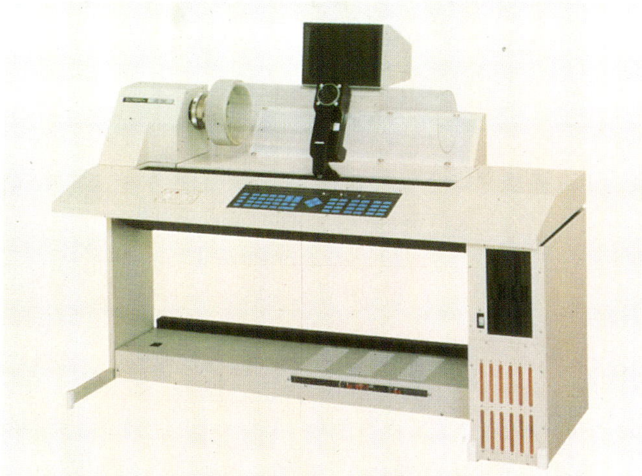

Figure 5.9. Data Setter DS-700

Royal Zenith 210-CM Color Monitor

Operating on-line to the newest RZ 210-L scanner, the Royal Zenith Color Graphics 210-CM Monitor provides a prescan view of the original with the operator visually verifying changes made via the scanner's keyboard prior to exposure onto film. After a quick scan of the original, the image can be displayed on the 210-CM. Among the capabilities of the unit which the operator can adjust in the scanner by viewing the monitor, are on-screen enlargement, cropping, density display, proof matching, ink and paper mapping, program storage, split screen function to compare changes made to the original, progressive display of proofs, and color correction. The user friendly operating system is tracker ball controlled ensuring that all monitor functions are easily selected from multilevel menus.

Courtesy Itek Colour Graphics

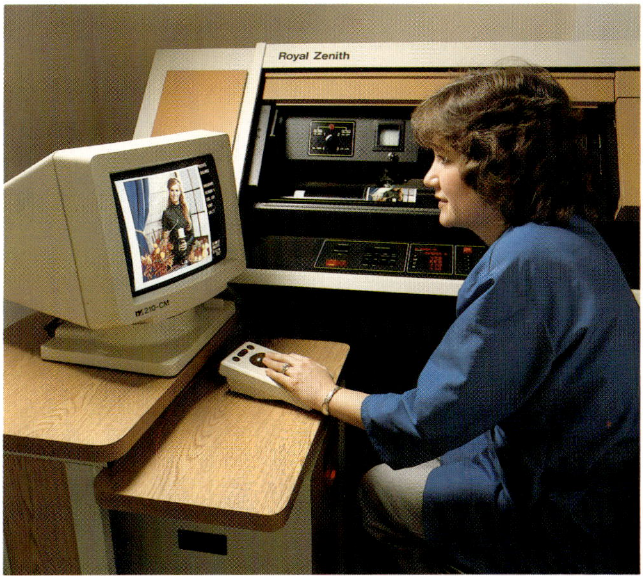

Figure 5.10. Royal Zenith 210-CM color monitor with the RZ 210L scanner in the background

Scan Proof

Made by a Japanese company named Toppan, Scan Proof is a previewer made exclusively for Dainippon Screen scanners. The previewer takes the image signal directly from the scanner and shows the operator exactly how the image will look when it will be reproduced. The manufacturer claims that the system provides a remarkable accurate simulation of the process colors and allows users to adjust for the specific printing characteristics of their own equipment.

Courtesy D.S. America, Inc.

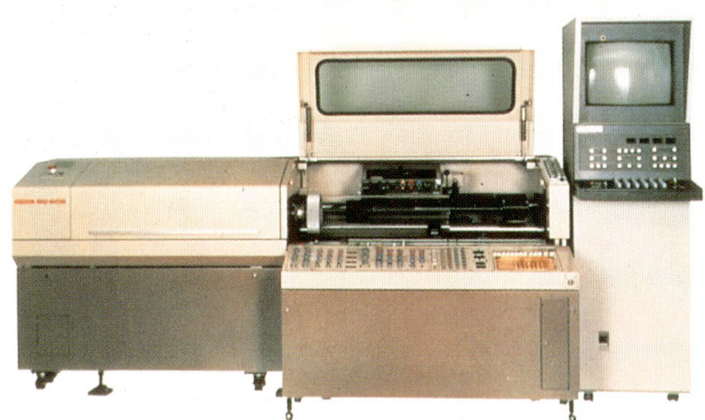

Figure 5.11. Toppan ScanProof SS-512

Scanvision

Gramag Ag, a Swiss company, introduced the Scanvision at Drupa 86. The unit can be connected to all standard color scanners and shows a soft proof before or after the separation films are exposed. The Scanvision receives its signals directly from the scanner computer. When the Scanvision is connected to the scanner, it memorizes the image signals electronically during scanning or recording and the image is then displayed on the color monitor. The colors and tone curves are then adjusted to the ink and printing conditions while viewing the image on the monitor.

Hell LP 307 Layout Programmer

This is an off-line system designed for the efficient operation of a scanner for the Hell Chromacom System. The LP 307 can also serve as the compact page make up system with a scanner. The components of the system include: a color monitor for layout display, a functional keyboard, a digitizer table with cursor, a control station with video display unit, two microprocessors, and three disk drives.

Geometric layout parameters of a page are entered off-line at the Layout Programmer and stored onto disks. The data of the prepared disks are then transferred to the scan station and undergo page make up processing. The color display monitor shows the progress of make up inputs in terms of signal colors. To distinguish and differentiate the masks, seven different colors clarify the display. The following are the main functions of LP 307:

1. Entering layout coordinates.
2. Generating mask for image positioning.

Courtesy Gramag Ag

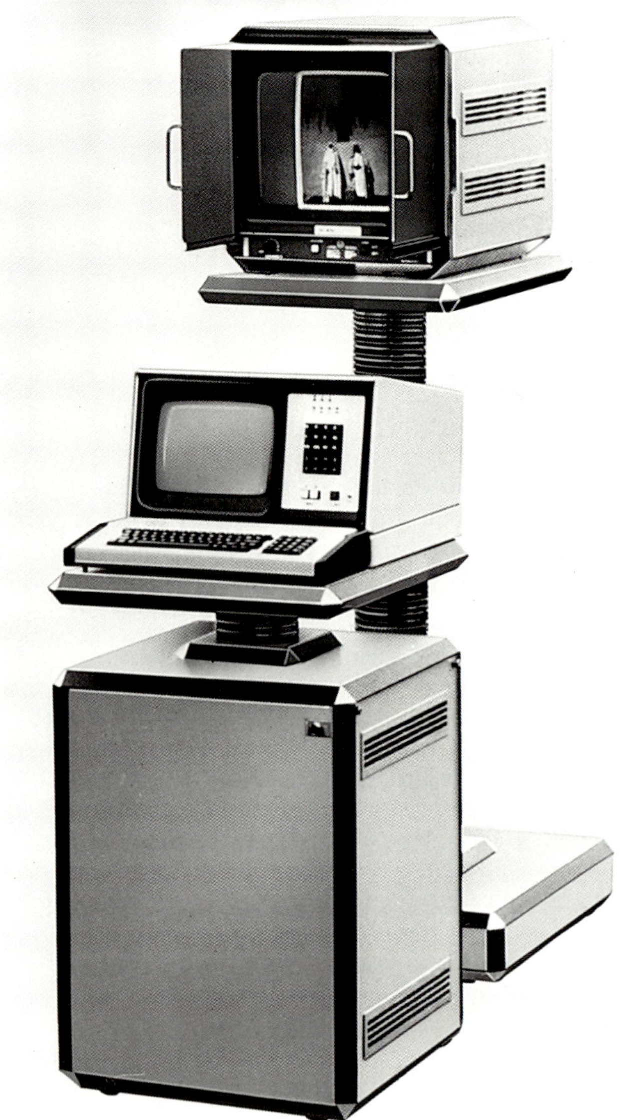

Figure 5.12. Gramag Scanvision

3. Allocating pictures to masks.
4. Carrying out the various construction functions.
5. Generating rules, circles, and other geometric shapes.
6. Generating borders, shades, and tints.
7. Coloring areas.

Scanview 600

Scanview 600 is an off-line job set up and correction terminal. The previewing terminal provides for the fast viewing and for correcting of scanned images on a high resolution color monitor for the Magnascan 600 series scanners. Scanview has the same operating keyboard as the 600 series scan-

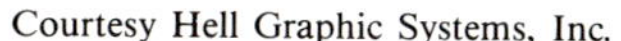

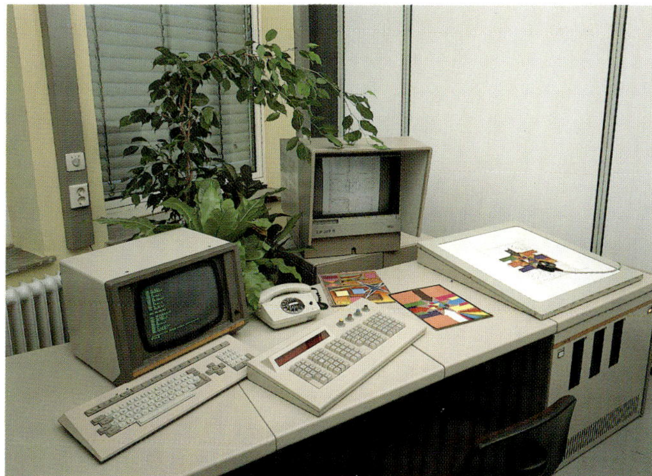

Figure 5.13. Hell LP 307S Layout Programmer

ners, and all job set up and editorial changes can be carried out on the Scanview. This unit is also compatible with Crosfield's Studio 800 series, the 600 can be used as a soft proofing facility for the image processing system.

Courtesy Crosfield Electronics

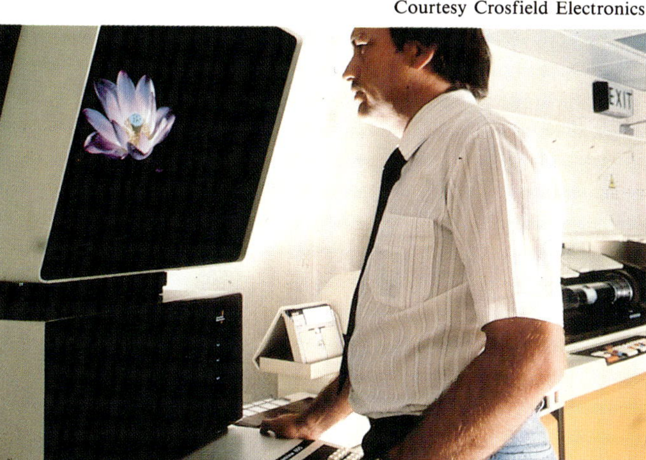

Figure 5.14. Crosfield Scanview 600

Scanner Data Terminal

The Scanner Data Terminal serves as a planning station for setting up the 600 series of Magnascan scanners. The unit consists of a twin floppy disk drive, a visual display and keyboard unit, and a hard copy printer. As an integral part of the Magnascan 645 unit, the Scanner Data Terminal can be used for storage and retrieval of all set up and job information including the color information. The Scanner Data Terminal provides limited page make up capabilities and the images can be accurately positioned on the output film.

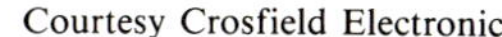

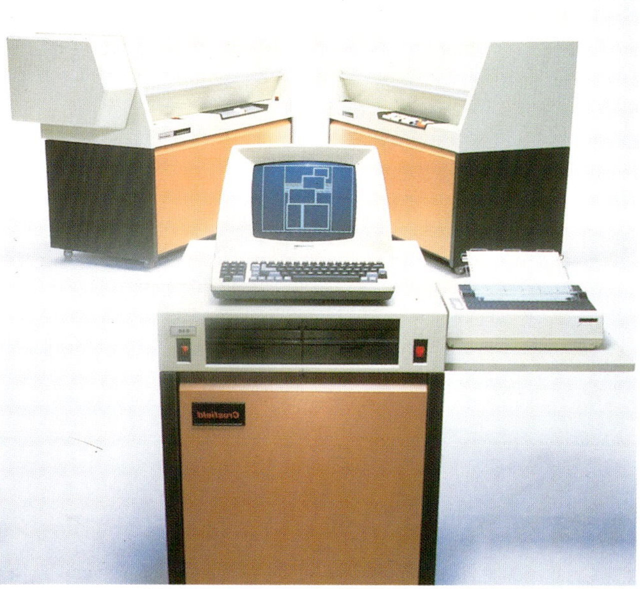

Figure 5.15. Crosfield Scanner Data Terminal

Courtesy Hell Graphic Systems, Inc.

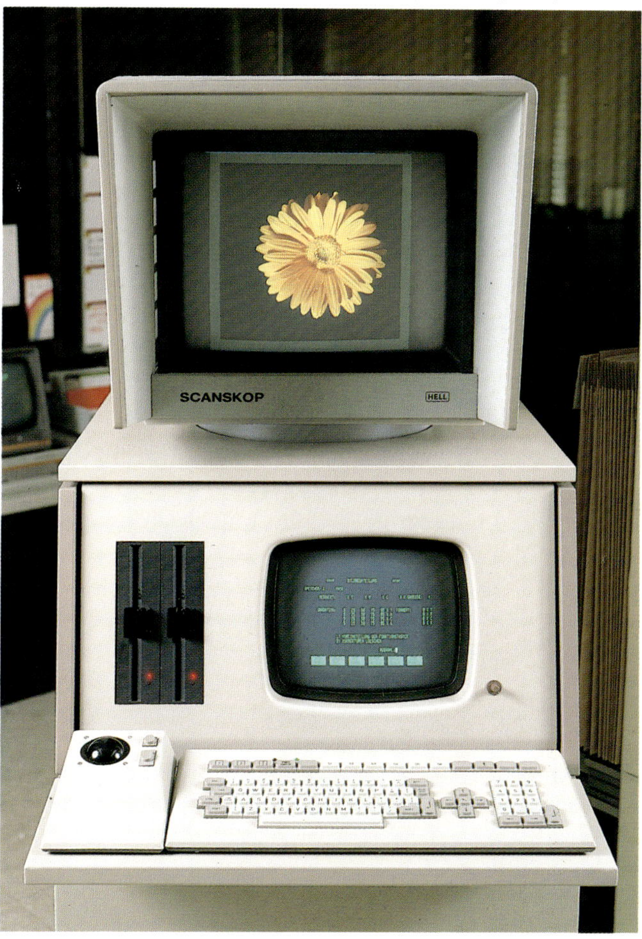

Figure 5.16. Hell Scanskop

Scanskop

This unit checks the quality of the images after they are scanned by the Chromagraph scanners and digitized. With the digitized data, the image manipulation is done at the Combiskop, the heart of the Hell's Chromacom Pagination System. Since the scanner is also used to generate the separations for the Chromacom System, the many features of the Scanskop make it an unique device for controlling the quality of the scanner output. The unit consists of a color video monitor, a keyboard, a trackball, dual floppy disk drives, and a data terminal. Many important features of the unit include — the operator defined skin tone display which may be positioned on the color monitor for comparison, displays of composite prints, white frame, and individual or progressive separation proofs; and split screen functions.

Scitex Pre-sponse Console

Scitex has developed this work station for its Response Pagination and Electronic Retouching Systems. However, the system can be interfaced with any type of scanner for controlling its output. The system lets the scanner operator view the scanned image instantly on a high resolution color video monitor in full color or as individual separation color. The operator then makes overall and selective color corrections on real picture data without rescanning. The scanner operator can see the colors as they would appear after printing in any of the customary ink/paper/press combinations. Before finalizing color changes, the operator compares the appearance of the corrected picture with the original by flipping a switch. In case of an error, the operator can always recall the original untouched image quickly and easily.

Courtesy Scitex America Corp.

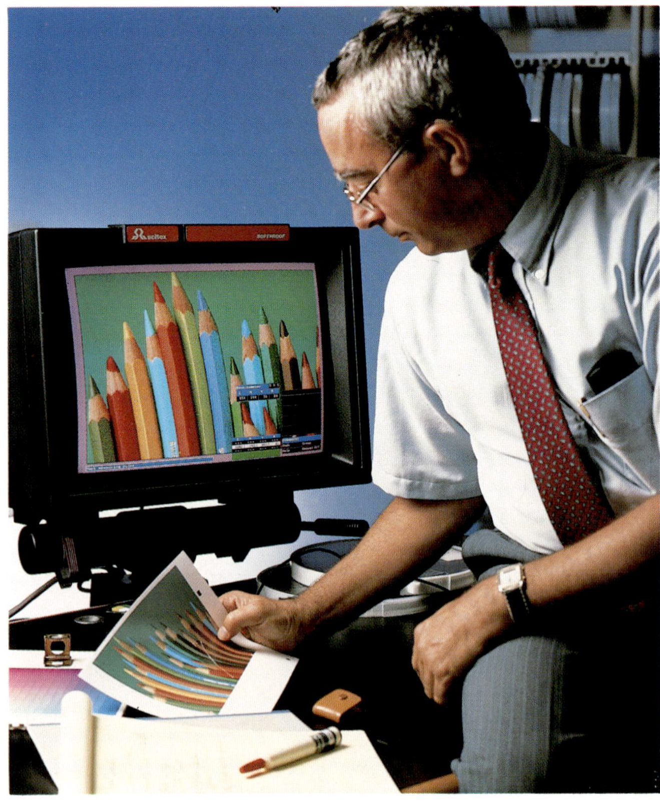

Figure 5.17. Scitex Softproof Viewer

Chapter 6
Basic Calibration

For day to day operation, the calibration of the scanner is of the utmost important for consistency and predictability in the separations. Frequent calibration is needed because of the changes in the equipment or materials that occur over a period of time. The effect of aging on the scanning or exposing lamp intensity, the change of colors of the scanning drum or fading of the gray scale, and the change of film emulsion will all affect the calibration. The purpose of calibration is to adjust the scanner for these changed values so that consistent and predictable results are obtained in each separation.

The basic calibration can be distinctly separated into two broad categories: Input and output calibration. The input calibration involves the calibration of the scanning and basic computer input sections. The objective of this calibration is to adjust the scanning light for the photomultipliers (also called multipliers) so that appropriate electrical values can be generated and fed into the color computer. The computer, in turn, will produce signals for the exposing lamp to record the desired tone or dot values on the film. The basic adjustment in the color computer includes the assignment of tone or dot values for the highest and lowest signals produced by the multipliers. The output calibration is used to adjust the exposing section of the scanner. This calibration consists of controlling the relationship between the exposing lamp intensity, film emulsion, and processor variables so that the required tone or dot values, which are set by the operator at the control panel of the computer are identical to those produced on the film.

INPUT CALIBRATION

Purpose

In most scanners, the light from each spot of the scanned copy transmits through the optical system of the scanning head. Depending on the brand of scanner, this beam is split into three or four beams and focussed onto the multipliers, one for each beam. The multipliers convert the light beams into electrical signals and are fed into the color computer for further processing.

To obtain consistent and predictable results, it is important that the electrical signals generated by the multipliers are all identical when similar light values are applied to them. The second important aspect is to adjust the electrical range of the multipliers for the highest and the lowest light values. In other words, the outputs from the multipliers must be adjusted to produce the highest and the lowest electrical signals for the equivalent light values. This is accomplished by the input calibration — first the multipliers are adjusted for identical output signal for a highlight, and then a range is adjusted for the brightest and the darkest light values. Once these values are set, an electronic circuit keeps track of the multiplier output and adjusts for any deviation. The input calibration of the scanner may be compared to the calibration of a densitometer — the densitometer is calibrated at the lowest density (zero) for the brightest light and the highest density for the darkest area. After the calibration of the multipliers is completed with the assigned light values, they will constantly produce the highest and the lowest signals within the density range of the original during the scanning of a copy.

Depending on the brand and model of the scanner used, different names are given to the basic input calibration. For example, in the Hell scanners, this calibration is called WHITE ALIGNMENT; whereas, in Crosfield, Dainippon Screen, and Royal Zenith, it is called AUTOBALANCE. Whatever the term used, the function and objective of this basic input calibration are the same in all scanners; it is used to set the multipliers so that they generate identical electrical signals for identical light values. The other adjustment is to set the range of the multipliers. This calibration is also referred to as electrical range adjustment of the multipliers and can be compared to the adjustment of screen range to match the copy range for a photograph in a conventional camera halftone technique. The range adjustment consists of assigning the lowest highlight and highest shadow density values to the multipliers so that they produce the electrical signals within that range. Subsequently, when the tone or dot values are assigned, the computer will automatically generate the highest and lowest tone or dot values for these two areas at the output.

In most scanners it is required that the above calibrations be performed every time that the scanner is set up for a new copy. This is because that the calibrations indicated above include values for certain mechanical, electrical, and optical factors, such as the scanning drums and apertures, the color and aperture of the unsharp masking beam, the focusing of the original, etc. As such, if changes are made in any of the above, the values for the calibration will also change and will necessitate a new calibration. For the same reason, separate calibrations are needed for transparency and reflection copy.

White Alignment and Autobalance

The initial calibration in most scanners is called WHITE ALIGNMENT or AUTOBALANCE. In some scanners this basic calibration for the highlight is carried out by first positioning a neutral bright area in the scanning light path and then pressing a calibration button which will automatically calibrate the multipliers for all the channels. A clear scanning drum or the highlight step of a gray scale is used as a neutral area. In the Hell and DS scanners, accurate balancing of the multipliers in each of the color channels is indicated by a numerical display on the front panel, and in Magnascan 645, it is indicated by a bleep sound. For example, proper white alignment in Hell scanners is indicated by the display of a numerical value of 60 for the color channels. Setting the meter switch to AUTO CAL and pressing the AUTO CAL button shows a numerical value of 100 in all the channels for the DS SG-608. In the Magnascan 645, a correct Autobalance is indicated by one bleep and an incorrect one with three bleeps. In the RZ 200-S, when the scanning light is positioned for a neutral white area, pressing a RESET button balances the multipliers automatically. In this scanner, a MASTER BALANCE CONTROL is provided to change the RESET values, if needed.

In the Hell 399ER scanner, after the multipliers are balanced for the highlight, range values of 100 are assigned for the highlight and 0 for the shadow, with the scanning light positioned for the highlight and shadow respectively. However, in the DS SG-608, the correct balancing shows a range value of 40 for the shadow. In the Hell and DS scanners, the maximum shadow is created by flipping a mirror, which is positioned at the scanning light path, to cut off the light to the multiplier. In the Magnascan 645, once started, the Autobalance functions for both highlight and shadow proceeds automatically. After the Autobalance for highlight is completed, the mirror in the scanning head flips, and the Autobalance for shadow takes effect. In this scanner, after the AUTOBALANCE is completed, the electrical range of the multipliers is adjusted by entering the brightest and darkest light values with pushbuttons labeled ENTER WHITE and ENTER BLACK. Similar HIGHLIGHT and RANGE controls are used in the RZ 200-S. Once the highest and lowest range values for the highlight and shadow are set, similar brightest and darkest points of any original, when scanned during the separations, will automatically determine the minimum and maximum recording densities on the film. However, this range setting can be changed to suit the individual need of a copy.

Assignment of dot values

In most analog scanners, the next step in the basic calibration is to enter the dot percentage for the calibrated highlight and shadow density values. Since the gray balance requirement calls for different dot values for each of the process colors, different sets of dots are assigned for these aim points. These are standard gray values and may vary according to the different printing conditions such as the quality of the ink, thickness of the printed ink layer, density, dot gain on the press, etc. Table 4 represents a typical example of dot values for the highlight and shadow steps for proper gray balance.

TABLE 4

	Highlight	Shadow
Cyan	6%	98%
Magenta	4%	95%
Yellow	4%	95%
Black	0%	85%

In an analog scanner, the above dot values are assigned by positioning the respective highlight and shadow steps and then assigning the values for each color with the respective highlight and shadow keys. During the subsequent production of a set of separations, the computer will automatically produce signals to generate identical dot values at the output for identical density values for highlight and shadow. These steps complete the basic calibration for balancing the multipliers and the color computer input. In most digital scanners, preprogrammed dot values for highlight and shadow are stored as gray balance values and are recalled when needed. Once the tone or dot values are programmed, they need not be repeated every time a calibration is performed. In most scanners, once the electrical range of the multipliers for any highlight and shadow are reset, these tone or dot values remain the same for the highlight and shadow for a new copy.

INPUT CALIBRATION IN DIFFERENT SCANNERS

Crosfield Magnascan 645

To balance the multipliers in this scanner, a clean area of the drum is positioned for the scanning or analyze light and the AUTOBALANCE button is pressed. Then the "AUTOBALANCE Y/N?" appears on the Alphanumeric display panel. Once the "yes" button is pressed, balancing the multipliers proceeds automatically for both highlight and shadow. At the end, a correct balance will be indicated by one bleep and the Alphanumeric display will revert to the monitor mode, indicating that normal operation may continue. An incorrect balance will be indicated by three bleeps. An incorrect balance may result from insufficient light reaching the scanning head or an electronic malfunction in the scanner.

To calibrate the multipliers for the highlight and shadow range of the original, the pushbuttons ENTER WHITE and ENTER BLACK are pressed while the scanning light is in the respective position. These values must be entered before other specific adjustments or editorial retouching controls are used. When ENTER WHITE and ENTER BLACK buttons are used in conjunction with MANUAL, AUTO, or AN (Auto Neutral) buttons, partial or complete removal of color cast is possible from the highlight and/or shadow areas of the copy. With the ENTER WHITE in the MANUAL mode, predetermined density values can be used for the highlight; in the AUTO mode a partial neutralization of the highlight is possible; and with AN mode, a total neutralization of the color cast is possible in the highlight of the original. With ENTER BLACK, in the MANUAL mode, predetermined density values can be used for the shadow; in the AUTO mode, the computer selects the highest density of any one color of the original and the other colors are automatically balanced for neutral; and in the AN mode, the shadow area will be completely neutralized. Precautions should be taken when the AN mode is used: if the spot selected in the original is not neutral for the AN mode, it will severely unbalance the colors in the output.

The above functions are performed while the scanning light is positioned at the appropriate areas of the original. However, predetermined values for highlight and shadow for the two aim points can be entered, regardless of whether the original is on the cylinder or not. It is necessary to recall the CUSTOMER VALUES(CV) prior to performing the ENTER WHITE and ENTER BLACK functions because the CUSTOMER VALUES contain the reproduction curve used to

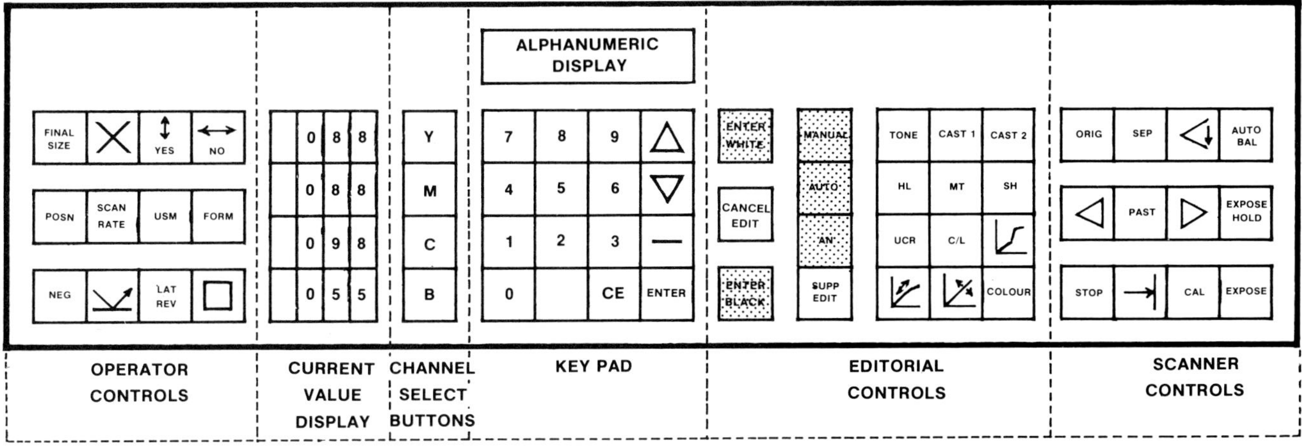

Figure 6.1. Panel of Magnascan 645 showing pushbutton controls for ENTER WHITE, ENTER BLACK, MANUAL, AUTO, and AN (Automatic Neutral). In the 645, ENTER WHITE and ENTER BLACK controls are used to enter the highlight and shadow density values of the original. When ENTER WHITE and ENTER BLACK buttons are used in conjunction with MANUAL, AUTO, or AN buttons, partial or complete neutralization of color cast is possible from highlight and/or shadow areas of the copy.

Courtesy D.S. America, Inc.

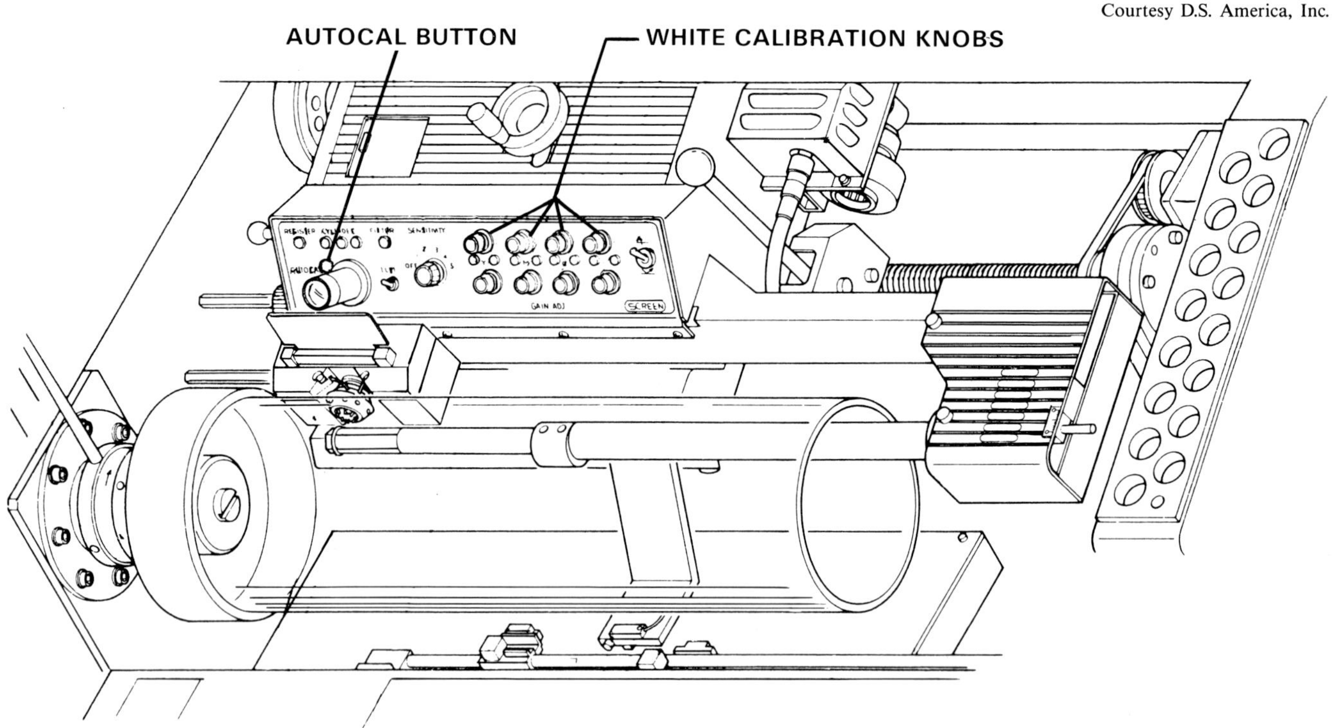

Figure 6.2 AUTOCAL button at the DS SG-608 scanning head. The button works in conjuction with the WHITE CALIBRATION knobs.These knobs can be used for adjusting the sensitivity of the photomultipliers. When any neutral highlight (copy highlight, gray scale, or the transparent cylinder) is placed in the scanning light path and the AUTOCAL button is pressed, an automatic calibration takes place. The correct calibration is indicated by the lights situated under the calibration control knobs going out. A value of 100 is also displayed on the digital meter for correct Autocalibration when the meter switch is at the AUTOCAL position. When a correct calibration is not possible because of un unusual highlight density, the sensitivity of the photomultipliers can be adjusted with the WHITE CALIBRATION knobs

assign tone values.

Dainippon Screen SG-608

In this scanner, the basic calibration is performed by first selecting a highlight, e.g. copy highlight, gray scale, or the clear cylinder and then the AUTOCAL button is pressed. An automatic calibration takes place and is indicated by the lights going out which are situated under the WHITE CALIBRATION control knobs. A value of 100 is also displayed in all channels on the digital meter for correct calibration when the METER is at the AUTOCAL mode. The HIGHLIGHT DENSITY set knob can be used to select an internal density for the calibration. The HIGHLIGHT DENSITY and SHADOW DENSITY set controls have ranges from 00 to .50 and from 1.3 to 3.3 respectively. For shadow, the scanning light is positioned for a shadow density, then the SHADOW DENSITY set knob is adjusted until the meter reads 40. When a correct calibration is not possible because of unusual highlight, the sensitivity of the photomultipliers can be adapted to a particular highlight with the WHITE CALIBRATION controls and then pressing the AUTOCAL button.

Once the multipliers are balanced and the range is set, the minimum and maximum dot percentages for cyan, magenta, yellow, and black are assigned. This is done by first positioning the Meter Switch to dot percentage, the Reference Switch I down, and setting the maximum shadow dot percentage with the shadow dot percentage control for each color. Similarly, with the Reference Switch II/III down, the minimum highlight dot percentage is set with the highlight dot percentage controls for each color.

Hell 399ER

In this scanner, the first step in the basic input calibration is called WHITE ALIGNMENT and consists of several controls; one is an eight-position Electronic Gray Scale. With this control, neutral density values ranging from 0.0 to .70 for a transparency highlight and from 0.0 to .20 for a reflective highlight can be simulated for the White Alignment.

A pushbutton called WHITE ALIGNMENT WITH COLOR CAST COMPENSATION KEY is used in conjunction with the copy highlight to neutralize a color cast. If the scanning light is positioned on the image highlight and the key is pressed, a color cast in the original will be neutralized. Otherwise, the WHITE ALIGNMENT is normally performed by positioning the scanning light on the clear scanning drum.

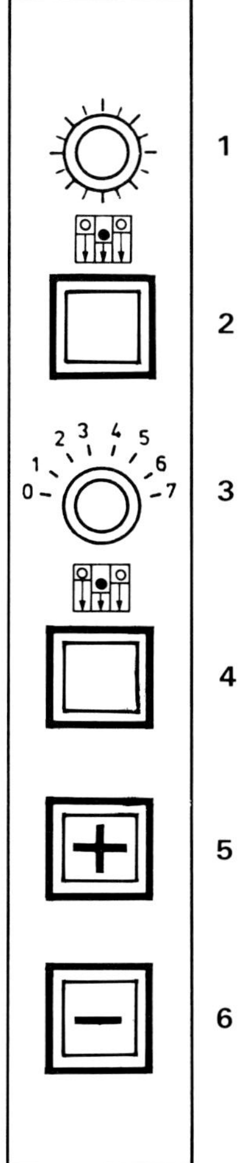

Figure 6.3. WHITE ALIGNMENT panel in the Hell 399ER. Control 1 is used to simulate neutral density for the WHITE ALIGNMENT. Control 2 is used in conjunction with Control 1 to reduce any color cast in the highlight during White Alignment. Control 3 is a color cast reduction switch. Pushbutton 4, when used in conjunction with Control 3, reduces various proportions of color cast while the scanning light is positioned on the image. Pushbuttons 5 and 6 are used to increase or decrease density or dot percent values after the White Alignment is performed.

In addition to the above, two more controls are provided, a seven-position COLOR CAST REDUCTION switch and a COLOR CAST REDUCTION key. The purpose of the COLOR CAST REDUCTION switch is to adjust the level of reduction of the color cast. At position 0, there will be no influence on the reduction, and at position 7, full color cast compensation will be effective. The color cast reduction function will be effective when the COLOR CAST REDUCTION key is depressed at the same time the scanning light spot is positioned on the image where the color cast is to be modified.

At the bottom of the panel, there are two WHITE SPOT ADAPTATION keys (plus and minus) that are used to increase or decrease the highlight density or dot percentage of the highlight after the White Alignment is performed.

After the WHITE ALIGNMENT, the electrical range of the multipliers are adjusted for the highlight and shadow with IMAGE ADJUSTMENT controls. The controls for IMAGE ADJUSTMENT consist of a set of four potentiometer controls, that are used for electrical adaptation of the photomultipliers to a white level selected by the operator. The value is adjusted to 100 while the scanning light is transmitted

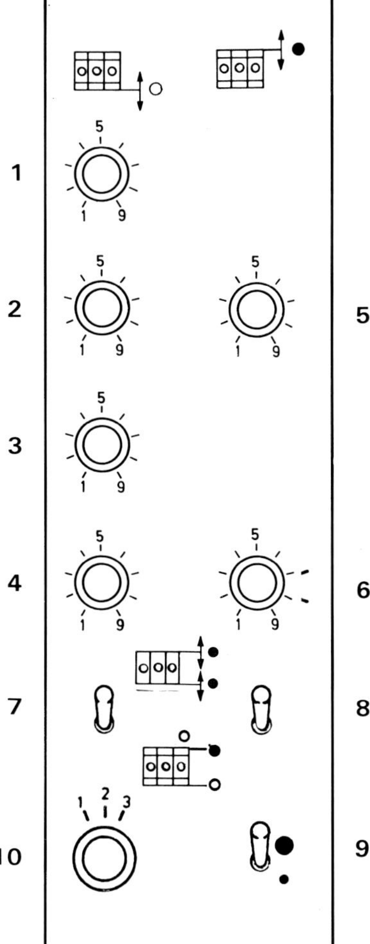

Figure 6.4. Hell 399ER PICTURE ADJUSTMENT panel. Controls 1 through 4 are used for electrical adaptation of the photomultipliers to a white level selected by the operator by assigning a value of 100. Controls 5 and 6 are used to assign a minimum value of 0 for the image shadow — Control 5 is for the cyan, magenta, and yellow separations and Control 6 is for the black separation. With toggle switches 7 and 8, the effects of the above controls can be deactivated, if necessary. With toggle switch 9, the density range of the original can be adapted for the computer — large dot for a large range and small dot for a small range. Control 10 is a 3-position black separation switch.

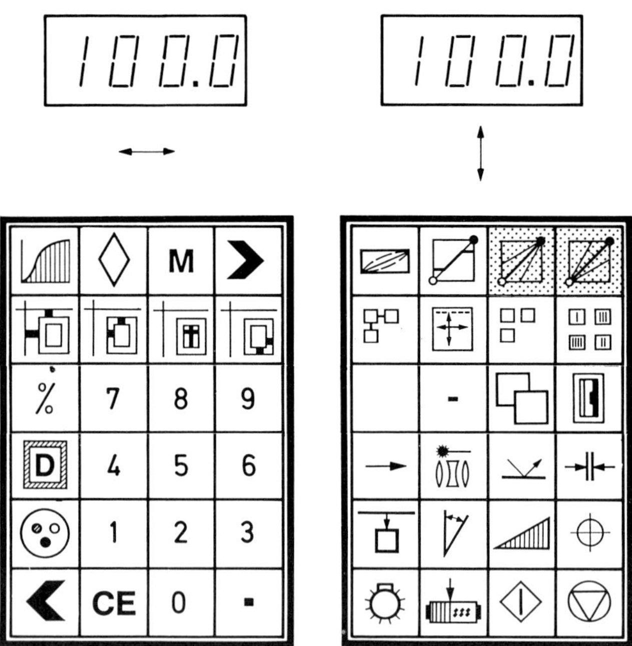

Figure 6.5. Hell 399ER Scale Computer panel showing the RECORDING DENSITY Highlight and RECORDING DENSITY Shadow buttons

through the selected neutral white. For the adaptation of the multipliers to a shadow, two controls are used — one for assigning a minimum value of 0 for the cyan, magenta, and yellow, and the other for assigning the same value for black. Two toggle switches activate or deactivate the effects of the above controls. With another toggle switch, the density range of the original can be adapted for the computer - large dot for a large range and a small dot for a small range.

The last step of the input calibration involves assigning the required dot percentages for highlight and shadow. These keys are located in the SCALE COMPUTER panel. The RECORDING DENSITY HIGHLIGHT and RECORDING DENSITY SHADOW keys are pressed, and the respective dot values for each color are entered for the highlight and shadow. During this adjustment, the Color Separation mode switch should be in the yellow channel, and the gray balance control deactivated.

Royal Zenith 200-S

In this scanner, a single RESET button balances the multipliers for color and unsharp masking output. When the scanner is in the set up mode, the scanning light is positioned for the clear drum, and the RESET button is pressed. The message "COMPUTING RESET" will briefly appear on the STATUS display panel while the scanner automatically balances the color input signals. Failure to achieve balance is indicated on the display panel by the message "RESET FAULT" and a signal that indicated which mode has failed to balance, e.g. Y SHARP.

To adjust the range of the highlight and shadow for the multipliers, the HIGHLIGHT and RANGE controls are used. The HIGHLIGHT control is used to adjust the highlight density, as well as to monitor and adjust for any color cast in the original. The RANGE setting allows the operator to adjust the scanner to the range of the original. However, before setting the HIGHLIGHT or RANGE, the program containing the gray balance, gradation, color correction, and other values which were previously programmed and stored must be recalled.

OUTPUT CALIBRATION: FILM LINEARIZATION

Purpose

The purpose of film linearization in a scanner is to control the relationship between the exposing light intensity and the results obtained on the film in order to produce consistent and predictable output. For example, when the operator adjusts a 50% dot value on the scanner for a certain tone, accurate

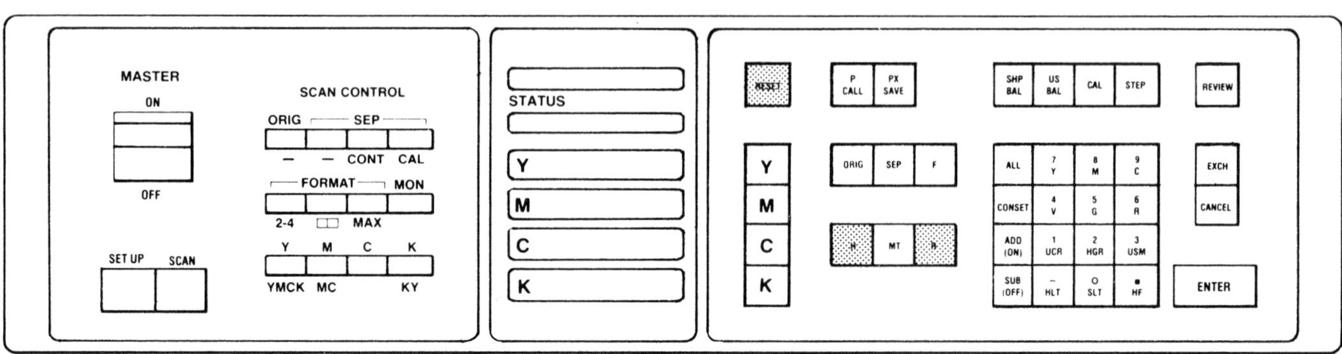

Figure 6.6. Control panel of the Royal Zenith 200-S showing the RESET, HIGHLIGHT, and RANGE pushbuttons

linearization assures that exactly a 50% dot will be produced on the film for the same tonal areas of the copy.

Linear Relationship

Linear relationship between the exposing current and the results obtained on the film can be explained with Figure 6.7. At 0 current at the exposing head, there is 0% of dot produced on the film, and for every 5 units of increment in the current, there is an increase of 5% of dots. That is, an increased amount of current assigned to the exposing lamp produces a proportional increase in the percentage of dots on the film. When these numbers are plotted, they make a straight line with a 45 degree angle. This line represents a linear relationship between the current, which produced various intensities at the exposing head, and the percentage of dots produced on the film.

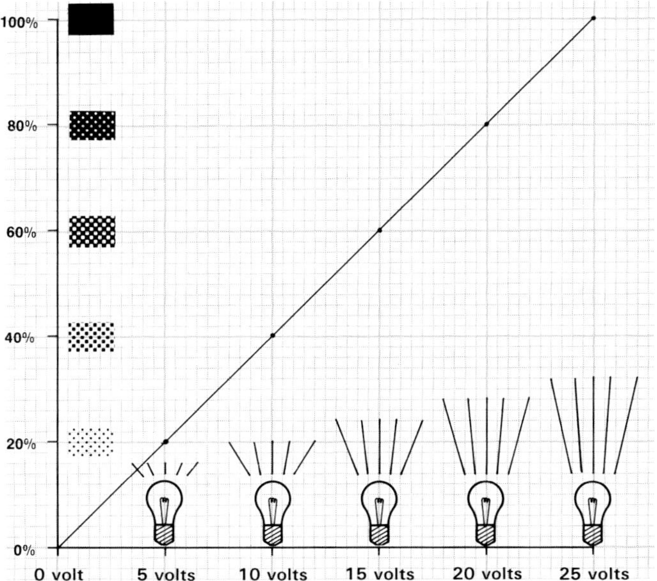

Figure 6.7. Linear relationship between various light intensities and the dots produced by the exposures

In practice, increments of current at the exposing head will not produce the same proportional increase of tone values on the film. This is because the film emulsion responds differently to the changing exposure and process conditions. The relationship may be compared to the speed of a car and the position of the accelerator; for example, depressing the accelerator twice as far will not double the speed of the car. Similarly, different proportions of currents are needed to produce the uniform increments of results obtained on the film. However, in a scanner these proportions are already internally set. Once the electrical signals from the multipliers are adjusted for the lightest and darkest tone values on the film with a suitable film processing condition, the intermediate tone values become accurate. Film linearization is the controlling the conditions which will produce the required tone values on the film for a specific film emulsion.

Linearization Procedure

The linearization procedure in a scanner will vary from one brand to the other. However, in most scanners the procedure consists of scanning a gray scale to determine the tone values produced by the exposing lamp with a suitable film processing condition. The first linearization is essentially a trial approach and consists of scanning the scale several times using a different current setting for each time. In all scanners, the current can be adjusted for the maximum and minimum output of the exposing lamp for the brightest and darkest tone values produced by the computer at the exposing head. A setting is selected which produces a series of predetermined tone or dot values for the shadow and highlight steps. The target for proper linearization may consist of obtaining tone or dot values for one or several steps on the scale. However, once the conditions for accurate linearization are obtained for a certain film emulsion, they are kept constant. In most situations, it is adequate to maintain developer strength, temperature, and gradient in the processor for predictability and consistency.

Instead of scanning a regular gray scale, most scanners with computer memory are equipped to produce exposing currents of various intensity. The results are similar to those obtained by scanning a gray scale. This internal current is more consistent because it is not affected by external variables such as aging of the gray scale, dirt, dust, etc.

Pre-exposure

A few conventional screen scanners have provisions for pre-exposing the film along with the main exposure. A pre-exposure is necessary to supplement the main exposing lamp to raise the sensitivity level of the film emulsion, especially when a low intensity lamp like a glow lamp is used for the main exposure.

The pre-exposure lamp is normally mounted on top of the main exposing assembly. The lamp produces a constant intensity of light and can be adjusted independently without affecting the main exposing lamp. After a suitable value is found, it is set to this position. Like a flash exposure in a conventional halftone, the pre-exposure will have very little effect on the shadow areas in a positive or the highlight areas in a negative. Figure 6.8 shows an exposing head assembly with the pre-exposure lamp mounted on top.

Courtesy Hell Graphic Systems, Inc.

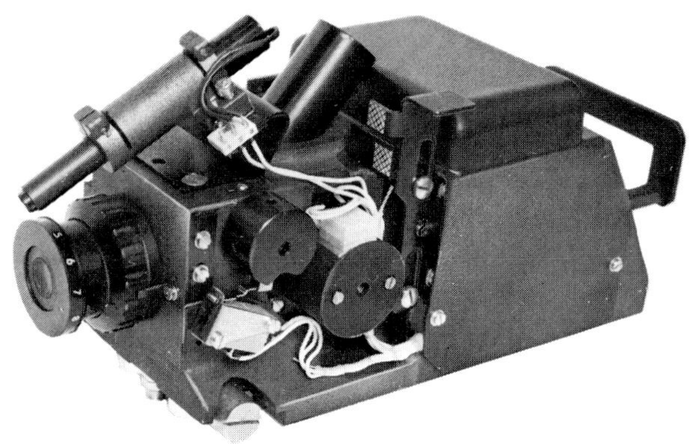

Figure 6.8. An exposing head assembly with the pre-exposing lamp mounted on the top

TYPES OF LINEARIZATION

Depending on the model used, a scanner may produce conventional screen halftones, continuous-tones, and direct electronic dots on the film. All conventional screen scanners produce both direct screen and continuous-tone separations. Some electronic dot generation scanners can be adapted to produce continuous-tone separations by changing the exposing head consisting a glow lamp or by using a different type of modulator that produces variable density on films with a laser light source.

Linearization in Conventional Screen Scanner

To determine linearization for contact screening in a conventional scanner, normally a gray scale is exposed with different settings to control the output current of the exposing lamp. When the film is developed in a controlled processing condition, scales with different tone values are obtained on the film, and the scanner is adjusted to produce the desired results. In some scanners, the dot values for each step of the scale must be entered into the computer's memory. The computer compares the results with preprogrammed target values and then corrects the results to ensure that all the preselected screen dot sizes are recorded on the film.

Linearization procedure for the direct screen and the continuous-tone separations in a conventional scanner are identical except that for the continuous-tone, varying density values are generated on the film in place of the screen dot values. This changeover is accomplished by some minor mechanical and/or electrical adjustments. The films used for continuous-tone separations are lower in contrast than those used in direct screening.

Linearization for Electronic Screening

In conventional screen scanner, the screen rulings are changed by changing the contact screens containing different rulings. However, the electronic dots generated by laser are controlled and produced by two distinct elements — electronics and optics. The shape, percentage value, and screen angle are calculated by the computer. Changing the screen rulings involves changing the size of dots, and is normally carried out by both the exposing optics system and the screen computer. For example, a 150 line screen will have four times as many dots as in a 75 line screen within the same area. Just like the zoom lenses in regular photographic cameras, the width of the dots are changed by zooming the optics at different focal points on the film. The exposed length of each dot element is controlled by the screen computer. Often more than one zoom lens is required to optimize the dots for different rulings.

In addition to locating the laser intensity, most of the electronic dot generation scanners need a few adjustments during the initial set up. These are focus adjustment, modulator alignment, zoom value adjustment, and similar mechanical, optical, or electrical adjustments. First a test pattern is exposed, and then adjustments are made after evaluating the pattern results on the film. Once the set up is optimized, the adjustments are normally saved on floppy disks. Later when

Courtesy Hell Graphic Systems, Inc.

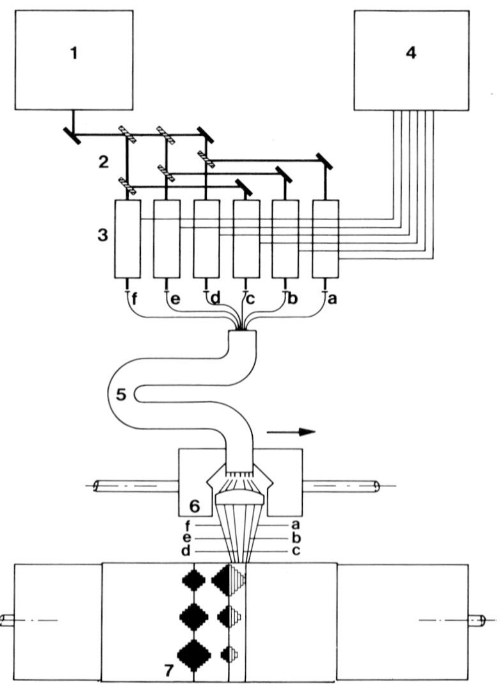

Figure 6.9. Electronic screening in a Hell scanner

the buttons are pressed for the desired line rulings, dot shape, etc., the functions are automatically adjusted by the computer.

Linearization for contact screen dots is more critical than electronic dots. The dots produced through the vignette patterns of each of the dot producing cells have soft fringe areas on the outer edges. If the exposure and developing conditions are not strictly maintained, the fringe areas will tend to lose or gain additional density, and the size of the reproducible dots become vulnerable to change. On the other hand, an electronic dot is exposed by a concentrated laser beam with a sharp cut off point between exposed and unexposed areas on the film. As a result, the dots produced by a laser beam are hard and have little fringe. With developing variables almost eliminated in generating electronic dots, the scanner predictability is achieved.

LINEARIZATION PROCEDURE IN DIFFERENT SCANNERS

Crosfield Magnascan 645

The exposing unit of the 645 is separate from the scanning/analyze unit. It is connected to the analyze unit by ribbon cables. The control panel of the expose unit consists of the following switches: Emergency-Off, Scanner, Vacuum, Laser, Stop, Expose, Traverse, Cal, and Load Film. The film loading is automatic.

The expose optics assembly consists of an optical system, a lens turret, and a laser unit. The light source is a 15mw argon laser. The light splits into six smaller beams which pass through a 6-channel polarizing modulator. The light is focussed by the lenses to form a fine spot on the output film. The size of the spot on the output film is selected by manual rotation of a 3-position lens turret in the light path. The turret position is selected in accordance with one of the three scan rates determined by the operator on the analyze unit. The system provides a wide range of screen rulings with the three scan rates. Four dot shapes are available — square, elliptical, round, and autotypical gravure. Various angle sets are also available. The angles in use are shown in the Current Value (CV) display.

The purpose of the output calibration is to determine the relationship between the light output, film emulsion, and processing conditions. The output calibration consists of exposing a 32-step gray scale and locating a 48% dot in the 16th step of the scale. If the step does not contain the required percentage of dots, then a program called CAL 46 is recalled, and the laser intensity is increased or decreased until the values are corrected.

Courtesy Crosfield Electronics

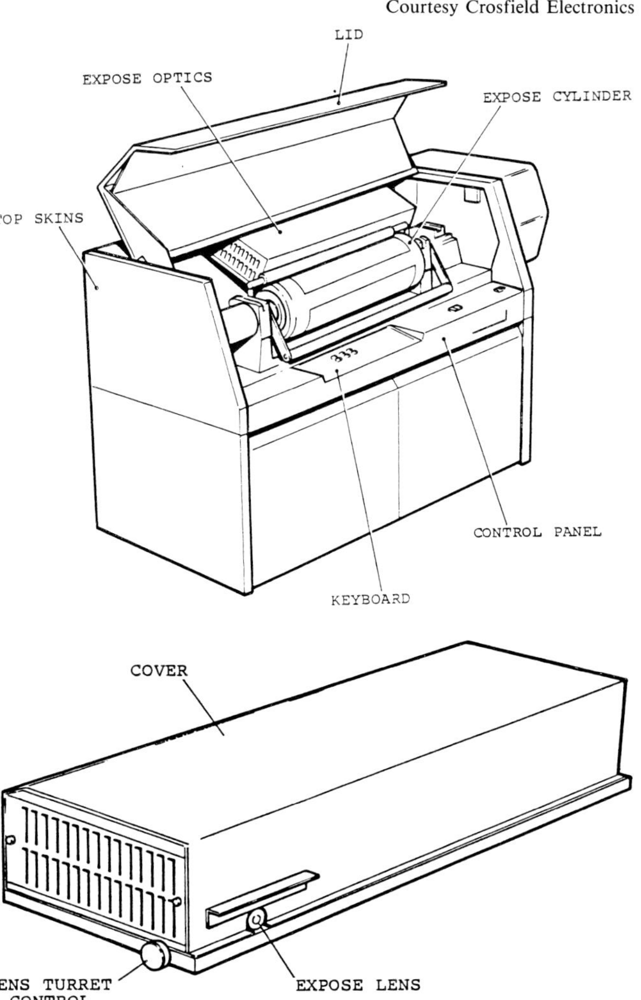

Figure 6.10. Magnascan 645 exposure unit and the exposing optics assembly

Dainippon Screen SG-608

The Electronic Dot Generator of the SG-608 consists of a recording head and a controller. The dot generator is controlled by a floppy disk drive located at the bottom right of the scanner cabinet. The switches for the dot generator are located on the front panel. During initial adjustment, first the ROM/RAM are checked and if found to be acceptable, the floppy disk is loaded. Then several functions of the dot generator are checked which include the selection of the screen angles and adjustment of the laser light level. Normally the laser light level is set in the factory, but if the linearization calls for a changed light level, it can be altered to suit the film emulsion and processing conditions.

The linearization procedure for the 608 is called DU Screen Gradation. The purpose of the DU Gradation is to "adjust the linearity of the gradation curve representing the relationship between the input and output dot percentage to make a correct exposure on film." Figure 6.12 explains the Screen Gradation Adjustment.

Courtesy D.S. America, Inc.

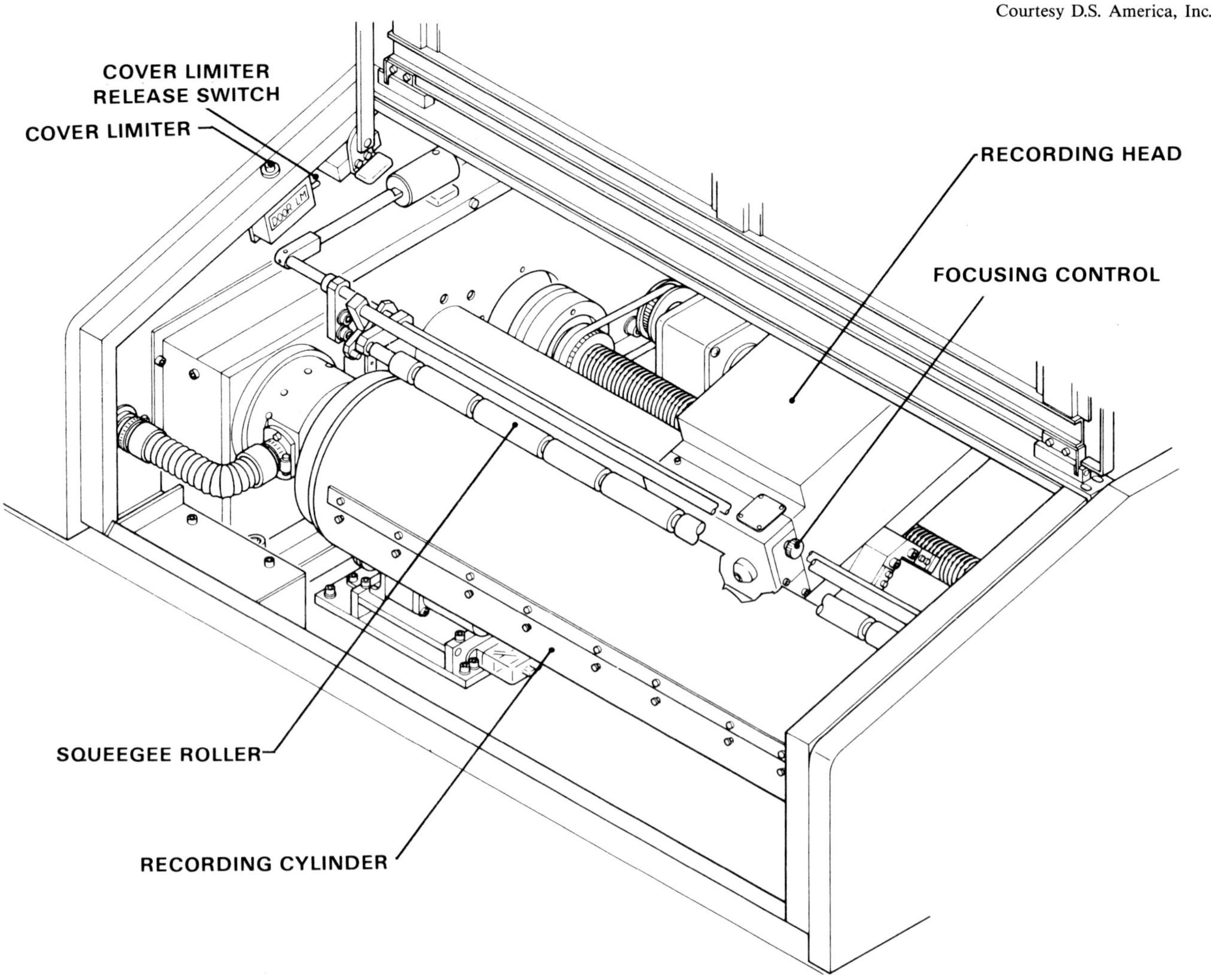

Figure 6.11. DS SG-608 exposing unit

The procedure consists of entering electronic data representing a 16-step gray scale and then entering the measured dot values for each step of the exposed gray scale into the computer. Once the values are entered, the computer adjusts the screen gradation in the entire screen range according to a set of data. An internal gray scale pattern can be generated to check the result of the adjustment. Once found to be acceptable, the screen gradation can be saved on a floppy disk. While the DU Screen Gradation is adjusted, the generated gradation curve can be observed through a synchroscope.

Once the above functions are completed for the dot generator, they need not be repeated as long as the film emulsion and processing conditions are not changed. During the scanning of any original, the operator simply checks the laser light level by viewing it on the display panel and selects the appropriate line ruling.

Courtesy D.S. America, Inc.

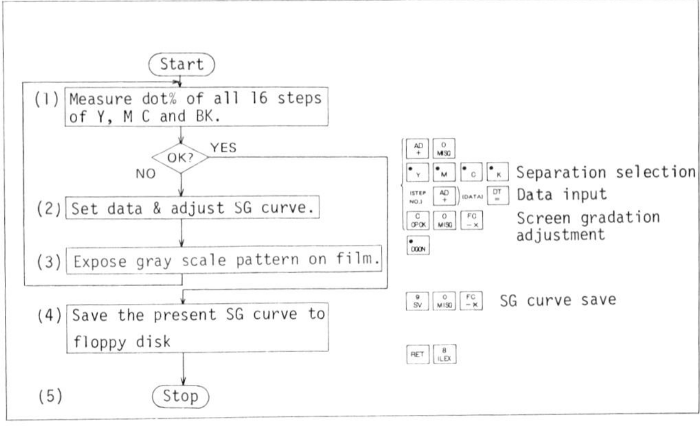

Figure 6.12. Procedure of DU Screen Gradation adjustment in the DS SG-608

Hell 399ER

In all the Hell electronic dot generation scanners, the steps for linearization are basically the same. At the initial stage of setting up the scanner, the procedure consists of adjusting the laser intensity, focusing the exposing optics, determining and adjusting the zoom values for different screen rulings, determining the light on film value by evaluating the density produced on the film, and adjusting the modulator.

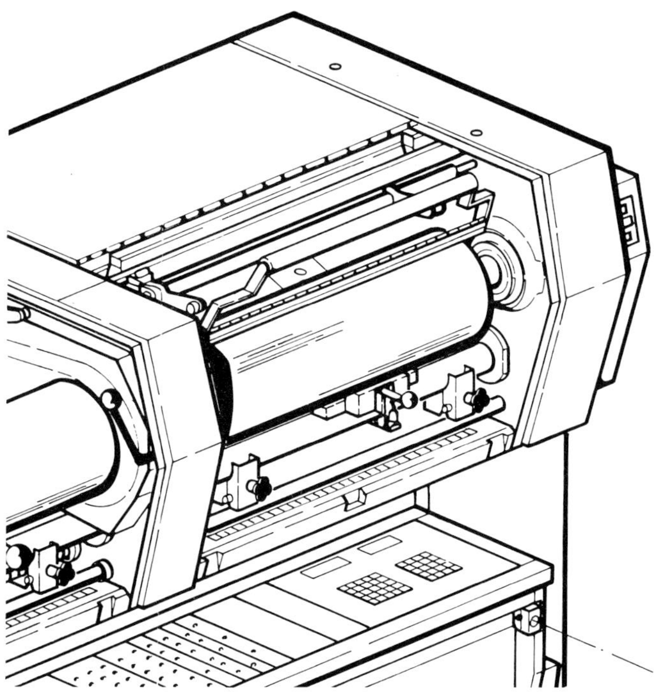

Figure 6.13. Exposing section of the Hell 399ER

By depressing the TEST key, located in the control panel of the Scale Computer, when a film is exposed, the program automatically generates a test pattern on the film which can be evaluated for the adjustment of the variables in linearization. The results on the film can be used for the following tests shown in Table 4a.

After all the elements of the exposing section are accurately adjusted, a linearization scale is exposed for all four screen angles. The dot sizes obtained for each step of the scale are entered into the computer by using the FILM LINEARIZATION key. Normally these values are identical for all the different screen angles. To enter the values, the color separation switch is positioned in the black channel, the FILM LINEARIZATION button is pressed, and the dot values for individual steps are entered. The values are then saved on a floppy disk for future use.

TABLE 4 a

Test No.	FUNCTION
1	Zoom Test 1
2	Zoom Test 2
3	Line Test
4	Light Test
5	Focus Test
6	Black Gradation Conversion
8	Zoom Test 8
10	Test Exposure
13	Voltage on output stage
14	Voltage on output stage variable
21	Fixed Gradation Input including the color computer (CCR operation)

Figure 6.14. Scale computer panel of the Hell 399ER showing the TEST PROGRAM push button and LINEARIZATION key.

Royal Zenith 200-S

RZ 200-S is a conventional screen scanner, and the same xenon lamp is used for both scanning and exposing light sources. The output of the lamp is of constant intensity; however, a modulator is used for controlling the intensity of light transmitting through the screen. The exposing light is collimated, passed through the modulator, and projected onto the exposing carriage (see Figure 2.7, page 49).

For linearization, the 200-S electronically generates a 32-step gray scale (screen or continuous-tone) on the film with marked steps which correspond to the adjustable horizontal points (steps 1-6) on the calibration curve. During calibration, the output in the scanner is adjusted until the six marked steps read 0%, 15%, 35%, 65%, 85%, and 100%. The equivalent continuous-tone reading will be 0.25, 0.49, 0.81, 1.29, 1.61, and 1.85 for the same steps (see Figure 6.16).

Once the gray scale is scanned and the film is processed, the six aim points on the gray scale can be checked for proper dot percentage or density values. Where the plotted curve disects the horizontal lines on the graph (steps 1-6), the correction needed is noted in the box provided in the graph. Then the calibration program is called and the correction figures are entered by adding or subtracting from the existing figures. There are nine memory areas available for storing screen calibration information.

After the initial calibration, and with a stable processing condition, the results will be fairly consistent. The daily calibration will include the scanning of a 32-step gray scale, reading dot percentage in each step, and entering the measured correction for step 1 and step 6. The 200-S has the facility to correct any slight imbalance in the screen.

Courtesy Itek Colour Graphics

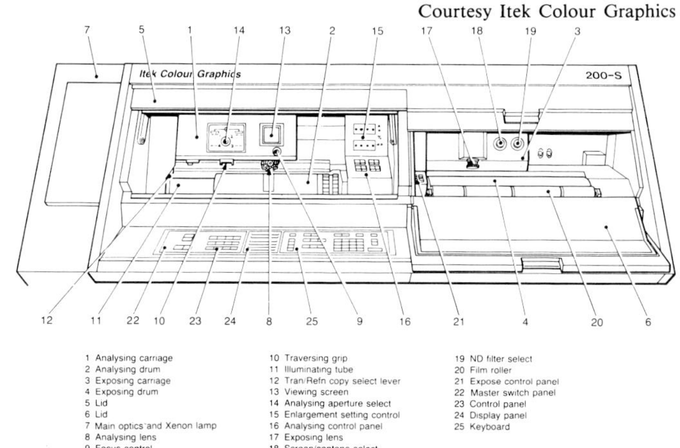

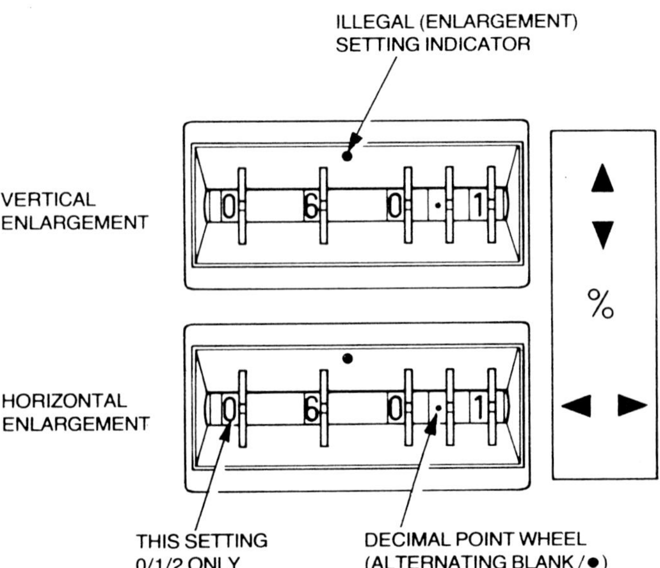

Figure 6.15. Front view of the RZ 200-S showing the analyzing and exposing sections; at the bottom is the enlargement setting panel

Courtesy Itek Colour Graphics

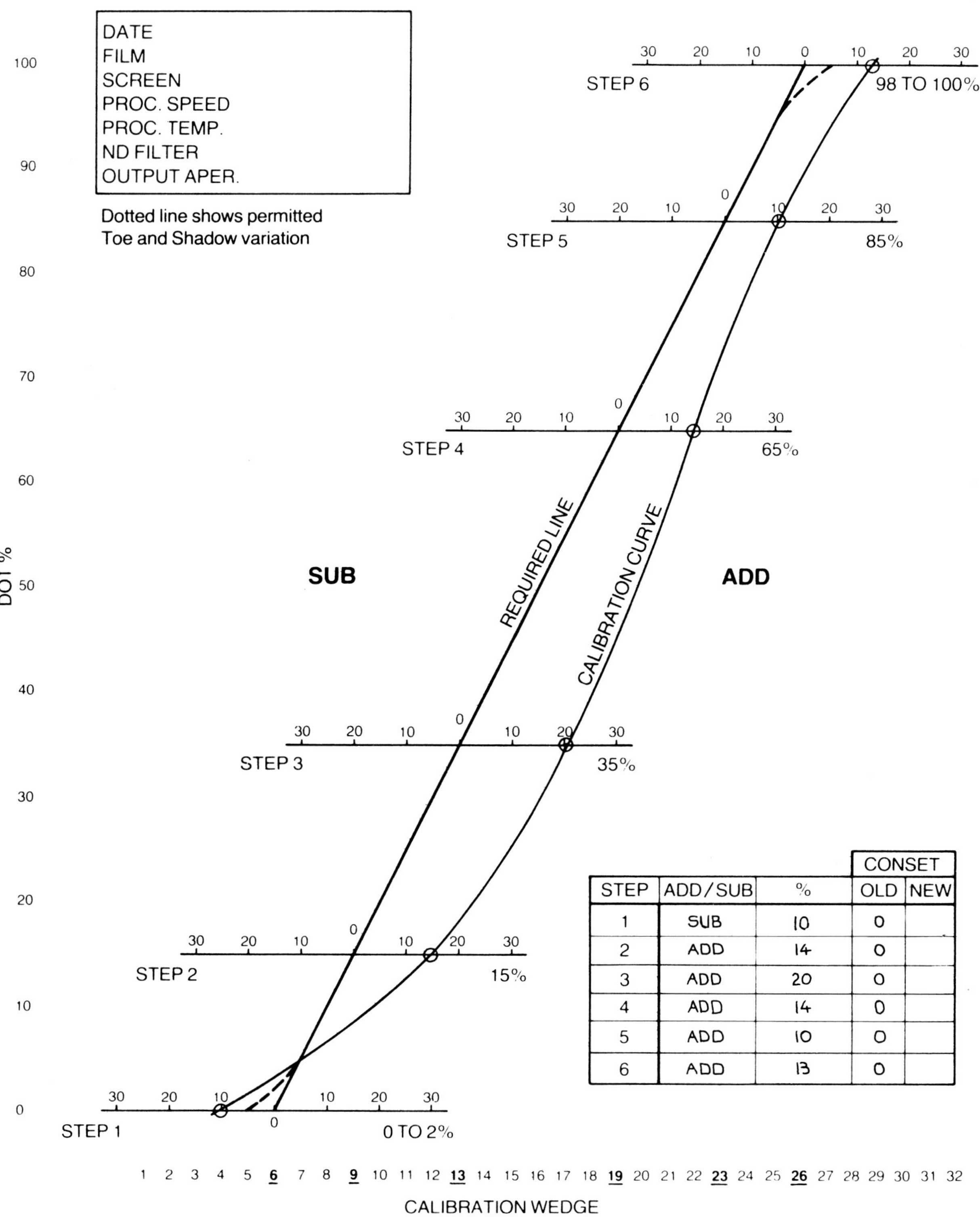

STEP	ADD/SUB	%	CONSET OLD	CONSET NEW
1	SUB	10	0	
2	ADD	14	0	
3	ADD	20	0	
4	ADD	14	0	
5	ADD	10	0	
6	ADD	13	0	

Figure 6.16. Example of screen calibration in the RZ 200-S

Chapter 7
Specific Adjustments

Each original is unique in its own way and needs special treatment for optimal reproduction. After the copy is evaluated for tonal range, color cast, and other requirements for the reproduction, specific adjustments are set on the basis of the special characteristics of each copy. These characteristics are determined only after a critical evaluation of the original is made. However, adjustments may also be necessary for special customer requirements, for example, to emphasize a tonal area or to change or maintain a specific hue. Most evaluations for specific adjustments are accomplished by viewing the originals with a standard viewing light, on a light table, and on the scanning drum. Modern scanners provide a special lighting system to view the transparency. However, evaluating copy while on the scanning drum provides additional advantages which are difficult to achieve by visual means. The various measuring devices in the scanner help to identify specific characteristics of the original which are difficult to interpret visually, such as color cast, neutrality of a gray tone, and the density values of highlight and shadow.

The densitometer is a valuable tool used to measure and identify special features of a particular original. For example, a densitometer fitted with red, green, and blue filters can compare and identify the presence of a color cast. This is not possible visually. It is also useful in locating the lightest highlight and the darkest shadow in a copy. But whatever is compared or measured, the aperture of the densitometer must be entirely covered by the area to be measured; otherwise error will occur.

During these specific adjustments, the scanner operator makes judgments and arrives at decisions based on the operator's background and expertise, the specific shop condition, the customer requirements, etc. The decision to be made is to what specific adjustments are required in the scanner to obtain optimal result for a particular original. At this point, some of the decisions regarding these adjustments may be subjective in nature and they must be made rationally. Adjustments without a proper understanding of the consequences may produce unacceptable results.

The following are the eight major specific adjustments provided in most scanners. In the following chapters, each of these specific adjustments are discussed with a detailed explanation of the concept, the related information for the conventional separation, an in-depth analysis of conventional and electronic separations, specific advantages of scanner over conventional separations, and instructions in setting up a scanner for optimal results. Also provided is a description of the controls and adjustments for these specific adjustments in four different scanners: Crosfield Magnascan 645, Dainippon Screen SG-608, Hell 399ER, and Royal Zenith 200-S. Wherever possible, related diagrams, charts, graphs, reproduction of actual scanner control panels, photographs, and illustrations are provided.

1. Correction for Color Cast: Sometimes originals have color cast in the entire picture or in particular areas of the picture. Unless specified, correction in the cast is required for accurate reproduction.

2. Tone Reproduction: Depending on the tonal characteristics of each copy and the emphasis to be made for different tonal areas, originals may require different contrast at the highlight, middle-tone, and shadow areas in the reproduction. In a scanner, contrast can be independently adjusted by selecting appropriate tone values for any aim point in the original.

3. Color Correction: Most modern scanners offer two types of color correction: basic correction and selective correction. The basic color correction adjustment allows the operator to adjust the main separation color and the unwanted density in that color. The basic adjustment affects the entire separation range. Selective color correction, on the other hand, provides adjustment for a specific color with minimum influence on the other colors. Color correction adjustments do not influence gray balance.

4. Gray Balance: Because of the ink impurities and other variables in process color reproduction, a gray scale will not reproduce as neutral gray with equal amounts of the three process colors. The gray balance is adjusted by assigning unequal dot values for cyan, magenta, and yellow separations throughout the entire range of the gray scale so that the reproduced gray scale becomes neutral gray.

5. Under Color Removal (UCR): Depending on the degree of under color removal desired, a set of controls is used to remove a proportional amount of cyan, magenta, and yellow from the neutral shadow areas and replace them with black in the separations. Under color removal does not affect any primary or secondary colors. In all scanners, additional program or control allows the operator to locate a point on the three color gradation curve from which under color removal will be effective.

6. Under Color Addition (UCA): In most scanners, these controls allow the operator to add colors in the shadow areas where a cast is present to render a neutral shadow so that under color removal can be effective. In some scanners, the function of UCA is used to add color under black for separations with gray component replacement (GCR).

7. Gray Component Replacement (GCR): This is a fairly old concept but revived recently in the reproduction of color. GCR is sometimes called achromatic color reproduction or by other names by different scanner manufacturers. The theory of GCR is based on the concept that it is unnecessary to use three colors to reproduce gray or achromatic component of the picture; instead, computed values of black are used.

8. Unsharp Masking: Unsharp masks are used to enhance details in the separations by producing exaggerated density or fringe at the borders of a density or color change. In conventional separation, the color correction mask is made unsharp for this effect. In a scanner, this is accomplished by both mechanical and electrical means. A separate signal is derived from the original during scanning and transmitted through a larger aperture than the main aperture, called unsharp masking aperture. Electronic controls are used for further enhancement or suppression of the details.

NOTE: It should be kept in mind that the above specific adjustments in a scanner provide the potential to customize or improve the quality of reproduction of any original. A thorough understanding of the concepts and underlying principles cannot be overemphasized. It should also be indicated here that the function of specific adjustments is to adjust for specific characteristics of a particular original. As such, after a set of separations is completed, all controls for specific adjustments must be turned back to the normal starting point before the next adjustment begins. Failure to do so will result in unacceptable result.

Chapter 8
Correction for Color Cast

SOURCES AND PROBLEMS

Both the transparency or reflective copy may have color cast in specific areas or in the entire original. These casts originate from the irregular processing of the film or paper and improper lighting conditions when the photographic emulsion was exposed.

Unless an exact reproduction of the original transparency or reflective copy is desired, the cast should be removed for a true color of the original scene. The presence of a cast in the reproduction will give improper hue, contrast, and lack of color saturation for the entire reproduction. However, quite often it is desirable to remove only a partial cast, either from the highlight, from the shadow, or from both, for a pleasing reproduction of the original. Often a cast removal reflects the customer's preference for a job and it is essential that the customer's wishes are communicated to the scanner operator.

Copy Evaluation

The evaluation of the copy for the presence of a cast is the first and most important step before adjusting the scanner for removing the color cast. Which color/colors are unwanted and need to be removed from the original is the critical decision to be made by the operator. To be accurate in making this decision, the copy must be evaluated visually with a balanced light source of 5,000°K in a viewing booth, on a light table, on the scanning drum, and, if necessary, with a densitometer.

A kit containing several finely graded color compensative transparent filters (CC filters) are available from Eastman Kodak Company to assess visually an original for a cast. The graded filters are simply placed over or looked through by positioning them at a certain distance from the original in different combinations, and the effect is observed by a reflected light source for a reflective copy and by a transmitted light source for a transparency (see Figure 8.1). These transparent filters are available in different colors, and for each color, various increments of graded density values are available. When a proper correction is established with a certain filter or combination of filters, the value of the filter(s), often called CC value, may be translated into dot percentage for certain color or colors. For example, if the placement of a .10 magenta filter appears to have corrected the cast, then the colors other than magenta, such as green, are dominant in the original. Similarly, if a combination of magenta and yellow filters corrects the cast, then the original has a cyan cast. Since the eyes have poor memory and tend to adapt to the imperfection of the copy, the evaluation will be accurate if it is compared with another standard original. For example, the grayness of an object in the transparency could be compared with the neutrality of a standard gray scale. However, for best results, they should be placed side by side and viewed at the same time. The original with a color cast may be analyzed on the scanning drum by placing the CC filters over the mounted transparency. It is also possible to perform the basic calibration of the photomultipliers, like Autobalance or White Alignment, with the color compensative filters placed over the gray scale or the scanning drum.

Courtesy Eastman Kodak Company

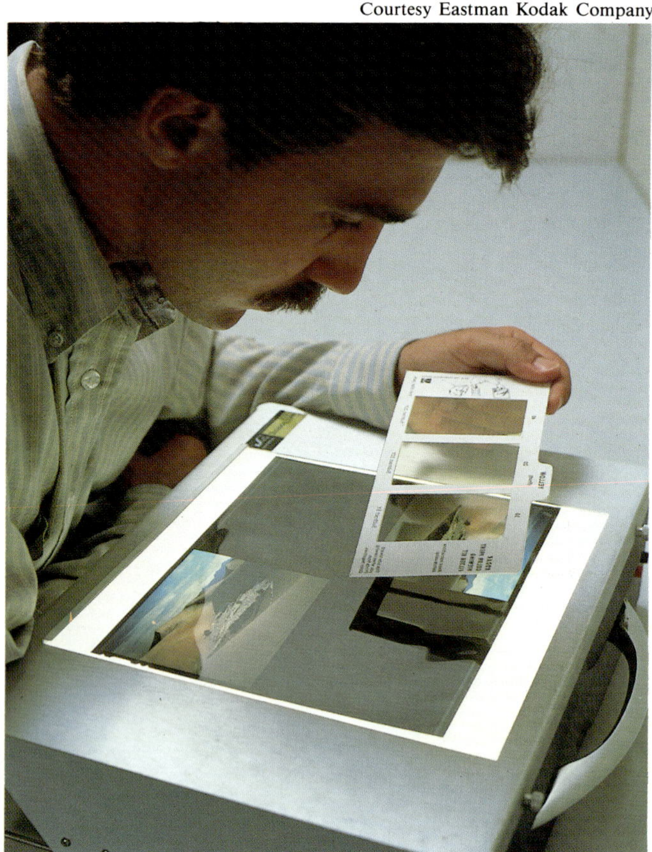

Figure 8.1. Viewing a transparency through Kodak Color Compensating filters

The Colortune Corporation manufactures a transparency viewer that changes the CC filtration by merely turning a set of knobs. Once the desired effect is achieved, the digital readout of the amounts of CC filtration is noted. A small calculator prints out the percentage dot target values to be used when programming the scanner. The target values incorporate the effects of CC filtration (see Figure 5.5 and related text on page 107).

Several prescanning devices are available in the market as an aid to the scanner operator for evaluating the originals. These devices can be effectively used to determine set up parameters for the scanner controls for color cast removal and other such variables in the original. There are two types of prescanning devices. One is used for the evaluation of the original before it goes to the scanner and is called an off-line device. The other prescan devices are used as integral parts of the scanner and are called on-line devices. A detailed discussion of the different types of prescanning devices is presented in the chapter "Copy Evaluation and Scanning Aids."

After a critical evaluation, the operator should make a decision regarding the removal of a cast on the basis of the following guidelines:

1. Some of the colors are called psychological reference colors or memory colors. They are generally seen and experienced everyday and remembered even if there is no copy to compare with. Any change of these colors in the reproduction are immediately noticeable and will be objectionable. Examples of memory colors are blue sky, green grass, red apples, yellow lemons, natural flesh tone, etc. The operator should carefully analyze the original to decide if total or partial removal of the cast will affect these memory colors.

2. In most cases, a partial removal of the cast will result in a better reproduction of the original than a complete removal. However, this decision is dependent on how the removal affects the memory colors.

3. Sometimes, identification of a cast may be deceptive. Although an area of the original seems to have color cast, it may be the result of reflection from an adjacent colored object. For example, a white shirt may have a color cast because of a light reflected from an adjacent blue suit. As such, if the blue cast is removed from the white shirt, the entire reproduction will be affected and will be deficient in cyan and magenta.

Although removal of cast in a scanner is relatively easy compared to removal in a conventional separation, appropriate precautions should be taken to identify the nature of the cast and the color or colors to be removed. An error in the adjustment of the controls may dramatically change the hue and contrast of the entire reproduction.

REMOVAL OF COLOR CAST IN CONVENTIONAL SEPARATION

In conventional separation, color cast can be removed by adjusting tone values during the separation and/or masking stages to affect highlight, middle-tone, and shadow dot values. Corrections by masking will involve changes in the standardized technique. There are limitations to the corrections that can be done by masking. Localized hue errors cannot be dealt with in this way and hand retouching has to be used. In the indirect separation, the removal of a cast can be accomplished by local dot etching, retouching the continuous-tone negatives, or changing the mask density during color correction. In direct-screening, color casts can be removed by changing the density of the color correcting masks and thus controlling the dot sizes during separation. However, color correction procedures in conventional separation are complex, and any changes required to deal with poor transparencies will cause delays, wasted materials, and higher costs. In conventional separation, it is easier to remove the cast at the photographic stage by changing the original, e.g. making a duplicate transparency from the original after compensating for the color cast or making another photographic print with different color filtration.

COLOR CAST REMOVAL IN A SCANNER

A scanner provides greater flexibility in removing color cast than in the conventional separation. With appropriate measuring devices on the scanner, the nature and precise measurement of the cast can be determined, and adjustments can be made accordingly. It should be remembered however, that faulty color cast removal adjustments in a scanner can produce disastrous results. Use of any color cast removal controls actually introduces a color at the input of the color computer. The effect may be compared to a person's putting on a pair of colored sunglasses. Just as placing a pair of sunglasses in front of the eyes changes the color of the objects seen, color cast removal controls change the way the computer "sees" the original. With an error in the adjustments, a false color can be easily introduced to change the quality of the entire separation.

It should be emphasized here that the adjustments of a color computer, such as for color correction, tone reproduction, gray balance, etc., are not independent and will have some effect on the overall color balance of the separations. Any faulty adjustments of one or more of these controls in the color computer may produce a color cast on the separations which may seem to be the result of inadequate removal of color cast. For example, a cast in the proof may be for a wrong gradation adjustment and not for inadequate color cast removal. As such, to correct the situation it is necessary that the gradation be adjusted properly rather than attempting to remove the cast from the separations.

Different Types of Color Cast Removal Controls in a Scanner

The technique of removing color cast from the original varies from one brand of scanner to the other. However, the cast removal controls can be classified into four general categories: (1) altering a standard gray value during gradation adjustment; (2) adding color in the shadow areas with under color addition controls; (3) neutralizing a color cast by using basic calibration of the photomultipliers, often called WHITE ALIGNMENT or AUTOBALANCE; and (4) using a standard set of color cast removal controls, especially designated for this purpose. More than one of the above techniques can be used to remove color cast in a scanner. A detailed explanation of each of the four techniques and how they are used in different types of scanners is presented below.

Altering Standard Gray Values

Color cast can be removed manually by altering neutral tone values during gradation adjustment. This is explained with Table 5. In this example, it is assumed that the original has a cyan color cast in the highlight which needs to be removed. Of the two sets of dot values presented, the first set is a standard gray value for a particular shop condition, and the other set is a corrected value to remove the color cast. The removal of color cast is accomplished by first selecting the five gradation aim points on the gray scale (highlight, quarter-tone, middle-tone, three-quarter-tone, and shadow); positioning each aim point for the scanning light; and then assigning the corrected set of dot values for each aim point.

TABLE 5

Aim Points	Standard Gray Value			Revised Gray Value		
	C	M	Y	C	M	Y
Highlight	5	4	4	3	4	4
Quarter-tone	21	17	17	18	17	17
Middle-tone	60	50	50	55	50	50
Three-quarter-tone	78	75	75	78	75	75
Shadow	98	95	95	98	95	95

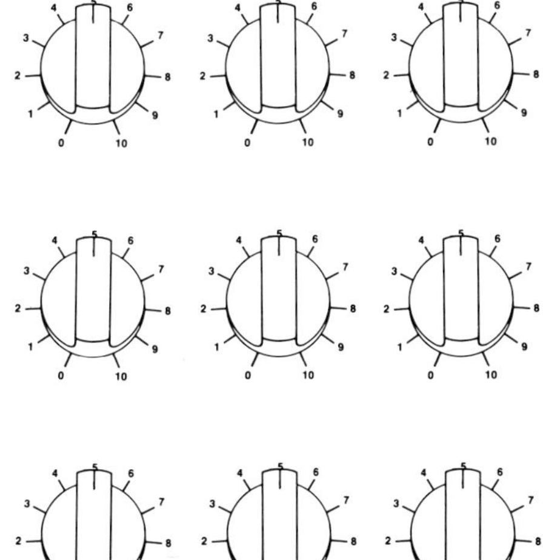

Figure 8.2. GRADATION panel of the DS SG-608. The highlight, middle-tone and shadow gradation knobs are used to adjust dot percent values for the cyan, magenta, and yellow separations in conjunction with a pair of Reference switches

This technique of changing the gray values during gradation adjustment can be used effectively to remove any amount of cast from highlight, middle-tone, and shadow. The deviation of tone or dot values can be located by first developing a standard gray balance curve for the three colors after a set of neutral values is found for a particular shop condition. Any deviation from the standard curve for one or more colors can be plotted and the numbers can be read off. Figure 8.3 contains the example of a curve representing neutral values for all colors.

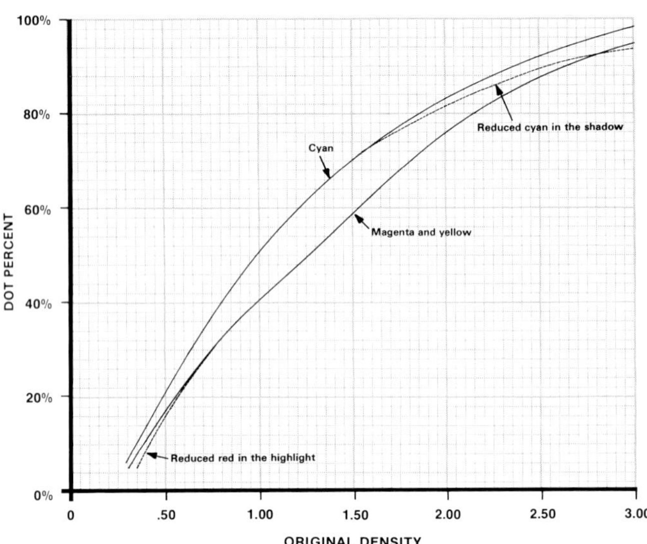

Figure 8.3. Example of neutral curves for the three colors drawn from the original aim point densities and dot percent. Note the possible deviations to remove color cast

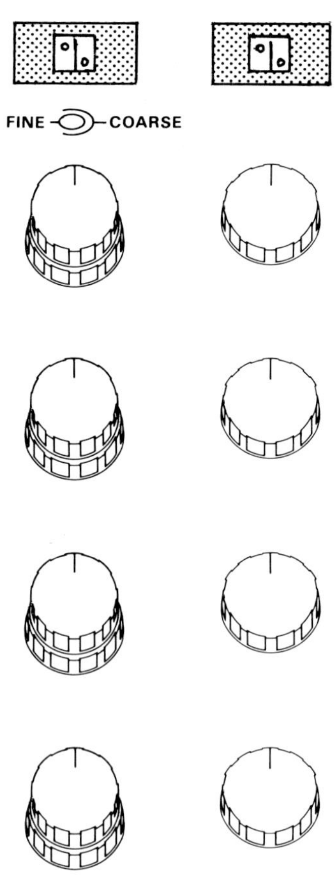

Figure 8.4. HIGHLIGHT and SHADOW Dot Percent set knobs in the DS SG-608 to set the highlight and shadow dot percent for the cyan, magenta, yellow, and black separations

In the DS SG-608, two sets of controls — the Highlight Dot Percent Set knobs and the Shadow Dot Percent Set knobs are used to set the appropriate dot percentage for a gray balance during gradation adjustment. Any deviation from the standard gray balance can be set with these controls to remove any color cast from the highlight and/or shadow areas.

Using Under Color Addition Controls

With this technique, colors are actually added to neutralize a cast in the shadow areas of the original. Most scanners offer a set of controls to add one or more colors to neutralize a shadow area. These controls, abbreviated as UCA, are mostly tied to the under color removal function of the scanner. Since under color removal takes place only in the neutral areas, one of the main purposes of under color addition is to create neutral shadow in an original so that under color removal takes effect for that original when scanned.

Most scanners, both analog and digital types, provide controls for under color addition (UCA). In the earlier Hell models, the UCA controls were used to neutralize shadow by adding one or more colors; however, in all recent Hell models, this designated control is used to add color under black during the CCR (Hell's version of Gray Component Replacement) function. A separate set of controls called COLOR CAST COMPENSATION-SHADOW is provided in this scanner for neutralizing a shadow area. In the DS SG-608, the controls for under color addition consist of a starting point control to select a point on the gradation curve from which the under color addition will be effective and three intensity controls for each of the cyan, magenta, and yellow channels. In the Crosfield Magnascan 645 scanners, two cast controls are provided that can be used independently. The cast control designated as CAST 2 can be used to subtract or add yellow, magenta, or cyan to neutral areas of a shadow without affecting any color. For example, if a neutral shadow area has a brown cast with dominant magenta and yellow, cyan can be added with CAST 2 to make it neutral. In this respect, this function of the CAST 2 control in the Magnascan is similar to UCA in other scanners except that a color can be both added or subtracted with this control. In the RZ 200-S, UCA is designated as reverse UCR, and the same set of controls can be used for both UCR and UCA. In this scanner, an increased percentage of one or more colors except black can be introduced in any tonal area/areas of the copy.

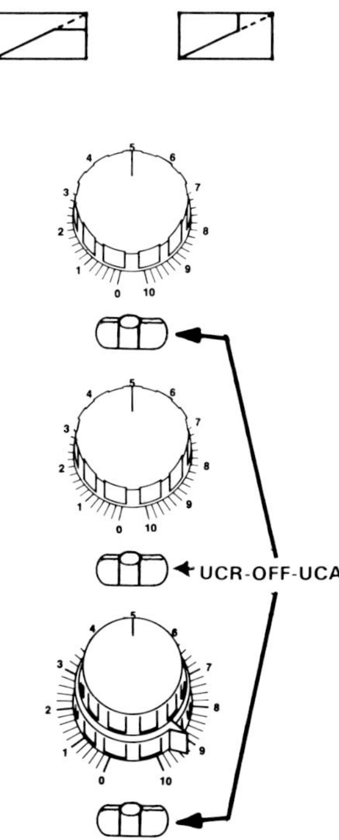

Figure 8.5. Control for UCR in the DS SG-608. In this scanner, the three knobs are UCR/UCA set knobs. The third UCR/UCA knob is also a pair of dual-function knob, the position of the outer knob determines the point on the gradation curve from which UCR/UCA will be effective. The three UCR-OFF-UCA select switches at the bottom of each knob are used to select UCR or UCA for the cyan, magenta and yellow separations

The steps for under color addition in an analog scanner include the following: the scanning light is positioned for the shadow areas in which a color cast is present; the position of the starting point control is determined and selected — for example, quarter-tone, middle-tone, etc.; the balance of the three colors are checked on the display panel; and the color or colors which are deficient are added with the individual controls while observing the amount on the digital panel. In a digital scanner, however, a specific program for color cast is recalled and each color can be increased or decreased, or specific values for any of the three colors can be entered.

Using White Alignment or Autobalance

With the basic input calibration technique for the photomultipliers, a color cast can be neutralized in the highlight of an original. In the Hell and DS scanners, during the basic input calibration, first the photomultipliers are adjusted for the brightest light, the darkest shadow, and then an electrical range value is assigned. In the final step of the calibration, neutral tone or dot values are allocated for the same highlight and shadow. Subsequently when the scanning light spot is positioned for the neutral highlight and shadow of a new copy and the above adjustments are reset, the previously set neutral values are automatically shifted to the new highlight or shadow. This technique can be successfully used to neutralize any highlight or shadow areas.

The main requirement for this type of color cast removal is that there must be a neutral highlight or a neutral shadow in the original. The area may not appear neutral in the copy because of the color cast, but the object can be identified as neutral in the original scene of the picture, e.g. a white dress, a gray rock, a gray background of a portrait, etc. If a color highlight or shadow is selected instead of a neutral area, unwanted colors will be introduced in the separations, and a satisfactory color correction will no longer be possible.

Inclusion of a gray scale in the original photograph can be effectively used to control this type of color cast removal. If a gray scale or a gray card is photographed in identical lighting conditions with the original, it can be used as a reference area for WHITE ALIGNMENT or AUTOBALANCE to neutralize any cast. This method is especially useful for roll films where an extra frame may be used to photograph the gray area. Since the original and the reference frame will contain the same type of film emulsion, lighting, and identical processing conditions, they will have the same color cast, if there is any. This method provides a faster and more accurate adjustment for color cast removal and gray balance in a scanner.

In the Hell 399ER, the technique for the removal of color cast in the highlight is different than that of the shadow area and consists of a panel of elaborate controls (see Figure 8.6). The knob at the top of the panel is used to simulate a neutral density ranging from 0.0 to .70 for the White Alignment. A second control is used in conjunction with the first control to reduce any color cast in the highlight during White Alignment. A third control is a color cast reduction switch, and when used in conjunction with a fourth control, it removes various proportions of color cast. There are two push-button controls at the bottom of the panel (+ or -), which are used to increase or decrease density or dot percent values after the WHITE ALIGNMENT is performed.

In the Magnascan 645, after the photomultipliers are initially calibrated by its AUTOBALANCE function, ENTER WHITE and ENTER BLACK functions can be used in con-

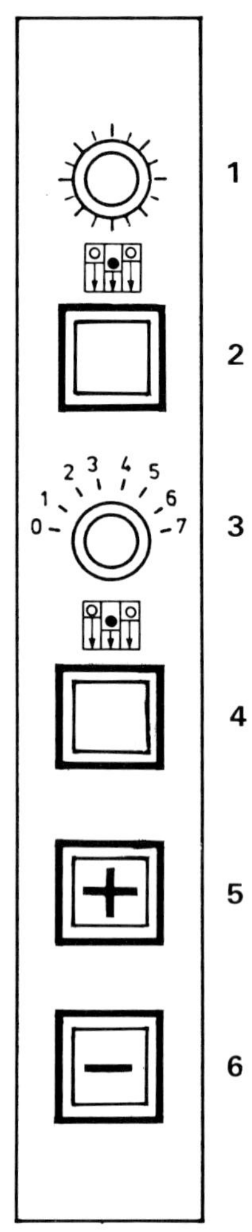

Figure 8.6. Hell 399ER WHITE ALIGNMENT panel

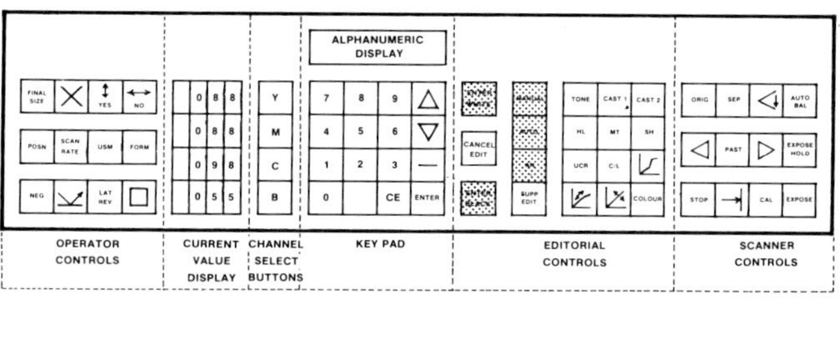

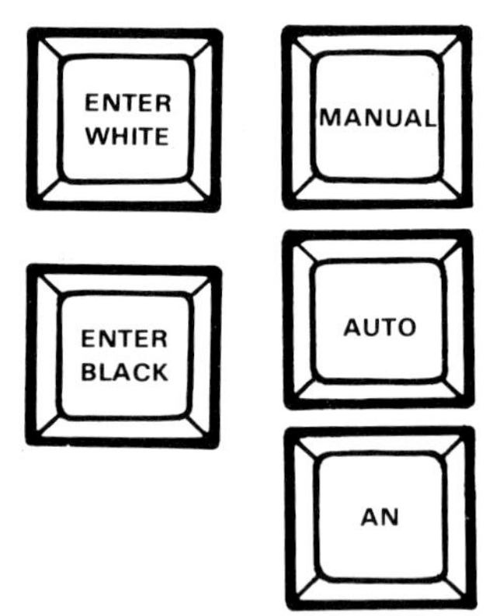

Figure 8.7. Magnascan 645 panel with pushbutton controls for ENTER WHITE, ENTER BLACK, MANUAL, AUTO, and AN (Auto Neutral) functions. When ENTER WHITE and ENTER BLACK buttons are used in conjunction with any of the MANUAL, AUTO, or AN buttons, partial or complete removal of color cast is possible from the highlight and/or the shadow

junction with the following programs to partially or completely neutralize the highlight and shadow areas of the copy: (1) MANUAL: for manual setting of dot percentage for highlight and shadow; (2) AUTO: For partial neutralization of casts in the highlight without affecting shadow; this function automatically sets the dot percentage to predetermined levels for both highlight and shadow; and (3) AN (Auto Neutral): this function provides total neutralization of color casts in both highlight and shadow. Further explanations of these functions are provided in Figure 8.7.

The MANUAL ENTER WHITE is performed after locating the lowest density value of the cyan, magenta, and yellow channels and then entering the dot percentage required for the channel with that value. The remaining two channels are automatically balanced for neutral. In the AUTOMATIC NEUTRAL ENTER WHITE mode, the channels are not selected, and the highlight of the copy is automatically given a predetermined gray value for neutralization. In AUTOMATIC NEUTRAL WHITE mode, the scanner will always neutralize any highlight cast. During this mode, density values of the two highest channels are selected and reduced so that all three channels become identical, and then gray values are applied to all the channels. This gray value may be chosen by the operator or it may be a preprogrammed value. MANUAL ENTER BLACK is used when the cyan channel contains the highest original density for the shadow aim point. Once the value is entered for the cyan, the other channels are automatically adjusted for neutral. AUTOMATIC ENTER BLACK is used when yellow or magenta is higher than cyan, and a predetermined neutral value is assigned to the highest channel other than black, regardless of the channel selected. The other two channels are automatically adjusted for neutral. AUTOMATIC NEUTRAL BLACK function will always neutralize any shadow cast. All the color channels are brought to the same value and then balanced for neutral. It is essential that the scanning light is positioned for a cast that is supposed to be a neutral shadow. For example, if a colored shadow like dark green is neutralized, other dark greens will also be neutralized or partially reduced in green content.

Using Standard Color Cast Removal Controls

Specific color cast compensation controls are provided in both the Hell 399ER and the Magnascan 645 series of scanners. As indicated earlier, in the Hell 399ER, the color cast removal control in the highlight is different from the removal of cast in the shadow. The technique of removal of cast from the highlight area has been presented earlier. In this scanner,

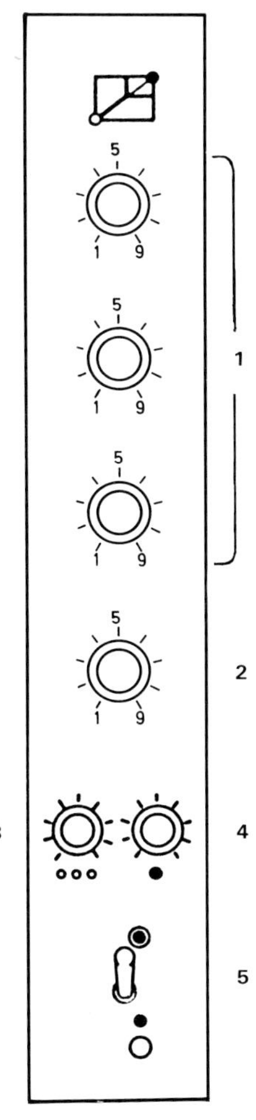

Figure 8.8. Hell 399ER COLOR CAST COMPENSATION-SHADOW panel. Control 1 is used to neutralize, partially remove, or set a color cast in the shadow. Control 2 is used to adjust image shadow for the black separation. Positions of the control 3 and Control 4 determine the points on the gradation curve from which the above adjustments will be effective for Control 1 and Control 2 respectively. The toggle switch (Control 5) activates or deactivates the effects of the above controls.

the removal of shadow cast has a set of elaborate controls and is called COLOR CAST COMPENSATION-SHADOW. With this set of controls, a color cast in the image shadow can be neutralized, or a desired color cast can be set. The elaborate set of controls consists of four intensity controls for each of the cyan, magenta, yellow, and black, two starting point controls for the three colors and black, and a toggle switch for activating or deactivating the effect of the controls.

As indicated earlier, in the Magnascan 645 series of scanners, two cast control programs, CAST 1 and CAST 2 are provided for the removal of color cast. This is a retouching feature and can be adjusted in any stage of the separations, that is, after or before the specific adjustments when a proof

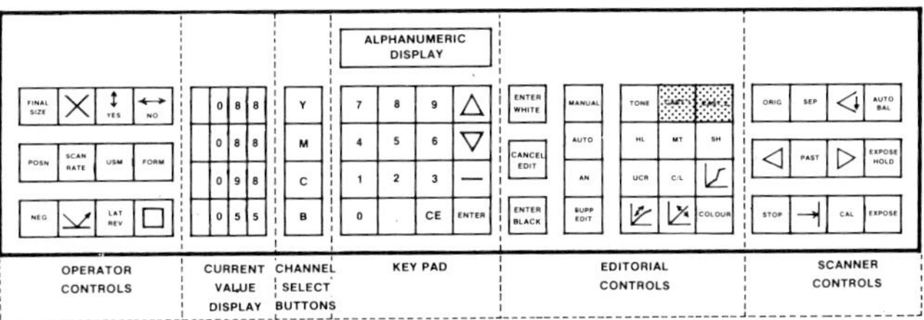

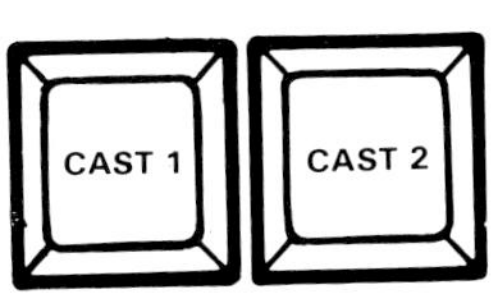

Figure 8.9. Magnascan 645 panel showing the CAST 1 and CAST 2 push-buttons.

is made from the separations and a color cast is detected. These are channel selective cast removal controls and CAST 2 must be adjusted before the CAST 1.

CAST 2 is used to remove or add yellow, magenta, or cyan individually to neutrals for the shadow areas only and it does not affect any color. For example, if the shadow has a brownish cast and needs some cyan to make it neutral, the CAST 2 control can be used to accomplish this.

CAST 1 is used for the removal or addition of yellow, magenta, or cyan casts independently in each color channel in the highlight, middle-tone and/or shadow areas. Unlike the CAST 2, it affects all areas of the subject simultaneously whether they are colored or neutral.

In the RZ 200-S, it is possible to remove color cast from the highlight, middle-tone and shadow areas with the appropriate programs. The color bias for a neutral highlight can be corrected by first calling the gray balance program and assigning the predetermined neutral dot percentages to a highlight that is required to be neutral in the reproduction. For a colored highlight where some color cast is to be introduced or maintained, the dot percentages for each color can also be set individually.

After balancing the highlight and adjusting the range of the original, if the middle-tone shows a color cast and is confirmed by the output readings, a pre-programmed gray value can be assigned to all colors of the middle-tone area. However, one or more colors can also be adjusted individually to maintain or introduce a color cast in the middle-tone area. The color cast in the shadow can be corrected during RANGE setting of the original and by calling the appropriate program. If a non-neutral shadow is to be reproduced as neutral, with the gray balance program, pre-determined dot percentages can be assigned to the area. However, it is also possible to keep or change the color cast in the shadow by adjusting the dot percentages of each color separately.

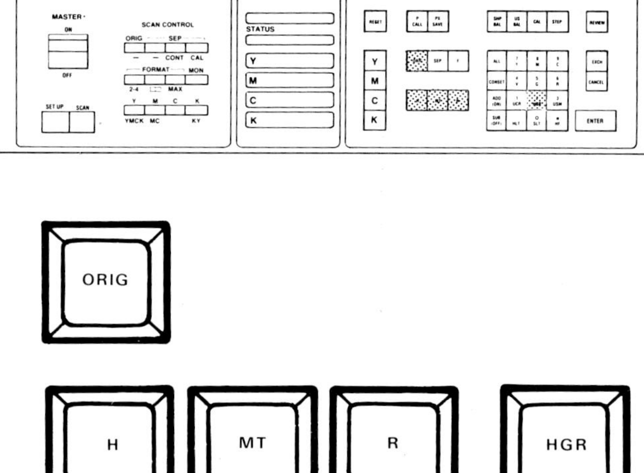

Figure 8.10. Panel of RZ 200-S showing ORIG, H, MT, R, and HGR pushbuttons

Chapter 9
Tone Reproduction

TERMS AND DEFINITIONS

Tone Reproduction and Gradation

Both the terms "tone reproduction" and "gradation" are used in the industry to explain the reproduction of tones. While the former term is general in nature, the term "gradation" is more specific and became widely known with the advent of electronic scanners. The terms "gradation" and "tone reproduction" may be defined as a distribution of a set of reproduced tone values in relation to a set of original tone values. These values may be in the form of density or dot sizes.

IMPORTANCE OF CONTROLLING TONES

Optimal tone reproduction for any original will render a pleasing contrast, preserve important details, and help in uniform gray balance for accuracy in the reproduction. Every color copy has a certain message for its viewer. Nothing can bring out the message better and more clearly than a suitable tone reproduction for that particular copy. Even a degraded original with unusual contrast and density values can be partially corrected in the reproduction with appropriate gradation for more pleasing contrast. However, the need to compress certain tonal areas of the original in the reproduction because of printing process limitations poses a problem. The decision as to which tonal areas are to be compressed will vary from copy to copy and often is subjective in nature.

The outcome of an improper tone reproduction can be easily recognized by the results obtained in the printed reproduction. The reproduction will look dull and will lack the natural *"sparkle"* of an optimal contrast. The highlights will be darker, or lack contrast, and the important areas will render a *"flat"* or washed-out effect and will lack good saturated colors.

Optimal tone reproduction is not dependent only on the separations. It also relies heavily on the result of other production processes and steps. Important among these are the quality of the ink and paper, the dot shape, the screen ruling, the density of solid ink on the paper, and the characteristics of press results such as dot gain, slur, trapping, and fill-in. For optimal tone in the separation stage, the separator must be aware of these limitations and their effect on the final result. Once the above conditions are standardized, they can be quantified and compensated for at the separation stage.

Improper reproduction of tones is also linked with other problems which may seem unrelated at the time. For example, improper tone reproduction may cause a lack of saturation in several areas of the reproduction, although one may think that this is because of an improper color correction adjustment. In extreme cases, a considerable shift in one or more colors may appear in the reproduction. Changes of this type cannot be corrected by means of color correction controls because the range of the correction controls lies outside the capabilities of the equipment. These color changes are not color errors; they are gradation errors, and may affect the gray balance of the three colors.

COMPLEXITY IN REPRODUCING TONES

An optimal reproduction of tone is possibly the most important factor for the quality of the final reproduction. However, there are two basic problems in obtaining predictable results: 1) tone reproduction is often a subjective decision to be made in the production flow, and 2) it is often difficult to visualize the effect of gradation adjustment in the reproduction for a specific original. For example, when adjustments are made for gray balance in a scanner, the balance of the three colors can be observed on the digital readout panel. If the film linearization and the gray balance values of the three colors were accurately established previously, the operator can predictably adjust the balance of the three colors. However, for gradation adjustments in a scanner, dot values are assigned to various aim points and the effect of the adjustments on the particular original will not be realized until a proof is made or the separations are printed.

The above factors make the approach of tone reproduction more critical. Although the decisions are often subjective, a thorough understanding of the different types of originals, the gradation curves and their effect on the originals, the limitations in the reproduction steps, and a systematic and objective approach will make the job easier.

GRADATION CURVES

An understanding of the graphs and curves is necessary for the understanding of tone reproduction. Curves represent and graphically show the relationship of two parameters at the same time. Figure 9.1 contains examples of curves showing the relationship of a set of two parameters — (1) the price of oranges during a period of ten years, and (2) the densities of an original and its reproduction. Two axes are drawn: axis X represents the year and original density and axis Y represents the price of oranges per pound and the reproduction density. After the numbers are plotted and the curves are drawn, the shapes of the curves represent the uniformity or the fluctuation of the price of oranges during the years, and the densities of the original versus the reproduction. Since tone reproduction deals mostly with the original tones and the reproduction of the same tones, a curve is a useful tool for demonstrating how much the tones in the reproduction have differed from those of the original.

When a set of separations is made from an original and printed, the tones may change in the reproduction. Original tone values between two aim points, such as middle-tone and shadow may expand, compress, or remain unchanged. Several possible examples are illustrated with Figure 9.2. The density values of the original and the density values obtained from the reproduction of the same original are at the X and Y axes respectively. In the figure, the density values of the

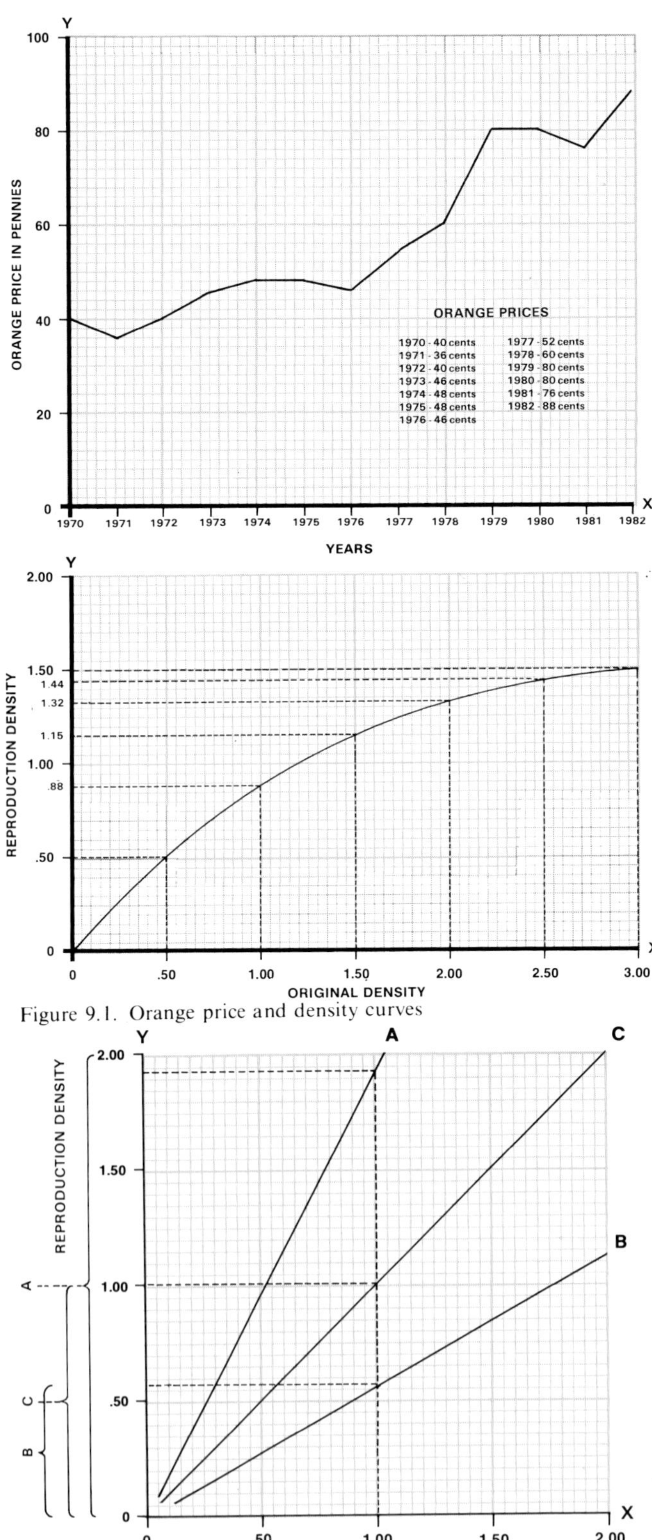

Figure 9.1. Orange price and density curves

Figure 9.2. Curves showing the relationship between the original density and the reproduced density. For curve A, the reproduced density is approximately twice the original density. For curve B, the reproduced density is about half of the original density. For curve C, the original and reproduced densities are identical

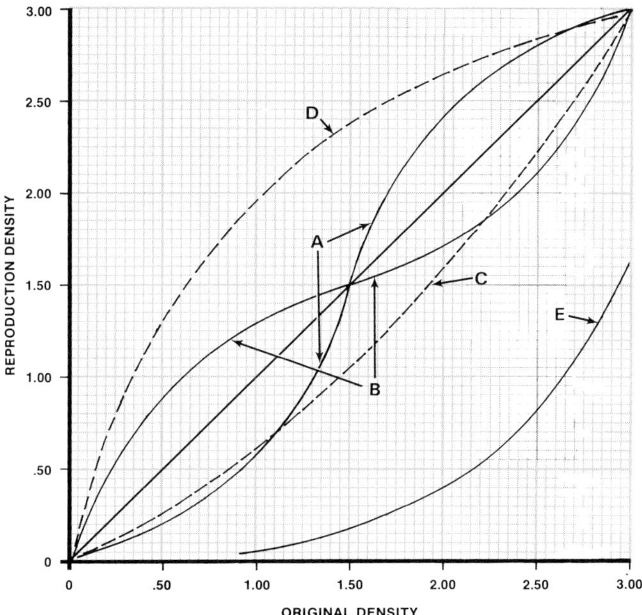

Figure 9.3. Examples of different gradation curves

reproduction are plotted against the density values of the original. When the tone values between two points expand more than the original, a steeper curve is obtained (Curve A). In this case, the reproduction is said to have more contrast than the original. In cases where the tones between two points are compressed, the curve, when plotted, becomes lower in profile, and the reproduction is said to be flat or lower in contrast than the original (Curve B). When tone values between two density points of the original and its reproduction are identical, plotting the curve will result in a straight line with a 45 degree angle between the X and Y axes (Curve C). In this case, the relationship between the original and the reproduction is considered to be perfect and linear.

Characteristic Curve, Gamma, and Contrast

A basic discussion on this subject relating to halftone reproduction is presented in the chapter "Halftone." The ratio of tone values between the original and the reproduction in a characteristic curve can be altered in various ways, and the resulting curves may take all different sizes and shapes, even for a curve obtained from the same original. Figure 9.3 shows several different curve shapes. In Curve A, after the density values of the original and the reproduction are plotted, the slope of the solid line became an elongated S-shaped curve which is flat in both the shadow and highlight areas. As such, the reproduced density values are lower in both the

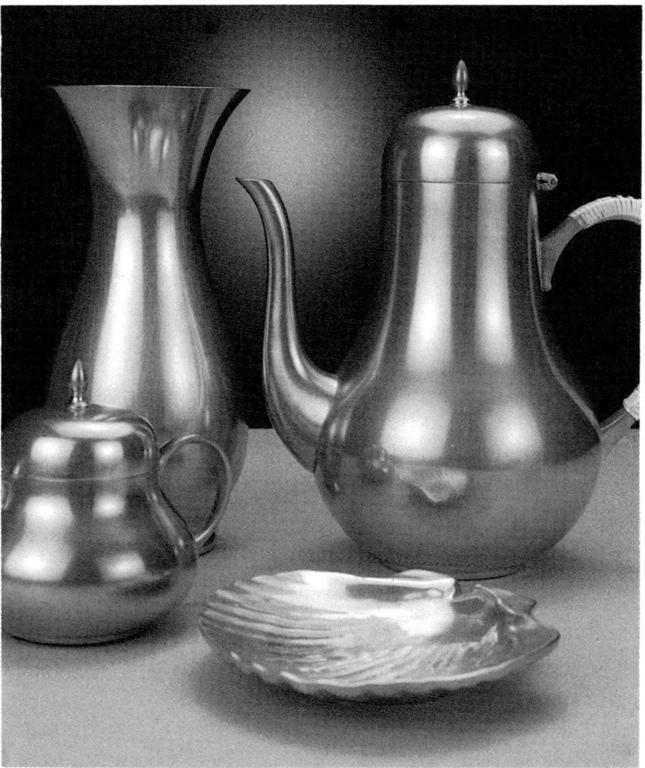

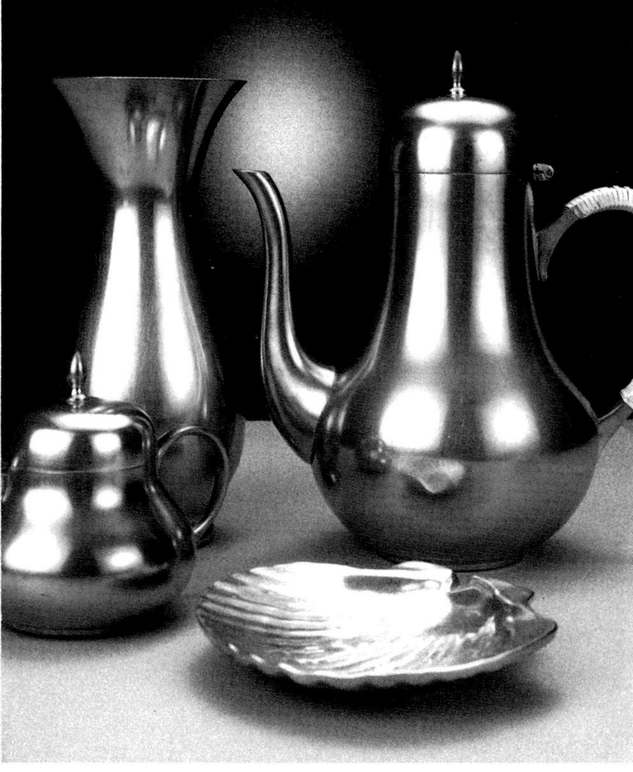

Figure 9.4. Examples of optimum and wrong tone reproduction. Note the difference of details/contrast in the various tones of the two reproductions

highlight and shadow areas than are those of the original and will result in a loss of details in these areas. The reproduction will be flat or pale in the highlight, the shadows will become "sooty" with little details, and the entire image will become "hard" without graduated soft rendering of tones. However, the middle-tone in the curve is steeper and, as such, will gain resolution. On the other hand, in curve B, a soft reproduction is achieved by increasing details in the highlight and shadow, but decreasing details in the middle-tone. Two more examples of dark and light gradations are represented by curves D and C. With light gradation, the contrast and details in the shadow areas have increased; however, the highlight and middle-tone areas become flattened and will lose details. Just the opposite has happened in the other curve; the gradation is dark with a boost in the highlight but is flattened at the shadow end. Curve E is called a skeleton gradation and is applied to a curve with no highlight, very little middle-tone, and an excessive shadow contrast. A skeleton gradation is applied mostly to black, both in the conventional and scanner separations.

IDEAL TONE REPRODUCTION

Copy Range versus Reproduction Range

Theoretically an ideal tone reproduction will be the one in which the tones of the reproduction match the tones of the original. However, because of the physical limitations of the printing process, this is almost an impossible task. For example, a normal color transparency has a highlight density of about .30 and a shadow density of 3.00 with a density range of 2.70. To match the original visually on a press sheet, the range of the printing density needed in the reproduction is also 2.70. However, the best quality white coated paper has a reflection density of about .06, and when printed with 4-color, the maximum printing ink density that can be obtained on this sheet is less than 1.80. These numbers get lower, about 1.50 when the reproduction is printed on uncoated paper, and even lower when newsprint is used, about 1.20. It is obvious that in most cases, the density range of the original is higher than the reproduction.

Tone Compression

The only way to solve the above problem is to compress the tones of the original so that they fit into the reproduction range of the paper and ink. This is done by altering the specific tonal areas of the original in such a way that they visually appear normal when reproduced. For optimal tone reproduction, two decisions of tone compression become critical - which tonal area(s) of the original need to be compressed and how much should the compression be. Since the reproduction not only depends on the separations, but other factors in the printing processes as well, a systematic approach will be to analyze and quantify the relationship between the original tone, the dot sizes of various tones in the separation negative or positive, and the printed results.

When any printed results are evaluated on the press sheet, they are evaluated as printing density rather than the dot percentage on the press sheet. However, a record is kept for different densities produced by different dot percentages in the negative or positive. It will provide information about the changes that take place during the intermediate steps between the separation and the final printing on paper, for example, dot gain during the press run. However, a meaningful evaluation can be made only after all the printing conditions are optimized and standardized.

Determining Press Variables

The initial step is to make a halftone negative from a standard gray scale and to print this under normal press conditions. Then the results can be compared by plotting a curve using the density values for each step of the reproduced gray scale and the percentage of dots in the negative or positive which produced these density values. This analysis can be made for a number of variables, such as coated or uncoated paper, ink, different press, etc. (see Figure 9.5).

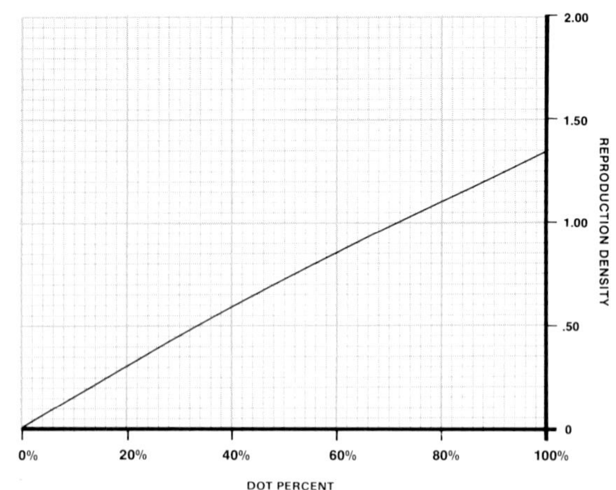

Figure 9.5. A curve drawn from the printed density and percent of dots showing the relationship of the two variables

The optimal tone reproduction using the press data can be determined by plotting another curve. This time the curve is plotted by using the original density versus the reproduction density for each step of the gray scale. For a more accurate visual comparison, the density values for both X and Y axes should be equally spaced. As shown in Figure 9.6, first a 45 degree line, consisting of Gamma (a detailed discussion of Gamma is presented in the chapter "Halftone") value 1 is drawn to show an ideal reproduction curve in which the original and the reproduction densities are identical. Then a shadow point is selected on the original and its equivalent printed density is also plotted on the graph. In the same way, an average highlight point is selected in the gray scale and its equivalent printed density is plotted on the graph. If a straight line is drawn on these two points, all the tones of the original are treated equally in the reproduction. The different approach taken for an optimal tone reproduction is explained next.

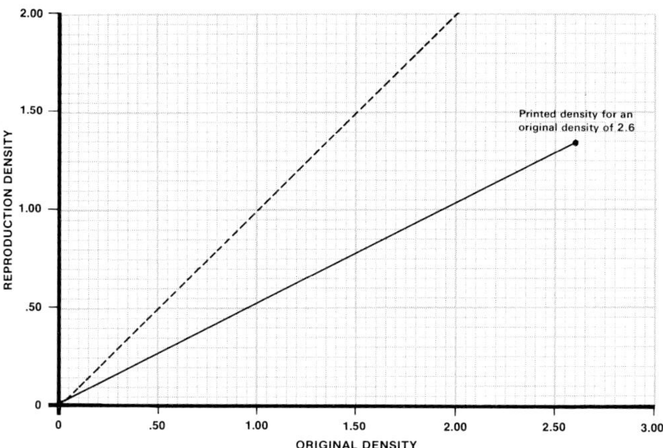

Figure 9.6. Linear and compressed tone reproduction curves within the printed density. In this example, tone compression is equal along the entire range of the compressed curve

Determining Optimal Tone Curve

The human eye is less sensitive to the dark areas, and consequently in a reproduction, the loss of details in the shadow areas would be less noticeable than the loss in the lighter areas. As such, for a normal original without any specific interest area, the identical or emphasized tone of the original is maintained in the highlight through the middle-tone areas, but the shadow areas of the original are compressed into the remaining narrow areas of the reproduction (see Figure 9.7). It is understood that the viewer will not be able to detect this less visible loss of detail in the shadow areas with most normal copy.

Because the ideal curve is based on the press data, standardized results are easier to achieve. The equivalent dot sizes in the halftone need to be determined in order to produce this optimal curve. Based on the data obtained from the original separation and press data, the printing dot sizes can be further optimized by using more than one curve — one for the original, one for the separation, and the other one for the press sheet. Curves of various interrelated parameters are drawn in different quadrants by using the values obtained by standardized printing conditions. These curves are then linked in

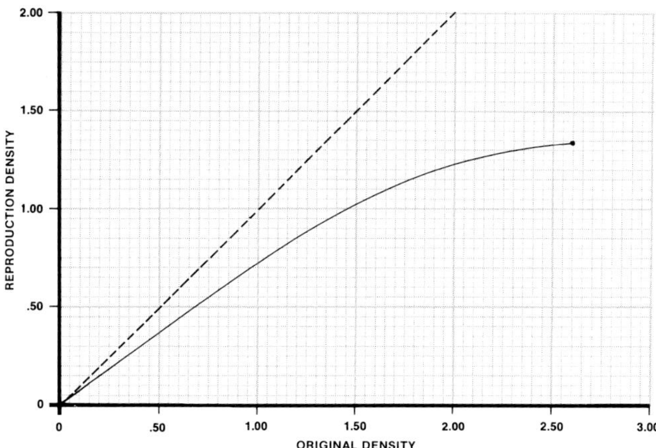

Figure 9.7. An optimum tone reproduction curve

such a way so that when an ideal separation curve is drawn, the unknown parameters for the required curve are obtained from another quadrant by drawing lines at the intersection points of the other curves. This is called a Jones Diagram and is presented in detail on page 143.

Change of Tone Curve for Change of Copy

The actual tone reproduction curve indicated above could work for all the originals if they have the same tonal characteristics. During production, however, the operator receives different types of copy. For example, originals which are overexposed (light with an overall washed-out effect), underexposed (overall dark with dark highlights), or are high-key originals (dominant highlights), low-key originals (dominant shadows), or originals with less weight in the shadow (lighter shadows) need different tonal emphasis in the reproduction for optimal results. If the same gradation is maintained for all different types of originals, in some cases most of the originals will lose their meaning. The intricate lacework of the bridal gown or a snow scene contains more important highlight details to be preserved in their entirety in the reproduction than does the picture of some dark vegetables.

In reality, all gradations have to be customized for each original so that the reproduction can convey the proper message. For different types of originals, tonal emphasis has to be placed at different areas for meaningful reproduction. For example, with a high-key original, more emphasis has to be placed in the highlight areas; emphasized tone values for highlight, quarter-tone, and middle-tone must be shifted towards the lighter end of the original to capture all the details of the highlight. Similarly, if the original calls for emphasis in the shadow areas for a low-key original, the emphasized tone values for highlight, quarter-tone, and middle-tone must be shifted towards the shadow end of the copy. A basic discussion of this tone reproduction principle is presented with Figure 4.6 under "Halftone" on page 83.

Tone Reproduction and Gray Scale

Since a gray scale contains all the possible tones any original may have, it is used as a standard tool to measure and adjust for appropriate tone reproduction. To standardize gradation for a particular shop condition, the original gray scale is photographed or scanned, and a set of separations is printed using normal ink and press conditions. The gradation of the original versus the reproduction is verified by plotting the densities for each step of the two scales. The gray scale is neutral in color, so it is also used to verify its neutrality in the reproduction for proper gray balance.

A gray scale with silver emulsion reads approximately 20% lower in density (brighter) on a densitometer than it does on a scanner. The reason is that the silver grains on the film scatter the incident light rather than transmitting it in the same direction. The densitometer evaluates all transmitted light including the scattered light, but the scanner reads only the transmitted light. A carbon dye gray scale scatters a minimum amount of light and is mostly used in a scanner for the accuracy of results.

TONE REPRODUCTION FOR BLACK AND WHITE HALFTONES

A basic discussion of black and white tone reproduction is presented in the chapter on "Halftone." Traditionally, the only criteria used for evaluating a halftone was to examine the tone values for the highlight and shadow aim points. However, it became evident that with the same highlight and shadow tone values, the change in the middle-tone dot placement can make dramatic changes in the appearance of the reproduction. Figure 9.8 contains three halftone reproductions made from the same original. In all three reproductions, the highlight and shadow dot values remain fixed, only the location of the middle-tone dots changed.

Basically, in conventional halftone technique, the placement of the dots is changed by changing the proportion of the main, flash, and bump exposures. The main exposure controls the highlight as well as the placement of the 50% dots, the flash exposure controls the shadow dot placement, and the bump or no-screen exposure can be used to reduce the size of the highlight dots. However, these exposures are interrelated. For example, the combination of reduced main

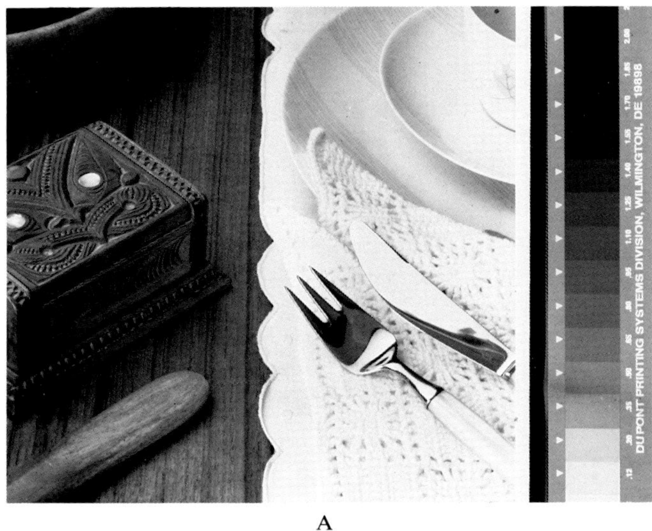

A

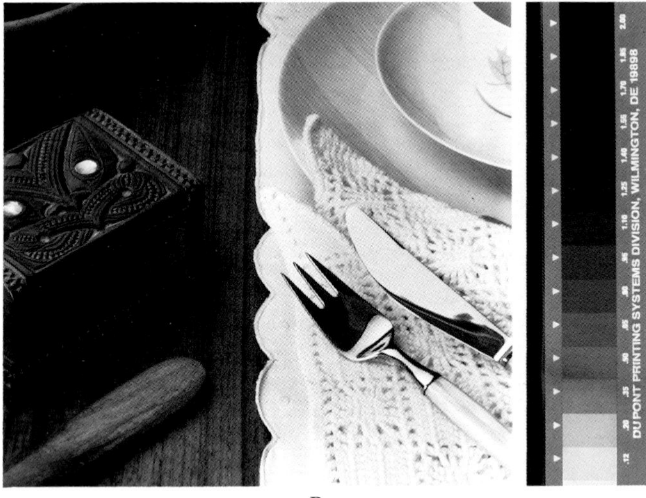

B

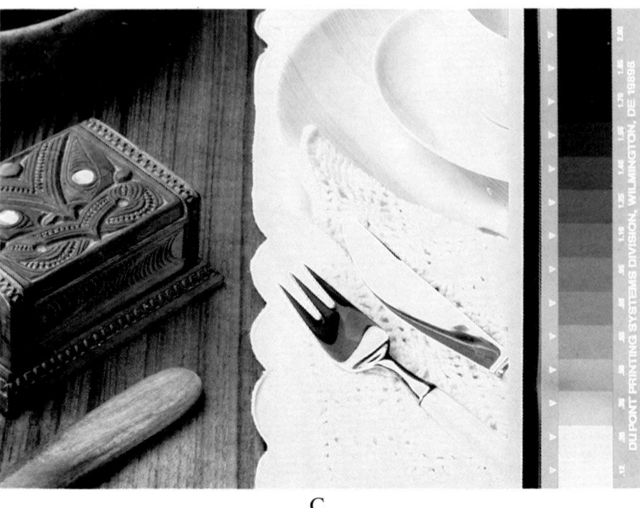

C

Figure 9.8. Three halftone reproductions — normal (A), with emphasized highlight (B), and with emphasized shadow (C). Note the change of dot values in the various steps of the gray scale.

and bump can produce the same size highlight dots as can be produced only by the main; however, the use of reduced main exposure underexposes the negative, and, as a result, the 50% dots are placed closer to the highlight end of the scale. Since the effect of bump is mostly on the highlight, it will have minimal effect on the middle-tone. There are exposure computers available in the market which can be precisely programmed to change the positions of the middle-tone dots in the tone reproduction scale for optimizing tone reproduction in a halftone. Such a device is the Carlson Sharpshooter (see Figure 4.11 on page 87).

The decision where to place the middle-tone dots is important in controlling the reproduction of tones. This decision is the same as deciding which tonal areas of the original have to be compressed or which ones have to be emphasized. However, it must be realized that since the entire tonal areas of a long range original have to be reproduced within the narrow range of the reproduction, one area can be emphasized only when the other areas are de-emphasized. In other words, while the contrast of one area is increased, the contrast of other areas become decreased or flattened. As indicated earlier, this decision is subjective and is often left up to the camera operator. However, a prior knowledge about the main interest area(s) of the picture will be more helpful in making these decisions. For example, in the three reproductions presented in Figure 9.8, if both the high and low key areas of the picture were important, reproduction A would have been appropriate. However, if the high key areas were more important than the low key, then reproduction B would have been more appropriate; if the low key areas were more important, reproduction C would have been more appropriate.

Jones Diagram to Determine Optimum Tone Curve for Black and White Halftones

To construct a Jones Diagram for black and white halftones, first a halftone negative is made from a gray scale with known density steps using standard exposure so that the smallest printable dots are obtained in the highlight and shadow areas of the negative. The negative is then stripped, plated and run in the press using the standard printing conditions, i.e. ink, paper, normal press adjustment, etc. Using a densitometer or dot area meter, dot percentages are recorded for each step of the gray scale negative; however, integrated density is recorded from the same printed steps of the gray scale. Since the original contains a continuous-tone density and will be compared with a printed reproduction, only the integrated density of the reproduction is required for evaluation. After plotting the parameters, a curve is drawn as shown in Figure 9.5.

The second step is to record the maximum density of ink on the press sheet and to plot this density point on the graph in relation to the original. In this example, a maximum density value of 1.35 is obtained on the press sheet from a continuous-tone density of 2.60 of the original. A 45 degree angle line is drawn that represents an identical reproduction of tone from the original (see Figure 9.7).

The tone reproduction curve must be within the limit of the maximum printing density. If a straight line is drawn from the highlight to the shadow points, the entire curve will be lower in contrast. As indicated earlier, the highlight area is more critical to the average viewer than the shadow. As such, an ideal curve is drawn in which the highlight through the middle-tone area is emphasized, but the contrast is reduced from the middle-tone to the shadow area (see Figure 9.7). However, the flattening of contrast in the shadow areas should be as smooth and gradual as possible. Abrupt compression will result in the loss of important details.

It should be emphasized here that the purpose of the first curve in Figure 9.5 is to record the changes that have taken place in the press during the printing of the negative, such as dot gain, ink, paper, and other printing characteristics. Figure 9.7 is an optimal tone reproduction curve drawn from the data. The curve is within the limits of the printing conditions. The main objective of drawing this curve is to obtain the halftone negative which will produce the curve with the printing conditions obtained in the curve of Figure 9.5.

The Jones Diagram is started by first making four quadrants on a graph paper. Since both of the aforementioned curves in Figures 9.5 and 9.7 have a common reproduction density data along the Y axis, the two curves are positioned on the top two quadrants; the curve in Figure 9.5 on the left, and the curve in Figure 9.7 on the right quadrant using Y as the common axis for both. On the bottom right quadrant, a 45 degree line is drawn which is designated as the transfer curve. Both the axes of this curve contain the original densities, and since both halves of the quadrants are identical, this curve will not influence the results. The remaining lower left quadrant will be used to draw the required curve for the halftone needed to produce the ideal tone reproduction curve.

The required halftone curve is drawn by finding the intersection points of the other three curves in this quadrant. For example, the .50 density from the original is traced to a point where it meets the ideal curve, left to the reproduction density and down to the quadrant at the bottom left. The point from the same original density is moved down until it intersects the transfer curve, turned left until it intersects with the line at the bottom left quadrant. A point is plotted at this intersection. This process is repeated for several original density points until the complete halftone curve is obtained at the bottom left quadrant.

Once the curve is obtained, the required dot percentages for each gray scale steps can be calculated from the curve. Different halftone exposures such as main, flash, and bump

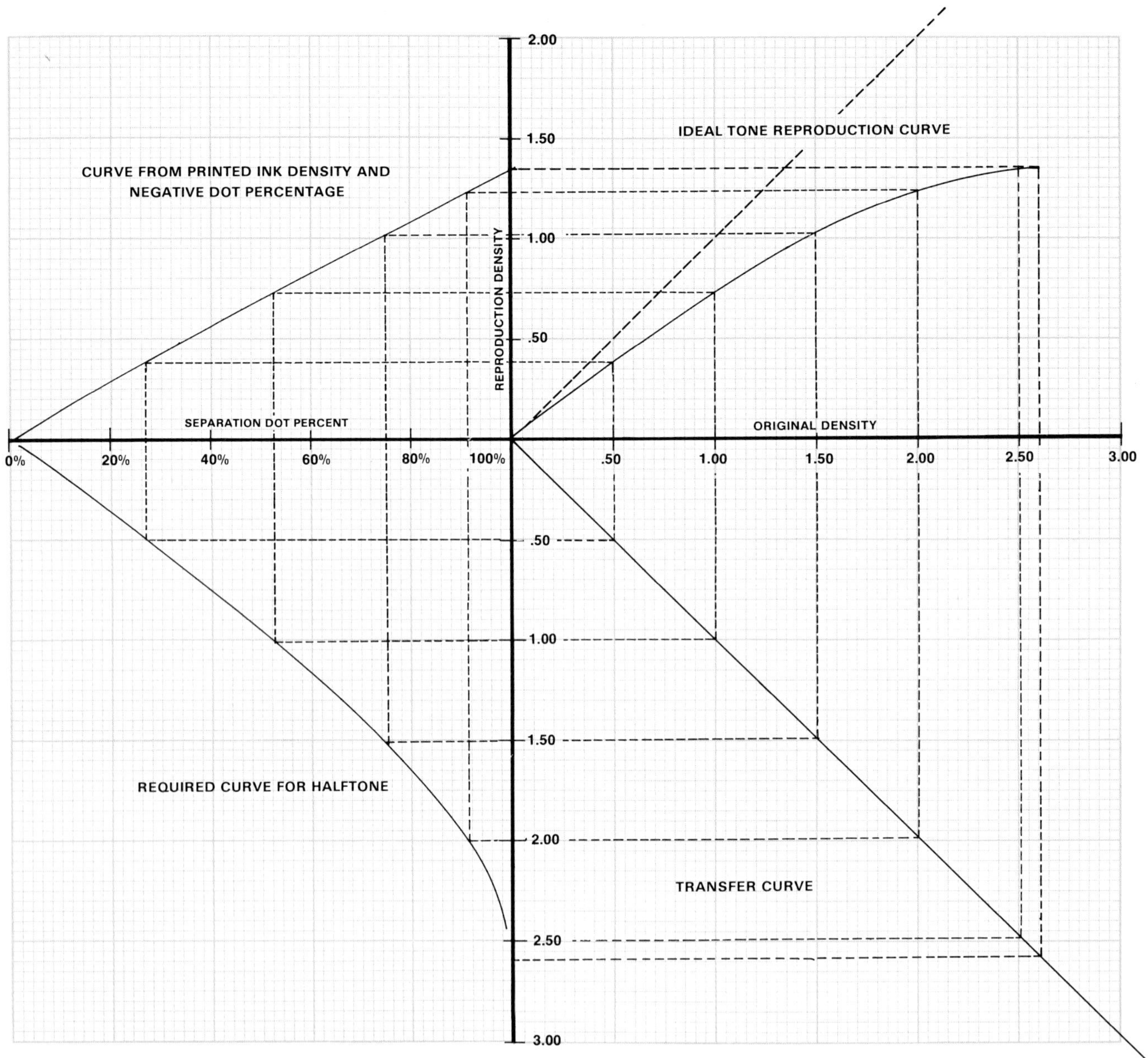

Figure 9.9. A Jones Diagram to determine an optimum halftone

can be calculated for a specific darkroom condition to obtain the required dots for the scale. There are automatic exposure control devices available to help the camera operator compute the bump and main to locate the different size dots in the curve.

TONE REPRODUCTION FOR PROCESS COLOR

The concept of tone reproduction for black and white halftone and color are the same — the tones of the original have to be compressed to fit into the limited density range produced by the ink on paper. The critical decision in both is to locate the tonal area or areas of the original within which the compression is to be effective in the reproduced tones.

Although the concept is the same, more variables are introduced for tone reproduction in color than in black and white because the reproduction is obtained with four colors instead of one. However, some of the printing characteristics, like solid ink density, dot shape, screen ruling, paper characteristics, and the press variables such as dot gain, slur, trapping, and fill-in, apply to color printing as well. Once the printing conditions are optimized, curves can be drawn using the printing characteristics data to analyze and locate an ideal set of separations.

One of the most important variables introduced in color reproduction is the gray balance of the three colors. Since each ink behaves as if it is contaminated with the other two inks by showing unwanted absorption and reflection characteristics, the inks are printed in different proportions to produce the original neutral as reproduced neutral for balancing the three process colors. A detailed discussion of gray balance is presented in the chapter "Gray Balance."

Jones Diagram to Determine Halftone Curve for Tone Reproduction in Color

The steps to determine tone reproduction for color using the Jones Diagram are the same as they are for black and white tone reproduction. First the existing printing conditions are optimized. Then a curve is plotted using the paper-press data, an ideal curve is drawn, and the required separation data is obtained by tracing lines along these curves. However, instead of only one negative and one set of dot

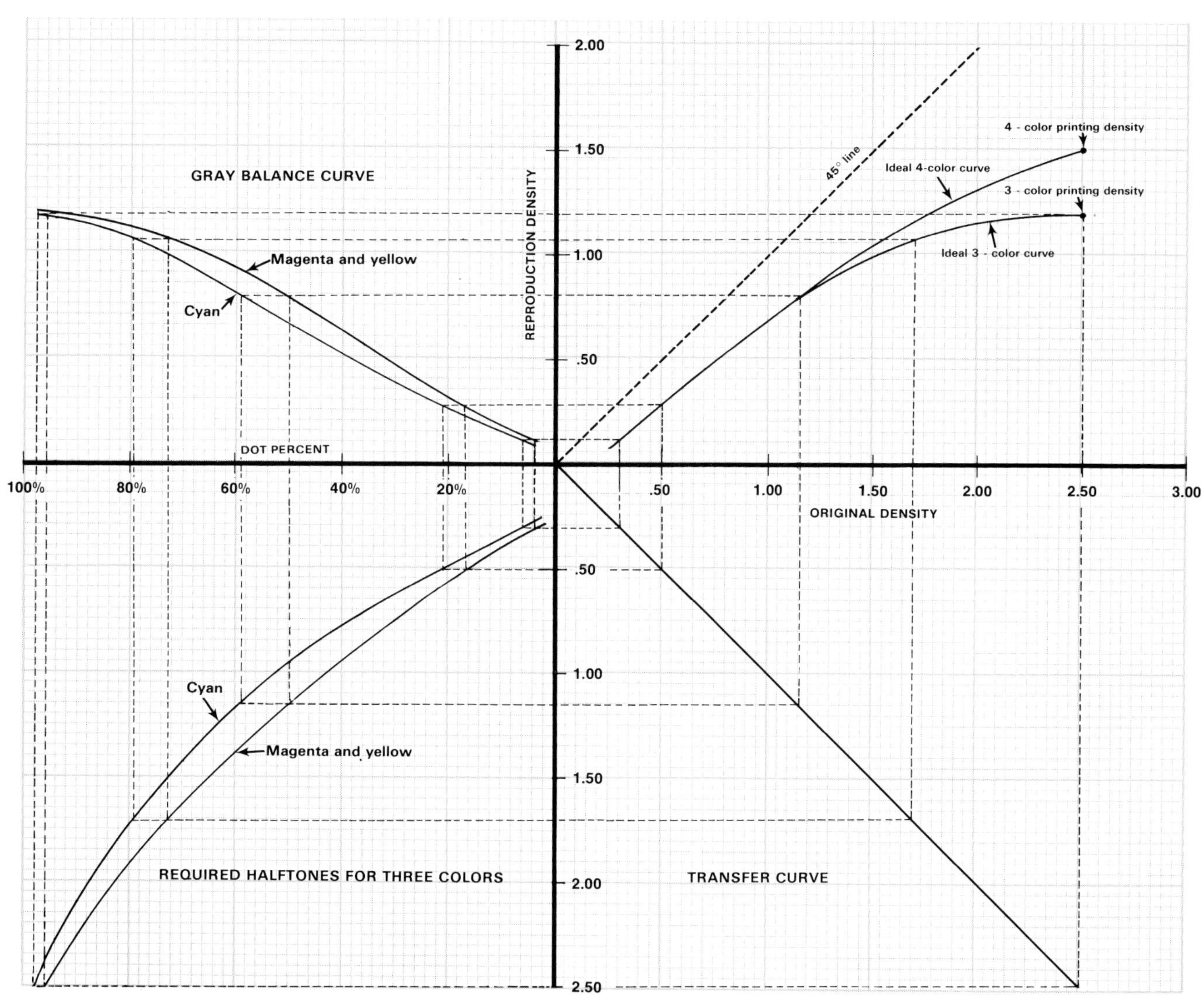

Figure 9.10. A Jones Diagram to determine the separation halftones required for the three colors

percentages for each step of the scale as in a black and white halftone, four sets of separations and dot values are used. These dot values for each color have to be different for maintaining a gray balance of the printing inks. In addition to the gray balance control, the thickness of the solid ink for each of the process colors also has to be optimized and maintained for consistency in the reproduction. For example, too much ink will plug-in the shadows and will cause excessive dot gain on the press. On the other hand, too little ink will cause a lack of saturation and a washed out effect.

Once the printing conditions are optimized, gray balance of the three colors can be established by trial or by using specific types of printing aids available for this purpose, such as the RIT TRAND Chart or the GATF Gray Balance Chart. (This topic is discussed in detail in the chapter "Gray Balance.") The optimal ink densities printed for the three colors, four colors, and the black can also be established for the same printing conditions. Once this information is quantified, the Jones Diagram can be plotted to find the separations needed for the optimal tone reproduction curve.

The first step for plotting a Jones Diagram is to find the separation dot sizes that were used to determine gray balance in each step of the negative or positive. This is obtained by a dot area meter or a transmission densitometer and a conversion chart. Then a reflection densitometer is used to determine the reflection densities for each step of the original gray scale as well as the printed densities for the three colors and black. This is calculated by using the respective complementary filters for each color. Theoretically, a neutral area reflects equal amounts of red, green, and blue, so the densitometer should also read equal values for red, green, and blue filters when a neutral area is measured. A good quality densitometer can be accurately calibrated to produce equal densities with the three filters when a neutral area is read. This is required to interpret the data for constructing the Jones Diagram.

As explained in Figure 9.10, the Jones Diagram is plotted on a graph paper into four quadrants. At the top left quadrant, the percent dot sizes are equally spaced at the base line X. The common Y axis for the two quadrants are calibrated for the reproduction density values of the gray scale, and the base line X at the top right quadrant is calibrated for the continuous-tone density values of the original. Each of the cyan, magenta, and yellow dot values are plotted against the integrated density values of the reproduced gray scale in the top left quadrant. This is the gray balance quadrant. In the top right quadrant, first a 45 degree line is drawn which is theoretically the ideal reproduction of the original. Then the three-color and four-color maximum density values obtained on the press sheet are plotted against the maximum density values found in the original. In Figure 9.10, the original density is 2.25 ,the maximum 3-color density obtained is 1.20 , and the maximum 4-color density obtained is 1.50

Similar to the black and white optimal tone reproduction curve, (see Figure 9.9) an ideal tone reproduction curve is drawn for the 3-colors in the top right quadrant. The highlight through the middle-tone section of the curve is kept parallel with the 45 degree line, but a gradual flattening of the shadow area has taken place to accommodate the curve within the reproduction range.

Once the ideal 3-color curve is drawn in the top right quadrant, the construction of the other two quadrants is identical to the black and white quadrants discussed earlier. The bottom right quadrant is the transfer curve. A 45 degree line is drawn, and the two axes of this quadrant represent the original density. Then a point on the original gray scale is selected and traced to the three-color curve located at the gray balance quadrant. The point is traced across the cyan, magenta and yellow curves and down to the required halftone quadrant. Then from the same point of the original gray scale, it is traced down to the transfer curve and left across to the required halftone quadrant. The point of intersection with the trace line coming from the three-color curve is plotted. Similarly, other points in the original gray scale steps are selected and traced until they intersect at different points in the required halftone quadrant. The process is repeated for several density steps of the gray scale until the required halftone separation curves for the three colors are obtained. From these curves, dot percentages needed at different aim points for the separations can be calculated.

TONE REPRODUCTION FOR BLACK

Theoretically three process colors are ideally suited to give an accurate reproduction of the black if they would absorb identical amounts of red, green, and blue. It seems that adding black ink to the reproduction would only darken the colors. However, because of the deficiency of the inks, when they are printed in combination, they produce reddish brown rather than black. As such, a black printer is needed to compensate for the deficiency of the three process colors. The following are the four main advantages of black in a color reproduction.

1. Shadows appear darker with better details with the addition of black.

2. The neutral balance of the three colors becomes less critical with the use of black, especially in the shadow areas.

3. When used with under color removal, the expensive process colors are replaced by the cheap black and thus makes the reproduction cost effective.

4. In wet on wet printing, when used with under color removal, the piling up of ink is avoided and ink drying problems are reduced.

An optimal tonal curve of the black separation is important for the accuracy in color reproduction. In practice, black will actually deteriorate the quality of the reproduction if the tone reproduction of the black does not match the original. The selection of a proper tone reproduction for black becomes more complicated because the tone curve for black can take many shapes. For example, when three colors are printed, there is only one combination for reproducing a certain color or a neutral area. However, when black is added, depending on the tone reproduction curve, a particular neutral tone may contain much black or little color, or inversely, much color and little black. The following are the three possible forms of black gradation:

1. In one form, the black printer may be used to simply extend the maximum density of the three colors.

2. In the second form, the maximum density for the three colors is increased by black; however, it will also replace the three colors in the neutral areas.

3. In another possible form, a full-scale black is produced along the entire tone reproduction curve. With the advent of gray component replacement (GCR), this black gradation seems to be more efficient if adapted to the existing printing conditions. Different types of tone reproduction curves for each of the above types of black are shown in Figure 9.11.

Among the three types of black gradation curves discussed above, type 2 is functionally more popular and will be discussed in detail. A detailed discussion of the full-scale black is presented under "Gray Component Replacement." The amount of black needed for the entire tone reproduction curve will depend on the difference between the three-color and four-color reproduction densities obtained for a given printing condition. However, another variable introduced at this stage, often termed as "additivity failure," is presented next.

Additivity Failure

When several inks are printed one at the top of the other, the added density measured through the respective complementary filters is often much less than individual densities of the same inks printed and measured separately. For example, when a blue filter is used to measure the densities of solid yellow, magenta, and cyan inks printed separately, they may show density values of 1.06, .69, and .42 respectively. When the same three inks are printed one at the top of the other, theoretically the combined density with the same blue filter should be 2.17. (1.06 + .69 + .42 = 2.17). However, the combined density will be much less, for example, about 1.35. This deficiency is called "additivity failure" of the three inks. This failure definitely limits the tone reproduction scale of the three colors in the shadow areas and needs to be compensated for by the black. The variables which affect this failure are paper surface reflection, internal reflection of the inks, opacity characteristics of the ink, ink trapping, scattering of light by the paper, and the halftone structure of the printed dots.

One important point that needs to be emphasized here is that the three-color gradation curve is not a straight line. The curve is flattened in the shadow. Because of this and the problem of additivity failure of the process inks, the black needs to be exaggerated more in the shadow than usual. A typical three-color, the black, and the four-color curves are shown in Figure 9.12.

To determine how much black is needed for the desired four color density, a graph similar to Figure 9.13 may be adapted to plot the values for black. First the highest density values for three-color, four-color, and only black are obtained by printing a gray scale. These values are then applied to the graph to obtain the required density for the black printer - at the Y axis, the densities of the three and four colors are plotted and at the X axis, the black printer density is plotted. The two spots, 1 and 2 are for the coated and uncoated paper respectively. Point x on the Y axis is the printed density of the three colors (in this example, 1.35) from which a straight line is drawn to spots 1 or 2 depending on the paper to be used. The

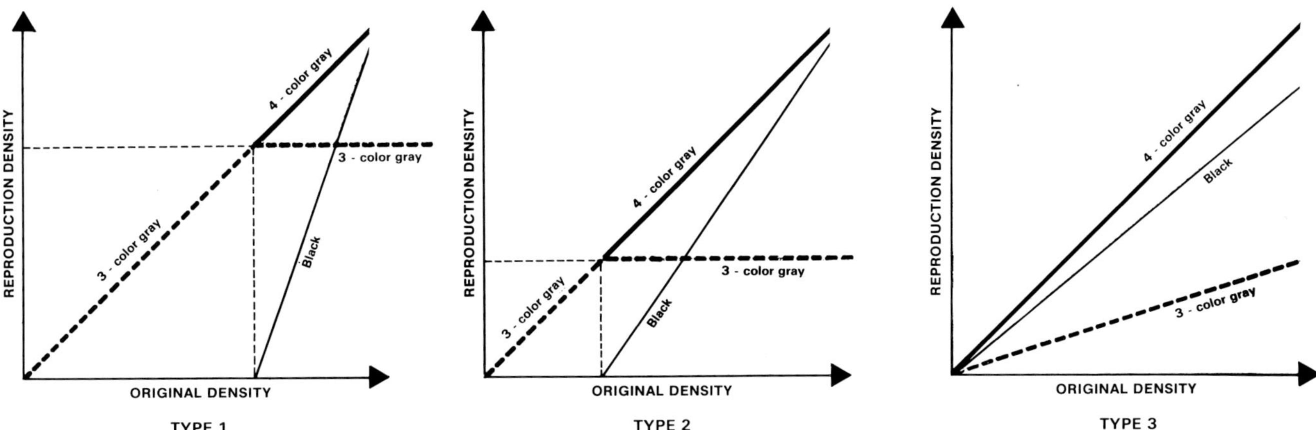

Figure 9.11. Examples of different forms of black gradation

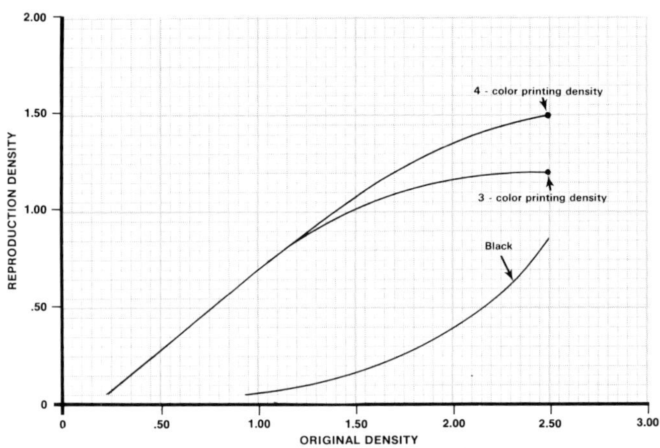

Figure 9.12. Three-color, four-color, and black gradation curves drawn from the original density and the densities obtained on a press sheet

maximum four-color density (in this example, 1.70) designated as o is also plotted on the Y axis. The required black density is obtained by drawing a horizontal line from o on the ordinate of the paper characteristic line and dropping a perpendicular from this point of intersection on to the abscissa. In this example, the black density value of .68 can be read off directly.

With the advent of Gray Component Replacement function in a modern scanner, full range black is becoming popular. One of the greater advantages of using the black throughout the scale is that the printing variables are easily controlled. However, with GCR, the color correction for the black becomes critical. The color correction requirement for the black is treated separately under "Color Correction." Black separation has also been discussed under "Under Color Removal," "Under Color Addition," and "Gray Component Replacement."

Determining Halftone Curve for Black Gradation with Jones Diagram

A Jones Diagram can be used to determine the black gradation for various shop conditions. The results obtained by printing a gray scale with three colors and four colors may be used to determine the black separation needed. This is explained in Figure 9.14. First the three-color printing density of the gray scale in relation to the original is entered into the top right quadrant. The desired four-color curve is drawn by extending the straight portion of the three-color curve. The percent dot sizes of the black printer for each step of the gray scale against the printed density is plotted in the top left quadrant. The ideal black curve found by using the "black addition diagram" (see Figure 9.13) is entered to the bottom of the

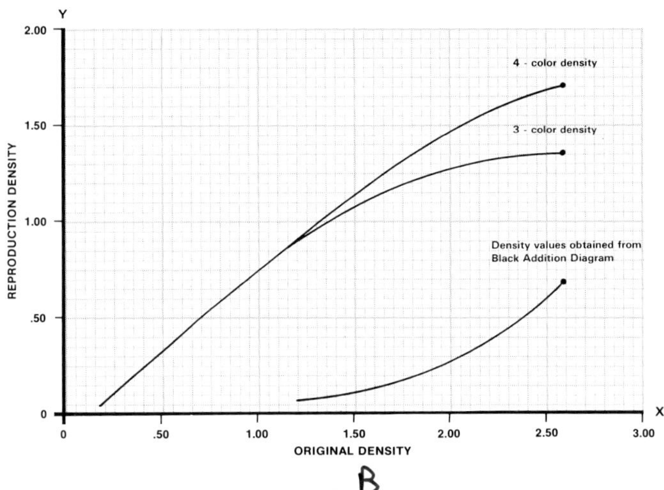

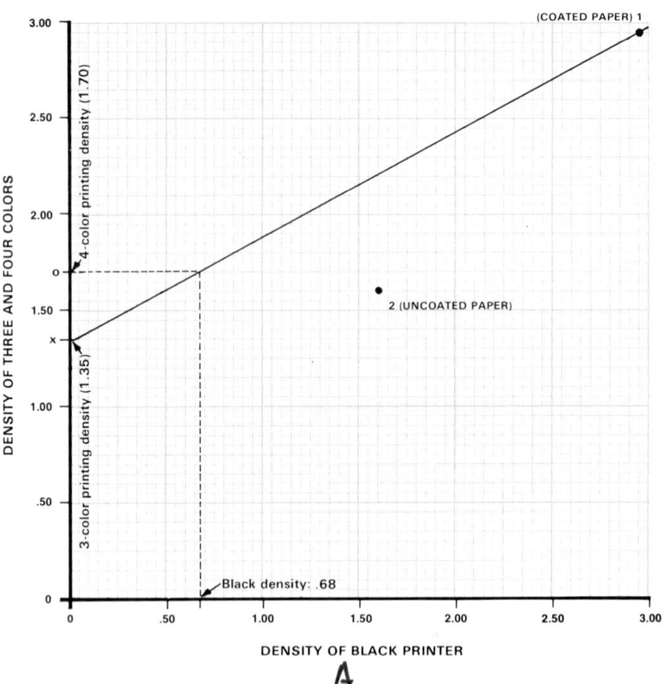

Figure 9.13. Determining black gradation for a specific shop condition. After the density values for black are obtained from the "Black Addition Diagram" in Diagram A, they are plotted in Diagram B to obtain the required curve

top right quadrant. The bottom left quadrant contains the transfer curve. From any point on the base of the top right quadrant, a vertical line is drawn. Via the black curve it is extended horizontally to the top left quadrant. From the point where the line intersects the curve at the top left quadrant, it is moved down to the transfer curve, and from the intersection point, moved horizontally to the bottom right quadrant. From the same original starting point at the base of the top right

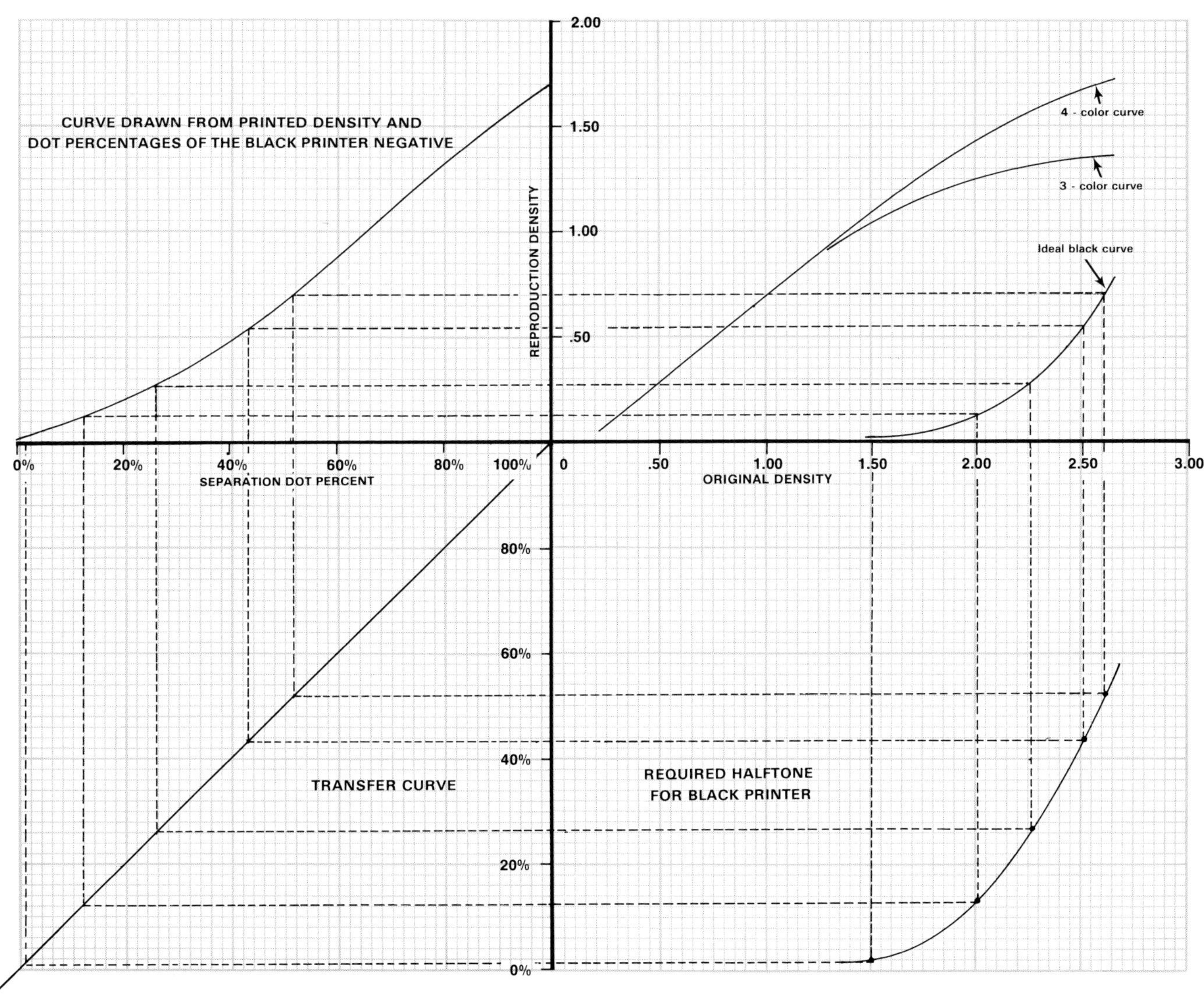

Figure 9.14. A Jones Diagram to determine the required halftone for an optimum black gradation

quadrant, a line is dropped perpendicularly to the bottom right quadrant where a point of intersection is found. Similarly, other points are selected and traced until they intersect at different points in the required black curve at the bottom right quadrant. The bottom right quadrant contains the required halftone curve. The original density and the dot percentages for each aim point can be obtained from the X and Y axes of this quadrant.

TONE REPRODUCTION IN THE CONVENTIONAL SEPARATION

For initial set up of the conventional equipment in a camera, an enlarger, or for the contact frame, a gray scale is placed beside the original and a set of separations is made. Three aim points — highlight, middle-tone, and shadow are selected on the gray scale, and the tone values for these aim points are checked in the separations for the accuracy in tone reproduction. During direct-screening, three different exposures are used to control the dot sizes of these aim points — the main exposure, the flash exposure, and the bump or no-screen exposure. Depending on the range of dots that can be produced by the screen with a single exposure (screen range), these exposures are adjusted to control dot sizes at various aim points. The cyan separation contains relatively larger dot sizes than the magenta and yellow separations for proper gray balance. The proportion is higher in the middle-tone than in the highlight and shadow. Similarly, in the indirect method, during screening of the continuous-tone separations, the sizes of the dots at different aim points are controlled by the

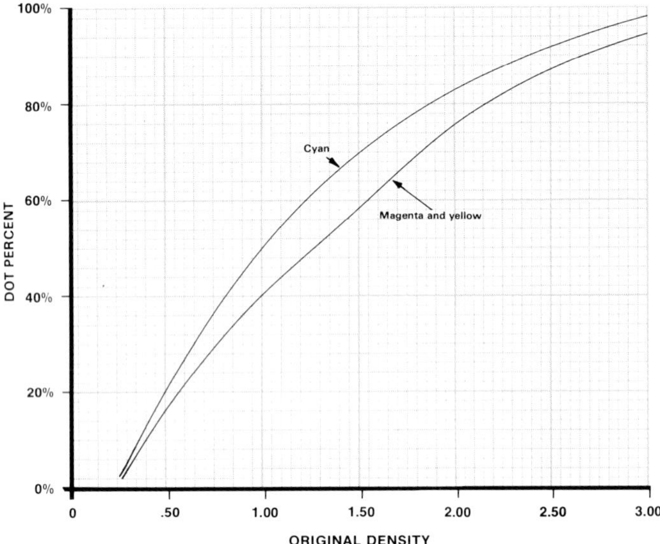

Figure 9.15. A typical gray balance curve drawn from the original densities and the dot percentages in the three-color separations

use of main, flash, and bump exposures. An ideal gray balance curve is shown in Figure 9.15.

Because the types of exposures used for color separation in the conventional equipment, it is difficult to control more than three aim points. However, they are proved to be adequate in a photographic process. In the earlier days, controlling the tone reproduction started with only two aim points: highlight and shadow. The addition of the middle-tone aim point was definitely a breakthrough (see Figure 9.16). However, controlling tones with only three aim points in a scanner is not adequate. Since scanning involves analyzing and separating the original a minute portion at a time, five aim points are necessary for accurate controlling of the entire tonal curve.

Another major problem in the conventional separation is the difficulty in achieving deliberate changes in contrast in the reproduction for different types of originals. There are two ways to accomplish the changes:

1. The middle-tone can be changed in relation to the highlight and shadow through adjustments of the exposure and development. The scope of these adjustments is very limited

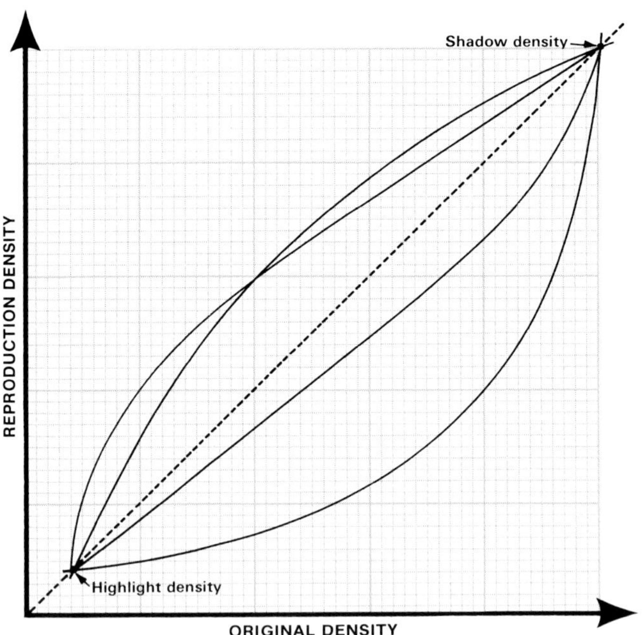

Figure 9.16. With the same highlight and shadow aim points, a drastic change in the gradation is possible by changing the middle-tone values.

and will depend on the experience of the worker.

2. The other change involves altering the mask aim points, and is accomplished by changing the tone relationship between the middle-tone and highlight and between the middle-tone and shadow. Normally a change of .05 will give approximately a change of .08 density in the middle-tone. These changes are made by adjusting exposure and development times and their scopes are also limited.

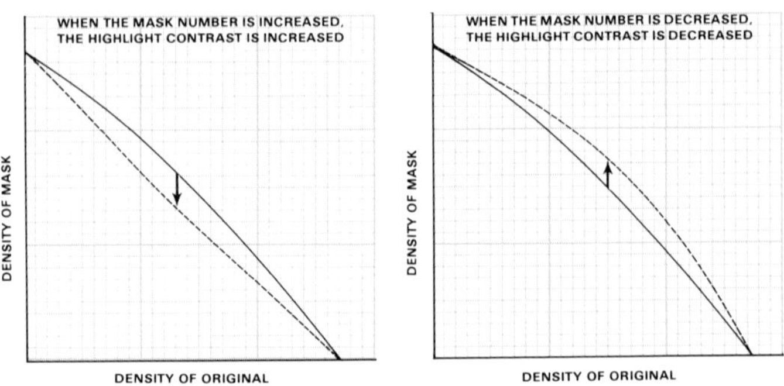

Figure 9.17. Curves showing the possible change of mask aim points to affect tone reproduction

TONE REPRODUCTION IN A SCANNER

The concept of tone reproduction in a scanner is similar to the reproduction of tones in conventional equipment. However, five aim points are normally selected in a scanner for controlling the tones instead of three as in the conventional separation. These five aim points are highlight, quarter-tone, middle-tone, three-quarter-tone, and shadow. The major advantage of tone reproduction in a scanner lies in its ability to control tone for one area of the original without significantly affecting the tones of the other area.

The tone reproduction in a scanner is more predictable than in the conventional system. Once the scanner is calibrated in relation to the film emulsion (called film linearization), the tones of the five aim points are selected, positioned for the scanning light, and then the operator simply dials in the tone values. In some of the latest programmable scanners, the operator can program and store dozens of different gradation curves. Each one can be selected for proper application. During operation, the computer automatically generates the identical tone values representing the selected gradation curve.

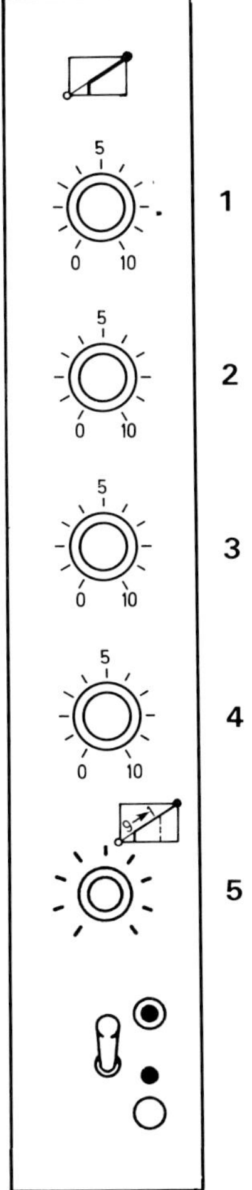

Figure 9.18. A CATCHLIGHT DROPOUT panel in the Hell 399ER. Controls 1 through 4 are used to adjust the dropout for highlight in each color. Control 5 is the starting point on the gradation curve from which the dropout will be effective. The toggle switch at the bottom is used to activate (when up) or to deactivate (when down) the effects of the catchlight controls.

CATCHLIGHT DROP OUT AND HIGHLIGHT LIMIT

A catchlight or a specular highlight should be reproduced with greater contrast than a normal highlight. If the specular highlight is used as a normal highlight to set up the scanner, it will render a dark reproduction. Examples of such specular highlights are sparkling reflection from water, shining lights from mirrors or glossy reflective surfaces such as the paint of a new car, etc. In general, these specular highlights do not contain any dot values in the reproduction, thus rendering the highest possible contrast showing the white of the paper. Most analog and digital scanners provide two types of controls for rendering the highest contrast for the specular highlights: one control consists of setting up the starting point or breakpoint in the tonal curve from which the drop out will be

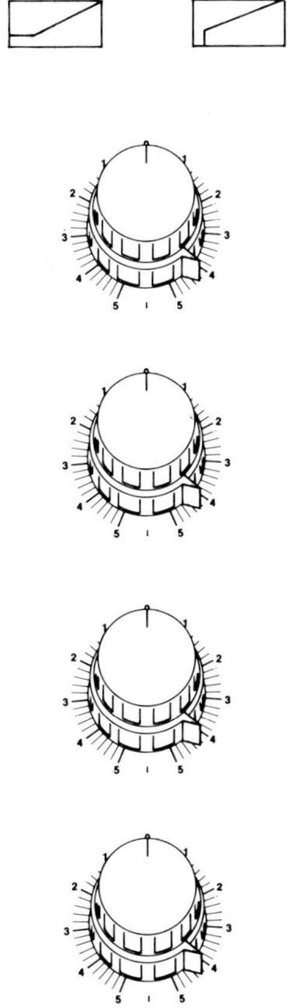

Figure 9.19. HIGHLIGHT CONTRAST CONTROL (HCC) with Highlight Boost-up (HBU) and Highlight Limit (HLM) in the DS SG-608. The outer control of each of the dual-function knobs sets the point on the gradation curve from which the HIGHLIGHT CONTRAST control will be effective. The clockwise turn of the inner control enhances the highlight tone to boost the highlight; counterclockwise turn of the same control flattens the highlight tone to achieve a limit of tone for the highlight.

effective. The other set of controls consists of the cyan, magenta, yellow, and black intensity controls to set the intensity of the drop out. Figure 9.20 shows the effect of catchlight dropout in the DS SG-608 scanner.

In letterpress or gravure printing, it is essential that the entire area of the picture contains tone or dot values. For example, if no highlight dots are present in a letterpress engraving, this non-printing area may pick up ink and print solid in the reproduction if this area is not shallow enough compared to the printing area. Similarly, the gravure and some web offset processes require that there should be no density in the separations higher than a specified maximum density. To be sure that the entire reproduction contains the tone or dot values, most scanners provide a set of controls with which the operator can set a limit of the tone or dot values in the separations. For example, the operator can set a limit of 10% dots in the highlight and 90% dots in the shadow. This limit means that no matter how light or dark the highlight or shadow density values in the copy are, the scanner will not produce less than 10% in the highlight or more than 90% in the shadow. In most analog and digital scanners, controls are provided to set the lower (highlight) or higher (shadow) limits which will prevent any lower or higher percentages of dots to be printed.

Courtesy D.S. America, Inc.

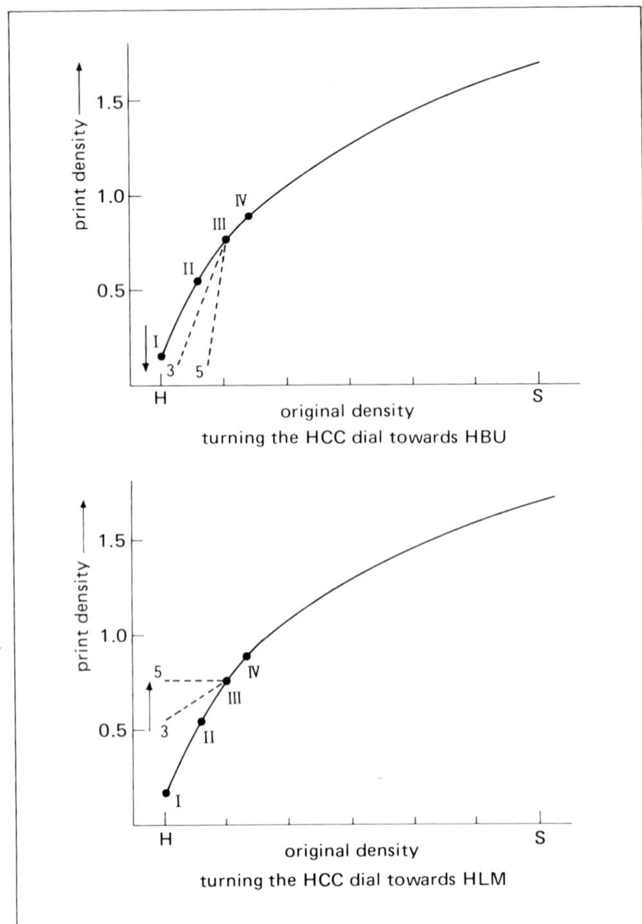

Figure 9.20. The effects of HIGHLIGHT CONTRAST CONTROL settings in the DS SG-608

EXAMPLES OF DIFFERENT TYPES OF GRADATION

There may be thousands of different types of originals received by the scanner operator; each may need a different gradation for optimal results. It is beyond the scope of this publication to discuss every possible type of gradation. However, it is easier to select only a few standard gradation curves for any originals. Each type of original is first identified in terms of tonal characteristics, and then a specific type of gradation is applied to that original. Each original may fall into any one of these categories: average, high-key, low-key, normal, overexposed, and underexposed. In the next few pages, examples of different types of gradation are presented with actual separations printed in four colors. A careful study of the examples will provide the operator with an understanding of the optimal application of gradation.

To adjust the gradation manually, first the operator selects the aim points on a dye gray scale with known density values. Fixed dot values are assigned to different aim points each time positioning the density step of each aim point for the scanning light. Alternately, a few scanners similar to the DS SG-608 offer fixed internal density values for the aim points. To change gradation, the dot values for various aim points are changed. A pair of four-position Reference switches are provided on the front panel of the SG-608 to select the fixed density values for the aim points and to adjust the dot percentages with the gradation control knobs. Other scanners offer a number of fixed preset gradation curves stored on a floppy disk. Each of these curves has fixed values for quarter-tone, middle-tone, and three-quarter-tone. First a normal curve is established by selecting the appropriate aim points and then assigning dot values for each aim point. Then the highlight and shadow aim points are selected for the new copy and the appropriate dot values are assigned for these two points. Each curve then can be produced by simply recalling any of these stored gradations. For example, in the Hell 399ER, a fixed gradation curve may have the following values: quarter-tone: -6%, middle-tone: -10%, and three-quarter-tone: 0%. This means that compared to a normal gradation curve which the operator has initially produced by assigning the dot values for each aim point, the fixed gradation will have 6% less dot values in the quarter-tone, 10% less in the middle-tone, and there will be no change of dot values in the three-quarter-tone aim point. If the standard dot values for these aim points are 21%, 60%, and 78%, then the fixed gradation values will be, in this example, 15%, 50%, and 78% respectively. According to the initial adjustment of gray balance, the tone values for all three colors will be automatically balanced. However, it should be kept in mind that regardless of the type of preset gradation used, the density values of the aim points will be changed whenever new highlight and shadow aim points are selected for each copy.

Table 6 is an example of preset fixed gradations available on a floppy disk for the Hell 399ER scanner. Table 7 is provided from the Magnascan 645 Manual. It contains examples of reproduced tonal characteristics needed for different types of originals. In Table 6, all 20 gradations are different in the quarter-tone, middle-tone, or in the three-quarter-tone areas. The difference in dot values is marked by + or – signs indicating that the dot sizes will be increased or decreased by that number in relation to the normal gradation which was preset by the operator. All the aim points of gradation #3 are designated 0, indicating that this is a normal gradation and the dot values assigned previously for each aim point will be reproduced the same with this curve.

TABLE 6
PRE-PROGRAMMED FIXED GRADATIONS

Gradation	Quarter-tone	Midtone	Three-quarter-tone
# 1	-6%	-10%	-7%
# 2	-3%	-5%	-4%
# 3	0%	0%	0%
# 4	+3%	+5%	+3%
# 5	+7%	+10%	+6%
# 6	0%	-7%	-7%
# 7	+2%	-4%	-4%
# 8	+5%	+1%	0%
# 9	+9%	+5%	+3%
#10	+12%	+9%	+6%
#11	-10%	-11%	-8%
#12	-7%	-6%	-4%
#13	-4%	-1%	0%
#14	-1%	+4%	+3%
#15	+4%	+10%	+6%
#16	-1%	-7%	-10%
#17	+1%	-5%	-7%
#18	+5%	-1%	-4%
#19	+9%	+4%	-1%
#20	+11%	+9%	+2%

(Chart courtesy of Hell Graphic Systems)

TABLE 7

Over Exposed Subject (thin transparency)	HL+	MT+	SH+
Under Exposed Subject (dense transparency)	SH-	MT-	HL-
Improve White Garments	HL+		
Improve Snow Scenes	HL+		
Improve Flat Subjects	SH-	HL+	
Improve Detail Overall	SH-	HL+	
Improve Shadow Detail	SH-		
Improve Midtone Detail	HL+	MT+	
Remove Detail Overall	SH+	MT-	HL-
Heavier Result Overall	HL+	SH+	

Example I: Standard Gradation for Average Copy

Courtesy Fuji Photo Film USA Inc.

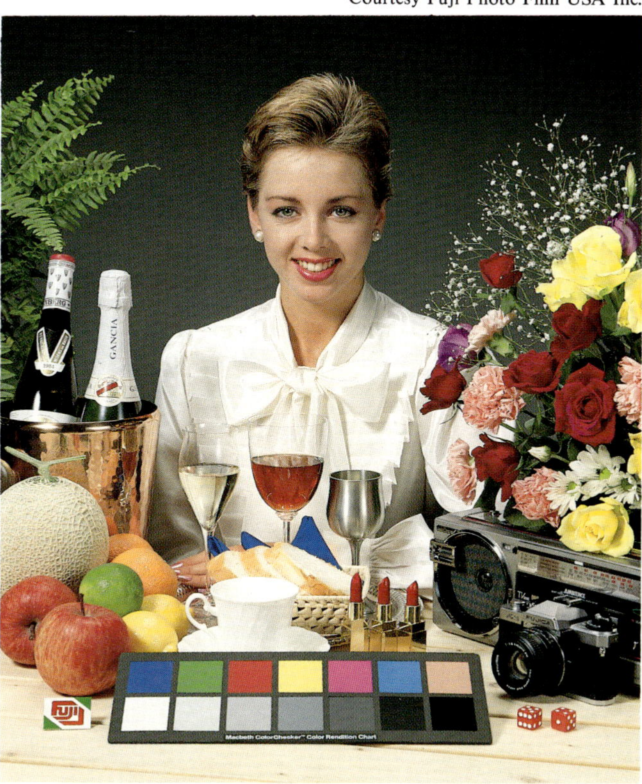

Figure 9.21. Reproduction of an average copy with a normal tone reproduction curve

An average copy contains no special "interest" area. In other words, the range of the entire original is equally important. A standard gradation may be defined as a normal gradation which is set up for an original with the following characteristics:

1. The reproduction curve is identical to an ideal curve. When plotted, the curve for the highlight through the middletone is parallel to a 45 degree line and a smooth compression takes place between the middle-tone through the shadow areas.

2. No special tonal emphasis is required in any area of the copy.

3. The gray balance of the three colors have been previously determined and is known to the operator.

4. The highlight and shadow density values of the original are known.

Standard gradation for an average copy is the most important adjustment for the subsequent gradation change in a scanner. The adjustment is based on the data obtained from the accurate reproduction of an average original. Since specific shop conditions affect tone reproduction, the initial or standard gradation setting is critical and must take into account all of the variables present in the shop. For example, dot gain in the press, or quality of the ink and paper will influence the initial setting of the scanner. If the reproduction of most average copy shows an unbalanced tone and needs frequent adjustments, it is strongly recommended that an ideal gradation curve is first selected and standardized using the optimized printing conditions.

For the data presented in Table 8, it is assumed that the original contains a highlight density of .30 and a maximum obtainable shadow density. In most scanners this maximum shadow density is obtained by simply blocking the scanning or analyze light to the photomultipliers. Figure 9.22 shows a normal gradation curve which was plotted from the original and the reproduction densities.

TABLE 8

Density Values of the Scale		Dot percent C	M	Y
Highlight:	.30	5	4	4
Quarter-tone	.50	21	17	17
Middle-tone:	1.20	60	50	50
Three-quarter-tone	1.70	78	74	74
Shadow:	No light (maximum shadow)	98	95	95

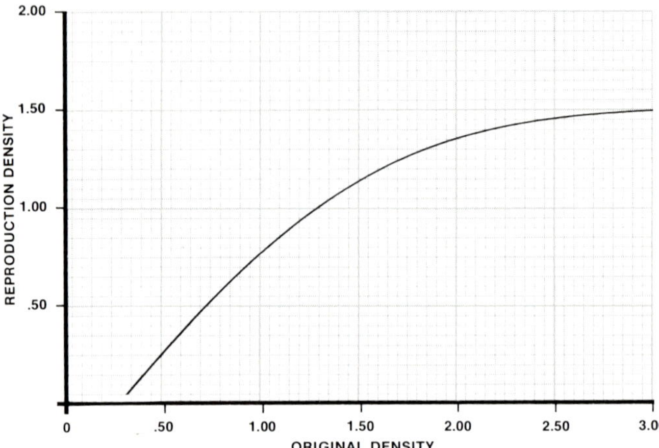

Figure 9.22. A normal gradation curve similar to the one applied to the reproduction in Figure 9.21

It should be emphasized here that the above aim points and dot values are purely hypothetical. The specific values will depend on the variables present in a particular shop — the kind of paper, ink, dot gain, ink trapping, etc. For example, a separation printed on newsprint normally prints darker in the middle-tone than when it is printed on other types of paper. As a result, the dot values for the middle-tone aim point may have to be lowered for separations used in newspaper printing.

The neutral values for the three process inks are adjusted during or before gradation settings. However, specific dot values for the five aim points will depend on the same variables as indicated earlier. For example, certain sets of process inks with warmer magenta may require a heavier cyan and yellow, or less magenta along the entire range of the scale. The quality or neutrality of the paper may also necessitate a different percentage of dots in the middle-tone for magenta, such as 45% instead of 50%.

Example 2: Gradation for Lighter Copy

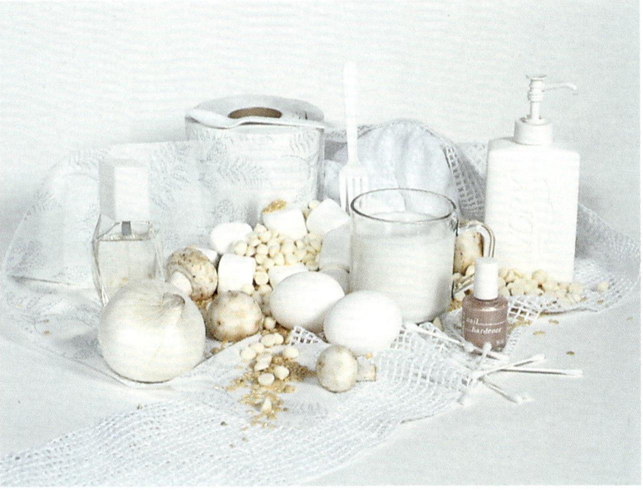

A

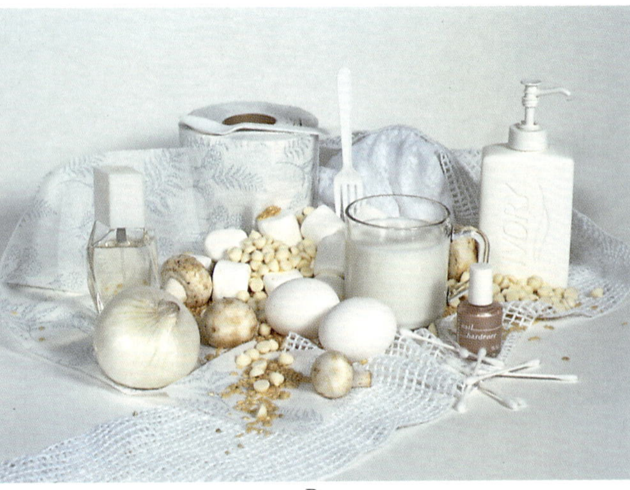

B

Figure 9.23. Two reproductions of a high-key original — a normal gradation is used for Reproduction A and a dark gradation is used for Reproduction B.

Lighter originals are those which have a brighter highlight and contain comparatively lighter middle-tones. An overexposed transparency or a high-key original are typical examples. If a proper reproduction of the original is required, a standard gradation with normal aim points will not render optimal contrast for this original. The emphasis of tonal values for the five aim points must be shifted towards the lighter end of the tone reproduction scale. This can be accomplished by selecting a set of aim points with lower density values compared to the normal aim points or by assigning higher dot values for each aim point, if the density values of the aim points are kept fixed. For example, compared to a set of normal aim points, the following lower density aim points may be assigned to a high key original while the dot values for each aim point remained the same.

Highlight density:	.10
Quarter-tone:	.30
Middle-tone:	.90
Three-quarter-tone:	1.30
Shadow:	1.80

Reproduction A is a normal reproduction and contains the same aim points as in the reproduction of Example 1. However, for reproduction B, the standard dot values are assigned to the five aim points whose density values are lighter (lower) than the normal aim points. The curve thus obtained is called a dark gradation curve. This is accomplished by positioning the scanning light spot for the aim points containing the lower density values and assigning the same dot values as used in the standard gradation. Reproduction B is darker than the reproduction A, and all the highlight details are emphasized.

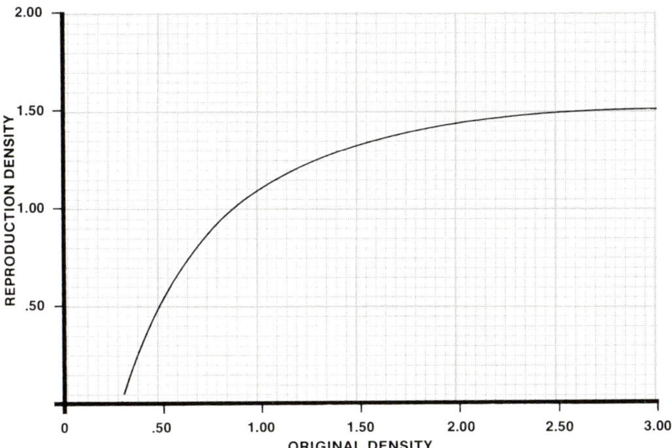

Figure 9.24. A dark gradation curve similar to the one applied to reproduction B in Figure 9.23.

If the scanner has selectable gradation curves, the operator, after selecting the appropriate highlight and shadow aim points, may recall a curve which will suit the copy. For example, from the list of 20 gradation data provided in Table 6, the operator can select Gradation #10, #20, or any similar curve for this type of copy.

Example 3: Gradation for Darker Originals

Photo courtesy Dale Brown

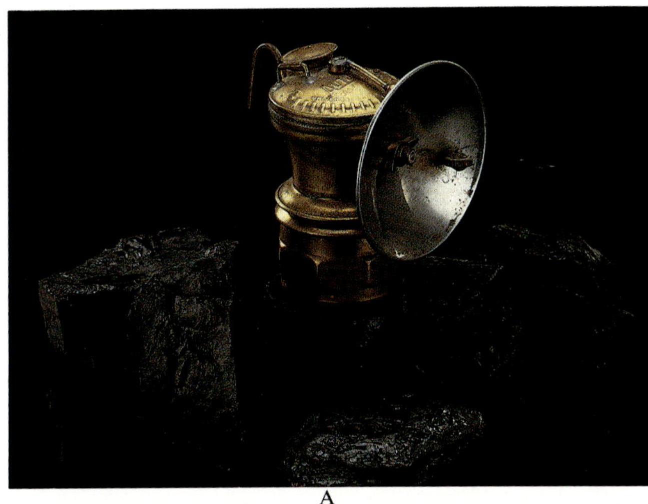

A

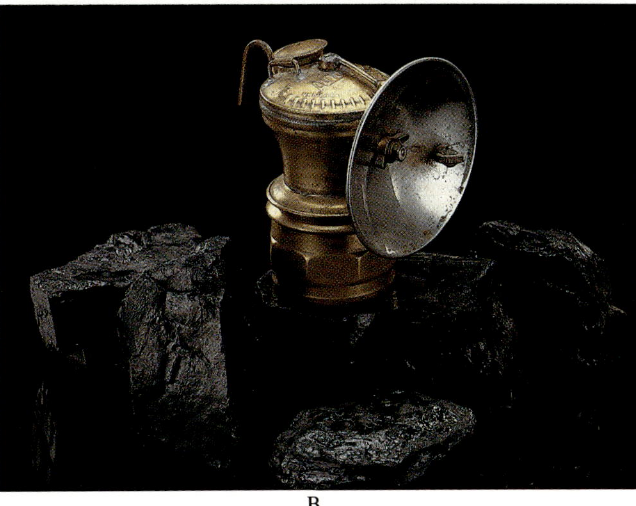

B

Figure 9.25. Two reproductions of a low-key original — a normal gradation is used for Reproduction A and a light gradation is used for Reproduction B.

Underexposed transparencies and low-key originals are typical examples of dark originals. These originals contain dark highlight, middle-tone, and shadow, with less defined details in the middle-tone through the shadow. Since the main interest lies mostly in the dark areas of the original, the following five aim points are typical choices for these types of originals compared to normal aim points. If the aim points are kept fixed, lower dot values may be assigned for each aim point compared to the normal dot values for the aim points.

Highlight:	.50
Quarter-tone:	.80
Middle-tone:	1.60
Three-quarter-tone:	2.20
Shadow:	3.00

Reproduction A represents a normal reproduction with the same aim points used for the reproduction in Example 1. However, for reproduction B the standard dot values are assigned to the aim points containing darker and higher density values than those of the normal aim points. The curve thus obtained is called a light gradation curve. Reproduction B contains more details in the darker shadow areas than it does in reproduction A.

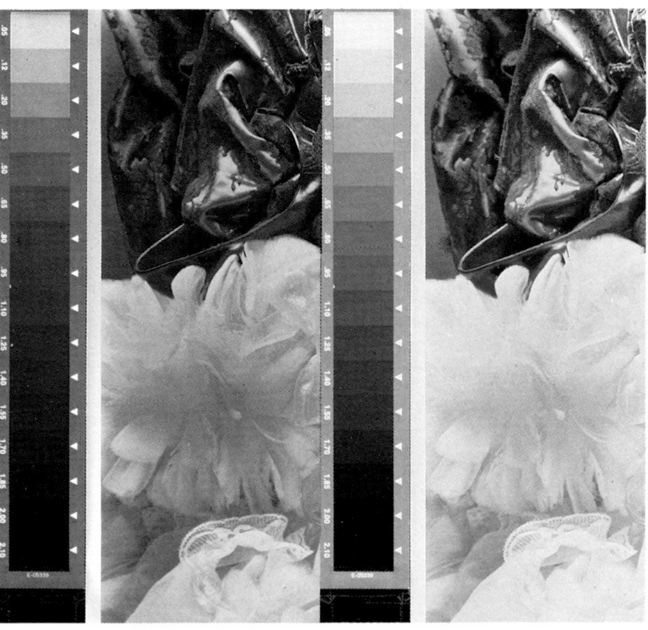

Figure 9.26a. A light gradation reduces the dot size in the shadow areas

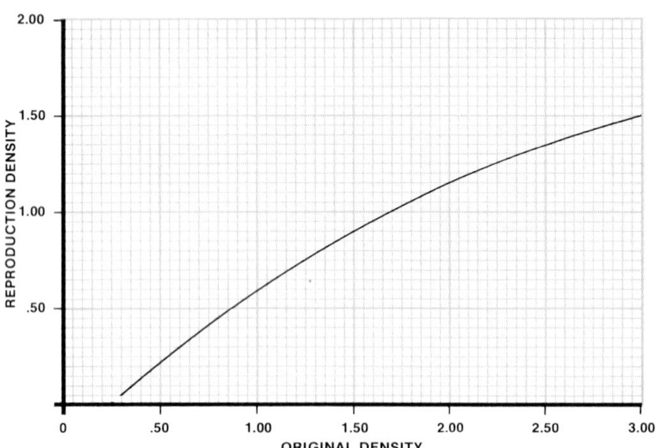

Figure 9.26. A light gradation curve similar to the one applied to reproduction B in Figure 9.25

If the scanner offers selectable preset gradation curves, the operator, after selecting the appropriate highlight and shadow aim points, may select an appropriate curve. For example, from the list provided in Table 6, gradation #6, #16, #17, or a similar curve may be selected for this type of original.

It should be noted here that a highlight area of the picture is emphasized by increasing the size of the dots in the highlight, but the details of the shadow areas are emphasized by reducing the size of the dots (printed solid area) in the shadow. For example, when a highlight aim point is moved from a higher to a lower density, say from .30 to .20, the dot sizes at .30 aim point will be increased. On the other hand, when a shadow aim point, say a three-quarter-tone is moved from 1.60 to 2.00, the sizes of the dots will be decreased at the original 1.60 density (see Figure 9.26a).

Example 4: "Opening Up" of Tones

Certain darker tonal areas of the original may contain details which are required to be more defined and visible. This is accomplished by opening up or lightening the tones in that area. The area is lightened by moving the aim point to a higher density value on the scale within which the tonal area falls. There may be a situation where the highlight and the shadow density values are fixed, but the aim points in the middle-tone, or the three-quarter-tone areas need to be shifted towards a darker value for the opening of tones. For example, in a copy the highlight and shadow density values are .30 and 2.50 respectively, but the middle-tone is unusually dark and needs to be "opened up." In this example, the situation is corrected by moving the normal middle-tone aim point from 1.20 to 1.50 and then assigning the normal middle-tone dot values for this aim point or to assign lower dot values for the fixed middle-tone aim point. This will lighten or open up the middle-tone. In Figure 9.27, reproduction A represents a normal reproduction with the same aim points used in the reproduction of Example 1, and reproduction B represents an opened-up tone of the same original. Table 9 presents the approximate guideline for opening up the middle-tone and three-quarter-tone areas when the fixed dot values are used.

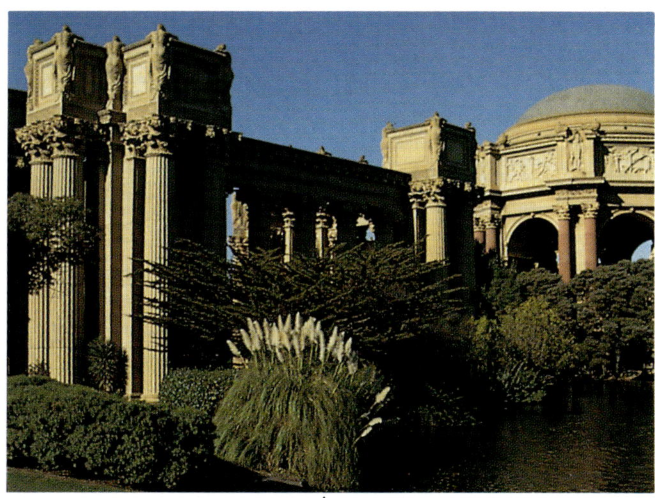

A

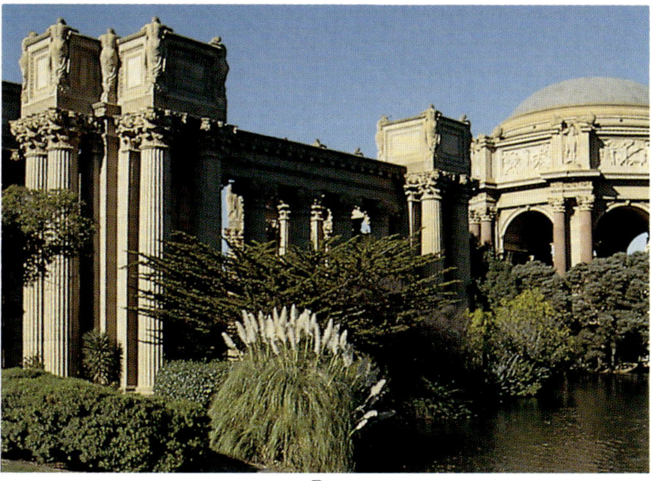

B

Figure 9.27. Two reproductions of an original - a normal gradation is used for Reproduction A and an "opened up" gradation is used in the middle-tone and three-quarter-tone areas for Reproduction B. Compare the contrast in these areas of the two reproductions

TABLE 9

Natural Aim Point		Changed Aim Points "Open Up Middle-tone"	"Open Up Three-quarter-Tone"
.30	Highlight:	.30	.30
.50	Quarter-tone:	.70	.50
1.20	Middle-tone:	1.50	1.40
1.70	Three-quarter-tone:	1.80	2.10
2.50	Shadow:	2.50	2.50

If the scanner has different types of fixed gradations in its memory, the opening up of tones in any area(s) of the copy is accomplished by selecting the appropriate tone curve. For example, if the middle-tone needs to be opened up, then #6 from the Table 6, or a similar gradation will be more appropriate.

From the above examples, it is apparent that the gradation can be easily changed to suit the special characteristics of the copy by lightening or darkening the tone values for one or

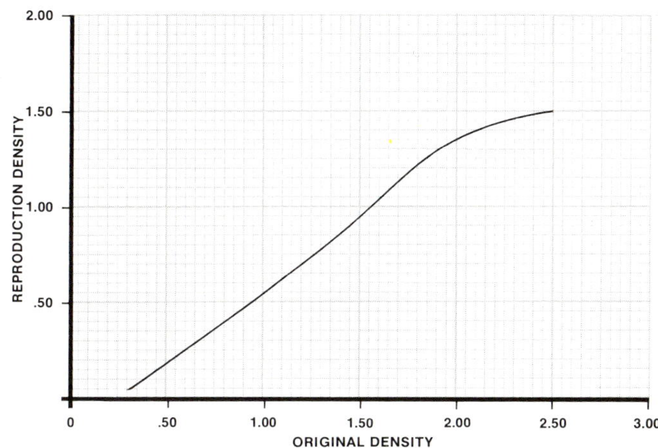

Figure 9.28. An "opened-up" gradation curve similar to the one applied to reproduction B in Figure 9.27

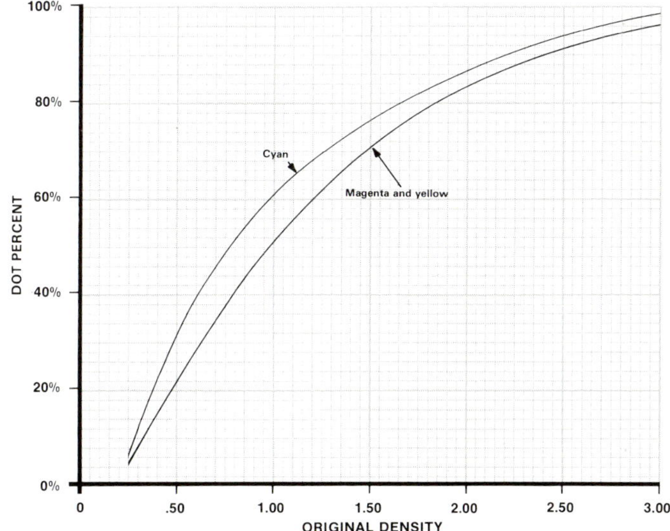

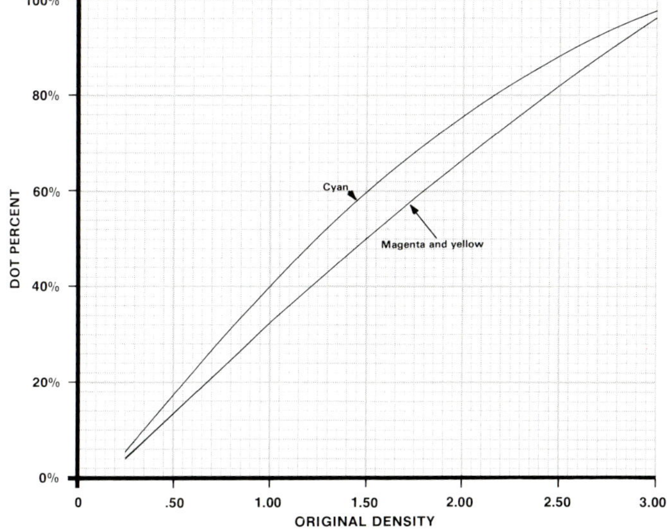

Figure 9.29. Two curves consisting of higher and lower contrast in the quarter-tone through the middle-tone areas

more of the five aim points. However, it should be kept in mind that when two aim points are brought closer together, the details between these two aim points of the copy will be enhanced in the reproduction, and also the contrast of that particular tonal area will be higher than the other areas. Conversely, when the two aim points are moved apart, there will be a loss of detail and the contrast will be decreased within the aim points (see Figure 9.29). For example, if the quarter-tone and middle-tone aim points are .50 and 1.20 respectively, moving the middle-tone towards the quarter-tone from 1.20 to 1.00 will increase contrast in the areas between the quarter-tone and middle-tone. On the other hand, when the middle-tone is moved from 1.20 to 1.40, the contrast will be reduced in the same tonal areas.

When tones in any of the aim points are emphasized, there are some effects on the adjacent aim points. This is because the gradation curve is essentially a bell-shaped curve. For example, in a dark original, when the normal highlight dot values are moved towards an aim point of higher density, the effect will be most apparent on the quarter-tone and to some extent on the middle-tone. When a light gradation is applied to a middle-tone, it also affects the three-quarter-tone aim point as well. The effects of a typical set of tone reproduction controls on the aim points are illustrated with Figure 9.30.

It should be reemphasized here that when the highlight and shadow aim points are fixed but the intermediate gradations are changed, the improvement of one area of the reproduction is achieved at the expense of the other. In other words, since the reproduction of tone has to be achieved within a fixed printing range, one area of the tone can be emphasized only when the other area is de-emphasized. For example, when a dark reproduction is made from a high-key or overexposed transparency, the highlights are emphasized, but the shadows are flattened. Conversely, when a light reproduction is made from a dark copy, the shadows are emphasized, but the highlight areas are flattened. In Figure 9.31, the following two curves demonstrate these examples. In curve A,

Courtesy D. S. America

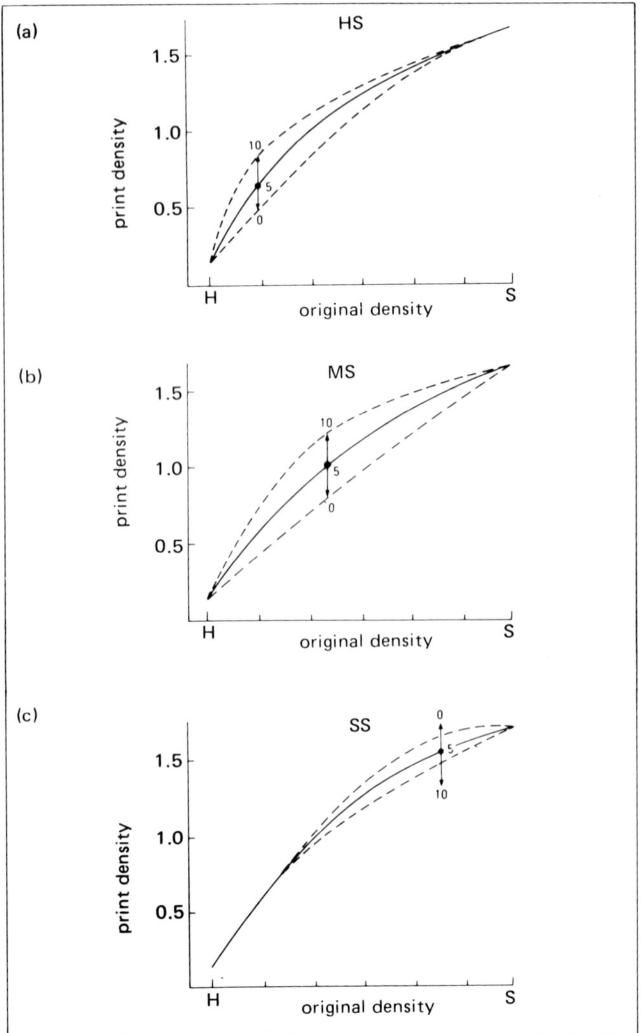

Figure 9.30. Effects of tone reproduction adjustment on the highlight, middle-tone, and shadow

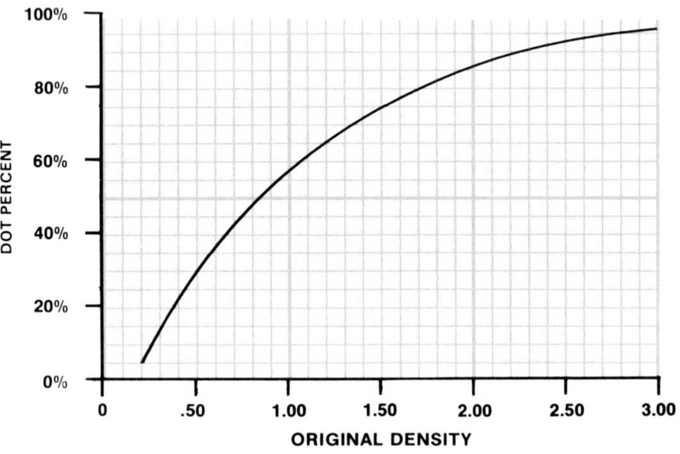

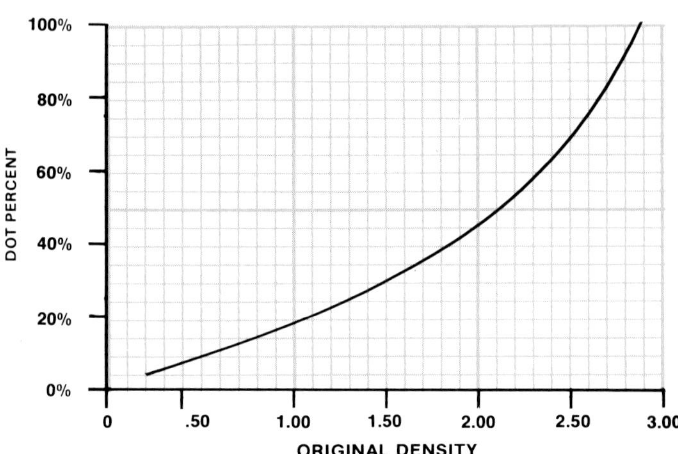

Figure 9.31. Dark and light gradation curves

the highlight is steep and contains a high degree of detail, but the shadow is flat and has minimum detail. In curve B, the shadows have a steep gradation, but the highlights contain minimum detail.

Example 5: Soft and Hard Reproduction

There are possibilities of selecting a soft reproduction from a hard original or a hard reproduction from a soft original. A typical hard original is a wedding scene: the bride in a white dress and the bridegroom in a black suit. To make a soft reproduction from this hard copy, the contrast of the highlight and shadow areas are emphasized; however, the contrast of the middle-tone areas are compressed. In this way, the transition of tones from the highlight to the middle-tone and middle-tone to shadow become gradual, depicting a soft rendering of tones. Figure 9.32 represents the related curve.

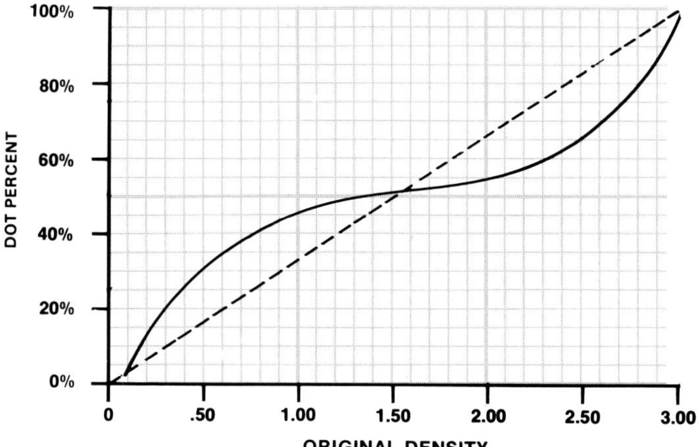

Figure 9.32. Gradation curve for a soft reproduction

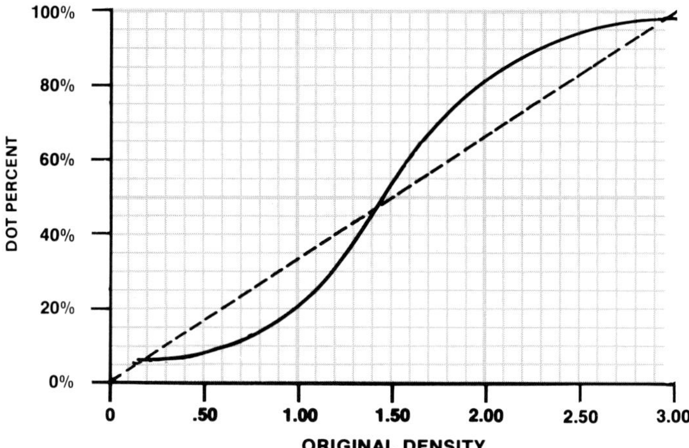

Figure 9.33. Gradation curve for a hard reproduction

In a similar way, a hard reproduction can be obtained from an unusually soft original by compressing quarter-tone and the three-quarter-tone areas; however, the middle-tone areas are emphasized. In practice, it is hardly necessary to apply hard gradation to an original because the various reproduction stages between the original and the finished product produce a hard reproduction. Figure 9.33 represents the related curve.

TWO ALTERNATIVES IN CHANGING GRADATION

From the above examples of gradation adjustment, it is apparent that a change of gradation can be accomplished by either of the two approaches:

1. In the first approach, different density values are selected for each aim point; however, the dot values for each aim point remain fixed. For example, the following dot values may be fixed for different aim points (the three numbers designate values for cyan, magenta and yellow): highlight: 5-4-4, quarter-tone: 21-17-17, middle-tone: 60-50-50, three-quarter-tone: 78-74-74, and shadow: 98-95-95. Only the density values for each aim point are changed to affect the change in the gradation curve. When adjusting the gradation, the operator selects an aim point on the basis of the tonal characteristics of a copy and assigns the fixed dot values.

2. In the second approach, the density values for each aim point are kept fixed, but different dot values are assigned from copy to copy. For example, the following aim points may be used as standard for all types of gradation: highlight: .30, quarter-tone: .50, middle-tone: 1.20, three-quarter-tone: 1.70, and shadow: 2.50. However, the dot values assigned for each of these aim points are different depending on the gradation curve desired. The operator simply assigns choices of dot values for the fixed aim points. For example, in the DS SG-608, the density values are fixed as reference values, only the dot values for each aim point are changed to change the gradation curve. However, the density values of the intermediate aim points will also shift every time when new density values for highlight and shadow are selected.

Both options can be used effectively to adjust gradation for any type of original. It should be emphasized here that although the approaches seem different, the end results are the same for both. Assigning higher dot values for a middle-tone is the same as moving the middle-tone aim point towards a lower density. For example, increasing dot values from 60% to 75% for a middle-tone is the same as moving the middle-tone aim point with fixed dot values towards the highlight. Similarly, assigning lower dot values to a quarter-tone is the same as moving the quarter-tone aim point towards the middle-tone.

OTHER FACTORS AFFECTING GRADATION

So far the discussion on gradation has been limited to the requirements for different types of originals. There are other factors; for example, the quality of the ink and paper also affect gradation. Figures 9.34 and 9.35 show the effects of the quality of paper on gradation. For a particular type of paper, the gradation is evaluated by measuring the reflection densities of the printed inks. For example, coated papers are of higher quality than newsprint, and a maximum density of up to 2.0 can be obtained in the shadow areas with the four solid colors. A middle-tone with a 50% dot size can be printed with an approximate density of 1.10 with the four colors.

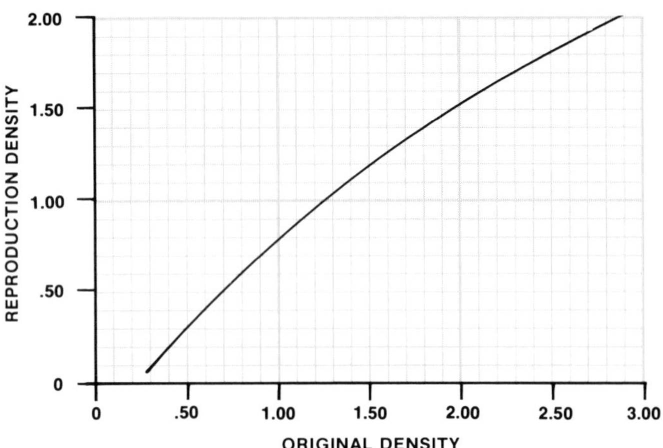

Figure 9.34. An optimum gradation curve for printing on a coated paper

On the other hand, when a newsprint is printed, the maximum density that can be obtained in the shadow area will be far less than when printed on the coated paper. The 50% dot size printed in four colors on the newsprint will also be lower

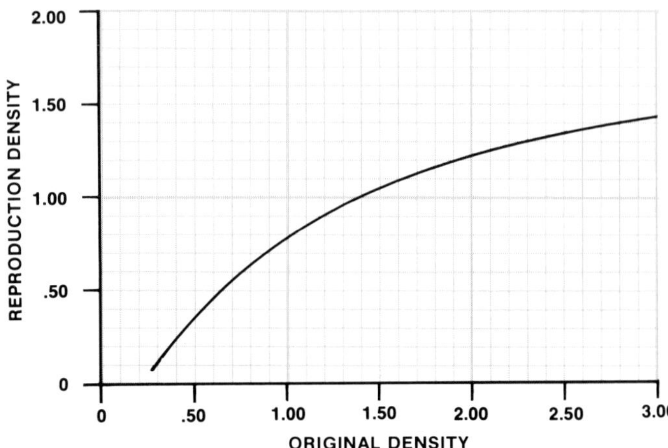

Figure 9.35. An optimum gradation curve for printing on a newsprint

in density. If both gradation curves of coated paper and newsprint are plotted as shown in Figure 9.35, the difference is immediately noticeable. The printing of the shadow areas on the newsprint is lighter than the same areas on the coated paper. However, the printing density of the middle-tone is darker for the newsprint in relation to the highlight and shadow end of the print. The densities at either highlight and shadow ends cannot be changed; however, the dark middle-tone can be made lighter by using a lighter gradation for the middle-tone. This can be achieved by assigning lower dot values for the middle-tone aim point or moving the middle-tone aim point to a higher density value.

STEPS TO ADJUST GRADATION IN A SCANNER

Scanner Calibration

The prerequisite for consistent and predictable gradation is the accuracy in the initial calibration of the scanner. A detailed discussion on basic scanner calibration is presented in the chapter "Basic Calibration." The quality of the separations, as well as the consistency and predictability of the output from the scanner will depend on the accuracy of the initial calibration. Because of the electrical and other external or internal factors, drifts in the calibration may occur from time to time. It is a good practice to check and adjust the basic calibration as often as possible.

MANUAL AND PRESET GRADATIONS

Depending on the model and brand of scanner, the adjustment for gradation may be entirely manual or it may be simply the selection of a preprogrammed curve. However, in all scanners, the operator first adjusts a normal gradation curve during the initial set up and assigns appropriate dot values to the selected aim points. In the scanners with a manual gradation adjustment, the operator uses an external or an internal gray scale for selecting the aim points and then assigns dot values for each aim point. For scanners which have provisions for preset or fixed gradations, the operator creates several gradation curves and stores them in the computer's memory.

Manual Gradation Adjustment

During the manual adjustment of gradations, the following points need to be considered to achieve accuracy in the results:

1. The standard or basic set up for normal gradation is critical. The selection of proper aim points and the dot values assigned for each aim point needs to be derived from the

existing shop condition. Table 10 shows the suggested normal aim points for transmissive and reflective originals. The suggested dot values for the above aim points are presented in Table 11.

TABLE 10

Aim Points	Transmissive Copy	Reflective Copy
Highlight	.30	.10
Quarter-tone	.45	.35
Middle-tone	1.20	0.95
Three-quarter-tone	1.70	1.60
Shadow	No Light	No Light

TABLE 11

Aim Points	Transmissive Copy				Reflective Copy			
	C	M	Y	K	C	M	Y	K
Highlight	5	4	4	0	5	4	4	0
Quarter-tone	21	18	18	0	21	18	18	0
Middle-tone	60	50	50	17	60	45	50	17
Three-quarter-tone	78	73	73	44	78	73	73	44
Shadow	98	95	95	85	98	95	95	85

The above values should be used as starting values only. The final values will depend on the results obtained in the shop with specific printing conditions. In some scanners, it is required that a basic set up is performed before deviations are made for different types of originals.

2. Proper highlight and shadow aim points should be determined by critical evaluation of the copy, both on and off the scanner.

3. If the shadow areas do not have enough density, more density should be added using basic calibration for black or shadow adjustment.

4. The gradation must be set prior to other specific adjustments, such as under color removal, under color addition, color cast removal, color correction, etc.

5. Highlight tone values for the black separation can be selected at any point of the three color gradation curve. For example, after the gradations for cyan, magenta, and yellow are adjusted, a spot of the gray scale is positioned which shows a 30% value for cyan; 1% dot for black may be assigned at this point.

Preset Gradation

In most scanners, selecting and recalling a preset gradation curve consists of the selection of proper highlight and shadow aim points and recalling any of the previously stored curves. It must be emphasized here that the stored curves are the deviations from a standard gradation curve which was initially set by the operator. As such, selection of the curve aim points and tone values for the standard curve are extremely critical. If the standard gradation curve is wrong, other preset gradations will also be wrong.

The selection of a gradation curve for a specific original to optimize reproduction calls for the operator to make judgments. The following are some of the guidelines and hints which can be used for the proper selection of a gradation curve:

1. Evaluation of the copy for tonal characteristics is the first and most important step. These questions may be asked: Does the copy need special tonal emphasis? If so, what tonal area? Can the copy be classified as high-key, low-key, or normal? Or should any of the tonal area(s) need to be opened up?

2. It will be helpful if the above decisions are made with an understanding that although the scanner provides the flexibility of gradation adjustment for each aim point individually, however, the gradation curve is essentially a bell-shaped curve. Emphasizing or de-emphasizing tone values for a certain aim point will also emphasize or de-emphasize the neighboring aim points to a certain extent. For example, lightening a middle-tone by about 10% will also lighten the quarter-tone and three-quarter-tone to some extent. When a density of .60 is selected for the highlight of a very dark copy, the quarter-tone and some middle-tone will be automatically lightened. There is no need to make drastic changes in those two areas.

3. Most of the originals which are received for reproduction can be successfully reproduced with only half a dozen or less programmed gradations. There is no need to look for one in forty! A few curves can be selectively and successfully standardized for day to day operation. However, still there will be a need for that special gradation curve for an unusual original.

4. Selection of the proper highlight and shadow aim points is important. If a catchlight or specular highlight is selected as a normal highlight, it will make a dark reproduction.

5. Selection of appropriate tone values for the middle-tone is most critical for successful gradation adjustment and will depend, in addition to the characteristics of a particular original, on pressroom variables.

6. Last, but not the least — everything should be standardized and kept as simple as possible. Too much use of the controls is the source of 90% of all the troubles in the operation of a scanner! There must be a reason for whatever controls the operator uses!

GRADATION ADJUSTMENT IN DIFFERENT TYPES OF SCANNER

Crosfield Magnascan 645

The controls for tone reproduction in this all digital scanner include three pushbutton controls: highlight (HL), middle-tone (MT), and shadow (SH). This is a retouching feature. The ENTER WHITE and ENTER BLACK functions must be set to enter copy highlight and shadow before this feature can be made effective. Tone adjustments in this scanner use the ENTER WHITE and ENTER BLACK as the pivot points. The change of tone values does not affect these points. Any of the three HL, MT, and SH buttons can be selected by depressing the appropriate pushbutton, and the tone values can be chosen for each of these points. However, simultaneous adjustments of all three points can be made effective by pressing the TONE button first.

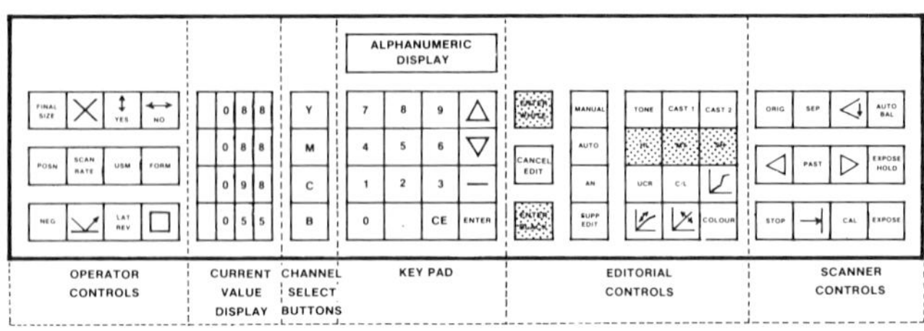

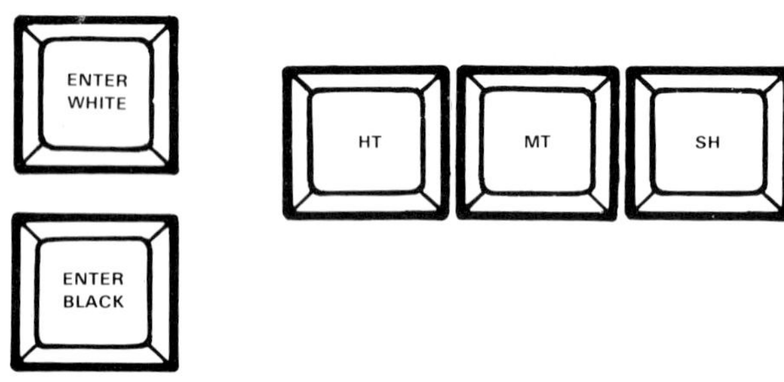

Figure 9.36. Magnascan 645 panel showing the ENTER WHITE, ENTER BLACK, and gradation control pushbuttons — HT, MT, and SH

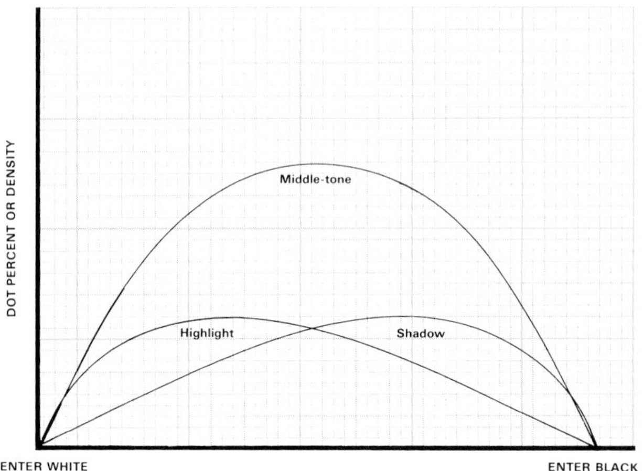

Figure 9.37. Curves showing the pivot points and the effect of change for one index number in gradation in the Magnascan 645

Changes in tonal values can be made by increasing or decreasing the index numbers as displayed in the alphanumeric display panel. The change of 1 index number changes 1% of dot in the highlight and shadow, but 2% in the middle-tone.

With the above gradation controls, any type of tone curve can be selected for a copy. However, if an unnatural curve is selected, the scanner computer will alter the entry to give the maximum permissible index number for the change sought, and will bleep three times.

A changed gradation curve can be stored as specific customer values and recalled later. Figure 9.38 shows the operating sequence of gradation adjustment.

Courtesy Crosfield Electronics

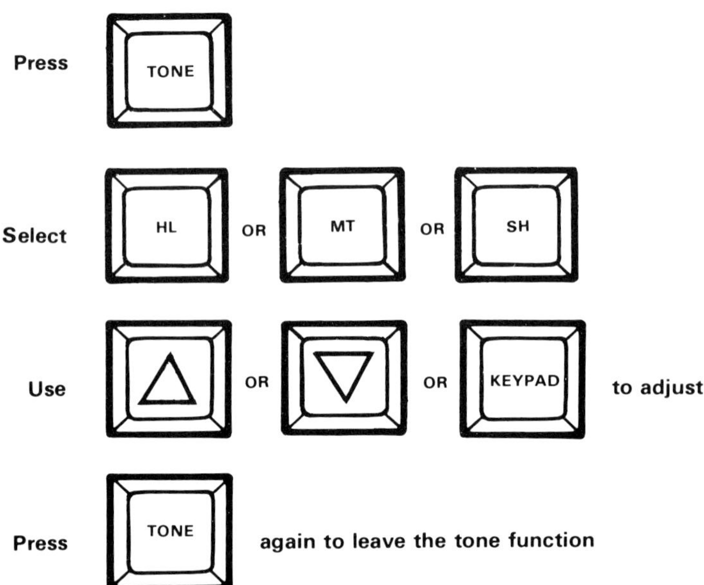

Figure 9.38. Operating sequence of gradation adjustment in the Magnascan 645

Programs are available for both catchlight drop out and highlight/shadow limit for the Magnascan 645. Once the breakpoint is selected on the tone curve, catchlight will be effective on all dot percentages below this point. As shown in Figure 9.39, there are five levels of slope: 0 = no slope; 1, 2, 3, and 4 = increasing levels of the slope. For example, selecting slope 4 will cause all the halftone dots to be eliminated below the break point.

Upper and lower limits can be set using LIMIT and the KEYPAD to set dot percentage for highlight and shadow. Applying LIMIT will prevent any dot percentage to reproduce either above the upper limit or below the lower limit. Individual limits can also be set in one or more color channels. Alternately common limits can be set for all three channels. Black limits are set separately (see Figure 9.40).

Courtesy Crosfield Electronics

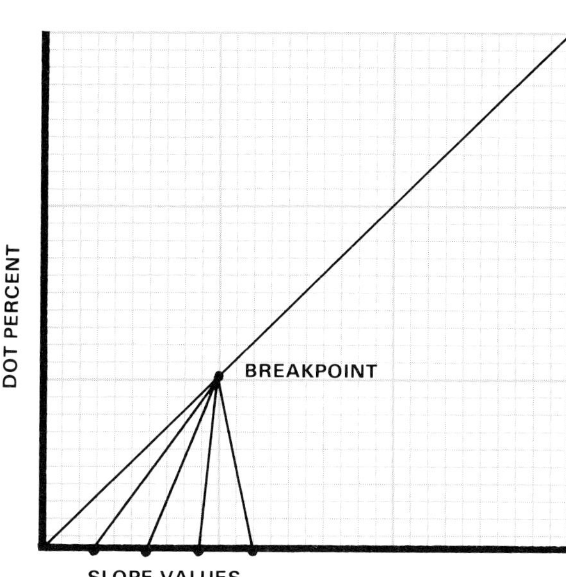

Figure 9.39. Different catchlight slope curves obtainable in the Magnascan 645

Courtesy Crosfield Electronics

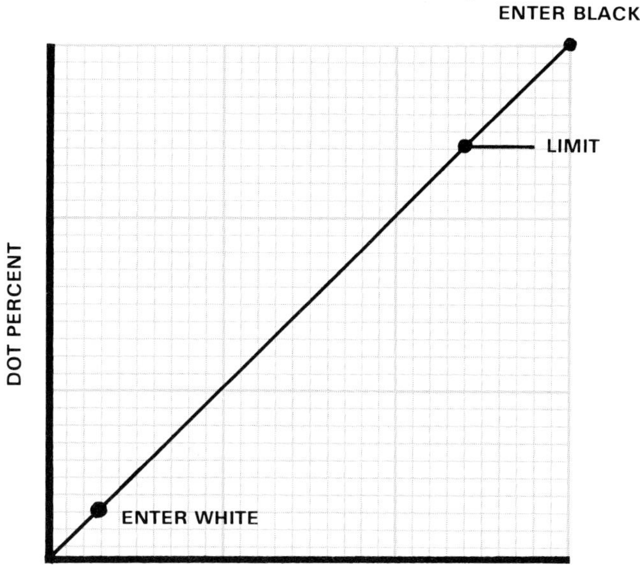

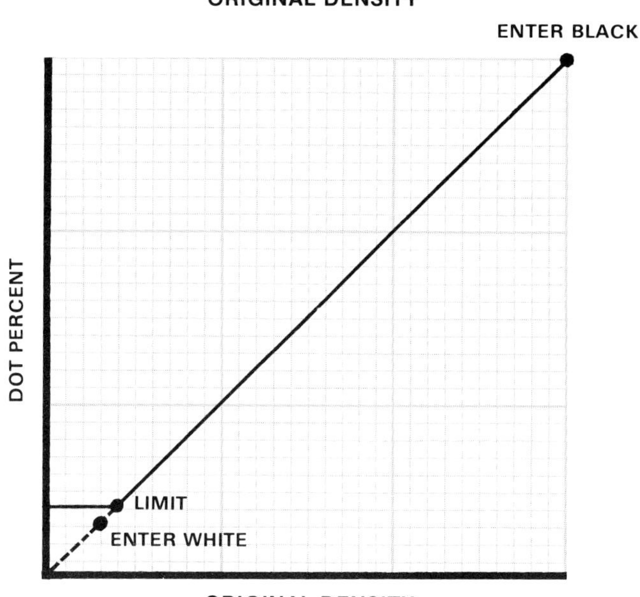

Figure 9.40. Effect of LIMIT controls in the Magnascan 645

Dainippon Screen SG-608

Among the several gradation controls in this scanner, one set of controls consists of two knobs — a highlight density set knob and a shadow density set knob. The highlight and shadow density for a particular copy can be set with these knobs. The highlight density is continuously variable from 0 to 1.0, and the shadow density can be varied in 11 graduated steps ranging from 1.3 to 3.3 to match the original highlight and shadow density points. There is also a set of HIGHLIGHT and SHADOW DOT PERCENT set knobs to set the highlight and shadow dot percent for the cyan, magenta, yellow, and black separations. With the four pairs of highlight dual-function knobs, the outer knobs are used for the coarse and the inner knobs are used for fine adjustment. The main gradation control consists of three sets of knobs to adjust the highlight, middle-tone and shadow contrasts for the cyan, magenta, yellow and black. With a set of two Reference switches, the fixed density values for the quarter-tone, middle-tone and three-quarter-tone are activated, and with the gradation knobs, dot values are assigned to these aim points while monitoring on the display panel.

The SG-608 is factory calibrated for a fixed standard gradation curve. This gradation curve is obtained when the cyan, magenta, and yellow controls are set at position 5 (as shown in Figure 9.41) and the black gradation control is set to 0.

In addition, a black gradation knob is provided to set the black tone reproduction curve. This control is a part of the under color removal and gray component replacement functions. By turning the black gradation control from 0 to 10, the black gradation changes from linear to full black. In conjunction with the ICR switch (GCR of DS), turning the black gradation knob causes the black separation curve to change from "linear" to "full" and the under colors of the cyan, magenta, and yellow are removed from 0% to 100% in step wise fashion.

For the DS SG-608, an optional function generator can be added to the main scanner unit. This is a memory unit and the main function of this unit is to store several gradation curves, color correction data, or other specific customer data in the memory which can be recalled and applied at a later time. With this unit, a set of 4 different preprogrammed gradation curves can be stored. With an auto/manual changeover switch, any of the gradation data can be changed if needed. Once the highlight and shadow density values for any original are selected, any of the stored curves can be recalled.

Both the Catchlight and Highlight Limit functions are inte-

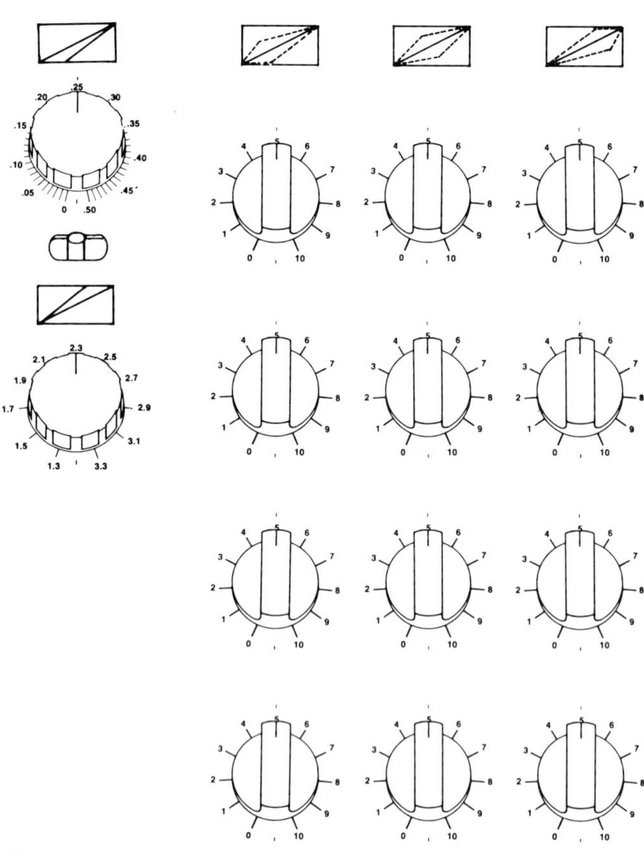

Figure 9.41. HIGHLIGHT DENSITY set knob, SHADOW DENSITY set knob, and the Gradation control panel in the DS SG-608

grated into a set of four controls, one each for the cyan, magenta, yellow, and black (see Figure 9.19). Labeled as HCC control (Highlight Contrast Control), each knob is a dual function control. The outer section of the knob sets the break point or the starting point from which the control will be effective. A clockwise turn of the inner knob enhances the highlight tone (Highlight Boost Up — HBU) and a counter-clockwise turn flattens the highlight tone (Highlight Limit — HLM). The effects of these controls are shown with Figure 9.20.

Hell 399ER

In this scanner, the gradation adjustment consists of the following three groups of controls:

1) In the scale computer panel, two separate pushbuttons are provided to enter the highlight and shadow tone values for each of the cyan, magenta, and yellow channels. For example, the following values are entered for highlight: C: 5%, M and Y: 4%, and K: -12%; and the following values are entered for shadow: C: 98%, M and Y: 95%, and K: 85%.

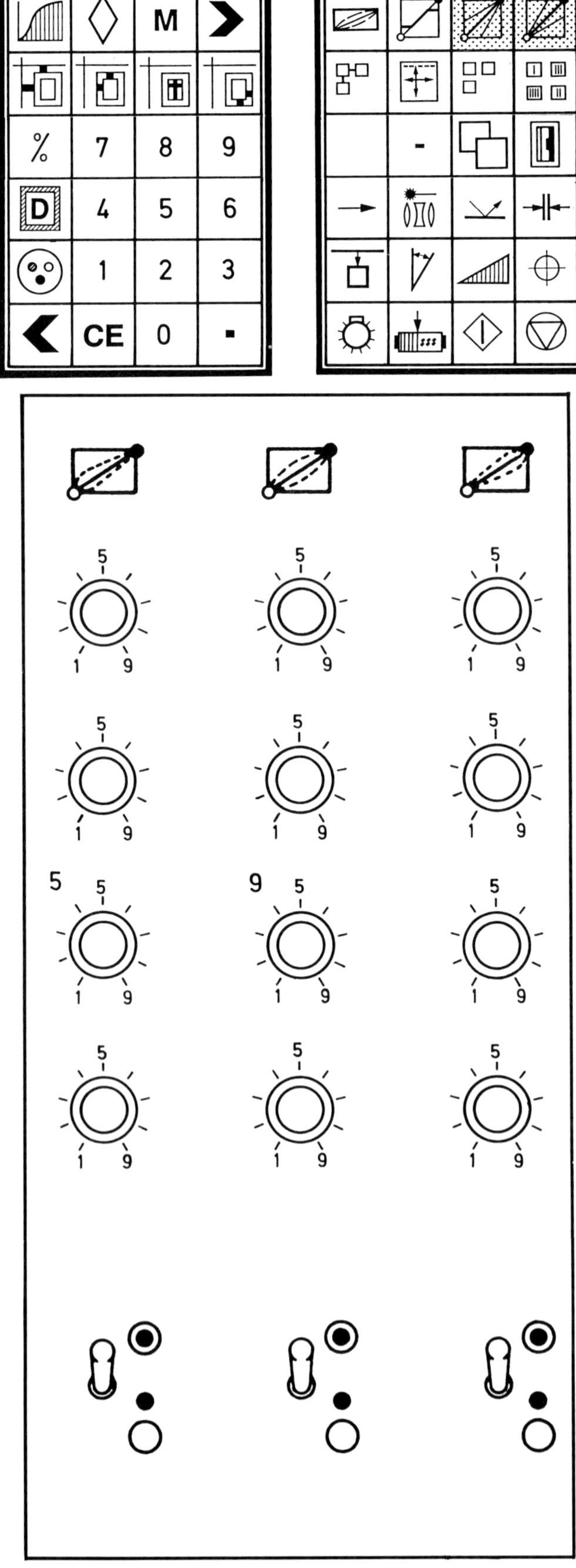

Figure 9.42. SCALE COMPUTER and GRADATION panel in the Hell 399ER. The shaded areas of the scale computer panel shows the buttons to enter highlight and shadow tone values.

2) Once the highlight and shadow tone values are selected for a particular copy, one of the 20 or more preprogrammed gradation curves is recalled from the floppy disk located in the electronics cabinet. A list of these fixed gradation curves was presented in Table 6, page 153. In addition to these fixed gradation curves, several custom curves can be developed by the operator and stored.

3) An elaborate panel of three groups of gradation controls for highlight, middle-tone and shadow are provided for each of the cyan, magenta, yellow, and black colors. After any one of the preprogrammed gradations is recalled, it can be individually changed or fine tuned using these manual controls. Three toggle switches are provided at the bottom of this gradation panel to activate or deactivate the effect of the manual gradation controls.

In addition to the above controls, a panel of four catchlight controls is provided for each of the cyan, magenta, yellow and black channels to adjust the gradation for catchlights. The Catchlight panel of the Hell 399ER is explained with Figure 9.18 on page 151.

Royal Zenith 200-S

The gradation control in this scanner consists of adjustments of several parameters with specially designated keys. First the range control is selected and the shadow for the specific original is assigned certain dot values for the three colors, e.g. 98%, 95%, 95% for cyan, magenta, and yellow respectively. The range control provides the correct setting of gradation for any original including the underexposed or overexposed. A middle-tone control is also provided to make special adjustments to suit an individual transparency. In addition to the above controls, a highlight gradation control (HGR) is provided to enhance the detail of any highlight area of the original. All the above controls have a control setting range of -128 to +127. Any attempt to key a value outside the control range will result in key error on the display.

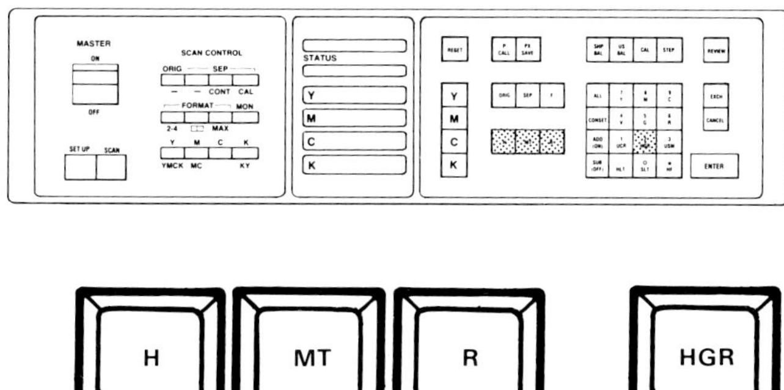

Figure 9.43. Panel of the RZ 200-S showing the position of the gradation control pushbuttons

Courtesy Itek Colour Graphics

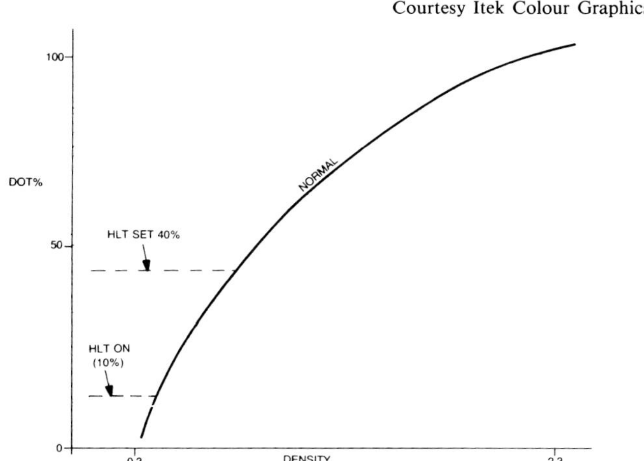

Figure 9.44. Effect of Highlight Limit control in the RZ 200-S

With a separate program, the black gradation can be adjusted independently using the same steps of the gray scale aim points which were used for the three colors. Once the black gradation is set in the program, the correct result will be produced automatically following the highlight and range adjustments of the three colors. During the program producing operation, the black channel is set in the same way as the color channels. The first printing tone required for the black may be monitored in the three-color highlight and entered. For a full-range black, the percentage needed for highlight and range can also be entered into the program by monitoring the gray scale steps.

Courtesy Itek Colour Graphics

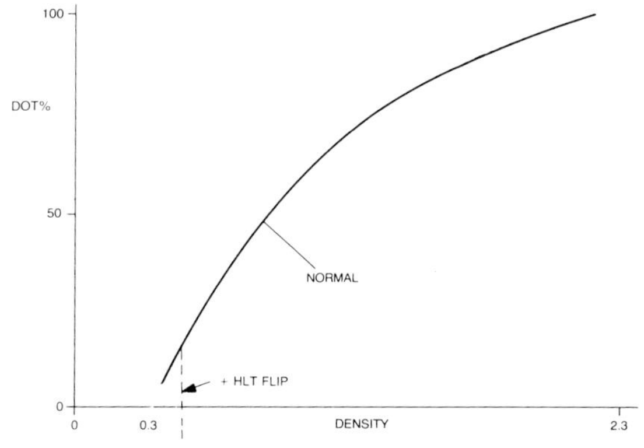

Figure 9.45. Effect of Highlight Flip control in the RZ 200-S

The highlight limit is programmable in dot percentage or density values within the range of -30% to 50% (-0.23 to 1.05 density). Optionally the limit may be set as a control setting number in the range of -128 to 127. The effect of setting a highlight limit on the gradation curve is illustrated with Figure 9.44 .

A Highlight Flip Control enables the operator to expand the difference between the first printing tone (highlight) and the next lower density tone (catchlight). The effect of this control is illustrated with Figure 9.45. The control can be selected for individual colors or for all colors at the same time.

Chapter 10
Color Correction

INADEQUACIES IN PROCESS COLOR REPRODUCTION

The problems in process color reproduction can be attributed to some of the basic inadequacies in the mechanics and materials. They are presented below in order of importance.

1. The most serious problem is the hue deficiencies of the standard process inks. The absorption and transmission characteristics of the yellow ink are nearly ideal. The magenta ink transmits red light fairly well, but is very deficient when transmitting the blue section of the spectrum. The cyan ink contains the worst hue deficiency. It absorbs a sizeable amount of blue and green lights which it should have transmitted completely. The situation is further complicated by the failure of the cyan ink to absorb the entire red section of the spectrum. The absorption and reflection characteristics of ideal and actual process inks are shown in Figure 10.1.

2. The original to be reproduced, normally has a far greater range of tones than the printing process can reproduce. As such, a tone compression is necessary in the reproduction. A compromise has to be reached as to which tonal area(s) of the original need to be compressed; however, any tone compression of the original will have some adverse effect on the reproduction.

3. The accuracy of the reproduction relies heavily on the correct overprinting of the three inks: cyan, magenta, and yellow. This requirement is hindered by the additivity failure: the total density of the colors printed is different than the added density of the individual colors.

4. The use of halftone dots in the separations introduces a proportionality failure. The small individual dots surrounded by white paper produce an integrated color which appears weaker and desaturated compared with the continuous-tone original.

5. Different brands of color transparencies like Agfachrome, Fujichrome, Kodachrome, Ektachrome, etc., use different dye materials for the emulsion. Although visually not noticeable, the spectral characteristics of each dye are different, and they behave differently in color sensitivity.

6. Because of the imperfect transmission and absorption characteristics of the separation filters, they fail to record accurately the unlimited number of mixed pigments and the intermediate colors produced by these pigments from the original. The result is a weak and desaturated color when printed.

Color correction for process color reproduction includes the correction for the above inadequacies and problems. However, problems associated with transmission characteristics of the filter, halftone technique, and the additivity and proportionality failures of the process inks are difficult to overcome, so hopefully, further research will contribute improvement in these areas. In recent years, however, significant progress has been made in the areas of color correction by correcting the proportion of the process inks to be printed in the reproduction. The discussion on color correction will be limited to the correction for the process inks.

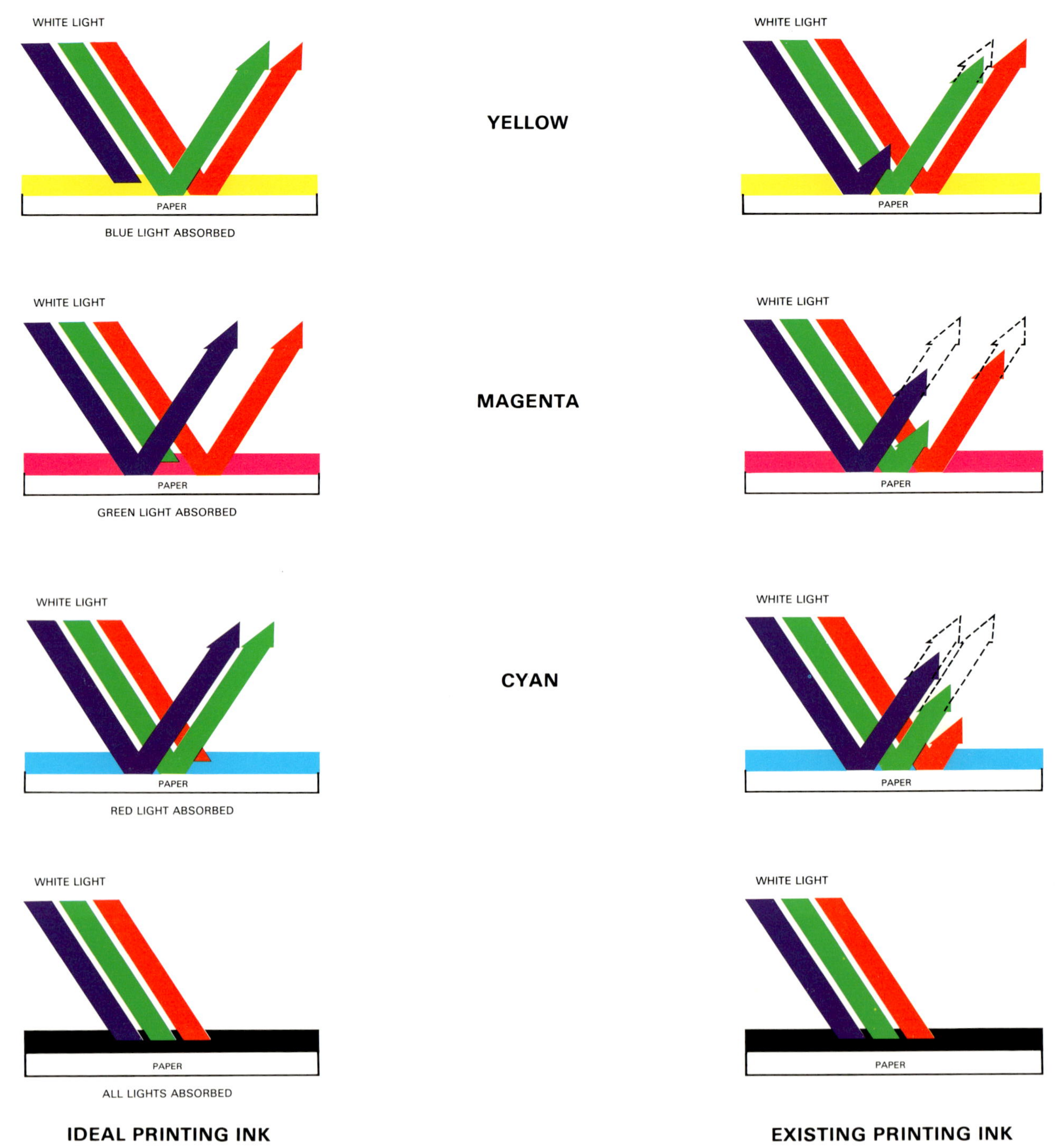

Figure 10.1. Reflection and absorption characteristics of the ideal and actual printing inks

Problems with Process Inks

The problems of the process inks are clarified in Table 12. Densities of standard and ideal process inks are shown when they are measured with a densitometer. When an ideal cyan ink is measured with red, green, and blue filters, the ink should record the highest density reading with the red filter and zero density reading with the green and blue filters. Similarly ideal magenta and yellow inks should record the highest density readings with the green and blue filters respectively and zero density readings with the other two filters. In practice, however, when the process inks are measured with individual filters, they produce different results. The values obtained from the standard process inks are shown in the table. The result indicates that in addition to the wanted densities, the inks also show a significant amount of unwanted densities with the other filters.

As seen in Table 12, the deficiency of the process inks can be thought of as being made up of perfectly pure pigments, contaminated with a small amount of each of the other two pigments, which are also pure. This concept may be expressed as follows:

TABLE 12

APPROXIMATE DENSITIES OF CONVENTIONAL AND IDEAL INKS

		Red Filter	Green Filter	Blue Filter
	Cyan	1.30	.50	.15
Conventional Inks:	Magenta	.10	1.10	.55
	Yellow	.01	.10	1.10
	Cyan	High	0	0
Ideal Inks:	Magenta	0	High	0
	Yellow	0	0	High

The cyan is a mixture of pure C + some pure M + some pure Y

The magenta is a mixture of pure M + some pure Y + some pure C

The yellow is a mixture of pure Y + some pure M + some pure C

To correct for the above imperfections for the process colors, they should be purified as follows:

Whenever cyan is printed, it is necessary to subtract some magenta and yellow.

Whenever magenta is printed, it is necessary to subtract some yellow and cyan.

Whenever yellow is printed, it is necessary to subtract some magenta and cyan.

When the above theory is considered, however, it is not possible to subtract the unwanted inks from the individual inks when each is printed alone. The unwanted inks can be subtracted only when more than one ink is printed to produce a secondary or tertiary color by the combination. For example, when magenta is printed alone, the unwanted colors cannot be subtracted. But when magenta and yellow are printed together to produce red, a lesser amount of the yellow can be printed with the result that as if the yellow contamination is subtracted from the magenta.

The concept of color correction for the process inks is further clarified in Figure 10.2. When the original is photographed through each of the color separation filters, the absorption and reflection characteristics of the colors from the original, reflected or transmitted through the color separation filters behave other than ideally. Section IA of Figure 10.2 shows an actual curve with the density produced by the pigments of the original with different filters and section IB represents a smoothed out curve for the same negative. As shown in the figure, each color is filtered through the red, green, and blue filters. The cyan should have been completely clear in the negative when filtered through red. The same applies when magenta is filtered through green and yellow through blue. On the other hand, when cyan is filtered through the green and blue filters, magenta through the red and blue filters, and yellow through the red and green filters, the three colors should have been completely dark in the negative as non-image areas. The results are shown at the bottom of IB — less saturation in the main separation color and a small amount of contamination in the other colors. As shown in part II of Figure 10.2, the arrows indicate the needed correction. When the arrow points up, the needed correction is for the white or unwanted absorption, and when it

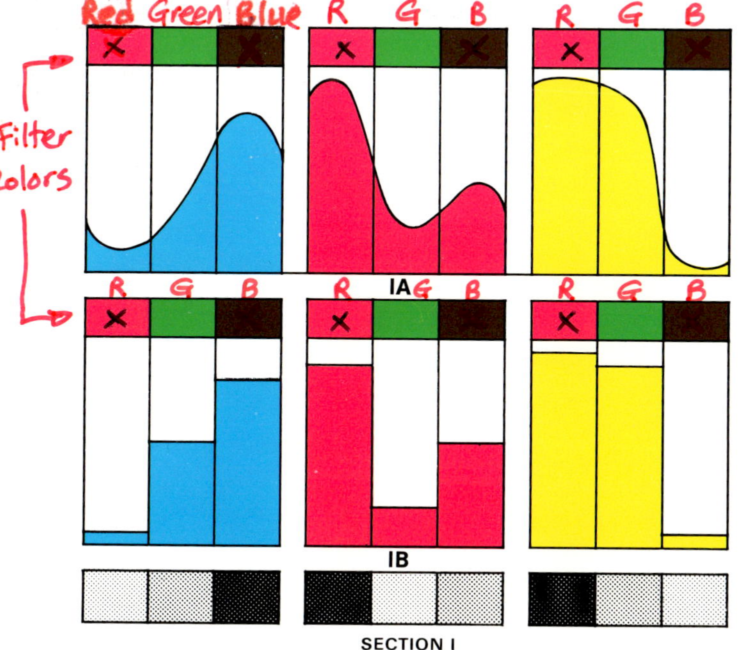

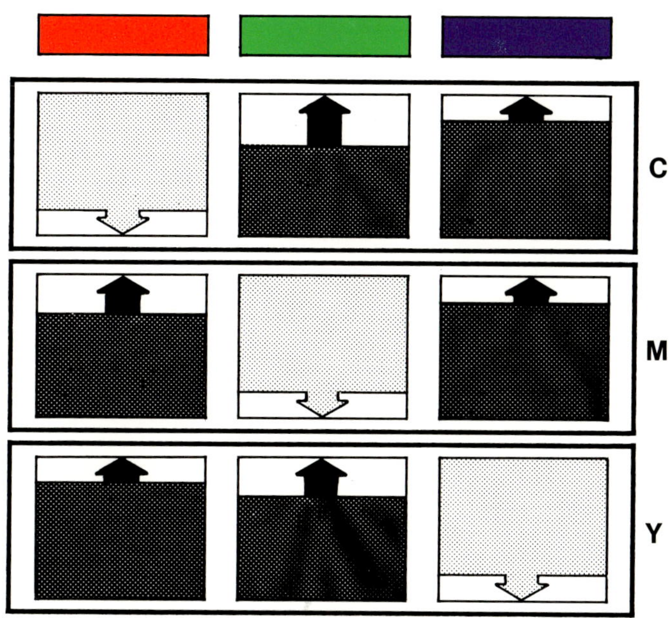

Figure 10.2. Section I of the figure shows the deficiency of the color separation filters, and Section II shows the correction needed in the process inks.

points down, the needed correction is for the black or wanted color correction. The arrows for the white colors indicate that a full density in the negative is needed for the white colors so that no colors are printed in these areas; whereas, the arrows for the black colors indicate that no density is required in the negative to print the full strength of color.

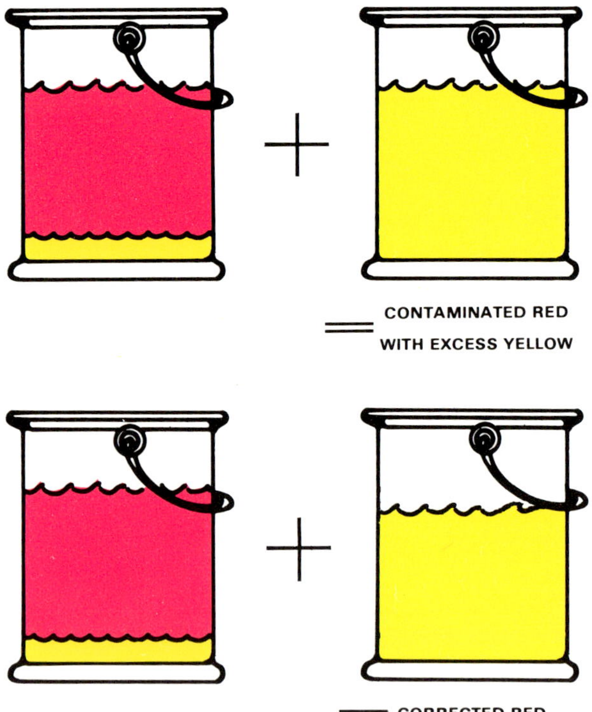

Figure 10.3. Cans of magenta and yellow inks showing the concept of contamination when these inks are mixed.

Color Correction by Masking

Traditionally, color correction for the ink deficiencies has been done by dot etching, a process of chemically reducing the size of the halftone dots manually. Manual color correction has some significant drawbacks: it is time consuming, expensive, and because each person works differently, the results may not be consistent. During the last three decades, however, the photographic masking method of color correction has been significantly improved and has gradually replaced manual color correction in the industry. It should be emphasized here that dot etching or masking does not correct the ink failures; instead it simply readjusts the proportions of their mixtures.

The masking principle is explained with a simple illustration in Figure 10.3. If someone is asked to paint a wall red with a can of magenta and a can of yellow process inks, the normal procedure would be to mix the inks in equal quantity to make the red paint. However, in practice, the yellow ink is almost perfect, but the magenta ink behaves as if it has already some yellow ink in it. As a result, equal quantities of magenta and yellow will have more yellow in the mixture and would make the mixed color look somewhat orange with the excess yellow, rather than pure red. Consequently, a reduced amount of yellow is needed to make the correct red. In principle, a proper mask will reduce yellow in the red areas to make it look normal red.

As explained earlier, when a separation is made for each color, the unwanted absorptions of the other two contaminant colors are removed from each ink by making two mask images for each color: cyan and yellow mask images for magenta, magenta and yellow mask images for cyan, and cyan and magenta mask images for yellow. Density range of the masks decide the extent of correction.

In conventional separation, the same masks are used for both wanted and unwanted colors, referred to as the black and white colors respectively. The process of correction for the black colors is opposite to that of the white color — the amount of tone values is to be increased for the black color by exposing less in a negative; whereas, the tone values are to be reduced for the white colors by increasing the exposure. In a conventional separation, when the original is exposed through the mask density and the exposure is adjusted to provide the appropriate tone values for the black colors, the white color areas are exposed proportionately more through the clear area of the mask to obtain the decreased tone values.

Figure 10.4 is an example of how a mask is used for the correction of color in a conventional separation. This illustration explains the correction of red, a secondary color produced by the mixture of magenta and yellow pigments. As indicated earlier, the magenta already contains some yellow, and the yellow ink needs to be reduced in the areas where it will be printed with magenta to make red. The correction should affect only the yellow in the red and not the other yellow areas.

First a light continuous-tone negative (approximately 1/3 density of the copy) is made from the original positive with the green filter. This is a magenta image of the original and consists of both the red and magenta areas. When this light image is placed in registration with the original during the yellow separation with the blue filter, the yellow transmitting through the clear magenta image of the mask will transmit more light compared to the same yellow transmitting through the mask density.

In a negative, more light means increased density with less image areas; less light means less density with more image areas. In other words, during the yellow separation, when the exposure is adjusted for the normal yellow (yellows which are not in red, for example, the center of the flower) through the regular density of the mask, the yellow which contains in the red will get more exposure because it is transmitting through the clear area of the magenta image on the mask (the

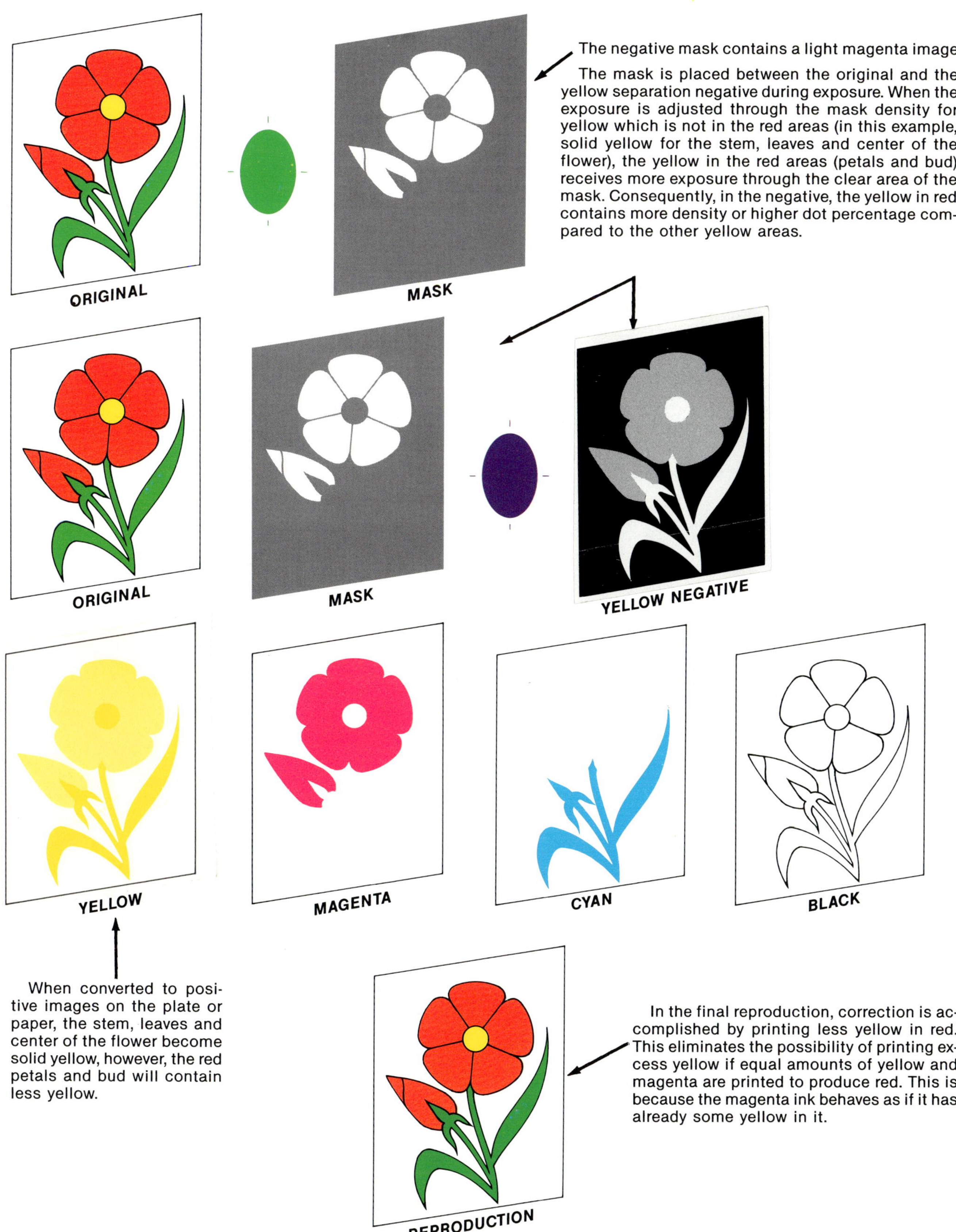

Figure 10.4. Principles of photographic mask. In this example, a mask made with green filter corrects the yellow separation for red by reducing the yellow in the red areas only

petals of the flower, in the example). As a result, there will be reduced dot values in the yellow of the red compared to the other yellows. The reduced dot values are proportional to the unwanted densities of red, produced by yellow contaminants in magenta. This is the reason why a green filter mask is used for correcting the yellow separation in the red colors. This reduction can be increased or decreased by controlling the density of the mask. With a denser mask, longer exposure will be needed for adjustment of the yellow which does not belong in red; however, longer exposure means more density through the clear magenta image, and less tone values in red with more correction.

Similarly, a red filter mask can be used to reduce the magenta in blue, and a blue filter mask can be used to reduce the cyan in green, etc. In fact, a combination of two filter exposures can be used in each mask to make corrections. For example, green and red filter exposures on a single mask can be used to reduce yellow in red and green; a red and blue filter exposures on a mask can be used to reduce magenta in blue and red; and a green and blue filter mask can be used to reduce cyan in blue and green.

When separate exposures are given on a single masking film with two filters, the resulting mask is called a split filter mask and is used effectively for direct and indirect separations. In the industry, the number of masks used for correcting the ink deficiencies in a set of separations varies. Normally two silver masks are used effectively for color correction in the conventional method of direct and indirect separations. A split filter mask made with red and blue filters is used for correcting cyan, magenta, and black separations and the other mask is made with a green filter for correcting the yellow separation only. A single mask consisting of three layers was also available to correct for the contaminants in all three separations. At one time this mask was very popular. It is Eastman Kodak's Tri-Mask and Agfa Gevaert's Varimask or Multimask.

Tone Compression and Unsharp Masking

In addition to color correction, a photographic mask offers some other advantages in the reproduction. Important among these are (1) the mask reduces the density range of the copy to accommodate for a narrow reproduction range of the printing process, and (2) when the mask is made unsharp and the separations are exposed through the unsharp mask, the result provides an enhancement of details in the reproduction. Both need further explanation.

Normally an original will have far greater density range than the reproduction range of a printing press. But when a mask is held in registration with the original for making a separation, the combined density range becomes lower than the range of the original and helps the reproduction process. In Figure 10.5, the original has a highlight density of .30, and a shadow density of 2.50, resulting in a copy range of 2.20. The mask has a highlight density of 1.20, and a shadow density of .40, resulting in a range of .80. When the original and the mask are combined for exposure, the resulting combined highlight density is 1.50 (.30 + 1.20), the combined shadow density is 2.90 (2.50 + .40), and the resulting range is 1.40 (2.90-1.50).

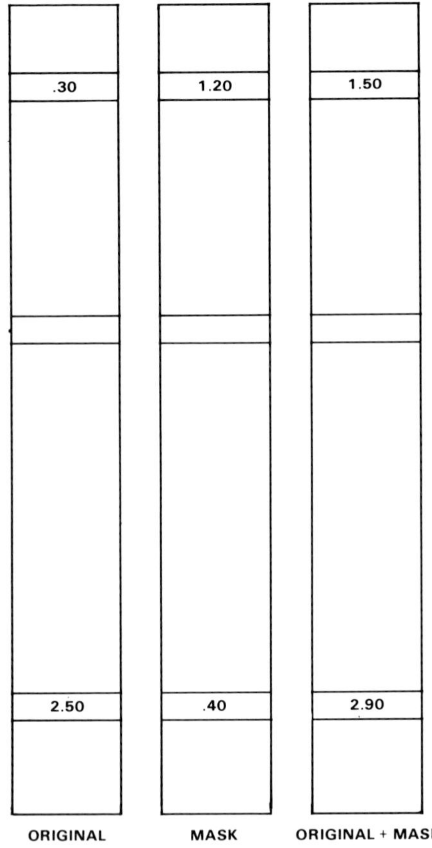

Figure 10.5. When a mask is added to the copy, the density range of the original is reduced.

In the conventional separation, the mask is made unsharp by exposing the mask through the base of the masking film or the original, or by placing a sheet of frosted acetate between the original and the masking film during exposure. All masking films have clear bases so that they can be exposed from the emulsion or through the base sides. The unsharpness of the mask results from the slight spread of light from the original onto the masking emulsion during exposure. When the separation negatives are made from the original using the unsharp masks, the edges of the images between light and dark areas are exaggerated and appear sharper than the original. A comprehensive discussion of unsharp mask is presented in the chapter "Unsharp Masking."

Mask Range and Mask Number

In the conventional color separation, mask range is responsible for the extent or intensity of color correction, and the mask number affects the tone reproduction. The extent of mask range is the extent of the density difference (range) between the highlight and shadow points of the mask. The higher this difference, the more correction will result. On the other hand, mask number is calculated from the position of the middle-tone aim point of the mask and will therefore influence the tonal curve of the separation. At first, three aim points, which are representatives of average copy for highlight, middle-tone, and shadow are selected from a gray scale. The scale is placed beside the original, a mask is made, and the mask range and mask number are calculated from the density values obtained from these aim points in the mask.

Mask range is calculated by subtracting the density values of the shadow from the highlight. The mask number is calculated by first subtracting the density values of the middle-tone from the highlight, then the shadow from the middle-tone, and finally, subtracting the two resulting values. For example, if the highlight, middle-tone, and shadow aim point densities of a negative mask are 1.20, .80, and .40 respectively, the mask number will be 0 (1.20-.80 = .40; .80-.40 = .40; and .40- .40 = 0). The normal mask range needed for average color correction is about one-third of the copy range, approximately .90 for a transparency and about .60 for a reflection copy. The mask number will vary from 0 to .20, depending on the printing condition and tone reproduction desired.

In both direct and indirect separations, a proper mask should allow the production of screened separations with suitable dot sizes in the highlight, middle-tone, and shadow areas. However, to change the tone reproduction curve, a change in the middle-tone dot sizes is normally adequate. This change can be affected in two ways: (1) by changing the relationship of the highlight/middle-tone and middle-tone/shadow in the separation negatives by adjusting the exposure and development; or, (2) by working a step further back and changing the mask aim points (see Figure 10.6).

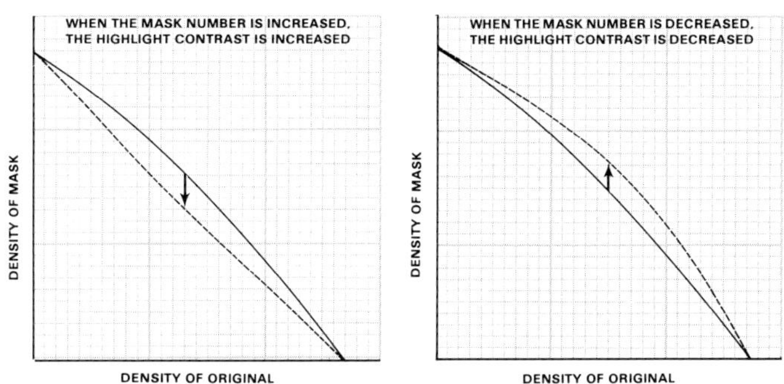

Figure 10.6. Different mask curves are obtained by changing the density of the mask aim points.

Positive and Negative Masks

A mask may be positive or negative; a negative mask is used for correcting a positive image, and a positive mask is used for correcting a negative image. In the indirect process, since color correction is done at a later stage from a continuous-tone negative, a positive mask is used. A positive overlay mask is a low contrast continuous-tone positive which is laid over a separation negative during exposure for the purpose of color correction. The positive masks are mostly made by contact or by projection. A negative mask is used in the direct-screen separation because the separation is done from a positive image. In the conventional separation, several other special types of masks are also used to improve the quality of the separations, such as highlight premask to increase highlight contrast, shadow detail mask to improve shadow detail, and under color removal mask to reduce the amount of process inks in the neutral shadow areas. Another type of mask, called a two-stage photographic mask, is also used for color correction. The density of the second stage positive mask corresponds to that of the initial negative color correction mask, thus compensating for the compression caused by the later. In other words, the second stage positive mask extends the density range of the original. In the photomechanical process of color separation, the steps for producing this mask are difficult and time consuming. However, in a scanner, this mask is easy to generate by the color computer because of electronic computation. This two-stage masking, often referred to as compensative mask, does not influence the quality of the color correction itself. Complete independence of color correction and gradation adjustment are its two main advantages.

ELECTRONIC COLOR CORRECTION

Computation in a Scanner

The concept of color correction for conventional and electronic separation is the same — the correction is necessary because of the basic inadequacies in the materials and equipment in the process color reproduction. The major function of the color computer is to compute the undesirable characteristics of the printing variables and compensate at the output stage. Once properly programmed and adjusted, the computer automatically compensates for these variables in the separations. This is accomplished by modifying the exposing signal in relation to the signals received from the original being scanned. This computation technique in a scanner involves a complex mathematical equation. The computation technique can be generally categorized into two types: Masking Equation and Neugebauer Equation. On Masking Equation, the color computer works on the same principle as the photographic masking. The position of the color correction controls in a scanner actually determines the characteristics of the color correction mask. On the other hand, the Neugebauer Equation approach is a point by point color correction approach. It assumes that if the primary, secondary and tertiary tonal values of cyan, magenta, and yellow are known for each and every possible point of an original and stored in the computer memory, then during scanning, the required dot values for each and every point of a new original can be searched, found, and generated at the output.

Masking Equations

Masking Equations are linear mathematical equations. They were derived from conventional photographic masking by John Yule in 1938. Most commercially successful scanners use this approach of color correction to determine the characteristics of the masks that are required to correct color separations for the unwanted absorptions of cyan, magenta, and yellow pigments.

The Masking Equation technique is mostly used in the analog scanners, and the position of the color correction intensity controls determines the strength of the color correction mask for both wanted and unwanted colors for each pigment to be printed. All analog signals in the computer are in electrical voltage and a continuous resistor type potentiometer is used to change the electrical signals to higher or lower values.

The Masking Equation technique uses an overall correction for the ink-paper-press conditions, instead of the point-by-point in Neugebauer Equation approach. This means that with a Masking Equation, the individual colors of the original are not corrected point by point. Rather compensation for the defects of the materials and printing conditions are made with the assumption that the subsequent color separations will be corrected for all colors within the original. The advantage of this masking technique is that the color correction is computed at the speed it takes for the electrical signal to travel from the photomultipliers to the exposing output, about 186,000 miles per second!

The problem of using the Masking Equation in color correction is that the dye of the original that is used for analyzing and calibrating the scanner is different than the inks used for printing the reproduction. As a result, pigments, which are mixed in different proportions in the reproduction to produce the secondary and tertiary colors, quite often do not match the original. To solve these problems in scanners similar to the Hell 399ER and the DS SG-608, which employ the Masking Equation technique for color correction, often two types of correction controls are provided. There is a set of basic controls for correcting the basic colors, and another set of selective controls for the correction of secondary and tertiary colors. The basic controls normally affect a wide band of colors influencing the entire separation; whereas, the selective controls affect a narrow band of colors without influencing the adjacent colors in the reproduction.

Neugebauer Equations

Hans Neugebauer first developed a set of equations in 1937 to solve the color correction problem. He considered the color halftone printed image as being made up of individual areas of white, cyan, magenta, yellow, red, green, blue, and black. These colors are formed by the subtractive principle, but they are additively fused together to form a uniform color tone. In his approach, he assumed that if the red, green, and blue values of the original are known, and if the red, green, and blue reflectance of the process colors and their overlaps are measured, it is possible to solve for cyan, magenta, and yellow dot values for each spot of the original during scanning. The Neugebauer Equation was modified several times to make it more practical.

The Neugebauer Equation is a point-by-point approach. For every point on the copy, the equivalent dots required for the cyan, magenta, and yellow are calculated by the computer from a set of standard values during scanning. A look up table, which consists of many of the possible cyan, magenta, and yellow dot values to be found in any original, is generated. The values are all digital and computed from actual printing conditions and stored in the digital computer, and later searched to find the point-by-point dot values for any original. However, the use of the Neugebauer Equation for a color computer in the early days had several restrictions. Earlier digital computers were not fast enough to compute the dot values from a look up table while the original mounted on the scanning drum was rotating at a fast speed. In addition, a look up table contains a large number of data and new look up tables had to be generated each time for any change in the printing conditions. However, recently the approach has been successfully adopted in the scanners with the advent of faster digital computers, newer and efficient light sensing devices, and modified application of the equation. In some of the latest digital scanners, a set of data for the characteristics of the printing process is taken, a solution is made, and a look up table is generated with limited data and stored in the computer's memory. These presolved "coarse" data are available as a software package with the scanner and stored in the form of red, green, and blue filter signals together with their cyan, magenta, yellow, and black printing dot values as computed by the color correction software program. When a new job is set up, the program is recalled and new values are entered for the characteristics of the original and printing conditions. These "fine" values are applied to the basic "coarse" values to come up with a set of new values. These new values are the final color correction values applied to the specific original. Interpolation techniques are often used by a digital computer which estimates the approximate values from two known values when the precise values are not found in the look up table.

In this chapter, an explanation of the concepts and principles of electronic color correction in a scanner will be presented. Computation to compensate for several deficiencies in process color reproduction consists of complex mathematical equations. However, only a general presentation will be made in the following paragraphs in order to discuss the concepts of electronic color correction.

Printing Ink Density

To understand electronic color correction, it is best to relate the correction to density values of solid printing inks when they are obtained through the red, green, and blue filters in a densitometer. This concept of unwanted absorption of the printing inks by different filters was discussed earlier in this chapter. Typical values obtained for each process ink with different filters are presented in Table 13. The values that are underlined are the black or wanted colors for each filter, and the values above which lines are drawn are the white or unwanted colors in the separation. For example, with the green filter separation, magenta, red, blue, and black are the wanted or black colors, and yellow, green, and cyan are the unwanted or white colors.

A photographic mask has about one-third the density of the original. Considering this mask, the cyan contaminant in the magenta is reduced by subtracting about one-third density of the red filter from the density of the magenta and is presented in the fourth line of Table 13. These values are very close to zero for the white colors (.05 for yellow, .02 for green, and -0.01 for cyan), whereas the densities of the black colors are decreased to give an almost uniform value which is comparable to an ideal magenta ink density (1.26 for black, 1.33 for blue, 1.30 for red, and 1.29 for magenta). This method of subtracting values for the white colors can be directly compared to conventional masking. In this example, a normal conventional mask with a one-third density range would subtract the unwanted density values from the magenta separation. A better correction can be obtained by also subtracting a small portion of the blue filter density. This would be exactly the same as a split filter mask made with red and blue filters to correct the magenta separation.

In the above example of a green filter separation, the original density value of the magenta may be called the main signal, and the unwanted density values obtained with the red and blue filters for the magenta separation may be called correction signals. The results obtained by subtracting the red and blue filter densities from the green filter density may be called corrected signal. In the same way in the cyan separation, the cyan density obtained with a red filter is the main signal. Densities produced by green and blue filters may be called correction signals, and when this density value is subtracted from the cyan density, it is called a corrected signal. In the yellow separation, density values of yellow produced by the blue filter is the main signal, density values produced by red and green filters are the correction signal, and the subtracted value is the corrected signal.

COLOR SPACE

A solution of color correction to minimize the unwanted absorptions of the three printing inks is based on the theoretical concept of color space. The first color correction computer for the scanners was constructed on the basis of this theoretical approach, and since then, it has been adapted with slight modifications by most of the scanner manufacturers. Since the density values of the printing inks are applied to this theory, it is practical in solving some of the most complex aspects of color correction.

In any reproduction, the printing values are expressed as halftone dot values ranging between 0% and 100%. Instead of using the density values, first the halftone dot values are used to draw the ideal three-dimensional color space. After plotting these values along the axes of the rectangular coordinate system, the color space becomes a cube, with white located at the zero point corner at the top and the black located at the bottom. The connected line ranging from black to

(Table 13)

Filter	Magenta	Red	Yellow	Green	Cyan	Blue	Black
Red filter	0.15	0.14	0.30	1.55	1.54	1.54	1.53
Green filter	1.34	1.35	0.06	0.54	0.6	1.84	1.77
Blue filter	0.6	1.55	0.8	0.92	0.22	0.76	1.56
Green filter minus 1/3 of red filter	1.29	1.3	0.05	0.02	0.01	1.33	1.26

white represents a continuous-tone gray scale (see Figure 10.7).

For example, if the magenta ink is viewed as an ideal cube as shown in Figure 10.7, the black, blue, red, and magenta are positioned at the corners of the lower cubic plane. At the upper horizontal plane of the cube, the printing quantity for

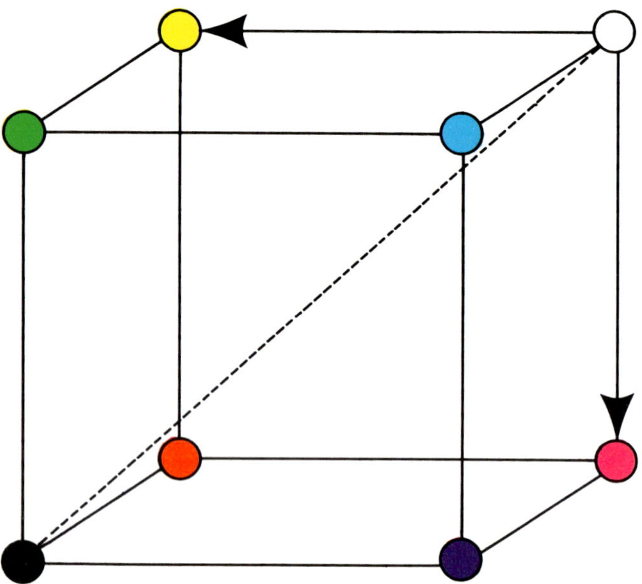

Figure 10.7. A three-dimensional color space

Figure 10.8. A distorted three-dimensional color space

magenta is zero, and the dot values for magenta at the four upper corners will also be zero. The colors at the lower plane, which should print solid magenta in magenta, red, blue, and black, can be termed as black colors for the magenta separation. On the other hand, the colors at the upper plane are white colors for magenta because magenta is printed without them. These colors are cyan, yellow, and green. The line which connected black and white points are the gray values presented by the magenta separation.

Now, if the percentages of solid inks are replaced by actual density values, the different colors in the color density space will have different positions. When magenta, red, blue, and black are measured through a green filter, ideally the density values should be identical because each of these colors contains the same amount of magenta. But they are different because of the deficiency and the unwanted absorptions coming from the cyan and yellow printing inks. Similarly, the colors at the upper plane — white, yellow, cyan, and green — when measured with the green filter ideally should be zero. However, they are also different for the same reasons and contain more densities than ideal. Now, if the density values of the colors are arranged in the coordinates, the perfect three-dimensional color space will take shape as a distorted rhomboid in the color density space as shown in the Figure 10.8. However, the black to gray diagonal line will remain unchanged.

The purpose of color correction calculation is to correct for these distortions of the color space because of uneven density, so that they resume their ideal cubic shape. The three-dimensional cube can be modified to a two-dimensional space for each of the process colors. In the two dimensional space, the white color line is at the top and through the gray line it reaches the black color line at the bottom. The objective of any color correction is to have a single value for each of the white and black colors. For example, all values should be zero for the white color line, and as such, the upper line should be positioned horizontally for the zero value. Similarly, all the black colors at the bottom line should have a uniform value which will correspond to the corrected value for the separation colors. To get the lines into the horizontal position, the correction color density must be subtracted or added so that the white and black colors will move towards the horizontal lines, closer to zero for the white colors, and closer to a corrected value for the black colors (see Figure 10.9). This principle is the same as the one explained on page 169 with Figure 10.2. When the white line is closer to 0, a full density will be produced on the negative so that no colors are printed in these areas. On the other hand, when the black colors are towards the horizontal line, full strength of the separation color will be printed.

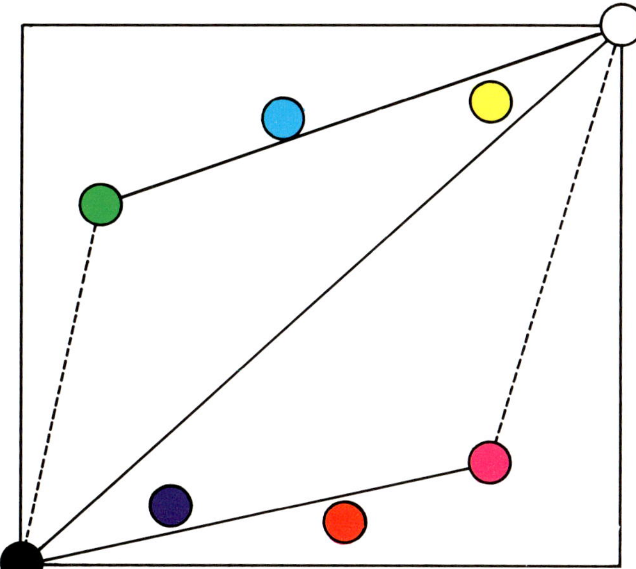

Figure 10.9. A two-dimensional color space

ELECTRONIC COLOR CORRECTION IN A SCANNER

In electronic correction, the correction color density is first subtracted from the separation color density. The resulting signal corresponds to a photographic compensative mask and does not contain any gray value. The gray values contained in the coordinate have identical values for all colors and become zero by subtraction. As explained in Figure 10.10, these values are positive for the color space above the gray line and negative for the color space below the gray line. In the color computer, they are in electrical voltage, and the gray line is separated by the negative and positive polarity. As shown in Figure 10.10, the horizontal lines above and below the gray line are white and black color lines respectively. In the color space, these lines can be moved up and down with the respective white and black color correction controls. For optimum correction, these lines should be in the horizontal position.

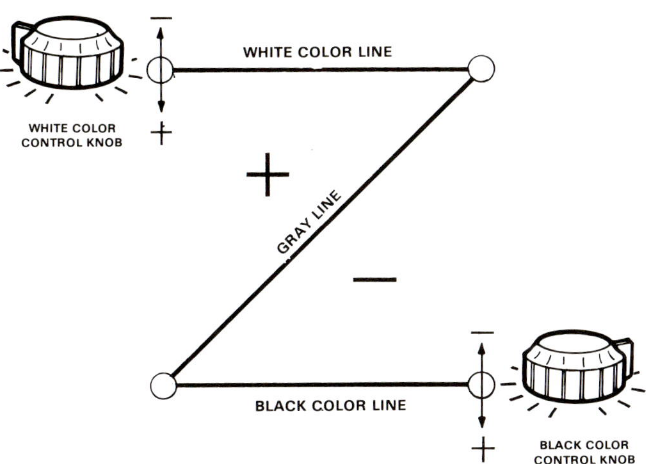

Figure 10.10. A two-dimensional color space showing values above and below the gray line; also shown are the effects of the color correction controls on white and black colors.

Electronic correction in a scanner can be better understood by studying Figures 10.11 and 10.12. The photomultipliers receive the uncorrected color separation signals from the color separation filters and, depending on the position of the color separation mode, (i.e. in cyan, magenta, or yellow), one of these three signals becomes the main signal. Figure 10.11 shows the white color correction for the magenta separation. A saturated green color patch is positioned for the scanning light, and the color separation mode is placed in the magenta separation. The correction signals for white colors are obtained by the same method as photographic compensative or multistage masking. While the magenta signal is being transmitted through the scanning head, the

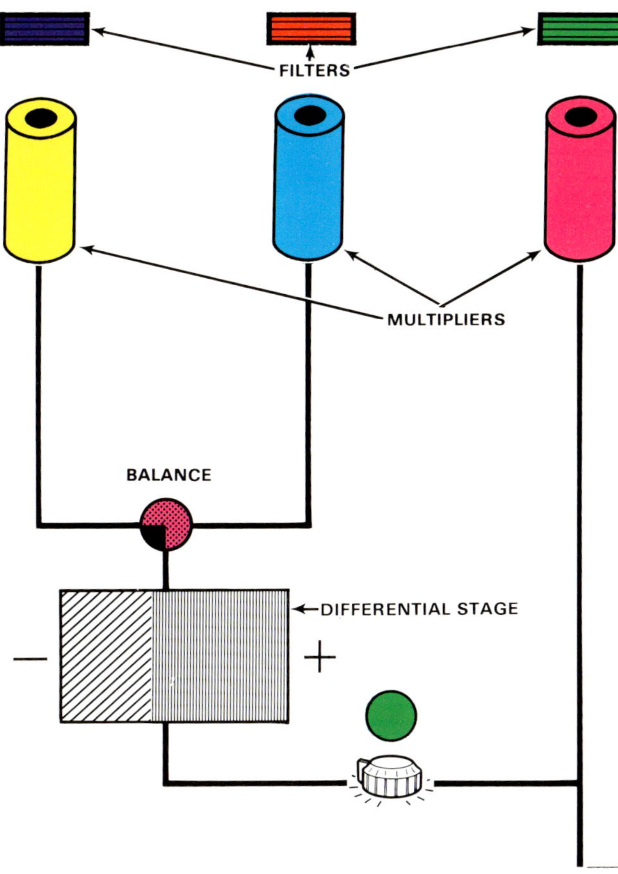

Figure 10.11. Concept of electronic color correction for the white colors in the magenta separation

exact ratio of the secondary absorption of the cyan and yellow printing inks coming through the red and blue filters is set with a balance setting as unwanted absorption for magenta. This setting determines the ratio of these two signals and can be compared to the ratio of the red and blue filter masking densities in a color correcting photographic mask. All three signals come to a position called the differential stage where the differences in the volumes of the three signals are electronically compared. In the diagram, the left section of the differential stage represents signals from the red, green, and blue filters, but on the right, the signal is only from the green filter. In other words, the left section contains the magenta, cyan, and yellow signals, and the right section contains only the magenta signal. Ideally, if there is no contamination or unwanted absorptions from the other colors, there should be no difference between the signals at the left and right sections and both should contain only the magenta signals. However, as shown in Figure 10.11, because of the unwanted absorptions in magenta, the magenta signal is larger than the combined signal. In this situation, the computer generates a positive sign indicating that the unwanted absorptions of cyan and yellow (green) in the magenta separation is excessive and need to be reduced by the white color correction control so that both sections contain equal values. Expressed in terms of color density, white color correction density is subtracted from the uncorrected separation density.

The black color correction for magenta is explained in Figure 10.12. The concept is the same as the white color correction except that a saturated magenta patch is placed in the scanning light path and the voltage generated by the computer is in negative form. Similar to the white color correction, a mixed signal is again formed via a balance control from the red and blue filter signals and added to the main signal at the differential stage. In the example of Figure 10.12, the magenta signal generated by the green filter (main signal) should be equal or lesser than the combined signals from the three filters unless there are some unwanted absorptions from the other colors. However, the magenta signal is less than the combined signals indicating that the magenta needs to be increased. In this situation, the computer generates a negative sign, indicating that the signals need to be increased by the black color correction controls. Expressed in terms of color density, more black color correction density is added. However, the magenta signal may be more than the combined signal indicating that the magenta needs to be decreased.

It should be emphasized here that the above principle of color correction is based on the theory of Masking Equation. Mostly the secondary color densities (unwanted densities) of the printing inks and their relationship determine the position of the balance controls. It will depend on the quality of the printing inks, their reflection and transmission characteristics and ratio of the corrections needed for each ink. As indicated earlier, in most scanners, the balance controls are internally set; however, these settings can be changed to suit the exacting need of a shop.

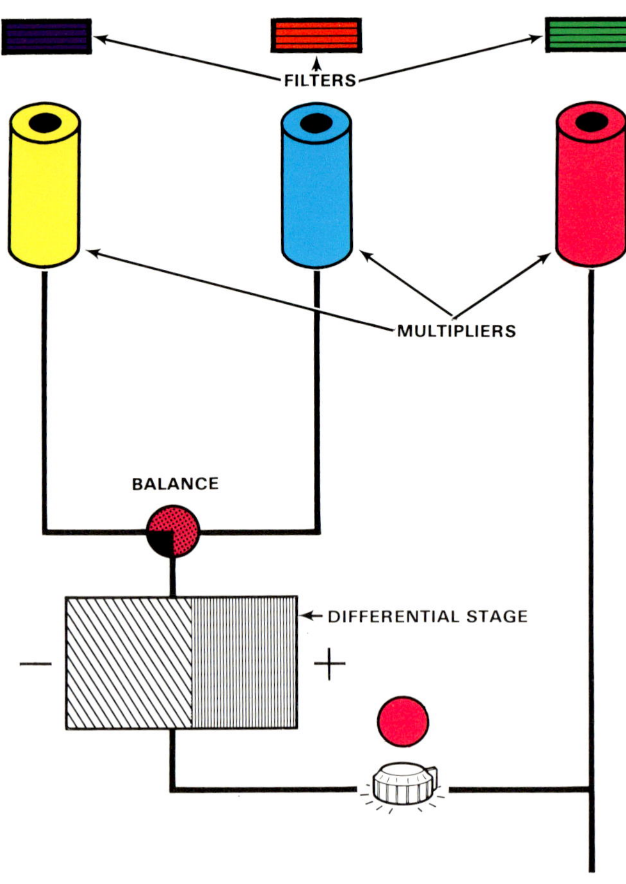

Figure 10.12. Concept of electronic color correction for the black colors in the magenta separation

Basic and Selective Color Correction

In most analog scanners, the color correction controls consist of basic and selective color correction. The basic correction involves in the correction of the major black and white colors. This correction involves the adjustment of those colors which are farthest from the gray line. For example, for cyan, red will be the basic white color and cyan will be the basic black color. Similarly, for magenta, green will be the basic white color and magenta will be the basic black color; and for yellow, blue will be the basic white color and yellow will be the basic black color.

As shown in Figure 10.13, after the basic white and black colors are corrected for cyan, the remaining two white and two black colors for cyan should be automatically corrected. However, in an actual situation these colors may need extra correction or fine tuning depending on the printing inks used in the press and the dye characteristics of the transparency.

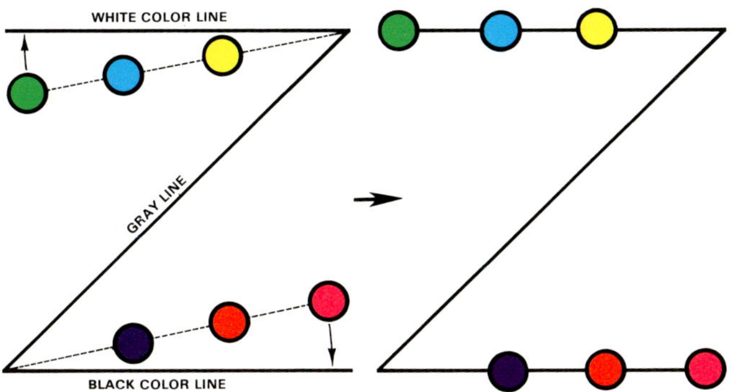

Figure 10.13. A basic correction control should correct all colors in the color space.

Figure 10.14 shows a normal, actual, and required correction for the other inks in the white and black color lines. It shows how the adjustment of the basic colors may over or undercorrect the other colors in the color space. For example, when green is corrected for white color in magenta to move to the horizontal position, yellow will be overcorrected and cyan will be undercorrected. Similarly, when magenta is corrected for black colors, red will be overcorrected and blue will be undercorrected. In this situation or where a change in certain secondary or tertiary colors is needed to improve reproduction, the selective correction is needed for the two white and two black colors to move in the horizontal lines.

The basic color correction in a scanner is carried out by adjusting the major white and black colors, the extent of which will depend on the secondary unwanted density for each color. This correction has a wide band effect and will influence the entire separation, whereas the selective correction normally has a narrow band effect and will have very little effect on the other colors. The selective color correction function can be effectively used to correct imbalances in specific secondary or tertiary colors without upsetting the color quality of the entire separation. As shown in the Figure 10.14, after the basic correction is set, the two white and two black colors may be out of balance. The selective controls are used to balance these colors individually so that they fall in their respective lines.

For normal originals reproduced with good printing inks, the basic correction is adequate. However, there is a great variety of originals and printing inks for which certain colors may require special correction. In these cases, considerable improvement can be accomplished by extending color correction with the additional selective correction adjustments. Figure 10.15 is a typical example of selective color correction panel layout in an analog scanner.

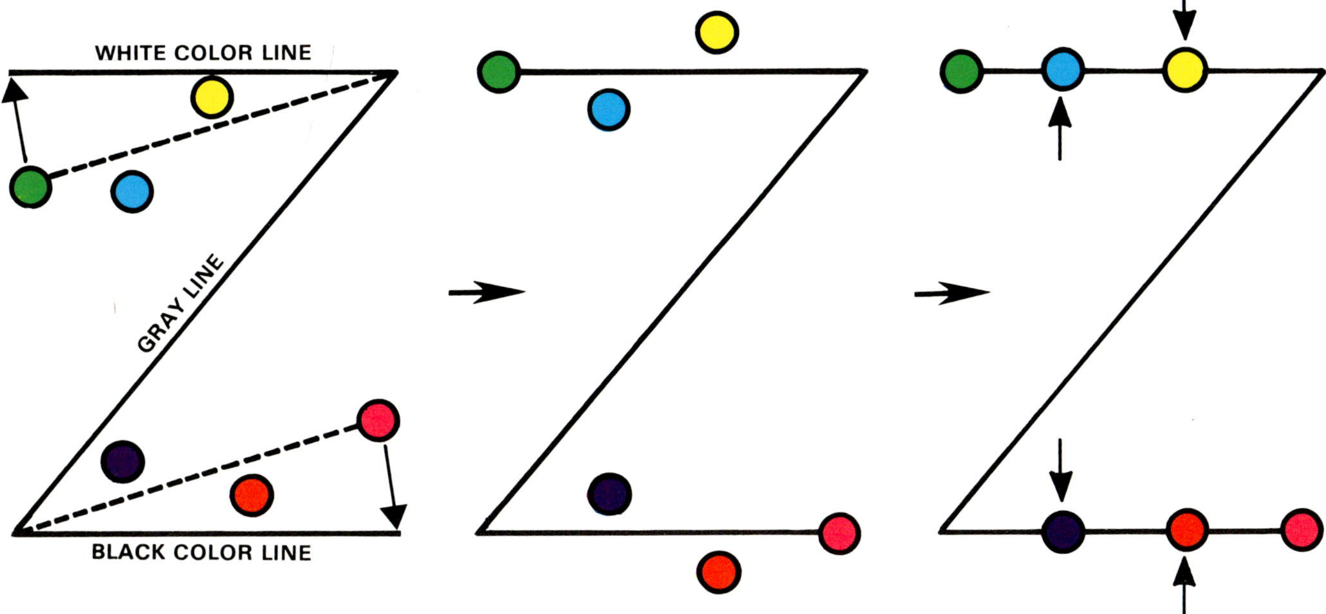

Figure 10.14. Selective correction is needed for colors other than the basic colors after the correction for the basic colors are set.

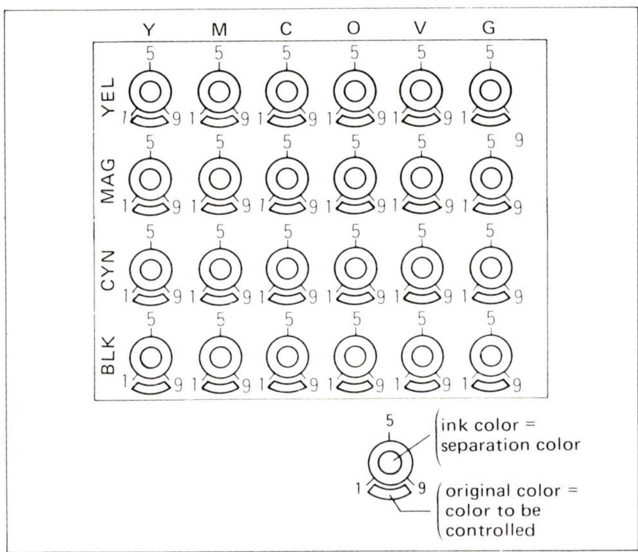

Figure 10.15. Selective Color Correction panel layout in the DS SG-608

Color Correction for the Black Separation

The computer for the black separation works in a different manner than the computer for the other three colors (see Figure 10.16). Whereas the color computer receives the signals from the photomultipliers, the black computer receives its signal from the three color signals. When the separations are in progress, the computer for the black separation keeps track of the signals in the three multipliers and deducts its black values from the overlapping of the other three colors. For example, when equal or proportional gray values of cyan, magenta, and yellow are printed, they will make gray or black. When the computer for black separation senses an area in which the tone values of all three separations are of the same proportion for gray or black, it automatically replaces the process inks with black. The extent of the replacement will depend on the under color removal adjustment.

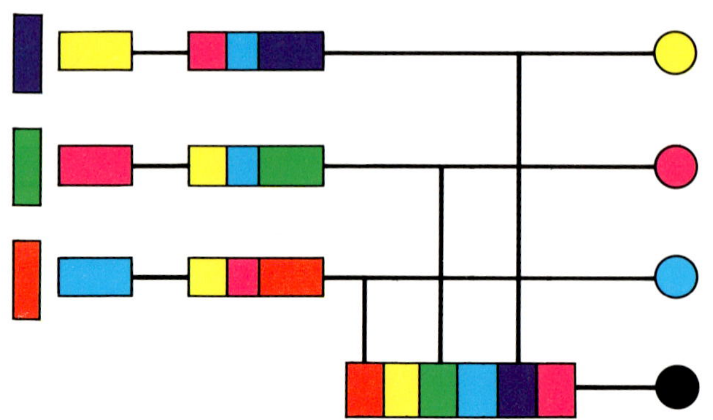

Figure 10.16. A black computer derives its signal from the other three color channels.

The concept of color correction for the black separation is explained with Figure 10.17. Theoretically, a neutral tone, gray or black, is composed of three equal amounts of cyan, magenta, and yellow inks. Since the smallest amount of the three colors is also present in the other two larger portions, the smallest amount of the three colors is a common black portion in the three colors. In an electronic signal, the hightest voltage corresponds to white and is identified in the figure as a white signal. The ink amount will be zero at this point. The decrease in voltage from the white signal of the three colors will correspond to the smallest amount of the inks as shown in Figure 10.17 (signal 1). This highest signal of the three colors can be replaced by black. This signal for the lowest ink amount is normally derived by the black computer from the white color correction values of the

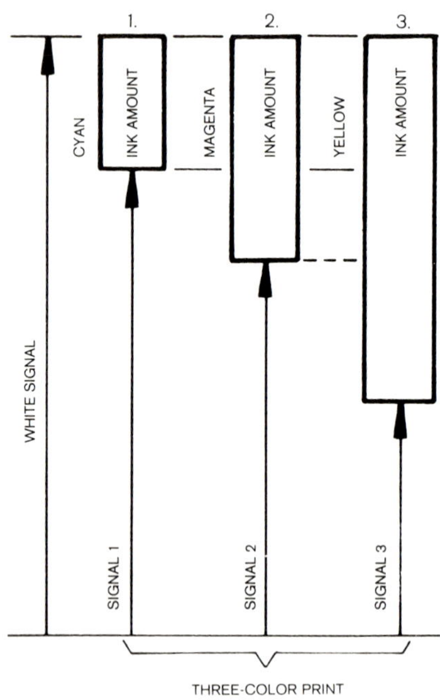

Figure 10.17. Diagram showing how different signal voltages are generated by the computer for different ink amounts

three colors. Consequently, the positions of the white color correction controls for the cyan, magenta, and yellow have direct relationship and will influence the black color correction. If the black color correction values are not found to be optimum, resetting the white color correction values for one or more colors normally solves the problem.

Selective Correction for Black

Most analog and digital scanners provide selective or special controls for black color correction. As indicated earlier, the amount of black is the smallest ink amount in the separations. However, the ink amount may have to be further increased or decreased for satisfactory results. The selective color correction control for black may be used to increase or decrease black in selected areas.

It may be indicated here that the curve shape for the black separation is determined by the settings of the under color removal (UCR) or gray component replacement (GCR) controls. This topic is discussed in detail in the chapters "Under Color Removal" and "Gray Component Replacement." When either a skeleton or a full range black is needed, the percentages required for the highlight and shadow can be entered into the computer by positioning a gray scale step, monitoring each step of the scale, and assigning the dot values. Once the black gradation is set, the correct result will be produced automatically when a new original is adjusted for highlight and shadow range.

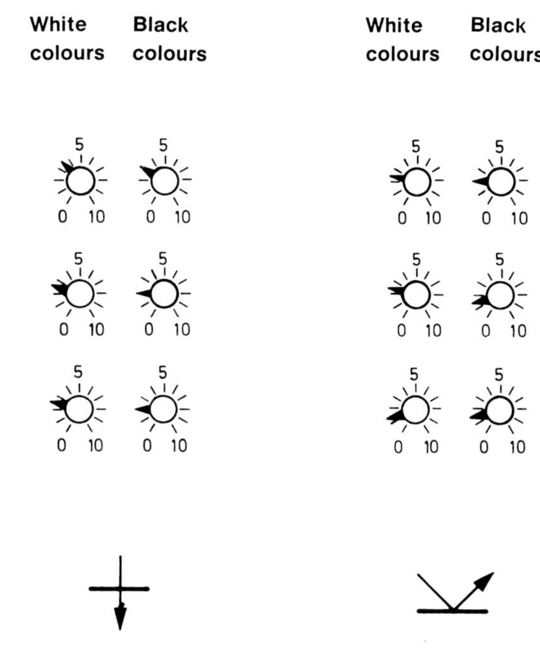

COLOR CORRECTION PROCEDURE IN A SCANNER

Unfortunately there is no standard method to adjust color correction for achieving consistent and optimal results because of the great diversity of originals and printing conditions that exist in the industry. Even identical originals may require different color correction settings depending on the picture areas to be emphasized or de-emphasized. Spectral sensitivity of the optical systems, the color filters, and the photomultipliers used in a scanner will greatly influence how the computer sees a color. Even the same brands and models of scanners may need different color correction settings. As a result, each scanner has to be custom calibrated for optimal color correction.

Another area which is subject to many misinterpretations in the industry is color saturation. Even the experts cannot agree as to the degree of saturation present in an original or to be obtained in the separations. Evaluation of the original, on and off the scanner, is possibly the most important step in determining the saturation needed for different areas of the original during color correction.

In the instruction manuals for a few scanners, standard color correction adjustment is offered. These adjustments are the mean values derived from the industry. Figure 10.18 contains the suggested basic and selective color correction settings in the Hell 299 and DS SG-608 scanners. The manuals recommend that when the first separation is made for the initial set up of the scanner, these color correction values may be used. However, when a deviation is needed, it is useful to check each basic color for its black color correction values

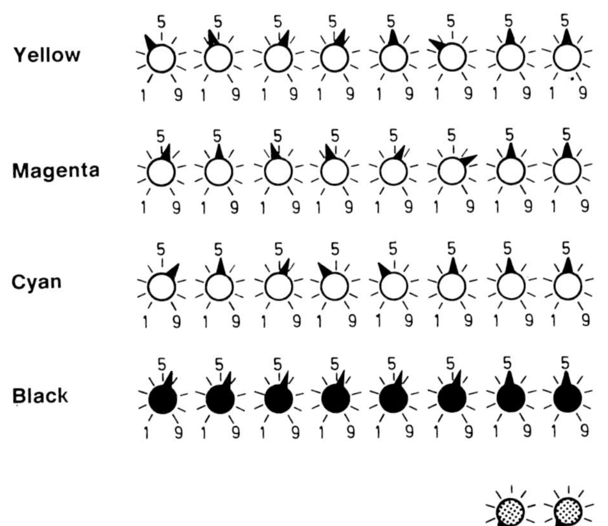

	Y	M	C	O	V	G
Y	4.6	5.7	5.5	5.7	4.7	4.9
M	4.9	4.7	4.8	5.3	6.3	4.7
C	5.1	4.6	5.3	4.7	5.3	5.8
BK	5.6	5.5	5.0	4.4	4.9	4.6

Figure 10.18. Recommended color correction control settings in the Hell 299L and the DS SG-608 scanners

and its complementary color for the white color correction values before the change in adjustments.

Most scanners offer a built-in standard color correction setting when the controls are set to a certain position. For example, in the Hell 399ER, a two-position toggle switch is provided to deactivate the color correction controls and to activate a fixed factory-calibrated color correction value. For their 645 scanners, Crosfield points out that each scanner is supplied with a standard program incorporating basic values which are typical values used for the appropriate printing process. These typical values are changed to suit customers' needs and stored in the computer's memory for future use. Crosfield refers to these changed values as CV (Customer Values). Most of the latest scanners provide some sort of programming and storage of several sets of such values.

INITIAL SCANNER SET UP FOR COLOR CORRECTION

The initial set up for color correction in a scanner is possibly the most important step for consistent and optimal colors in the reproduction. As such, it should be approached as objectively as possible. Although there are no universal guidelines, fortunately several aids are available for the scanner operator to make an objective decision in this respect.

Two basic approaches can be taken for the initial set up: (1) to color correct for the ink and printing process deficiencies, and (2) to color correct for originals with different types of dyes or emulsions. Further clarification on these two points is in order.

Initial set up for ink, paper and Press Conditions

A precise adjustment of the scanner is possible for any printing condition by first printing solids and tints in different combinations and then using this print as an original to set up the scanner. Negatives or positives of similar guides are offered by the Graphic Arts Technical Foundation for the initial color correction set up in a scanner. First, a set of color patches is printed using the normal process inks and printing conditions in the plant for which the scanner is to be set up. Then the printed image is wrapped around the scanning drum and is used to adjust the scanner's basic and selective color correction controls. Figure 10.19 is a reproduction of the GATF Color Reproduction Guide.

For proper color correction set up in a scanner, it is also necessary to establish gray balance requirements for a given ink set. First the scanner needs to be adjusted for determining the proportions of the ink set to produce neutral gray. It should be emphasized here that color correction does not affect the gray balance. Along with a GATF Color Reproduction Guide, a Gray Balance Chart is also printed to determine the printing dot percentages for cyan, magenta, and yellow that will produce neutral gray. The chart normally consists of several combinations of cyan, magenta, and yellow tints. A proportion of dot percentages are selected from the printed chart which produces the gray. These dot percentages are then assigned to the cyan, magenta, and yellow at various aim points during gradation adjustment. A detailed discussion on the subject is presented in the chapter "Gray Balance." The GATF Gray Balance Chart and the RIT Tone Reproduction and Neutral Determination Chart (TRAND) are presented with Figures 11.4a and 11.4b on pages 196 and 197.

In addition to the above, a reflection gray scale similar to the Kodak SR-37 Scanner Gray Scale and an original color print should be mounted beside the Color Reproduction

Courtesy Graphic Arts Technical Foundation

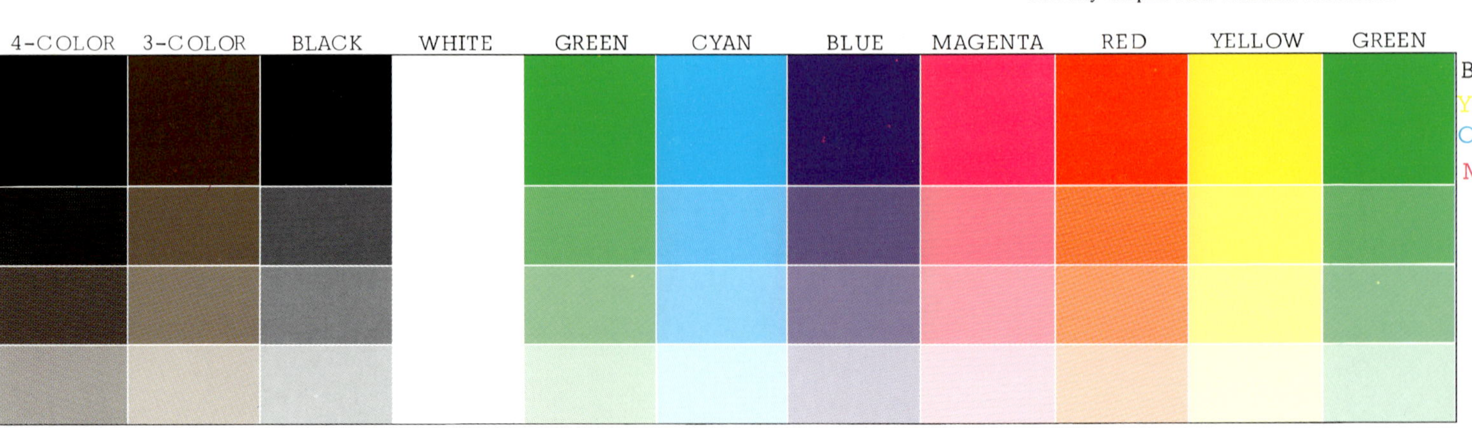

Figure 10.19. GATF Color Reproduction Guide

Guide. The color print should be a standard print with neutral gray and well-saturated colored areas.

The first step for the initial set up using the GATF Guide includes a normal gradation and gray balance adjustments for the three process inks using the data from the previously printed gray balance chart. The printed guide, a reflection gray scale, and an original are mounted on the scanning drum. Then the color correction controls or values are set in the scanner to correlate to a standard built-in correction provided by the scanner manufacturer. Next the scanning head is positioned for the printed solid cyan, magenta, and yellow on the Color Correction Guide and the saturation is adjusted by the black color control with the color separation modes in their respective positions. Unwanted absorption of these colors is also adjusted with the white color control, each time positioning the head for the respective complementary colors (e.g. red for cyan, green for magenta, and blue for yellow). Once the primary colors are corrected with the basic correction controls, then the scanning head is positioned for the other white and black colors, and with the respective selective controls, each color is corrected or fine tuned.

After the scanner is set up for gray balance and color correction, the original is scanned and printed using a normal paper-ink-press condition. Then the color correction adjustment is checked by evaluating the results obtained in the reproduction. If press proofs are hard to justify, a high quality off-press proof can be made which closely resembles a press proof. This procedure, if followed carefully, will ensure proper gray balance and color correction settings in the scanner for a given ink set, paper, and press conditions. However, it will be necessary to readjust the tone reproduction and color correction for originals with different characteristics.

The importance in determining the color correction set up with a normal range good quality original cannot be overemphasized. This original should have good color saturation, neutral areas, and no color cast. Most scanner manufacturers and companies like Eastman Kodak and Fuji offer such original. Once the optimum color correction is established using one of these standard originals, any deviations are easy to accomplish for other types of originals.

Initial Set Up for Different Emulsion Characteristics of the Original

For Kodak transparency and print materials, Eastman Kodak Company has developed a test kit that facilitates precise calibration of a color scanner for different emulsion and dye characteristics. With the Kodak kit, once a good set of separations is obtained on one type of color emulsion, the test image of that material is placed on the scanner and the color values on the color squares are noted. Test images of the other color materials are then mounted on the scanning drum

Courtesy Eastman Kodak Company

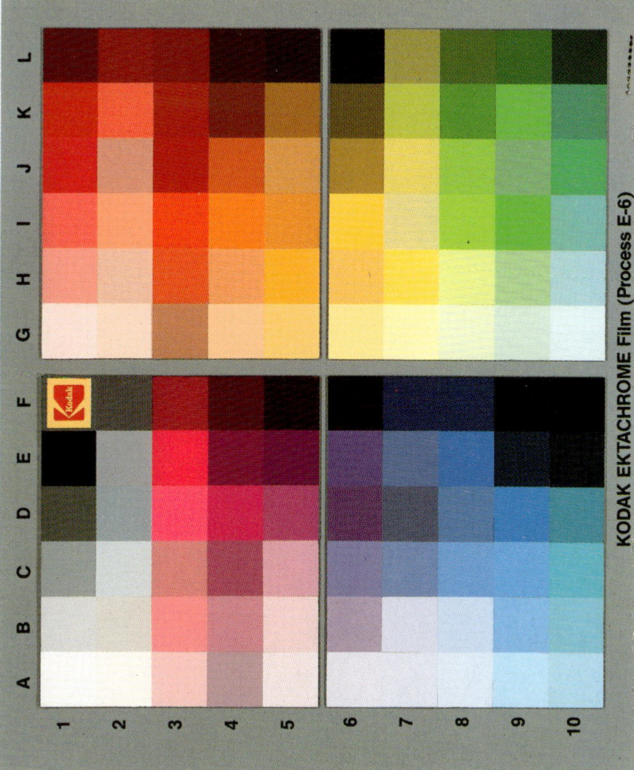

Figure 10.20. Kodak Emulsion Guide

and the SELECTIVE COLOR CORRECTION, PASTEL COLOR BOOST, or similar controls are adjusted until the color values for a specific area are the same as those recorded from the original color emulsion. In this respect, the scanner works as an analyzer or a comparator; the difference of the two emulsions as seen by the scanner is adjusted with the color correction controls until they are of equal value. The scanner is now adjusted for the other dye or emulsion characteristics.

The initial setting in the scanner for color correction must not be based on a limited number of separations done from one subject only. The operator should run as many jobs as possible with different types of originals and make several proofs before a decision can be made for the final setting. This will also give the operator a clear understanding of how the optics and other scanner functions react to different copy, such as different dye materials, original vs. duplicate chromes, etc. In the long run, it will be well worth the time spent for the initial set up. Some operators prefer to use several normal range transparencies containing different emulsions (Kodachrome, Ektachrome, Fujichrome, etc.) for the initial set up. They can evaluate the scanner's response by looking at the results of identical colors in the different transparencies. For example, if the green is identical in the identical proofs of four transparencies, but not in others, possibly a change in gradation or gray balance is needed for the emulsions which were not corrected.

Some people in the industry rightfully argue that the scanner operator needs to possess more background in the photographic aspects of the original rather than more background in the printing process. The printing conditions, after all, can be standardized, but the originals for scanning are never the same. There are hundreds of different types of originals, each of which may need different adjustments for optimal reproduction. For example, there are high-key, low-key, and normal originals; each may need a different gradation adjustment. Then there are some originals with a variety of color cast. Casts are to be removed from some, but in others, the cast cannot be removed because of its influence over the saturation. Then again, there are differences in emulsion between different chromes, and there are originals and duplicate transparencies with completely different dye and grain characteristics. It is estimated that 90% of all the changes in a scanner set up are due to different characteristics of the originals. A thorough understanding of the different types of originals and duplicates, the characteristics of different emulsion and dye, and how the scanner differs in response to these variables will be of much help to the operator. A detailed discussion of the subject is presented in the chapter "Copy Evaluation and Scanning Aids."

If a Color Correction Control Guide discussed earlier is not available for the initial set up, any original transparency or color print with solid patches of primary and secondary colors can be used instead. Scanner manufacturers normally supply a set of transparency and reflection copy with the scanner which can be used for initial set up as well as for a reference original. These originals contain several saturated color patches and gray areas. Figure 10.21 is the reproduction of a transparency from the Scanner Reproduction Guide by Hell Graphic Systems, Inc.

Courtesy Hell Graphic Systems, Inc.

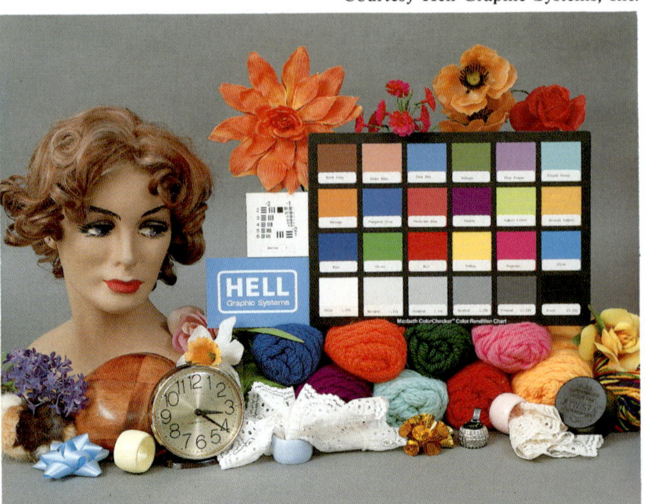

Figure 10.21. Hell Scanner Reproduction Guide transparency

STEPS FOR COLOR CORRECTION IN A SCANNER

Whatever method is used for the initial color correction set up, the operator must understand the objectives of each step of the set up. For example, the purpose of the color correction for the black colors is to check the saturation of the color in question. For white colors, the adjustment is for the removal of unwanted absorption in that color. As such, for a black color adjustment, the color to be checked and corrected must be positioned for the scanning light so that the color transmits through the scanning head. For example, to increase or decrease yellow in green, the green patch in which the yellow is to be added or subtracted must be positioned for the scanning light, and then the BLACK correction control in the yellow channel is used to increase or decrease the yellow. On the other hand, when the unwanted absorption of the white colors are to be adjusted for the same yellow, the color to be transmitted must be cyan and magenta (blue), because the unwanted absorptions for yellow will come from these colors. The WHITE color correction control in the yellow channel is used to increase or decrease these unwanted absorptions in the yellow. To avoid any confusion in the basic set up, the following steps of basic and selective color correction steps are presented with a detailed explanation of each.

Basic Correction for Cyan

Black Color: the scanning light spot is positioned on a pure and saturated cyan. The percentage of cyan content is determined. The final percentage of cyan will depend on the color patch used and the degree of saturation needed for a specific shop condition. It may vary from 90% to 100%. However, the operator may start with 100% and reduce the amount depending on the results obtained. The other two secondary black colors for cyan — blue and green — will be precision adjusted later with the selective or similar controls.

White Color: the scanning light spot is positioned for a saturated red patch. The percentage of white (unwanted) colors for the cyan separation is determined. In theory, the white color value for red in cyan should be zero. However, in all practical purposes, cyan will contain a small percentages of magenta and yellow. If they are adjusted to zero, the cyan will look unnatural. The approximate starting point to set the white color content will be the same as the percentage of smallest highlight dots assigned during the basic set up. For example, if the highlight dot percentage is 5%, it is set at 5%. This value, however, can be changed later depending on the results obtained in the reproduction. The other two white colors for cyan - yellow and magenta — will be precision adjusted with the selective or similar controls.

Basic Correction for Magenta

Black color: the scanning light spot is positioned on a pure and saturated magenta. The percentage of magenta dots is determined according to the previous setting of cyan, for example, 100%. The other two black colors for magenta — red and blue — will be precision adjusted later with the selective or similar controls.

White Color: the scanning light spot is positioned for a pure saturated green patch. The percentage of white colors is determined for magenta, for example, 4%. The other two white colors for magenta — cyan and yellow — will be precision adjusted with the selective or similar correction controls.

Basic Correction for Yellow

Black Color: the scanning light spot is positioned on a pure and saturated yellow. The dot percentage of yellow is determined and adjusted, for example, 100%. The other two secondary black colors for yellow — red and green — will be precision adjusted with the selective or similar controls.

White Color: the scanning light spot is positioned for a pure saturated blue. The percentage of white colors is determined and adjusted for yellow, for example, 4%. The other two white colors for yellow — cyan and magenta — will be precision adjusted with the selective correction or similar controls.

Selective Correction

Selective controls can be effectively used to increase or decrease hue content in any secondary or tertiary colors. As indicated earlier, the selective controls have a narrow band effect and will have minimal influence on the colors other than the one which is corrected. In most of the analog scanners, the controls for selective correction also include identical controls as the basic black and white colors. They can be used to fine tune a spot of color where a narrow band effect of the adjustment is desired. Editorial correction control similar to the selective correction control in an analog scanner is also offered in most digital color computers. For example, Magnascan 645 offers a program labeled as "Pastel Color Boost." This control affects all colors of limited saturation while leaving the neutrals and highly saturated colors unaffected.

The six primary and secondary colors, i.e. cyan, magenta, yellow, red, green, and blue, can be selectively adjusted for the cyan, magenta, and yellow separations. However, the required values for the black and white colors in the following set ups will be mostly influenced by the values set during the basic color correction. The six corrections for each separation are explained below with diagrams of a two-dimensional color space showing the effect of these corrections.

Cyan Separation

CONTROL OR PUSH-BUTTON (Black or white color)	EFFECT (Reduces or increases)
Blue (Black color)	Cyan in blue
Cyan (Black color)	Cyan in cyan
Green (Black color)	Cyan in green
Yellow (White color)	Yellow in cyan
Red (White color)	Red in cyan
Magenta (White color)	Magenta in cyan

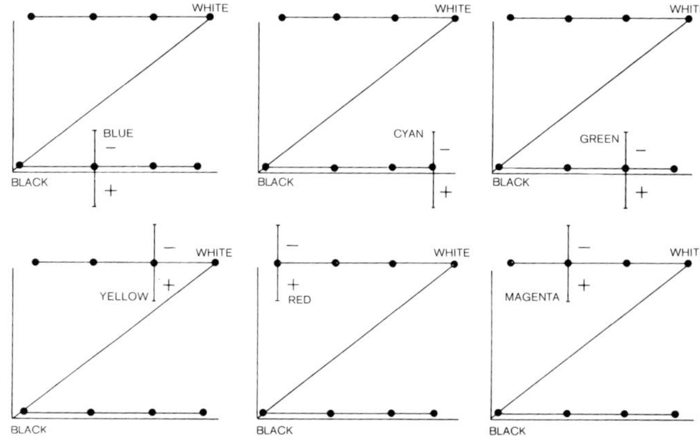

Figure 10.22. Selective correction for the cyan separation

Magenta Separation

CONTROL OR PUSH-BUTTON (Black or white color)	EFFECT (Reduces or increases)
Blue (Black color)	Magenta in blue
Cyan (White color)	Cyan in magenta
Green (White color)	Green in magenta
Yellow (White color)	Yellow in magenta
Red (Black color)	Magenta in red
Magenta (Black color)	Magenta in magenta

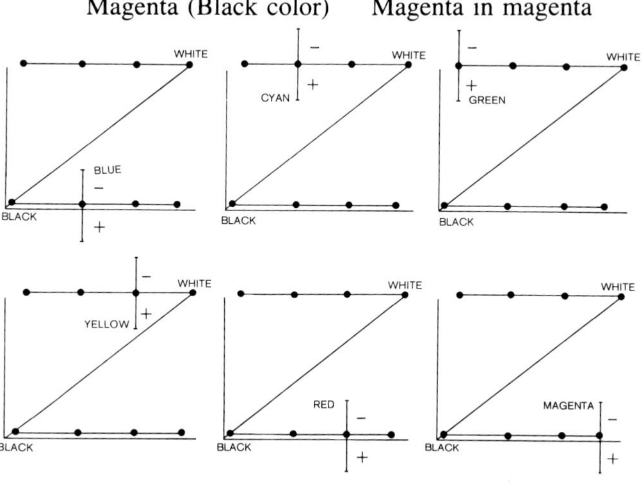

Figure 10.23. Selective correction for the magenta separation

Yellow Separation

CONTROL OR PUSH-BUTTON (Black or white color)	EFFECT (Reduces or increases)
Blue (White color)	Blue in yellow
Cyan (White color)	Cyan in yellow
Green (Black color)	Yellow in green
Yellow (Black color)	Yellow in yellow
Red (Black color)	Yellow in red
Magenta (White color)	Magenta in yellow

Courtesy Hell Graphic Systems, Inc.

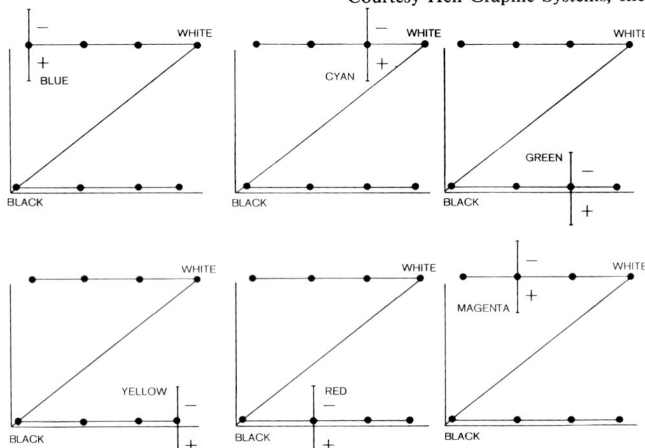

Figure 10.24. Selective correction for the yellow separation

Black Separation

CONTROL OR PUSH-BUTTON (Black or white color)	EFFECT (Reduces or increases)
Blue (White color)	Black in blue
Cyan (White color)	Black in cyan
Green (White color)	Black in green
Yellow (White color)	Black in yellow
Red (White color)	Black in red
Magenta (White color)	Black in magenta

Courtesy Hell Graphic Systems, Inc.

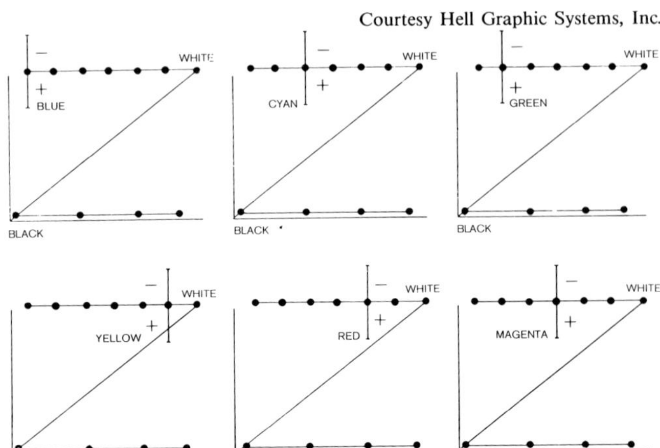

Figure 10.25. Selective correction for the black separation

IMPORTANT CHECKS AND TIPS

Tips and important points to remember for color correction:

1. One has to be careful about original dyes and retouched dyes. The scanner will respond differently for these two dyes although visually there may be no difference between the two.

2. If considerable adjustments of the selective controls produce only a very small correction, the correction should be set at the original values recommended in the manual.

3. After the color correction adjustment, the approximate middle-tone and three-quarter-tone values of the original should be checked for color values. If the desired values are not attained, the gradation setting is wrong.

4. No one color can be set in complete isolation; it will have some effect on the other colors. Correction for the basic colors should always be done before the selective correction. Sometimes, the adjustments of the basic correction controls are offset by selective controls. Frequently, wrong adjustments of this type may result in inversions.

5. The final result of the color correction setting will also depend on the correct gradation setting. More often, a wrong color in the reproduction results from a wrong gradation setting rather than from the adjustment of color correction.

6. If the customer requests some color changes in the original, there should be no guessing. Samples of printed colors of particular inks and screen ruling should be used to communicate and to produce the requested color.

7. Always standard viewing light should be used to communicate color. A 5,000°K light source is the standard in the industry.

8. Theoretically, the value of a white color is 0 and the value of a black color is 100%. However, the white color values and the black color values need to be changed for natural results. The extent of change will depend on a particular shop condition.

9. Changes in tone, gray balance, color cast removal, and similar specific adjustments will change the color correction. Before altering any color correction values, the highlight, middle-tone and shadow range controls should be checked to ensure that they are set correctly. For example, if the middle-tone is altered, this can have an effect on the color correction. Any movement of the aim points of the three colors would alter the color content of that color.

10. All steps should be standardized and kept simple. Frequent changes in color correction will cause confusion resulting in the incorrect assessment of the real problem. For example, most of the time a wrong gradation setting is thought of as a color correction problem.

11. The black correction should always be made after the correction for cyan, magenta, and yellow. Changes in the correction of process colors will result in the change in the correction for black.

COLOR CORRECTION CONTROLS IN DIFFERENT SCANNERS

Crosfield Magnascan 645

There are six dual-function color correction buttons on the panel of this scanner. For color correction function, the CC (color correction) facility must be selected beforehand by pressing COLOR. The six buttons are for the correction of the three primary and three secondary colors — cyan, magenta, yellow, red, blue, and green. If a direct entry is not acceptable by the computer, for example, monitoring a blue area and trying to use the red button in the cyan channel, an error message will appear in the display panel. Pressing the same COLOR button twice exits the function from the color correction mode.

As shown in Figure 10.27, the following sequence is used to enter a change in color correction:

For example, to increase yellow in green, the green color is positioned for the scanning light and the green CC button is presssed. The values are then changed by the INCREASE or DECREASE button while monitoring the displayed values. However, a direct entry of the predetermined values is also possible.

By pressing the SUPP EDIT button, the operation temporarily suspends the selected CC edit to show the value before the edit was applied. Again by pressing COLOR mode, the CC mode is entered.

Each scanner is supplied with a standard program incorporating Basic Values (BV). Facilities are provided to store a specific value, called Customer Values (CV), to suit one's need and the customer requirements. A detailed explanation of Basic values, Job Values, and Customer Values for Magnascan 645 is provided in the chapter "Basic Mechanics of a Scanner."

In addition to the above color correction controls, an editorial control — PASTEL COLOR BOOST, provides the correction of colors of limited saturation while leaving neutrals and highly saturated colors unaffected. Figure 10.28 illustrates the operating procedure of pastel color boost in the Magnascan 645.

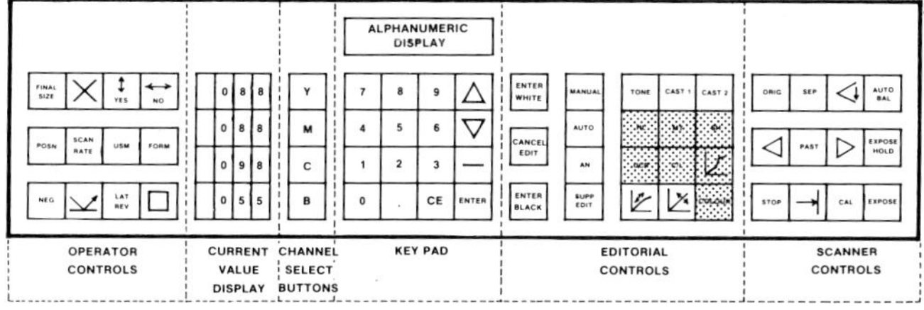

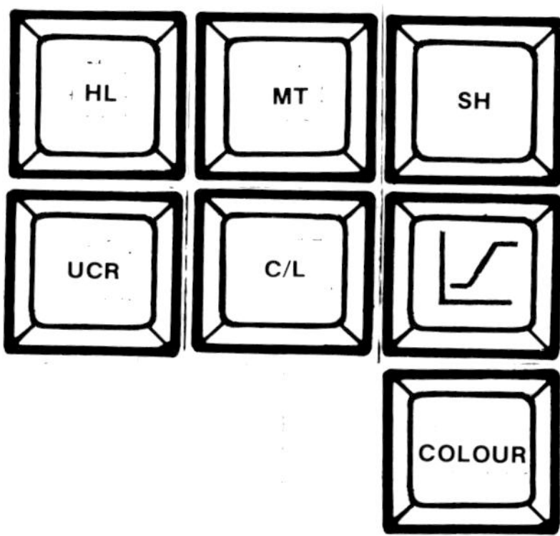

Figure 10.26. Panel of Magnascan 645 showing pushbutton controls for color correction. The six buttons shown have dual functions: HL: Red; MT: Yellow; SH: Green; UCR: Cyan; C/L: Blue; and ⟋ Magenta. The color correction function is activated by pressing the pushbutton COLOUR. Otherwise they operate according to the functions marked on their faces. Each of the six buttons specify which color in the original is to be adjusted and the position of the channel select buttons Y, M, C, or B specify the separation which is affected by the adjustment.

Courtesy Crosfield Electronics

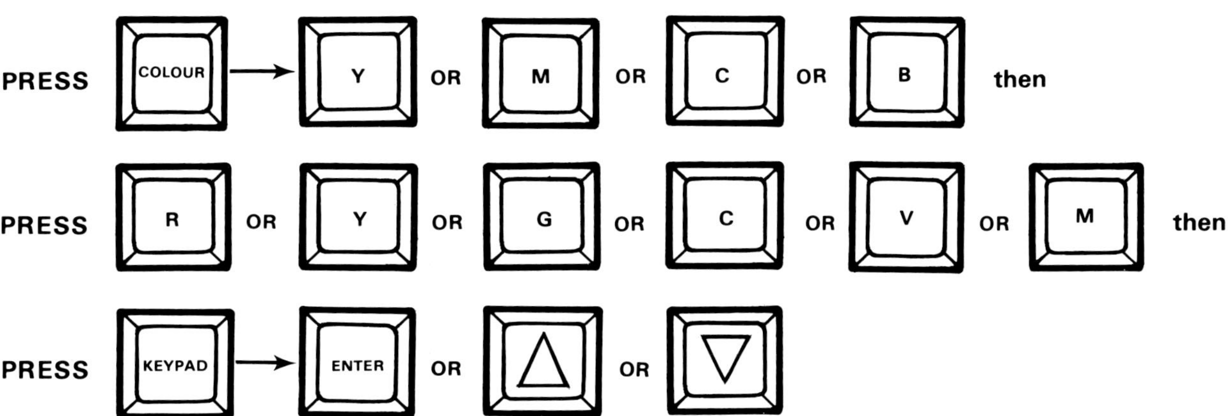

Figure 10.27. Sequence of color correction functions in the Magnascan 645

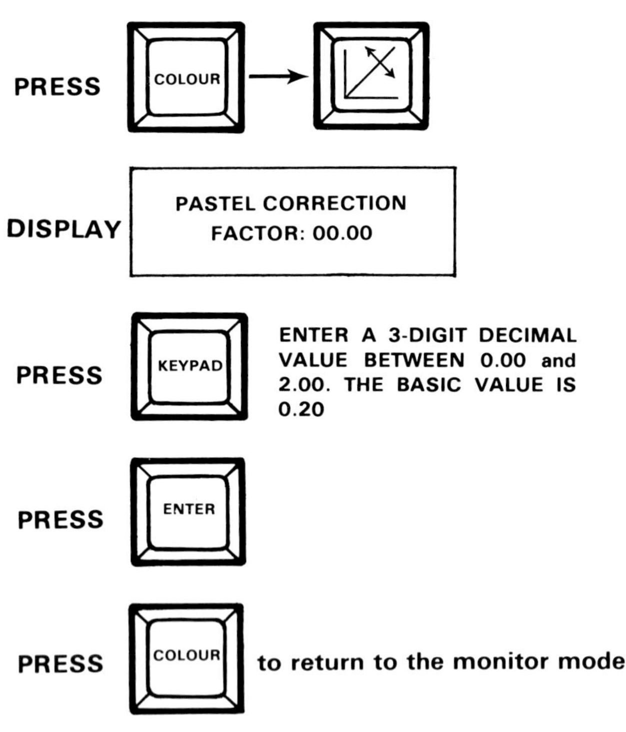

Figure 10.28. Operating procedure of "Pastel Color Boost" in the Magnascan 645

Dainippon Screen SG-608

As a typical analog scanner, the SG-608 has two separate panels — Color Control I and Color Control II. Color Control I consists of six controls. Three of them are for the correction

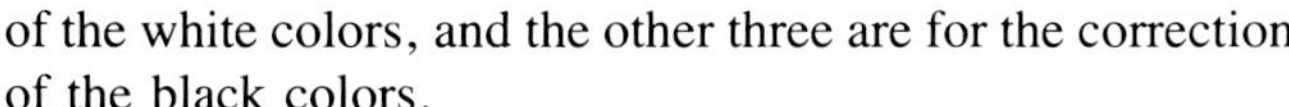

of the white colors, and the other three are for the correction of the black colors.

Color Control II consists of six rows of controls with 4 controls in each row. The color of each control knob represents the separation color (ink color), and the color shown in the window below the control represents the color to be controlled or corrected. A counterclockwise turn of each control increases the amount of the ink (Y, M, C or BK) to be included in the output color, and turning the control clockwise decreases the amount of the ink. A table of suggested settings has been provided for the operator as a guideline.

COLOR CONTROL I

WHITE BLACK

COLOR CONTROL II

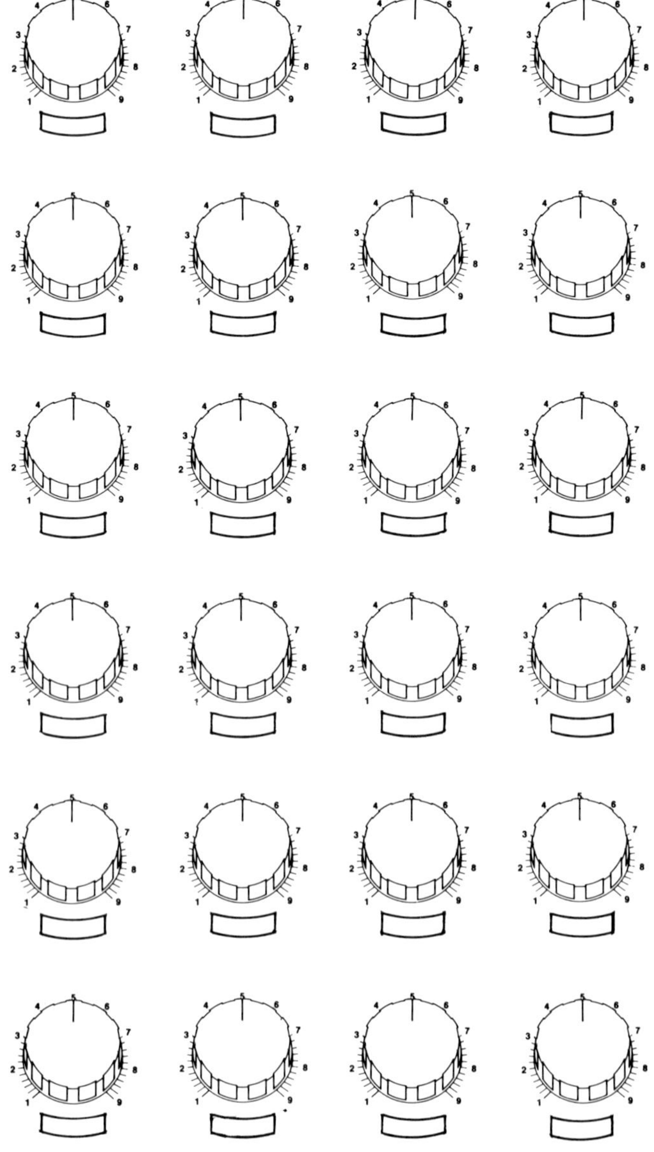

Figure 10.29. Basic and Selective color correction control panels in the DS SG-608

Hell 399ER

The color correction panels in the Hell 399ER consist of two separate sets of potentiometer type controls: a set of six basic color correction controls and a set of 24 selective correction controls. Three of the six basic correction controls are for the white colors, and the other three are for the black colors. At the top of each of the basic controls, there are three different size dots designating the effect of correction on the respective colors. The correction which affects the color most is the largest dot of that color; the color with the smallest dot is the least affected by the control. These colored dots can be directly related to the concept of color correction in a color space as shown in Figure 10.30. In addition to the six controls for the basic correction, there is a dual-function toggle switch at the bottom of the panel. The switch has two positions. When the switch is up, the individual settings for each of the six controls are activated, and when it is down, the effect of the individual correction controls are deactivated and the scanner's fixed standard basic correction value is applied to the separations. This is a highly desirable feature to compare the effects of the two settings instantly by activating or deactivating the controls for the standard and the changed color correction settings.

Six controls are provided for each of the cyan, magenta, yellow, and black selective color corrections. These six controls are for the three primary and three secondary colors. The controls can also be directly related to the concept of color correction in a color space as shown in Figures 10.13 and 10.14. In addition to these controls, two toggle switches are provided at the bottom of the panel. Both are dual-function switches. One has two positions — either the individual controls for selective correction are activated, or alternately, the scanner's fixed color correction values are selected by deactivating this control. The other switch increases the intensity of the selective color correction when it is positioned for the larger dot and decreases the intensity when it is positioned for the smaller dot.

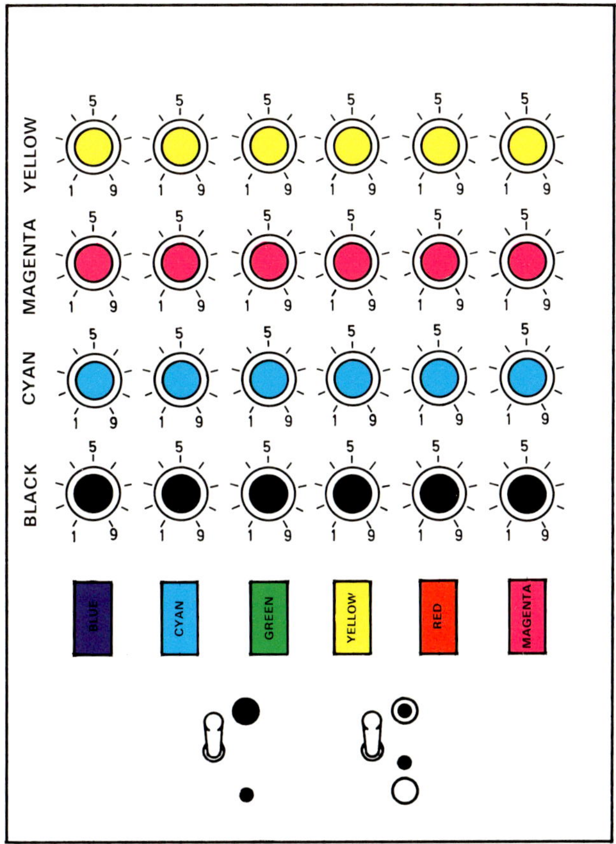

Figure 10.31. Selective color correction panel in the Hell 399ER

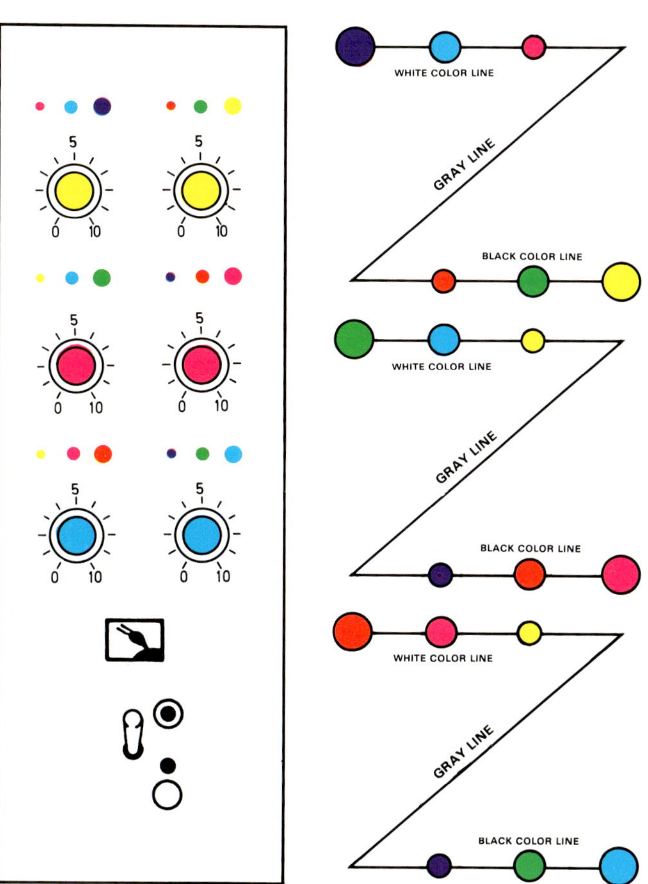

Figure 10.30. Basic color correction controls in the Hell 399ER. The diagram on the right shows how the colors in the space are affected by the controls.

Royal Zenith 200-S

At the time of installation, all basic color corrections are set up and entered into the scanner via a program by a technician. As a result, the scanner operator has a preset start point to work from.

There are six pushbutton controls corresponding to cyan, magenta, yellow, red, green, and blue. These colors can be adjusted in each separation including the black. A standard correction value is also included in the scanner. The color correction program is recalled by pressing "F", the function key and then increasing or decreasing the correction setting within a range of — 128 to + 127.

As for example, suppose the scanning light is positioned on a dark blue portion of the transparency. The reading on the display panel is Y: 20%, M: 75%, C: 90%, and K: 28%. Without moving the scanning light, the following corrections are made:

Y F V SUB 5%
M F V SUB 5%
C F V ADD 5%
K F V SUB 8%

The following change will be on the display panel:

Y: 15%, M: 70%, C: 95%, and K: 20%

This change can now be saved as a new program and the operator can check this setting with old settings for comparing the effect of color correction. The operator may move the scanning light to any spot of the transparency and switch back and forth between the old and the new program to check the changes which may have taken place because of the new settings. This is further simplified by pressing the EXCHANGE key which will display the old setting for all colors at once.

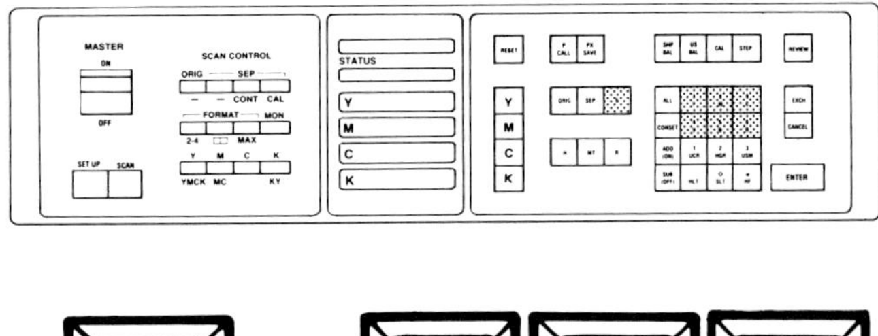

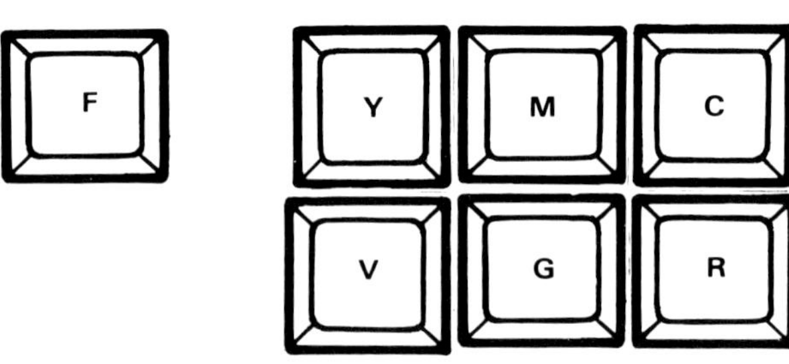

Figure 10.32. Panel of RZ 200-S showing the pushbuttons for color correction

Chapter 11
Gray Balance

DEFINITION

Gray balance occurs when an original gray scale can be reproduced with the process colors as a neutral gray scale. But the meaning and functions of gray balance go much further than this simple stated definition.

FUNCTIONS OF GRAY BALANCE

There are two reasons for reproducing a gray scale as neutral. One of them is that if the original has gray or neutral areas, these areas have to be reproduced as neutral if an accurate reproduction is desired. However, if the process color reproduction had not been printed on white paper, this would not be a serious problem. The human eye and brain can compensate within reason for any error in the neutrality of white or gray as long as there is no other point of reference in the field of view. Since the white paper area surrounding the reproduction is the reference area in the field of view, any imbalance in the neutrality of the white or gray becomes immediately visible and objectionable.

The second major purpose for gray balance is more important and carries the implication much further. When equal amounts of red, green, and blue lights reflect from a surface, it is viewed as neutral. When a balanced white light is used for viewing a neutral gray scale, it reflects or transmits (depending on whether it is a reflective or a transmissive copy) equal amounts of red, green, and blue to the eye (see Figure 11.1). Because of the impurities in the process inks, when equal proportions of cyan, magenta, and yellow are printed on white paper, they do not reflect equal amounts of red, green and blue to produce gray. This is because each of the process inks absorbs or reflects an unequal amount of its share of the red, green, and blue of the spectrum. As such, if equal amounts of cyan, magenta, and yellow are printed, they would make a brownish color rather than neutral. For example, 20% cyan, 20% magenta, and 20% yellow would make light brown rather than light gray; the yellow and magenta would dominate the reproduction. This is because the cyan behaves as if it already has some magenta and yellow, and magenta behaves as if it has some cyan and yellow contaminants in it. The amount of these contaminants are different in different inks and normally when the three inks are

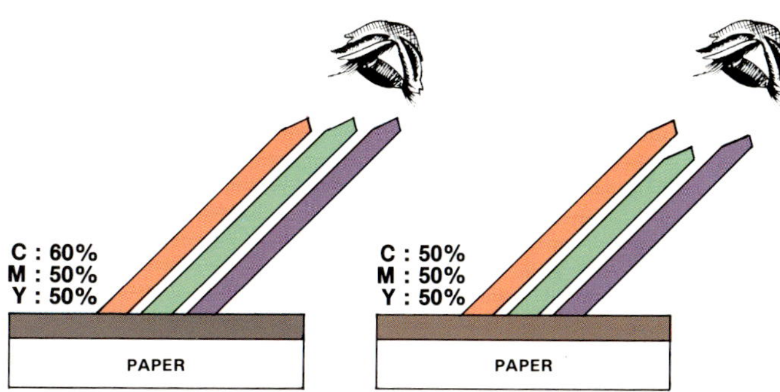

Figure 11.1. Because of contamination, an unequal amount of cyan, magenta, and yellow inks are needed to reflect equal amounts of red, green, and blue for producing gray.

printed in equal quantities, there are more magenta and yellow than cyan. So it is apparent that in order to reproduce a neutral gray as neutral gray, the process colors have to be printed in different proportions on the white paper to compensate for these contaminants. To find the correct proportion, a set of separations is made of the gray scale with different dot sizes for cyan, magenta, yellow, and reproduced. The proportion will be correct when the combination of the three inks, after printing, will reflect neutral color to the eyes from the entire gray scale. When the three process inks are balanced for the neutrality of the gray scale, they also affect the balance of the entire set of separations for an accurate recording of cyan, magenta, and yellow in the three separations. If both the original and the reproduced gray scales reflect or transmit equal amounts of red, green, and blue to the eyes, the red, green, and blue lights from every point of the reproduction will also match the reflection or transmission of the red, green, and blue lights of the original. This will ensure the accuracy of the reproduced color, point by point, compared to the original.

USE OF GRAY SCALE FOR GRAY BALANCE

One advantage to using the gray scale as a reference color is that it actually compares the balance of the three process colors at once. Another major advantage in checking the gray scale for accuracy in color balancing is that the human eye can detect any shift in neutrality when neutral areas are compared side by side. Comparing just by looking at the neutrality of two gray scales is much easier than comparing the purity of the reproduced process inks with a color in the original. The eyes can quickly detect if there is any color cast in the neutral area. In this respect, the eyes become the most sensitive instrument for checking gray balance.

TONE REPRODUCTION AND GRAY BALANCE

A gray scale is used as a control device for checking both tone reproduction and gray balance. To check for the accuracy in tone reproduction, the reproduced tone values of the gray scale are compared with the original tone values. For gray balance, only the neutrality of the reproduced gray scale is compared with the original gray scale. Although it seems that there is no relationship between the two, inconsistency in one will affect the accuracy in the other. During the adjustment of gradation in a scanner, the tone values of gray are independently set for each color. If these settings do not compensate for individual characteristics of each ink and do not take into account the press and paper variables, there will be an uneven gray balance - the entire or certain portions of the gray scale will have a color cast. In this situation, one or more colors may be out of balance, and the tone values for the three colors will have to be readjusted after the evaluation of the color cast area of the reproduced gray scale.

COLOR CORRECTION AND GRAY BALANCE

Confusion exists regarding the relationship between color correction and gray balance. Gray balance can be legitimately thought of as correcting the inks for contamination because the adjustment compensates for the unwanted absorption and reflection of lights by the contaminated inks. The question may be asked at this point that if balancing for the gray compensates for the contamination of the process inks, then why is further color correction necessary for an accurate reproduction? The answer to this question may be summarized as follows:

1. In the conventional separation or electronic scanning, a set of separations is made of an original gray scale and they are printed to check the neutrality of the reproduction. The three exposures are adjusted in the conventional separation and during the basic calibration in a scanner, the photomultipliers are balanced for equal output. If the exposures are correct and the photomultipliers are accurately balanced, all three light values coming from the original neutral scale should be equal. Consequently, gray balance is purely a printing function, e.g. the light values for the three colors reaching the film emulsion are identical, only the dot values for the three inks are adjusted for a neutral result. However, the colors other than gray in the original will produce unequal output during the exposure adjustment in the conventional separation and balancing the multipliers in a scanner. Consequently, balancing the three pigments for the gray will not automatically balance all the pigments in the other areas of the original.

2. When the three inks are properly balanced for gray, the combination of three will reflect equal amounts of red, green, and blue to the eyes. However, most of the visual problems in process color printing arise from the reproduction of secondary colors, a combination of two inks. The peculiar absorption and reflection characteristics of the printing inks, along with the superimposition of halftone dots and the patterns created by them make additional problems for the secondary colors which cannot be solved by correcting for gray balance alone.

3. Because of the additivity and proportionality failures in color reproduction, the colors reproduced on a press sheet lack the saturation compared to the original. Enhancement in the saturation of some specific colors is needed for a more pleasing effect. This enhancement is accomplished by the adjustment of color correction controls but without affecting the gray balance for the three colors.

FACTORS AFFECTING GRAY BALANCE

There are several factors which affect gray balance. Important among these are impurities in the process inks, the thickness of printed ink film on paper, dot gain on the press, and the quality and color of the paper surface on which the image is printed. They all contribute to the complexity in gray balance. To compensate for the impurities in process inks, the cyan dots are made comparatively larger than the magenta and yellow dots along the entire tone curve. However, because of the effect of proportionality and additivity failures, the difference in the proportion of cyan dots is not uniform throughout the scale. Proportionality failure refers to the three ink dots and the white of the paper, when combined, fail to produce the required saturation and tone values as the continuous-tone original. On the other hand, in the darker areas, the combination of the three solid or near-solid inks does not add up to the density of the individual inks if they were printed separately. This is additivity failure. For the cyan dots, there is a difference of about 10-15% in the middle-tone, 1-2% in the highlight, and about 5-10% in the shadow areas. When printed with standard process inks, magenta and yellow dots are normally kept the same size throughout the entire scale.

Other factors which affect gray balance can be measured and compensated for during the separation stage. For example, Figure 11.2 shows the effect of paper quality and the printing ink quality on gray balance. The figure shows the relationship between the required dot sizes on the halftone positive and the equivalent neutral density or END obtained under different conditions. A detailed presentation of equivalent neutral density (END) is made later in this chapter. As shown in part A of Figure 11.2, less yellow and magenta inks are needed for uncoated paper which is normally warmer in hue than coated paper. Part B of the same figure shows that if strong yellow and magenta inks are used, less yellow and magenta inks are necessary in neutral hues. In solids, a thick ink film produces correspondingly dominant yellow and red hues.

The effect of dot gain is a common problem for proper gray balance. Dot gain is referred to as the change of halftone dot sizes during the production steps. The dots usually get larger because of several mechanical and optical factors such as the pressure of the blanket on the press, the exposure factor during platemaking, tack, viscosity, opacity and internal reflection of the inks, etc. However, the distribution of dot gain over the tonal range varies, the greatest being in the middle-tone area. The amount of dot gain will also vary depending on the type of dot pattern and the printed stock. For example, square dots will have more gain on the press than the elliptical dots, especially in the middle-tone. Similarly, there is less dot gain for good coated stock and more on an uncoated stock. The greatest dot gain occurs on a soft

Courtesy Hell Graphic Systems, Inc.

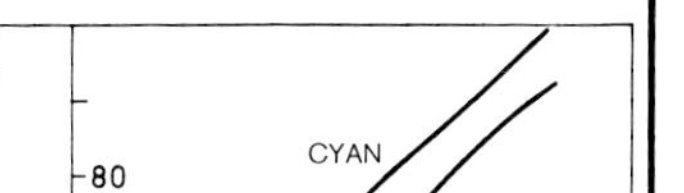

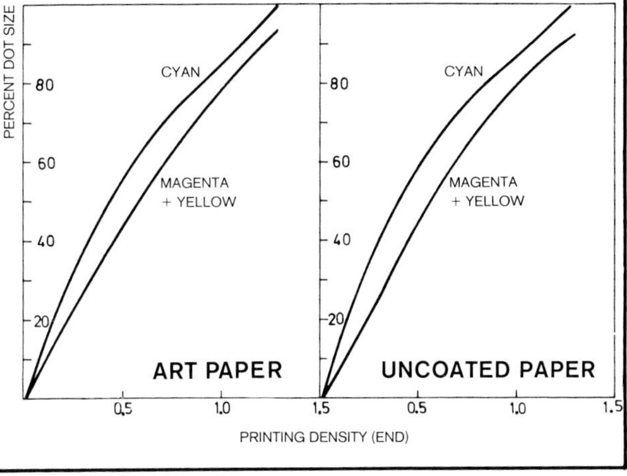

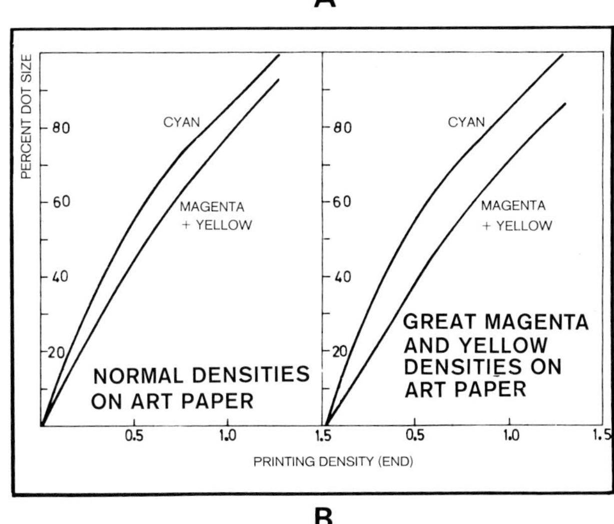

Figure 11.2. Effect of paper and ink quality on gray balance

and rough stock such as newsprint. The scanner operator should know what setting for each color in the scanner will produce neutral gray after compensating for these factors. To accomplish this, a basic calibration is needed for gray balance for different types of screens and/or paper. A test target similar to the GATF Gray Balance Chart or the RIT TRAND chart may be printed on different types of paper using the normal ink and press conditions. These test targets consist of blocks of tints of the three colors printed in different proportions (See Figures 114a and 114b). The tint values for the different colors are selected which produce gray. If the printing condition is optimized and standardized, these variables can be easily quantified and compensated for at the separation stage.

Maintaining the difference in dot sizes for the three process colors along the entire tone values of the gray scale to achieve accuracy in gray balance is critical. As indicated earlier, it is a common practice to assign the same size dot values for magenta and yellow separation at various aim points. But sometimes, depending on the purity of the magenta ink (reddish or bluish) or the color of the paper (a coated paper renders a different color than uncoated), there may be slight variations of dot sizes needed between magenta and yellow in relation to the cyan. To fine tune the gray balance, a reproduction of the gray scale should be made using the specific ink or paper, and the entire range should be checked and readjusted for accuracy.

A point to consider is that the combination of paper and ink quality affects gray balance in the lighter areas of the reproduced scale whereas the ink quality alone mostly affects the gray balance in the shadow areas. This is because the lighter areas of the reproduction are affected by proportionality failure - the reflection of light from the highlight through the middle-tone of the reproduced scale is an additive mixture of the white of the paper and the individual ink dots. The added proportions of the lights reflected from the colored dots and the white of the paper fail to match the color saturation of the original continuous-tone original, no matter how accurate the reproduction is. However, in the darker tones, the three-color overlap will be predominant. This will mainly depend on the quality of the ink — there will be less reflection of light from the dark areas and less interference by the white of the paper on the reflected light. In this area, the additivity failure will affect the darker tones — the density of each individual ink will not add up when they are printed one at the top of the other. As a result, no matter how accurate the gray balance is, the reproduction will have a reddish brown cast in the shadow areas with dominant magenta and yellow. However, the black overprint will generally compensate for this problem in the dark shadow areas printed by the three colors.

GRAY BALANCE IN CONVENTIONAL SEPARATION AND SCANNER

The methods and purposes of gray balance in both conventional and electronic separations are to compensate for the unwanted absorption and reflection characteristics of the process inks. Both systems use the reproduction of a gray scale with the process inks to check and adjust for its neutrality.

During the initial adjustment of gray balance in the conventional method of color separation, three appropriate aim points, such as highlight, middle-tone, and shadow, are selected at different density steps of the gray scale. In direct screening, three exposures — main, flash, and bump — are used to obtain the proportional dot sizes in the three separations. In the indirect method, proportional dot sizes are maintained during the screening stages using the same types of exposures. Since the cyan negative requires a higher percentage of dots in the middle-tone than in the highlight and shadow compared to the magenta and yellow negatives, the cyan is comparatively exposed less than the other two colors to maintain the difference at the middle-tone. The difference is narrowed at the highlight by the no-screen or bump exposure and in the shadow by the flash exposure. After the separations are completed, plates are made and printed using the standard press, paper, and ink. If the result is not acceptable, each separation is evaluated and remade after proper adjustment in the exposures and/or processing conditions.

The major difference in the gray balance between conventional equipment and the scanner is that in the scanner, five different density aim points are used for setting up the difference of dot sizes for proper balancing of the three colors rather than using the three aim points in the conventional separation. In the scanner, these five aim points on the gradation curve along with the technique of scanning and exposing one fine line at a time provide a more accurate and predictable adjustment of tone or dot values along the entire length of the gray scale. During the gradation adjustment in a scanner, the aim points which are representative of average copy, are selected on the gray scale. These aim points consist of highlight, quarter-tone, middle-tone, three-quarter-tone, and shadow. Different tone or dot values are then assigned for different colors for these aim points on the gray scale. Some of the latest scanners offer options in selecting several preset gradations to match the type of the copy to be used. Because of the proper adjustment of gray balance control, these preset gradations result in the same unequal tone or dot values for the three colors. Figure 11.3 shows a curve and a table of

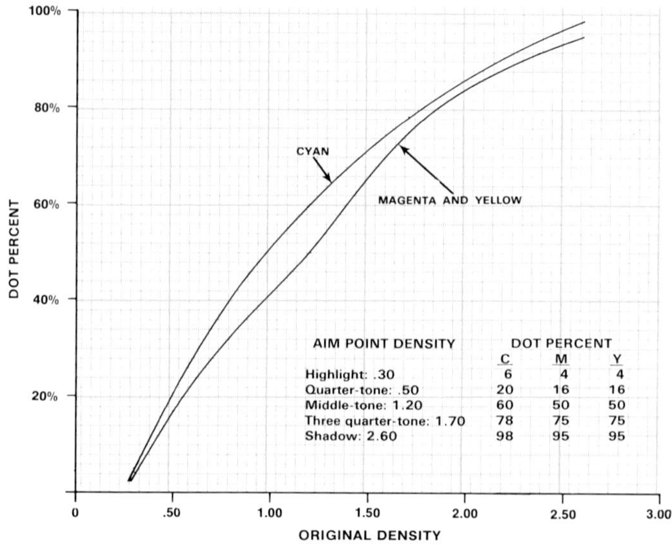

AIM POINT DENSITY	DOT PERCENT C	M	Y
Highlight: .30	6	4	4
Quarter-tone: .50	20	16	16
Middle-tone: 1.20	60	50	50
Three quarter-tone: 1.70	78	75	75
Shadow: 2.60	98	95	95

Figure 11.3. Neutral balance of the three colors for offset printing

standard set of normal aim points and dot values for gray balance for the three process inks. This set of values may be used as starting values to set up the scanner during initial calibration for press, ink, and other variables in a plant.

EVALUATING THE ACCURACY IN GRAY BALANCE

Evaluating the accuracy of gray balance consists of checking for the neutrality of the entire range of the gray scale steps, from the brightest highlight to the darkest shadow, viewed under standard viewing light. Although the eyes are good tools for evaluating gray balance, sometimes, because of fatigue and other factors, eyes may not be relied on to make an accurate comparison. Even worse, the eyes are known to be the least dependable memory device for colors or tones. If the eyes look at one gray scale once and then look at another gray scale, they may not be able to compare accurately the neutrality of the two. So the reproduction and the original have to be positioned in such a way that both of them are visible at the same time. Densitometers can also be used for comparing the original and the reproduced gray scale. As indicated in the chapter "Tone Reproduction," after a gray scale has been properly reproduced, a densitometer can be used to read tone values at several points of the reproduced scale through the red, green, and blue filters. Once the densitometer is calibrated using a gray calibration tablet or an original gray scale, readings through different filters at the identical points on the reproduced scale should result in identical values. However, only a high quality densitometer with these adjustment capabilities can give such results.

At this point it should be emphasized that the densitometers are press control instruments. They can be used to compare the density values of two colors, but they are not suitable for color measurement. Color can be more objectively measured with a colorimeter or a spectrophotometer. A colorimeter is a special densitometer with three broad band filters. The spectral response of these filters closely match the spectral response of the human eyes. Any densitometer can be converted to a colorimeter by adding these filters. However, colorimeters are also available as special equipment for measuring color. For the most accurate color measurement, spectrophotometers are used that separate the visual color into specific wave lengths. However, a majority of the printing plants successfully use a good quality densitometer for evaluation and comparison of colors after the equipment is critically calibrated.

STEPS TO DETERMINE GRAY BALANCE FOR A SPECIFIC PRINTING CONDITION

Accurate gray balance does not depend on any single factor, in fact, it relies heavily on some closely related variables. Change or alteration of any one of these variables can alter the accuracy in gray balance. The scanner operator will be unable to establish and maintain an accurate gray balance for a particular shop unless the persons involved in the production steps understand each other's functions, capabilities, and limitations. For example, if the magenta ink has changed in the press for a bluer hue, the tone values of all the three inks need to be readjusted for maintaining the gray balance. No other area of process color printing needs more in-plant communication than gray balance. The scanner operator must be informed about the changes in ink, press, paper, and other such variables that take place from time to time if the accuracy of the reproduction is to be maintained.

Before attempting to establish accurate gray balance, interrelationships of several variables in process color printing need to be understood and examined. One of these is Equivalent Neutral Density or END and is discussed next.

Equivalent Neutral Density

END or equivalent neutral density of a pigment may be defined as the amount of pigment required to convert to a neutral gray by superimposing the required amount of the other pigments. END is an accepted method in keeping a record of the proportional dot sizes of the three separations for maintaining gray balance. This record can be used as a reference standard by the scanner operator when the END is plotted against the separation dot percentages for each color.

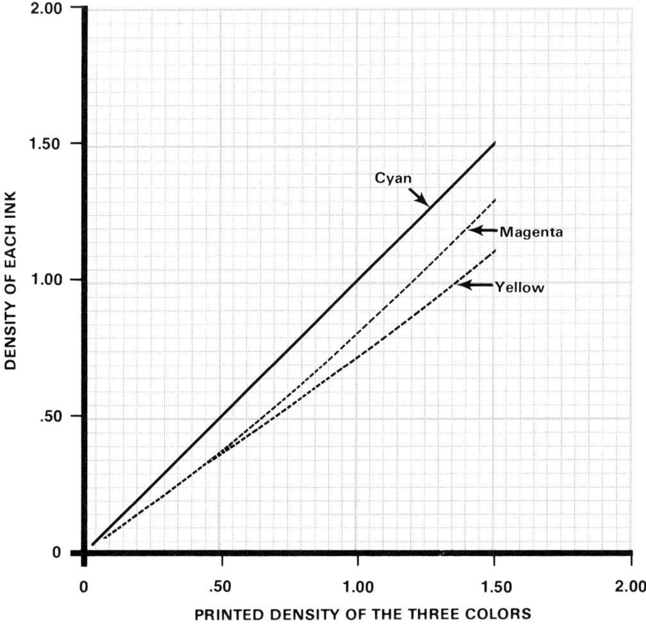

Figure 11.4. Relationship of END with each of the three-color ink densities

Courtesy Graphic Arts Technical Foundation

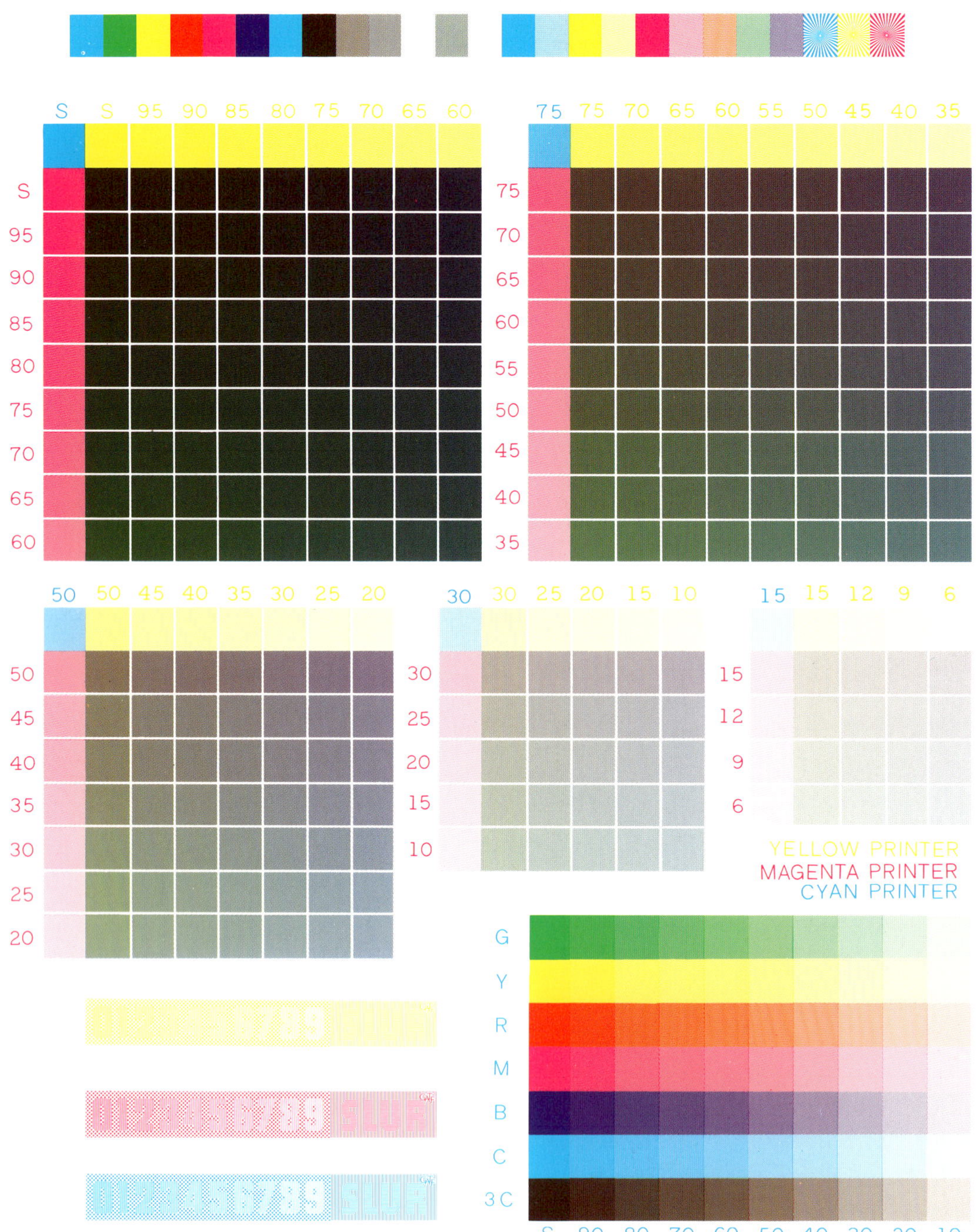

Figure 11.4a. GATF Gray Balance Chart

When the END is plotted against the individual printed density of each ink through the complementary filters, the press operator can use this information to check and adjust each printing color density for the accuracy of gray balance on the press sheet. To make an END curve, a gray scale is reproduced as neutral, then the dot values of the entire reproduced scale for each of the separations and printed density of each of the process colors are plotted against the combined density of the reproduced gray scale.

The reproduced gray scale is measured twice, once for the integrated density with a visual filter and once for each individual color with red, green, and blue filters. Once the curve is plotted and drawn, the scanner or press operator can pick up any density or percentage of dots of any one ink on the scale and find the exact equivalent density or dot percentage of the other two colors for a gray value. Conversely, the operator can pick up any point on the integrated density and locate the dot percentage required for any of the three colors to produce this density. An example of such curves is shown in Figure 11.4. The density values measured from a single ink film will be different than when the same ink film is measured from the integrated density reproduced with other colors. Normally the individual inks will read a lower density than when read from the integrated density because of the additivity failure. In this example, however, the density readings for cyan have been kept identical for both readings.

Courtesy T & E Center, Rochester Institute of Technology

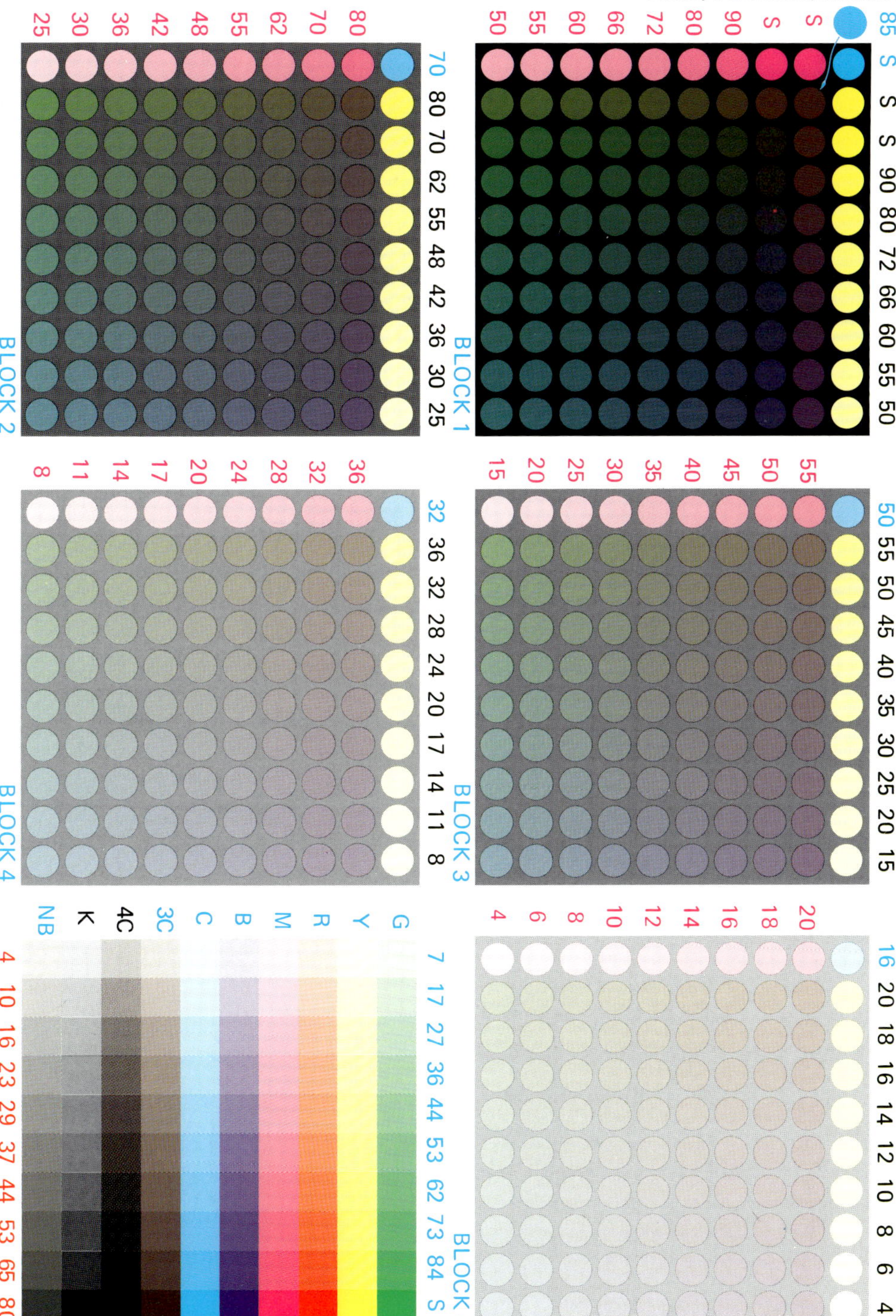

Figure 11.4b. RIT Tone Reproduction and Neutral Determination (TRAND) Chart

Methods for Determining Gray Balance

Several test targets are available to determine the amounts of cyan, magenta, and yellow needed to produce gray for a particular shop condition. Most printing processes achieve gray balance by varying the dot sizes for the three colors along the entire tone reproduction curve. Once the printing conditions are standardized, the correct printing dot sizes for gray balance can be determined with specially designed test targets such as the GATF Gray Balance Chart and the RIT Tone Reproduction and Neutral Determination Chart (TRAND). These targets consist of patches printed with different amounts of three dot percentages. Once the patches are printed, they are evaluated with standard viewing light and a patch is selected that produces neutral gray. After the gray patches are located for each gray level, the dot percentages for the three negatives are selected which produced the gray. The five aim points on the gray scale may produce the following data as shown in Table 14.

Table 14

Aim Points	Dot Percentage		
	C	M	Y
Highlight	5	4	4
Quarter-tone	21	18	18
Middle-tone	60	50	50
Three-quarter tone	78	73	73
Shadow	98	95	95

The major factors which influence END are the ink film thickness and the ink trapping problems on the press. When density readings are obtained by a densitometer, the readings are likely to change with the change of the ink film thickness, especially in the shadow areas. As such, the control of ink-film thickness and ink trapping are necessary for the consistency of the END. It should be emphasized here that no matter what charts or test targets are used to determine gray balance, its values will be entirely dependent on the printing variables. As such, it is important that no special press conditions are created to print these targets or charts. They should be printed alongside a regular production job using the standard press conditions. Otherwise the purpose will not be served. Once an optimum gray balance condition is determined, it can be plotted as a curve and recorded for use in the production steps.

When special targets such as GATF Gray Balance chart are not available to determine gray balance, the data obtained from END can be successfully used to determine gray balance. This is especially helpful when the three colors did not produce neutral when printed. Once the density of the three overprinted inks, individual density of each printed ink, and the dot percentages in the separations which produced these values are plotted, approximate values of the separations for gray balance along the entire length of the gray scale can be obtained from this data. Figure 11.5 is such an example. The base of the left quadrant is the printed density of the three colors. The middle line is the density values of each ink obtained by the complementary filters. The base of the right quadrant is the percentages of dots in the separations. The curves on the left quadrant are constructed from the data of the three color integrated printing density and the individual ink density. The readings are taken after the densitometer is calibrated for each color with a complementary filter to obtain equal density values for a neutral point. The calibration is normally done using a neutral plaque or an original gray scale. The curves on the right quadrant are plotted from the separation dot percentages and printed density for each color. With the assumption that each density point selected on the three color density will have equal values for all the three colors, any density point can be selected on the scale and the equivalent dot sizes can be found for the three colors for that density point. As in Figure 11.5, for a .50 density, the dot percentage for cyan is about 52, and for magenta and yellow are 46 and 44 respectively. Similarly in the same figure, for a three-color integrated density of 1.00, the cyan, magenta, and yellow separations contain 92%, 88%, and 80% dots respectively.

STEPS TO ADJUST GRAY BALANCE IN A SCANNER

Although the purpose is the same, the steps to adjust gray balance in a scanner vary from one brand of scanner to another. In most of the earlier models, after a neutral gray scale is reproduced and the tone values are obtained, adjustment for gray balance is performed manually during gradation adjustment. Three or more gradation aim points are selected on a dye gray scale. Each aim point is positioned for the scanning light, and then the predetermined tone values are assigned for each color.

With the advent of more sophisticated computers and memory devices, programs can be created and stored for gray balance by assigning unequal dot values for the three colors. Some scanners even have provisions to create and store additional gray balance programs for different requirements like coated or uncoated paper, different kinds of ink, dot gains in different presses, etc. Any of these programs can be recalled at any time to suit the need. During the creation of a basic program, average aim points are selected and gray balance tone or dot values are assigned.

Once the appropriate dot values for each aim point are stored in the computer for the three colors, the proportional dot values for gray balance will remain the same for any type of gradation. For example, some advanced scanners offer several fixed gradations to be stored in the computer's memory which can be recalled at any time for a specific type of

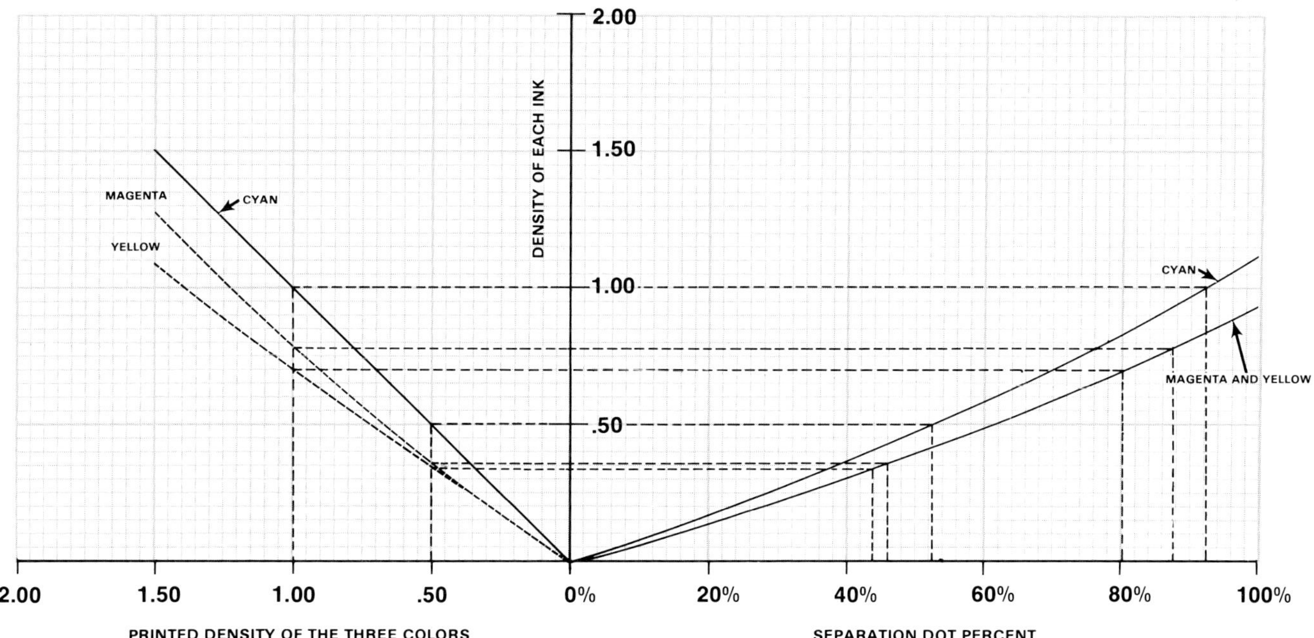

Figure 11.5. Relationship of END, individual ink densities, and halftone dot percentage

original. These gradations differ only in the curve shapes in quarter-tone, middle-tone, and three-quarter-tone values. Once the desired highlight and shadow aim points are selected for a specific original, any type of fixed gradation curve can be recalled and generated. This is true for both analog and digital types of scanners. However, no matter what type of curve shape is introduced, the difference in the proportional dot values for the three colors remain the same.

A few scanners provide three controls for cyan, magenta, and yellow to adjust tone or dot values for each color independently. Others offer one and sometimes two to adjust magenta and yellow tone values in relation to cyan. Some of the current scanner models like the Hell 399ER, offer a switch to activate or deactivate the gray balance adjustment. This provision allows the operator to adjust gradation or some other functions of the scanner without the effect of gray balance. For example, after the gray values are introduced by activating the switch, the operator deactivates the gray balance switch during the gradation adjustment. He/she then selects any aim point and assigns same size dot values for the three colors for each aim point without having to worry about the proportional dot values for each color. The gray values will take effect as soon as the gray balance switch is activated.

Some programmable scanners such as the Magnascan 645 provide up to a 16-step reference point density scale for gray balance. Others offer the normal five — highlight, quarter-tone, middle-tone, three-quarter-tone, and shadow. With the 16-step reference scale, for each fixed cyan values in the steps, the magenta and yellow values are entered into the computer. During the subsequent operation of the scanner, the gray balance will be effective for any gradation curve.

GRAY BALANCE CONTROLS IN DIFFERENT SCANNERS

Crosfield Magnascan 645

In this digital scanner, the gray balance tone values for the three colors are already programmed in the software and available as Basic Values (BV). This Basic Values consist of a tone-value curve for each color against a 16-step reference print density scale. This 16-step basic gray balance values can be generated as an electronic gray scale by using Calibration # 54. This electronic scale contains fixed values for cyan. The scale is printed under normal printing conditions, and the results are assessed for neutrality. If change is necessary, the magenta and yellow dot values are changed in relation to the cyan for proper gray balance. The following are the cyan dot percentage values for the entire 16-step scale:

0-5-10-15-20-25-30-40-50-60-70-80-85-90-95-100

After the new magenta and yellow values for the above cyan values are entered, they are stored as Customer Values

(CV) as a specific program. Several different programs for gray balance can be stored as Customer Values for different printing conditions such as change of paper or ink quality, etc.

Dainippon Screen SG-608

In this scanner, the gray balance is set and maintained with the Highlight and Shadow dot percent set knobs and the gradation control knobs in conjunction with two Reference switches. With the pair of Reference switches, fixed density values are generated for quarter-tone, middle-tone, and three-quarter-tone aim points. After the photomultipliers are calibrated with the Autobalance function, first the gray dot values for highlight and shadow for the three colors are selected with the Highlight and Shadow dot percent set knobs. Then the Reference switches are placed in different positions for the different aim points, and then unequal dot values are assigned for the three colors with the gradation control knobs. Figure 11.6 shows the Highlight and Shadow dot percent set knobs. The Reference switches are located at the left bottom section of the color computer panel. The gradation panel is presented with Figure 9.41 on page 164.

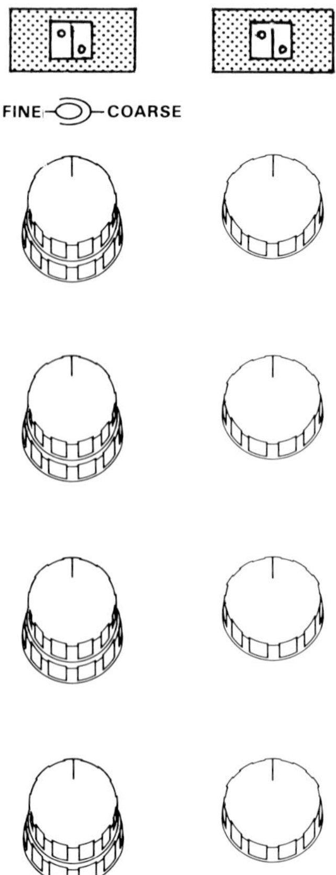

Figure 11.6. HIGHLIGHT and SHADOW DOT PERCENT set knobs in the DS SG-608 to set the highlight and shadow dot percent for the four colors. There are four highlight dual-function knobs; the outer knobs are for coarse and the inner knobs are for fine adjustments

Hell 399ER

The gray balance controls in this scanner consist of three specially designated knobs for cyan, magenta, and yellow and a toggle switch. The functions of the three knobs include independent adjustment of dot values for each color in relation to the other colors for accurate gray balance. During the initial gradation adjustment, each aim point is positioned for the scanning light and these controls are used to adjust the dot values. The toggle switch is used to activate or deactivate the effect of the gray balance controls.

The percentage of dots for all the colors are identically set during the basic gradation adjustment by assigning identical dot values for each aim point of the gray scale. However, the effect of gray balance control is deactivated with the toggle switch. During the operation of the scanner, the gray balance control must be activated for unequal dot values in the three colors.

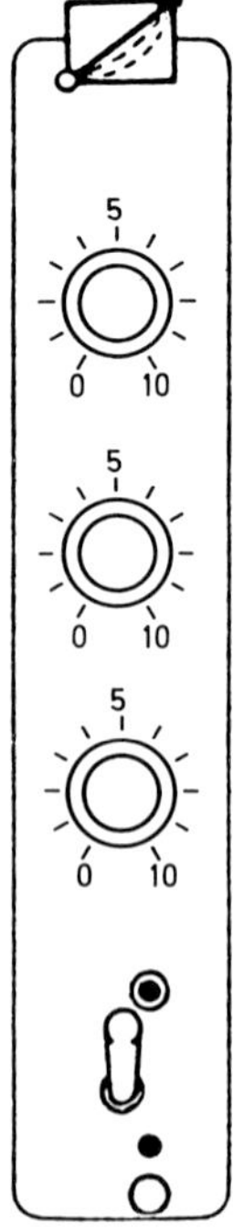

Figure 11.7. Gray Balance panel in the Hell 399ER

Royal Zenith 200-S

In this scanner a single curve for tone reproduction and gray balance can be programmed and stored in the computer for future use. If a gray scale with known density steps was reproduced and found to have produced satisfactory tone and gray values, the separation dot percentage values for each step can be used to produce the program.

The steps to produce the program include monitoring each step of the scale and entering the dot values for cyan, magenta, and yellow. After all the values for the three colors are entered, the black values for the entire scale can also be entered by monitoring the same scale steps. When programming is completed, the control setting values (CONSET) for each color can be displayed and recorded on a program sheet. This part of the program is then stored. A gray scale can then be generated using the program and printed, to verify the accuracy of gray balance. Once the program is finalized and stored, and once the highlight and range for an original is set, the gray balance values will be automatically generated by the computer.

Chapter 12
Under Color Removal (UCR)

TERMS AND DEFINITIONS

Experts agree that in color reproduction black can be beautiful if used wisely. Black can add details and contrast in the reproduction which is impossible to achieve with the three process colors. However, if the black is not used judiciously, it will do more harm than good. It will make the colors look dirty and create an unnatural contrast.

One way to use black to the best advantage is to remove some of the cyan, magenta, and yellow inks from the dark neutral areas of the reproduction to make room for a strong and rich black. This process is called under color removal and is abbreviated as UCR.

ADVANTAGES OF UCR

Theoretically, when all the process colors — cyan, magenta, and yellow are printed on the same area of the paper, they should absorb all the colors reflected from the white surface of the paper and produce black. However, because of the impurities in the ink, the combination of equal amounts of three colors become brownish with dominant magenta and yellow hues, and the reproduction cannot match the contrast of the original. As a result, the black ink is added to the three colors to compensate for the deficiency of the printing inks. However, addition of the black has a far reaching effect on the reproduction that goes beyond compensating for the ink problems. Some of the advantages of black in the process color reproduction are:

1. Black brings out better detail and contrast in the photograph than is possible with process colors. Black will make the white appear whiter and will add density, resulting in improved contrast in the shadow areas. Higher contrast usually also increases the image sharpness.
2. Substantial amounts of the process colors removed from the areas where black is to be printed allows better ink trapping during press run.
3. Process colors are more expensive than black. Substituting three process colors with a cheaper black makes under color removal more economical.
4. With under color removal, the total deposit of ink on paper is much less, and as such, the ink set off problem is reduced.
5. For the reason indicated above, drying time is also reduced through the use of under color removal.
6. Because of the use of black, balancing the other three colors is less critical, especially in the shadow areas.

UCR IN THE CONVENTIONAL SEPARATION

Until the introduction of electronic scanners, under color removal had been a time consuming and difficult technique. Only in the indirect method of color separation has under color removal achieved a certain degree of success. With the introduction of the direct-screening in an enlarger or in a process camera, a separate mask was needed for under color removal. This is a time consuming step and undermined the advantages of direct-screening.

In the indirect separation, under color removal is applied by using a positive mask made from the black printer separation negative. During the exposing of the positives from the corrected three-color separation negatives, the mask is placed in register with each of the three process color negatives, one at a time. In the direct-screen separation, the mask is exposed with the split filters to record the black image. This under color removal and the color correction masks are then placed in register with the original when separations are exposed. In the indirect separation, correction of the black separation is critical when it is used for making an under color removal mask. This is especially true when the separations are for high speed wet-on-wet printing where maximum under color removal is needed. Failure to do so will make the black image print in the dark color areas of the reproduction.

In a camera or an enlarger, the process of creating an image which will substitute the neutral areas of the copy has some serious obstacles. Under color removal is achieved by removing the cyan, magenta, and yellow inks from the neutral areas of the original. However, because of the delicate nature of the processes and materials, the gray value obtained in the conventional separation is only an average value and often contains dark color areas. Although the characteristics of the color computer in a scanner can be adjusted to suit various conditions, however, the scope of adjustments in a photomechanical exposure is limited. As a result, when a black separation is exposed, in addition to the neutral shadow areas of the copy, the separation will also record some dark color areas of the original. To minimize this problem, it has been a practice in the industry to expose the black separation through the red, green, and blue separation filters in turn. This is called split filter black, and the purpose is to obtain the average darkest value for each of the process colors. As a consequence, the split-filter black will produce a density which will be more accurate in the darkest neutrals and will print on the dark colored areas if it is extended beyond the darkest shadow. As a result, split filter black has a very limited success and to avoid printing black on colored areas, the black printer in the conventional separation is made to print only in the darkest shadow areas of the reproduction. This type of black gradation is called skeleton black.

UCR IN A SCANNER

Compared to a conventional separation, the capabilities of a modern scanner offer a radical change in the application of under color removal. Among its numerous advantages, the scanner scans the original point by point and thus offers better control for effective under color removal. All scanners, in addition to having three computers for cyan, magenta, and yellow, have a separate computer for the black separation. During scanning, when the separations are in progress, the computer for the black separation keeps track of the three colors where an equal or proportional quantity of the three inks are producing neutral. Depending on the extent of under color removal desired and the appropriate controls set, the three process inks are automatically weakened or reduced in these neutral areas. During the black separation, the computer generates images only in the areas where the three process inks were reduced or weakened, i.e. the neutral areas. No black appears in areas where any of the primary or secondary colors are present. The result is an improvement of the black image in the entire range of the reproduction — an intense and clean black without affecting the purity of the other colors.

Further explanation on the electronic generation of a black printer is in order. It was indicated earlier that theoretically a neutral tone is composed of three equal amounts of cyan, magenta and yellow. As shown in Figure 12.1, the smallest portion of the three color ink amounts producing black or neutral is also present in the other two inks. In this particular example, the smallest portion is cyan, which is also present

Courtesy Hell Graphic Systems, Inc.

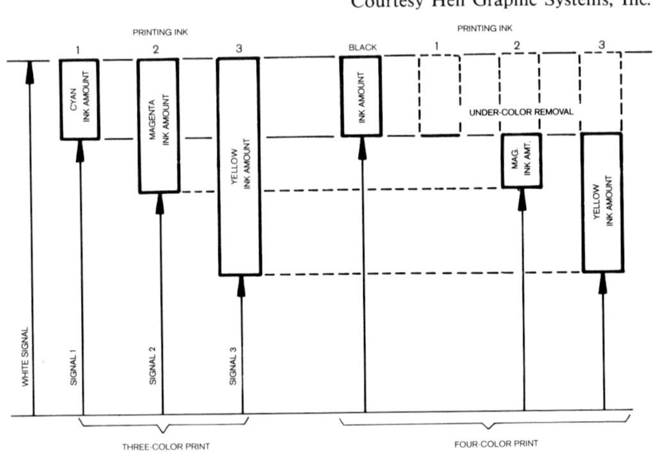

Figure 12.1. Three and four-color printing ink density produced by the exposing light and the black portion of the ink amount

in magenta and yellow. Theoretically, when the smallest portion of the cyan and the same amount of magenta and yellow are combined, they make black or neutral gray. As shown in the figure, when an electrical signal is generated from a picture, the maximum voltage will produce the maximum intensity for the exposing lamp. In a negative it will be the dense black portion or the non-image area and will correspond to the white signal in the diagram. The ink amount will be zero at this point. A decrease in voltage will increase the ink amount, and the lowest voltage will produce the highest ink amount. The highest of the three color signals (signal 1 in Figure 12.1) corresponds to the smallest amount of the process inks. This smallest signal from the three photomultipliers can be easily selected electronically by the black computer.

The discussion in the chapter "Color Correction" indicated that the settings of the basic and selective color correction controls for white colors play a major role in the generation of the black printer. As explained with Figure 10.17 on page 180 , the smallest amount of the three colors is a common black portion. The black computer monitors the smallest ink amount in the three colors and replaces this amount with black ink. However, if required, adjustments other than the smallest signal or lowest ink amount can also be selected by means of the selective color correction or similar controls in the analog and digital scanners.

EXTENT AND PERCENTAGE OF UCR

The degree or extent of under color removal may vary. It may be moderate to extensive depending on whether a lot or a little of the process colors are removed from the shadow areas and replaced by black. The extent of under color removal to be applied will depend on the type of original and the printing process. For example, originals with plenty of shadow details similar to a low-key original need more under color removal than a high-key original. In high speed wet-on-wet printing, like newspapers, where all colors are printed without allowing time to dry before the next ink is applied, it is not possible to print a large amount of the colors in the shadow areas. In this situation, a considerable amount of under color removal is applied. On the other hand, when each ink is allowed to dry before the next color is applied, a much smaller amount of under color removal may be used. However, certain paper, ink, and press conditions cannot print with good results more than a limited percentage of dots in an area. In fact, the SWOP Committee for web offset printing in 1986 revision states that 300 percent of a possible 400 percent is the absolute maximum for four color process printing to accomplish proper ink trapping.

The volume or extent of under color removal is normally expressed and measured in percent values. The higher the percentage, more under color removal is applied. It should be noted that when under color removal is applied, it compresses the range of the separation in the neutrals; the higher the percentage of under color removal, the more compression results. The percentage and the tone compression resulting from under color removal are explained with the following example.

It is assumed that a 30% under color removal is applied to a transparency having a highlight density of .30 and shadow density of 2.70. First it will be necessary to locate the three-color printing density values obtained from these two original density values. It is assumed that the .30 and 2.70 density values on the original produced the printing density values of .10 and 1.30 on the press sheet respectively.

The range of the printing density is: 1.20 (1.30-.10).

For a 30% under color removal, the approximate shift of the shadow density of the three colors will be .36 (30% of the printing density of 1.20).

When the density of .36 is subtracted from the three color printing density of 1.30, the revised three-color density will be .94 (1.30-.36) because of 30% UCR. The range of the reproduced neutral scale is reduced from 1.20 to .84 (.94-.10) for a 30% under color removal.

DETERMINING BLACK SEPARATION

The under color removal and the black separation are closely related and one cannot be discussed without referring to the other one. A detailed discussion of color correction and tone reproduction for the black separation is presented in the chapters "Color Correction" and "Tone Reproduction." Although the purpose of the black is to make up for the deficiency of the three process inks, still it is difficult to obtain a four-color print which will be optically equivalent to a multicolored original. The quantity of black required for a certain reproduction will be dependent on the printing technique, the paper, the printing speed, and the printing colors being used. These factors may make the required level of black to fluctuate for different jobs, and the precise value of standard black can be obtained by trial for individual operating conditions.

In most scanners it is possible to produce a flexible black gradation ranging from a typical skeleton to a full range black. The two most important adjustments for the black separation are: (1) to select an appropriate range of the black, in other words, to select the proper tone values for the highlight and shadow; and (2) to determine the appropriate curve shape for the black gradation. For most scanners, selecting the range is performed by positioning the scanning light spot on a gray scale or copy and entering the appropriate dot values. For example, if the black is required to start in the light area where 30% cyan dots are present, the operator first positions the gray scale for a 30% cyan, and then a 1% dot value for black is entered. Normally 80 to 90 percent black dots are printed in the shadow area. In addition to assigning dot values for highlight and shadow, various aim points can be selected manually on the gray scale and different types of gradations for the black can be created by assigning different dot values. In most scanners, various types of black gradation curves can be programmed and stored for different applications.

As indicated earlier, the impurities and the additivity failure of the three process inks cause considerable flattening in the shadow areas causing a color cast. The black is used to increase the density at the extreme shadow end, thus compensating for the additivity failure of the three inks. As a result, the gradation for the black separation is adjusted to produce more contrast with a steepened curve at the shadow so that it compensates for this flattening effect caused by the three process inks.

Using a Jones Diagram to Determine Black Gradation for Different Percentages of UCR

A Jones Diagram can be effectively used to determine the black separation required for a specific printing condition. This was explained earlier in the chapter "Tone Reproduction" with Figure 9.14 on page 149. Once the printing conditions are optimized and standardized, a Jones Diagram can also be used to determine the curve shape of the black, as well as the three-color separation curves for different percentages of UCR. Several gradation curves with different percentages of UCR can be calculated and applied in the separations for different printing conditions. In some of the modern scanners with memory banks, various curves can be stored for different types of paper, ink, original, or any other printing characteristics which call for different percentages of UCR.

The data needed for plotting the Jones Diagram is the same as the data which was used previously to obtain an optimum black gradation. First the percentage of under color removal needed is determined, and then the density shift for three-color overprints is also calculated from the printing data. As in the example cited on page 205, the UCR is 30% and the density shift of the three-color print caused by the 30% UCR is .94 from the original shadow density of 1.30. The shift or change is 0.36.

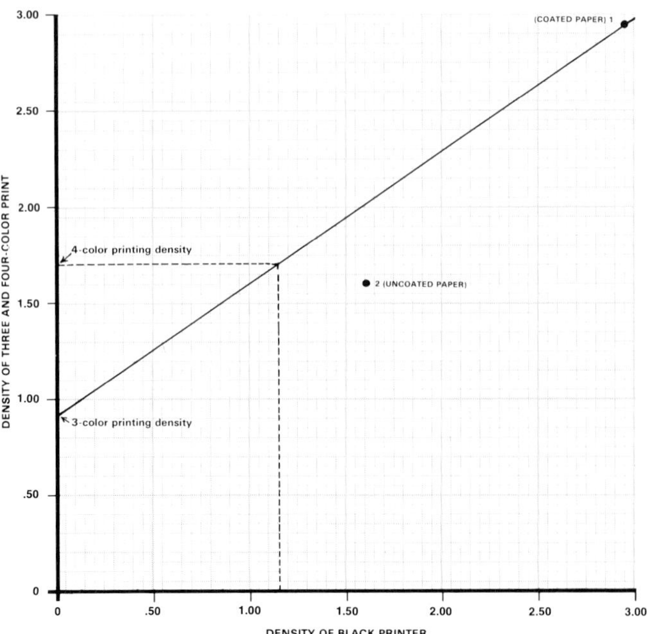

Figure 12.2. Determining the black printer for a 30% UCR

As shown in Figure 12.2, the revised three-color printing density (in this example .94) and the four-color density values are applied to the ordinate of "Black Addition Diagram" to locate the black printing density. In Figure 12.3, these density values are applied to the top right quadrant from which the black gradation curve is obtained. The procedure to plot the halftone positives for black in the bottom right quadrant is the same as previously described with Figure 9.14 on page 149 in the chapter "Tone Reproduction."

CONTROLS FOR UCR IN A SCANNER

Depending on the brand of scanner, the controls for under color removal will vary from one scanner to another. Analog scanners with variable potentiometer type controls normally consist of starting point control and intensity controls for cyan, magenta, and yellow colors. The effects of these controls on a separation are explained in Figure 12.4. With the starting point control, the operator selects a point on the three color gradation curve from which the under color removal will be effective. In Figure 12.4, three different starting points at different density values on the gradation curve are indicated by P1, P2, and P3. After the starting point is selected on the gradation curve, the intensity controls for cyan, magenta, and yellow are adjusted for the required degree or percentage of under color removal.

First the scanning light spot is positioned on a shadow point of the original or a step of the gray scale. From this point towards the shadow, under color removal will be effective. The starting point control is set for the particular density selected, and the removal of the process colors are affected by adjusting a single control or a set of individual controls for each color. If the shadow area has a color cast, it must be corrected to make it neutral so that under color removal can be effective. But several scanners including the Crosfield Magnascan 645 and the Hell 399ER provide UCR adjustment facilities in a color cast area, if required.

Some scanners provide an additional pushbutton or toggle switch to turn off the effect of under color removal adjustment on the separations to check the adjustment effect on the important colors. A faulty adjustment of the under color removal control will affect the hue of certain colors. To find if there is any change of color because of the under color removal adjustment, first the scanning light spot is positioned for a tone value or color to be checked, and the effect of under color removal is turned off by the push button or the switch provided. By releasing and depressing the pushbutton or turning the switch on and off in quick succession, a difference in values will indicate that the color is affected by under color removal adjustment. No change indicates that the color is not affected by this adjustment. This control is especially

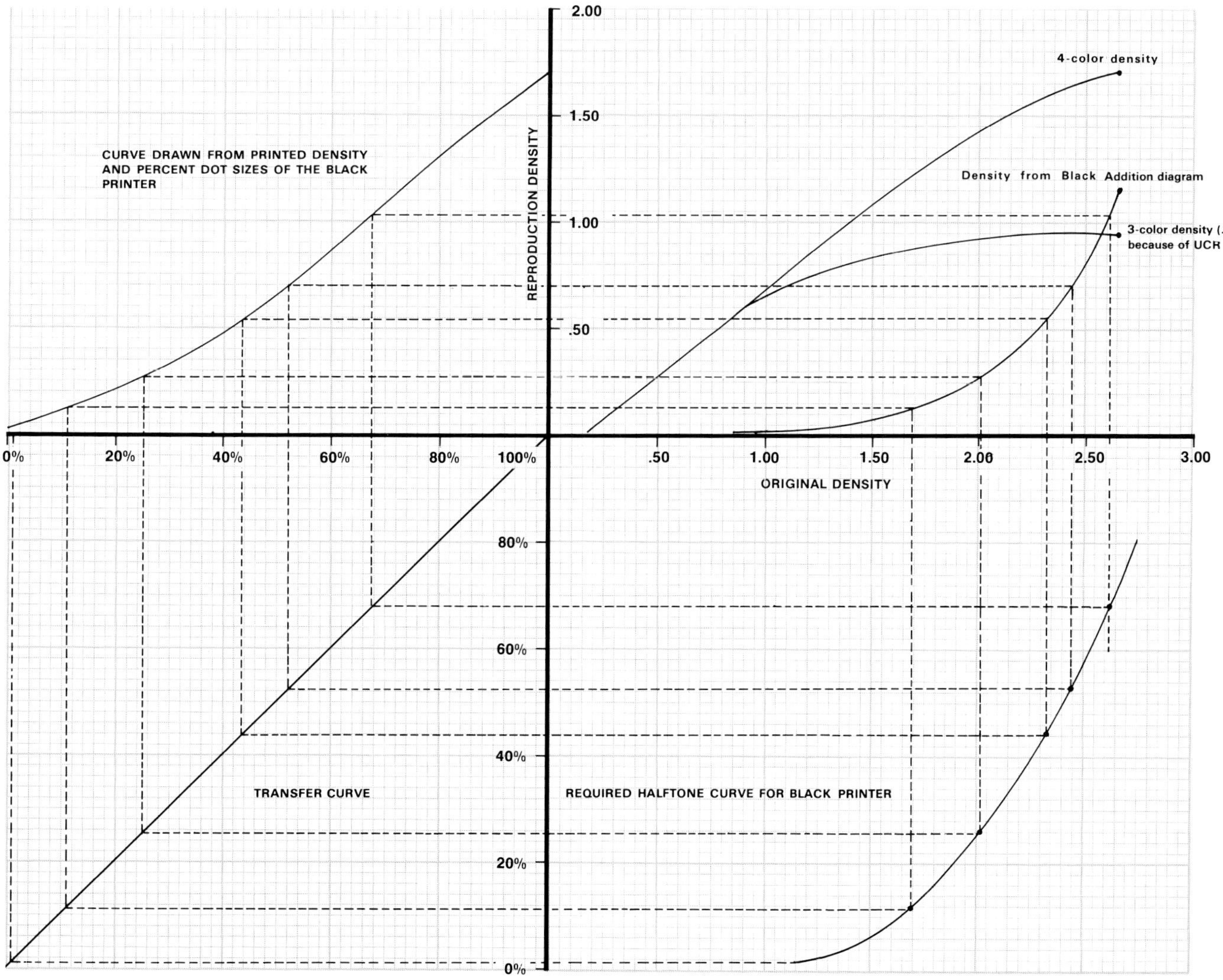

Figure 12.3. A Jones Diagram to determine the required halftone for black with 30% UCR

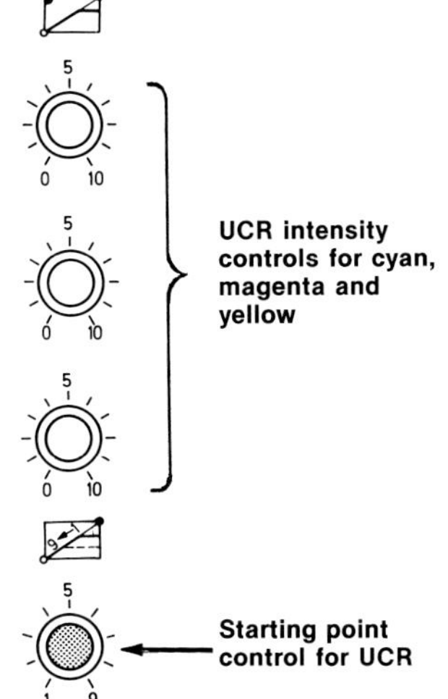

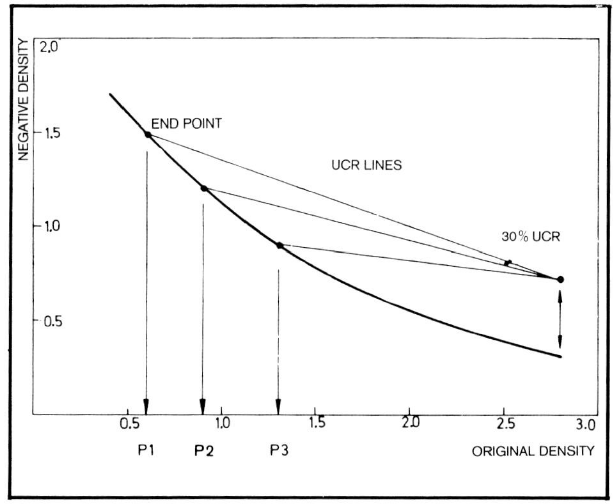

Figure 12.4. Effect of starting or break point control on the UCR

useful for checking critical colors like flesh tones, wood tones, etc.

If the tone values of certain critical colors are shifted because of the adjustment of UCR, repositioning the starting point control towards the shadow density normally solves the problem. However, if the situation still persists, the white color correction adjustment for the three colors should be checked. If this does not solve the problem, color correction for the black separation needs to be readjusted.

The digital scanners allow the operator to use a fixed under color removal program or to develop a program and assign certain values for the amount of under color removal. With this program, it is also possible to adjust the range and slope of the black gradation curve and store the program for later use. The operator simply recalls the specific program values during operation. In the Magnascan 645, a basic UCR program (called Basic Values or BV) is supplied with the scanner for normal originals. The program can be recalled by using a Calibration number. However, the operator may create new programs and store these as Customer Values for specific application. In some of these scanners, under color removal and under color addition functions are combined in one set of controls.

UNDER COLOR REMOVAL AND GRAY COMPONENT REPLACEMENT

Since the introduction of gray component replacement (GCR) (discussed in the chapter "Gray Component Replacement") in various scanners, the functions of UCR and GCR have been somewhat integrated in these scanners. For example, in the DS SG-608 scanner, when the ICR (Integrated Color Removal — GCR version of DS) is activated, the UCR and the black separation curves are coupled. The UCR controls cease to function, and turning the black gradation knob changes the black gradation curve from a skeleton to a full range black and at the same time the UCR amount of C, M, and Y changes from 0% to 100% in a step wise fashion (see Figure 12.5). In the Hell 399ER scanners, the control for UCR and UCA has double functions — it is used to determine the intensity of under color removal as well as to determine under color addition of neutral tones in the cyan, magenta, and yellow separations. However, when the CCR (Complementary Color Reduction, Hell's version of GCR) switch is activated, the function of the UCR is switched to UCA. With this control, the UCA intensity of cyan, magenta, and yellow can be added to reinforce the image shadows. This technique of adding process colors to the black is often called black color addition or BCA.

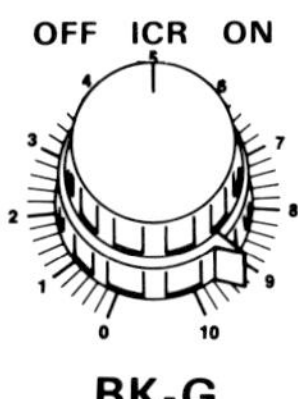

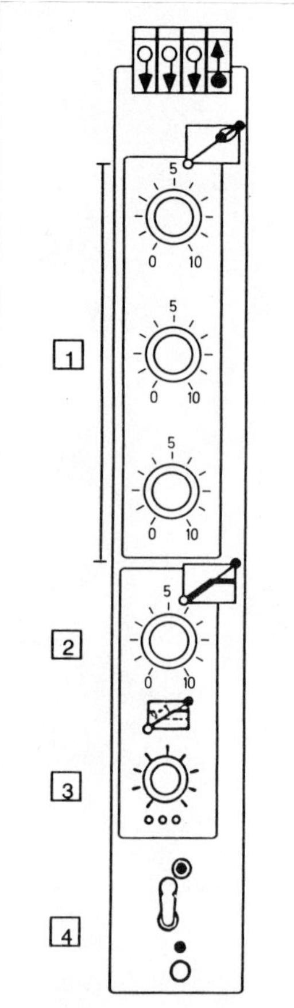

Figure 12.5. ICR/Black gradation knob in the DS SG-608 (top); and the Dominant Color Control (1) and UCR/UCA panel in the Hell 399ER showing UCR/UCA intensity control (2), starting point control (3) and toggle switch to activate either UCR or UCA (4)

UCR CONTROLS IN DIFFERENT SCANNERS

Crosfield Magnascan 645

In this all digital scanner, UCR is accessed via a calibration number. The operator selects the appropriate calibration number (CAL 515), answers "yes" to the prompt shown in the alphanumeric display and enters a break point and a slope of the black gradation curve. The break point is achieved by entering a starting dot percentage for the black by monitoring the cyan separation, and the slope is achieved by entering the maximum dot percentage for black while monitoring cyan

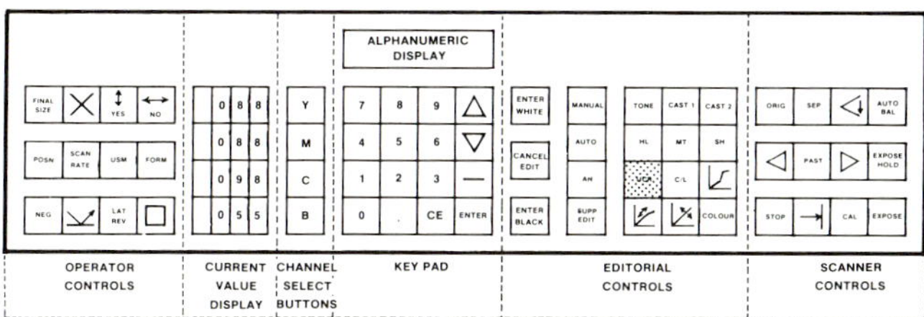

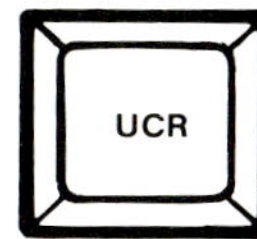

Figure 12.6. Magnascan 645 panel showing the UCR pushbutton control

separation and a neutral shadow area of the original. This shadow area should be the same as the one used for ENTER BLACK during the basic calibration of the multipliers.

Dainippon Screen SG-608

The controls for UCR in this scanner (see Figure 12.5) consist of a set of three intensity controls for cyan, magenta, and yellow to reduce the three colors independently in the shadow areas. The third control is a dual-function knob. The outer knob is a starting point control to determine the point on the gradation curve from which UCR will be effective. Each control can be switch-selected for UCR or UCA. If there is any cast, it is first corrected with the UCA controls. Then the UCR controls are activated, and the desired amount of UCR is set with the respective controls.

In addition, a black gradation knob is provided at the bottom of the panel. This control is used to determine the shape of a black gradation curve. At the 0 position, the curve is linear, and becomes full range when this control is at the highest intensity.

Hell 399ER

In this scanner, the controls for UCR, UCA and CCR are integrated into an elaborate and functional control panel (see Figure 12.5). There are three intensity controls for cyan, magenta and yellow called the DOMINANT COLOR CONTROL. When the positions of these controls are set at 0, any color cast in the shadow, for example, a dark green or a dark brown including the neutral will be affected by UCR. In other words, at position 0, the UCR will be effective in the darkest shadow areas regardless of whether the shadow is neutral or has a dominant color cast. When the intensity of any one or more of these controls is increased, there will be less effect by UCR on a color cast in the shadow. Consequently, the position of these dominant color controls determines the color or colors of the shadow cast to be affected by UCR.

The UCR and UCA consist of a single intensity control with dual functions. This control determines the intensity of under color removal (UCR) of neutral tones in the cyan, magenta, and yellow separations. The position of the starting point control for the UCR/UCA determines the point on the gradation curve from which the UCR/UCA will be effective. Any one function of the UCR/UCA is selected by a toggle switch. Another toggle switch is used to activate or deactivate the UCR/UCA intensity and starting point controls.

The toggle switch which selects the functions of UCR/UCA automatically activates the CCR control when the UCA is activated, and simultaneously the UCR intensity and starting point control become the UCA intensity and starting point control for the CCR. With these controls, the printing colors of cyan, magenta, and yellow can be added to reinforce the picture shadows for the CCR function.

The UCR function of this scanner works closely with another set of controls called COLOR CAST COMPENSATION-SHADOW (see Figure 8.8). With these controls, the color cast of a shadow can be neutralized if necessary. The panel consists of a set of cyan, magenta, and yellow control knobs that can neutralize the picture shadow, and another intensity control for adjusting the intensity of the black shadow. There are two starting point controls — one for the three-color shadow, and the other one for the black shadow. The positions of these controls determine the position on the gradation curve from which the color cast compensation for shadow will be effective. In addition, there is a toggle switch at the bottom of this panel that activates or deactivates the effect of the above controls.

Royal Zenith 200-S

In this scanner, adjustments for UCR is made with the F and UCR keys and then changing the control setting numbers within the range of +128 and -127 to increase or decrease the effect of UCR on the three colors. The plus numbers reduce

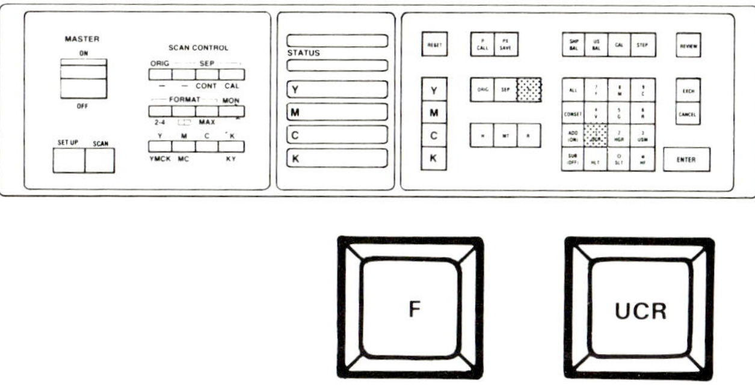

Figure 12.7. Panel of RZ 200-S showing the pushbutton control for UCR

and minus numbers increase the density or dot percentage. The UCR can be adjusted for all colors at once or individually for each color. The same keys can be used for UCR and for UCA individually for a single or for all colors. Adjustments for black UCR is made with the K and UCR keys.

Normally a program is produced for the black in the same way as the color channels, and once the black gradation is programmed and stored, the correct black will be automatically produced when the highlight and range of the transparency are set. After the highlight dot percentage for the cyan, magenta, and yellow are set using the gray scale, the first printing dot required for the black can be set by monitoring any color on the gray scale and entering the percentage for black. A full range black can also be obtained by first selecting the highlight and range of the original and entering the black values using the gray scale steps. Adjustments for the black UCR can be made with special keys designated for this purpose. Unlike the UCR for the colors, positive control setting numbers in UCR for the black separation increase the density, and negative numbers decrease density.

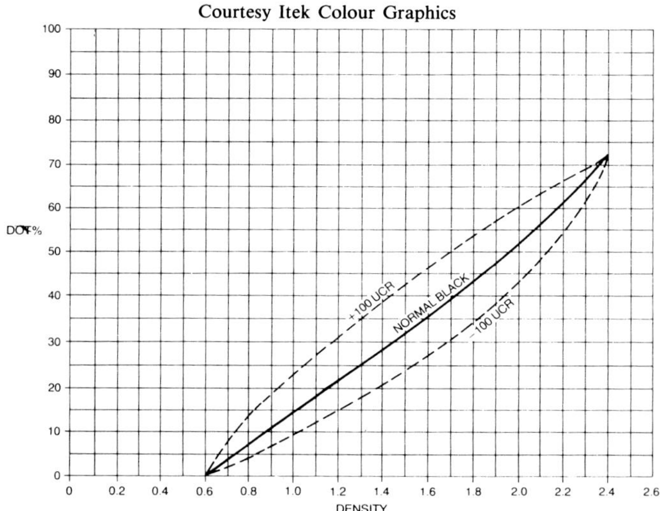

Figure 12.8. Adjusted black curve for UCR in the RZ 200-S

Chapter 13
Under Color Addition (UCA)

TERMS AND DEFINITIONS

A number of scanners offer controls to add colors in shadow areas of the original, if there is any, for insufficient density or a color cast due to lack of one or more of the three colors. Actually the addition of color is needed to eliminate a color cast so that a neutral shadow can be produced and the three colors of the original become balanced. As such, the blacks or neutrals are increased by addition rather than decreased as in the case of under color removal. Under color addition strengthens only the neutral shadow areas and does not affect any color components. In this respect, under color addition is closely tied with under color removal — since under color removal takes place only in the neutral areas. One of the main purposes of under color addition is to create neutral areas in the shadow of an original so that under color removal takes effect for that original. In the industry, under color addition is normally abbreviated as UCA.

UCA AND GRAY BALANCE

The addition of color introduces a color cast in the selected tonal areas of the original, and if a true gray scale is reproduced with the original, the neutrality of the gray will change, and the reproduction will show color cast in the shadow areas. Figure 13.1 shows the effect of under color addition on a reproduced gray scale. The curve on the left is plotted from a normal reproduced gray scale, and the curve on the right shows the effect at the shadow end of the gradation when UCA is introduced. In some scanners, the addition of color controls are effectively used to remove color cast from the shadow areas.

DIFFERENCE BETWEEN THE UCA AND COLOR CAST REMOVAL CONTROLS

Some analog scanners offer specific controls to remove color cast from the original, if there is any. Normally there are two sets of controls — one for the highlight and the other for the shadow areas. The major difference is that the color cast removal controls are used to subtract colors from the original; whereas the main purpose of under color addition is to add colors in the shadow areas of the original to make a neutral shadow. In addition, most color cast removal controls do not have controls for starting points. However, the overall chromatic effect on the separation is the same for both UCA and color cast removal controls. Adjustment of these controls changes the way the separation computer "sees" the original; that is, the chromatic input of the color computer is changed.

Courtesy Hell Graphic Systems, Inc.

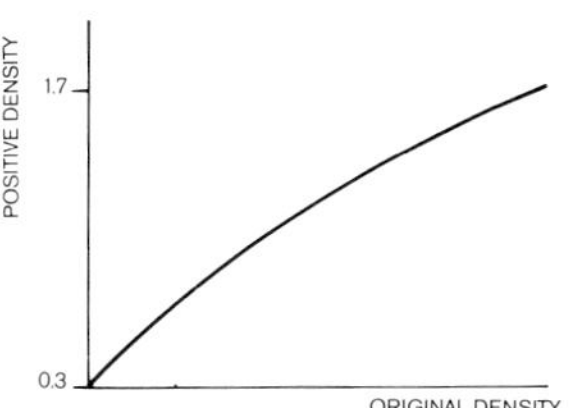

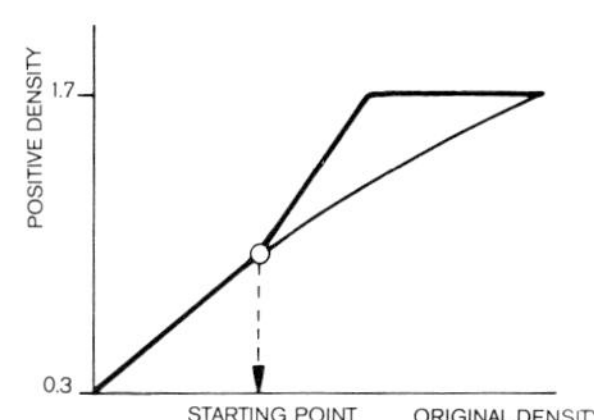

Figure 13.1. Effect of UCA on a gray scale curve

UCA IN DIFFERENT TYPES OF SCANNERS

A set of switch-selected dual function knobs is provided for both UCR and UCA in the DS SG-608 scanner. The outer knob in one of these controls can be used to select a starting point on the gradation curve from which the UCR/UCA will be effective. With the three intensity controls, the cyan, magenta, and yellow can be adjusted to neutralize a shadow area if a color cast is present. The adjustment is carried out by positioning the shadow area of the original for the scanning light spot and then individually balancing the colors with the three intensity controls.

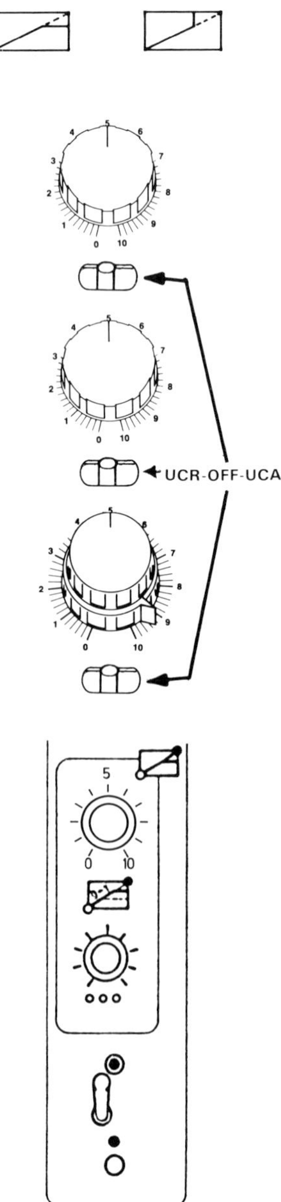

Figure 13.2. UCA controls in the DS SG-608 and Hell 399ER

In the Crossfield 645 scanners, two cast controls are provided which can be used independently for each of the three colors. CAST 1 is used for the removal or addition of cyan, magenta and yellow casts independently in each color channel in the highlight, middle-tone, and shadow areas. It affects all areas of the subjects simultaneously whether they are colored or neutral. CAST 2 control can be used to remove or add cyan, magenta, and yellow individually to neutral only in the shadow without affecting colors. The cast can be corrected by first positioning the scanning light for the shadow area affected by the cast, monitoring the different tone values on the Alphanumeric display, calling the CAST 2 program, and entering either the appropriate index number or using the INCREASE/DECREASE button.

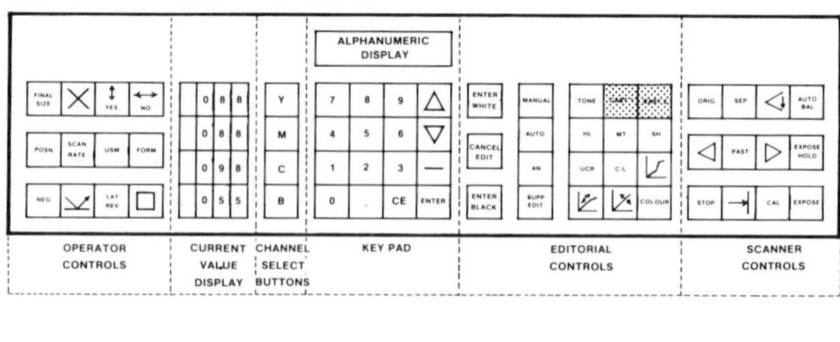

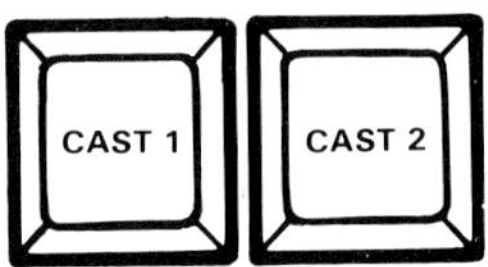

Figure 13.3. Control panel in the Magnascan 645 showing the pushbutton controls for CAST 1 and CAST 2

In the Hell 399ER, the UCA is a dual-function control. When the CCR (Complementary Color Reduction, GCR version of Hell) function is activated, the UCA is used to add color under black. However, a separate set of controls called COLOR CAST COMPENSATION-SHADOW is used to neutralize a shadow cast. The set consists of a panel of three controls, one each for the cyan, magenta and yellow, and a separate control for the black. The three intensity controls are used to neutralize a color cast, and the control for black is used to adjust the intensity of black for the picture shadow. Both the colors and black have starting point controls which are used to select a point on the gradation curve from which these controls will be effective. In addition, a toggle switch is provided at the bottom of the panel to deactivate the effect of the above controls, if needed. These adjustments are explained with Figures 8.8 and 12.5 in the chapters "Correction for Color Cast" and "Under Color Removal" on pages 135 and 208

In the RZ 200-S scanner, the UCA is called a Reverse UCR, and the same UCR program is used to increase the percentage of dots individually or for all the colors except black in the shadow areas. First, the standard UCR program is called, the scanning light is positioned for the shadow area in which the color needs to be added, the dot percentage for each color is monitored on the display panel, and then one or more colors are increased or decreased for neutral results.

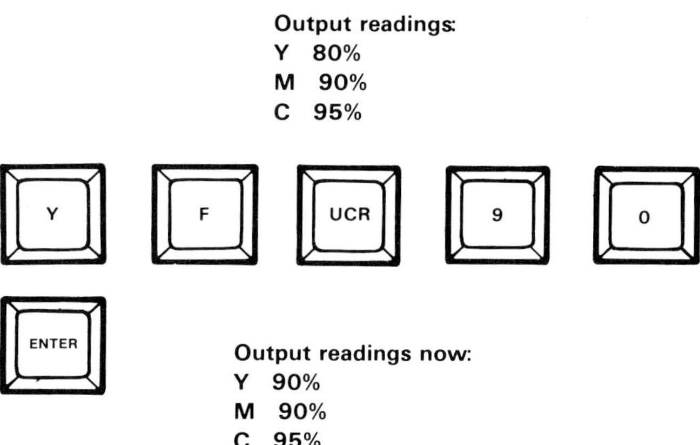

Figure 13.4. Sequence of Reverse UCR in the RZ 200-S

Chapter 14
Gray Component Replacement (GCR)

TERMS AND DEFINITIONS

An old concept related to under color removal and gradation of the black printer has been recently revitalized. Gray Component Replacement or GCR is the official name given to this concept by the US printing industry. The function of GCR is included in most of the latest scanners. Scanner manufacturers are using various terms for GCR in process color reproduction. For example, PCR is Crosfield's Polychromatic Color Removal; ICR is Dainippon Screen's Integrated Color Removal; CCR and PCR are Hell's Complementary Color Reduction and Programmed Color Reduction; and PIR is Royal Zenith's Programmed Ink Reduction.

BACKGROUND INFORMATION

More than twenty five years ago, most color reproductions were done by using a long range black in the letterpress printing to increase details and to create colors which are difficult to produce by the three process inks. In addition to the photographic process, considerable manual skills were needed to remove under colors and to produce the long range black. With the introduction of photographic masking, color correction was accomplished with the photographic process, and hand retouching of the negatives or positives became limited. In the photographic process, under color removal is achieved by making a mask from a split-filter black separation. However, this method provided only an average value of the neutrals for the three process colors, and as a result, the black separation had certain limitations in that if a long range black was used, it contaminated the dark color areas. Consequently, the introduction of photographic mask prohibited the use of a long range black, and the industry was forced to use a skeleton or short range black for the darkest shadow areas of the copy.

Electronic color scanners replaced many of the steps in conventional separation; however, some principles of conventional separation have been transferred to the electronic scanners and have limited the potential of electronic scanning. One of these limits is the use of a skeleton black. A long range black has many advantages over the skeleton black in that certain shades are produced better with black ink than with the overprinting of cyan, magenta, and yellow. In process color reproduction, it is difficult to control colors on press, particularly browns, purples, reds, and other two-and-three color overprints. A slight change in the balance of the inks will shift the hues. With the advent of modern offset printing, it was found that certain shades are reproduced better with one or two process colors and the black ink than with the three colors. Only recently, with the incorporation of advanced computers in electronic scanners has this concept been revitalized, and reentered the industry as the achromatic system, gray component replacement, or GCR.

CHROMATIC AND ACHROMATIC COLOR

To understand GCR, one has to understand the difference between chromatic and achromatic color reproduction. Chromatic color reproduction is a normal reproduction proc-

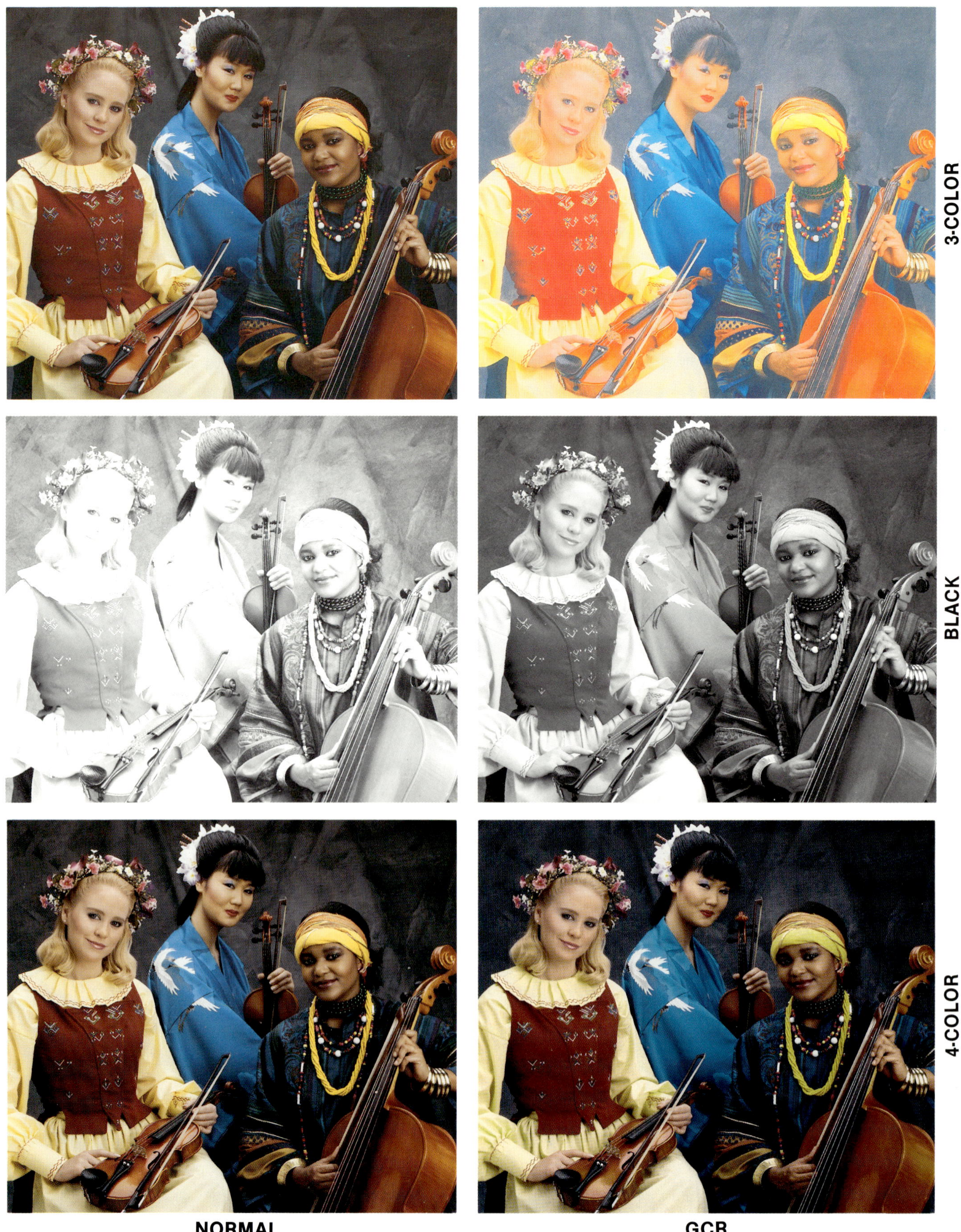

Figure 14.1. Examples of normal chromatic and GCR (achromatic) reproduction. Note the difference in the three-color and black reproductions

ess practiced by the industry. This reproduction is based on the theory that it is necessary to print cyan, magenta, and yellow inks to reproduce any color, and reinforce their overprints with black ink where necessary. The black will give neutrality, depth, and extend the maximum density of the three colors. In practice, the three colors cannot produce a satisfactory black on their own, and the black ink is used mainly to assist the color inks. The meaning of achromatic is colorless, and the term "achromatic color reproduction" is mostly used in Europe in place of Gray Component Replacement. The achromatic color reproduction is based on the theory that it is unnecessary to use yellow, magenta, and cyan to produce the black or achromatic component when a single black color can be used. In achromatic composition, the primary and the secondary colors are the same as the chromatic colors. The tertiary colors, which can be formed by mixing together the three process inks, are generated by a maximum of two colors and black. This is explained with Figure 14.1a.

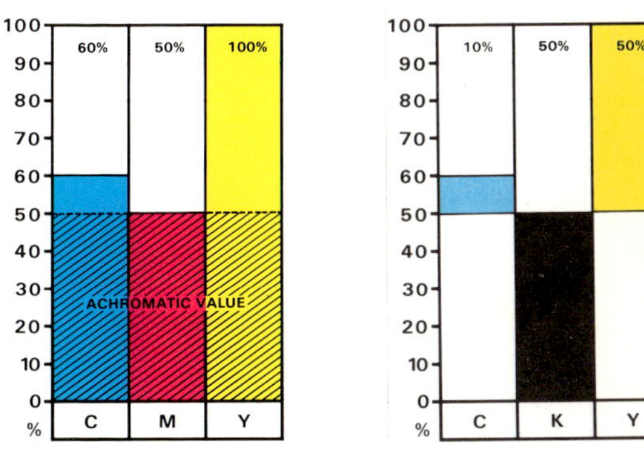

Figure 14.1a. The concept of achromatic reproduction - the achromatic value of magenta is replaced with black.

In this example, the achromatic value is controlled by the amount of magenta and is replaced by black. Whenever a color is produced by some combination of cyan, magenta, and yellow primaries, the two predominant colors determine the hue of that area. The least dominant color darkens and provides the "details" of the predominant hue. For example, a brown is produced with halftone values of 40% magenta, 55% yellow, and 30% cyan. The cyan becomes the least dominant primary color as shown in Figure 14.2. In principle, cyan will appear to be black in a red area, magenta will be black in a green area, and yellow will be black in a blue area. These darkening effects of the third or tertiary colors can be called gray value. Therefore, the printing of cyan, magenta, and yellow can be separated into two distinct components: the color component and the gray component. In GCR, the gray component of a given color is removed and is replaced with black. Figure 14.2 compares the traditional chromatic and achromatic treatment of a brown color and relative values of

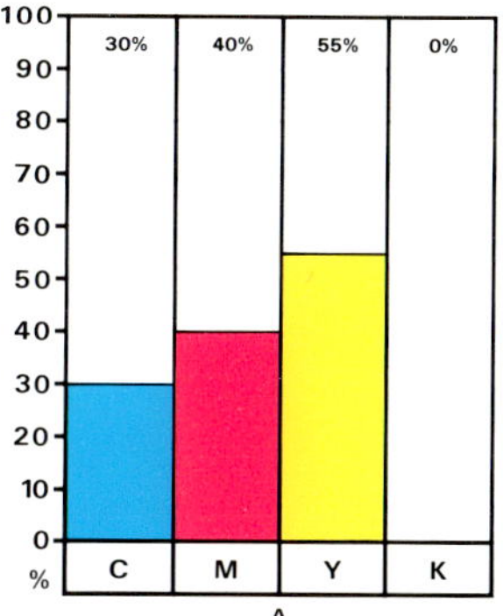

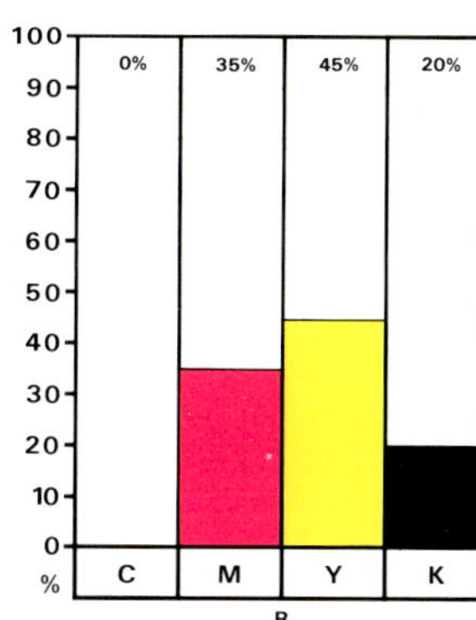

Figure 14.2. Reproduction of a brown color with chromatic and achromatic methods

each ink can be seen in the figure. In part A of the figure, a brown color is formed with its balance of yellow, magenta, and cyan. This is a normal chromatic separation. With the achromatic separation, the cyan ink is totally removed and replaced by a computed value of black. So for achromatic separation, to reproduce brown, the values needed are yellow, magenta, and black as shown in part B of the figure.

GCR AND GRAY BALANCE

Producing neutral grays with the three process inks is one of the most complex variables in process color reproduction. When the neutral gray tones are examined in a chromatic or traditional reproduction, the tones are reproduced by a delicate balance of the three process inks. The proportion of the inks in the tone scale must vary precisely throughout the press run to render the gray tones in different parts of the reproduction. The situation becomes more complicated with the addition of other variables like dot gain, ink trapping, fluctuation of the ink film thickness, reflection characteristics of the process inks, etc. However, using achromatic reproduction, the gray tones are principally reproduced by black, and its neutrality cannot vary with ink fluctuation. If

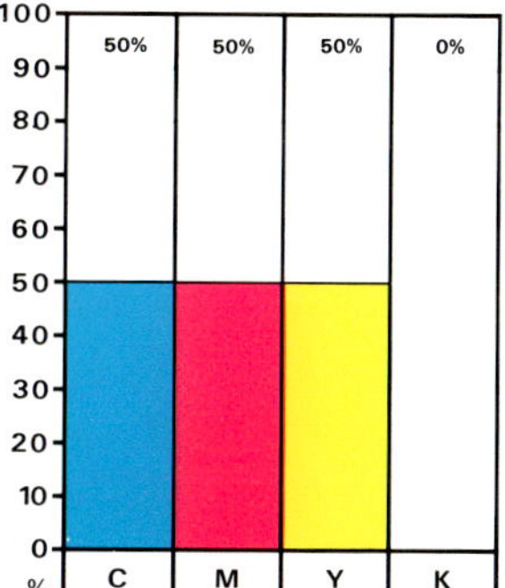

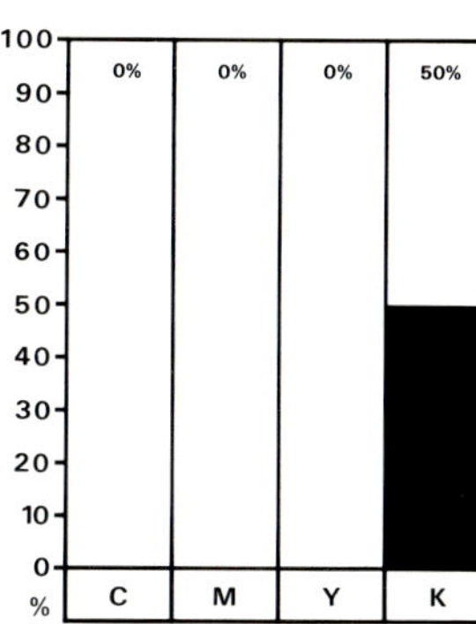

Figure 14.3. Reproduction of gray with chromatic and achromatic methods

the black is slightly off gray, for example, warm gray or cold gray, then one or two of the process inks can be added to provide any emphasis for the black.

GCR, UCR, AND UCA

With the introduction of GCR, the function of UCR has become less prominent in the separations in a scanner. However, to better understand GCR, one has to understand the difference between these two concepts. The UCR is mainly concerned with the removal of cyan, magenta, and yellow from the neutral areas of the original and replacing the three balanced pigments with black. Their quantity is controlled through masking techniques in conventional separation and by electronic computation in scanners. Originally UCR was referred to as the reduction of the process inks in the dark or near neutral areas of the printed picture. Electronic UCR works satisfactorily with gray, but is deficient in colors close to the gray. This deficiency leads to an undesired loss of color saturation, to reversals, and to contours which cannot be covered adequately with the black printer.

In addition to the function of removing cyan, magenta, and yellow from the neutral areas of the copy, with GCR it is also possible to remove the gray component from all colors in the separation, right from the highlight through the shadow, and replaces them with black. The GCR part is formed with the parts of the three color components, and when combined, they neutralize each other. In other words, GCR consists of those components of the three colors in a reproduced color, which would have produced gray if it had been separated from the reproduction. When GCR controls are in operation, in most scanners the UCR control is deactivated. In the Hell 399ER scanner, activating the CCR (Hell's version of GCR) automatically cuts off the UCR and simultaneously switches to UCA with the starting point control. Any combination of color or black can be adjusted with the CCR intensity and the UCA controls. In the DS SG-608, when the ICR (GCR version of Dainippon Screen) is activated, the dual function UCR and the black gradation functions are coupled. With the black gradation knob, the gradation curve of the black can be changed from a skeleton to a full range black, and the UCA knobs can be used to increase or decrease the amount of cyan, magenta, and yellow under black. In the RZ 200-S, the PIR (GCR version of Royal Zenith) program can be called and when the proportion of color under black is changed by altering the proportion of any one color, the other colors are automatically computed and adjusted. The black program is produced and stored in the computer, and when a full range black is needed, the range and the percentage needed for the highlight and range are entered into the program. In the Magnascan 645, a special program can be selected to increase or decrease the weight of color under black. With another program, the weight of the black can also be balanced with the weight of the color under black.

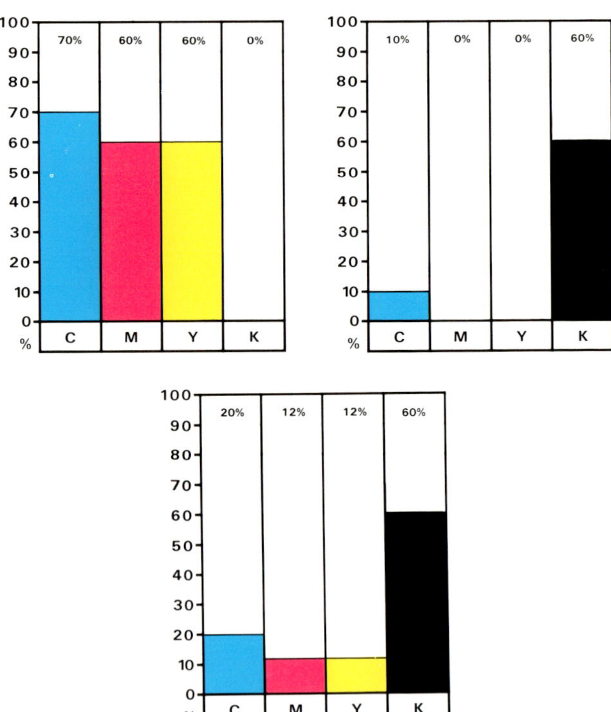

Figure 14.4. Conventional chromatic, ideal GCR, and practical GCR values

Although UCA is mostly used to introduce a color to neutralize a shadow area, it has emerged as a dominant force in the production of GCR separations. With GCR, black is prominent, critical, and the ink requirement is of the highest quality for proper density and gloss. However, for all practical purposes, the reproduction with even a 100% black may lack saturation and gloss. This can be overcome with a strong pigmented black ink, or any desired value of cyan, magenta or yellow introduced to reinforce the black ink. The process of black color addition (often referred to as BCA) is confined to the neutral tones only and does not affect any colors. Certain percentages of colors are added to the neutrals to compensate for lost gloss or to add a color cast where the black ink is deficient. The three examples in Figure 14.4 illustrate the chromatic, ideal GCR, and practical GCR reproductions.

PERCENTAGE OF GCR

In the separations with GCR, the tertiary colors or the smallest ink proportion are either completely removed or reduced to different percentages for certain printing characteristics. The interpretation of GCR percentage values has still not been standardized in the industry. However, one way to interpret is to accept the entire percentage of the tertiary or the smallest ink amount among the three colors as the GCR percentage. When this ink amount is completely removed and replaced with the same proportion of black, the separation is said to contain a 100% GCR.

In the theory discussed above, the different percentages of GCR depend on how much of the tertiary color or the smallest ink amount is reduced or replaced by black. If the tertiary color including the chromatic values are reduced, for example, if reduced to 50%, the GCR value is said to be 50%. Examples of conventional chromatic and different percentages of GCR are shown in Figure 14.5.

The above theory of GCR could have been ideal, but it has been complicated by the fact that the average process color inks are not pure and have unwanted absorptions and reflections. The situation becomes even more complicated with the variables in different printing conditions such as dot gain, ink

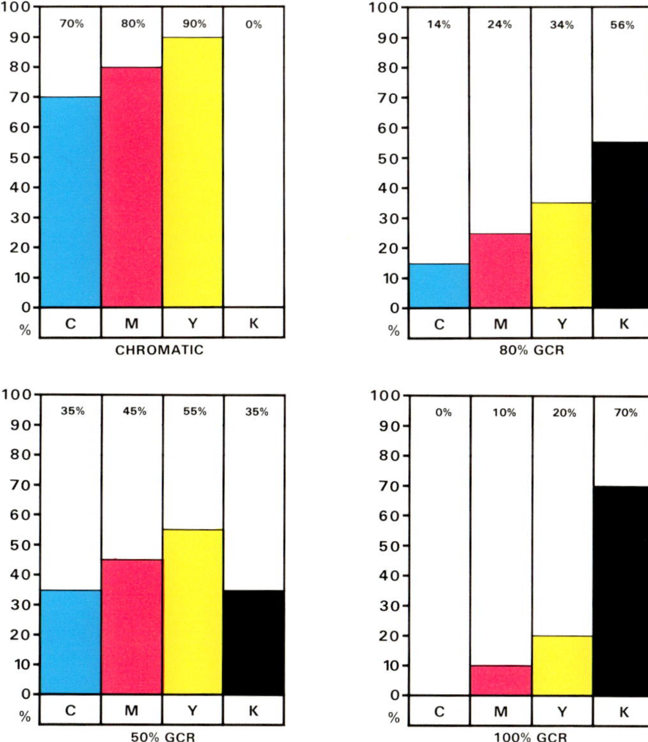

Figure 14.5. Examples of chromatic, 50%, 80% and 100% GCR values

trapping, ink film thickness, etc. As such, merely eliminating the least predominant primary color and replacing it with a black will not produce the desired results. In fact, if the achromatic value is replaced by black without changing the chromatic value, then the hue and saturation characteristics of the colors will change at various percentages of GCR. In practice, for different percentages of GCR, the values for cyan, magenta, yellow, and black have to be adjusted differently, and the values will vary for different printing conditions.

Although the balance of the three colors is less critical because of the use of black, in order to obtain an accurate reproduction of the primary and secondary colors with the least proportion of chromatic value, the balance should be made according to the printed results. This is because of the printing variables as well as the spectral characteristics of the different types of black ink. The higher the GCR percentage, the more critical is the requirement for the accuracy of the balance. An example is the production of gray with GCR. With most black ink, it is difficult to print the scale with only black to match the original neutral. A small proportion of the other three colors is also added to the black for the desired reproduction of the neutral. For successful and consistent GCR results, it will be important to find the delicate balance of the colors with the black for different printing conditions. Hell's Programmed Color Reduction (PCR) is a solution in this direction. The technique uses precalculated color transformation tables which consider all relevant printing data like gradation, dot gain, paper, printing inks, gray balance, etc. The operator simply sets up the color separation controls in the usual way when using the PCR hardware. The PCR is automatically carried out by the hardware extension of the scanner.

A SUMMARY OF COMPARISON BETWEEN TRADITIONAL CHROMATIC AND GCR REPRODUCTION

The chromatic and GCR process steps are again compared in the following table with appropriate figures:

TABLE 15

	CHROMATIC PROCESS	GCR
PRIMARY COLOR Cyan Magenta Yellow	Darkening is accomplished with equal quantities of the other two primary colors	Darkening is accomplished with black

Figure 14.6. Chromatic and achromatic processes

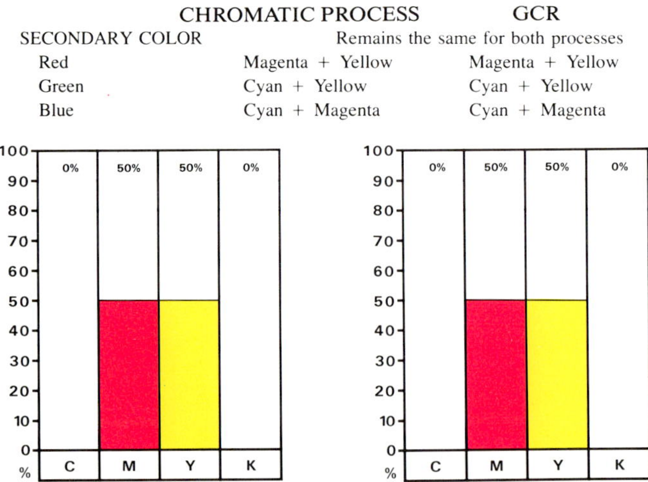

Figure 14.7. Secondary color in the chromatic and achromatic processes

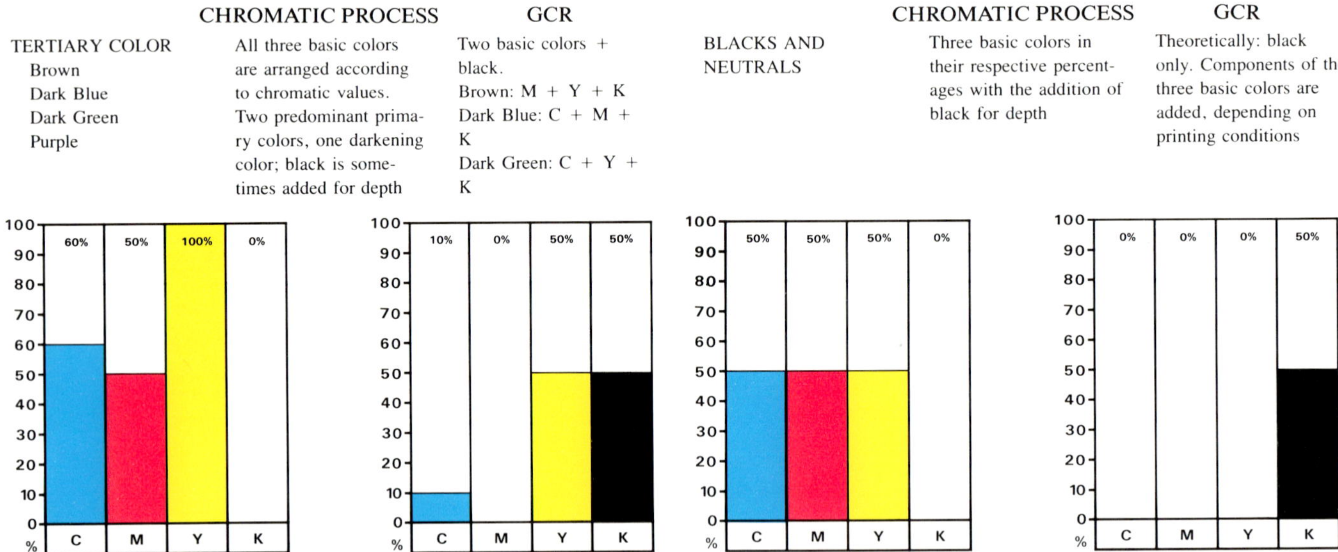

Figure 14.8. An olive green color produced by the chromatic and achromatic processes

Figure 14.9. Neutrals in chromatic and achromatic processes

ADVANTAGES OF GCR

Gray Component Replacement has many economic and technological advantages. The following list is a summary of these advantages:

Economic Advantages

1. Color ink consumption is reduced.
2. Because of less ink film thickness, faster makeready with quicker up to color and less paper waste are possible.
3. Because of less ink on paper, lighter paper is suited to print materials which would have required heavier stock.
4. Because of less ink on paper, drying expense is also reduced.

Technological Advantages

1. Dot gain fluctuation is generally less critical because most color shades are darkened with black.
2. Neutral grays will stay neutral, because grays are primarily made with black ink.
3. Moiré patterns, particularly common to four color browns are eliminated because brown shades are made with two colors and black. However, in some colors, patterns are

reported to be more prominent.

4. The reproducible color space is better; colors darkened with black show the changes in tonal range better compared to hue shifts caused when a third primary color is used for darkening.

5. The effects of metamerism seen by viewing the print under different lighting conditions are minimized because black is not affected by metamerism.

6. Register problems are reduced because black is dominant and covers most outlines.

7. Trapping problems in wet on wet printing are minimized because the quantity of ink is reduced in all colors.

8. The use of lighter stock with the full advantage of four color process is made possible because of the reduced ink coverage.

9. Color control is often less critical because color is generally composed of two colors plus black for darkening. However, in some cases, GCR reproduction shows more variability.

GCR COLOR REPRODUCTION CONCERNS

1. Changes in the reproduction process, particularly the departure from the familiar three color separation process, is difficult. Proofs look different and progressive proofs are often difficult to interpret.

2. Should the black be moved from the first to the last unit in the sequence of printing colors?

3. Intermixing of standard and achromatic separations are not advisable.

4. The black ink may need a higher density, should be neutral, and must have adequate coverage at an ink film thickness of one micron.

5. Dot gain control of the black printer is essential.

In addition to the above, recent surveys show some interesting features of the use of GCR in process color reproduction. Less critical makeready with less time is being experienced with GCR separations. Once the press is running, there seems to be greater consistency and less color shift in longer runs. GCR seems to work better where denser colors and color saturations are required, as in food subjects such as tomatoes, green vegetables, and meat. In lighter colors, such as cosmetic advertisements, the advantages are still realized, but not as much.

One major characteristic of GCR is that when used on lower-grade paper stocks, results are found to be outstanding. Color saturation and details, especially in shadow areas are enhanced. GCR is being successfully used for high speed web printing on lower-grade stocks.

The percentage of GCR applied will depend on individual shop conditions, paper, ink, subjects, etc. Separations with 40-60% GCR seem to be optimum at this point. It has been indicated that 100% GCR may create problems such as a white line around an object if the registration on the press sheet is not perfect. A higher percentage of GCR may also be responsible for the lack of editorial change facilities and a severe loss of maximum density.

GCR CONTROLS IN DIFFERENT SCANNERS

Crosfield Magnascan 645

In this digital scanner, to enter PCR, the UCR button is first pressed and after the YES button is pressed to answer question, the PCR gain value between 0.0 and 1.00 appears on the Alphanumeric display. With the KEYPAD, a 3-digit decimal value is selected and entered for the proportion of PCR required.

Most of the functions in this scanner are operational from software within the scanner. Each program can be called by entering the appropriate number; for example, 524 and 523 designate the weight of black and the weight of color under black respectively. There are several options in adjusting the black or color values for PCR.

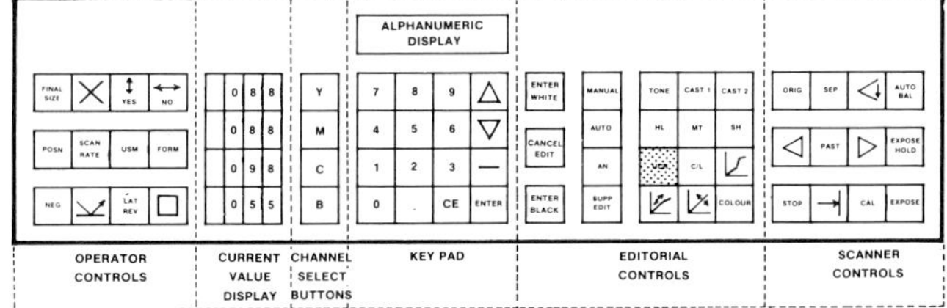

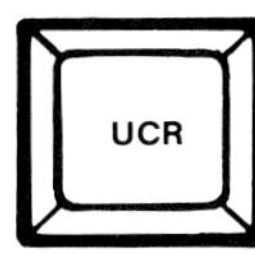

Figure 14.10. Magnascan 645 panel showing the pushbutton controls for PCR

A program is available to overprint the maximum percentages of dots for each color for the PCR. However, changing from low to a high value will also alter the proportion of PCR.

The editorial control of the PCR consists of adjusting or balancing the weight of black and the weight of color under black. To increase or decrease the black or color, specific programs are called and new values are entered.

In the Magnascan 645, a separate program to adjust PCR only for the highlight is available. However, it applies to a maximum of 40% dot and then automatically cuts off. The PCR at the highlight end is not selective, e.g. it does not work with a single color and cannot be used with full PCR.

Dainippon Screen SG-608

In the SG-608, an ICR switch is provided to activate the GCR function of the scanner to generate achromatic color separation. When the ICR is activated, turning the black gradation knob causes the black separation curve to change from a "linear" black to a "full" range black. However, at the same time, the amount of cyan, magenta, and yellow under the black are automatically reduced from 100% to 0% in a step wise fashion. The effect of ICR, black gradation control and the three colors are shown in the curves in Figure 14.12.

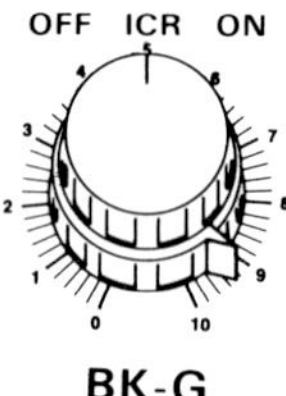

Figure 14.11. ICR control in the DS SG-608

In addition to the above controls, the scanner is equipped with a color correction function for the ICR. When the ICR switch is activated, the conventional color correction function is converted to ICR color correction. This function is helpful in setting up the best combination of the black gradation and the three colors for a true achromatic reproduction for various printing conditions such as different paper, ink, etc.

Hell 399ER

All color corrections, gradation adjustments, and other specific adjustments have to be completed before the CCR function is activated in this scanner. The controls for the CCR consist of a set of 3 Dominant Color Controls to maintain a dominant color cast in the shadow, a set of intensity and starting point controls for the addition of color under black, and the CCR intensity control. A toggle switch activates the functions of the CCR and UCA. With the CCR intensity control, tertiary color or the lowest amount of the three colors can be infinitely reduced to 0. With the CCR control at 0, there will be no achromatic effect on the separations. The higher the position of this control, the more CCR will take place, and at the highest position of 10, 100% CCR will be effective.

With the CCR intensity control set to a higher position, the chromatic colors under the black are automatically decreased and the black is increased. However, for certain printing conditions, specific quantities of the chromatic colors are added to the black with the UCA intensity control. The position of the starting point of the UCA determines the point from which UCA will be effective on the three-color gradation curve.

Courtesy D.S. America, Inc.

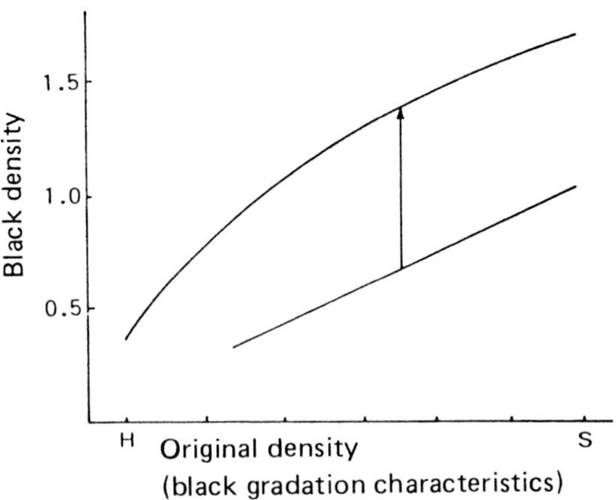

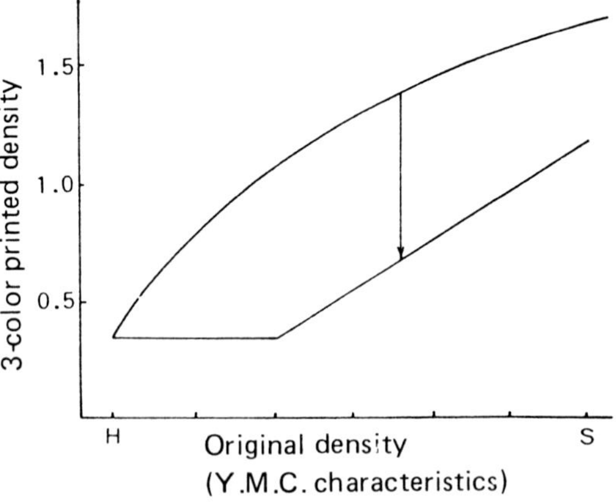

Figure 14.12. The effect of ICR control settings

Programmed Color Reduction or PCR is a different approach for the adjustment of GCR in some Hell scanners. The important prerequisite for the system is that first a set of test targets or color charts are printed using the optimized printing conditions, and the data obtained is integrated into the color computer. The data on the test color chart are accurately measured by a spectrophotometer for specific requirements such as gray balance, gradation, dot gain, paper, ink, etc. The results are then calculated for the separation values required for the different percentages of CCR. The calculated results are then stored on floppy disks. The operator simply continues to set up the scanner in the conventional manner; however, once the PCR unit is activated, the dot sizes required for different percentages of PCR are automatically calculated. The system can be used in the Hell Chromacom Pagination System, as well as in some selected scanners including the 399ER by using the PCR software extension.

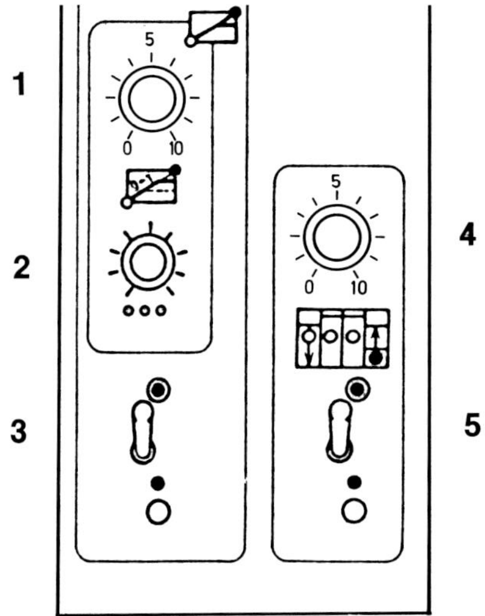

Figure 14.13. Hell 399ER UCR/UCA/CCR panel showing UCR/UCA intensity control (#1); starting point control for UCR/UCA (#2); toggle switch to activate UCR/UCA (#3); intensity control for CCR (#4); toggle switch to activate CCR (#5)

Royal Zenith 200-S

In the RZ 200-S, PIR (Programmed Ink Reduction) is selected by the F EXCH key sequence and the amount of PIR is set by the F UCR controls. However, a program is first developed and stored. The procedure to make a new program for PIR is similar to the one used to develop a standard tone reproduction curve, except that the gray balance for the three colors is established by the SEP R control without the use of UCR, and secondly the curve shape for the black separation is made for a full range black.

Once the PIR program is stored, it can be recalled and adjusted by increasing or decreasing dot percentage or control setting (CONSET) values. The control setting values are applied to all colors including black. The PIR adjustments must be made after all the specific adjustments such as gradation, color correction, etc. are completed.

PIR is selected by the F EXCH key sequence and the amount of PIR is set by the F UCR controls. First the PIR program is called and the dot values of all colors are checked when monitoring the black. The amount of PIR is decided by keying the F EXCH. Alternately, the PIR amount may be based on the strongest printing ink in the shadow.

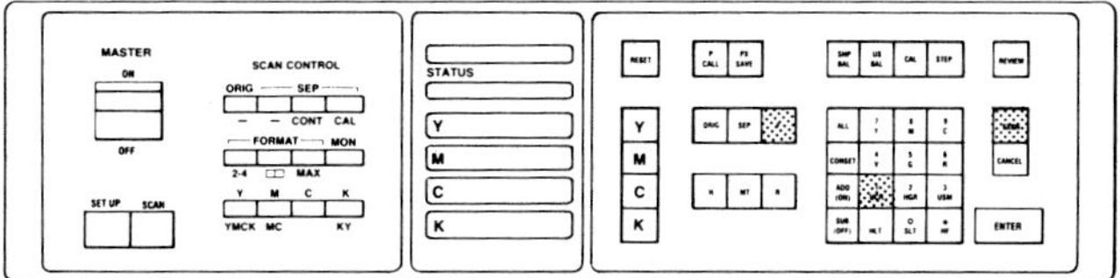

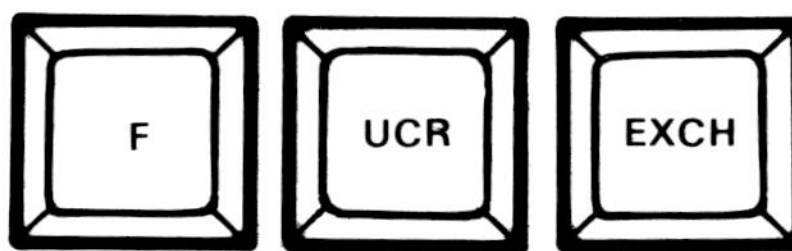

Figure 14.14. Panel of RZ 200-S showing the pushbutton controls for PIR

Chapter 15
Unsharp Masking (USM)

PURPOSE

When the color correction masks for direct and indirect separations were introduced about thirty years ago, the main concern at that time was to register the mask with the original during separation, especially when the original was a small 35 mm transparency. Initially, the masks were made unsharp to solve this registration problem. However, it became apparent that the unsharpness of the masks did more than just solve the problem of registration; it enhanced the details of the reproduction more than if a sharp mask was used.

EFFECT OF UNSHARP MASK ON HUMAN EYES

The retina of the human eye consists of light-sensitive sensory cells, and they can adapt to a bright or dark environment. When there is a sharp jump in the brightness, for example, from a bright highlight to a dark shadow, the eye adapts itself to the shift and sees the transition in sharp focus. However, if there is a gradual transition of tone values, which are closely related, the retina fails to adapt to the transition and the tones appear as out-of-focus. As a consequence, sometimes the retina can hardly differentiate between adjacent delicate tones. This problem in the reproduction can be remedied by increasing the contours, lines, or fringes at the edges of the adjacent tones. With the effect of unsharp masks, these lines produced at the edges of the transitional tones appear focused by providing more details to the retina.

UNSHARP MASKING IN CONVENTIONAL SEPARATION

In conventional separation, the combination of sharp images of opposite signs, for example, a positive transparency and a sharp negative mask made from the same transparency, will reduce the contrast and the sharpness. On the other hand, an unsharp mask will decrease the contrast during separation, but because of its unsharp nature, it will mask the critical detail without flattening it. An unsharp mask tends to emphasize the density change between the two tones producing an emphasis in the form of a slight transitional hump of increased density.

In describing unsharp masks in his book *"Principles of Color Reproduction,"* Yule indicated that in the photographic process, two factors are responsible for the increased sharpness: 1) the tone compression of the copy resulting from the mask and 2) the unsharpness of the mask. When a positive color transparency is held in registration with a negative mask, or vice versa, the density range or contrast of the original is lowered, but the sharpness is increased. The reason is that in the unsharp mask, larger tonal differences are maintained, but the fine details are lost. As a result, during tone compression, the large scale tone differences in the original are lowered by the mask, but has little effect on the fine details. As a result, the fine details of the original remain intact and appear sharper than they would if a sharp mask had been used. In addition, when the contrast of the reproduction as a whole is increased during the intermediate reproduction steps to make up for the flattening effect of the mask, the fine details in the reproduction appear sharper than in the original.

The effect of sharp and unsharp masks are shown in Figure 15.1. When a combination of a positive original with a negative mask is used, at the edge where two different tones are adjacent, the change of density at the edge (often called gradient) is higher with the unsharp mask. In addition, there is a slight hump so that the density difference at the edge is greater. However, if this hump is too excessive because the mask is excessively unsharp, an objectionable edge effect may be produced showing a dark outline on one side of the edge and a light one on the other side.

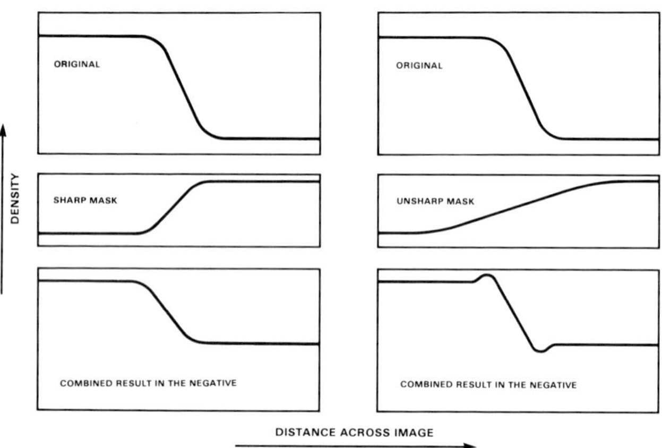

Figure 15.1. Concept of unsharp mask to improve image sharpness in the conventional separation

In a conventional separation, an unsharp mask can be made in the following ways:

1. By exposing through the back of the transparency using a large diffuse light source.

2. By introducing a "spacer" - a matt surfaced diffusion sheet between the two surfaces, the matt side being positioned away from the emulsion on to which the mask image will be exposed.

3. Degrees of unsharpness can be controlled by the rotation method. A suitable contact frame is rotated while a point source of light, which is positioned away from the vertical center, exposes the emulsion at an angle, thus spreading the mask image in an unsharp manner.

UNSHARP MASKING IN A SCANNER

The concept of unsharp mask is used effectively in the scanner to enhance details; however, the technique is different than that used in a photographic process. In the scanning head of most scanners, pairs of normal scanning and unsharp masking apertures are provided. The unsharp masking aperture is larger in size than the main aperture; however, the size variation is different for different pairs of apertures. When a copy is scanned, the light signal transmits through both the scanning and the unsharp masking apertures (see Figure 15.2). The light is focussed onto the respective photomultipliers which convert them into electrical signals. When the apertures travel on the smooth area of the original containing no tonal or density change, there is no change in the signals

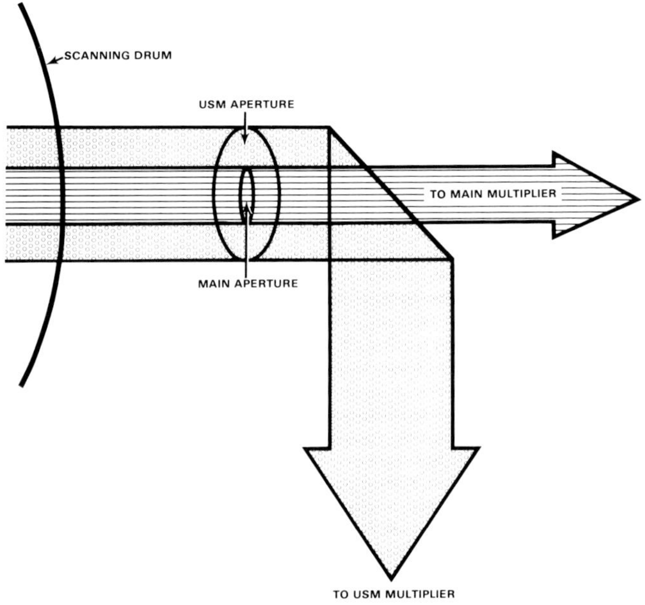

Figure 15.2. Main and unsharp masking beams

between the two apertures, and consequently, nothing happens to the main signal. The unsharp masking signal becomes superfluous. However, when there is a change of density in the copy during scanning, light signals transmitting through the two apertures will be different because the unsharp masking aperture is larger than the scanning aperture and therefore, will react to changes in density sooner. The difference of the main and unsharp masking signals are calculated and added electronically to the main scanning signal. This will result in whitening or blackening in the lighter and darker areas at the edge of the tonal change of the reproduction to create an illusion of sharper detail (see Figure 15.3). The concept is explained next in detail with Figure 15.4.

In Figure 15.4, the rectangles are originals with sharp tonal changes from white to black at the center, and the series of circles at the top are the two apertures shown at different positions during the travel of the scanning head. The small and the large circles are the main and unsharp masking apertures respectively. Different positions of the apertures are numbered to show the locations of the apertures during scanning when they are moving horizontally. Both the apertures travel together while the scanning light transmitting through or reflecting from the copy passes simultaneously through them.

In Figure 15.4, if the processing of the signal through the scanning aperture is considered first, it will be observed that

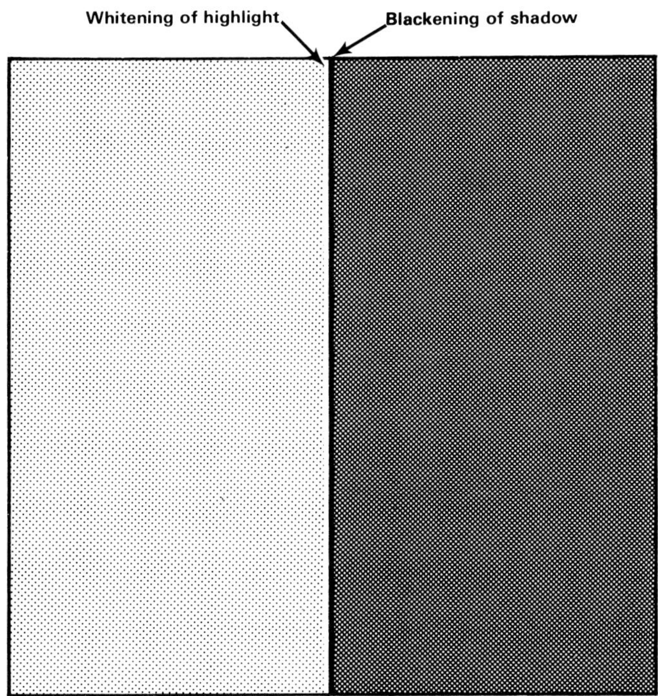

Figure 15.3. The whitening and blackening of lighter and darker edges in the areas of density change.

when the aperture is moving from left to right, the lights entering from the clear area of the original do not change until the aperture is closer to the area where there is a change of tone from light to dark. Since the main aperture is small, the tonal change will not be apparent until the aperture is very near to the area of the change. On the other hand, the change of lights transmitting through the larger unsharp masking aperture will be gradual or slower compared to the light transmitting through the smaller main aperture. As shown in Figure 15.4, at position 1, the main and the unsharp masking apertures are in the white range and if the light values generated by both the apertures are considered to be equal, they have the same values - the difference between the signals is zero. However, in position 2, 1/3 of the unsharp masking aperture is in the black range while the entire main aperture is still in the white range. Thus the signal produced by the unsharp masking aperture contains 1/3 or 33% less white value than the main aperture. In position 3, both the main and the unsharp masking apertures are in midpoint between the white and black ranges, and as such, the difference between the signals is again zero at this point. From this point, the signals are moving towards the minus range. In position 4, the main aperture is completely in the black range, whereas 1/3 of the unsharp masking aperture is still in the white range. As such, the unsharp masking aperture contains 1/3 or 33% less black value than the main aperture. In position 5 both the main and the unsharp masking apertures are completely in the black range of the original, and as such, the difference between the signals is zero.

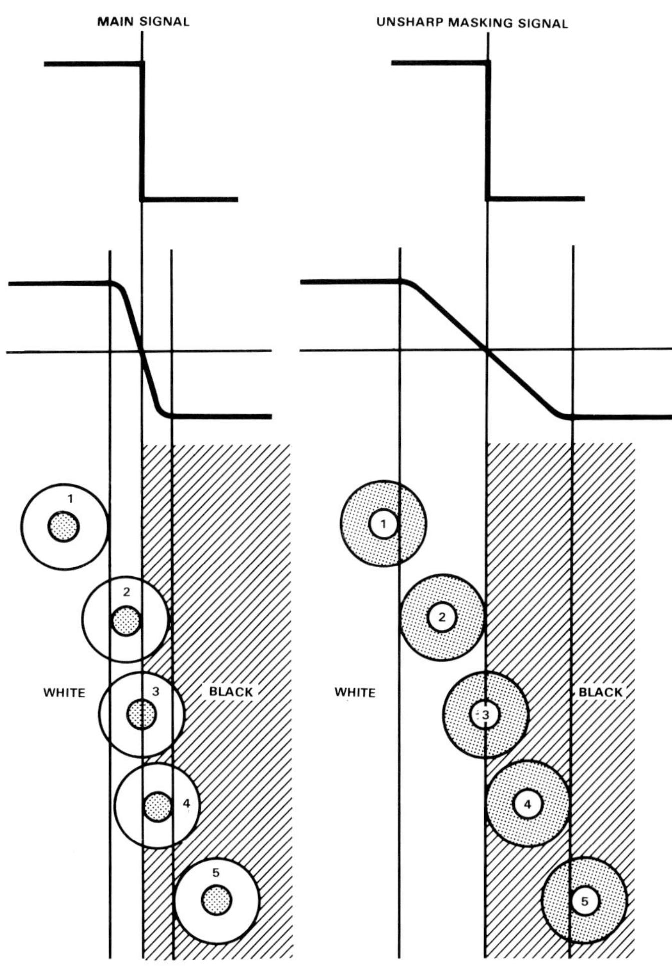

Figure 15.4. The effect of density change on the main and USM apertures

Positive and Negative Peaking

The light values from the main and unsharp masking apertures are converted into density values. When the values at the position of the density change of the original are averaged, the main aperture will produce less density in position 2 and more in position 4 than the unsharp masking aperture. However, when both lenses are travelling across the white or black areas only, there will be no density change between the two apertures. As a consequence, a differential signal arises (difference between the two signals) which is split according to positive and negative amplitudes. The difference is then added to the main signal, the positive signal will increase the amplitude at the edge of the light area, and the negative signal will decrease the amplitude at the edge of the dark area (see Figure 15.5). This will result in more density in a negative with less density at the lighter edge in the reproduction (a white line) and less density in a negative with more density at the darker edge (a black line) in the reproduction. Consequently, this will create an illusion of increased sharpness that is sometimes referred to as peaking. These effects are less noticeable in an area where the change of density is much higher, for example from a bright highlight to a dark shadow. However, the effects will be apparent in the areas where the density change is subtle.

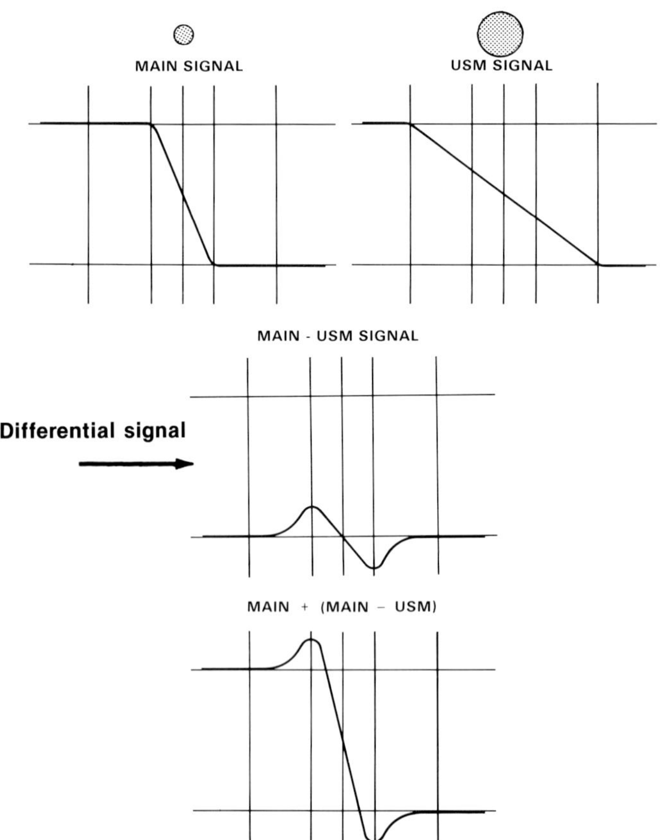

Figure 15.5. Positive and negative peaking affected by the addition of differential signal

The positive peaking will result when the main and most of the unsharp masking apertures are in the white area, and it will be negative when the main aperture and most of the unsharp masking aperture are in the shadow area. When both apertures are midway between the white and shadow areas, the difference between the signals is zero, and there will be no peaking. This is the point where the transition occurs from positive to negative peaking.

Controls for Unsharp Masking in Analog and Digital Scanners

In scanners which employ analog color computer like the Hell 399ER and DS SG-608, controls for unsharp masking include the following: selection of the main scanning aperture in relation to the unsharp masking aperture, selection of a color filter to influence the color of the unsharp masking beam, independent controls to increase or decrease the intensity of positive or negative peaking, and another set of controls to suppress the effect of unsharp masking in selected areas of the separation. In a digital scanner similar to the Magnascan 645, the functions are similar, but they are controlled in a different way. A preprogrammed software allows the operator to select the appropriate program and adjust any value with increasing or decreasing intensity. In this scanner, several apertures are provided to control the size of the scanning light spot; however, the amplitude or intensity of detail enhancement is independent of the main scanning aperture and controlled electronically. In addition, no color filter is provided for the unsharp masking signal in the Magnascan 645. A digital electronic circuit derives the unsharp masking signal from the main color separation signal and creates the detail enhancement. Programs are also available to suppress the unsharp masking effect in the selected areas of the reproduction. Similarly in the RZ 200S, no color filter is used, the color of the unsharp masking beam is the same as the separation color.

Types of Controls for Unsharp Masking in a Scanner

Controls for the unsharp masking signals in a scanner can be divided into two categories: manual and electronic. Manual controls include the selection of a pair of main and the unsharp masking aperture and the selection of a color filter for the unsharp masking beam. The electronic controls include the adjustment of the unsharp masking intensity or peaking at various points on the gradation curve and the suppression of the unsharp masking effect in the selected areas of the reproduction.

Manual Unsharp Masking Controls

The extent or amplitude of unsharp masking in an analog scanner will depend on the difference in the volumes of signal between the main aperture and the unsharp masking aperture. This will depend on the size differences between the main aperture and the unsharp masking aperture. The higher the difference, the more detailed enhancement will result, and vice versa. Two unsharp masking effects are obtained at the edge of the density difference — the contour intensity and the contour width. Contour intensity is actually the extent of density produced by the black and clear lines along the border of the density shift. This density can be increased or decreased with the electronic intensity control. These lines may not be apparent at the edges where there is a high density shift, but the effect is more visible at the lower density shift in the copy. The secondary effect is the widening of the white and black lines. The width of the contour will represent an increase in contrast. The higher the value of the unsharp masking signal, the wider the lines will be. These effects are obtained by mechanically changing the ratio of the main and unsharp masking apertures and explained in Figure 15.6.

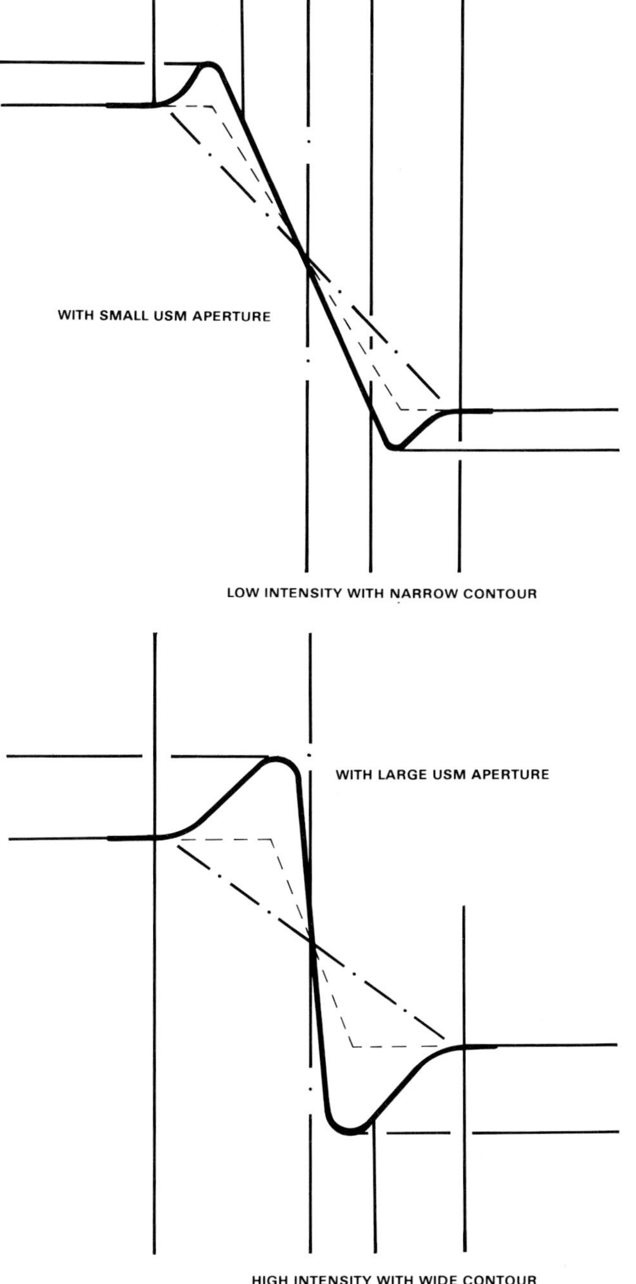

Figure 15.6. The effect of different main and USM aperture ratios

Most digital and analog scanners provide several combinations of main and unsharp masking apertures to control the effect of unsharp masking. In the Hell 399ER and DS SG-608, several sets of main and unsharp masking aperture combinations are provided. Selection of any one pair will depend on the enlargement and reduction scales, the type of the original, the screen ruling, the drum, the required resolution, and the screen system. A detailed discussion on the guidelines for the selection of the main aperture is presented under "Selection of the Main Aperture" later in this chapter. Figure 15.7 is a diagram of an aperture wheel containing 10 sets of apertures taken from a Hell scanner. A table containing the ratio of the main and unsharp masking aperture sizes of the ten apertures follows the figure.

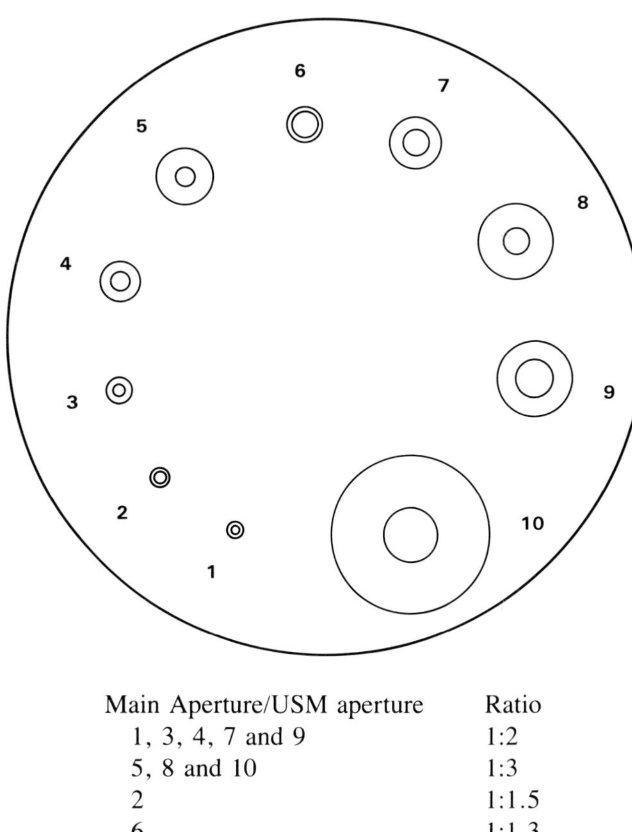

Main Aperture/USM aperture	Ratio
1, 3, 4, 7 and 9	1:2
5, 8 and 10	1:3
2	1:1.5
6	1:1.3

Figure 15.7. Aperture wheel of the 399ER

ADVANTAGES AND DISADVANTAGES OF VARIOUS MAIN AND UNSHARP MASKING APERTURE RATIOS

Effect of Small main with Small and Large USM Apertures

When smaller apertures are selected for both the main and unsharp masking signals, a high resolution of the reproduction with narrow detail contrast will result. If the original is unsharp, very little detail contrast will result. If high resolution with strong detail contrast effect is desired, a combination of a small main aperture with a large unsharp masking aperture may be selected. However, the main disadvantage with this combination is that the imperfections in the original like film grain, skin blemishes, and scratches will also be emphasized.

Effect of Large Main with Small and Large USM Apertures

A large main aperture with a small unsharp masking aperture will provide the smoothness in the reproduction for originals with apparent grains or other small imperfections; however, the result will be a low resolution and a minimum detail contrast effect. A combination of a larger main aperture and comparatively a larger unsharp masking aperture will provide more smoothness and a higher detail contrast effect with unsharp originals. However, the result will be of lower resolution and wider detail contrast contours.

EFFECT OF COLOR FILTER ON THE USM SIGNAL

The use of a larger aperture for the unsharp masking signal compared to the main aperture increases the sharpness only in the areas where there is a change of density or tones. However, this method does not affect the edges of a color change unless the shift is seen as the jump in density by the unsharp masking photomultiplier. Most analog scanners use color filters for the unsharp masking signal for enhancement in the borders of a color shift. If there is a change of hue in an area of the original, a detail enhancement will increase contrast, and differences in the colors will be more apparent.

To understand the effect of color filters on the detail enhancement, it is necessary to understand the production of black and white colors by the use of three separation filters - red, green, and blue. The light from the unsharp masking aperture transmits through any one of the red, green, or blue filter to the unsharp masking photomultiplier. Table 16 shows the corresponding black and white colors that are being produced by the filters.

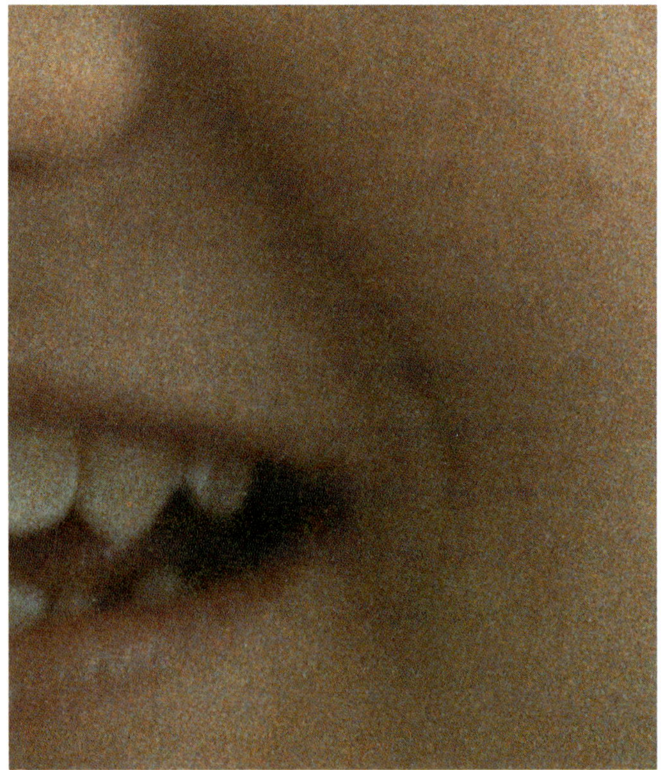

A

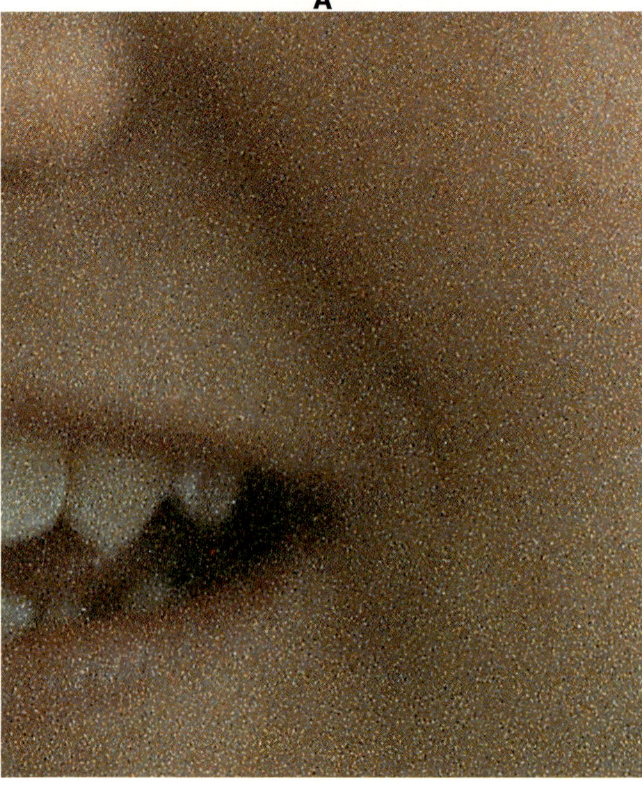

B

Figure 15.8. Effect of large (Reproduction A) and small scanning apertures (Reproduction B) on a grainy original

A **red** USM filter was used for this separation. Note the darker and lighter lines at the borders of color change in the colors except red (including magenta and yellow). For example, compare the words "Tropicana" and "Comet" in the three reproductions. With the red USM filter, there are no dark lines around these words and they appear smooth, however, in the other two reproductions, the dark lines around the same words created an illusion of increased sharpness.

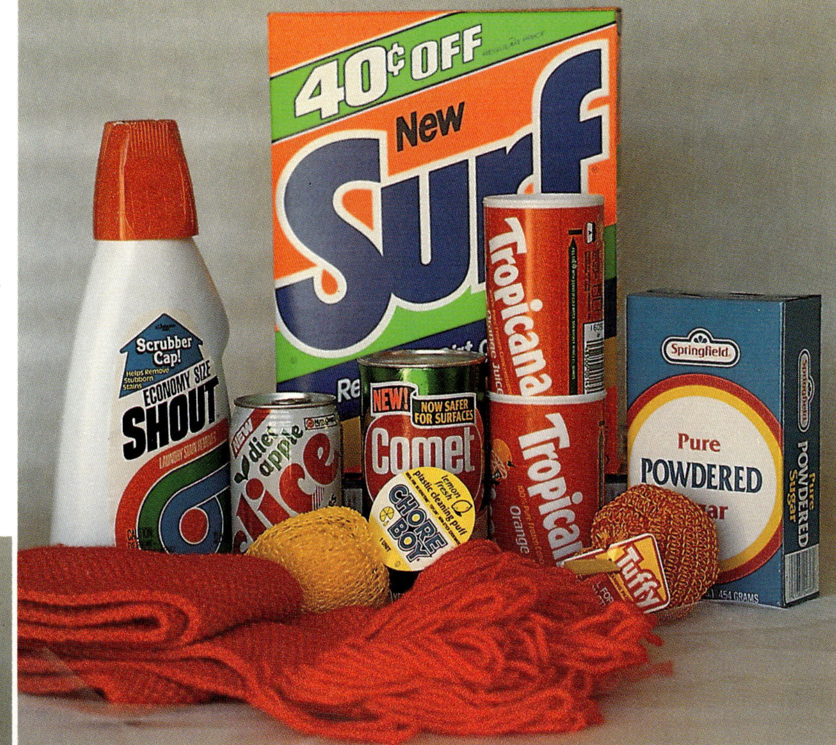

A **green** USM filter was used for this separation. Note the darker and lighter tones at the borders of color change in the colors except green (including cyan and yellow). For example, note the outline details of the red-yellow Tuffy plastic scrubber at the bottom right compared to the same reproductions with red and blue USM filters.

A **blue** USM filter was used for this separation. Note the darker and lighter lines at the borders of color change in the colors except blue (including cyan and magenta). For example, note the dark line at the border of the yellow circle in the box of sugar when compared to the other two reproductions.

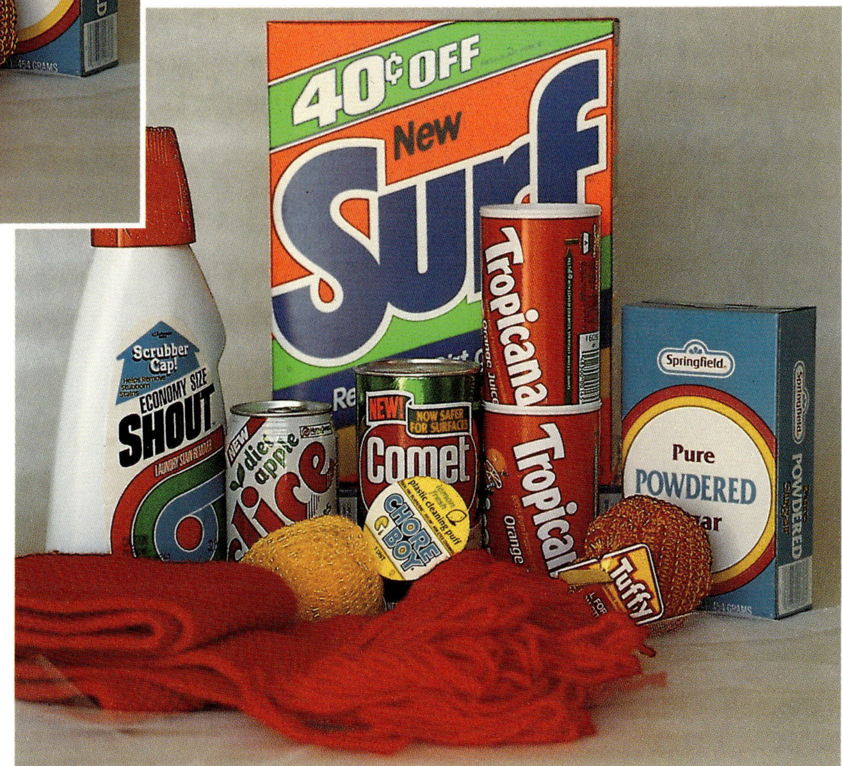

Figure 15.9. Reproductions showing the effects of different USM color filters at the edges of color change. All three separations were made in identical scanner set up except the USM color filters were changed each time for the three separations

TABLE 16

FILTER	WHITE COLOR	BLACK COLOR
	Red	Cyan
Red	Magenta	Green
	Yellow	Blue
	White	Black
	Green	Magenta
Green	Cyan	Red
	Yellow	Blue
	White	Black
	Blue	Yellow
Blue	Cyan	Green
	Magenta	Red
	White	Black

The above black and white colors generated by each color filter can be used effectively to determine the sharpness required in the borders of colors. With the respective filters, when there is a change of color and if the change is from white to white or from black to black, there will be a minimal density shift. For example, a red filter will not recognize a difference in density at the transition point of the following white colors: red, magenta, yellow, white; or the following black colors: cyan, green, blue, and black. In other words, if there is a transition from magenta to yellow or cyan to green, there will be a minimum effect of unsharp masking on the borders of these colors with the red unsharp masking beam. However, when a green filter is used for the same color transition, the yellow will be white and the magenta will be a black color. The sharpness is achieved in the borders of yellow and magenta — light contour or line for the yellow and dark contour or line for the magenta.

A combination of different color filters can be used creatively to enhance details in selected areas of the original. For example, if there is a white writing on a red background and if a green filter is used for unsharp masking, red will be the black color, and it will increase the contrast between red and white in each separation. As a result, sharp black lines will appear around the letters for increased contrast when printed.

In situations where the black or white lines are not desirable for an original, the unsharp masking color filter may be changed for each separation so that enhancement will result only in the respective colors and will eliminate unwanted dark or light borders at the edges when there is a transition from one hue to another. For originals where natural intensification at the borders of the separation colors are required, the unsharp masking color must be set at the same color as the separation color, i.e. a green filter for magenta separation, a red filter for cyan separation, and a blue filter for yellow separation. Conversely, a rule of thumb will be to use a red filter for important red areas where no black borders are needed at the red edges. The same is true for the green and blue filters. The main disadvantage, however, is that for each separation, the scanner needs to be stopped to change the unsharp masking filter. This is a disadvantage for scanners which produce multiple separations in one pass. In addition, when an unsharp masking filter is changed, the photomultipliers need to be recalibrated. As a result, a new White Adjustment or Autobalance has to be performed during each time the color of the unsharp masking filter is changed.

Electronic Unsharp Masking Control

In most analog and digital color computers, there are usually two types of computer controls to adjust the effect of unsharp masking. These are intensity controls for the white and black contours or lines, and a control to suppress the unsharp masking effect in selected areas of the reproduction.

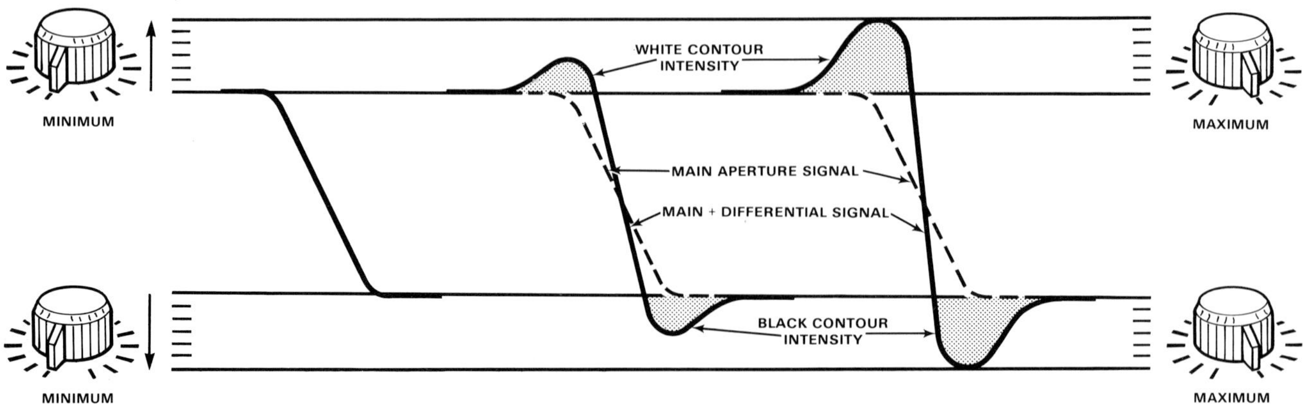

Figure 15.10. Effect of electronic USM intensity controls on positive and negative peaking

The second process is often called Grain Suppression or USM Smooth.

The intensity controls affect the white and the black contours or lines over the entire density range of the image. These changes influence the density (more dense black lines for the shadow contours and clearer lines for the highlight contours). This will also effect the width of the contour. Figure 15.10 explains the effect of this control in an analog scanner. Both controls for the white and black contours have

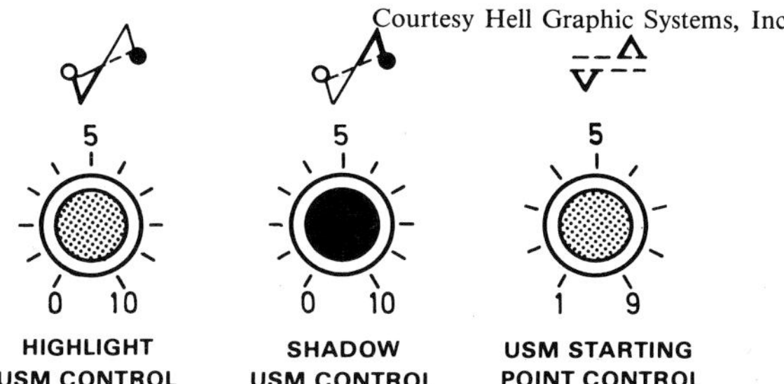

Figure 15.11. A typical set of electronic USM controls in an analog scanner

ranges from 0 to 10. When a control is set at 0, there is no effect of unsharp masking intensity. Setting the control at position 10 provides the maximum intensity of the white and black contours.

It should be noted here that the contour intensity and width depend not only on the intensity control settings, but also on the ratio of the main and unsharp masking aperture sizes. As such, the intensity controls should be used with caution to avoid any undesirable effect due to an excessive unsharp masking adjustment. For example, when the ratio between the main and the unsharp masking aperture is larger, a lower intensity control position should be used, and vice versa for a lower aperture ratio. In most scanners, separate controls are provided for each of the white and black contours to set the intensity individually. The controls in Figure 15.11 represent a typical set of electronic controls for unsharp masking in an analog color computer.

The setting of the electronic intensity control will depend on the original, the scanning aperture, and the ratio of the two apertures. It should be emphasized that the primary importance is the original itself, the contrast and sharpness contained in it, and the desired increase in contrast. Originals containing a lot of details such as script, fine patterns, etc. need a stronger detailed contrast effect. A metallic object will need more relief effect at the edges of the tonal change to render a three-dimensional view of the object than a portrait will. As for enlargement and reduction, a high enlargement needs a lower detail contrast setting in a scanner than is needed for a low enlargement or reduction. Originals with high image contrast need a lower value than originals with low image contrast.

The level of enhancement will also depend on the dye and other characteristics of the emulsion of the transparency. For example, the sharpness setting for an original Kodachrome and a duplicate made from the same transparency will be

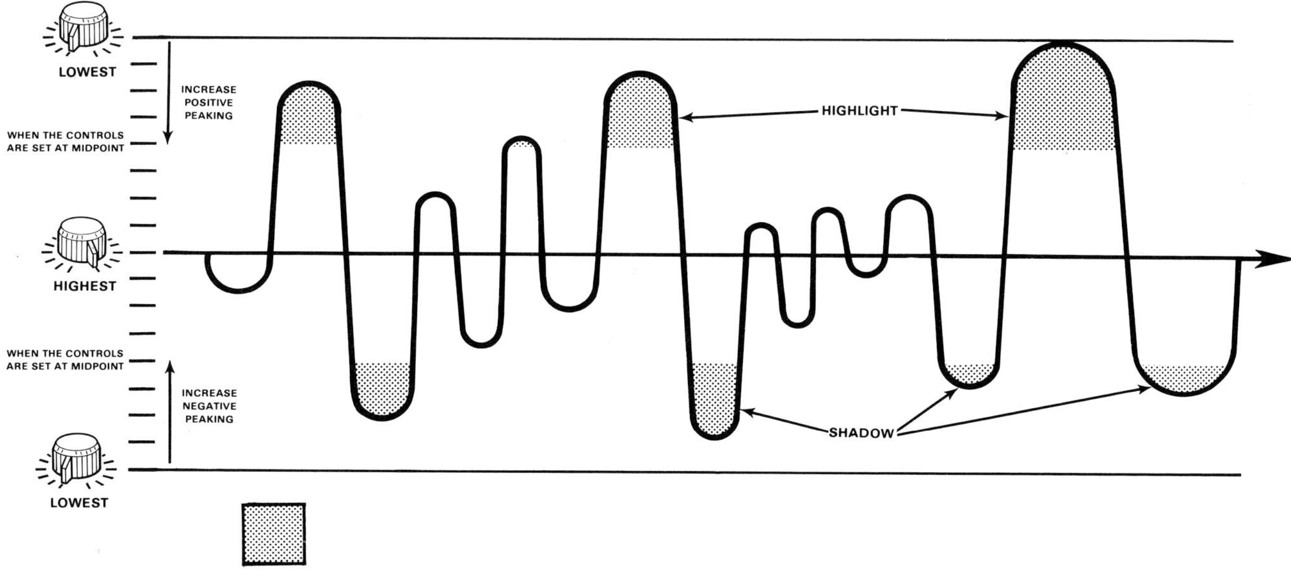

Figure 15.12. The effect of Starting Point/Suppression control. As shown in the diagram, when the control is set at midpoint, the smaller peaking effect in both highlight and shadow created by the smaller differential signals are not apparent in the reproduction. These differential signals arise from small density jumps in the copy such as skin blemishes, film grains, minor scratches, etc. When the control is at the lowest setting, the detail enhancement will be totally suppressed. When the same control is at the highest setting, all types of peaking generated by the differential signals will be preserved

different. The grain of an original Kodachrome will be much finer than the duplicate and the sharpness may be increased without having an adverse effect in the reproduction. A grain suppression adjustment may be used for certain areas of a duplicate transparency, but other areas of the transparency may show an unnatural enhancement effect in the reproduction. Most scanner manufacturers provide specific charts, tables or guidelines for using different apertures for optimal unsharp masking adjustments for various original or duplicate emulsions at different scales.

Depending on the brand and model of scanner, the other type of electronic control is usually called Starting Point control, Grain Suppression or USM Smooth. When an optimum level of sharpness is adjusted for an original, the effect in some specific areas of the reproduction may not be desirable. For example, when an original is enlarged, the difference of the main and unsharp masking apertures on a film grain structure, blemishes on a skin tone, or dirt and scratches on the emulsion may create light and dark contours around these imperfections and may result in unwanted exaggeration. The Starting Point, Grain Suppression or USM Smooth controls provide the limit of the formation and application of the differential signals to the main signal at a certain level of density change. As shown in Figure 15.12, although various amplitudes of differential signals are formed, with the starting point control set at midpoint, only the selected higher amplitudes are effective on the separations. In this example, there is an effective control range from minimum to maximum. By adjusting the control at different positions, the maximum limit of a differential signal can be set so that the smaller amplitudes are suppressed. The smaller contours, which are the result of smaller density variations in the copy, will not be recorded on the film. The main disadvantage of this adjustment is that no detail enhancement will result in the original where there is a small density jump or small differences of tone values.

As a general guide, low starting point control values should be used for a small scanning spot with higher enlargement; and high control values should be used for a large scanning spot with reduction or same size duplication. To achieve a finer recording of very small details, a combination of a small unsharp masking aperture, a lower unsharp masking intensity setting, and a higher value of the starting point or suppression control can be used effectively.

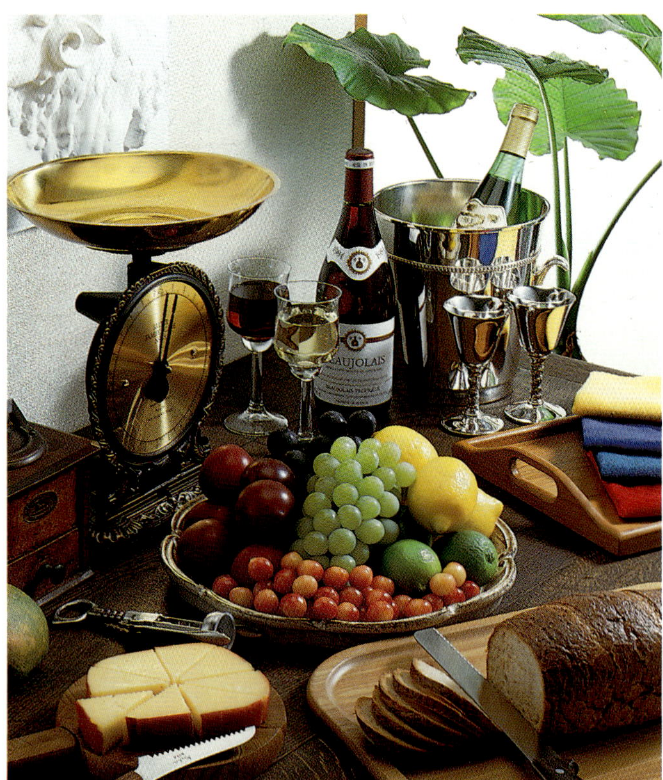

A

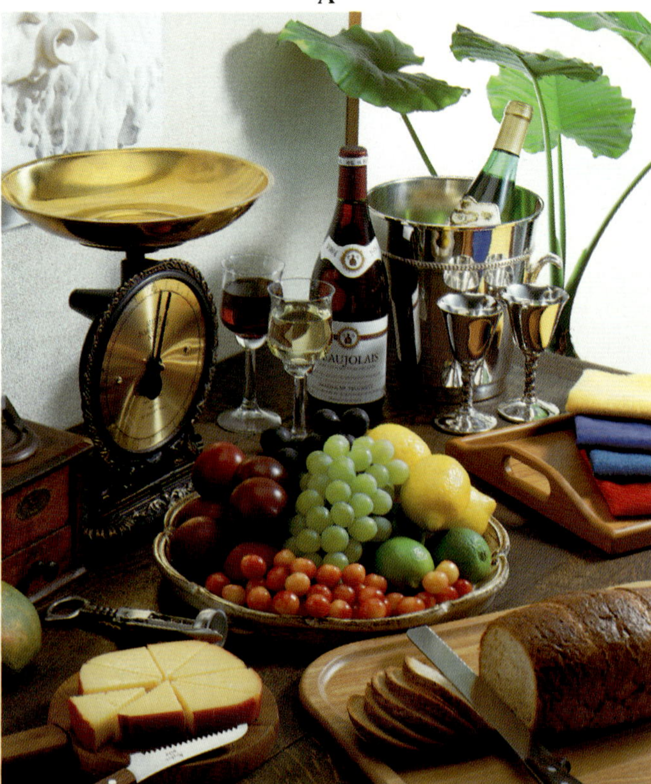

B

Figure 15.13. Effects of small and large main apertures on the reproduction. In both reproductions, the ratio between the main and unsharp masking apertures remained the same, however, the main aperture is smaller in reproduction A than in reproduction B.

SELECTION OF THE SCANNING APERTURE

As indicated earlier in this chapter, the detail enhancement with unsharp masking will depend on several factors: the ratio of the main and unsharp masking apertures, the electronic intensity adjustment, and the position of the suppression control adjustment. However, factors other than the effect of the unsharp masking affect the selection of the main aperture. These are scanning feed rate and resolution, and discussed next.

Scanning Feed and resolution

The scanning feed is the width of the scanning lines that are scanned for each revolution of the scanning drum. The smaller the width, the higher the resolution. The fineness of this line will depend on the number of the scanning lines (this in turn will depend on the speed of the scanning head in a horizontal direction) and the size of the scanning spot.

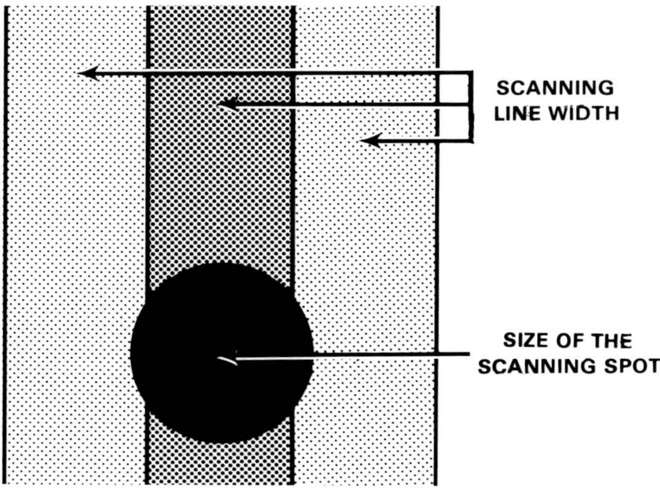

Figure 15.14. Scanning spot size and the width of the scanning line

The width of the scanning line will be dependent on the size of the scanning light spot selected. Usually the diameter of the scanning light spot is 50% more than the width of the scanning line width. This provides a slight overlapping of the scanning line during the scanning of the original, as shown in Figure 15.14.

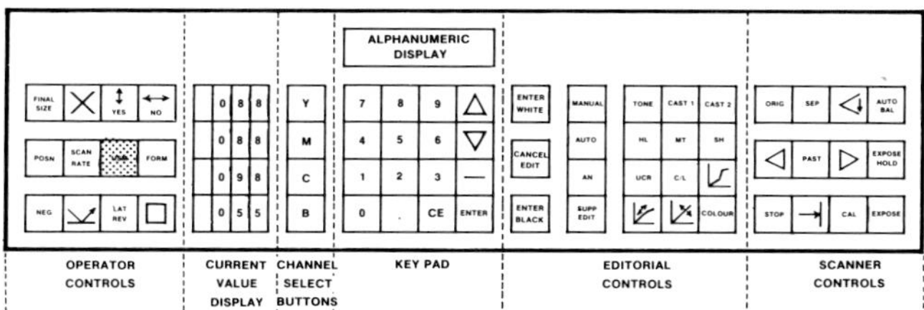

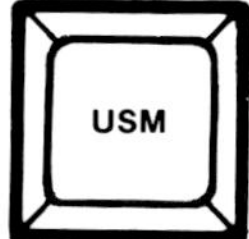

Figure 15.15. The control panel of Magnascan 645 showing the pushbutton control for unsharp masking

Small and large scanning feeds are needed for different enlargement and reduction requirements. At the exposing section, the exposing line width remains the same for a specific screen ruling unless it is changed for special requirements. But at the scanning end, the scanning line width has to be changed to accommodate for different feed rates for different enlargement and/or reduction requirements. The concept is explained with Figure 5.1 on page 99 .

The resolution of the separation can be increased or decreased through the selection of different sized main apertures. Just as a process camera lens offers choices of f-stops, several scanning apertures of different sizes are available in a scanner. When an aperture is small, the scanning light spot is also small. The effect of a smaller main aperture along with an adjustment for finer scanning width results in higher resolution because the scanning light spot is smaller and more lines are scanned with this spot than with a larger spot. Although the resolution will be low when a larger main aperture is used for the same scanning width, the result will be a smooth overall effect on the final reproduction. If choices are provided in a scanner, smaller scanning apertures should be selected for sharp originals and larger scanning apertures should be selected for unsharp and grainy originals. Normally as a general rule, however, for an enlargement, a small feed is needed, and consequently, a small scanning aperture is selected. Conversely, for a reduction, a large scanning aperture is selected for the large feed. This selection is automatic when the suggested guidelines by the scanner manufacturer are followed.

A small main aperture is desirable for optimum resolution, but it has other negative consequences. With a high resolution, the important details of the original undergo sharpness; however, any film grain, scratch, skin blemishes, dirt, and other such imperfections will also gain the same effect. As a result, although small main apertures provide higher resolution, the selection of the aperture will also depend on the quality of the original. A small aperture should be used only for the sharp originals. Originals that contain imperfections or are going to be greatly enlarged, should have a larger aperture setting.

Low light intensity for the scanning light spot can cause problems during the initial calibration of the multipliers like White Alignment or Autobalance. The highest possible intensity of light should be used for the scanning spot. In most scanners, a neutral density filter is positioned to cut down the intensity of the scanning light before it reaches the multipliers. Unless a problem occurs with input calibration, no neutral density filter should be used in the path of the scanning lamp so that the maximum intensity is available for the multipliers. Dirt at the scanning head optics, stray light, misadjustment of the scanning light, and dirty drums may also cause similar problems and affect the quality of the separations.

It should be emphasized that the scanner provides the creative tool to increase or decrease the details in the reproduction by the simple turn of a knob or the push of a button. However, too much use of the unsharp masking controls may result in an unusual enhancement, producing visible borders at the edges of the tones or colors. An unnatural sharpness in any area of the copy will create an unpleasant contrast and may cause a major distraction from the main subject.

UNSHARP MASKING CONTROLS IN DIFFERENT SCANNERS

Crosfield Magnascan 645

The operator controls all the functions in this digital scanner by entering data into the keyboard. The keyboard carries two displays, Alphanumeric and Current Value, and a number of pushbuttons are arranged in groups. Some of the buttons have more than one function.

The scanning or analyze head of the Crosfield 645 consists of a turret with five apertures. A table is provided for the optimum selection of the appropriate aperture. There is no color filter at the analyze or scanning head for the unsharp masking signal. The USM MK3 has incorporated a special circuit to provide greater flexibility in unsharp masking. Following are the main features:

Courtesy Crosfield Electronics

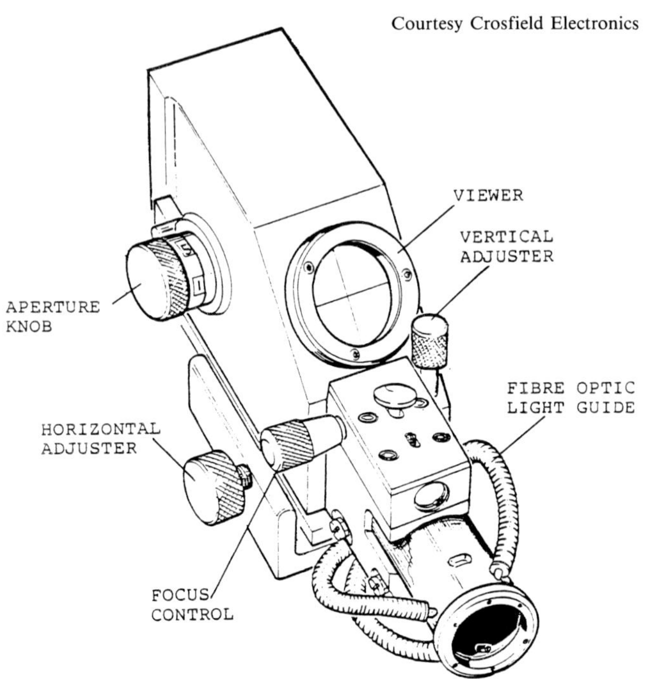

Figure 15.16. Analyze head of the Magnascan 645 showing the aperture knob

1. All output color channels can use any unsharp masking channel of yellow, magenta, and cyan as the source for the detail enhancement.

2. In the black printer, there can be only normal low density enhancement or black high density enhancement.

The controls for the unsharp masking include several functions which the operator can select via the panel:

USM Sharp and USM Smooth: USM Sharp will enhance details where there is a distinct change of density. Values can be entered in the range of 0-9 units in steps of 1. USM Smooth is a facility which smooths out small unwanted density variations, such as grain or skin blemishes. Depending on the value chosen for USM Smooth, it will reduce, neutralize or reverse the effect of USM Sharp over the selected range of density variations.

USM Threshold: the USM Threshold separates those density variations where USM Sharp has full effect, from those where USM Sharp is reduced, neutralized, or reversed by USM Smooth. Smaller variations due to grain can be smoothed while larger variations due to picture detail can be enhanced.

USM Density 1/2: There is little detail in the high density areas of an original but usually the dyes are grainy. With this control the detail enhancement can be reduced from the full value to 0.

Negative Gain: When contact copies are made from negative separations, "fill-in" of the highlight details occur. To compensate, the details in the highlight should be made considerably larger than the details in the shadow. With the negative gain control it is possible to increase the gain in the highlight more than the shadow.

Dainippon Screen SG-608

On the scanning head of the SG-608, a knob is provided to select either one of the two unsharp-masking filter colors, green or red. A light indicates the color of the filter being selected. A total of twelve apertures are provided for different magnification ranges, ten for transparencies and two for reflective copies. All the apertures are stored in an aperture magazine positioned at the right hand side of the operator panel. When any aperture is changed, it must coincide with a predetermined position on the sensitivity switch for the photomultiplier. The sensitivity switch must be turned off when an aperture is changed, a proper sensitivity number for the photomultiplier is selected from a table, and the switch is positioned at that point. It is recommended that signals through the red filter are used to enhance the sharpness of cool colors in a copy where similar colors are dominant; the signal through the green filter is used for dominant warm colors.

Table 17

SG-608 Aperture List

Original Type	Slit No.	Magnification Range (%)	Sensitivity Select SW Setting
Trans-parency	I 01	25 – 75	1
	I 02	75 – 150	2
	I 03	100 – 200	2
	I 04	180 – 350	2 or 3
	I 05	300 – 500	3
	I 06	400 – 700	4
	I 07	600 – 900	4
	I 08	800 – 1200	4
	I 09	1000 – 1600	5
	I 10	1400 – 2000	5
Reflection Original	I 11		3 or 4
	I 12		

Courtesy D.S. America, Inc.

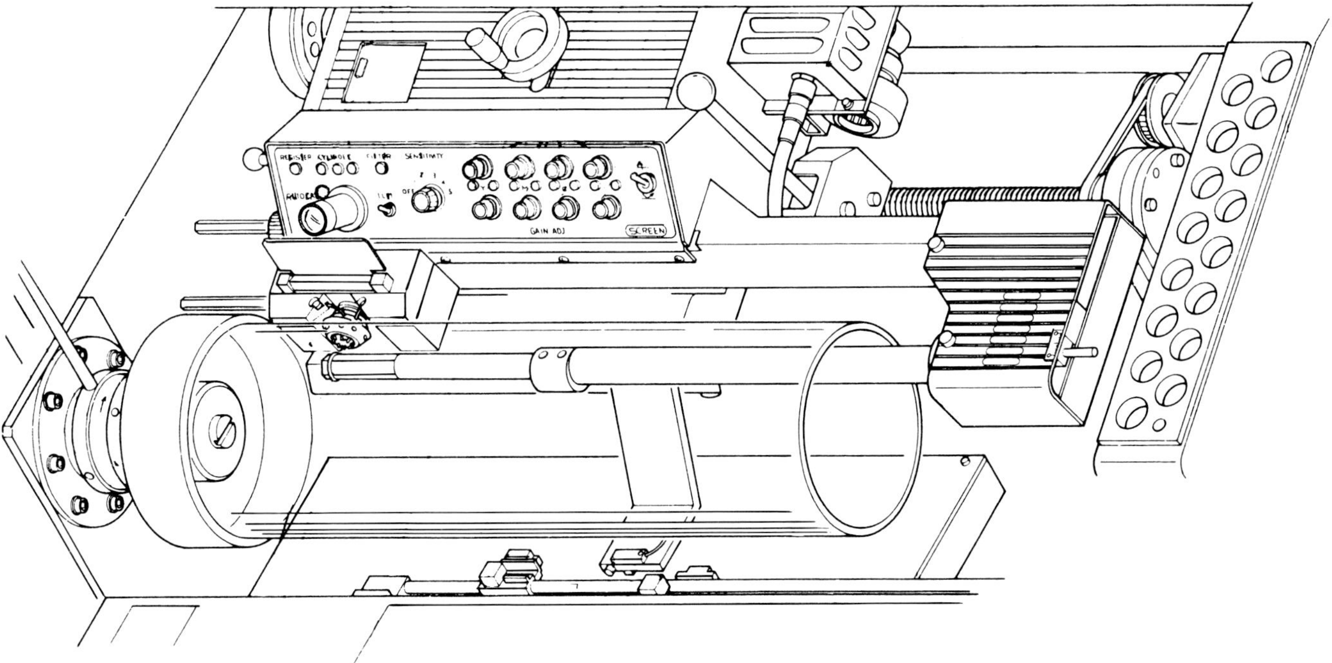

Figure 15.17. Scanning head assembly of the DS SG-608 showing controls for unsharp masking

In addition to the mechanical adjustments for the unsharp masking signal on the scanning head, three controls are provided at the operator panel for the electronic control of the detail enhancement. This is shown in Figure 15.18.

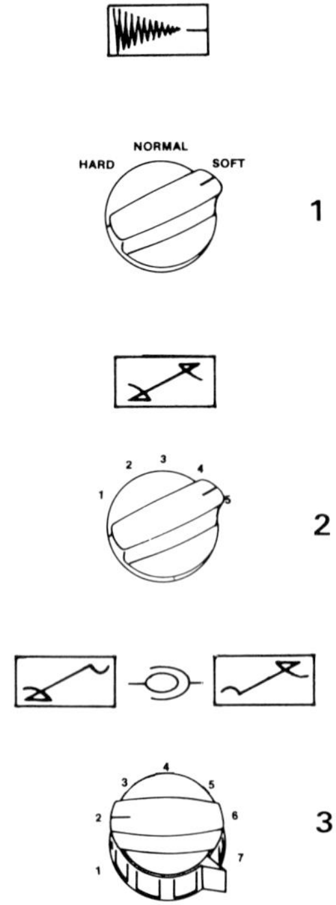

Figure 15.18. Unsharp masking panel in the DS SG-608. Control 1 is used for the adjustment of graininess in 3 steps; with Control 2, adjustment can be made for both highlight and shadow details; Control 3 is a pair of dual-function knobs, the inner knob controls the enhancement in the highlight and the outer knob controls the shadow

Setting the Amount of USM: A set of two controls is provided for controlling the detail enhancement. One knob controls both the highlight and shadow details. The second set is a dual-function knob. The inner knob controls the highlight contour while the outer knob controls the shadow contour. Higher settings of these two controls produce higher contour or density values. The following guidelines are provided for the operator:

Low USM Settings: Portraits and similar images which need to be scanned with high magnification and have a problem of graininess.

Medium USM Settings: Typical images such as still life and natural scenes.

High USM Settings: Images where metallic objects are included and a certain degree of relief is required.

A graininess switch is provided to limit the undesirable effects of emulsion grain, scratches, and other such imperfections in the original or the effects of an unsharp masking setting. There are three selectable positions for the switch — Normal, Hard, and Soft. The graininess is improved when the switch is set at Soft position and vice versa for the other positions.

Hell 399ER:

In all Hell scanners, two adjustable wheels, one with a different combination of scanning/unsharp masking apertures and the other one with color filters, are positioned at the top of the scanning head. The scanning aperture wheel is numbered, the smallest number for the largest aperture and vice versa for the larger numbers. In the Hell 399ER, there are ten scanning/unsharp masking aperture combinations and a table is provided that indicates the size of each light spot for the apertures to be selected for different scanning drums. Guidelines are also provided for selecting different combinations of apertures for different types of originals, scales, scanning feeds, and screen rulings.

Courtesy Hell Graphic Systems, Inc.

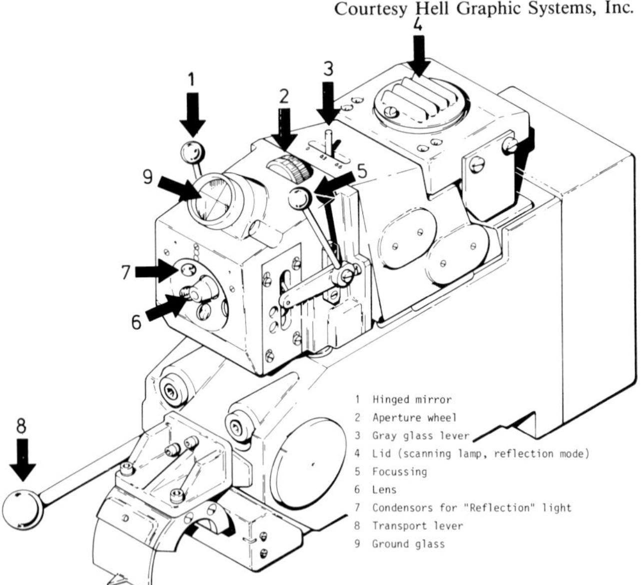

Figure 15.19. Scanning head of the Hell 399ER with aperture and color filter wheels for unsharp masking

The other rotating wheel is to select color for the unsharp masking beam with three color spots — cyan, magenta, and yellow, each designating red, green, and blue filters. Any one filter can be selected by rotating and positioning the respective spot. It is recommended that when scanning a normal original, the unsharp masking filter wheel should be set to the magenta symbol (green filter). However, when scanning originals with fine colored lines, for example, maps, ornaments, etc., the unsharp-masking filter wheel should be set to the respective color channel during separation, i.e. green for magenta, red for cyan, etc.

In addition to the above mechanical adjustments on the scanning head, five controls are provided in the control panel for an electronic adjustment of the different functions of the detail contrast as shown in Figure 15.20.

Highlight Detail Contrast: With this control, the contour intensity and the width can be adjusted for a lower or higher value for the light tones. The control has 0 as the lowest adjustable value and 10 as its highest adjustable value.

Quarter-Tone Detail Contrast: Similar to the highlight detail contrast control, this control is used to decrease (when turned anti-clock wise) or increase (when turned clock wise) the effect of detail contrast in the quarter-tone areas.

Shadow Detail Contrast: With this control, the contour intensity and width can be adjusted for a lower or higher value for the dark or black tones. The control too goes from 0 to 10.

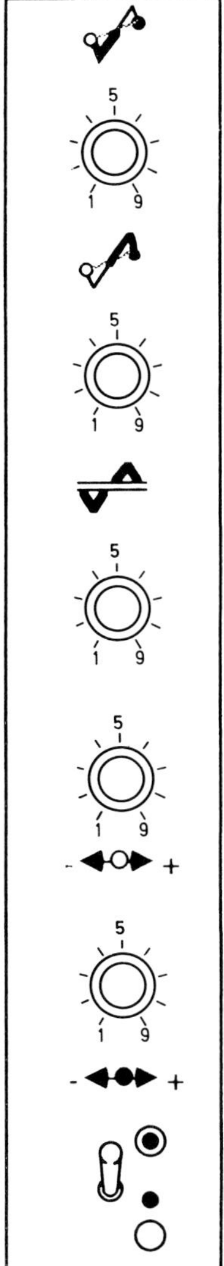

Fugure 15.20. Unsharp masking panel in the Hell 399ER

Three-Quarter-Tone Detail Contrast: Similar to the shadow detail contrast control, this control is used to decrease (when turned anti-clockwise) or increase (when turned clockwise) the effect of detail contrast in the three-quarter-tone areas.

Starting Point for Detail Contrast: The position of this control sets the threshold value for the detail contrast intensity, light and shadow controls. The control has a position from 1 to 9. Rotation towards a higher value decreases the threshold value, thus increasing the effect of intensity controls.

In addition to the above controls, a toggle switch is provided in the same panel to activate or deactivate the effect of the above controls. If required, the effects of the above adjustments can be bypassed or eliminated by turning this switch off.

Royal Zenith 200-S

A feature in this scanner has eliminated the need of a color filter for the unsharp masking signal — a single photomultiplier is used for all the three color signals and the color of the unsharp masking signal is the same as the separation color. In other words, unsharp masking is color selective, it is generated individually for each color. It is claimed that this feature eliminates unwanted detail enhancement at the edges of some colors.

Four apertures are available to control the extent of unsharp masking. A table is provided to select the appropriate aperture for different enlargements and reductions. It is recommended that for duplicate transparencies and transparencies with visible grain structure, a larger aperture (a lower aperture number) be used to decrease detail enhancement. The electronic control of the unsharp masking signal in the RZ 200-S includes several programmable key command sequences.

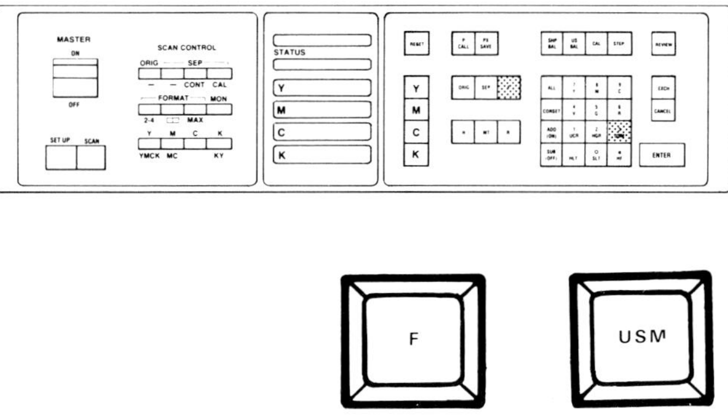

Figure 15.21. Panel of RZ 200-S showing unsharp masking control pushbuttons

The electronic USM control in the RZ 200-S has triple functions, which are selected by control setting number groups in the following control command structure:

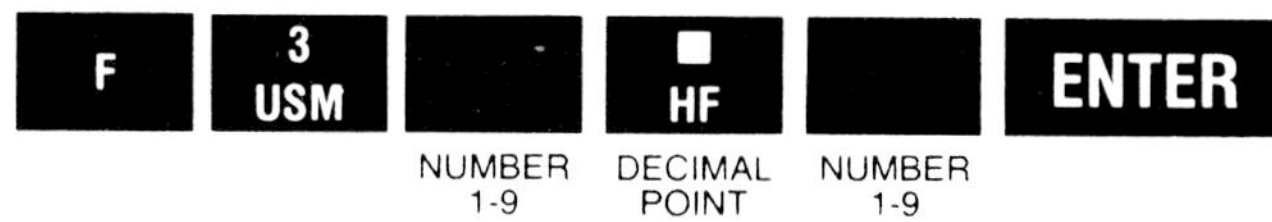

The first group of numbers defines the amount of unsharp masking that can be changed from 1 through 9; the standard setting is 5. If more or less enhancement is required, the control numbers can be altered accordingly. The second group, consisting of the decimal points, selects varying mixes of shaped/unshaped mask responses and assists in automatically reducing noise and grain problems in highlight, in large dense areas and in shadow, while retaining significant USM enhancement. This is defined according to the control number selected as follows:

Conset	USM Shaping	SNL
0 1	100% Unshaped	OFF ON
2 3	25% Shaped	OFF ON
4 5	50% Shaped	OFF ON
6 7	75% Shaped	OFF ON
8 9	81% Shaped	OFF ON

Chapter 16
Color Communication

IMPORTANCE

It is a common knowledge that a set of separations plays only a small but significant role in the complex steps of process color reproduction. The final result will depend on the optimal placement of the four inks on paper. This process involves a number of other skills and personnel. To obtain quality results, a careful control of the processes and techniques must be maintained at all stages of the reproduction. The results of the control must also be communicated to all other personnel involved in the reproduction for consistency and predictability. For example, in order to maintain a consistent result, it is necessary that the pressman optimizes and controls the printing conditions, and the platemaker maintains the quality of the image on the plate. However, it is equally important that the scanner operator or the proofer understand the limits of these controls in order to produce separations or proofs which are equally competent with the other steps in the production line.

Basically printing is a service industry. Every printed job is different and needs careful planning for optimal results. This is even more true in process color printing. For successful planning and maintaining a high standard of reproduction in color, communication is the primary requirement. Most scanner operators, platemakers, proofers, or the pressman can do a good job, but none of them can do it in isolation. It must be a joint effort among all those involved. The chances of communication breakdown, however, is greater in color reproduction than in any other area of production. Two reasons can be attributed to this problem. One is the complexity of the process itself. Each step of the production needs a thorough and critical quality control for optimal results. The other problem stems from the rapid advancements that have taken place in only one area of the technology without parallel developments in other areas. For example, the research and development in electronic separation and related areas have taken place almost in isolation without parallel growth in other areas such as plate, press, stripping, etc. Although research has continued in these areas, they remain inadequate compared to the work that has gone into electronic color separation and page makeup systems. As a result, a scanner operator, compared to other personnel, needs to possess superior knowledge in the theories and practices of color reproduction. In addition to this, the operation of a color scanner provides glamour and a superior environment which are not present in other production areas in the shop. Naturally it gives a sense of superiority to the scanner operator, and often as a result, instead of resolving discrepancies mutually in the production flow, he creates his own standards and sets the conditions for optimal results. Quite often in a shop it seems that the stripper, platemaker, and the pressman work towards a goal — to meet the standard set by the scanner operator. If anything in the production line does not measure up to the expected quality, the last person to be blamed is the scanner operator. However, instances contrary to the above are also there — the scanner operator is frequently blamed for all the shortfalls in other production steps and processes. This creates a production environment which destroys the concept of team effort.

The scanner operator who understands all the steps of correction, proofing, and the printing processes that will be used is invaluable. A good production supervisor will also insist that the retouching, proofing, stripping, and press department personnel be trained to become familiar with the capabilities of the scanner. Awareness of how the scanner operates will ensure proper communication between departments and will frequently save time and money in the retouching and stripping functions. Furthermore, feedback from the proofing department often gives the scanner operator the data that allows valuable fine tuning with respect to the set ups being used in various types of separations. Good scanner results will depend on the cooperation and good communication among everyone in the shop.

AREAS OF COMMUNICATION

The areas of communication may involve in a wide range of personnel and departments ranging from the sales to the production people and finally to the customers. However, the discussion in this chapter will be limited to the areas of personnel, specific production steps, and materials which directly or indirectly influence the quality of separations in a scanner. These are classified into four sections: (1) areas of mutual communication — production processes, steps and materials; (2) conditions for visual communications; (3) prepress proofs as a communication tool; and (4) techniques of communication.

PRODUCTION PROCESSES, STEPS AND MATERIALS FOR COMMUNICATION

The objective areas of communication involving the scanner operator and the other areas of color reproduction are the paper surface efficiency, hue error and grayness of the ink, ink film thickness, dot gain, gray balance, trapping and printing sequence of the process colors, color control targets, platemaking control, and the quality of the originals. A detailed discussion of these areas follows.

Paper

The quality of the paper contributes significantly to the final quality of the reproduction. The scanner operator and the other personnel in the prepress areas must know the type of paper to be used to print the job. The whiteness, ink absorbency characteristics, and gloss of the paper all have a very significant effect on the appearance of the reproduction. The effect of the available ink on the paper must be taken into account when color correction and gradation adjustments are done for a correct balance between the individual separations. For example, a set of color separations produced for a gloss coated paper will not be suitable for a mat finished surface. Similarly, it is important that when proofs are made they should be made on a similar substrate with similar hue and grain characteristics so that it will simulate the printed result. The results on various substrates will help the scanner operator to quantify and adjust the controls of the scanner for optimum results.

Inks

There are dozen brands of process inks available in the market with different hue characteristics. The scanner operator can adjust the scanner for the different types of inks for optimum results in the reproduction. However, the use of a large variety of primary colors may create confusion since the scanner operator and the proofer will be constantly changing their conditions in order to produce satisfactory results. For this reason, the use of a standard set of inks should be maintained as long as possible, and any change should be communicated to the involved persons immediately. This communication eases the problems of all the production personnel concerned. When all the persons know that they are working with the same inks, then a standard set of conditions can be maintained. With a standard set of ink, the chances of proof and print matching are increased with less problems for the pressman.

Ink Film Thickness

The color of the ink alone is not responsible for a good reproduction. The hue and strength of an ink will be dependent on the amount of ink film thickness printed on paper and it will be controlled by the pressman. With different ink film thickness, the light reflected from the paper will change and so will the reproduction. A measurement of the reflected light can be used to control the press run and the proof. A reflection densitometer can be employed for this purpose with good success.

Controlling the press run for a particular job will be no problem for the pressman. He/she can measure the color on the subsequent printed sheets by a quality reflection densitometer as the run progresses and compare the readings. If a significant change in the reading takes place, he/she can make the necessary adjustments to correct the press conditions. However, different densitometers may respond differently to colors which may result in different readings. It is essential that the printer, proofer or the scanner operator does not communicate with the density figures alone unless their equipment is precalibrated against one another.

Dot Gain

It is a fact that identical reproduction of the separation dots of a halftone is not possible. This is because that the dot area is affected by a number of complex optical and mechanical variables such as opacity, of the paper, internal reflection of the inks, plate, blanket, type of paper, roller pressures, cylinder packing, ink film thickness, and the tack and viscosity of the ink. Obviously, if consistent results are to be obtained, the dot gain must be maintained at a certain level and standardized for the specific printing conditions. If it fluctuates from one press run to another or from color to color in a four-color run, the reproduction will be unpredictable. Current SWOP specifications recommend that the difference must not exceed 4% between the colors with the highest and the lowest dot gains. However, the information regarding these variables in the production steps must be available to the scanner operator and the proofer for compensating these factors in the respective equipment. A densitometer may be used to measure and evaluate the dot gain for consistency. For example, if the density of the solid area remains constant during a press run but the halftone area changes, this suggests that a variation in dot area is taking place. Dot gain scale and similar quality control devices are valuable to the press operator for visual evaluations during the press run. These control devices may be reproduced along with the job and checked periodically during the press run (see Figure 16.1).

Courtesy Graphic Arts Technical Foundation

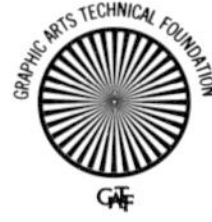

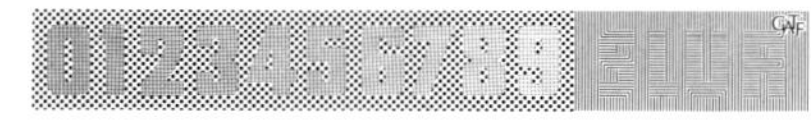

Figure 16.1. GATF Star Target, Dot Gain Scale and Slur Gauge

Gray Balance

Once the set of inks, ink film thickness and dot gain are defined, then one of the most important parameters of color reproduction to be controlled is the amount of cyan, magenta, and yellow inks required to produce a range of neutrals from white through the different shades of gray and black. Because of ink impurities, the cyan normally needs larger halftone dots than the magenta and yellow. In addition, the difference will be much larger in the middle-tone than in the highlight and shadow. The proportion will depend on the ink film thickness and the dot gain associated with each color.

An accurate gray balance ensures that the three primary colors in the reproduction are in balance with each other. With the advent of gray component replacement (GCR), the neutral colors in the reproduction can be partially achieved by the addition of black; however, gray balance still remains a crucial factor. Any deviation of gray balance leads to an imbalance of all colors in the reproduction with a pronounced color cast. For the control of color during the press run, the pressman can make visual assessment of a neutral tone produced from the three color separations. If the inks lose their initial relationship, the neutral will take a color cast and the direction of deviation indicates which adjustments are required in the machine.

Trapping and Sequence

Ink trapping refers to the ink film thickness of a wet ink superimposed on a previously printed ink which may be wet or dry. Ideally the thickness should be identical to the ink film produced alone on the same stock. However, the previously printed ink normally refuses to accept the wet ink film completely. As a result, poor trapping causes the color(s) which are first printed to dominate in the reproduction, and a different sequence of printing the colors may produce different results in the reproduction. For example, the printing of yellow and magenta first may cause a reddish cast in the reproduction. On the other hand, if yellow and cyan are printed first, the reproduction will have a greenish cast.

Ideally the inks are transparent, and as such, the sequence of printing should not have any effect on the results. Unfortunately, some scattering of the light takes place because of the impurities in the vehicle which give a degree of opacity to the ink. As a result, different sequences may also produce different results or cast in the reproduction. In order to maintain color consistency, these parameters must be controlled and taken into consideration.

Color Control Targets

As an aid to the pressman and proofer, a number of targets are available from several companies which consist of small areas of each of the primary colors, an overprinting of the solid colors, and some neutral patches printed with the three or four colors. These targets, when printed, help the operator to take density measurements or make visual judgments and adjust wherever needed. Printed quality control devices include color bars, step wedges, various target devices, scales for indicating dot gain and/or slur, and register marks. Graphic Arts Technical Foundation, Technical Research Center of the Rochester Institute of Technology, Printing Research Division of the DuPont de Nemours and Company,

Courtesy Graphic Arts Technical Foundation

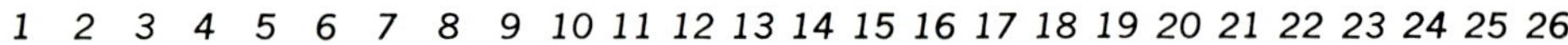

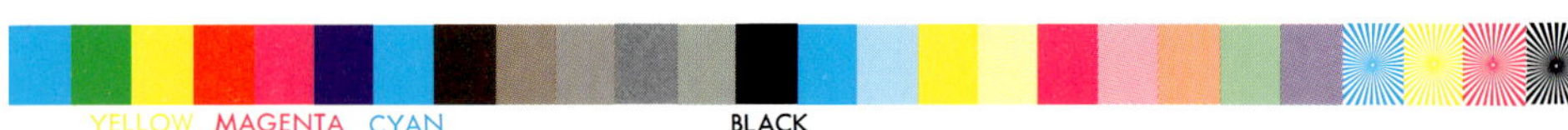

Figure 16.2. GATF Compact Color Test Strip

and 3M Company are but a few organizations among others that manufacture these devices. The functions of the targets are to allow measurement for the purposes of control and communication to the separator. The areas of control are (1) hues and densities of the single colors, i.e. cyan, magenta, yellow, and black; (2) hues and densities of the overprints, i.e. red, green and blue; (3) dot resolution and deformation, i.e. slur, doubling, dot gain, etc.; and (4) color reproduction efficiency, such as gray balance.

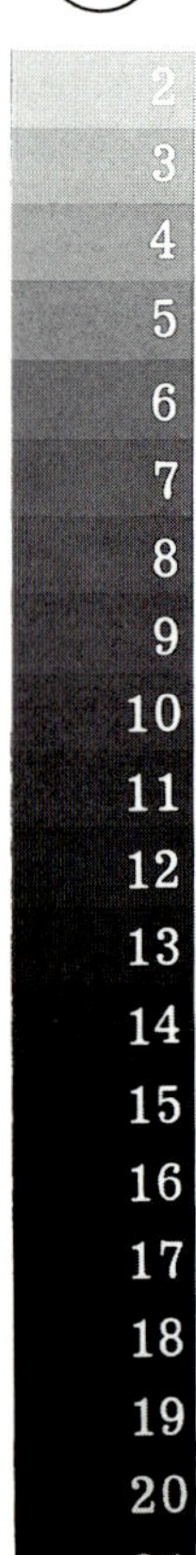

Figure 16.3a. Stouffer-Enco 21-step Sensitivity Guide

Platemaking Control

Variation in the exposure, development, and etching will affect the dot area on the plate. Standardization is the key to controlling the quality of the plates. Special control targets are available to help the platemaker in maintaining an optimum quality by standardizing exposure and development. Two major factors are important to the platemaker: 1) an identical reproduction of the photographic image on the plate without loss of quality; and, 2) production of a plate which will give the maximum press life without deterioration of the image quality. The above factors are directly related to the image resolution, vacuum frame contact during exposure, exposure control, halftone dot gain or loss, and press dot gain and slur. To control these variables, various manufacturers produce and market control devices such as the GATF Star Target, the Dot Gain Scale, Stouffer Continuous-tone Sensitivity Guide, Pira Electronic Planimeter, the GATF color control bar, to name a few.

Originals

The scanner is a flexible and highly versatile color separation device, however, still it has limits to its capabilities. The quality of the separation and reproduction will still depend on the quality of the original. Ideally a copy should have no color cast, should be sharp with a fine grain, and have an acceptable density range with a highlight density of approximately .30 for a transparency and .15 for a reflective copy. It must be clean and free from scratches, fingermarks, and uneven processing characteristics. Deviation from any of these factors is likely to reduce the quality of the reproduction.

Courtesy 3M Company

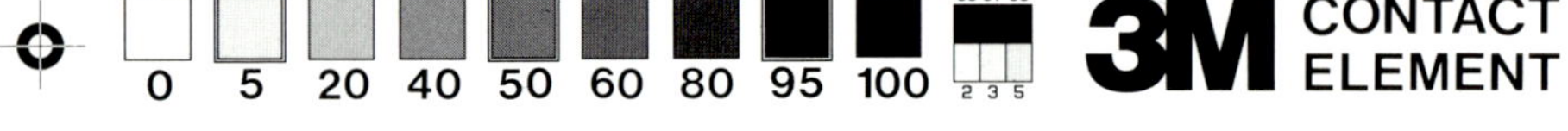

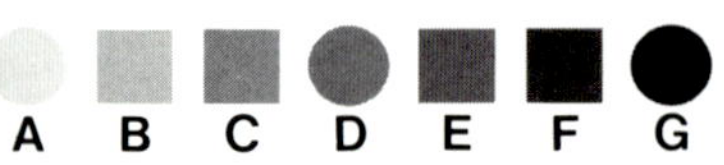

Figure 16.3. 3M Contact Element

Memory Colors

Because of the personality and psychological factors, people may respond differently when they are exposed to various aspects and properties of color. However, there seem to be consensus about *"memory"* colors. These are the colors which are seen in everyday activities and remembered. Even a slight imbalance in these colors become immediately noticeable and objectionable. Colors like blue sky, a yellow banana, green grass, a normal flesh tone, etc. are in this category. With a standardized viewing condition, people seem to agree on the accuracy of these colors. As such, it is important that these colors be thoroughly checked for accuracy in the reproduction.

VISUAL COMMUNICATIONS

In a shop, most of the production steps and processes, from evaluating the original to quality determination of the finished printed results, are evaluated visually. Each person involved in the production steps communicates with one another from his/her own visual impression about how well the step has been performed. In fact, one of the main objectives of process color printing is to satisfy the visual need of the customer. As such, in the production steps, the visual method of evaluation provides more objective results than with other methods, no matter how accurate they are. For example, if the label of a soup looks mushy and unappetizing when it goes to the grocery shelves, the entire process has failed to meet the visual and resulting psychological need of the customer even if the processes were performed accurately. Visual evaluation remains, in effect, the most important tool for evaluating a printed sheet.

Viewing Light

Simply stated, there is no color without light and the quality of the color will be dependent on the quality of the light. The viewing light should be as neutral as possible. Since the reproduction will reflect various proportions of red, green, and blue lights derived from the source, any color bias in the light will affect the evaluation. This color bias in the reproduction will be mostly noticeable in the highlight through the middle-tone areas. If two different lighting conditions are used for viewing the same reproduction at the pressroom and at the customer's office, it will look different. The entire personnel in the scanner, proof and pressroom may think that they have done an accurate job, but because of the different lighting condition, the customer may question the quality and refuse to approve the job. Another phenomenon is that certain colors will match under one lighting condition, but not under a different lighting condition. This is designated as the metameric color matching problem. Small portable viewers fitted with standard 5000°K light source can be used to avoid these problems.

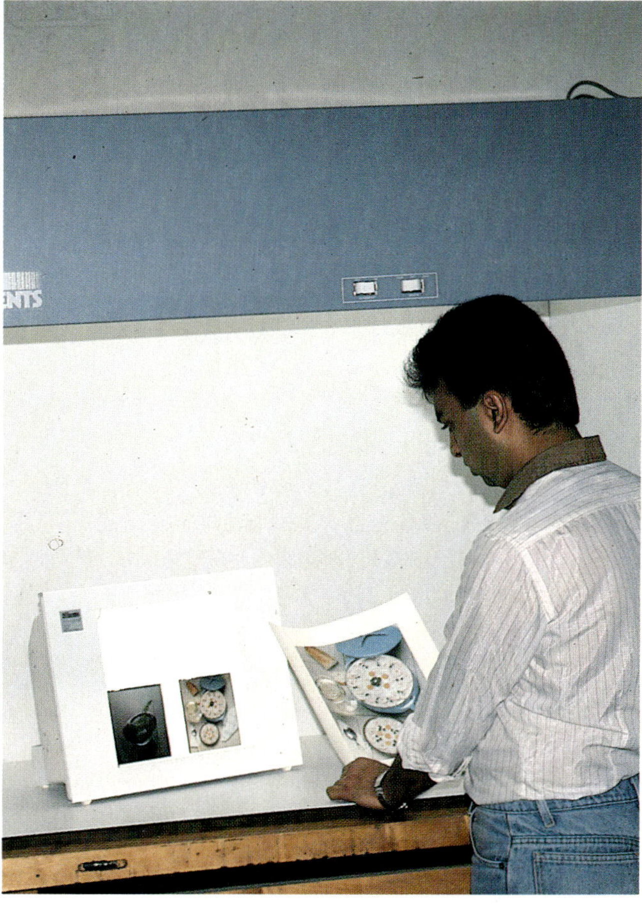

Figure 16.4. A color viewing booth with transparency viewer

Problems with Human Eyes

Human eyes do fairly well at discriminating between small differences in hue, saturation, and brightness when they are observed under identical viewing conditions. When two different reproductions are viewed at once, the eyes can easily recognize the difference between the two. However, one of the major problems with the eyes is that when they are exposed to only one viewing condition, they tend to adapt to that condition. Although there may be a defect in terms of color cast or other improper balancing of the reproduction, because the eyes have adapted to certain condition, the viewer will fail to recognize the problem.

Another problem with visual evaluation is that visual memory of the human being is very poor, and the memory is even worse for colors. A viewer who looks at one reproduction, then looks at another, will have difficulty in evaluating the differences accurately. By the time the eyes are turned, some of the visual memory is lost. However, the eye can do a better job as a comparator when the subjects are seen at the same time. To use the eyes as an accurate comparator, the subjects are placed as close as possible under identical lighting conditions and viewed at once.

Standard Viewing Conditions for Copy and Reproduction

The American National Standards Institute (ANSI) has established a set of conditions for appraising color quality in the graphic arts. They recommend different viewing conditions for the large and smaller transparencies. For 4 X 5 inches or larger transparencies it is recommended that the transparency should be illuminated from behind by diffuse light and surrounded by at least two inches of illuminated area. The surround area should not exceed four times the transparency area. When viewing a small transparency, any illuminated area in excess of this ratio should be covered with an opaque gray border of about 60% reflectance. The transparency illuminator should be placed within the illuminated area provided for viewing the reflection copy or reproduction.

Viewing a small transparency does not always give a true indication of how the contrast and color will look when it is enlarged. Using a magnifier may provide a wrong evaluation. The ANSI recommends that the small transparency should be enlarged not less than four times or not more than 12 times and then viewed in identical conditions as the larger transparency for evaluation. A number of separators build special viewers to project the transparencies to the reproduction size. The viewers can be fitted with neutral density filters or color filters to adjust the general illumination level or the color balance of the transparency.

The spectral power distribution illuminating both the reflection copy and the transparency viewing area has been recommended to be 5000°K. This viewing standard is now accepted worldwide as a standard for viewing color in the graphic arts industry. There are color-viewing booths commercially available that meet the ANSI standards for 5000°K viewing.

It should be realized that the appearance of a transparency or a print strictly depends upon the way they are viewed. Although standards are set up, but they are frequently ignored, particularly by the customer who prefers to view the print by the window light or in all types of artificial lights. Everybody in the production process must ensure that they are using similar conditions when making a judgement on the quality of the reproduction. The sources of illumination must be similar both in terms of brightness and spectral emission, and there should be no glare or intrusion of light from other sources or by reflection from the colored walls.

PREPRESS PROOFS

Prepress proofs are universally used as a strong communication tool by the scanner operator and other personnel responsible for the production of color. Proofs are used for both as an internal, as well as an external communication tool. As an internal tool it is used to communicate with various departments to evaluate the results, as well as a guide and corrective tool. For example, it is difficult to visualize the subtle changes in the reproduction from the adjustments made in a scanner for color correction, gradation, etc. Once the proof is made, the scanner operator can evaluate the separations for further corrective adjustments in the scanner. The proofs provide an objective way to evaluate the results in a scanner for subsequent corrections. In the same way, the stripper or the printer can use the proof as a guide to crop, size, and run the set of separations in a press.

The other function of the proof is more critical in terms of resemblance of the final printing when it is shown to the customer to explain how the job is going to look when it will be printed. In this situation the press proof could have served the purpose best. However, the cost involved in the stripping, making plates, and then running all the four colors in a press for making a proof is prohibitive, especially if changes are required at this stage. Press proofs have their disadvantages too. Since the proof will be done by a slow press run, it may not look the same as the finished product. However, a prepress proof is an inexpensive alternative for a press proof to predict for the customer what the final job will look like. This is the first time the customer sees the result from the original presented and on the basis of this he approves the separations produced, perhaps with corrections. As such, a more cautious approach should be undertaken when these prepress proofs are presented to the customer for approval.

Various Types of Prepress Proofs

There are dozens of different types of prepress proofs available under different brand names. However, these can be generally categorized into four distinct types: overlay system, superimposed system, photographic print system, and electronic proofs.

Overlay Systems

The overlay system consists of a set of light sensitive transparent films with pigments similar to the four process colors. Both negative and positive acting emulsions are available for both negative and positive separations. Each separation is exposed on the respective color films and developed. The unexposed areas wash away for a negative and the exposed areas for a positive, so that the final result is a set of positives for each of the process colors. The four color images are then superimposed one above the other in registration. A piece of paper is placed under the image and the integrated image is then viewed with reflected light. DuPont has introduced a dry overlay color proofing system called Cromacheck. It is an inexpensive dry proofing system which does not need chemical processing. Using a set of separation negatives, the color material is exposed by a high intensity UV light source. The top layer from each color materials is peeled, and all the four layers are registered for the finished proof (see Figure 16.5). In addition to their popular NAPS/PAPS overlay proofs, Enco's newest overlay system on the market is the Colorlink system. The materials are available for both negative and positive working emulsion. The material is exposed emulsion to emulsion and processed manually or in a processor with water-based chemistry (see Figure 16.6). Example of another popular overlay proof is the 3M Color Key.

Courtesy E. I. Du Pont De Nemours Co.

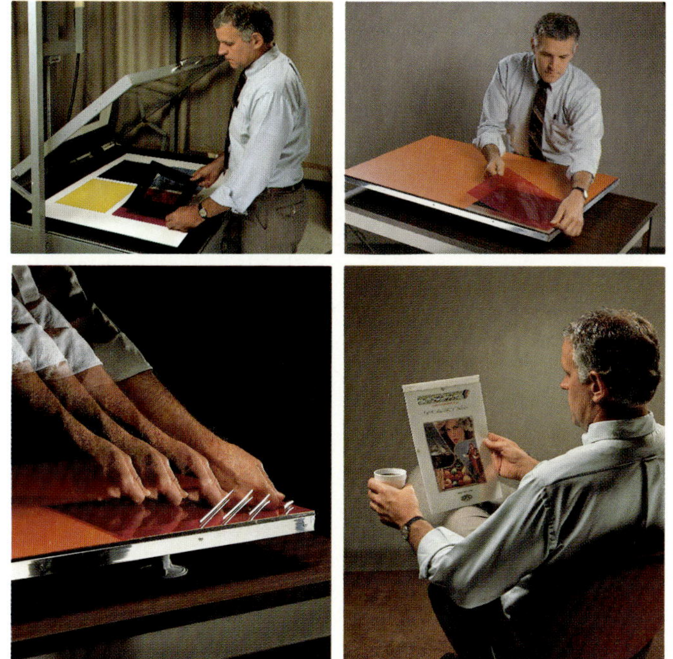

Figure 16.5. DuPont Cromacheck dry proofing system

Overlay proofs are easy to make, and inexpensive to produce. Only a minimal equipment is needed. Other advantages of overlay proofs include a progressive proof that can be simulated by using only the respective color layers. The separations can be evaluated by comparing them with the respective color layers. Dot etchers can use these proofs effectively to see the result of dot etching in any one of the separations and compare the overall effects by laying over

Courtesy Hoechst Celanese Corp.

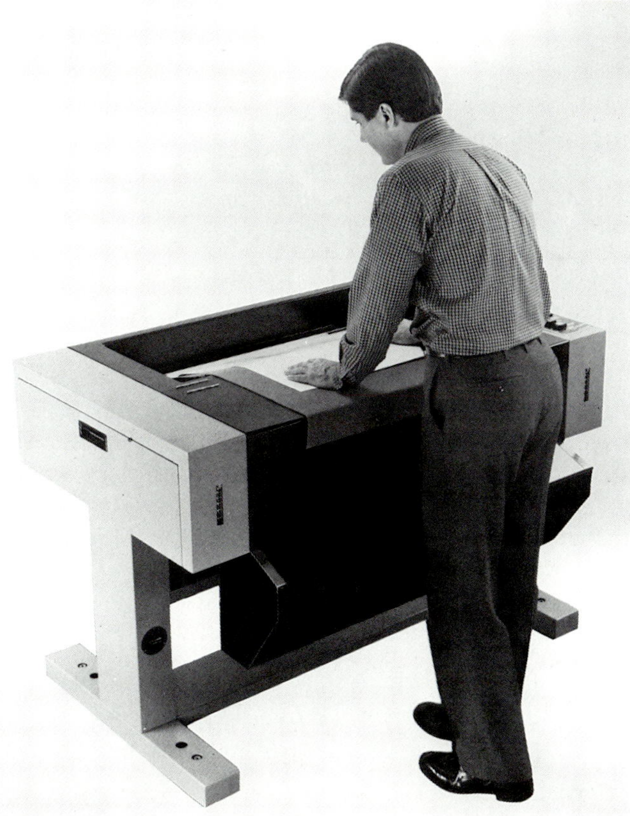

Figure 16.6. Enco Colorlink CF-262 processor for overlay and Pressmatch single sheet proofs

the others. The major disadvantage, however, is that these proofs bear little relation to the press print in appearance because they are glossy and suffer from internal reflections which cause color changes. As an inexpensive internal communication tool, they are highly desirable and valuable, but as customer proofs they have limitations. Because of the type of pigment, the presence of density in the carriers, and the absence of press variables in the proofs, such as the effects of dot gain, trapping, etc., these proofs hardly match the final printed sheet. However, depending on the situation, it can be accommodated in a particular customer-proofer-printer relationship where the client fully understands the difficulties and limitations.

Superimposed Systems

This is a general term used to describe systems in which the image is produced on an integral backing sheet either specific to the process or of the type on which the print will be produced. The best known of this type of proof is the DuPont Cromalin system. Basically Cromalin consists of a tacky polymer which is hardened by the action of light. Exposure to a positive leaves only the image areas tacky. The image areas are then dusted with color toner. By the successive application of polymer, exposure, and dusting, the complete four color proof is produced. Cromalin is available for both positive or negative working polymers. This system is versatile and can be set up to compensate for the variables in the press run. Toners are available in variety of process colors and they

Courtesy E. I. Du Pont De Nemours Co.

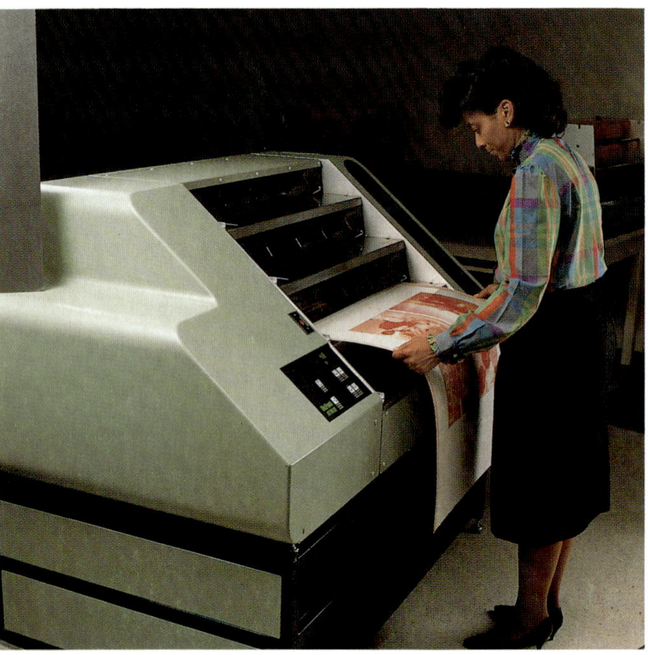

Figure 16.7. DuPont Cromalin Autotoner

can be blended to duplicate the process inks. However, the success of this system depends on the basic calibration steps, finding the exact exposure to compensate for the press variables and the blending of the toners to match the printing inks. Recently DuPont has introduced their Cromalin Masterproof system in which a new receptor enhances the negative to positive match which was difficult in the earlier Cromalin system. The main characteristics of the Cromalin Masterproof system include a wider range of process colors, which can be exactly matched to the SWOP color inks for web offset publications, and a built in dot gain. DuPont has also announced its new Electrostatic Master Proofing (EMP) system. The system will offer fine resolution (2% to 98% dots, 150 lines per inch), positive/negative working, selectable dot gain from 15% to 22%, and SWOP proofing stock. A high resolution liquid color toner is deposited on the appropriate stock in an electrostatic printing machine. No date has been announced about the availability of this unit.

The 3M Matchprint II is a negative acting single-sheet proofing system which simulates the inks for commercial sheet-fed printing. The films use a thermal lamination process and bond the films to Matchprint II Commercial Low-Grain Base in the MR-447 Matchprint Proofing Laminator. 3M has also developed the Matchprint II Publication SWOP/GAA VI color proofing system for web offset and gravure applications. The system simulates the SWOP/GAA VI requirements for ink tonal response and incorporates dot gain,

Courtesy 3M Company

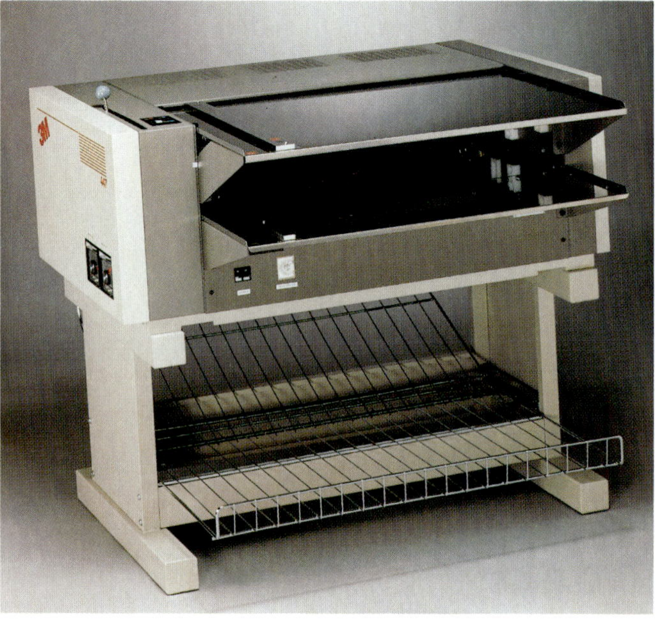

Figure 16.8. 3M MR-447 Laminator

color density specifications, as well as the brightness characteristics of publication paper stocks. Identical to the Matchprint II negative system, the Matchprint II Positive Publication Proofing Film uses a thermal laminator process and is

Courtesy 3M Company

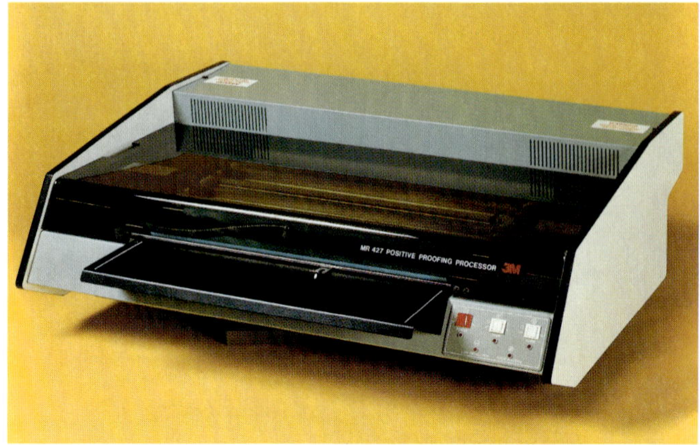

Figure 16.8a. 3M MR 427 Positive Proofing Processor

bonded to Matchprint II SWOP Publication (or Commercial) Base in the MR 447 Laminator. The 3M Matchprint system eliminates the variables of other systems by coating the color at the factory.

Current entry in the market is Enco's Colorlink Pressmatch, a single-sheet proof which meets SWOP off-press proof specifications. The three available receivers offer high brightness, commercial, and SWOP publication stocks. A simulation of the final press finish is achieved with a choice of high gloss, gloss, or matte finish. The dot gain characteristics can be adjusted to suit any press needs. The process uses a thermal laminator (Figure 16.9) to bond a factory coated color sheet to the appropriate receiver stock. The sheet is then exposed, and developed in a water-based chemistry. The chemistry and processor can also be used for the negative or positive Colorlink overlay proofing materials.

Courtesy Hoechst Celanese Corp.

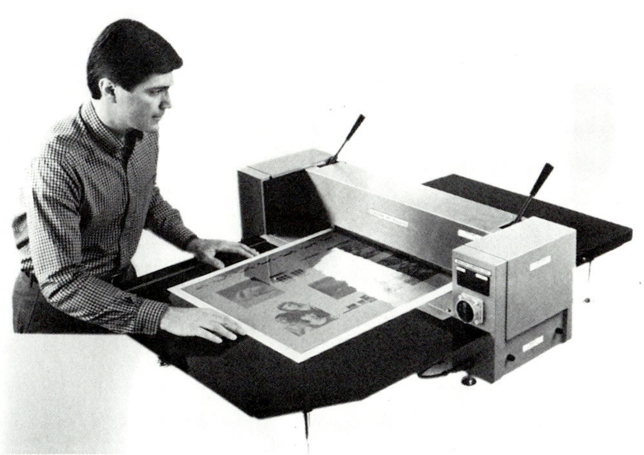

Figure 16.9. Enco Colorlink LAM-1 laminator for the Pressmatch single sheet proofing system

Photographic Proofs

A new direction of proofing has emerged during the last few years using the conventional color photographic paper as a base material for proofing. A large number of firms are exploring the possibilities of this idea. The main advantage of the system is that it is inexpensive. The three color dyes are already present on the paper, and after exposure, a simple two-step processing is all that is needed for the image. However, the main disadvantages are that the separations are to be exposed through the complementary filters, the quality will depend on accurate filtration and exposure, and the characteristics of the dye present in the photographic emulsion is different than that of the printing ink.

Chesley F. Carlson Co. of Minneapolis, MN, markets a similar product called Proofmaster. The Proofmaster exposes the color print photographic paper through specially de-

Courtesy Chesley F. Carlson Co.

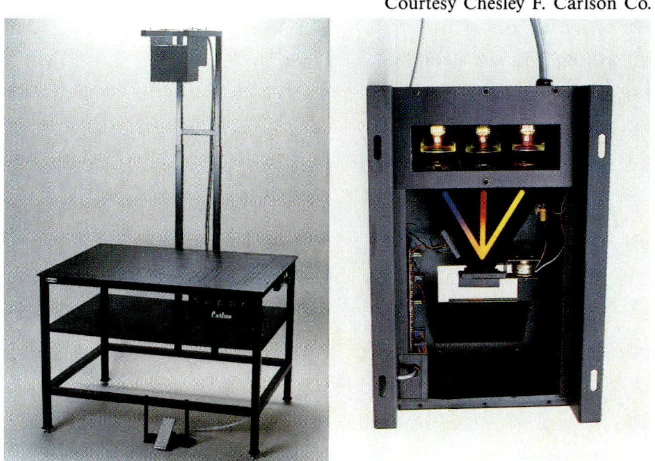

Figure 16.10. Carlson Proofmaster

signed narrow band filters. A unique mixing chamber blends the light from the three filters to create the color needed for the proof (see Figure 16.10). The company claims that an eight-page proof can be exposed and ready for processing in less than five minutes, and costs less than ten dollars.

The Hell CPR 403 is a digital system which exposes directly on the color photographic paper (see Figure 5.1). The unit uses two light sources, a helium/neon laser and an argon/ion laser to image photographic material directly from the stored color data. It is possible to program the proof recording unit to simulate the dot gain, trapping, and the ink color of the final print. The 403 fills the need in the process sequence of the Hell electronic page-makeup — the Chromacom System. After the digital data is manipulated, a duplicate proof of the entire assembly can be recorded on a color photographic paper or color transparency material. Because of the high resolution offered by the system, the assembled duplicate image often exceeds the quality of the original copy and it may be used as an original for separation on the scanner.

Recoprint by Agfa-Gevaert is a similar new off-press color proofing system which can be used in conjunction with the Carlson Proofmaster, Kreonite Color Proof, or the Hell CPR 403 unit. The system consists of a color film, color paper, and special chemicals. The Recoprint can be used in variety of applications including position proofing, pre-scan full page makeup proofs, and second generation originals when used with the Hell CPR 403 unit.

Video Proofs

Designated as soft proofs, electronic color video monitors are becoming popular as a type of prepress proofing. These visual terminals extend the scope of the scanner far beyond the color separation and correction. Over the years, there

Courtesy Itek Colour Graphics

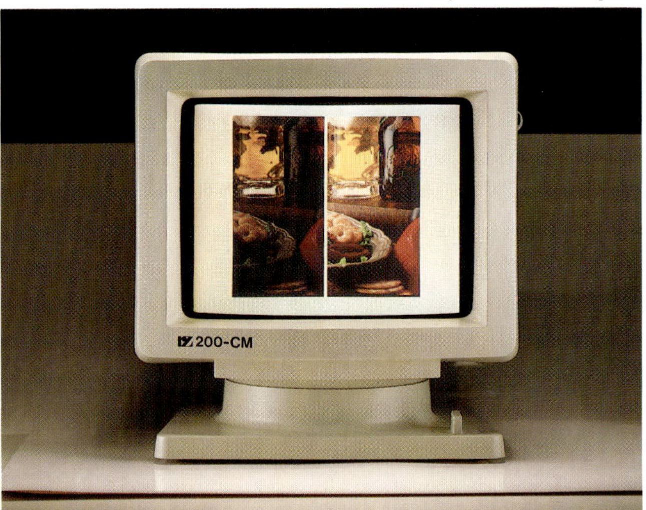

Figure 16.11. RZ 200-CM Color Monitor

have been a number of such viewers introduced, but recently some color scanner models have incorporated visual display terminals successfully as an integral part of the scanner and extended the function of the scanner considerably. As an integrated terminal it takes only a few minutes to program and generate the image on the terminal.

The main disadvantage in this type of proofing is that there is no hard copy, and the proof has to be for internal use only. The scanner operator, after receiving the job data, can make a speedy set up of the scanner with the aid of these terminals for an optimal result on the film. The latest of these units include such facilities as on screen enlargement or reduction, cropping, density display, matching of the screen to the users paper and ink characteristics, adjusting the monitor screen to match the proofed result, split screen function to compare changes, visual checking of color correction, and even progressive display of color proofs simulating the press results. However, the accuracy of this proofing will depend on the environmental lighting conditions. Moreover, these units work on the additive color principle and the images have to be interpreted with the printed sheet which is produced on the subtractive principle.

Digital Proofs

The role of color proofing has expanded with the greater use of color electronic prepress systems (CEPS). After the images are manipulated in the CEPS system, they need to be checked for accuracy and acceptance before they are recorded on the film. Otherwise, it would be expensive and time consuming to have to produce separations and a hard copy

Courtesy E. I. Du Pont De Nemours Co.

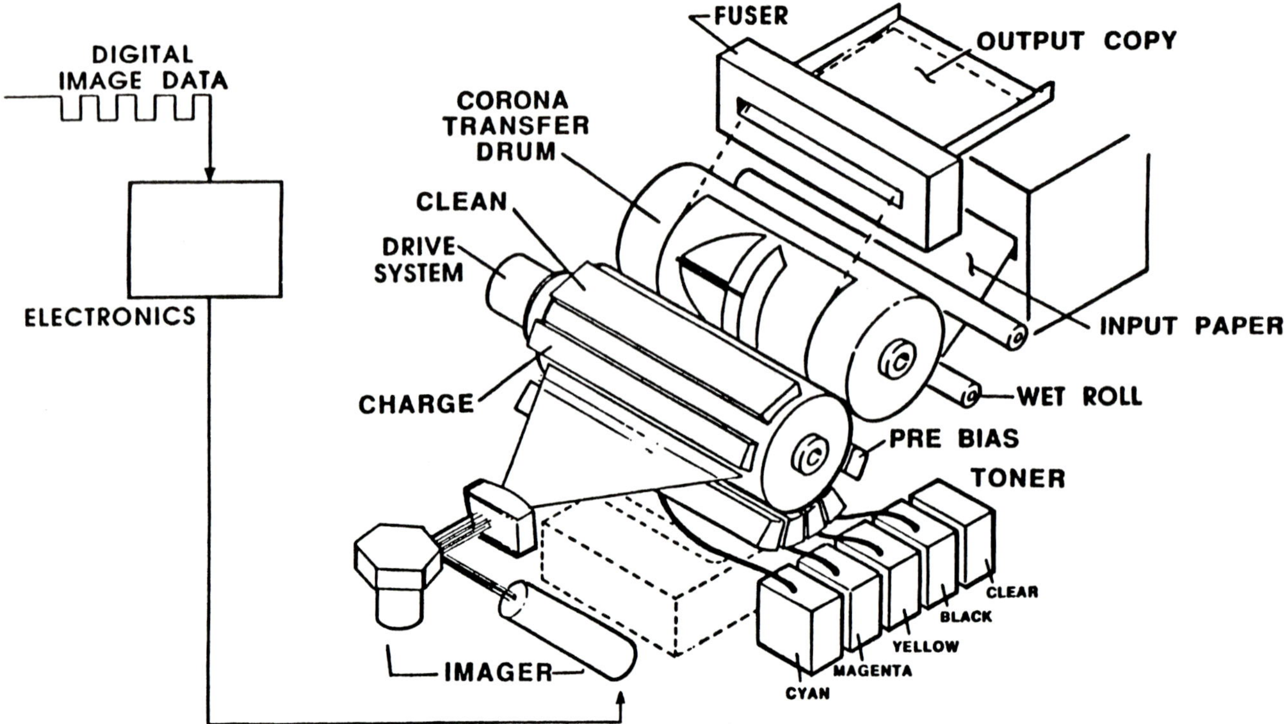

Figure 16.12. A simplified concept of DuPont's Direct-Digital Color Proofing (DDCP) System

color proof before client changes can be identified. Several new digital proofing methods have been introduced and are in operation within the industry. They all make use of color photographic paper. The software transforms the cyan, magenta, yellow, and black digital picture data into exposure values. An example of successful digital proofing technology is the Hell CPR 403 system mentioned earlier. However, the unit produces only continuous-tone image on a color photographic paper or transparency materials.

Several new digital halftone proofing systems are in the developmental stages. Most of them are based on the existing photopolymer, ink-jet imaging, and thermal transfer technology. However, high quality digital color proofs for customer-approval are under development by Eastman Kodak and DuPont. Both systems are based on electrophotographic principle — Kodak's is on the existing Signature technology, and DuPont's on the Electrostatic Master Proofing System (EMP). If the digital proof is to be helpful, it must simulate the same high image quality as the press, faithfully reproduce the hues, as well as simulate the effect of dot gain and other variables.

Other Types of Proofing Systems

In Drupa '86, a number of manufacturers unveiled their prepress proofing systems. Significant among these is Kodak's Signature Color Proofing System. The system offers production of negative or positive color proofs that are more like an actual press proof. The main features of the Signature System are that the proof can be made on a coated press sheet from a positive or negative, variable dot gain and printing density can be adjusted independently, and that four-color SWOP proofs are possible. It takes about 20 minutes for a full size proof. The proofing film is electronically charged in the toning unit. Then the sensitized film is exposed through the film support to the first of four-color separations. After each exposure, the film is moved to a toning station where a liquid toning solution is dispersed across the film's surface. The tonal particles are attached by the charge pattern on the photoconductive layer of the film. As the liquid developer carriers evaporate, the "self-fixing" toners adhere to the film, which then goes back for the additional charging and exposures. When all the four-color images are built into the film, it is removed from the toning console and carried to the laminating unit where the film is placed in contact with the substrate. The film/substrate "sandwich" is put inside the laminator. When the "sandwich" is removed and pulled apart, 100 percent of the image has been transferred to the substrate.

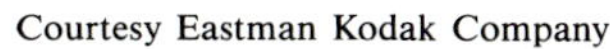
Courtesy Eastman Kodak Company

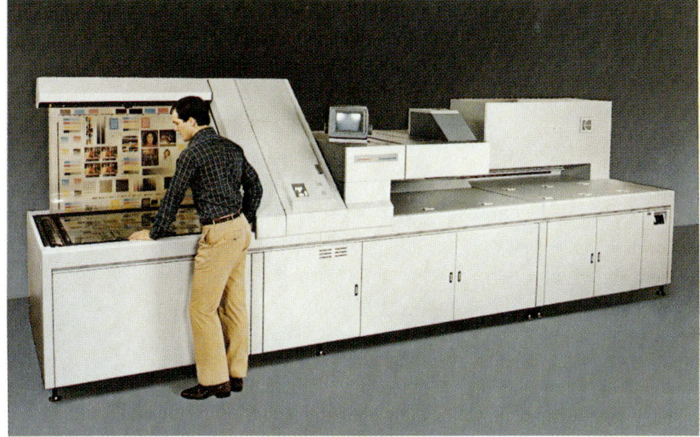

Figure 16.13. Kodak Signature Proofing System

Fuji Color-Art System is a new prepress overlay color proofing system from either negative or positive film using the same chemicals and equipment. The Hoechst Company of West Germany unveiled their Ozasol Transproof System using a receiver system and color films. First the color film is laid on a receiver sheet and placed on a laminator. Next the color separation film and the corresponding laminated color film are exposed, and then the receiver sheet is fed into a special processor which develops and rinses automatically. The process is repeated with the four colors for the finished proof.

There is little doubt that prepress proofing is widely used in the industry for good reasons. The primary reason is the cost. After a separation is generated, an acceptable proof ensures that the set of separations meet the required standard before it goes to the stripper and the press. Regardless of its relationship to the final print, it gives the scanner operator or retoucher a useful guide to determine whether or not the set of separations is acceptable. However, consistency is the key factor in using these proofs as a valuable tool for internal evaluation. The main problem is that these prepress proofs will never match the final print and some interpretations will be necessary. These interpretations come from experience. However, when these proofs are used for the customer, there are limitations, and they should be used with caution. If a customer expects to see the press results looking like the prepress proof he has approved earlier, he may be disappointed if the variation is significant.

COMMUNICATION TECHNIQUE

The technique of communication in color may range from an informal verbal exchange to a more precise sophisticated electronic measuring device. There is no hard and fast rule as to which communication technique will be the most effective; however, the success of communication will not depend on the technique alone. Factors like human relations, behavior, rapport among the production people, the dedication and sincerity of the personnel involved are also considered to be major factors for effective communication. However, it should be emphasized here that to be effective, communication should be always a two-way street. This will help in better understanding and create better rapport among the persons involved to reach the common objectives in the optimum reproduction of color.

Courtesy Graphic Arts Technical Foundation

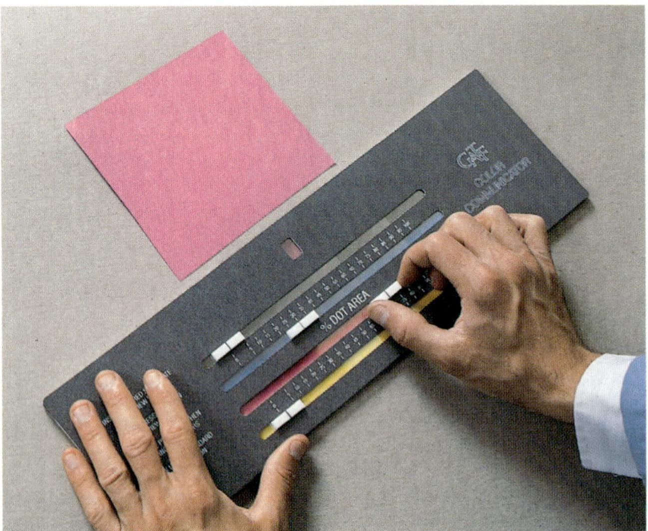

Figure 16.14. GATF Color Communicator

Verbal Communication

Verbal communication can be very specific or vague depending on its uses. Expressions like "the color needs a little more snap," and "the rose needs to stand out more" are very informal and bear little meaning unless the communicator and the listener have established a meaning for these expressions within themselves. However, in everyday shop conditions these words are frequently used in the informal evaluation and expression of color. The effectiveness of such informal expressions will depend on the rapport of the persons involved.

Verbal color communication can be more objective if used with acceptable and standardized terminologies used in the industry. This will make the communication reasonably unambiguous. These terms are listed and explained below.

Hue: Hue shifts can be specified with any of the six primary or complementary colors — cyan, magenta, yellow, red, blue, and green. For example, if the apple looks orange rather than red, it can be corrected by adding magenta or reducing yellow.

Saturation: Only two terms should be used for specifying saturation — cleaner or grayer. To increase saturation, gray value has to be removed from the color. For example, if a red looks dirty and needs more saturation, the cyan has to be removed or magenta and yellow have to be added. In other words, saturation can be increased by removing complementary colors or adding the primary or secondary colors. Conversely, for specifying less saturation more complementary colors or less basic colors need to be added.

Lightness: Only two terms, lighter or darker can be used for specifying lightness. A pale color can be made darker or lighter by increasing or decreasing dot values or adding or removing black.

Communication using Physical Samples

Physical samples are extremely important tools for communication in color. A color communication which employs a visual method, provides greater acceptance and confidence among people in the communication process. Special solid ink colors like the Pantone® system provide an unambiguous meaning to all concerned who have the same book. Various types of color charts are also available from different manufacturers specifying different color changes using different combinations of tints and solid colors. These charts can be successfully used to specify color. DuPont Color Communicator, a small color chart printed with the reproduction, can be used effectively for this purpose. The desired color in the chart can be indicated by reference to the printed color chart. Another device for the specification of color is the GATF Color Communicator. The device consists of sliding wedges of cyan, magenta, yellow, and black. Each of these colors can be continuously varied from 0% to 100% to match a specified color.

Communication using Measuring Instruments

A measuring instrument provides the most objective method of color communication. Spectrophotometers, colorimeters, densitometers, and glossmeters all can be used for quantifying and communicating color. However, a densitometer is the most widely used instrument for measuring and comparing originals, proofs, and printed sheets. The current line of a few densitometers can read the dot percentages directly from a set of separations or print. Using a reflection and a transmission densitometer, the techniques and processes can be standardized for the optimal production of color. Densitometers are extremely useful tools; however, they should be accurate and calibrated as precisely as possible for an accurate reading. Density numbers are often communicated between the proofer, scanner operator, the platemaker, and the pressman. The densitometers used by different departments must be calibrated for the same response if the communication is to be successful.

Chapter 17
Introduction to Digital Image Processing

Although a scanner plays a significant role in the prepress areas, its efficiency can be enhanced or severely limited by the other prepress area activities. For example, the efficiency of the prepress production will also depend on the quality of stripping, dot etching, and typesetting functions in the production flow. The following are some of the areas which can restrict efficiency in the prepress areas.

1. Color stripping has been mostly a manual function, and the critical assembly of the films is required for exact image placement on the paper. This is a time consuming step and it is not uncommon to employ several strippers to assemble separations produced by a single scanner.

2. Because of the diversified needs of the customer and various types of copy being received for scanning, dot etchers are frequently needed to correct specific areas in the separations. The method is time consuming, expensive, and may create a backlog in the prepress areas.

3. Where a page or format calls for the assembly of several pictorial images, size changes and retouching are often needed for the originals. Normally photographic duplicates are made from the original after they are retouched to fit them into the spaces provided in the layout. Because of the limitations of the photographic steps, a duplicate is often inferior in quality to the original.

4. If the page to be reproduced involves the production of different geometrical shapes and sizes, inclusion of tints, lineworks, etc., the time and expense involved in the manual assembly of these functions may be prohibitive. In some cases, the manual work may not produce the desired results.

5. An integration of types and images is frequently needed for a majority of the jobs. This is a manual operation and may become complicated in terms of space, size, and positions.

The above are just a few examples of limitations in the prepress areas where the scanner alone cannot increase productivity or efficiency. However, with the advent of digital technology, all of the above functions and more are now being effectively handled in the image processing equipment. An entire page consisting of various elements can now be modified or changed in almost limitless ways by the press of a few buttons while the operator can watch the effect on the color monitor in real time, i.e. simultaneously. The corrected image then can be saved on a floppy disk and color separated in the scanner as a composite image on four pieces of films.

Image processing, in its simplest sense, means the manipulating of an image. An example would be to adjust or change the contrast and color in a color television with the respective controls. With the advent of digital technology, a number of exciting things can be done with the image which was not previously possible. With this technology, images are broken down into a series of digital values representing such things as the brightness (luminance) and color (chroma) at every given point in the image. By manipulating this data with a computer, images can be improved, changed, and even merged by the press of a few buttons.

Image processing, once handled only by large and expensive computer systems, is now possible at home with a small personal computer, similar to a word processor. Special image processing software for the home computer is now available from companies such as American Telegraph and Telephone Company, Atronics International, and others. Personal computers can be used to process an image using an input from a video camera or a video cassette recorder. The image can be instantly captured in full color, frozen, and enhanced feature by feature and stored on a floppy or hard disk. These pictures can even be transmitted to any remote computer via a modem. American Telegraph and Telephone Company's True Vision Image Processing System, a plug-in board and software combination, uses a video camera, an IBM personal computer or a compatible, and a graphics tablet or mouse to capture, digitize, and manipulate images on a color monitor. However, it should be emphasized here that there is a distinct difference between an "expensive computer system" which is used for graphic arts pagination systems and the image processing with the personal computer. The amount of data, resolution, flexibility, output quality, and ease of operation needed for the graphic arts industry is not there when the image is processed with a personal computer with limited memory.

BACKGROUND

The theories and practices of electronic image processing are not new. One dimensional signal processing was used extensively during the World War II to clean up radar signals. Linear system theory was well-known in applied mathematics. The makers of page readers were working in the areas of optical character recognition. And researchers in chromoscope analysis had experimented with image analysis and pattern recognition as early as 1960s. However, as one of the major sources, the current thrust of the digital image processing technology has possibly emerged from the research by NASA's Jet Propulsion Laboratory.

The signals and pictures sent by the early space program by the United States and Soviet Union were in analog form. The photographs captured and sent back to the earth by the analog cameras were grainy, out of focus, and distorted by signal noise. However, one person, Dr. Robert Nathan of Jet Propulsion Laboratory who came from the California Institute of Technology, applied his knowledge of digital techniques to the image sent back from America's early space probes. The success came with the lunar mission of Ranger 7. Ranger 7's cameras transmitted the first highly detailed images of the moon to the earth.

Dr. Nathan suggested digitizing the analog video images and adopting the technique of one-dimensional signal processing to process the two-dimensional images with the help of computers. The image enhancement techniques developed by Dr. Nathan and others at the Jet Propulsion Laboratory were used successfully on the images from Rangers 7,8, and 9, which returned a total of 17,267 images of the moon. Dr. Nathan also developed an image enhancement technique known as deconvolution, which deblurred the images and improved resolution dramatically. In 1965 Jet Propulsion Laboratory established an image processing laboratory with its own computing facility. Dr. Nathan was also responsible for completing his work on a VLSI chip in 1985 with five multipliers and accumulators. The chip uses a pipeline architecture so that each component performs certain functions and passes its intermediate results to the next component. It is estimated that the chip could enhance images 50 to 1000 times faster than the computers available at that time. This chip was responsible for the spectacular pictures of Uranian moons transmitted from the Voyager 2 in January 1986.

Parallel developments in digital technology have also taken place in the medical field. Researchers began adapting digital techniques to such analog technologies as X-rays and Ultrasound. Magnetic resonance imaging (MRI) uses a strong magnetic field and the response of certain atomic nuclei (such as hydrogen) in the body to generate images. The computerized tomographic (CT) scanning uses an X-ray tube that travels around the body and transmits a thin X-ray beam. A computer then reconstructs the digitized data to create a highly detailed "slice" through the body. At the Johns Hopkins Medical Institutions, volume-rendering techniques (VRT) are employed on a Pixar Image Computer to re-create three-dimensional images of elusive imaging problems such as the acetabular (hip socket) fractures. Researchers at Pixar have developed a system that merges computer graphics with image processing and lets physicians view high resolution images of patient's internal structures.

The image processing technology is also being used in the conservation of art. In most of the ancient arts, paints fade and varnishes darken with time and exposure to heat, light, and other chemical reactions. Art conservation is beginning to benefit from the exploration of the image processing technology. Another later use of the technology is to color the old black and white classic movies.

THE TECHNIQUE

An image processing technique consists of an acquisition device for capturing the image, an image memory, a computer with disks and keyboards that can have access to the memory, and a device that can display the contents of the memory. The image acquisition device puts an image into the image memory. This usually involves digitizing — scanning a continuous-tone image such as a photograph and breaking into an array of digital values called pixels (picture elements). Most image processing systems have an analog to digital converter which transforms the analog signal from the video cameras or photomultipliers of the scanner into a pixel array in the image memory. The acquisition device can write to the image memory unit. The data can be accessed by the computer's central processing unit (CPU) and displayed on a monitor screen. For acceptable intensity and detail resolution, an average monochrome image must be represented by an array of pixels, and each pixel must have a minimum number of bits. The computer processes the pixels in the image memory and the display device converts the processed pixels back into spatially organized image intensities. The display device uses a digital to analog converter (D/A) that drives a monochrome or color television monitor.

The two components of a signal consists of luminance (the black-and-white values) and chrominance (the color information). The chrominance consists of hue (the actual color) and saturation (the amount of color). Any pixel of the original may have one or more of these characteristics. A look up table changes a pixel's value based on the values in a table. This hardware consists of a memory that has a storage location for each possible pixel value. An input pixel value is used as an address into this memory, and the output is the value at that address. The input value "looks up" the output value. These look up tables generate values to the red, green, and blue channels of a color monitor, based on the input pixel value.

IMAGE PROCESSING IN THE GRAPHIC ARTS INDUSTRY

Electronic image processing is used for two distinct purposes in the graphic arts industry: (1) composition of pages or images where different elements are required to be assembled, and (2) electronic retouching, sometimes referred to as air brushing, to improve or change the elements or the finished pages. The creative and fast production capabilities of electronic image processing are amazing. If a multi-image magazine cover or the page of a catalog is analyzed, it will be found that assembly of numerous elements are required to produce those pages. In addition to the assembly, a creative approach is also necessary to position and modify those elements so that the page appears attractive, both visually and psychologically. Almost limitless modifications are made possible with electronic composition and retouching. In fact, the creative potential in an electronic image processing system is only limited by the imagination of the operator. The technology saves effort and time, and it often cuts costs and offers increased productivity with such precision that it is often impossible to accomplish the same results manually. A page may consist of numerous elements, such as photographs, types, border, line illustrations, etc., with different geometrical shapes and sizes. Producing the page with the conventional photographic methods may prove to be a stripper's nightmare, apart from the fact that most of the elements needed for the page have to be duplicated. When an original transparency is retouched and duplicated photographically, the quality of the duplicated image will suffer. However, in the electronic image processing system, once an image is stored as digital data, the potential for manipulation of the images is limitless, without losing any quality.

In the hands of an expert and creative technician, the possibilities of the page make up and retouching systems are almost limitless. The various functions of the page make up operations, such as tint laying, vignetting, the creation of cutout mask in any geometrical shape for image assembly, borders, etc., are easy to accomplish electronically. In addition, color and tone changes, the removal of undesirable features in the original, airbrushing, mosaics, multiimage montages, image combination, merging, and host of other retouching functions give the operator a tool to match any imagination.

The five major manufacturers of electronic image processing systems designed for printing production applications are Crosfield from Great Britain, Dainippon Screen from Japan, Eikonix-Kodak in the USA, Hell GMBH from West Germany, and Scitex from Israel. All systems are modular and can be configured to meet individual requirements. The equipment is expensive. The price starts at under half a million dollars, and a full scale production system runs from approximately one million to over 2.5 million dollars depending on how extensive or powerful the image processing facilities are.

The Concept

All electronic image processing systems are based on an easy to understand concept. Any image including photographs, drawings, paintings, types, etc. can be broken down into binary patterns of electrical impulses such as "yes," "no" or "1" and "0," so that they can be read by a computer. Once each and every spot of the original is translated into electrical impulses, they can be stored on a number of electronic media — most commonly are the magnetic tapes or disks.

With enough computer power and sophisticated software, this electronic information can be copied and rearranged almost endlessly. Once the manipulations or corrections are completed, the image data can be recorded in a number of different ways. The most common method is a set of screened separation films for platemaking and printing with the process colors.

The Systems Technology

Electronic image processing works within a system, which consists of computers and programs. The entire system consists of a number of computer units which are dependent on each other and are controlled from a central unit. The hardware or the computer units are of high performance with great adaptability, and the software within these units can be used to manipulate the hardware in various ways. The computer performs the functions of controlling and regulating the central units. It calculates, controls, monitors, and checks with lightning speed and extremely high precision.

An electronic system for image processing solves the task of image design, assembly, and retouching functions using electronic means. The intelligence that makes all of these functions possible is embodied in the software, which is actually the life and blood of the hardware. Images which are to be processed in this way must be available as electronic information stored in digital form. High capacity magnetic disk storage fulfills this task.

How Do Images Arrive on the Disks

Images from any source can be recorded on a magnetic media as digital data. The most popular method for generating the digital data is to use a conventional scanner. When a scanner is used as an input source, the original is scanned in a rapid sequence of consecutive image lines. The image data thereby produced are stored on the tracks of the magnetic disks until the whole image is electromagnetically "preserved." This data storage may be compared to the storage of materials on floppy disks in a microcomputer. Originals can also be recorded in the digital form using other media as well, such as the flat-bed scanners or video cameras.

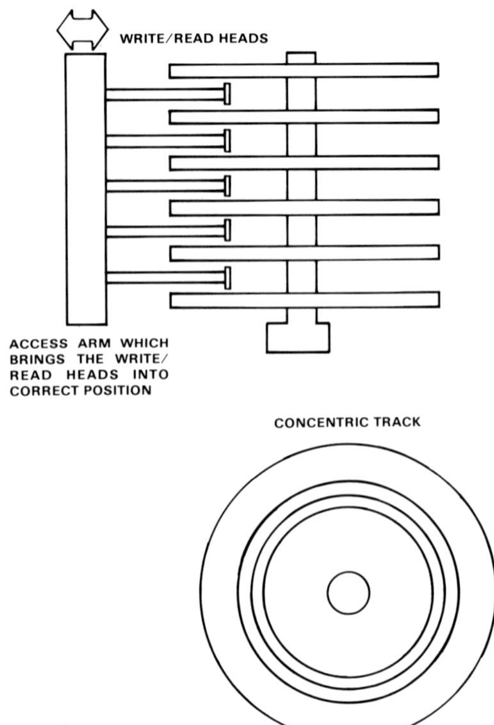

Figure 17.1. The concept of storing and retrieval of data on and from magnetic disks

Magnetic Disks

Magnetic disk storage units look like LP records piled on top of one another with a small gap between each one (see Figure 17.1). Magnetic disks do not have any spiral-shaped groove like a record does. The disks are coated with a magnetized layer on which the data can be stored. In contrast to a magnetic tape, the data is not stored on parallel tracks but on many concentric ones.

Normally a magnetic disk pack is used for a large amount of data. The disks of the pack rotate together and an access arm which passes through the spaces in between the disks writes onto or reads from the concentric tracks. On the top and the bottom side of every prong of the access arm is a write/read head. The magnetized layer which is the storage medium of the disk surface is not touched by the write/read head. The advantage is that there is no mechanical wear even with constant operation and that all data can be safely stored or called back at any time.

Electronic Assembly and the Layout

In the electronic image processing system, the scanners serve as data acquisition and output units. The display units are used for visual control and monitoring of the assembly work. After the computer receives the instruction from the operator, all image information is processed into a complete page assembly according to the parameters of a layout. The images may be of many types and categories as found in the page of a mail-order catalog or a fashion magazine.

The first technical step towards the printed page is the page design. With unlimited possibilities, this creative work can be produced at the monitor of the design station. It should be emphasized that electronic imaging technology has emerged into dual operational concepts, one in the production and the other in the art and design. However, there are low-cost systems available which are used exclusively for layout and design by the art departments and studios. These systems are normally lower in resolution and do not have the capabilities of the fully configured pagination system used in the graphic arts industry. Both systems are used directly by the systems operator/artist to create electronic artwork, rather than using the conventional drawing techniques. An electronic layout has certain advantages over the traditional layout. The layout is produced right on the monitor of the design station, and can be altered or changed at will by the press of a few buttons. Moreover, the manually produced layout cannot render so accurate an idea of the eventual outcome of the printed product as the layout produced by the electronic process. At the design station, the operator can check the work visually at the color monitor and store the images digitally. Each page can be created separately and assembled together as an entire section. Electronically assembled layouts can be matched to

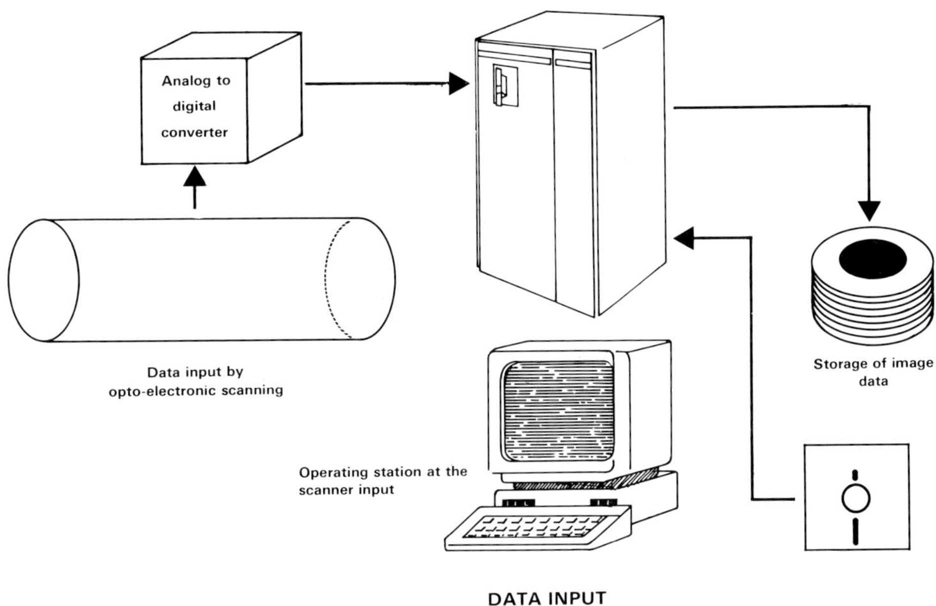

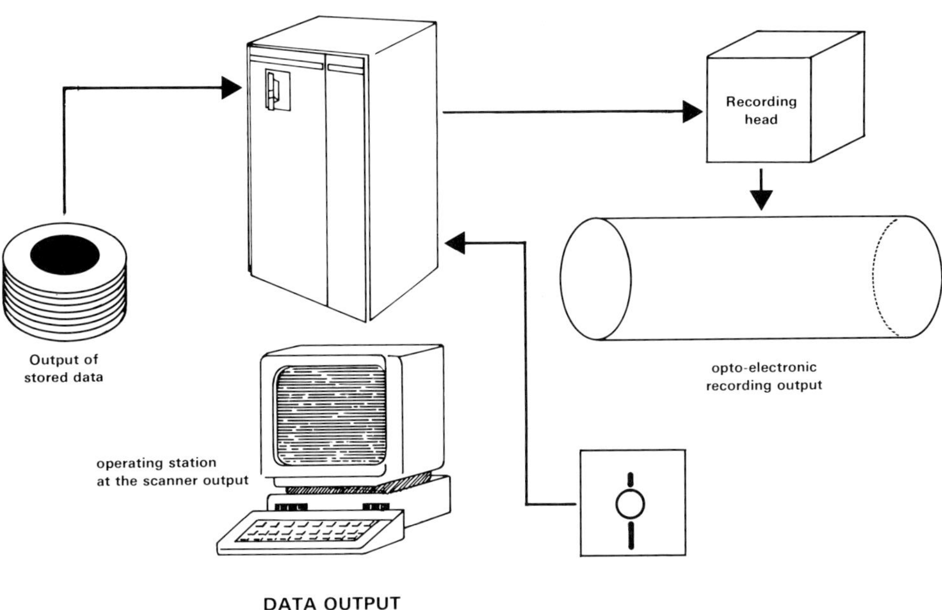

Figure 17.2. A block diagram of data input and output

reproduction requirements and need no additional treatment as in the case with a conventional layout.

A Digitizer

The digitizer is an electronic drawing pencil (Figure 17.3); the graphic work is carried out with the digitizer according to the layout while the operator is viewing the result on the monitor. With the digitizer, the operator can assign X and Y coordinates and thus limit the area within which he/she applies the layout data. First, the basic outline of the layout, the "mask," is produced on the color monitor. Next the images required are called up at the press of a key and then moved to the correct location using the digitizer. They can then be cropped or inserted into geometric shapes or any contour.

Production of Proofs or Originals for Further Reproduction

When a duplicate is made with the conventional photographic method, normally it is inferior in quality to the original because of the limitation in the photographic process. However, the resolution inside a digital processing system can be incredibly high, exceeding 1,500 lines per inch. As a result, the resolution at the output is only limited by the limited range of the recording material. Now digital image processing is being used to produce high resolution photographic transparencies and prints which are very close to that of the optically produced photographic images. Even when the final image is a combination of several heavily retouched components, it is almost impossible to detect the difference between those transparencies and photographically produced transparencies. These transparencies or prints, in turn, can be used for separation and reproduction by other systems. Hell has developed a system for generating a processed image straight onto photographic transparency film or photographic paper with the Hell CPR 403 Proof Recorder. The hard copy produced by the CPR 403 is no longer inferior in reproduction quality to the image it was copied from. In fact, often times, the digitally processed copy appears to be superior to the originals in terms of separation quality. The CPR 403 serves as an output station for both the layout design and image processing stations — the output from the recorder can be used as a proof, or as an original for scanning. Thus the image processing system of Hell Chromacom not only produces pages with multiple elements, but also produces second originals. The continuous-tone recording head of the Hell CPR 403 works with color laser beams, is controlled individually, and can expose all color layers of the photographic material. The sketch in Figure 17-4 shows the production flow of second originals in the Hell CPR 403 unit. Similar imaging called Studio-Proof and Magnatran are developed by Crosfield to make hard proofs on instant imaging materials such as Kodak Ektaflex and Agfachrome-Speed, and high quality transparencies from their page composition systems. Simple to operate and cost effective, the Studio-Proof provides a quick previewing of the image without having to output the final separations. The Magnatran is a high resolution color film recorder capable of exposing images in the negative or positive forms on transparency materials at a very high recording rate.

Courtesy Hell Graphic Systems, Inc.

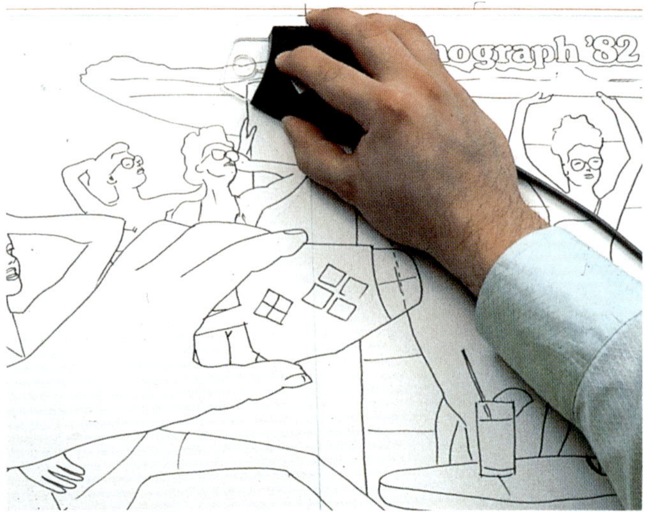

Figure 17.3. A digitizer

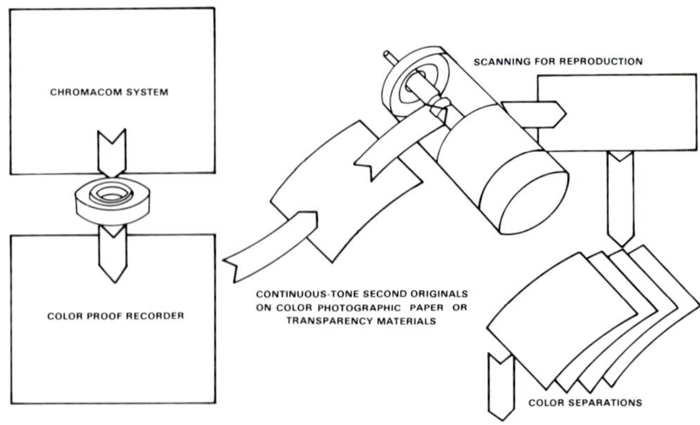

Figure 17.4. Application of second originals in the Hell Chromacom System

A FEW POPULAR PAGINATION SYSTEMS

Several imaging systems are currently available from several manufacturers. A brief description of only four of the top models manufactured by these companies are presented here:

Crosfield Studio 800, Dainippon Screen's Sigmagraph System 6000, Hell's Chromacom, and the Scitex Response System. The Kodak Eikonix Designmaster 8000 was presented in Chapter 1 under History of Scanner.

Crosfield Studio 800

The Studio 800 series are the top models of digital image processing systems offered by Crosfield. These are highly flexible systems utilizing modular components which can be configured to suit operation requirements.

System Architecture:

The top of the line in the Studio 800 system are the Studio 870/880 models. The computing power is harnessed in the file manager system where high speed data processing and multi tasking operation ensure fast page assembly. On Studio 880 this power is enhanced with the embodiment of a second PDP 11/73 processor in the composition console to provide dual high speed operation. Scanned images and completed pages are held on removable 300MB disk drives with up to four drives possible on line.

The ergonomically designed color composition console with an integrated high definition color display and monochrome planning monitor places the operator at the center of all functions. The 1024 line monitor displays color images full screen size to provide an accurate representation of input scans held on disk. The graphic display is used alongside the color monitor for constructing the key line page grid and also to show alphanumeric data and system messages. The Studio operator works with the page layout positioned on the accurate full size digitizing table with all planning instructions implemented by simple electronic cursor operation. A floppy disk drive is provided for convenient storage of page layout information.

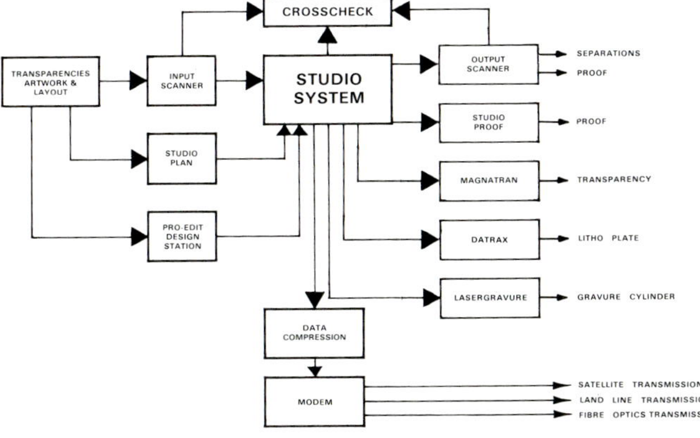

Figure 17.5. Possible pre-press configurations based on the Crosfield Studio 845/865

Page Composition with Studio 870/880:

Input from the Magnascan scanning station is converted into digital picture information and recorded onto magnetic disk. The Scanview terminal can also be used to enhance input scanning productivity and image correction. Viewfiles are created to allow examination and manipulation of the images on the color monitor immediately after the scanning is completed.

Page planning is accomplished using the cursor and command menu on the digitizing table. A wide range of editorial and creative functions are available in the menu to the operator including borders, regular or irregular shapes, tints, vignettes, grip, detail zoom, image merge, pixel, edit, image retouching, etc.

A split screen command permits the operator to see retouched work compared with the original scanned data or the image created immediately prior to enhancement. The operator can then readily decide which correction achieves the required effect.

For magazine work, by taking advantage of a snap-to-grid function, standard page layout grids can be generated and displayed on the screen to speed up planning images and text into position.

The Textran capability is a major feature of Studio 870 and 880. Textran provides high quality text output and the generation of fine lines and rules, as well as applying sharp edges to features using the Textran electronic-dot-slicing technique.

Courtesy Crosfield Electronics

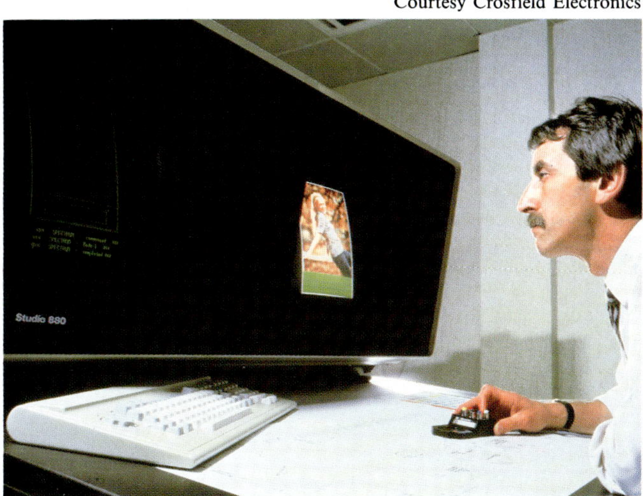

Figure 17.6. Crosfield Studio 880

Several sets of software are available as optional accessories to enhance the system. Airbrushing can be electronically simulated to limitless effect with the Airbrush option. The Image Transform option enables the Studio operator to deal with the more demanding image handling tasks. Image rotation and re-sizing, for example, are useful additional capabilities in coping with difficult layouts, and correcting errors made at the input scanning stage with small format originals. The Tape Achieving module provides a quick and simple alternative for the retention of scanned image or assembled page information held on disk. Where accurate mechanical drawings of the page plan are required, an optional A2 Pen Plotter is available. Also available as an additional option is the DCT Text Interface which provides high speed type font conversion of text information from digital front-end systems for display on the color monitor.

STUDIO OPTIONS:

Several pieces of optional equipment are available to enhance the capability of the Studio 800 models. Studioplan 805 is an off-line layout station for the production of all page planning information for the color monitor systems. Completed layouts are stored on floppy disks for transfer to Studio 870/880, where image related operations such as cropping, color retouching and soft proofing are undertaken. Crosfield Studio proof imager offers the 870/880 user immediate access to hard copy proofs straight from the color monitor. Magnatran is a high resolution color film recorder for the direct transparency output of images created on Studio 870/880 up to a maximum size of 220 X 254 mm. Recent developments of data compression techniques enable the economic transmission of color data as in the Crosfield Studio Systems.

Courtesy D.S. America, Inc.

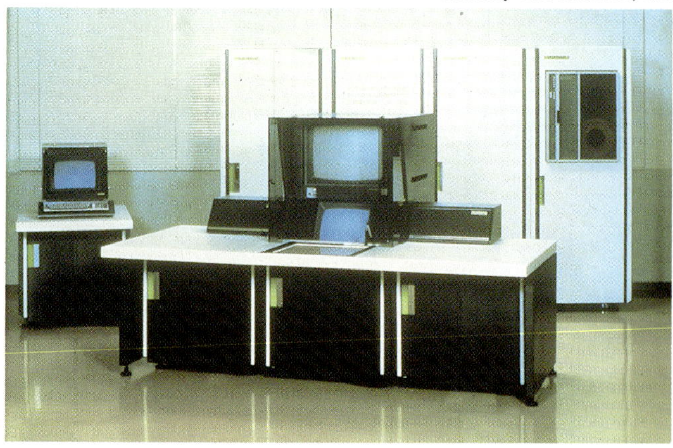

Figure 17.7. Dainippon Screen Sigmagraph 6000

Dainippon Screen Sigmagraph System 6000

Sigmagraph System 6000 is the top of the line digital image processing systems offered by Dainippon Screen. The wide array of processing functions of the unit include:

1. Graphics — creation of graphics in the shape of circles, ellipses, rectangles, and other geometric figures.

3. Image retouching and modification — tone change, color change, air brushing, dot modification, cutouts, montages, image combination, etc.

4. Layout — image assembly, flat tint laying, vignetting, superimposition, key line generation, etc.

5. Graphic modification — offset, dashed line generation, etc.

6. Four-color composite monitoring — Cyan, magenta, yellow, and black separation data are converted to R, G and B monitor data, lending greater accuracy to retouching and ICR (DS's version of GCR) processing.

To increase speed in both processing and data transfer, the Sigmagraph System 6000 utilizes an exclusive hardware for internal image processing calculations. Another is a special-purpose data bus which allows for parallel transmission of 4-color (Y, M, C, and K) data. Easier operation is maintained by employing a stylus with a one-touch menu for entering the commands, following instructions presented on the character display. Data processing efficiency is also increased by employing two data processing modes: (1) a full-resolution mode that reproduces images onto the screen using all the pixels stored on the magnetic disk, and (2) a data compression mode that reproduces images using a reduced number of pixels. Ultimately, the mode to be used by the operator will depend on the accuracy requirements.

Courtesy D.S. America, Inc.

DIRECT SCANAGRAPH
SG-888II
SG-608
SG-818

Scanner Input/Output Unit

Disk Unit

Magnetic Tape Unit

Operation Processor

Processor Unit

Work Station

Data

Command

Figure 17.8. Sigmagraph 6000 flowchart

A SYSTEM CONFIGURATION FOR THE SYSTEM 6000

The Sigmagraph System 6000 configuration consists of a scanner input/output station, host computer, work station, operation processor, and disk unit.

Work Station: page make up and retouching work, such as the creation of graphics and key lines, tint and vignette laying, and cutout mask creation. Retouching and modifications are performed from this station using a rough layout.

Scanner Input/Output to the scanner: image data from the scanner is directly recorded onto disks.

Operation Processor: this unit performs high speed computations in response to commands from the processor unit. These computations are essential to the make-up and retouch operations done at the work station, as well as the operations necessary for monitor display and output film storage.

Disk Unit: hard disks allow greater stability in data processing and transfer. Up to four units can be incorporated to provide parallel execution of scanner input/output and work station processing.

Magnetic Tape Unit: data processed on the system can be stored on 6250-bpi magnetic tape.

The processing capabilities of the System 6000 can be increased by adding several pieces of optional equipment to the system. The Cadograph 500 series automatic drafting/mask cutting system can be used to create graphic design from the data loaded into the system via floppy disks. Extra disk units can also be added to increase productivity by allowing parallel processing of input/output and work station operations. Any of the Dainippon Screen's Direct Scanagraph series scanners can be used as an input/output scanner.

Hell Chromacom

The Hell Chromacom is the top of the line digital image processing system manufactured by Hell. Since its introduction at the GEC show in Milan in 1979, the Chromacom System has enjoyed the reputation as one of the most sophisticated and flexible unit of its kind. The unit offers functions ranging far beyond the simple assembly of individual images. A few functions are listed below.

1. Seamless image composing;
2. Soft homogeneous edges when composing several originals;
3. Color retouching in all variations under visual control such as transparent, spray-gun effect, opaque, duplicate, softening, and contrast modifying;
4. Removal of scratches and cracks;
5. Continue background tones or images without seams;
6. Enlarge or reduce final pages, with same or different screen resolution;
7. Allow image and text portions to run out to paper white;
8. Retint image portions while retaining all tonal gradations.

SHORT DESCRIPTION OF THE CHROMACOM

The Chromacom System consists of a powerful multitasking computer, an option of up to two scanners/recorders connected to the system, and a 16-300MB disk drive. Magnetic tapes and Combiskop work stations can be interfaced and run simultaneously with the system. The SCAN/RECORD station records digitized images as job elements on a 300MB disk pack during scanning. A job is organized and the elements belonging to this job are scanned and digitized for recording on a disk pack at the scanning station. The disk pack, with the digitized image data, is then taken to the Combiskop for page make-up in accordance with the customer layout for this job. The various elements for this job are used during the page make-up, and in many cases the scanned image elements on this disk pack are viewed and is called up for positioning on the page and appears on the color monitor. The operator corrects the deficiencies on the Combiskop through data processing functions available for geometry or color correction; however, if a Scanskop is available, it is used to detect any fault at this stage. The Scanskop provides the operator with a previewing color monitor for the purpose of reviewing a scan as it occurs or after completion of the scanning.

Courtesy Hell Graphic Systems, Inc.

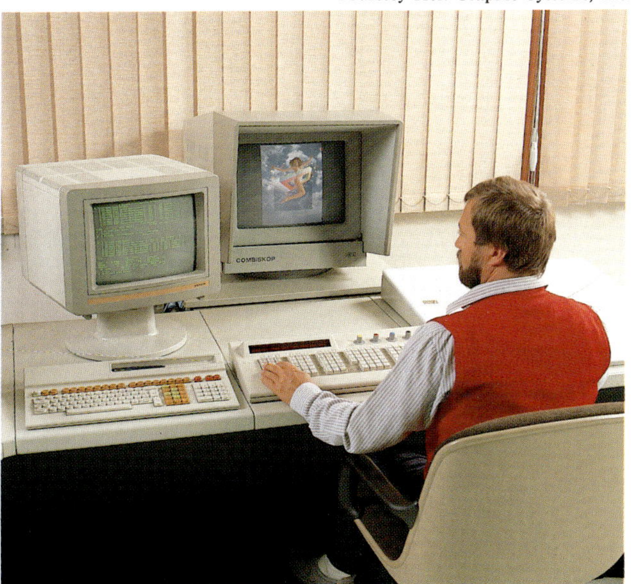

Figure 17.9. Hell Chromacom System

In the Chromacom the image originals are acquired by a Chromagraph scanner. The scanned image data are buffer-stored on magnetic disks. They can be called up when they are required. The operator performs all work under visual control on the color monitor. He/she can see at any time what the assembly or retouching result will look like, or change quickly from the old status to the current one for comparison purposes. Finally the result is output by the recorder as a final page film through electronic screening. Alternately, new integrated originals can be generated via the color image recorder, CPR 403.

The Chromacom System is available in 4 extension stages corresponding to its 4 levels of performance:

1. Chromacom I, Assembly System: this configuration consists of the LP 307S Layout Programmer, a combined scanning/recording station, one computer and the Magatape station. The entire page structure is prepared on the LP 307S. In addition, other images can be scanned and "filed" onto magnetic disk via the computer. The stored image data is then combined with the layout parameters and the areas and vignettes to be tinted. Finally the film is exposed with the scanner.

2. Chromacom II, the Compact Assembly and Retouching System: this is the same as the Chromacom I configuration, except that the Combiskop has been added for interactive image processing with all conceivable functions. Any retouching function can be performed and the effects of the retouching operation can be immediately seen on the color monitor.

3. Chromacom III, the Large Assembly and Retouching System: in addition to the configuration of Chromacom II, this system consists of an additional Combiskop II, two computers in the dual-port network, a CS 410 scanning station, a CR 402 recording station, and the facilities to connect an additional Chromagraph scanner.

4. Chromacom IV, Assembly and Retouching Network System: the Chromacom IV consists of a coupling network for the network system, several scanning stations, several Combiskop workstations, several recording stations, additional data memories, and more than two computers in the network system.

It may be noted that the Chromacom I configuration can be fully expanded to the Chromacom IV without any fixed intermediate stages. Several improvements were introduced to the Chromacom System and they were exhibited at DRUPA '86. Significant among these are new computers with increased capacity, the incorporation of a Digital Color Converter (DCC) to adapt the monitor for the most diverse printing conditions, new software for the data compression, and a remote data transmission, to name a few.

Scitex Response System

Scitex is in the forefront in the field of digital image processing for the graphic arts industry. At the top of the Scitex line is its Response Systems. With its sophisticated, computerized image handling capabilities, the Response System can assemble numerous small images in a montage type layout. It is possible to create ghost effects and transparent images, extend pictures by cloning, sharpen or blur picture outline as desired, mirror images, vignette tints to an infinite number of possibilities, and graft picture elements for unusual special effects.

CAPABILITIES

With the Response System, complex page assembly, color correction, retouching jobs, high-resolution line work, shrinks and spreads, typeset text, laying tints, and perfect registration can be done with its advanced computer imaging and data handling techniques. Prep work takes place at Scitex's interactive color page production station. This includes the high resolution Imager console and the compact Pixel color console. The Imager console, at the heart of the Response System, is designed for simple operation of the system. With the dial and track ball, it is possible to enlarge, reduce, rotate, and move pictures automatically, even through a mask or window. An electronic airbrush permits the operator to draw, paint or airbrush in full color and to create all kinds of masks and borders. Results appear instantly on the high resolution color screen.

Scitex's building block approach makes it easy to custom design a Response configuration according to price/performance and production needs. Each component of the Response

Courtesy Scitex America Corp.

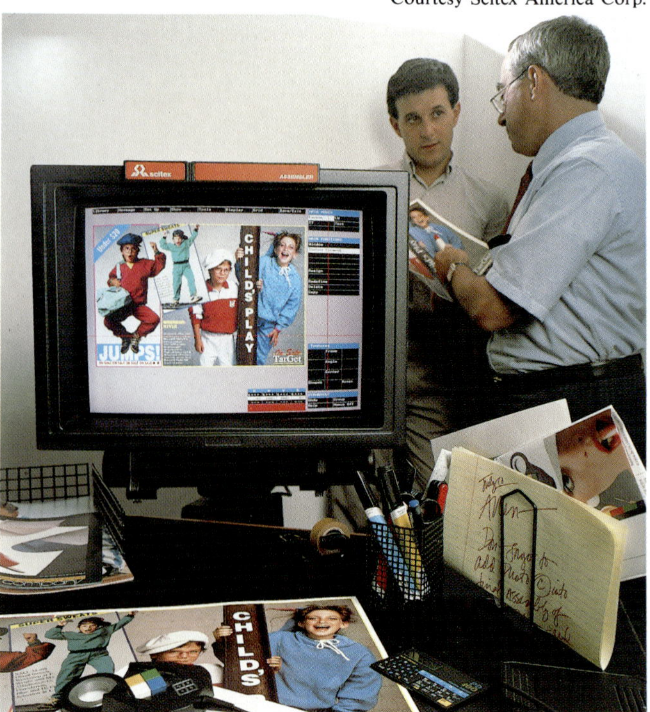

Figure 17.10. Scitex Assembler

System is compatible with other system elements, so upgrading is easier. The following are some of the standard configurations.

Pixet: This is an entry-level Response configuration tailored to meet the need of small and medium-sized prepress operations. Built around the compact Pixet Console, these configurations can include one or more computer sets. Page elements are scanned into the system for retouching and assembly. Separations are exposed on the scanner output drum.

Imager: The interactive Imager console for rapid page makeup can serve as the basis for more powerful entry-level configurations. These are driven by one or more computer sets. Input for color page production comes from a scanner. Film separations are exposed on the scanner output drum.

Pixet with ELP: These configurations can include the large format laser plotter (ELP) for top-quality output. Dual computer sets enable simultaneous operation of the scanner and either the PIXET console or the ELP. These configurations provide the basis for large-scale page assembly operations on a medium-sized budget.

Imager with Eray: A Response system configured with the interactive Imager Console and high-speed, high-resolution Eray laser plotter for film output boosts productivity for any large volume color trade house for a full-service printer. Three computer sets provide for the simultaneous operation of scanning, page makeup, and film exposure.

One important feature of the Scitex Response System is that it can be adapted to all modern color separation scanners. This has been made possible by a unique universal interface designed and built by Scitex.

To improve scanner performance and reduce the frequency of rescans, Scitex has developed the Pre-Sponse Console post-scanning workstation. This Response subsystem lets the scanner operator view the scanned image instantly on a high resolution color video screen, in full color or as individual separations.

FILM EXPOSURE

Any images handled by the Response System can be transferred electronically to one of Scitex's film exposure units: the Eray Laser Plotter (ELP). The ELP produces electronically screened films for offset or continuous-tone films for gravure at the push of a button. For smaller Response configurations, Scitex offers the high-resolution, large format ELP. Both plotters offer standard and unconventional screen angles, electronically screened exposure on line or litho film, a variety of screen dots, and unscreened exposures on continuous-tone films.

Courtesy Scitex America Corp

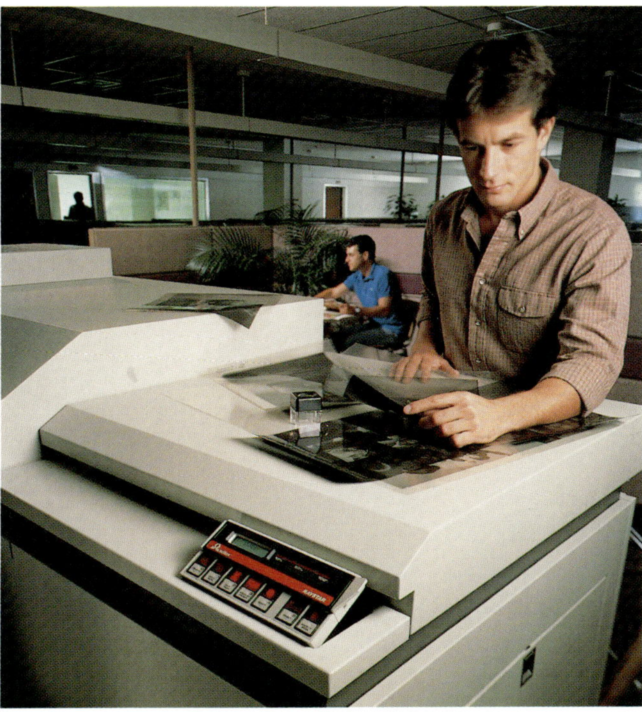

Figure 17.11. Scitex Raystar.

Courtesy Scitex America Corp.

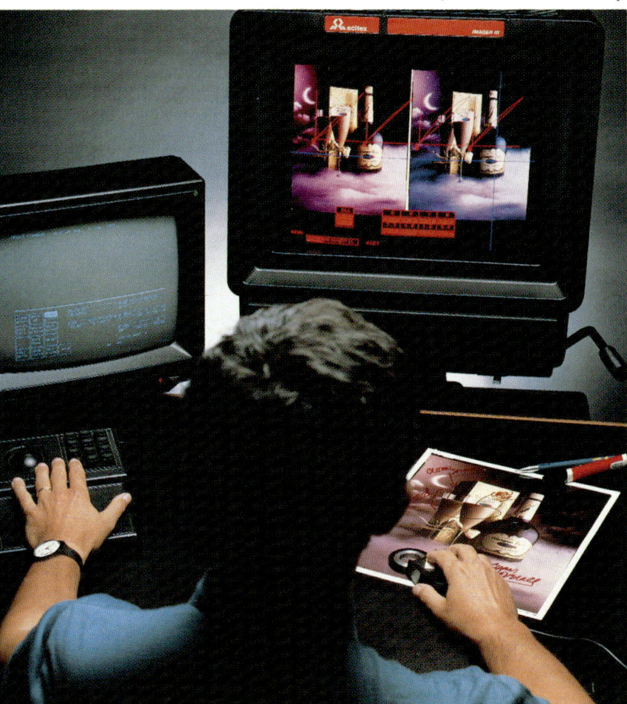

Figure 17.12. Scitex Imager III.

Glossary

- A -

Access: To locate an area of the computer memory for the purpose of storing or retrieving data to and from that location.

Achromatic: Colorless.

Achromatic color removal: To reduce the gray component of the three colors in the separations and replacing them with black. This is a popular term in Europe, however, in the United States, gray component replacement (GCR) is the standard term in the industry for the same function.

Actinic: The invisible, chemically active light rays which react with the photographic emulsion to produce an image.

Additive color theory: Colors produced by adding other colors. Applies to red, green and blue lights which are the major components of the visible white light (spectrum). Two of each of these primary additive colors can be combined to form secondary additive colors, i.e. blue and green lights are combined to produce cyan (blue-green) light. When equal proportions of all three colored lights are combined, they produce white or shades of gray.

Additivity failure: The combined density of the overprinted ink films is not equal to the sum of the individual ink densities.

Airbrush: Similar to the use of airbrush to design a mechanical, the term is used in the color electronic prepress systems (CEPS) to remove or add color or tone values in specific areas of the image. When the image is called up on a color monitor, using a digitizing pen and a tablet, the operator checks every point of the image. Dot percentage can be read from any area, and then the color or tone content can be changed by simultaneously viewing the effects of change on the screen, e.g. in real time.

Algorithm: A mathematical process of solving a problem that involves a definite number of steps in the operation. In the color electronic prepress system (CEPS), involves the application of a mathematical formula to transform a value or function to another.

American National Standards Institute (ANSI): An United States agency responsible for establishing and sustaining industry standards. Decisions on the issues of the standards are made by committee members that meet at a specific time.

American Standard Code for Information Interchange (ASCII): The general designation of bits in a computer to input, store, process and output characters.

Analog: Continuous or nondiscrete values, opposite of digital. In the simplest terms, analog is what happens in the "real world," digital is what happens in a "computer." Examples are voltages, continuous-type volume controls in a stereo system, mercury thermometer, etc. A color computer of a scanner can be both analog and digital. The analog computers use potentiometer type controls to adjust and change values.

Anamorphic: Unequal scale changes in the circumferential and axial directions in a scanner. For example, the ratio of enlargement in the horizontal and vertical directions of the original may be made differently to stretch the image in one direction while compressing the image in the other direction. Usually done for special effects.

ANSI: See American National Standards Institute.

Apochromatic: A color corrected optical system used to avoid chromatic aberration during color separation. If a lens is not color corrected, unequal wavelengths of the red, green and blue lights may converge at different focal points of the optical system producing a different image size for each color.

Archival storage: A storage system for keeping permanent records of images which may be recalled, altered and reused. Examples of such a storage media are photographic films, magnetic tapes and optical disks.

Argon laser: A directional, coherent blue-green light source with only one wavelength and a spectral output of 470 nanometers. In the graphic arts industry, it is used to expose images onto blue sensitive photographic emulsions such as orthochromatic films, papers, or plates.

Array: A regular or orderly arrangement of elements. A CCD (charge coupled device) chip may contain a single line, or a pixel (picture element) may contain an array of rows or columns of different color and tone values.

ASCII: See American Standard Code for Information Interchange.

Assembly: A process of placing several files in specific positions relative to each other.

Average: A processing function in the color electronic prepress systems (CEPS) where the computer creates a new CT (continuous-tone) file from the original file normally at a reduced size. As the size is enlarged, however, the details are lost. The color and tone values of the pixels in the new file are average of the original file values.

- B -

Bandwidth: The rate of information transfer in the telecommunications and computer industry. Examples are, the rate of change of electrical voltages within a time period and the velocity of a scanner drum in relation to the size of the scanning spot.

Baud: The rate of data transmission similar to the bandwidth. However, baud is the bandwidth of the shortest pulse in the data stream.

Beam splitter: An optical device to split a beam of light and to redirect the beams in various directions. In the scanning head of most color scanners, beam splitters split the scanning light to direct towards each of the photomultipliers through the red, green and blue filters. In most electronic dot generation scanners, a single laser light source is split into six or more beams and are directed to the crystal modulators for producing dots on the film.

Binary: A coding or counting system with only two symbols such as yes or no, 0 and 1, on and off, etc. It is the normal format for storing and processing data in a computer.

Birren color notation system: A color notation system developed by American colorist, Faber Birren, who maintains that there are three basic forms of sensation: white, black and color. The system consists of thirteen hues and nine steps from black to white. Four basic hues, which can be regarded as psychological primaries, are red, yellow, green, and blue. In describing colors, hues are designated by letters and are followed by two numerals, the first referring to white content, the second to black content.

Bit: An abbreviation for binary digit which is the smallest stored information in a computer in binary form. It takes eight bits to make a byte for creating a value or a character.

Black: The absence of all colors.

Black body: A body whose spectral energy output depends on its temperature - used to describe Kelvin temperature. At different temperatures, the output of the light will be different in quality. Also see color temperature.

Black color: A color which should be in other specific colors and is often called wanted color. For example, yellow is a black color for yellow, green and red.

Black printer: Black ink is used as one of the process colors to compensate for the deficiency of the inks. The black ink, when used properly, will increase contrast in the reproduction and replaces the process inks in the neutral shadow areas. In normal chromatic reproduction, usually a skeleton or short range black is used, however, in the current GCR reproduction, a full scale black is used that replaces the gray component from the three colors along the entire range of the reproduction. With the advent of GCR (Gray Component Replacement), black printer has played a dominant role in four-color process printing.

Blur: The function of reducing the contrast of a continuous-tone file to yield a softer result in a local area. This function is generally used to reduce contrast at the adjoining lines of two images or for special effects in the reproduction such as soft scenes.

bpi: Abbreviation for bits per inch.

bps: Abbreviation for bits per second.

Brightness: One of the three dimensions of color; the other two being hue and saturation. The term is used to describe differences in the intensity of light reflected from or transmitted through an image regardless of its hue and saturation.

Brushing: The modification of the shape or color of an image using a stylus-like instrument in the color electronic prepress systems (CEPS). Brush work is normally done in a small area of the image without affecting the entire image area and with maximum detail on the screen.

Bump exposure: A short no-screen exposure from the copy that supplements the main exposure. Bump exposure compresses the screen range and reduces the size of the highlight dots in a negative.

Buffer: A specific memory location of the computer where data can be temporarily stored for further processing.

Bus: A connection between computers to move data from one computer or peripheral to another.

Byte: Eight bits of stored information make one byte to represent a value or a character.

- C -

CAD: Abbreviation for computer assisted design or drafting. CAD technology is used to produce engineering or technical illustrations.

Carbon wedge: A continuous-tone strip of film made by varying the deposit of carbon dye. An insignificant amount of light will be scattered and lost when transmitted through a carbon wedge; however, when the same light transmits through a silver wedge, about 20% will be lost by scattering. Consequently, when a wedge is used during the basic calibration of a scanner for transparent original, a carbon wedge provides more accurate results than a silver wedge.

CCD: (Charge Coupled Device) An array of light sensitive solid state devices, usually silicon chips, that react electronically to light. The CCD will generate a voltage relative to the light it senses and functionally can be compared to a photomultiplier. CCDs are now being used in most of the flat-bed scanners and some page make-up systems as light sensing devices.

CEPS: Abbreviation for Color Electronic Prepress Systems. Dr. S. Thomas Dunn of Dunn Technology, Inc. has a copyright on this term. Refers to a computer based color image manipulation and page makeup system for the graphic arts industry.

Chroma: A term used to distinguish the strength, intensity and purity of a color.

Chromatic: Relating to color, color phenomena or sensations.

Chromatic aberrations: Disorder caused by the differences in the wavelengths of the color components of the spectrum. Also see apochromatic.

Chrome: A slang term meaning color transparency.

CIE: Commission Internationale de l'Eclairage, an organization for setting standards for color measurement.

Clone: The function of creating an exact duplicate of certain image data.

Coarse data: A set of data with low resolution. Often referred to as Low Resolution File, the coarse data is used for video displays to make noncritical judgements regarding the final output.

Cold color: A color that appears psychologically cold such as blue or green. Examples of warm colors are red, orange, etc.

Color: The property of light which causes various objects to have different appearance to the eye.

Color balance: The proportions of the three process colors are printed in such a way that the red, green, and blue lights reflecting from every point of the reproduction matches to those of the original. Because of the impurities in the process inks, color balance is a complicated process. Usually a gray balance of the three inks is required for proper color balance. This is accomplished by color separating and printing a gray scale as neutral gray in the reproduction with cyan, magenta and yellow inks in different proportions along the entire tonal range.

Color cast: An unwanted dominant color present in the original or in the reproduction usually caused by improper lighting during exposure or processing conditions.

Color Compensating Filters: Abbreviated as CC filters, used to change the color balance of the photographic prints or transparencies. Finely graded CC filters are also used to view prints and transparencies to decide on the color cast compensation required for optimum reproduction of the original.

Color circle: Colors are assembled in a circle to show their relationship. An example is the GATF Color Circle.

Color computer: The section of a color scanner or the color electronic prepress system (CEPS) that computes the various proportions of cyan, magenta, yellow and black pigments necessary to reproduce the spot of copy being analyzed or scanned. A color computer may be analog or digital. In the analog color computer, the output voltage is modified by changing the position of each potentiometer type control; the computation is based on Masking Equations. In the digital computer, on the other hand, for each and every spot of the copy being scanned, the color computer derives the value from a look up table which is previously calculated and stored in the memory of the computer. Digital color computers are based on Neugebauer Equations.

Color control bar: A strip with measurable colors and gray patches printed usually in the non-image areas on a substrate to control the variables in the printing process visually or with a measuring device.

Color correction: The adjustment of the proportion of the three process inks to compensate for their deficiency and/or contamination.

Color Electronic Prepress System: See CEPS.

Color gamut: A term usually referring to various hues that can be obtained by combining all different dot values from a given set of colorants.

Color scanner: A device that uses rotating drums or flat beds, light beams, optical devices, color filters and computer assisted electronic circuitry to scan an original point by point and to produce a set of color corrected separations.

Color separation: The photographic or electronic means to separate an original into the components of cyan, magenta, yellow and black halftone negatives or positives so that plates can be made to print the colors in register to simulate the original.

Color sequence: The order of printing the four process colors, usually in order of yellow, magenta, cyan and black.

Color space: A theoretical three dimensional color space in which the three dimensions of color, hue, saturation and brightness, can be represented.

Color temperature: The temperature assigned to any light source by matching it visually against a light radiating from a heated black body. When the black body is heated, the spectral distribution emitted by the body depends on its Kelvin temperature. The higher the color temperature, the bluer the light; the lower the temperature, the redder the light. A standard viewing light, which should be neutral, is obtained with equal amounts of red, green and blue lights at a color temperature of approximately 5,000 degrees Kelvin.

Colorant: A dye or pigment which causes an object to appear colored.

Colorimeter: Color measuring and control equipment with filters designed to provide same response as the human eyes.

Colorimetry: The science of color measurement.

Complementary color: In both additive and subtractive color mixing, when the primary colors are combined in pairs, each combined color becomes complementary to the third color. For example, in the additive process, cyan light (combination of blue and green lights) is complementary to red light; in the subtractive process, red (combination of magenta and yellow pigments) is complementary to cyan.

Compression: In the graphic arts industry, usually refers to the compressing of data and tones for transmission and reproduction purposes respectively.

Computer program: A set of instructions that directs a computer to perform a series of specific operations.

Console: The workstation in a color electronic prepress system (CEPS) where the operator performs interactive work that can be viewed on a color monitor on real time.

Continuous-tone (CT): Tone values of different densities without halftone dots. In the color electronic prepress system (CEPS), a CT refers to a picture file with the assumption that screening can be performed on the file.

Contrast: The relationship between the tones of an original and the tones in the reproduction of the same original. However, contrast may also refer to the tonal values within the same picture, differences between light and dark tones.

CPU: Abbreviation for Central Processing Unit. Area where the data processing takes place.

CRI: Abbreviation for Color Rendering Index, also called color quality index, usually measured in percentages. For example, the standard ANSI viewing light must have a CRI index of 90-100, meaning that the source must contain 90 to 100 percent of all wave lengths of visible spectrum from 400 to 700 nanometers.

Cross feed: The horizontal or axial speed of the scanning or recording optics assembly. In a scanner, the scaling functions are accomplished by stretching or compressing the image signal in the circumferential direction of exposing and the speed functions of the optics in the cross feed direction of scanning.

CT: See Continuous-tone.

Crossover: A reproduction that extends beyond the two facing pages and crosses over the binding.

CT Merge: The process of combining two continuous-tone files in such a manner that they appear smooth and without noticeable break between images.

Cursor: A location marker on the computer display screen.

Cyan: One of the subtractive pigments that absorbs the red light of the spectrum and reflects the green and blue when printed on white paper. Cyan light is a secondary additive color.

- D -

Data base: A file of information that meets specific processing needs.

Data compression: A process in which the data is reduced to its essential content when large data volumes are transmitted for economical reasons. For example, the image information on a newspaper page can be reduced to less than one tenth of the original data volume. Data compression technique enables one to transmit only the needed data and the original can be reconstructed at the receiver end.

Data file: Electronically represents picture or line images and parameters for description, usually digital.

Data transmission: Sending electronic digital data from one place to another by cable, fiber optics, microwave or satellite.

DDES: Abbreviation for Digital Data Exchange Standards. A set of standard formats or values that allows the use of several vendor's equipment for passing of files from one vendor's color electronic prepress system (CEPS) to another's.

DEG: An abbreviation of the term "Degraday," used to describe a computer generated vignetting CT file.

Demodulate: The conversion (usually from digital to analog) of a signal to its original state after transmission.

Density: The ability of an object to stop or absorb light. Density values are obtained by measuring the proportion of the incident to the reflected or transmitted light values. When both light values are the same, the density value is 0. The less the light is reflected or transmitted relative to the incident light, the higher will be the density value. The density values are expressed in logarithmic terms similar to the increments of 1, 10, 100, 1000, etc. This is because the eye does not recognize equal increments of density values by the illumination or exposure time in intervals between the increments of 1, 2, 3, 4, etc.

Desaturated color: When a color appears to show a more grayer value, it becomes desaturated. A desaturated color may look faded when it is close to a light gray value and may look dirty or dark when it is close to a dark gray value.

Dichroic filter: An optical filter that may reflect light of one color and transmit light of another color.

Diffuse highlight: The whitest or lightest area in an original within the copy density range that is part of the highlight details. Normally the smallest printing dots are printed in this area.

Diffuse reflection: The reflection of light in all different directions from an area caused by the uneven surface characteristics of the area upon which the incident light falls.

Digital: A system or device in which the discrete or stepped information is stored or manipulated by on/off, 0/1, or similar impulses instead of varying continuously as in analog devices. Examples of discrete or stepped values are pulses, coins, etc. Most digital scanners have digital computers that convert the analog signal from the photomultipliers or charge coupled devices (CCDs) and process them digitally. Almost all modern scanners use digital computers for processing such functions as scaling, electronic dot generation, electronic gray scale, registration marks, etc.

Digital Data Exchange Standards: See DDES.

Digitizing tablet: A smooth rectangular surface that is sensitive to the location of the stylus. When the stylus is moved on the tablet, the same movement on the x, y coordinates are displayed on the video monitor.

Direct Digital Color Proof (DDCP): A proof directly made on a color video monitor (soft proof) or a substrate (hard proof) from the digital data without the intermediate steps of producing a set of separations. The proofs can be made by photographic exposure, ink jet printer, or other recording devices.

Direct screen separation: A method of producing color separation negatives or positives directly from the original in one step. Normally a camera, enlarger, or a contact frame is used for the separations with panchromatic films and gray contact screens.

Disk: A flat circular plate coated with magnetic material on which data can be recorded by magnetization of the surface. However, optical disks are capable of storing data by optical means. A disc may be flexible, "floppy" or "hard."

Discrete value: Discontinuous or stepped values, usually used in digital devices.

Distortion: The change of size of a file in nonproportional manner in a color electronic prepress system (CEPS). For example, distortion results when different enlargement ratios are used in the vertical and horizontal directions of an original. Also see anamorphic.

Dither: A technique of filling the gap between two pixels with another pixel with an average value of the two to minimize the difference or to add detail for a smooth result.

D max: Maximum density that is obtained in a photographic negative or positive.

D min: Minimum density that is obtained in a photographic negative or positive.

DOS: Abbreviation for Disk Operating System. Computer program instructions controlling storage and utilization of information that are stored on magnetic disks.

Dot area: An area of the reproduction covered by halftone dots.

Dot etching: Manual or photographic technique to change the halftone dot size. Manual dot etchings, often referred to as wet etchings, are done to reduce the size of the halftone dots with chemicals. Photographic dot etchings or dry etchings are done by photographic masks.

Dot gain: The gain in the printing dot size resulting from the variables in the prepress and press operations. Dot gain may be both mechanical and optical. Most common causes of dot gain are in the plate exposure, tack and viscosity of the ink, ink film thickness, internal reflection of the ink, pressure between the blanket and impression cylinder, etc.

Downlink: The communication link transmitting the data from a satellite to an earth station.

Dropout highlight: Highlight areas that should appear to be whiter than the normal highlight and will contain no detail. It is necessary to reproduce specular highlights with reduced dot size or no dots to render more contrast than a normal highlight. Examples of specular highlights in an original are reflections from water, shine from the paint of a new car, etc.

DRUPA: The largest international printing show convening once in every five years in Dusseldorf, West Germany. The last show was held in 1986.

Dry etching: See dot etching.

Dupe: A slang used for a duplicate transparency.

Duplex: A mode for simultaneously transmitting and receiving data.

Duplo: A term used in some scanners when two color separations are produced simultaneously on a single pass. "Two-up" is identical term used in other scanners.

Dye: A soluble coloring material used as a colorant in photographic prints or transparency materials.

- E -

EDG: Abbreviation for Electronic Dot Generation. The production of halftone dots directly on the film by a laser light source without the use of any contact screens.

Edge enhancement: An optical illusion of what appears to be increments of details at the edges of density or color change created by producing a black line at the edge of the darker tone and a white line at the edge of the lighter tone. This is accomplished in a scanner by both mechanical and electrical means. Mechanically, it is set by changing the size ratios of the main and unsharp masking apertures and electronically by turning up the detail enhancement controls.

Editorial changes: Specific changes of color or tonal areas of the reproduction to improve its appearance. Usually these modifications are requested to meet the customer's requirement.

Electromagnetic spectrum: The range and chart of electromagnetic waves based on their wavelengths.

Electromagnetic waves: Waves of varying electric and magnetic fields that travel at about 186,000 miles per second through space.

Electronic color scanner: See color scanner.

Electronic dot generation: See EDG.

Electronic gray scale: A stepped gray scale generated by the internal digital computer of a scanner. These scales are normally produced to conform to a standard set of values during the initial output calibration of the scanner for proper linearization.

END: Abbreviation for Equivalent Neutral Density. The amount of dot values required for each process color (cyan, magenta and yellow) to produce various density steps of a reproduced neutral scale.

Error diffusion: A process of minimizing the difference of adjoining pixels to smooth out an area.

Etch: An operation of increasing or decreasing the color or tone values of a continuous-tone (CT) file.

Exposure level: The amount of light that is permitted to expose the light sensitive photographic materials.

- F -

Facsimile: A duplicate image that is identical to the original in every respect.

Facsimile transmission: The transmitting of data for a duplicate image that is identical to the original in every respect.

Fake color: Various colored areas in an illustration produced by means of several flat colors.

File: See data file.

Fill: In the color electronic prepress system (CEPS), the function of turning a closed line work area into a new discrete color area. Any specific color tint values can be assigned to this area.

Flat: A lack of contrast in an original. Properly stripped negatives on goldenrod for exposing the plates are also called flats.

Flat color: A single ink, solid or tint, used to produce a desired hue.

Flat-bed scanner: A device in which the scanning and exposing devices are on the flat planes rather than the normal revolving cylinders as on a drum scanner.

Fluorescence: The property of emitting invisible portions of the spectrum which is mixed with the visible portion of the spectrum.

Focus: Adjusting the elements of an optical system so that the image is formed on the exact focal plane for the sharpest detail.

Format: An arrangement or organization of images, data or computer codes that enables the data to be stored properly.

Frame: Often referred to as a single picture element.

Frequency: The number of times that a periodic function repeats the same sequence of values.

Full-scale black: A black separation that prints over the entire tonal range. In contrast, skeleton black prints only in the darkest shadow areas.

- G -

Gamma: A value obtained by dividing the reproduced density with the original density of the straight line portion of a slope developed by exposing and developing a sensitive film emulsion. Normally the slope has three sections: a toe, a straight line, and the shoulder. The straight line portion is the usable portion with usually a 45 degree slope and a gamma value of 1.

GCR: Abbreviation for Gray Component Replacement. The removal of the gray components of the three colors and replacing them with black. In GCR reproduction, all the primary and secondary colors remain the same as the normal chromatic reproduction, however, the blackening effects by the tertiary colors along with the gray components of the other two colors are removed and replaced with black. Various percentages of GCR can be applied to the separation for economical reasons and visually more pleasing results. Various vendors use different terms for GCR. For example, PCR is Crosfield's Polychromatic Color Removal; ICR is Dainippon Screen's Integrated Color Removal; CCR and PCR are Hell's Complementary Color Reduction and Programmed Color Reduction; and PIR is Royal Zenith's Programmed Ink Reduction. Also see achromatic color removal.

Gigabyte: One thousand megabytes or one billion bytes.

Gigahertz: A determinant of frequency equivalent to one billion cycles per second.

Ghost: In the color electronic prepress system (CEPS), the process of overlaying two images in such a manner that both images are seen on the monitor at the same time. The strength or percentage of each image can be varied so that one appears visually dominant.

Global work: Work that involves the entire area of the image rather than local areas only.

Gloss: The property of an object which causes it to reflect light specularly.

Glow lamp: A crater discharge lamp which responds instantaneously by changing its intensity when different voltages are applied. It is mostly used in the older contact screen and continuous-tone scanners.

Gradation: The distribution of a set of tone values in the reproduction in relation to the original tone values.

Grain: Cluster of silver particles in the photographic emulsions. Emulsions with faster speed have larger grains than emulsions with slower speed.

Gray: A visual perception that appears under a neutral light (approximately 5000 degrees Kelvin) when the proportions of different wavelengths of the visible spectrum are equal. The gray level may vary from white to black depending upon the amount of the red, green and blue content; the highest content will produce white, and the lowest will produce dark gray or black.

Gray balance: To reproduce a neutral original as neutral with the three process inks. Gray balance is the primary requirement for accurate process color reproduction. Also see color balance.

Gray Component Replacement: See GCR.

Gray level: The different gray values that are seen in an image through the color separation filters. Most of the scanners and color electronic prepress systems (CEPS) are capable of visualizing and storing up to a maximum of 256 levels of gray for an image. In the CEPS, 256 is a chosen number because it is the amount that can be represented in a byte.

Gray scale: Small wedges of continuous-tone images with orderly and progressive densities. They are available in various sizes and shapes to control halftones, color separations, and printing characteristics.

Gray stabilization: The term is often used by System Brunner to emphasize the importance of maintaining gray balance during color reproduction. As opposed to normal chromatic reproduction, it is easier to maintain gray balance with GCR and is considered to be one of the important functions of GCR.

Gray wedge: An image that varies continuously from the lightest to the darkest, often used for color scanner set up. It is a gray scale but does not have the specific tone steps.

- H -

Halftone: The technique of breaking a continuous-tone copy into various size dots to make it printable. It is a reproduction of a photograph, drawing, print, or other object having a gradation of tones and when viewed from a normal distance, simulates continuous-tone. Contact screens are used for producing a halftone. However, in the electronic dot generation scanners, dots can be produced directly on the film with a laser light source and without the use of any contact screen.

Handshake: The initial signal exchange between two computers to determine if the computers are compatible and whether they will be able to communicate or not, usually done by a modem.

Hard proof: A proof made on a substrate such as paper. A soft proof refers to a proof produced on a video screen.

Helium neon laser: A red laser with a wavelength of 632.8 nanometers. In addition to the Argon laser (blue), the Helium neon laser is used in certain electronic dot generation scanners and certain black and white input scanners to expose a film. A special red-sensitive film emulsion is needed to expose the film with the Helium neon laser. It is claimed to be less expensive and easier to maintain than the blue laser.

Hertz: A unit of frequency, one cycle per second, often used to measure radio and electronic signals.

High Key: An original that contains the important details in the highlight area.

High resolution: An image in a file or on the video screen with a resolution sufficient enough to capture all the details of the original.

Highlight: The lightest point on the copy within the reproducible density range. The smallest printing dots are normally printed in these areas. Specular highlights are not to be confused with normal (diffuse) highlight. Small or no dots are printed for specular highlights so that they appear brighter than the normal highlight.

Hue: One of the three attributes of color. With different wavelengths, the name of each hue places the various colors in their correct positions in the spectrum and are distinguished from one color to another, i.e. yellow, blue, red, etc.

Hue error: The contamination in a process ink. Each process ink absorbs one of the three colors of the spectrum, e.g., cyan absorbs red, magenta absorbs green and yellow absorbs blue. However, because of the contamination, the inks do not absorb and reflect their proper share. Consequently, when printed, the appearance of the colors will be distorted or flawed causing hue error.

- I -

Image processing: In the color electronic prepress system (CEPS), the manipulation of the electronic data in a picture to change or improve the characteristics compared to the original. CEPS performs its processing through digital image processing.

Indirect separation: A technique with which the continuous-tone separations are made on a low contrast film. The screening is made at a later stage from these separations. The indirect process provides flexibility in the retouching for color correction or other changes. On the other hand, the direct separations are made directly on a high contrast panchromatic film with a gray contact screen.

In-line: Often used as an adjective. When a device is connected between other devices and when the signals are passed through, it is said to be an in-line device.

Ink film thickness: The thickness of the printed ink when printed on a substrate. When printed on paper by an offset process, the thickness of the ink film is approximately 1 micron. However, with the rotogravure process, it is much less.

Ink trapping: See trapping.

Input scanner: An input device used for the color electronic prepress system (CEPS). Normally a copy is scanned on the scanner and the data for each pixel is converted into analog or digital signals and stored on a magnetic disk for use in the CEPS. Rotary drum scanners can function as either an input and/or output device as well as produce separations conventionally.

Interactive work: Work done by an operator in which the results of his work appear instantaneously (often called "real time") on the monitor as he or she performs the activity.

Interface: When two independent devices are connected by a hardware or software so that the two devices can communicate with each other, the hardware or software being used is called the interface. Also, the monitor on a color electronic prepress system (CEPS) can be called the "human interface" between the system and the operator.

IPA: Abbreviation for International Prepress Association.

- J-K -

Jaggies: The ragged edge of an image in the color electronic prepress system (CEPS). Examples of other terms used are stairstepping, chainsawing, etc.

Jones Diagram: Named after the inventor, Lloyd Jones, a graphical analysis of the reproduction steps by plotting graphs in a quadrant. The information at each step is linked to the next step in such a way that the effect of each successive step is displayed on each graph.

Kelvin: The temperature of a black body plus 273 degrees Celsius. When a black body is heated, the spectral distribution emitted by the body depends on the Kelvin temperature of the black body. The system is named in honor of its developer Lord Kelvin. Also see color temperature.

Kilobit: 1024 bits of data.

Kilobyte: 1024 bytes of data.

- L -

L*a*b: Numerical values of color in a three-dimensional space. L* is the lightness and darkness value; a* and *b give reference points to the hue and chroma values.

Laser: A laser beam is the result of amplification of only one frequency of light and hence the acronym LASER (Light Amplification by Stimulated Emission of Radiation). A laser beam is directional, coherent with a single phase, and is polarized. In an electronic dot generation scanner, these properties of laser are used electro-optically or electro-acoustically with a modulator to switch the beam on and off during exposure to produce the dots directly on the film.

Lightness: The degree of lightness or darkness of an area..

Linearization: Controlling the relationship between the exposing light intensity, film emulsion, and processing conditions in order to produce consistent and predictable results. For example, when the operator adjusts a 50% dot value on the scanner for a certain color or tone, accurate linearization assures that exactly a 50% dot will be produced on the film for the same tonal or color areas of the copy during scanning.

Line: Line art or line work refers to images that contain only a solid image without any graduated tone values.

Local work: Work done in specific areas of a picture without affecting the entire original.

Look up tables: In digital computers, look up tables are values generated and stored in the memory of the computer for future use. In the digital color computer of a scanner, a look up table contains all possible values for cyan, magenta, yellow and black inks and their overprints of different combinations. During scanning, the computer looks up the values of cyan, magenta, yellow and black for each point of the original being scanned and sends signals to the exposing section to produce these required dot or tone values.

Low key: An original with the important details in the shadow areas. During gradation adjustment in a scanner for this type of copy, emphasis is placed on the shadow areas by moving the major aim points towards the shadow with fixed dot values, or, in the case of fixed aim points, the size of the dots are reduced in these areas.

Luminance: The lightness or darkness of a picture (same as brightness).

LPI: Abbreviation for lines per inch, meaning the number of scan lines or exposed lines in the cross feed direction of the scanning or exposing heads.

Lux: A measure of illumination in Metric.

LW: Abbreviation for line work. When used in the color electronic prepress system (CEPS), they are stored differently in the computer than the CT (continuous-tone) file.

- M -

Magenta: One of the four primary subtractive pigments used in the four-color process printing. Magenta absorbs the green light of the spectrum. In the additive color mixing process, magenta is a secondary color; when red and blue lights are combined, they produce magenta light.

Mask: In the color electronic prepress system (CEPS), it is an electronic outline silhouette used to isolate a picture element from the rest of the pictures to perform local corrections and isolate the final image. In the conventional separation, a photographic mask is used for color correction, tone compression and detail enhancement.

Masking Equation: As linear mathematical equations, they are derived from conventional photographic masking. Most analog scanners use this equation in the color computer to determine the characteristics of the masks that are required to correct color separations for the unwanted absorptions of cyan, magenta, and yellow process inks.

Megabyte: One million bytes of data.

Menu: A function display of a program that lists the production steps.

Memory color: The colors which are seen in everyday activities and are remembered by the viewer in the reproduction. A slight imbalance of these colors in the reproduction becomes immediately noticeable and objectionable. Colors like the blue sky, a yellow banana, green grass, a normal flesh tone, etc. are in this category.

Metameric colors: Colors that make a perfect match under one lighting condition, but look quite different under another. Many printers carefully match colors in the pressroom, but after comparing the finished job in sunlight, find that it did not look like the color sample at all. To solve metamerism, viewing lights with 5,000 degrees Kelvin have been standardized in the industry.

Middle-tone: Tone values located approximately midpoint between the highlight and shadow. In color separations, a density value of .65 for a reflective original and 1.20 for a transparency are considered to be optimum middle-tone aim points for normal originals. The dot value for a middle-tone aim point is 50%.

Mirror: Generating a copy of a file that has been flopped or rotated 180 degrees vertically or horizontally.

Modem: A set of input and output devices that are connected into two computer systems. The output signal from one computer is modulated and sent to another modem of a second computer which demodulates the signal for input.

Modulator: Used in an electronic dot generation scanner to modulate a laser source and produce halftone dots on the film. It is a crystal polarization filter that can be activated by electrical or acoustical signals. A modulator will allow a directional light similar to a laser to pass through it or to stop it. When a defined electrical or acoustical signal is connected to the modulator, it will let the light pass through; however, when another signal is applied, it will stop the light. Modulators are also used to vary the intensity at the output for contact screen and continuous-tone separations.

Moiré: An undesirable pattern resulting from the overlapping of two or more grid patterns such as the halftone dots produced by a screen. The moiré can be minimized by placing the screens 30 degrees apart. An accepted set of screen angles for process color reproduction are Cyan-105 degrees, Magenta-75 degrees, Black-45 degrees, and Yellow-90 degrees. Because there are not enough angles for the four screens, the yellow is placed 15 degrees from the cyan and magenta. This causes the yellow to produce moiré, however, it is least noticeable among the four colors.

Monitor: Usually refers to a video screen.

Mouse: A small hand held device which when moved on a flat surface causes a corresponding movement of a cursor on the display monitor.

Munsell color notation system: A three-dimensional system of color notation, devised by Albert H. Munsell that has gained wide commercial use. Munsell's three dimensions of color are hue, value, and chroma. Scales for these three colors are part of a sphere. Hue is the method of segregating one color from another. The ten basic hues are red, yellow-red, yellow, green-yellow, green, blue-green, blue, purple-blue, purple, and red-purple. These hues form a circular scale on the outer surface of the sphere. The axis of the Munsell sphere is a gray scale in ten steps from black to white. This is known as the value scale. Value defines whether a color is dark or light. Zero on the scale represents black and ten represents white. Chroma defines the strength or weakness of a color as a color. As value is the vertical scale, hue the circular scale, and chroma is the horizontal scale of the Munsell sphere. The further away from the vertical axis the color appears, the stronger is it in chroma, having proportionately more of the hue and less of the gray. Lower numbers on the chroma scale begin at the center or value shaft of the sphere.

- N -

Nanometer: A measuring unit, one billionth of a meter, used to describe the wavelengths of various color components in an electromagnetic spectrum. The visible spectrum containing red, green and blue lights have a range of wavelengths from approximately 400 to 700 nanometers.

Network: An assembly of several system components interfaced together to perform a specific function.

Neugebauer Equations: Set of equations developed to solve the color correction problem. In the process color reproduction, the color halftone printed image is made up of individual areas of white, cyan, magenta, yellow, red, green, blue and black. These colors are formed by the subtractive principle, but they are additively fused together to form a uniform color tone. If the red, green, and blue values of the original are known, and if the red, green and blue reflectances of the process colors and their overlaps are measured, it is possible to solve for the cyan, magenta, and yellow dot values for each spot of the original during scanning. The Neugebauer Equation was modified several times to make it practical and usable in a digital computer.

Neutral Density: An optical density without any apparent hue. A perfect neutral density such as white or gray will reflect equal proportions of red, blue and green lights. Also see gray.

Neutral gray: Any neutral spot that appears without any color cast.

Newton rings: Irregular shaped patterns which appear in the separations caused by prismatic actions of the two surfaces in contact, such as the scanning cylinder and the transparency surfaces. In the scanner, the problem is solved by applying a coat of oil or a thin mist of powder in the two contacting surfaces.

Noise: An unwanted signal that causes interference in the main signal and increases errors during receiving, processing and storing of data.

North pulse: The starting point on the scanning cylinder, usually indicated by a small lamp. This is used to line up the scanning cylinder with the exposing cylinder so that the copy and exposing films have the same horizontal starting points.

- O -

Off-line: Used as an adjective referring to a device that is used in a system; however, the device is not interactively connected to the system. For example, in some of the latest scanners, an original may be set up separately on a scanning drum away from the scanner with a separate computer terminal, and all the settings may be recorded on a floppy disk. On the scanner, the scanning drum and the floppy disk are replaced to perform the normal scanning and exposing functions.

Off-press proof: A proof that is made without the printing press.

Oil mounting: Mountings of transparencies required to minimize the effect of Newton rings, dust, dirt, etc., in the separations. Clear paraffin or mineral oils are used for this purpose. Sometimes, clear jelly or a coat of vaseline may be used on the base side of the transparency to minimize the effects of scratch.

On-line: An adjective describing a device that becomes an integral part of the system. On-line storage devices can store large amounts of data which become permanent parts of the network and permit rapid retrieval of data. In some computer texts, this would be an interactive operating environment.

Optical disk: A disk that is capable of storing data by optical means. As a medium for archival storage of digital data, this device offers high-speed random access to data. Numerous optical disk memory systems are in the developmental stage.

Ostwald color notation: Based on the principles similar to those employed in the Munsell color notation system, Ostwald uses a double-cone solid to locate and categorize his colors. It works on the principle that all colors seen by the eye are composed of varying combinations of hue, white and black. The central pole of the double cone is a vertical scale of eight steps from white to black, each step being designated by a letter. The circumference is a scale made up of twenty-four chromatic hues. While the Ostwald system has more hues in its circumference than the Munsell design, it is inflexible in that the end points are fixed and cannot be extended to accommodate new colors as can be done in the Munsell system.

Output: When referred to a scanner, the entire optical and electronic systems that make up for the exposing unit. In the color electronic prepress system (CEPS), output refers to the information that comes from the computer as a result of processing.

Over correction: This results when colors are corrected more than necessary resulting in desaturated or faded color with lack of details in the reproduction.

Overlay proof: An off-press proof consisting of a set of light sensitive transparent materials with pigments similar to the four process colors. Each separation is exposed on the respective color films and then processed. The four color positive images are then superimposed one above the other in registration. A white paper is placed under it, and then viewed with a white light.

- P -

Parallel processing: A computer's capability of doing multiple processing simultaneously.

Pastel colors: Colors that appear to be desaturated and weak.

Peaking: The unsharp masking function of a scanner in which additional signals are added to the positive and negative main signals to create white and black lines on the edges of a density change. These lines create an illusion of detail enhancement. A positive peaking results when the signal is added to the highlight, and a negative peaking results when the signal is added to the shadow area. Also see edge enhancement.

Peripherals: Any additional device that is added to a computer system for additional use or storage. A peripheral such as an extra disk drive may be added to a personal computer.

Photodiode: A light sensitive photocell, normally used on a computer chip to measure the strength of light to perform certain related operations.

Photomultiplier: The most commonly used light sensing device in a drum scanner. Another device that is used on the flat bed scanner is the CCD (charge coupled device). A photomultiplier can sense very low levels of light, amplify them and convert them into relative electronic signal. In a scanner, the output from the photomultiplier is connected to the color computer and used for further processing.

Pivot point: A point from which an object turns, oscillates or rotates. An example will be the highlight point from which various tonal curve shapes can be drawn.

Pixel: An abbreviation for picture element. The smallest visual picture element that can be handled in a file.

Plotter: A device that exposes photographic materials from digital data under the control of a computer.

PMT: See photomultiplier.

Preangled screen: A set of screens with different screen angles used for separations in a scanner or with conventional methods. It usually consists of a set of four screens, one each for the cyan, magenta, yellow and black.

Prepress proof: See off-press proof.

Prescan analyzing device: A type of device used to examine the original so that a correct scanner set up is possible for an optimum separation. These devices may range from simple visual to complex electronic. Some of those can be programmed to automatically calculate the optimum set up in a scanner.

Primary colors: These colors cannot be produced by mixing colors from the same family of additive or subtractive principles. In the additive principle, red, green and blue lights are the primary colors. In the subtractive principle, cyan, magenta, and yellow colorants are the primary colors.

Process color: Producing a variety of colors by superimposing different proportions of a set of four color pigments - cyan, magenta, yellow and black.

Process inks: A set of four transparent process inks - cyan, magenta, yellow and black.

Processing: The computer process where the interactive and/or preprogrammed instructions from the computer are carried out.

Progressive proofs: Proofs made from the separate plates used in process color work, showing the sequence of the printing and the result after each additional color has been applied. Sometimes progressive proofs are used to evaluate the results of dot etching.

Prompt: A signal from the computer meaning it is waiting for a reply. Usually, the prompt will remain on the monitor until a reply is made.

Proportionality failure: In four color process printing, when the cyan, magenta and yellow ink dots are fused with the white paper, the red, green and blue reflectances from the area do not match the color or tone of the continuous-tone original. Proportionality failure is mostly evident in the highlight through the middle-tone areas of the reproduction.

Pulsed xenon lamp: See xenon lamp.

Psychological reference colors: See memory colors.

- Q -

Quadracolor: The function of certain scanners that can produce all four separations in one pass. "Four-up" is another term often used.

Quarter-tone: Tonal values which are situated approximately midpoint between highlight and middle-tone.

Quartz-halogen lamp: A small gas-filled lamp used in some scanners for scanning and analyzing purposes.

- R -

RAM: Abbreviation for Random Access Memory. The section of the computer's memory that is used for temporary storage of data. The data is accessible for processing and is independent of the position of the data on the storage medium.

Raster: A series of lines of information that are recorded by writing each line following the previous line working off of a digital signal. The series of scanning lines and exposing lines that form an image are examples of raster imaging.

Read: The function of copying a file from one medium to another, e.g. tape to disk.

Real time: An image processing device works in real time when the image changes instantly on the display unit as the operator manipulates the data on the keyboard.

Register: When two or more images are printed in predetermined alignment.

Resolution: A term used for measuring the number of pixels per unit. For example, if there are 12 pixels per mm, then the RES is 12. The resolution is counted both vertically and horizontally, e.g. RES 12 will have 12 X 12 = 144 pixels per mm. The higher the resolution, the better the image detail appears, but the file will be larger. More computer memory and longer processing time are needed for higher resolution.

RGB: Abbreviation for red, green and blue, the additive primaries.

RIP: Abbreviation for Raster Image Processor. Also see Raster.

ROM: Abbreviation for Read Only Memory. Computer memory that can be read by the Central Processing Unit (CPU) but cannot be altered or processed.

Rotation: An operation of rotating an image to fit in the prescribed angle in the color electronic prepress system (CEPS). It is a slow and expensive process and can unnecessarily tie up the system. However, with some CEPS software, this problem may not be as apparent because the image can be scanned at the proper angle before it is used on the CEPS.

- S -

Saturation: One of the three attributes of color. The closer a color is to gray, the less saturation there is, and the further it is from gray, the more saturation there is.

Scale: In a scanner, the scale designates the enlargement and reduction size. In the color electronic prepress system (CEPS), the term refers to the change in the dimensional size of a file without a change in data which make up the file.

Scan data terminal: A monitor and a keyboard used for a page makeup system. However, the terminal can be used for other functions as well. For example, a terminal is connected to the Crosfield 645 and 646 scanners for limited page assembly functions.

Scan rate: A rate of scan lines per inch or centimeter. Depending on the enlargement, reduction, or resolution desired in the separations, scan lines vary in numbers. The higher the scan rate, the greater the resolution but slower the scan will be. The scan rate will also depend on the optical system of the exposing assembly.

Screen angle: Refers to different screen angles for the cyan, magenta, yellow and black.

Screen Ruling: Number of lines of dots per inch or centimeter of a halftone screen. For example, for 120 lines per inch, there will be 120 lines of dots per each inch, and the total number of dots per square inch will be 120 X 120 = 14,400.

Secondary colors: Colors produced by combining two primary colors. For example, in the additive process, red and blue lights may be combined to produce magenta light; in the subtractive process, cyan and yellow pigments are printed on white paper to produce green.

Sequential storage: Data that is stored in a linear mode. It is often less expensive to store data than the random access storage, but it takes more time to locate and recover the data.

Signal to noise ratio: The strength of the wanted signal in relation to the unwanted signal.

Simulation: Creating something which looks like something else. For example, halftones printed with small dots simulate the continuous-tone. Another example is a prepress proof which simulates actual printing.

Skeleton black: A short range black derived in the middletone through the shadow to increase contrast and to replace the three colors in the neutral shadow areas in the reproduction.

SNAP: Abbreviation for the Specification for Non-Heat Advertising Printing. These are specifications developed for printing on newsprint and uncoated stock.

Soft proof: A proof that is made on a color video monitor from the scanned data of an image or from working on a color electronic prepress system (CEPS).

Specular highlight: See dropout highlight.

Spectrophotometer: An instrument for measuring the relative intensities of light in different parts of the spectrum.

Spectrum: The series of colors from red to violet produced when white light is passed through a prism. The white light being dispersed into rays of different color and wave length, the rays of longest wave length producing red, and the rays of shortest wave length producing violet.

Spray brush: Electronic air brushing - depositing of color over a certain area or areas of the picture.

Standard viewing conditions: American National Standards Institute developed a standard set of viewing conditions for viewing originals and reproductions to avoid metamerism. Among the many criteria for viewing conditions prescribed by the ANSI, two of them are the use of viewing lights and the CRI index. The viewing light must have a color temperature of 5,000 degrees Kelvin and the color rendering index (CRI) 90-100, meaning that the viewing light source must contain 90 to 100 percent of all wave lengths of the visible spectrum from 400 to 700 nanometers. The other criteria mostly deal with the viewing distance for different types of originals or reproductions and the quality of the surroundings.

Subtractive color theory: Colors produced by subtracting colors. In color reproduction, cyan, magenta and yellow inks are printed on white paper to absorb the red, green and blue portions of the visible spectrum. These inks are printed in different proportions on the white paper to selectively absorb and reflect the various proportions of red, green and blue lights to simulate the original.

Superimpose: In the color electronic prepress system (CEPS), the insertion of one CT file into another in such a manner that the first image visually appears to lay on top of the second.

Swatching out: A technique for evaluating a set of separation films and proofs to ensure that the desired results are achievable with a certain printing condition.

SWOP: Abbreviation for Specifications for Web Offset Publications. A standard set of specifications for separations, proofs and color printing usually for magazine production.

System: An integrated assembly of hardware and software desìgned for a certain application or a set of applications.

System Brunner: A set of theories and controls developed by Felix Brunner dealing with the optimization of color proofing and printing.

- T -

Terminal: The keyboard used by the operator to give instructions to the computer.

Tertiary colors: Colors that are produced by mixing any two secondary colors.

Text: Letters and symbols that are stored in text files using ASCII and EBCDIC codes.

Three-quarter-tone: A tone value located approximately midpoint between middle-tone and shadow.

Tone compression: Compressing the original tones to fit the range of the reproduction. Even when the whitest paper and the darkest inks are used with most normal originals, the range of the reproduction is still much lower than the range of most originals. For a normal copy, the tones from the highlight through the middle-tone of the original are kept about the same in the reproduction. However, most of the tones between the middle-tone and the shadow are compressed to fit the narrow reproduction range. The human eye is less sensitive to the loss of details in shadow areas, and, consequently, the compression is less noticeable.

Tonal curve: The curve showing the relationship between the original density and the density or the percent dots in the reproduction.

Tone reproduction: The various processes and techniques of reproducing tones of an original. Also called gradation.

Track ball: A computer control device, usually in the shape of a sphere, used to move images around on the screen in two dimensions.

Transmission rate: The amount of data that can be transmitted over a period of time, usually per second.

Transparency: Any color slide with a positive image. Examples are Agfachrome, Fujichrome, Kodachrome, etc.

Trapping: Color trapping means slightly overlapping two adjoining colors to minimize the effect of misregister. In color printing, the trapping problem occurs when a second layer of ink is printed on the first layer, and the first layer does not take all the ink of the second layer.

Two-stage masking: In photographic color separations, a mask reduces the range of the original. However, another mask may be made to counter the effect of the first mask, thus expanding the range. The purpose of the second mask is to make reproduction of tones more flexible, it does not in any way affect the original. In most analog color scanners which use Masking Equations, a two-stage mask is computed and applied by the computer electronically. A two-stage mask is difficult to produce and apply in conventional camera separations.

- U -

UCA: Abbreviation for under color addition. A technique of adding cyan, magenta, or yellow inks in the neutral shadow areas to remove color cast so that under color removal can be effective. With the advent of GCR (gray component replacement), UCA is used to add colors under black for the required neutrality and to increase the quality of the black, e.g. gloss or neutrality.

UCR: Abbreviation for under color removal. The technique of reducing the cyan, magenta, and yellow inks from the darkest neutral shadow areas in the reproduction and replacing them with black. UCR has several advantages: it is economical, uses less process ink, and the drying time of the ink is reduced because of the reduced ink coverage in the dark shadow areas.

Under color addition: See UCA.

Under color removal: See UCR.

Undercorrection: When the process colors are not properly corrected for unwanted absorptions and reflections due to contamination.

Unsharp masking (USM): The term is adopted from unsharp masks. In the conventional separation, it is used to increase sharpness at the edges of density change. In a scanner, the sharpness at the edges of density or color changes are possible with the use of an unsharp masking aperture and electronic controls. The unsharp masking aperture is made larger than the main aperture; they travel together during scanning and produce white and black lines on the lighter and darker edges producing an illusion of extra sharpness. Color filters for unsharp masking signals are used to increase sharpness along the border of a color change. In addition, in most scanners, electronic controls are available to enhance or suppress the effects of unsharp masking. Also see edge enhancement and peaking.

- V -

Vehicle: Ink solvent in which the pigment is added.

Video analyzer: A device similar to a television screen used to analyze the original for proper set up in the scanner.

Video disk: See optical disk.

Video monitor: A monitor similar to a television screen that displays texts, picture data or graphics.

Visible spectrum: That part of the spectrum that is visible to human eye. The range of the visible spectrum or white light is approximately between 400 and 700 nanometers.

- W -

White: The presence of equal proportions of the components of the visible spectrum.

White Alignment: A procedure in a scanner to generate equal electrical output from the photomultipliers when they are exposed to identical neutral light source. This technique of balancing the photomultipliers is used at the initial calibration stage.

White colors: A color which should not be in other specific colors and often called an unwanted color. For example, yellow is unwanted color in cyan, magenta and blue.

Wideband filter: A special color filter that transmits a wideband of the visible spectrum.

Winchester: A hard disk drive that can store up to 300 megabytes. It is mostly used in the page make up systems. A winchester disk is not removable from the drive but is very durable.

Work station: A set of computer equipment that can be used by one person at one time. It normally consists of an input and a display and output devices.

WORM: Abbreviation for Write Once, Read Many. Applied to optical disks where data was once recorded and cannot be erased or altered.

Write: The function of copying a file.

- X-Y -

Xenon lamp: A high pressure gas-filled lamp that is pulsed 120 times a second and appears to transmit a continuous emission of light. The color temperature of the xenon lamp is approximately 5400 degrees Kelvin. It is an ideal and balanced light source for illuminating and evaluating a copy for separations in the conventional method or scanning.

Yellow: A subtractive primary color used in the four color process printing technique that absorbs the blue light of the spectrum. In the additive principle, yellow light is produced by overlapping red and green lights.

YMCK: An abbreviation for the process colors: yellow, magenta, cyan and black.

Bibliography

Allen, E. M. *Harper's dictionary of the graphic arts*. New York: Harper & Row, 1963.

Billmeyer, F. W., Jr., & Saltzman, M. *Principles of color technology*. New York: Interscience Publishers, 1967.

Birren, F. *Principles of color*. New York: Van Nostrand Reinhold Company, 1969.

Birren, F. *The story of color*. Westport: The Crimson Press, 1941.

Brooks, D. Which color slide film is right for you? *Photo-Graphic*, December 1982, 11(8), 45-48, 51-53, 66, 67.

Burgstein, M. *Gray component replacement*. Wilmington: Printing Systems Division, E. I. Du Pont De Nemours & Co.

Burnhal, R. W., Hanes, R. M., & Bartleson, C. J. *Color: a guide to basic facts and concepts*. New York: John Wiley & Sons, Inc., 1967.

Chambers, E. The art and science of colour. *British Printers*, June 1979, 92(6), 47-50.

Chambers, E. Colour separation: what it is and how to do it. *British Printers*, December 1979, 92(12), 51-54.

Chambers E. The principles and practice of colour separation. *Printing Trade Journal*, July 1975, (1061), 17-21.

CCR/PCR. Kiel, West Germany: Dr. -Ing. Rudolf Hell GMBH, D2300 Kiel 14.

Chromagraph, gradation and color correction. Kiel, West Germany: Dr. -Ing. Rudolf Hell GMBH, D2300 Kiel 14.

Chromagraph 299L Operating Manual. Kiel, West Germany: Dr. -Ing. Rudolf Hell GMBH, D2300 Kiel 14.

Chromagraph 399ER Operating Manual. Kiel, West Germany: Dr. -Ing. Rudolf Hell GMBH, D2300 Kiel 14.

Clulow, F. W. *Color, its principles and their applications*. New York: Morgan & Morgan, 1972.

Cogoli, J. E. *Photo-offset fundamentals*. Bloomington: McKnight Publishing Co., 1973.

Coulson, M. G. Global influences on the graphic arts. Pittsburgh: *GATF Market Research Newsletter*, Number 6, October, 1984.

Coulson, M. G. The search for digital proofs. *Printing Impressions*, January 1987, 29(8), 47-49.

Cox, F. L. Considerations for scanner setup. *GATF/RIT Color Scanner Users Conference*. Conducted jointly by GATF and RIT Graphic Arts Research Center, March 18 & 19, 1975.

Dawson, B. M. Introduction to Image Processing Algorithms. *BYTE*, March 1987, 12(3), 169-186.

Direct Color Scanner SG-608 Instruction Manual. Kyoto, Japan: Dainippon Screen Mfg. Co. Ltd., 1985.

Direct Scanagraph Technical Guide. Kyoto, Japan: Dainippon Screen Mfg. Co. Ltd., 1985.

Electronic color scanners make their mark. *Australasian Printer*, May 1978, 29(4), 34-35.

Ettinger, M. A. What scanner technology can do for the '80s. *Printing Impressions*, February 1980, 22(9), 13.

Field, G. G. The Significance of recent developments in colour scanner technology. *Printing Technology*, January 1973, 17(1), 20-25.

Fuller, R. The impact and trends in color scanning. *The Photoplatemakers Bulletin*, June 1976, 66(1), 7-10.

Fuller, R. What scanner technology will do for the '80s. *Printing Impressions*, February 1980, 22(9), 12.

Gast, I. U. Electronic screening for color separations. *Photoplatemakers Bulletin*, January 1975, 64(8), 7-12.

Glanville, M. What scanner technology will do for the '80s. *Printing Impressions*, February 1980, 22(9), 12.

Goodacre, C. Carry on scanning. *Printing Today*, November 1979, 16(188), pp. 34-35; 39-40; 43; 81.

Guide for Discussion Leaders Color Electronic Prepress Systems. A video program for sales and service personnel. Edina: International Prepress Association, 1987.

Hubl, A. F. V. *Three-colour photography*. London: A. W. Penrose & Co., 1904.

Hunt, R. W. G. *The reproduction of colour*. Hartfordshire: Fountain Press, 1975.

Itek 200-S Operation Manual. Cheltenham, England: Itek Colour Graphics Limited, 1984.

Johnson, A. J. Colour scanning. *British Ink Maker*, February 1976, 18(2), 48-51.

Knowles, P. Colour separation. *British Printer*, February 1975, 82(2), 48-51.

McMains, C. Low-cost Image Processing. *BYTE*, March 1987, 12(3), 191-195.

Magnascan 645 IE/M Operator's Manual. London, England: Crosfield Electronics Limited, 1984.

McGuire, R. R. Undercolor removal — a key to better printing. *Graphic Arts Monthly*, January 1977, 49(1), 30-34.

Munsell, A. H. *A color notation*. Boston: Munsell, 1947.

Nelson, R. D. *Fundamental techniques of direct-screen color reproductions*. Rochester: Eastman Kodak Company, 1980.

Optimization of the recording quality on ER Chromagraphs. Kiel, West Germany: Dr. -Ing. Rudolf Hell GMBH, D2300 Kiel 14.

Preucil, F. M. Some new and old trends in color reproduction. *Graphic Arts Monthly,* June 1973, 45(6), 76-79.

Pritchard, E. J. How to Select a Colour Transparency for Graphic Reproduction. *Pira Self-Instruction Manual No. 3.* Surrey: Printing Industry Research Association.

Pugsley, Peter C. *Colour correcting image reproducing methods and apparatus.* US patent literature. Assignee: Crosfield Electronics Limited, 1974.

Radebaugh, J. *The color separation scanner.* Rochester: Eastman Kodak Company, 1981.

Rainwater, C. *Light and color.* Racine: Western Publishing Co., Inc., 1971.

Rhodes, W. L. Tone reproduction in the graphic arts processes. Color problems in the graphic arts. *Symposium of the Inter-Society Color Council,* Inc., 1959.

Rogers, M. C. Color printing methods in the graphic arts. Color problems in the graphic arts. *Inter-Society Color Council and Pacific Printer,* Publisher and Lithographer, 1959.

Roth, J. GCR separates color shop from the rest. *American Printer,* October, 1985, 196(1), 50-53.

Schaub, G. & O'Connor, T. Slow down for ultimate quality chromes. *Popular Photography,* January 1986, 93(1), 42-50 and 102.

Sheldon, K. Probing Space by camera. *BYTE,* March 1987, 12(3), 143-148.

Southworth, M. *Color reproduction techniques.* Livonia: Graphic Arts Publishing, 1979.

Southworth, M. Electronic scanners: How they work, what their future is. Printing Impressions, *November 1972, 15(6), 12-13.*

Southworth, M. Color separation: Why the day of the scanners has arrived. Printing Impressions, June 1977, 20(1), 8G-8P.

Suddenly its all color. *British Printer,* November 1979. 92(11), 19-30.

Ultraviolet Absorption in Color Reproduction. Rochester: Eastman Kodak Company, 1980.

Using Kodak Ektachrome and Kodachrome Film Transparencies on Color Scanners. Color Notes No. 5. Rochester: Eastman Kodak Company, 1980.

Walker, M. What scanner technology will do for the '80s. *Printing Impressions,* February 1980, 22(9), 13.

Wood, P. J. New Development in colour scanning. *Professional Printer,* January 1977, 21(1), 2-4.

Ynostroza, R. Color scanners, today and tomorrow. *Graphic Arts Monthly,* August 1975, 47(8), 38-42.

Yule, J. A. C. Color separation photography, In R. Blair & C. Shapiro (Eds.), *The lithographers manual.* Pittsburgh: The Graphic Arts Technical Foundation, Inc., 1980.

Yule, J. A. C. *Principles of color reproduction.* New York: John Wiley & Sons, Inc., 1967.

Addresses of vendors, business and professional organizations whose equipment and services are indicated in this publication

Agfa-Gevaert, Inc.
Graphic Systems
100 Challenger Road
Ridgefield Park, NJ 07660, USA
Phone: 201-440-2500

American National Standards Institute
1430 Broadway
New York, NY 10018, USA
Phone: 212-354-3300

Chesley F. Carlson Co.
2700 Campus Drive
Plymouth, MN 55441, USA
Phone: 612-553-7800

Colortune Corporation
5 S. Rt. 12
Fox Lake, IL 60020, USA
Phone: 312-587-2177

Commission Internationale de l'Eclairage
57 Rue Curier
Paris 5, France

Crosfield Electronics Limited
Three Cherry Trees Lane
Hemel Hempstead
Herts HP2 7RH, England
Phone: 0442-218311

Crosfield Electronics, Inc.
65 Harristown Road
Glen Rock, NJ 07452, USA
Phone: 201-447-5800

Dainippon Screen Mfg. Co. Ltd.
12-2, Bohjoh-cho Chudoji
Shimokyo-ku, Kyoto 600, Japan
Phone: 075-365-3111

Dr. -Ing. Rudolf Hell GMBH
Postfach 6229
2300 Kiel 14, West Germany
Phone: 0431/211-0

DS America, Inc.
5110 Tollview Drive
Rolling Meadows, IL 60008, USA
Phone: 312-870-1960

Eastman Kodak Company
Graphic Imaging Systems
343 State Street
Rochester, NY 14650, USA
Phone: 716-724-4558

Eikonix Corporation
23 Crosby Drive
Bedford, MA 01730, USA
Phone: 617-275-5070

E. I. Du Pont De Nemours Co.
Printing Systems Div.
Barley Mill Plaza
Wilmington, DE 19898, USA
Phone: 302-992-2295

Flexographic Technical Association
95 West 19th Street
Huntington Station, NY 11746, USA
Phone: 516-737-6020

Fuji Photo Film USA, Inc.
Graphic Arts Products
1000 Pratt Blvd.
Elk Grove Village, IL 60007, USA
Phone: 312-569-3500

Graphic Arts Technical Foundation
4615 Forbes Avenue
Pittsburgh, PA 15213, USA
Phone: 412-621-6941

Gravure Association of America
90 Fifth Avenue
New York, NY 10011, USA
Phone: 212-255-0070

GTI Graphic Technology, Inc.
211 DuPont Ave.
Newburgh, NY 12550, USA
Phone: 914-562-7066

Hell Graphic Systems, Inc.
25 Harbor Park Drive
Port Washington, NY 11050, USA
Phone: 516-484-3000

Hoechst Celanese Corporation
Enco Printing Products
3070 Route 22 West
Somerville, NJ 08876, USA
Phone: 201-231-3829

International Prepress Association
552 West 167th Street
South Holland, IL 60473, USA
Phone: 312-596-5110

Inter-Society Color Council
US Army Natick RD&E Center
Natick, MA 01760, USA

Itek Colour Graphics Ltd.
Princess Elizabeth Way, Cheltenham
Glos., England
Phone: 0242-582182

Macbeth
Rt. 207, P.O. Box 230
Newburgh, NY 12550, USA
Phone: 914-565-4440

Printing Industry Research Association (PIRA)
Randall's Road
Leatherhead
Surrey KT22 7RU, England

Printing Industries of America
1730 North Lynn Street
Arlington, VA 22209, USA
Phone: 703-841-8100

Royal Zenith Corporation
Scanner Division
2 Oxford Drive
Moonachie, NJ 07074, USA
Phone: 201-641-7200

Scitex America Corporation
Eight Oak Park Drive
Bedford, MA 01730, USA
Phone: 617-275-5150

Screen Printing Association International
10015 Main Street
Fairfax, VA 22031, USA
Phone: 703-385-1335

Technical Association of the Graphic Arts
T&E Center, Rochester Institute of Technology
1 Lomb Memorial Drive
Rochester, NY 14623, USA
Phone: 716-272-0557

3M Printing Publishing Systems
Bldg. 223-2N-01, 3M Center
St. Paul, MN 55144, USA
Phone: 612-733-6785

Westvaco Corporation
299 Park Avenue
New York, NY 10171, USA
Phone: 212-688-5000

X-Rite, Inc.
3100 44th Street, SW
Grandville, MI 49418, USA
Phone: 616-534-7663

Index

About the author

Rafiqul K. Molla is a Professor of Printing Technology, West Virginia Institute of Technology. He was born and received his early education in Bangladesh. After receiving B.S. in Chemistry, he became interested in printing and started his own business in photoengraving, color printing and advertising in Dhaka, Bangladesh. He came to the United States in 1963 on a Fulbright Scholarship to earn a masters degree in Printing Management at South Dakota State University. After completing his degree, he returned to Bangladesh (erstwhile East Pakistan) in 1967 and founded and became the principal of Graphic Arts Institute, the only printing school in the country. At this government institution, he developed and implemented a three-year diploma program in printing technology.

Molla and his family emigrated to the United States in 1973. He joined the West Virginia Tech faculty in 1975, started his doctoral study at West Virginia University in Technology Education in 1979 and completed the degree in 1983. His doctoral dissertation topic was on color scanners. In fact, the concept of writing this book originated from his experience with the doctoral research. After about three years of study with the Graphic Arts Technical Foundation, he completed his dissertation entitled "Identification of the Concepts, Principles and Skills for the Optimum Operation of a Color Scanner." More than three hundred scanner operators, trainers, and color separation experts from this country and abroad participated in the study.

Among his many accomplishments, Dr. Molla is singularly responsible for developing one of the finest color curriculums at West Virginia Tech. Through his efforts, industry has donated equipment and materials including two latest color scanners to set up a modern color separation laboratory. In addition to teaching color, Dr. Molla also taught process camera, copy preparation, and offset press for many years. He taught various adult printing and photography courses sponsored by the Continuing Education department at West Virginia Tech. He was a Visiting Professor at the Department of Graphic Communication, California Polytechnic State University, San Luis Obispo, California, during the 1986-87 academic year. He has conducted many seminars on color scanner for the industry at West Virginia Tech and California Polytechnic State University. Molla has extensive experience in color photography. He owns a professional portrait studio and a color photographic laboratory. Recently he was awarded a Graphic Arts Education and Research Foundation Grant for developing a training module on color scanner.

Dr. Molla lives in Montgomery with his wife Faizun. He has five children, the eldest Khaled is a printing graduate from West Virginia Tech and works for U.S. News and World Report in Washington, D.C. The second son, Ziaus, is an electrical engineer who also graduated from West Virginia Tech and works for Signetics, a computer company in San Jose, California. The third son, Farid, graduates in May 1988 in Printing Management from West Virginia Tech. Daughter Sheila and son Mithu are in high school.